EXPERIENCING
Race, Class, and Gender
in the United States

Sixth Edition

ROBERTA FISKE-RUSCIANO
Rider University

The McGraw·Hill Companies

Connect
Learn
Succeed™

EXPERIENCING RACE, CLASS, AND GENDER IN THE UNITED STATES, SIXTH EDITION

Published by McGraw-Hill, a business unit of The McGraw-Hill Companies, Inc., 1221 Avenue of the Americas, New York, NY, 10020. Copyright © 2013 by The McGraw-Hill Companies, Inc. All rights reserved. Printed in the United States of America. Previous editions © 2009, 2005, and 2000. No part of this publication may be reproduced or distributed in any form or by any means, or stored in a database or retrieval system, without the prior written consent of The McGraw-Hill Companies, Inc., including, but not limited to, in any network or other electronic storage or transmission, or broadcast for distance learning.

Some ancillaries, including electronic and print components, may not be available to customers outside the United States.

This book is printed on acid-free paper.

1 2 3 4 5 6 7 8 9 0 DOC/DOC 1 0 9 8 7 6 5 4 3 2

ISBN: 978-0-07-811161-7
MHID: 0-07-811161-7

Senior Vice President, Products & Markets: *Kurt L. Strand*
Vice President, General Manager, Products & Markets: *Michael Ryan*
Vice President, Content Production & Technology Services: *Kimberly Meriwether David*
Editorial Director: *William Glass*
Publisher: *Gina Boedecker*
Development Editor: *Amy Mittelman*
Marketing Specialist: *Alexandra Schultz*
Director, Content Production: *Terri Schiesl*
Lead Project Manager: *Jane Mohr*
Buyer: *Susan K. Culbertson*
Cover Designer: *Studio Montage, St. Louis, MO.*
Cover Image: *Royalty-Free/CORBIS*
Media Project Manager: *Sridevi Palani*
Typeface: *10/11 Garamond Light*
Compositor: *Laserwords Private Limited*
Printer: *R.R.Donnelley*

All credits appearing on page or at the end of the book are considered to be an extension of the copyright page.

Library of Congress Cataloging-in-Publication Data

Fiske-Rusciano, Roberta.
    Experiencing race, class, and gender in the United States/Roberta Fiske-Rusciano.—6th ed.
      p. cm.
    ISBN 978-0-07-811161-7 (alk. paper)
      1. United States—Social conditions—1980- 2. United States—Race relations. 3. United States—Ethnic relations. 4. Social classes—United States. 5. Cultural pluralism--United States. 6. Women—United States—Social conditions. 7. Gays—United States—Social conditions. 8. Discrimination—United States. I. Title.
    HN59.2.E96 2013
    305.800973—dc23

                                                                                                    2012025326

The Internet addresses listed in the text were accurate at the time of publication. The inclusion of a website does not indicate an endorsement by the authors or McGraw-Hill, and McGraw-Hill does not guarantee the accuracy of the information presented at these sites.

www.mhhe.com

Dedicated to Luca, bringer of light

CONTENTS

Change   355

PREFACE

The first several years of the new millennium have been saturated with debate concerning fundamental ideals and principles by which people live worldwide. Large migrations of populations, due to shifts in economic opportunities, natural disasters, and especially war, have put into sharp relief the need for reassessing who we are and where we are headed as a society. Each nation, each identity group, does this in its own way, focusing on what seems most urgent, most potentially divisive, or on a shared opinion that a group wants to voice. The sixth edition of *Experiencing Race, Class, and Gender in the United States* offers an opportunity to look at many of these issues as experienced by the diverse population of this country. Collecting details of the "American experience" is an ongoing effort that requires each of us to keep our eye on the shifts and different reflections of this richly varied and complex society. Learning more about the past and present through many voices will help us all problem solve with balance and wisdom as valuable, participating members of this country and of the world.

Experiencing Race, Class, and Gender in the United States, sixth edition, introduces students to basic concepts of multiculturalism and to seminal debates taken up by social scientists, physical scientists, and political commentators. Some points, however, can be made only by the poets and literary writers included herein. This text encourages readers to examine their own lives by challenging notions of hierarchy and stereotypes that often seem so natural and largely go unchallenged. Such a journey is transforming and lengthy and is part of an ongoing American experience. *Experiencing Race, Class, and Gender* is a guide for students in thoughtful exploration of issues that surround personal and institutionalized bigotry. It encourages informed debate and avoids being doctrinaire, for learning to think through these issues is a far greater commitment than carefully agreeing with the professor.

Organization of the Book

This book is divided into three main divisions: *Identity* (Parts I–III), *Power* (Parts IV–VII), and *Change* (Parts VIII–IX). The first division, *Identity*, guides the reader to examine his or her own life and those of others by exploring the many layers that make up our selves and how those layers are affected by the lived experience of race, ethnicity, religion, gender, sexuality, and socioeconomic class.

The text then shifts its focus to a wider context in the second division, *Power,* in order to examine how our lives are shaped by specific social powers. Understanding one's social skin includes an acknowledgment of how we are all tied to institutions, groups, ongoing conflicts, and supportive networks. Exploring the differing circumstances and seeing patterns that reflect groups' varying experiences within our society gives us a better intellectual grip on inequalities that persist in the United States, made more clear after natural and man-made disasters.

As some of us have become used to the idea that only governmental institutions or business conglomerates can change social policies and broad economic circumstances, the acknowledgment of inequities and human rights abuses leaves many feeling powerless, angry, and concluding "there will always be poverty (or racism, sexism, etc.), so I just have to take care of myself." The third division of this text, *Change,* guides students to the knowledge that they can indeed effect change. Part VIII, *Taking Action,* introduces students to the stages of identifying a problem, visualizing the needed change, and going forward with a collective plan of action while armed with the knowledge of how to handle resistance. Part IX, *Change Makers,* brings the reader into the experiences of ordinary people who have changed many lives by refusing to give up their human rights and those of their community.

The introductions to the text's three main divisions and nine parts are intended to situate the concepts of the readings in a particular context, but students and instructors are encouraged to challenge the editor's and authors' assumptions. Some theoretical terms are highlighted by boldface type, and term definitions follow some of the readings. Each reading is followed by a set of "Understanding the Reading" questions to aid in critical thinking and classroom discussion and by "Suggestions for Responding," which encourages further study for those who are interested.

Web site: Visit the sixth edition Web site at www.mhhe.com/fiske6e for comprehensive student and instructor resources, including an instructor's manual on the password-protected instructor portion of the Web site and self-quizzes for students on the student side.

New to the Sixth Edition

The sixth edition has twenty-three new readings. As with the last edition, the text remains a combination of social science and the humanities, drawing on the strengths of a multidisciplinary approach that hopefully will add to the flexibility of the collection's use and provide broader exposure to knowledge as we grapple with these most basic questions in our society. Other new readings focus upon divisions in our understanding of U.S. history and the consequences. A future U.S. president and a musician/educator write about their very personal American stories. The question of how to define a "real Indian" is not new, but one author points out the irony of how it is being decided of late. The changed military policy of "Don't Ask, Don't Tell" and more information about transgender rights have been added. Using a Pew Research

Center article we learn about Black Americans' attitudes during the recession and the impact of immigration raids on families and children. There is updated U.S. Census information on urban Indians and a discussion of citizenship and violence, focusing upon the Violence Against Women Act. As we explore the portion of the text devoted to classism, we consider the new articles about minimal taxation for the super-rich, the United States' bulging jails, and the expansion of health care to employees of small businesses, due to Obamacare. Two articles are added on environmental justice as "unfinished business." An article on religion and mental health needs focuses on American Muslims. In the Change section, there are new essays and editorials that reflect some of the salient issues of our time: voting rights, the marriage equality struggle for same-sex couples, Occupy Wall Street demands, and a hate crimes prevention act. A famous activist remembers challenging the Elks Club over segregation when he was a teenager, and Caddo Indians fight for respect for their ancestral remains.

Acknowledgments

I am deeply grateful to colleagues at Rider University who have either directly guided me to readings or helped me think through ideas that have somehow found their way into this book: Frank Rusciano, Pearlie Peters, Bosah Ebo, Nancy Schluter, Rebecca Basham, Barbara Franz, Minmin Wang, Mathew Goldie and Don Brown. My special thanks go to Reverend Nancy Schluter's Race, Class, Gender, and Ethnicity in America students at Rider University, who gave me specific suggestions as to what should be changed within the text.

My gratitude goes to Peter Shungu, a longtime friend who shared his changing racial identity as he traveled from the United States to the Congo and to South Africa. I would also like to thank the following reviewers for their helpful comments and suggestions: Adann-Kennn J. Alexxandar, Valdosta State University; Carolyn Black, Indiana University-Purdue University, Indianapolis; Hillary Hazan-Glass, SUNY Rockland Community College; Gloria P. Martinez-Ramos, Texas State University-San Marcos; Nancy Schluter, Rider University; Corina D. Segovia-Tadehara, Weber State University; and Sharlene Toney, Indiana University–Bloomington.

My heartfelt thanks go to everyone at the McGraw-Hill Companies, Inc., who helped in innumerable ways and patiently waited as I crafted the book, including Lisa Pinto, executive director of development; Jessica Cannavo, sponsoring editor; Amy Mittleman, developmental editor; Karyn Morrison, permissions editor; and Jane Mohr, project manager.

Finally, I thank my husband, Frank, who not only contributed an essay but also wrestled with my computer files and kept me happy during this process; and my son, Francesco, who is a good listener, sharp critic, and a citizen of the world.

Roberta Fiske-Rusciano

Experiencing Race, Class, and Gender in the United States

The public image of America* that existed fifty years ago has little similarity to the American public image of the twenty-first century. In the 1950s and 1960s Americans were associated with being White, middle class, speaking English, and living in a nuclear family where Father works outside the home and Mother works "inside" the home, caring for children, cleaning, shopping, and cooking. While this image reflects some of the postwar ideals of our country, it definitely was not descriptive of most American families. Most importantly, this media-driven portrait denies the country's diversity of that time: one-quarter of Americans were poor in the 1950s, and one-third of native-born, White families could not get by with two incomes (Coontz, S., *The Way We Never Were,* c. 1992, pp. 27–28). Contrary to television depictions of the fifties and sixties, Blacks, Puerto Ricans, Mexicans, and other immigrant groups were flocking into American cities looking for work.

Although today we are much more aware of the vast differences among us, this recognition presents us with many challenges. One-quarter of the U.S. population is either Hispanic or Black, and the majority of Californians are no longer Caucasian. The nuclear family as the predominant social unit has given way to a varied list of family constellations, such as single female-headed household with children, divorced parents with half-siblings and stepchildren in the household, and gay or lesbian couples with or without children. Whatever arrangement, whomever is included as family, married couples comprise only about one-half of American households.

Gender roles have changed enormously since World War II, most obviously for women, as they have come to occupy more and more public space. Although many women worked during World War II, filling positions of men who were sent to war, once the soldiers reentered U.S. society women were expected to "make way" as men needed jobs. Women also were chosen for college admission only after male veteran applicants were chosen. Following World War II fewer than one-third of all women were in the labor force, while today approximately 60 percent are in the labor force and make up 58 percent of all college students. Will American males keep the edge on earnings, power, and general entitlement, or are their roles shifting

---

* *America* is used in this book in the vernacular sense, referring to the United States; it is not intended to detract from or dismiss the many other cultures and citizens of the Western Hemisphere.

as we all redefine and reposition ourselves in a globalizing world? If a higher percentage of women than men (among Whites, Blacks, and Latinos) are achieving higher educational attainment, what does this mean for leadership in public office, private business, and personal lives? How exactly does this redefine manliness (if in fact, it does)?

It is hoped that this text will ignite classroom discussion and help students integrate and explore the great questions of our century that surround race, class, gender, and religion as we go through rapid social changes within the boundaries of the United States and as a globalizing entity. The more interdependent we become as global citizens, the more our relationships change and the more porous our boundaries become, changing our national and personal identities forever. Becoming increasingly aware of our individual connections to larger social constructs is one of the hallmarks of a liberal education and a strong building block on which to situate an increasing understanding of our obligations as members of a civil society. Hopefully, this book will challenge and stimulate students to act on their knowledge and empowerment to effect social change.

Names and Labels

In a course where one speaks of many different people grouped according to skin color, country of origin, class, ethnicity, region, religion, or profession, one must take special note of names and labels that we have inherited from years gone by. The general rule of respect is: Call people what they want to be called, and do not be surprised if everyone from one group does not agree. In some universities it is protocol to address the professor as "Professor," while elsewhere professors prefer "Doctor," and elsewhere they prefer to be called by their first names. As another example, a young American man whose father is originally from the Congo and whose mother is Caucasian American visited Africa recently. "In America I am considered Black, in the Congo I was considered White, but in South Africa I was Colored." You may have noticed that the term *third-world people* is often avoided, as it implies a lower status. *Developing countries* is one of the terms that has replaced it for now. There has been an unhelpful tradition of lumping peoples together such as Hispanic, which is supposed to include South America, Central America, Mexico, and much of the Caribbean. However, that excludes those who do not speak Spanish from these regions, but speak Portuguese, French, and indigenous languages. It also annoys those in the Southwest who often prefer to be called Latino or Latina, Spanish American, Latin American, La Raza, Mexican American, MexAmerican, Chicana, or Chicano. Others prefer specific appellations such as Cuban American or Puerto Rican American, Haitian, and so on. The term *Asian American* lumps billions of people, whose groups have little to do with one another. Whereas U.S. Native Americans (a term preferred by academicians) often refer to themselves as Indians, Apache, Winnebago, Comanche, and so forth, according to their nations' names, Canadians use the terms *First Nations* and *First Peoples*.

Understanding labels does not only require us to take notice of people's preferences, but also gives us the responsibility of recognizing pejorative terms and ethnic, sexist, and racist slurs. If a word is chosen to deliberately antagonize and hurt, or to share a kind of solidarity against one group, it is important as members of a civil society to openly object. For example, calling a female colleague *little lady* or *girlie* is disrespectful and considered harassment. Sometimes those around us simply need to have it pointed out that they are being offensive. In other cases the offenders need to be reported to a superior at work, or avoided if the setting is social.

Theories About Diversity and Group Interaction

In addition to considering appropriate labels for various American groups, we need to explore how groups interact with one another and how they fit into the totality of American culture. Whether our ancestors came across a land bridge 10,000 years ago, were on the *Mayflower,* survived the Middle Passage on a slave ship, or endured steerage or whether we have just arrived, all Americans originated somewhere else. Where each of us or our ancestors came from affects not just who we are individually but what America is.

Three **theories,** systematic ways of organizing knowledge to explain a variety of occurrences, have been proposed to explain the impact that heterogeneous immigrant cultures have had on one another and on the American way of life. The **assimilation theory** argues that American culture demands that new arrivals become absorbed into the dominant culture, that they assimilate. According to this theory, early European immigrants—in particular, Protestants from England—created a society that reflected their roots. As new immigrants arrived or were transported here, as in the case of Africans, and as the native populations lost power and autonomy, all were forced to discard the unique features of their former cultures and adopt the values and norms of the European American culture. Even today, many people believe that current immigrants must assimilate in order to survive here.

Another theory rejects the idea of British or even European supremacy and describes America as an **amalgamation** or a **melting pot.** According to this theory, all the various heritages have influenced one another, blending together to create a unique American culture in which no group or single set of values is dominant. Everyone is equally American.

Today, many people consider America to be multicultural. The **pluralistic** or **multicultural theory** views American culture as a combination of many subsocieties. It claims that each group retains some of its customs and traditions, that these are accepted as valid and valuable, and that all groups coexist and interact with the larger system. This is obviously an overly optimistic picture of our society, but like the other two theories it does contain elements of truth. We are not all alike or assimilated, and it is obvious that some groups and values dominate American culture, whereas others are marginalized, devalued, or repressed. There are also some groups within the United States who wish to remain, as much as possible, apart from the dominant American culture. Nonetheless, we must learn to live with our differences.

Any theory is, of necessity, an abstraction. Thus, no single theory can adequately account for all specific, real experiences. In general, a combination of the three theories is needed to describe American society realistically. Clearly, European Americans played a central role in establishing American social institutions that served their interests. Although other groups have been shaped and controlled by these institutions, we cannot ignore the ways in which these "others" have helped shape social policies and practices as well. We all influence and are influenced by the larger society, yet we cannot fully escape our distinctive heritages, either.

Sociopolitical Positions

Recently, some people have expressed the worry that recognition of the multicultural dimension of society results in a devaluation or destruction of traditional values. According to these people, ethnic, racial, and gender perspectives distort and may even corrupt America's cultural and intellectual traditions. They are worried that advocates of the inclusion of these nontraditional perspectives are intolerant, extremist advocates of a radical program. However, multiculturalists value diversity and feel that examining society and ideas from multiple perspectives, including the traditional one, enhances and enriches our lives, our society, and our understanding of the world. All healthy cultures grow and adapt without losing their essential core. Following the wisdom of the Micmac Indians of Canada, the degree of flexibility of a society is a good index of its strength. The author Carlos Fuentes once observed that cultures that exist in isolation perish, and only cultures that communicate and give things to one another survive.

To describe the various positions people take on social issues in the United States, the terms *conservative* and *liberal* are often used. It is often claimed that conservatives favor less government involvement in people's lives, whereas liberals favor more government involvement. However, the social reality is more complex. Generally speaking, conservatives in the United States believe in government intervention to regulate social behavior (pornography, abortion, gay relations, gender roles), but they do not favor government intervention in economic relations (welfare, minimum wage, environmental regulations on businesses or consumers, etc.). Liberals tend to believe in government intervention in economic relations, but not to regulate social behavior, unless it is a matter of civil rights. For example, conservatives may oppose a minimum wage law because they believe the market should set wages, whereas liberals support a minimum wage law. Conservatives advocate the banning of abortion, whereas liberals believe it should be a matter of personal choice. It is not uncommon to see a mixture of liberalism (or left wing) and conservatism (or right wing) within one person. Regardless of where we position ourselves on the political spectrum, this book raises issues that we need to consider and debate with open minds.

Ideological Principles

Each position reflects a different response to the traditional ideology of our culture. An **ideology** is a system of assumptions, theories, and beliefs characterizing a particular group or culture; the system supports and reinforces or questions political, social, and economic arrangements. Three ideological tenets of traditional American culture are relevant to our interests here, and all three have at one time or another been challenged by those who are disadvantaged by their consequent prejudices.

The first ideological principle is ***Eurocentricity,*** the assumption of the supremacy of European Americans and their values and traditions. For example, like most Europeans, most Americans are Judeo-Christian monotheists (believers in one god). If one were from this background and belittled Asian religions that worship multiple gods or gods in many forms, such as Hinduism or Shintoism, that describes being Eurocentric or ethnocentric. Most Americans also value the European principles of objectivity and scientific methodology and believe that verifiable truth can be established by measurement of physical phenomena and confirmed by repeatable experiments. In the past many European Americans tended to devalue mysticism or a personalistic explanation of events—the belief held by many Native Americans and African and Asian cultures that unseen, intangible spiritual forces animate and influence the natural world and human interactions with it. Today one can see Americans from many backgrounds fascinated by these different worldviews, religions, and practices by visiting university classrooms. One example is the practice of Falun Dafa, forbidden in China but practiced all over the world.

The second ideological principle is that traditional American culture is a **patriarchy,** a hierarchical system of social organization in which structures of power, value, and culture are male-dominated. Under patriarchy, men are seen as "natural" heads of households, presidential candidates, corporate executives, college presidents, and so on. Women, on the other hand, are men's subordinates, playing such supportive roles as homemaker, mother, nurse, and secretary. As we know, patriarchy has been under serious attack during the past quarter century.

The third important principle of American ideology is the belief in our economic system, capitalism. Any economic system defines the production and distribution of goods in a society and beyond. Capitalism advocates individual ownership of production and distribution according to whoever can pay for the goods and services. One of the problems with unregulated capitalism is that it tends to concentrate wealth at the top. One of its virtues is that it has enormous productive capacity to create goods and services. An important feature of this system, in the context of this book, is that, in times of economic downturn, it can lead to poverty in the midst of wealth. Our culture, which holds each individual responsible for his or her own welfare, contrasts with cultures that make priorities of cooperation and mutual responsibility, as many European, African, Asian countries and many Native American communities do.

The unique multiple-dimensionality of America that gives our country its rich texture also lends itself to divisiveness and inequity. All three ideological principles have been used to rationalize **prejudice,** negative attitudes about certain groups of people, and to justify **discrimination,** actions that flow from those prejudices and disadvantage members of "other" groups. In our country's history, Eurocentric prejudice and discrimination have resulted in **racism,** the subordination of certain groups of people based on their origins and physical characteristics. Patriarchal values have led to **sexism,** the subordination of women and the assumption of the superiority of men solely on the basis of sex. The **classism** that our capitalist society fosters has stigmatized poor and working-class people and their cultures and has assigned high status to the affluent and their culture solely because of their relative wealth.

As mentioned before, each of these ideological beliefs has been challenged by individuals who either act alone or organize united action. Racism has been under siege throughout much of our history, from the abolitionist crusade in the nineteenth century through the civil rights movement of the 1950s and 1960s to current activism by such groups as the National Association for the Advancement of Colored People and the Southern Poverty Law Center. From suffragists to modern **feminists,** advocates of equality between the sexes and of the value of females, women and men have struggled to combat the sexism in our society. Likewise, classism has been challenged by social reformers, labor unions, and Marxist socialists. Efforts by all these activists teach us that we do not have to resign ourselves to life in a society we think could be improved.

This book is intended to increase our awareness and understanding of the complexities of American society and culture. The readings have been selected to help us get inside the lives, minds, and hearts of the many peoples of America, so we can appreciate one another's interests, values, and concerns. The various authors speak in many distinctive voices, but despite their diversity they reveal common themes that connect us as members of American society. Some voices will sound familiar and speak to our background, values, and experiences. Others may seem alien and will challenge us, as the saying goes, to walk a mile in another's moccasins. Collectively, they will help us gain insight into who we are and what has shaped our identity. The readings will also enhance both our understanding of some of our social problems and our appreciation of the rich diversity of American life.

W ho are you? The way you answer this question depends on many factors, not the least of which is the context in which it is asked. Most frequently—meeting a professor, for instance—you give your full name, but when you arrive at your dorm, you might instead respond that you are the new roommate. At a big family reunion with lots of relatives you have never met, you might identify yourself as Stan and Ruth's daughter. Think about the many other ways you could respond. "I'm a college student." "I'm an economics major." "I'm a big fan of yours." "I'm your new neighbor." "I'm Tony's spouse." "I'm Puerto Rican." "I'm the place kicker." "I'm the babysitter." "I'm a New Yorker." "I'm an American." The list is almost endless.

Identity

In fact, you are all these things. Your individual identity is a unique blend of the many aspects of your life. These elements include your gender, your age, your placement in your family, your religion and your devotion to it, your race, your ethnic heritage and how (or even whether) your family has preserved it, your sexual orientation and experience, your education, your employment history, your socioeconomic background. What else would you add?

Identity incorporates both those personal characteristics by which we recognize an individual and those that define one's affiliation with a group. American culture puts considerable emphasis on the former. From Daniel Boone to Rambo, we make heroes of the nonconforming loner who acts independently, often in opposition to or in defiance of society. Advertisers promote their products as having what it takes to set us apart from the crowd and demonstrate our unique individuality.

This view of identity seems to make some sense, in that some psychologists suggest that a personal sense of identity begins when a child first recognizes his or her mother as a separate being, who in turn recognizes the child as an individual. From there, however, we go through innumerable developmental stages, as we perceive and accept or reject the values and distinctions established by our particular lifestyle.

Despite the myth of American individualism, our **identity**—our self-definition or sense of selfhood—actually is shaped not by separation but by affiliation, by bonding and identifying with others. As children, we observe the people around us and learn the qualities associated with those who seem like us, especially in terms of such characteristics as gender, race, age, and religion. For example, we learn what it means to be female or male by our interactions with the women or men around us. Then we **internalize,** accept as part of our own thinking, the characteristics that we recognize as appropriate to various facets of our identities.

Psychologists have differing theories about how this internalization takes place. Some see it as a cognitive process by which we learn how people are labeled and accept those labels for ourselves. Others think it is behavioral, that we learn how to act in response to rewards and punishments. Still others believe internalization to be the emotional desire to feel connected with others like us.

Whatever the process may be, all agree that what we learn about who we are in childhood is central to how we perceive ourselves and act as adults. Even though most of us continue throughout our lives to develop new and more inclusive identities, the "new me" is most accurately understood as an integration of some new or newly discovered facet of ourselves with our previous identifications and self-images. Our individuality, our identity, is actually a constellation of the various affiliations we accept and that are attributed to us.

In this division, "Identity," we look at how race and ethnicity, gender, and socioeconomic status influence identity formation in American culture. Part I, "Racial and Ethnic Identity," explores the nature of race and ethnicity by considering them from both theoretical and personal perspectives and in both historical and contemporary contexts. Part II, "Gender and Sexual Identity," examines how we learn to be male or female in our society and how gender roles affect the way we relate to and interact with one another. Because of the complexity of this topic we shall focus on the physicality and the accompanying social forces of sexual experiences, through several case studies. Part III, "Economics and the American Dream," shows that, despite the belief that America is a classless society or that everyone is middle class, sharp disparities in the distribution of wealth determine individual and group values and access to opportunity.

The purpose of the "Identity" division is to help us consider our own identity in the context of race, ethnicity, class, and gender. Even though any single reading selection may not speak specifically to your personal experience, the themes the readings explore will help you recognize and evaluate your place in the overall mosaic. As we come to realize that we actually have a great deal in common with some people who initially seemed different from us, when we discover that they and their experiences are more like our own than we had thought, we are more capable of understanding and sympathizing with the discrimination to which some people are subjected.

I

Racial and Ethnic Identity

YOU MAY BE SURPRISED TO LEARN IN PART I, "RACIAL and Ethnic Identity," that race and ethnicity are not as easily distinguished from each other as is commonly assumed. Even though we use these terms in everyday conversations, most of us don't have an accurate understanding of what they really mean and how imprecise they actually are.

In the United States, when we identify someone as a member of an **ethnic** group, we mean that he or she belongs to some identifiable group with common ancestral or geographical origin.

Ethnic subgroups are defined by many complex, often variable traits, such as religion, language, culture, customs, traditions, physical characteristics, and, probably most important in this country, ancestral origin. Ancestral origin is the reason we often label ethnic groups as "compound Americans": African Americans, German Americans, Filipino Americans, Chinese Americans, and so on.

"Wait a minute," you are probably saying, "some of those groups are racial, not ethnic." Do not be so sure.

One definition of **race** in *The American Heritage Dictionary* is "any group of people united or classified together on the basis of common history, nationality, or geographical distribution." In this sense, race does not differ substantially from ethnicity. Traditionally in the United States, people identify race solely in terms of physical characteristics, such as skin color, texture and color of hair, and other attributes, especially facial features. However, these attributes are not as discrete or self-evident as it might seem at first. From earliest times, human populations have migrated and intermingled, mixing and blending their biological makeup. Precise lines of racial demarcation are blurred, so that, at best, systematic classifications of race are complex and must be carefully qualified and questioned.

For this reason, scientists and an increasing part of the general public have come to believe that race is less a scientific actuality than it is a **social construct**—a classification based on social values. "Racial" lines are blurry as shown by genetic analysis, yet remain deep in the psyche of Americans. Originally articulated and ordered as a way to cement a hierarchy on this continent, our history is a record of official policy discrimination against certain groups in the United States. In the twenty-first century we continue to see the results of the inequities originally assigned approximately four hundred years ago. While many laboratories now offer DNA testing kits and analyses, where a simple swab of one's mouth reveals the geography of one's ancestral origins, our cities and their schools reveal the surface color of urban poverty. What effect will

3

genetics testing have on our future understanding of ourselves and others?

Today, many of us tend to think of African Americans, Asian Americans, and Native Americans as racial groups and Jewish Americans, Italian Americans, and Irish Americans as ethnic groups. In the early part of the twentieth century, however, each of the latter three was called a race and was said to have distinctive physical features that marked group identity, a belief that now strikes us as quaintly absurd.

Although we tend to consider both ethnic and racial identity to be fixed and unalterable, in fact, they are fluid and quite subjective. You may call yourself German American because your forebears came from what is now Germany, but they may have seen themselves instead as Prussian or Bavarian, or members of one of the many other nation-states that only later were united to form the Germany we know today.

Our current racial and ethnic groupings reflect another blind spot in social thought: our insensitivity to the realities of cultural heritage. The label *European American,* for example, camouflages the differences between Scandinavians and the French and between those two groups and the Poles, the British, and the many other distinct European cultures. While the term "Native American" is most often used by non-Indians and academicians, most Indians identify themselves as Sioux, or Lakota Sioux, Arapaho, and so on, or simply Indian.

Similarly, when we classify all African Americans as one homogeneous group, we ignore the extreme divergence of African cultures. The Ethiopian Plains culture differs tremendously from that which developed in Morocco or West Africa; moreover, like Native Americans, Africans are more likely to consider themselves Zulu, Ibo, Hausa, or Yoruba than South African or Nigerian—or even African. Finally, today there are at least nineteen Asian and Pacific Island populations lumped together under the *Asian American* label. These include the Hmong, Cambodians, Laotians, Sikh, and Burmese in addition to the more widely recognized groups representing Japan, China, Korea, India, and the Philippines.

Finally, it is important to note that all these subgroups exist within the American context,
and every subgroup has been transformed by the influences of this larger society. Nevertheless, even when many historical features of the subgroup have been lost or altered, members may continue to identify with the re-created group. These are the compound Americans.

The readings in Part I present a sampling of the innumerable accounts that are part of this evolutionary process. Some of them and some of the themes they present may reflect your heritage; others may not. However, each of them is part of the American experience, and we need to understand them if we are to understand what it means to be American. This is where we are now, learning about and becoming sensitive to the multiplicity and complexity of the ethnic and racial cultures that have shaped the America we know today and that will mold our nation in the future.

Reading 1 is by Afro DZ ak, the poet/musician and educator presently working and performing in the Boston area.

Reading 2, the American Anthropological Association "Statement on Race," introduces some social scientists' recent position on the theoretical and practical questions surrounding our understanding and use of race as a category.

Reading 3 provides a general perspective on ethnic identity and explores several related issues. John Hope Franklin discusses historical changes in Americans' attitudes about and treatment of immigrants and ethnic groups, illuminating the distance between the American ideal that "all men are created equal" and the reality of exclusion. The fourth article, by then-Senator Barack Obama, focuses on our need and ability to form a more perfect union, as we promised in the U.S. Constitution. The following article, by David von Drehle, discusses how central slavery was to the building of the United States, and that both Northerners and Southerners profited from and paid for slavery. The sixth article, by James Baldwin, is of his leaving America and his sense of betrayal of those he loved.

Readings 7 and 8 describe the effects of **assimilation,** the process by which minority groups—under overt or subtle pressure from the majority group—abandoned the unique features of their former cultures and adapted to the values and norms of European American culture, which was dominated by the Anglo-Protestant ethic. In Grace Paley's story, Jewish immigrant parents see that their daughter's selection as the narrator of her public school's Christmas play is a difficult but necessary part of assimilation into American society. Polingaysi Qoyawayma, renamed Elizabeth Q. White by White missionaries, tells of a similar conflict when she returns for a visit to her traditional Hopi parents after her conversion at the Christian mission; her rejection of her parents' beliefs about the spiritual power of nature is painful to all three members of her family.

In Reading 9, by Darryl Fears, "People of Color Who Never Felt They Were Black," he describes the experience of many immigrants from Latin America and Brazil who were never considered Black until they entered the United States. Similarly, in her interview with John Langston Gwaltney in Reading 10, Rosa Wakefield describes what being Black means to her, but her contemplation of the differences between Blacks and Whites and among Blacks exposes how complex and subjective ethnic identification is.

Reading 11 by Thomson American Health Consultant considers the debate concerning racial profiling in a doctor's office:essential or dangerous to the patient's health?

Many second-generation Americans struggle to understand their distinctive identity, achieving self-acceptance in different ways. Shanlon Wu (Reading 12) tells of his lifelong search for positive Asian American role models, none of which really fit him until he realizes he must mold his own life.

Readings 13 and 14 explore the impact of recent population changes on American culture and society. As a Hindu, Bharati Mukherjee discusses the values she has developed as a naturalized American and how they differ from those held by many Indians and Indian Americans. Elizabeth Gordon addresses the issue of racial intermarriage. She remembers growing up in the hills of West Virginia with a White father and a Vietnamese mother.

Final Readings 15 and 16 directly address the complexities of living in our diverse nation. Eugenia Kaw writes of Asian American women and cosmetic surgery—choosing to erase racial markers, such as distinctively Asian eyes and nose. Then Chicano poet Carlos Cumpián reflects on Thanksgivings past and present.

Reading 17 ("Race in a Genetic World") explores how recent DNA uses have situated themselves in the debate on the meaning of race, amongst scientists, politicians, and the public. Finally, in Reading 18, K. N. Maillard, a member of the Seminole nation of Oklahoma, writes of the long-held debate over who is a "real Indian" and how skin color can affect a nation's politics.

By the time you have finished the readings in Part I, you will have some sense of the elements most central to ethnic identity and may have thought about your family and your life in light of those factors.

Racism
multidential
underline

1

Just 'Cause I'm Mixed

AFRO DZ ak (PETER SHUNGU)

Just 'Cause I'm Mixed, that don't mean that
*   I'm mixed up*
Inherently confused or I need to be fixed up
Just 'Cause I'm Mixed, that don't mean I'm a
*   mule*
So don't call me mulatto *thinkin it's cool*
Just 'Cause I'm Mixed, that don't mean I'm
*   adopted*
Yes, she's white, and yes, she's my biological
*   mama*
But whether or not I was adopted, you ain't
*   got the right*
To stare or make comments 'cause my mother
*   is white*
Just 'Cause I'm Mixed, that don't mean I'm
*   'not Black'*
Cuz the concept we can have only one iden-
*   tity is wack*
And I stand proudly with all my people of
*   color*
Painting broad concepts of 'sister' and
*   'brother'*
Just 'Cause I'm Mixed, that don't mean I'm
*   ill-conceived*   *look up*
As words like miscegenation *would have you*
*   believe*
Just 'Cause I'm Mixed, that don't mean I'm
*   ashamed*
Cuz the 'race' of my mom and my dad ain't
*   the same*
Just 'Cause I'm Mixed, that don't mean I'm
*   predictable*
So sayin 'mixed people all do this' or 'mixed
*   people are all like that' is despicable*
Just 'Cause I'm Mixed, and I rock a big fro
Don't mean I'm Maxwell, Lenny Kravitz, Bob
*   Marley, Jimi Hendrix, or 'that guy in that*
*   commercial for jeans, beer, or cologne'*
Just 'Cause I'm Mixed, that don't mean that
*   I'm 'Other'*
Miscellaneous, Oreo, or the 'half & half
*   brother'*

© Eric Whitney.

Just 'Cause I'm Mixed, that don't mean rac-
*   ism has ended*
As some ignorant conservative politicians
*   have pretended*
Just 'Cause I'm Mixed, that don't mean that
*   I'm perfect*
Like some kind of 'hybrid vigor*' has made my*
*   genes superior to mere earthlings*
Cuz being Multiracial *is a blessing and a curse*
It's better and it's worse, it's last and it's first
It's nothing and it's everything, it's yin and
*   it's yang*
It's the apocalypse, the creation, and the big
*   bang*
It's a subject that inspires me to write
It's a commonality which has helped me unite
With other Mixed people who can relate all
*   across the earth*
But being Mixed does not define my personal
*   worth*   [2011]

Understanding the Reading

1. Why does the poet defend his being "mixed"?
2. Discuss "Cuz the concept we can have only one identity is wack."
3. Do you recognize the stereotypes to which he is referring? Give examples.
4. Discuss "Cuz being Multiracial is a blessing and a curse."

Suggestions for Responding

1. Speak to friends who are multiracial; bring ideas to the class.
2. Research "miscegenation" and its history in the United States. ◆

2

Watch for the chain
rate of Being

American Anthropological Association "Statement on Race"

The following statement was adopted by the Executive Board of the American Anthropological Association, acting on a draft prepared by a committee of representative American anthropologists. It does not reflect a consensus of all members of the AAA, as individuals vary in their approaches to the study of "race." We believe that it represents generally the contemporary thinking and scholarly positions of a majority of anthropologists.

In the United States both scholars and the general public have been conditioned to viewing human races as natural and separate divisions within the human species based on visible physical differences. With the vast expansion of scientific knowledge in this century, however, it has become clear that human populations are not unambiguous, clearly demarcated, biologically distinct groups. Evidence from the analysis of genetics (e.g., DNA) indicates that most physical variation, about 94%, lies *within* so-called racial groups. Conventional geographic "racial" groupings differ from one another only in about 6% of their genes. This means that there is greater variation within "racial" groups than between them. In neighboring populations there is much overlapping of genes and their phenotypic (physical) expressions. Throughout history whenever different groups have come into contact, they have interbred. The continued sharing of genetic materials has maintained all of humankind as a single species.

Physical variations in any given trait tend to occur gradually rather than abruptly over geographic areas. And because physical traits are inherited independently of one another, knowing the range of one trait does not predict the presence of others. For example, skin color varies largely from light in the temperate areas in the north to dark in the tropical areas in the south; its intensity is not related to nose shape or hair texture. Dark skin may be associated with frizzy or kinky hair or curly or wavy or straight hair, all of which are found among different indigenous peoples in tropical regions. These facts render any attempt to establish lines of division among biological populations both arbitrary and subjective.

Historical research has shown that the idea of "race" has always carried more meanings than mere physical differences; indeed, physical variations in the human species have no meaning except the social ones that humans put on them. Today scholars in many fields argue that "race" as it is understood in the United States of America was a social mechanism invented during the 18th century to refer to those populations brought together in colonial America: the English and other European settlers, the conquered Indian peoples, and those peoples of Africa brought in to provide slave labor.

From its inception, this modern concept of "race" was modeled after an ancient theorem of the Great Chain of Being, which posited natural categories on a hierarchy established by God or nature. Thus "race" was a mode of classification linked specifically to peoples in the colonial situation. It subsumed a growing ideology of inequality devised to rationalize European attitudes and treatment of the conquered and enslaved peoples. Proponents of slavery in particular during the 19th century used "race" to justify the retention of slavery. The ideology magnified the differences among Europeans, Africans, and Indians, established a rigid hierarchy of socially exclusive categories, underscored and bolstered unequal rank and status differences, and provided the rationalization that the inequality was natural or God-given. The different physical traits of African-Americans and Indians became markers or symbols of their status differences.

As they were constructing U.S. society, leaders among European-Americans fabricated the cultural/behavioral characteristics associated with each "race," linking superior traits with Europeans and negative and inferior ones to blacks and Indians. Numerous arbitrary and fictitious beliefs about the different peoples were institutionalized and deeply embedded in American thought.

Early in the 19th century the growing fields of science began to reflect the public consciousness about human differences. Differences among the "racial" categories were projected to their greatest extreme when the argument was posed that Africans, Indians, and Europeans were separate species, with Africans the least human and closer taxonomically to apes.

Ultimately "race" as an ideology about human differences was subsequently spread to other areas of the world. It became a strategy for dividing, ranking, and controlling colonized people used by colonial powers everywhere. But it was not limited to the colonial situation. In the latter part of the 19th century it was employed by Europeans to rank one another and to justify social, economic, and political inequalities among their peoples. During World War II, the Nazis under Adolf Hitler enjoined the expanded ideology of "race" and "racial" differences and took them to a logical end: the extermination of 11 million people of "inferior races" (e.g., Jews, Gypsies, Africans, homosexuals, and so forth) and other unspeakable brutalities of the Holocaust.

"Race" thus evolved as a worldview, a body of prejudgments that distorts our ideas about human differences and group behavior. Racial beliefs constitute myths about the diversity in the human species and about the abilities and behavior of people homogenized into "racial" categories. The myths fused behavior and physical features together in the public mind, impeding our comprehension of both biological variations and cultural behavior, implying that both are genetically determined. Racial myths bear no relationship to the reality of human capabilities or behavior. Scientists today find that reliance on such folk beliefs about human differences in research has led to countless errors.

At the end of the 20th century, we now understand that human cultural behavior is learned, conditioned into infants beginning at birth, and always subject to modification. No human is born with a built-in culture or language. Our temperaments, dispositions, and personalities, regardless of genetic propensies, are developed within sets of meanings and values that we call "culture." Studies of infant and early childhood learning and behavior attest to the reality of our cultures in forming who we are.

It is a basic tenet of anthropological knowledge that all normal human beings have the capacity to learn any cultural behavior. The American experience with immigrants from hundreds of different language and cultural backgrounds who have acquired some version of American culture traits and behavior is the clearest evidence of this fact. Moreover, people of all physical variations have learned different cultural behaviors and continue to do so as modern transportation moves millions of immigrants around the world.

How people have been accepted and treated within the context of a given society or culture has a direct impact on how they perform in that society. The "racial" worldview was invented to assign some groups to perpetual low status, while others were permitted access to privilege, power, and wealth. The tragedy in the United States has been that the policies and practices stemming from this worldview succeeded all too well in constructing unequal populations among Europeans, Native Americans, and peoples of African descent. Given what we know about the capacity of normal humans to achieve and function within any culture, we conclude that present-day inequalities between so-called "racial" groups are not consequences of their biological inheritance but products of historical and contemporary social, economic, educational, and political circumstances.   [1998]

Understanding the Reading

1. How do anthropologists argue that human populations are never biologically distinct groups?
2. What was the Great Chain of Being?
3. How did we ever come to believe in the superiority and inferiority of races?

1. Have a debate on whether U.S. society should collect data on "racial" and ethnic groups. ✦

3

Ethnicity in American Life: The Historical Perspective

JOHN HOPE FRANKLIN

The United Slates is unique in the ethnic composition of its population. No other country in the world can point to such a variety of cultural, racial, religious, and national backgrounds in its population. It was one of the salient features in the early history of this country: and it would continue to be so down into the twentieth century. From virtually every corner of the globe they came—some enthusiastically and some quite reluctantly. Britain and every part of the continent of Europe provided prospective Americans by the millions. Africa and Asia gave up great throngs. Other areas of the New World saw inhabitants desert their own lands to seek their fortunes in the colossus to the North. Those who came voluntarily were attracted by the prospect of freedom of religion, freedom from want, and freedom from various forms of oppression. Those who were forced to come were offered the consolation that if they were white they would some day inherit the earth, and if they were black they would some day gather their reward in the Christian heaven.

One of the interesting and significant features of this coming together of peoples of many tongues and races and cultures was that the backgrounds out of which they came would soon be minimized and that the process by which they evolved into Americans would be of paramount importance. Hector St. Jean de Creve-coeur sought to describe this process in 1782 when he answered his own question, "What, then, is the American, this new man?" He said, "He is either an European, or the descendant of an European, hence that strange mixture of blood, which you will find in no other country. . . . He is an American, who, leaving behind him all his ancient prejudices and manners, receives new ones from the new mode of the life he has embraced, the new government he obeys, and the new rank he holds. He becomes an American by being received in the broad lap of our great *Alma Mater.* Here individuals of all nations are melted into a new race of men, whose labours and posterity will one day cause great changes in the world."

This was one of the earliest expressions of the notion that the process of Americanization involved the creation of an entirely new mode of life that would replace the ethnic backgrounds of those who were a part of the process. It contained some imprecisions and inaccuracies that would, in time, become a part of the lore or myth of the vaunted melting pot and would grossly misrepresent the crucial factor of ethnicity in American life. It ignored the tenacity with which the Pennsylvania Dutch held onto their language, religion, and way of life. It overlooked the way in which the Swedes of New Jersey remained Swedes and the manner in which the French Huguenots of New York and Charleston held onto their own past as though it was the source of all light and life. It described a process that in a distant day would gag at the notion that Irish Catholics could be assimilated on the broad lap of Alma Mater or that Asians could be seated on the basis of equality at the table of the Great American Feast.

By suggesting that only Europeans were involved in the process of becoming Americans, Crevecoeur pointedly ruled out three quarters of a million blacks already in the country who, along with their progeny, would be regarded as ineligible to become Americans for at least another two centuries. To be sure, the number of persons of African descent would increase enormously, but the view of their ineligibility for Americanization would be very slow to change. And when such a change occurred, even if it merely granted freedom from bondage, the change would be made most reluctantly and without any suggestion that freedom qualified one for equality on the broad lap of Alma Mater. It was beyond the conception of Crevecoeur, as it was indeed beyond the conception of the founding fathers, that Negroes, slave or free, could become true Americans, enjoying that fellowship in a common enterprise about which Crevecoeur spoke so warmly. It was as though Crevecoeur was arguing that ethnicity, where persons of African descent were concerned, was either so powerful or so unattractive as to make their assimilation entirely impossible or so insignificant as to make it entirely undesirable. In any case Americanization in the late eighteenth century was a precious commodity to be cherished and enjoyed only by a select group of persons of European descent.

One must admit, therefore, that at the time of the birth of the new nation there was no clear-cut disposition to welcome into the American family persons of any and all ethnic backgrounds. Only Europeans were invited to fight for independence. And when the patriots at long last relented and gave persons of African descent a chance to fight, the concession was made with great reluctance and after much equivocation and soul-searching. Only Europeans were regarded as full citizens in the new states and in the new nation. And when the founding fathers wrote the Constitution of the United States, they did not seem troubled by the distinctions on the basis of ethnic differences that the Constitution implied.

If the principle of ethnic exclusiveness was propounded so early and so successfully in the history of the United States, it is not surprising that it would, in time, become the basis for questioning the ethnic backgrounds of large numbers of prospective Americans, even Europeans. Thus, in 1819, a Jewish immigrant was chilled to hear a bystander refer to him and his companion as "more damned emigrants." A decade later there began a most scathing and multifaceted attack on the Catholic church. On two counts the church was a bad influence. First, its principal recruits were the Irish, the "very dregs" of the Old World social order; and secondly, its doctrine of papal supremacy ran counter to the idea of the political and religious independence of the United States. Roman Catholics, Protestant Americans warned, were engaged in a widespread conspiracy to subvert American institutions, through parochial schools, the Catholic press, immoral convents, and a sinister design to control the West by flooding it with Catholic settlers. The burning of convents and churches and

the killing of Catholics themselves were indications of how deeply many Americans felt about religious and cultural differences for which they had a distaste and suspicion that bordered on paranoia.

Soon the distaste for the foreign-born became almost universal, with Roman Catholics themselves sharing in the hostility to those who followed them to the new Republic. Some expressed fear of the poverty and criminality that accompanied each wave of immigrants. Some felt that those newly arrived from abroad were a threat to republican freedom. Some saw in the ethnic differences of the newcomers an immediate danger to the moral standards of Puritan America. Some feared the competition that newcomers posed in the labor market. Some became convinced that the ideal of a national homogeneity would disappear with the influx of so many unassimilable elements. Soon, nativist societies sprang up all across the land, and they found national expression in 1850 in a new organization called the Order of the Star Spangled Banner. With its slogan, "America for Americans," the order, which became the organizational basis for the Know-Nothing party, engendered a fear through its preachments that caused many an American to conclude that his country was being hopelessly subverted by the radical un-Americanism of the great variety of ethnic strains that were present in the United States.

If there was some ambivalence regarding the ethnic diversity of white immigrants before the Civil War, it was dispelled by the view that prevailed regarding immigrants in the post-Civil War years. The "old" immigrants, so the argument went, were at least assimilable and had "entered practically every line of activity in nearly every part of the country." Even those who had been non-English speaking had mingled freely with native Americans and had therefore been quickly assimilated. Not so with the "new" immigrants who came after 1880. They "congregated together in sections apart from native Americans and the older immigrants to such an extent that assimilation had been slow." Small wonder that they were different. Small wonder that they were barely assimilable. They came from Austro-Hungary, Italy, Russia, Greece, Rumania, and Turkey. They dressed differently, spoke in unfamiliar tongues, and clung to strange, if not exotic customs. It did not matter that Bohemians, Moravians, and Finns had lower percentages of illiteracy than had the Irish and Germans or that Jews had a higher percentage of skilled laborers than any group except the Scots. Nor did it matter that, in fact, the process of assimilation for the so-called "new" group was about as rapid as that of the so-called "old" group.

What did matter was that the new nativism was stronger and more virulent than any anti-immigration forces or groups of the early nineteenth century and that these groups were determined either to drive from the shores those who were different or to isolate them so that they could not contaminate American society. Old-stock Americans began to organize to preserve American institutions and the American way of life. Those who had been here for five years or a decade designated themselves as old-stock Americans and joined in the attack on those recently arrived. If the cult of Anglo-Saxon superiority was all but pervasive, those who were not born into the cult regarded themselves as honorary members. Thus, they could celebrate with as much feeling as any the virtues of Anglo-Saxon institutions and could condemn as vehemently as any those ideas and practices that were not strictly Anglo-Saxon. Whenever possible they joined the American Protective Association and the Immigrant Restriction League; and in so doing they sold their own ethnicity for the obscurity that a pseudoassimilation brought. But in the end, they would be less than successful. The arrogance and presumption of the Anglo-Saxon complex was not broad enough to embrace the Jews of eastern Europe or the Bohemians of central Europe or the Turks of the Middle East. The power and drive of the Anglo-Saxon forces would prevail; and those who did not belong would be compelled to console themselves by extolling the virtues of cultural pluralism.

By that time—near the end of the nineteenth century—the United States had articulated quite clearly its exalted standards of ethnicity. They were standards that accepted Anglo-Saxons as the norm, placed other whites on what may be called "ethnic probation," and excluded from serious consideration the Japanese, Chinese, and Negroes. It was not difficult to deal harshly with the Chinese and Japanese when they began

to enter the United States in considerable numbers in the post-Civil War years. They simply did not meet the standards that the arbiters of American ethnicity had promulgated. They were different in race, religion, language, and public and private morality. They had to be excluded; and eventually they were.

The presence of persons of African descent, almost from the beginning, had helped whites to define ethnicity and to establish and maintain the conditions by which it could be controlled. If their color and race, their condition of servitude, and their generally degraded position did not set them apart, the laws and customs surrounding them more than accomplished that feat. Whether in Puritan Massachusetts or cosmopolitan New York or Anglican South Carolina, the colonists declared that Negroes, slave or free, did not and could not belong to the society of equal human beings. Thus, the newly arrived Crevecoeur could be as blind to the essential humanity of Negroes as the patriots who tried to keep them out of the Continental Army. They were not a part of America, these new men. And in succeeding years their presence would do more to define ethnicity than the advent of several scores of millions of Europeans.

It was not enough for Americans, already somewhat guilt-ridden for maintaining slavery in a free society, to exclude blacks from American society on the basis of race and condition of servitude. They proceeded from that point to argue that Negroes were inferior morally, intellectually, and physically. Even as he reviewed the remarkable accomplishments of Benjamin Banneker, surveyor, almanacker, mathematician, and clockmaker, Thomas Jefferson had serious doubts about the mental capabilities of Africans, and he expressed these doubts to his European friends. What Jefferson speculated about at the end of the eighteenth century became indisputable dogma within a decade after his death.

In the South every intellectual, legal, and religious resource was employed in the task of describing the condition of Negroes in such a way as to make them the least attractive human beings on the face of the earth. Slavery was not only the natural lot of blacks, the slaveowners argued, but it was in accordance with God's will that they should be kept in slavery. As one sanctimonious divine put it, "We feel that the souls of our slaves are a solemn trust and we shall strive to present them faultless and complete before the presence of God. . . . However the world may judge us in connection with our institution of slavery, we conscientiously believe it to be a great missionary institution—one arranged by God, as He arranges all moral and religious influences of the world so that the good may be brought out of seeming evil, and a blessing wrung out of every form of the curse." It was a difficult task that the owners of slaves set for themselves. Slaves had brought with them only heathenism, immorality, profligacy, and irresponsibility. They possessed neither the mental capacity nor the moral impulse to improve themselves. Only if their sponsors—those to whom were entrusted not only their souls but their bodies—were fully committed to their improvement could they take even the slightest, halting steps toward civilization.

What began as a relatively moderate justification for slavery soon became a vigorous, aggressive defense of the institution. Slavery, to the latter-day defenders, was the cornerstone of the republican edifice. To a governor of South Carolina, it was the greatest of all the great blessings which a kind Providence had bestowed upon the glorious region of the South. It was, indeed, one of the remarkable coincidences of history that such a favored institution had found such a favored creature as the African to give slavery the high value that was placed on it. A childlike race, prone to docility and manageable in every respect, the African was the ideal subject for the slave role. Slaveholders had to work hard to be worthy of this great Providential blessing.

Nothing that Negroes could do or say could change or seriously affect this view. They might graduate from college, as John Russwurm did in 1826, or they might write a most scathing attack against slavery, as David Walker did in 1829. It made no difference. They might teach in an all-white college, as Charles B. Reason did in New York in the 1850s, or publish a newspaper, as Frederick Douglass did during that same decade. Their racial and cultural backgrounds disqualified them from becoming American citizens. They could even argue in favor of their capacities and potentialities, as Henry Highland Garnet did, or they might argue their right to fight for union and freedom, as 186,000 did in the Civil

War. Still, it made no sense for white Americans to give serious consideration to their arguments and their actions. They were beyond the veil, as the Jews had been beyond the veil in the barbaric and bigoted communities of eastern Europe.

The views regarding Negroes that had been so carefully developed to justify and defend slavery would not disappear with emancipation. To those who had developed such views and to the vast numbers who subscribed to them, they were much too valid to be discarded simply because the institution of slavery had collapsed. In fact, if Negroes were heathens and barbarians and intellectual imbeciles in slavery, they were hardly qualified to function as equals in a free society. And any effort to impose them on a free society should be vigorously and relentlessly resisted, even if it meant that a new and subordinate place for them had to be created.

When Americans set out to create such a place for the four million freedmen after the Civil War, they found that it was convenient to put their formulation in the context of the ethnic factors that militated against complete assimilation. To do it this way seemed more fitting, perhaps even more palatable, for the white members of a so-called free society. And they had some experience on which to rely. In an earlier day it had been the Irish or the Germans or the free Negroes who presented problems of assimilation. They were different in various ways and did not seem to make desirable citizens. In time the Irish, Germans, and other Europeans made it and were accepted on the broad lap of Alma Mater. But not the free Negroes, who continued to suffer disabilities even in the North in the years just before the Civil War. Was this the key to the solution of the postwar problems? Perhaps it was. After all, Negroes had always been a group apart in Boston, New York, Philadelphia, and other northern cities. They all lived together in one part of the city—especially if they could find no other place to live. They had their own churches—after the whites drove them out of theirs. They had their own schools—after they were excluded from the schools attended by whites. They had their own social organizations—after the whites barred them from theirs.

If Negroes possessed so many ethnic characteristics such as living in the same community, having their own churches, schools, and social clubs, and perhaps other agencies of cohesion, that was all very well. They even seemed "happier with their own kind," some patronizing observers remarked. They were like the Germans or the Irish or the Italians or the Jews. They had so much in common and so much to preserve. There was one significant difference, however. For Europeans, the ethnic factors that brought a particular group together actually eased the task of assimilation and, in many ways, facilitated the process of assimilation, particularly as hostile elements sought to disorient them in their drive toward full citizenship. And, in time, they achieved it.

For Negroes, however, such was not the case. They had been huddled together in northern ghettoes since the eighteenth century. They had had their own churches since 1792 and their own schools since 1800. And this separateness, this ostracism, was supported and enforced by the full majesty of the law, state and federal, just to make certain that Negroes did, indeed, preserve their ethnicity! And as they preserved their ethnicity—all too frequently as they looked down the barrel of a policeman's pistol or a militiaman's shotgun—full citizenship seemed many light years away. They saw other ethnic groups pass them by, one by one, and take their places in the sacred Order of the Star Spangled Banner, the American Protective Association, the Knights of the Ku Klux Klan—not always fully assimilated but vehemently opposed to the assimilation of Negroes. The ethnic grouping that was a way station, a temporary resting place for Europeans as they became Americans, proved to be a terminal point for blacks who found it virtually impossible to become Americans in any real sense.

There was an explanation or at least a justification for this. The federal government and the state governments had tried to force Negroes into full citizenship and had tried to legislate them into equality with the whites. This was not natural and could not possibly succeed. Negroes had not made it because they were not fit, the social Darwinists[1] said. Negroes were beasts, Charles Carroll declared somewhat inelegantly. "Stateways cannot change folkways," William Graham Sumner, the distinguished scholar, philosophized. The first forty years of Negro freedom had been a failure, said John R. Commons,

one of the nation's leading economists. This so-called failure was widely acknowledged in the country as northerners of every rank and description acquiesced, virtually without a murmur of objection, to the southern settlement of the race problem characterized by disfranchisement, segregation, and discrimination.

Here was a new and exotic form of ethnicity. It was to be seen in the badges of inferiority and the symbols of racial degradation that sprang up in every sector of American life—in the exclusion from the polling places with its specious justification that Negroes were unfit to participate in the sacred rite of voting; the back stairway or the freight elevator to public places; the separate, miserable railway car; the separate and hopelessly inferior school; and even the Jim Crow[2] cemetery. Ethnic considerations had never been so important in the shaping of public policy. They had never before been used by the American government to define the role and place of other groups in American society. The United States had labored hard to create order out of its chaotic and diverse ethnic backgrounds. Having begun by meekly suggesting the difficulty in assimilating all groups into one great society, it had acknowledged failure by ruling out one group altogether, quite categorically, and frequently by law, solely on the basis of race.

It could not achieve this without doing irreparable harm to the early notions of the essential unity of America and Americans. The sentiments that promoted the disfranchisement and segregation of Negroes also encouraged the infinite varieties of discrimination against Jews, Armenians, Turks, Japanese, and Chinese. The conscious effort to degrade a particular ethnic group reflects a corrosive quality that dulls the sensitivities of both the perpetrators and the victims. It calls forth venomous hatreds and crude distinctions in high places as well as low places. It can affect the quality of mind of even the most cultivated scholar and place him in a position scarcely distinguishable from the Klansman or worse. It was nothing out of the ordinary, therefore, that at a dinner in honor of the winner of one of Harvard's most coveted prizes, Professor Barrett Wendell warned that if a Negro or a Jew ever won the prize the dinner would have to be canceled.

By the time that the Statue of Liberty was dedicated in 1886 the words of Emma Lazarus on the base of it had a somewhat hollow ring. Could anyone seriously believe that the poor, tired, huddled masses "yearning to breathe free," were really welcome here? This was a land where millions of black human beings whose ancestors had been here for centuries were consistently treated as pariahs and untouchables! What interpretation could anyone place on the sentiments expressed on the statue except that the country had no real interest in or sympathy for the downtrodden unless they were white and preferably Anglo-Saxon? It was a disillusioning experience for some newcomers to discover that their own ethnic background was a barrier to success in their adopted land. It was a searing and shattering experience for Negroes to discover over and over again that three centuries of toil and loyalty were nullified by the misfortune of their own degraded ethnic background.

In the fullness of time—in the twentieth century—the nation would confront the moment of truth regarding ethnicity as a factor in its own historical development. Crevecoeur's words would have no real significance. The words of the Declaration of Independence would have no real meaning. The words of Emma Lazarus would not ring true. All such sentiments would be put to the severe test of public policy and private deeds and would be found wanting. The Ku Klux Klan would challenge the moral and human dignity of Jews, Catholics, and Negroes. The quotas of the new immigration laws would define ethnic values in terms of race and national origin. The restrictive covenants[3] would arrogate to a select group of bigots the power of determining what races or ethnic groups should live in certain houses or whether, indeed, they should have any houses at all in which to live. If some groups finally made it through the escape hatch and arrived at the point of acceptance, it was on the basis of race, now defined with sufficient breadth to include all or most peoples who were not of African descent.

By that time ethnicity in American life would come to have a special, clearly definable meaning. Its meaning would be descriptive of that group of people vaguely defined in the federal census returns as "others" or "non-whites." It would have something in common with that magnificent term "cultural pluralism," the consolation prize for those who were not and could not be assimilated. It would signify the same groping for respectability that describes that group of people who live in what is euphemistically called "the inner city." It would represent a rather earnest search for a hidden meaning that would make it seem a bit more palatable and surely more sophisticated than something merely racial. But in 1969 even a little child would know what ethnicity had come to mean.

In its history, ethnicity, in its true sense, has extended and continues to extend beyond race. At times it has meant language, customs, religion, national origin. It has also meant race; and, to some, it has always meant only race. It had already begun to have a racial connotation in the eighteenth century. In the nineteenth century, it had a larger racial component, even as other factors continued to loom large. In the present century, as these other factors have receded in importance, racial considerations have come to have even greater significance. If the history of ethnicity has meant anything at all during the last three centuries, it has meant the gradual but steady retreat from the broad and healthy regard for cultural and racial differences to a narrow, counter-productive concept of differences in terms of whim, intolerance, and racial prejudice. We have come full circle. The really acceptable American is still that person whom Crevecoeur described almost two hundred years ago. But the true American, acceptable or not, is that person who seeks to act out his role in terms of his regard for human qualities irrespective of race. One of the great tragedies of American life at the beginning was that ethnicity was defined too narrowly. One of the great tragedies of today is that this continues to be the case. One can only hope that the nation and its people will all some day soon come to reassess ethnicity in terms of the integrity of the man rather than in terms of the integrity of the race.   [1989]

Notes

1. SOCIAL DARWINISM: The theory that applied Darwin's theory of evolution, "survival of the fittest," to society; it assumed that upper classes were naturally superior, and the failure of the lower classes was the result of

their natural inferiority, not of social policies and practices.

2. JIM CROW: Laws and practices, especially in the South, that separated Blacks and Whites and enforced the subordination of Blacks.

3. RESTRICTIVE COVENANTS: Codes prohibiting members of some groups—often Blacks, Jews, and Asians—from buying real estate in certain areas.

Understanding the Reading

1. Today, why do we find de Crevecoeur's 1782 definition of "the American, this new man" inadequate or inappropriate?

2. How did the principle of ethnic exclusion that omitted people of African descent affect later immigrant groups in the nineteenth century?

3. What does nativism mean?

4. How was the exclusion of African Americans from American society justified?

5. How was it maintained?

6. How did the treatment of African Americans affect other groups in the twentieth century?

Suggestions for Responding

1. According to Franklin, America has not lived up to its ideals. Do you think his pessimistic views are justified? What arguments would you offer to support or refute his analysis?

2. Is the "really acceptable American" today still that person whom de Crevecoeur described, as Franklin claims? Why or why not? ✦

4

Toward a More Perfect Union

BARACK OBAMA

"We the people, in order to form a more perfect union."

Two hundred and twenty one years ago, in a hall that still stands across the street, a group of men gathered and, with these simple words, launched America's improbable experiment in democracy. Farmers and scholars; statesmen and patriots who had traveled across an ocean to escape tyranny and persecution finally made real their declaration of independence at a Philadelphia convention that lasted through the spring of 1787.

The document they produced was eventually signed but ultimately unfinished. It was stained by this nation's original sin of slavery, a question that divided the colonies and brought the convention to a stalemate until the founders chose to allow the slave trade to continue for at least twenty more years, and to leave any final resolution to future generations.

Of course, the answer to the slavery question was already embedded within our Constitution—a Constitution that had at its very core the ideal of equal citizenship under the law; a Constitution that promised its people liberty, and justice, and a union that could be and should be perfected over time.

And yet words on a parchment would not be enough to deliver slaves from bondage, or provide men and women of every color and creed their full rights and obligations as citizens of the United States. What would be needed were Americans in successive generations who were willing to do their part—through protests and struggle, on the streets and in the courts, through a civil war and civil disobedience and always at great risk—to narrow that gap between the promise of our ideals and the reality of their time.

This was one of the tasks we set forth at the beginning of this campaign—to continue the long march of those who came before us, a march for a more just, more equal, more free, more caring and more prosperous America. I chose to run for the presidency at this moment in history because I believe deeply that we cannot solve the challenges of our time unless we solve them together—unless we perfect our union by understanding that we may have different stories, but we hold common hopes; that we may not look the same and we may not have come from the same place, but we all want to move in the same direction—towards a better future for our children and our grandchildren.

This belief comes from my unyielding faith in the decency and generosity of the American people. But it also comes from my own American story.

I am the son of a black man from Kenya and a white woman from Kansas. I was raised with the help of a white grandfather who survived a Depression to serve in Patton's Army during World War II and a white grandmother who worked on a bomber assembly line at Fort Leavenworth while he was overseas. I've gone to some of the best schools in America and lived in one of the world's poorest nations. I am married to a black American who carries within her the blood of slaves and slaveowners—an inheritance we pass on to our two precious daughters. I have brothers, sisters, nieces, nephews, uncles and cousins, of every race and every hue, scattered across three continents, and for as long as I live, I will never forget that in no other country on Earth is my story even possible.

It's a story that hasn't made me the most conventional candidate. But it is a story that has seared into my genetic makeup the idea that this nation is more than the sum of its parts—that out of many, we are truly one.

Throughout the first year of this campaign, against all predictions to the contrary, we saw how hungry the American people were for this message of unity. Despite the temptation to view my candidacy through a purely racial lens, we won commanding victories in states with some of the whitest populations in the country. In South Carolina, where the Confederate Flag still flies, we built a powerful coalition of African Americans and white Americans.

This is not to say that race has not been an issue in the campaign. At various stages in the campaign, some commentators have deemed me either "too black" or "not black enough." We saw racial tensions bubble to the surface during the week before the South Carolina primary. The press has scoured every exit poll for the latest evidence of racial polarization, not just in terms of white and black, but black and brown as well.

And yet, it has only been in the last couple of weeks that the discussion of race in this campaign has taken a particularly divisive turn.

On one end of the spectrum, we've heard the implication that my candidacy is somehow an exercise in affirmative action; that it's based solely on the desire of wide-eyed liberals to purchase racial reconciliation on the cheap. On the other end, we've heard my former pastor,

Reverend Jeremiah Wright, use incendiary language to express views that have the potential not only to widen the racial divide, but views that denigrate both the greatness and the goodness of our nation; that rightly offend white and black alike.

I have already condemned, in unequivocal terms, the statements of Reverend Wright that have caused such controversy. For some, nagging questions remain. Did I know him to be an occasionally fierce critic of American domestic and foreign policy? Of course. Did I ever hear him make remarks that could be considered controversial while I sat in church? Yes. Did I strongly disagree with many of his political views? Absolutely—just as I'm sure many of you have heard remarks from your pastors, priests, or rabbis with which you strongly disagreed.

But the remarks that have caused this recent firestorm weren't simply controversial. They weren't simply a religious leader's effort to speak out against perceived injustice. Instead, they expressed a profoundly distorted view of this country—a view that sees white racism as endemic, and that elevates what is wrong with America above all that we know is right with America; a view that sees the conflicts in the Middle East as rooted primarily in the actions of stalwart allies like Israel, instead of emanating from the perverse and hateful ideologies of radical Islam.

As such, Reverend Wright's comments were not only wrong but divisive, divisive at a time when we need unity; racially charged at a time when we need to come together to solve a set of monumental problems—two wars, a terrorist threat, a falling economy, a chronic health care crisis and potentially devastating climate change; problems that are neither black or white or Latino or Asian, but rather problems that confront us all.

Given my background, my politics, and my professed values and ideals, there will no doubt be those for whom my statements of condemnation are not enough. Why associate myself with Reverend Wright in the first place, they may ask? Why not join another church? And I confess that if all that I knew of Reverend Wright were the snippets of those sermons that have run in an endless loop on the television and YouTube, or if Trinity United Church of Christ conformed to the caricatures being peddled by some commentators, there is no doubt that I would react in much the same way.

But the truth is, that isn't all that I know of the man. The man I met more than twenty years ago is a man who helped introduce me to my Christian faith, a man who spoke to me about our obligations to love one another; to care for the sick and lift up the poor. He is a man who served his country as a U.S. Marine; who has studied and lectured at some of the finest universities and seminaries in the country, and who for over thirty years led a church that serves the community by doing God's work here on Earth—by housing the homeless, ministering to the needy, providing day care services and scholarships and prison ministries, and reaching out to those suffering from HIV/AIDS.

In my first book, *Dreams from My Father*, I described the experience of my first service at Trinity:

"People began to shout, to rise from their seats and clap and cry out, a forceful wind carrying the reverend's voice up into the rafters. . . . And in that single note—hope!—I heard something else; at the foot of that cross, inside the thousands of churches across the city, I imagined the stories of ordinary black people merging with the stories of David and Goliath, Moses and Pharaoh, the Christians in the lion's den, Ezekiel's field of dry bones. Those stories—of survival, and freedom, and hope—became our story, my story; the blood that had spilled was our blood, the tears our tears; until this black church, on this bright day, seemed once more a vessel carrying the story of a people into future generations and into a larger world. Our trials and triumphs became at once unique and universal, black and more than black; in chronicling our journey, the stories and songs gave us a means to reclaim memories that we didn't need to feel shame about . . . memories that all people might study and cherish—and with which we could start to rebuild."

That has been my experience at Trinity. Like other predominantly black churches across the country, Trinity embodies the black community in its entirety—the doctor and the welfare mom, the model student and the former gang-banger. Like other black churches, Trinity's services are full of raucous laughter and sometimes bawdy humor. They are full of dancing, clapping, screaming and shouting that may seem jarring to the untrained ear. The church contains in full the kindness and cruelty, the fierce intelligence and the shocking ignorance, the struggles and successes, the love and yes, the bitterness and bias that make up the black experience in America.

And this helps explain, perhaps, my relationship with Reverend Wright. As imperfect as he may be, he has been like family to me. He strengthened my faith, officiated my wedding, and baptized my children. Not once in my conversations with him have I heard him talk about any ethnic group in derogatory terms, or treat whites with whom he interacted with anything but courtesy and respect. He contains within him the contradictions—the good and the bad—of the community that he has served diligently for so many years.

I can no more disown him than I can disown the black community. I can no more disown him than I can my white grandmother—a woman who helped raise me, a woman who sacrificed again and again for me, a woman who loves me as much as she loves anything in this world, but a woman who once confessed her fear of black men who passed by her on the street, and who on more than one occasion has uttered racial or ethnic stereotypes that made me cringe.

These people are a part of me. And they are a part of America, this country that I love.

Some will see this as an attempt to justify or excuse comments that are simply inexcusable. I can assure you it is not. I suppose the politically safe thing would be to move on from this episode and just hope that it fades into the woodwork. We can dismiss Reverend Wright as a crank or a demagogue, just as some have dismissed Geraldine Ferraro, in the aftermath of her recent statements, as harboring some deep-seated racial bias.

But race is an issue that I believe this nation cannot afford to ignore right now. We would be making the same mistake that Reverend Wright made in his offending sermons about America—to simplify and stereotype and amplify the negative to the point that it distorts reality.

The fact is that the comments that have been made and the issues that have surfaced over the last few weeks reflect the complexities of race in this country that we've never really worked through—a part of our union that we have yet to perfect. And if we walk away now, if we simply retreat into our respective corners, we will never be able to come together and solve challenges like health care, or education, or the need to find good jobs for every American.

Understanding this reality requires a reminder of how we arrived at this point. As William Faulkner once wrote, "The past isn't dead and buried. In fact, it isn't even past." We do not need to recite here the history of racial injustice in this country. But we do need to remind ourselves that so many of the disparities that exist in the African-American community today can be directly traced to inequalities passed on from an earlier generation that suffered under the brutal legacy of slavery and Jim Crow.

Segregated schools were, and are, inferior schools; we still haven't fixed them, fifty years after *Brown v. Board of Education*, and the inferior education they provided, then and now, helps explain the pervasive achievement gap between today's black and white students.

Legalized discrimination—where blacks were prevented, often through violence, from owning property, or loans were not granted to African-American business owners, or black homeowners could not access FHA mortgages, or blacks were excluded from unions, or the police force, or fire departments—meant that black families could not amass any meaningful wealth to bequeath to future generations. That history helps explain the wealth and income gap between black and white, and the concentrated pockets of poverty that persists in so many of today's urban and rural communities.

A lack of economic opportunity among black men, and the shame and frustration that came from not being able to provide for one's family, contributed to the erosion of black families—a problem that welfare policies for many years may have worsened. And the lack of basic services in so many urban black neighborhoods—parks for kids to play in, police walking the beat, regular garbage pick-up and building code enforcement—all helped create a cycle of violence, blight and neglect that continue to haunt us.

This is the reality in which Reverend Wright and other African-Americans of his generation grew up. They came of age in the late fifties and early sixties, a time when segregation was still the law of the land and opportunity was systematically constricted. What's remarkable is not how many failed in the face of discrimination, but rather how many men and women overcame the odds; how many were able to make a way out of no way for those like me who would come after them.

But for all those who scratched and clawed their way to get a piece of the American Dream, there were many who didn't make it—those who were ultimately defeated, in one way or another, by discrimination. That legacy of defeat was passed on to future generations—those young men and increasingly young women who we see standing on street corners or languishing in our prisons, without hope or prospects for the future. Even for those blacks who did make it, questions of race, and racism, continue to define their worldview in fundamental ways. For the men and women of Reverend Wright's generation, the memories of humiliation and doubt and fear have not gone away; nor has the anger and the bitterness of those years. That anger may not get expressed in public, in front of white co-workers or white friends. But it does find voice in the barbershop or around the kitchen table. At times, that anger is exploited by politicians, to gin up votes along racial lines, or to make up for a politician's own failings.

And occasionally it finds voice in the church on Sunday morning, in the pulpit and in the pews. The fact that so many people are surprised to hear that anger in some of Reverend Wright's sermons simply reminds us of the old truism that the most segregated hour in American life occurs on Sunday morning. That anger is not always productive; indeed, all too often it distracts attention from solving real problems; it keeps us from squarely facing our own complicity in our condition, and prevents the African-American community from forging the alliances it needs to bring about real change. But the anger is real; it is powerful; and to simply wish it away, to condemn it without understanding its roots, only serves to widen the chasm of misunderstanding that exists between the races.

In fact, a similar anger exists within segments of the white community. Most working- and middle-class white Americans don't feel that they have been particularly privileged by their race.

Their experience is the immigrant experience—as far as they're concerned, no one's handed them anything, they've built it from scratch. They've worked hard all their lives, many times only to see their jobs shipped overseas or their pension dumped after a lifetime of labor. They are anxious about their futures, and feel their dreams slipping away; in an era of stagnant wages and global competition, opportunity comes to be seen as a zero sum game, in which your dreams come at my expense. So when they are told to bus their children to a school across town; when they hear that an African American is getting an advantage in landing a good job or a spot in a good college because of an injustice that they themselves never committed; when they're told that their fears about crime in urban neighborhoods are somehow prejudiced, resentment builds over time.

Like the anger within the black community, these resentments aren't always expressed in polite company. But they have helped shape the political landscape for at least a generation. Anger over welfare and affirmative action helped forge the Reagan Coalition. Politicians routinely exploited fears of crime for their own electoral ends. Talk show hosts and conservative commentators built entire careers unmasking bogus claims of racism while dismissing legitimate discussions of racial injustice and inequality as mere political correctness or reverse racism.

Just as black anger often proved counterproductive, so have these white resentments distracted attention from the real culprits of the middle-class squeeze—a corporate culture rife with inside dealing, questionable accounting practices, and short-term greed; a Washington dominated by lobbyists and special interests; economic policies that favor the few over the many. And yet, to wish away the resentments of white Americans, to label them as misguided or even racist, without recognizing they are grounded in legitimate concerns—this too widens the racial divide, and blocks the path to understanding.

This is where we are right now. It's a racial stalemate we've been stuck in for years. Contrary to the claims of some of my critics, black and white, I have never been so naïve as to believe that we can get beyond our racial divisions in a single election cycle, or with a single candidacy—particularly a candidacy as imperfect as my own.

But I have asserted a firm conviction—a conviction rooted in my faith in God and my faith in the American people—that working together we can move beyond some of our old racial wounds, and that in fact we have no choice if we are to continue on the path of a more perfect union.

For the African-American community, that path means embracing the burdens of our past without becoming victims of our past. It means continuing to insist on a full measure of justice in every aspect of American life. But it also means binding our particular grievances—for better health care, and better schools, and better jobs—to the larger aspirations of all Americans—the white woman struggling to break the glass ceiling, the white man who's been laid off, the immigrant trying to feed his family. And it means taking full responsibility for own lives—by demanding more from our fathers, and spending more time with our children, and reading to them, and teaching them that while they may face challenges and discrimination in their own lives, they must never succumb to despair or cynicism; they must always believe that they can write their own destiny.

Ironically, this quintessentially American—and yes, conservative—notion of self-help found frequent expression in Reverend Wright's sermons. But what my former pastor too often failed to understand is that embarking on a program of self-help also requires a belief that society can change.

The profound mistake of Reverend Wright's sermons is not that he spoke about racism in our society. It's that he spoke as if our society was static; as if no progress has been made; as if this country—a country that has made it possible for one of his own members to run for the highest office in the land and build a coalition of white and black, Latino and Asian, rich and poor, young and old—is still irrevocably bound to a tragic past. But what we know—what we have seen—is that America can change. That is [the] true genius of this nation. What we have already achieved gives us hope—the audacity to hope—for what we can and must achieve tomorrow.

In the white community, the path to a more perfect union means acknowledging that what ails the African-American community does not just exist in the minds of black people; that the legacy of discrimination—and current incidents of discrimination, while less overt than in the past—are real and must be addressed. Not just with words, but with deeds—by investing in our schools and our communities; by enforcing our civil rights laws and ensuring fairness in our criminal justice system; by providing this generation with ladders of opportunity that were unavailable for previous generations. It requires all Americans to realize that your dreams do not have to come at the expense of my dreams; that investing in the health, welfare, and education of black and brown and white children will ultimately help all of America prosper.

In the end, then, what is called for is nothing more, and nothing less, than what all the world's great religions demand—that we do unto others as we would have them do unto us. Let us be our brother's keeper, Scripture tells us. Let us be our sister's keeper. Let us find that common stake we all have in one another, and let our politics reflect that spirit as well.

For we have a choice in this country. We can accept a politics that breeds division, and conflict, and cynicism. We can tackle race only as spectacle—as we did in the OJ trial—or in the wake of tragedy, as we did in the aftermath of Katrina—or as fodder for the nightly news. We can play Reverend Wright's sermons on every channel, every day and talk about them from now until the election, and make the only question in this campaign whether or not the American people think that I somehow believe or sympathize with his most offensive words. We can pounce on some gaffe by a Hillary supporter as evidence that she's playing the race card, or we can speculate on whether white men will all flock to John McCain in the general election regardless of his policies.

We can do that.

But if we do, I can tell you that in the next election, we'll be talking about some other distraction. And then another one. And then another one. And nothing will change.

That is one option. Or, at this moment, in this election, we can come together and say, "Not this time." This time we want to talk about the crumbling schools that are stealing the future of black children and white children and Asian children and Hispanic children and Native American children. This time we want to reject the cynicism that tells us that these kids can't learn; that those kids who don't look like us are somebody else's problem. The children of America are not those kids, they are our kids, and we will not let them fall behind in a 21st century economy. Not this time.

This time we want to talk about how the lines in the Emergency Room are filled with whites and blacks and Hispanics who do not have health care; who don't have the power on their own to overcome the special interests in Washington, but who can take them on if we do it together.

This time we want to talk about the shuttered mills that once provided a decent life for men and women of every race, and the homes for sale that once belonged to Americans from every religion, every region, every walk of life. This time we want to talk about the fact that the real problem is not that someone who doesn't look like you might take your job; it's that the corporation you work for will ship it overseas for nothing more than a profit.

This time we want to talk about the men and women of every color and creed who serve together, and fight together, and bleed together under the same proud flag. We want to talk about how to bring them home from a war that never should've been authorized and never should've been waged, and we want to talk about how we'll show our patriotism by caring for them, and their families, and giving them the benefits they have earned.

I would not be running for President if I didn't believe with all my heart that this is what the vast majority of Americans want for this country. This union may never be perfect, but generation after generation has shown that it can always be perfected. And today, whenever I find myself feeling doubtful or cynical about this possibility, what gives me the most hope is the next generation—the young people whose attitudes and beliefs and openness to change have already made history in this election.

There is one story in particularly that I'd like to leave you with today—a story I told when I had the great honor of speaking on Dr. King's birthday at his home church, Ebenezer Baptist, in Atlanta.

There is a young, twenty-three-year-old white woman named Ashley Baia who organized for our campaign in Florence, South Carolina. She had been working to organize a mostly African-American community since the beginning of this campaign, and one day she was at a roundtable discussion where everyone went around telling their story and why they were there.

And Ashley said that when she was nine years old, her mother got cancer. And because she had to miss days of work, she was let go and lost her health care. They had to file for bankruptcy, and that's when Ashley decided that she had to do something to help her mom.

She knew that food was one of their most expensive costs, and so Ashley convinced her mother that what she really liked and really wanted to eat more than anything else was mustard and relish sandwiches. Because that was the cheapest way to eat.

She did this for a year until her mom got better, and she told everyone at the roundtable that the reason she joined our campaign was so that she could help the millions of other children in the country who want and need to help their parents too.

Now Ashley might have made a different choice. Perhaps somebody told her along the way that the source of her mother's problems were blacks who were on welfare and too lazy to work, or Hispanics who were coming into the country illegally. But she didn't. She sought out allies in her fight against injustice.

Anyway, Ashley finishes her story and then goes around the room and asks everyone else why they're supporting the campaign. They all have different stories and reasons. Many bring up a specific issue. And finally they come to this elderly black man who's been sitting there quietly the entire time. And Ashley asks him why he's there. And he does not bring up a specific issue. He does not say health care or the economy. He does not say education or the war. He does not say that he was there because of Barack Obama. He simply says to everyone in the room, "I am here because of Ashley."

"I'm here because of Ashley." By itself, that single moment of recognition between that young white girl and that old black man is not enough. It is not enough to give health care to the sick, or jobs to the jobless, or education to our children.

But it is where we start. It is where our union grows stronger. And as so many generations have come to realize over the course of the two hundred and twenty-one years since a band of patriots signed that document in Philadelphia, that is where the perfection begins.   [2008]

Understanding the Reading

1. Why does Barack Obama state that the Declaration of Independence of 1787 was "ultimately unfinished"?
2. What were the gaps between the ideals of the U.S. Constitution and the reality of living those ideals? (Trace from the 18th century to the 21st century).
3. Why was Obama's former pastor so controversial and why during Obama's first presidential campaign does he not simply disown him?
4. What are some of the legacies of slavery and Jim Crow according to this article?

Suggestions for Responding

1. Discuss how some politicians and talk show hosts build their careers by exploiting people's fear of crime and unemployment.
2. Have a classroom discussion that responsibly focuses upon racial injustice and the working class immigrant experience. ✦

5

150 Years after Fort Sumter: Why We're Still Fighting the Civil War

David Von Drehle

A few weeks before Captain George S. James sent the first mortar round arcing through the predawn darkness toward Fort Sumter, South Carolina, on April 12, 1861, Abraham Lincoln cast his Inaugural Address as a last-ditch effort to win back the South. A single thorny issue divided the nation, he declared: "One section of our country believes slavery is right and ought to be extended, while the other believes it is wrong and ought not to be extended. This is the only substantial dispute."

It was not a controversial statement at the time. Indeed, Southern leaders were saying similar things during those fateful days. But 150 years later, Americans have lost that clarity about the cause of the Civil War, the most traumatic and transformational event in U.S. history, which left more than 625,000 dead—more Americans killed than in both world wars combined.

Shortly before the Fort Sumter anniversary, Harris Interactive polled more than 2,500 adults across the country, asking what the North and South were fighting about. A majority, including two-thirds of white respondents in the 11 states that formed the Confederacy, answered that the South was mainly motivated by "states' rights" rather than the future of slavery. The question "What caused the Civil War?" returns 20 million Google hits and a wide array of arguments on Internet comment boards and discussion threads. The Civil War was caused by Northern aggressors invading an independent Southern nation. Or it was caused by high tariffs. Or it was caused by blundering statesmen. Or it was caused by the clash of industrial and agrarian cultures. Or it was caused by fanatics. Or it was caused by the Marxist class struggle.

On and on, seemingly endless, sometimes contradictory—although not among mainstream historians, who in the past generation have come to view the question much as Lincoln saw it. "Everything stemmed from the slavery issue," says Princeton professor James McPherson, whose book *Battle Cry of Freedom* is widely judged to be the authoritative one-volume history of the war. Another leading authority, David Blight of Yale, laments, "No matter what we do or the overwhelming consensus among historians, out in the public mind, there is still this need to deny that slavery was the cause of the war."

It's not simply a matter of denial. For most of the first century after the war, historians, novelists and filmmakers worked like hypnotists to soothe the posttraumatic memories of survivors and their descendants. Forgetting was the price of reconciliation, and Americans—those whose families were never bought or sold, anyway—were happy to pay it.

But denial plays a part, especially in the South. After the war, former Confederates wondered how to hold on to their due pride after a devastating defeat. They had fought long and courageously; that was beyond question. So they reverse-engineered a cause worthy of those heroics. They also sensed, correctly, that the end of slavery would confer a gloss of nobility, and bragging rights, on the North that it did not deserve. As Lincoln suggested in his second Inaugural Address, the entire nation, North and South, profited from slavery and then paid dearly for it.

The process of forgetting, and obscuring, was long and layered. Some of it was benign, but not all. It began with self-justifying memoirs by defeated Confederate leaders and was picked up by war-weary veterans on both sides who wanted to move on. In the devastated South, writers and historians kindled comforting stories of noble cavaliers, brilliant generals and happy slaves, all faithful to a glorious lost cause. In the prosperous North, where cities and factories began filling with freed slaves and their descendants, large audiences were happy to embrace this idea of a time when racial issues were both simple and distant.

History is not just about the past. It also reveals the present. And for generations of Americans after the Civil War, the present did not have room for that radical idea laid bare by the conflict: that all people really are created equal. That was a big bite to chew.

The once obvious truth of the Civil War does not imply that every soldier had slavery on his mind as he marched and fought. Many Southerners fought and died in gray never having owned a slave and never intending to own one. Thousands died in blue with no intention to set one free. But it was slavery that had broken one nation in two and fated its people to fight over whether it would be put back together again. The true story is not a tale of heroes on one side and villains on the other. Few true stories are. But it is a clear and straightforward story, and so is the tale of how that story became so complicated.

BLEEDING KANSAS

History textbooks say the Civil War began with the shelling of Fort Sumter. The fact is, however, that the Founding Fathers saw the whole thing coming. They walked away from the Constitutional Convention fully aware that they had planted a time bomb; they hoped future leaders would find a way to defuse it before it exploded. As the Constitution was being written, James Madison observed, "It seems now to be pretty well understood that the real difference of interests lies not between the large and small but between the Northern and Southern states. The institution of slavery and its consequences form the line."

As long as the disagreement remained purely a matter of North and South, the danger seemed manageable. But then North and South looked to the west. All that land, all those resources—the idea that the frontier might be closed off to slavery was unacceptable to the South. It felt like an indictment and an injustice rolled into one. Slave owners were not immune to the expansionary passion of 19th century America. They too needed room to grow, and not just to plant more cotton. Slaves could grow hemp and mine gold and build railroads and sew clothes. The economic engine of slavery was immensely powerful. Slaves were the single largest financial asset in the United States of America, worth over $3.5 billion in 1860 dollars—more than the value of America's railroads, banks, factories or ships. Cotton was by far the largest U.S. export. It enriched Wall Street banks and fueled New England textile mills. This economic giant demanded a piece of the Western action.

In 1854, the Kansas-Nebraska Act proposed to let territorial settlers decide the future of slavery. Never in U.S. history had so much depended on so few so far beyond the rule of law. There was a footrace to the distant prairie, and Kansas, where the racers clashed, was where the war started, not Fort Sumter. And everyone involved knew exactly what the killing was about.

It was on May 21, 1856, that a proslavery army, hauling artillery and commanded by U.S. Senator David Rice Atchison of Missouri, laid waste to the antislavery bastion of Lawrence, Kans. "Boys, this is the happiest day of my life," Atchison declared as his men prepared to teach "the damned abolitionists a Southern lesson that they will remember until the day they die."

One of those abolitionists was John Brown, who tried to come to the aid of Lawrence but arrived too late. Three days later, as Brown pondered what to do next, a messenger arrived with news from far-off Washington: an antislavery leader, Senator Charles Sumner of Massachusetts, had been clubbed nearly to death by South Carolina Congressman Preston Brooks while sitting at his desk in the Senate chamber after delivering a fiery speech titled "The Crime Against Kansas." Brown went "crazy—crazy" at the news, his son reported. That night he led a small group, including four of his sons, to a proslavery settlement on Pottawatomie Creek. Announcing themselves as "the Northern army," Brown's band rousted five men, led them into the darkness and hacked them to death with swords.

Two contending armies, artillery fire and flames, bloodshed in the Senate and corpses strewn over dew-damp ground. People at the time knew exactly what to call it: civil war. Kansas Territorial Governor Wilson Shannon used the phrase himself in a warning to President Franklin Pierce. "We are standing on a volcano," Shannon added.

The reason for the eruption was simple. As Brown explained, "In Kansas, the question is never raised of a man, Is he a Democrat? Is he a Republican? The questions there raised are, Is he a Free State man? or Is he a proslavery man?" This is why armies marched and shells burst and swords flashed.

THE FRACTURE

From there, the remaining steps to Fort Sumter seemed to follow inexorably. The Supreme Court, in its infamous *Dred Scott* decision, tried to answer the question in favor of slave-holders. The backlash was furious. In Kansas, settlers passed competing constitutions, one slave and one free, and the battle over which one Congress should accept splintered the Democratic Party. When Stephen A. Douglas failed to reunite the Democrats in 1860, he opened the door to a Lincoln victory.

Meanwhile, Brown organized a quixotic plot to invade the South and stir up an army of slaves. Quickly captured at the armory in Harpers Ferry, Va., tried for treason and hanged, he was hailed by abolitionists as a martyr. After that, the idea that Northern Republicans supported slave rebellion became the defining theme, for Southerners, of the 1860 election. A vote for Lincoln was in many minds a vote for the sort of blood-soaked insurrection that had freed the slaves of Haiti and left thousands of white slave owners dead.

Abolitionists had "inspired [slaves] with vague notions of freedom," explained President James Buchanan as he prepared to leave office. "Many a matron throughout the South retires at night in dread of what may befall herself and her children before morning," making "disunion . . . inevitable." As Southern states began to declare their independence, they echoed this theme. South Carolina's leaders indicted the North for encouraging "thousands of our slaves to leave their homes, and those who have remained have been incited by emissaries, books and pictures to servile insurrection." Mississippi affirmed, "Our position is thoroughly identified with the institution of slavery—the greatest material interest of the world," adding, "There was no choice left us but submission to the mandates of abolition, or a dissolution of the Union." Georgians declared, "We refuse to submit."

Even as the conflict turned to all-out war, many people still hoped for a way to put things back as they had been. As George McClellan, General in Chief of the Union Army, wrote to a friend in 1861, "I am fighting to preserve the integrity of the Union & the power of the [government]—on no other issue. To gain that end, we cannot afford to raise up the negro question—it must be incidental and subsidiary." His words go to the root of a persistent question: How could slavery be the cause of the war when so many in blue had no interest in emancipation? McClellan was speaking for the millions whose goal was not to free the slaves but to preserve the Union.

What McClellan did not perceive, though, was that the Union and slavery had become irreconcilable. The proposition on which the revolutionaries of 1776 had staked their efforts—the fundamental equality of individuals—was diametrically opposed by the constitution of the new Confederacy. "Our new government is founded upon exactly the opposite idea; its foundations are laid, its cornerstone rests, upon the great truth that the negro is not equal to the white man; that slavery, subordination to the superior race, is his natural and normal condition," explained Confederate Vice President Alexander Stephens. In other words, the warring sides had stripped their arguments to first principles, and those principles could no longer be compromised.

FOGGING MEMORY

The forgetting began with exhaustion. "From 1865"—the year the war ended—"until the 1880s, there was a paucity of writings about the war that really sold," says Harvard historian John Stauffer. "Americans weren't ready to deal with the reality of the war because of the carnage and the devastation." When an appetite for the story began to return, readers embraced only certain kinds of memories. There was no market for books of war photographs. Ulysses Grant's 1885 memoirs were a best-seller, but the

Union general gave almost no attention to the events leading up to Lincoln's call for troops, while his touching account of the Confederate surrender at Appomattox strongly conveyed the idea that it was best to move on. There was an avid audience for essays by military leaders in the magazine *The Century,* describing their battles in minute detail but paying scant attention to the big picture. This "Battles and Leaders" series spawned an endless literature that, some critics say, treats the terrible conflict as if it were America's original Super Bowl, Yankees vs. Rebs, complete with watercooler analysis of the play calling, fumbles and Hail Marys.

The first publishing success to really engage the reasons for the war was a strange and rambling book by Confederate President Jefferson Davis. Twenty years earlier, Davis had framed the choice to secede in simple terms: "Will you consent to be robbed of your property"—meaning slaves—or will you "strike bravely for liberty, property, honor and life?" But looking back, he preferred to say that the slavery issue had been trumped up by "political demagogues" in the North "as a means to acquire power."

Davis' book, *The Rise and Fall of the Confederate Government,* became a polestar for the Lost Cause school of Civil War history, which takes its name from an 1866 book by Richmond newspaper editor Edward Pollard. Highly selective and deeply misleading, the story of the Lost Cause was immediately popular in the South because it translated the Confederacy's defeat into a moral victory. It pictured antebellum life as an idyll of genteel planters and their happy "servants" whose "instincts," in Davis' words, "rendered them contented with their lot. . . . Never was there happier dependence of labor and capital on each other."

But then: "The tempter came, like the serpent of Eden, and decoyed them with the majic word of 'freedom.'" Though outgunned and outnumbered, the South fought heroically to defend itself from aggressors whose factories up north were the true slave drivers. And though God-fearing warriors like Robert E. Lee and Thomas "Stonewall" Jackson outgeneraled their foes at every turn, ultimately the federal swarm was too large and too savage to repel.

The Lost Cause story required a massive case of amnesia. Before the war, Southerners would have scoffed at the idea that the North was overwhelmingly stronger. They believed that King Cotton was the dominant force on earth and that powerful Britain—where roughly 1 in 5 people depended on cotton for a living—would intervene to ensure Confederate victory.

But people were eager to forget. And so Americans both Southern and Northern flocked to minstrel shows and snapped up happy-slave stories by writers like Thomas Nelson Page and Joel Chandler Harris. White society was not ready to deal with the humanity and needs of freed slaves, and these entertainments assured them that there was no need to. Reconstruction was scorned as a fool's errand, and Jim Crow laws were touted as sensible reforms to restore a harmonious land.

A QUARREL FORGOTTEN

Instead of looking back, postwar Presidents stressed the future, adopting the reconciling tone of Grant at Appomattox. William McKinley, assassinated in 1901, was the last Civil War veteran to lead the country. His successor, Theodore Roosevelt, was the living embodiment of reconciliation and moving forward. His father had served the Union cause; his plantation-raised mother had supported the South; his childhood was a master tutorial in leaving certain things unsaid in the pursuit of harmony.

By the 50th anniversary of Gettysburg, it was nearly impossible to know from the commemoration why the war had happened or who had won. The year was 1913, and the President was Woodrow Wilson, the first Southerner to hold the office since 1850. Wilson had been a historian before entering politics, and his book *A History of the American People* was tinged with Lost Cause interpretations. He described the Ku Klux Klan as "an empire of the South" created by men "roused by a mere instinct of self-preservation." It was no surprise, then, that his remarks at Gettysburg completely avoided slavery. Instead he chose to talk about "gallant men in blue and gray . . . our battles long past, our quarrels forgotten."

So what was remembered? Two years after Wilson spoke at Gettysburg, partly influenced by Wilson's book, filmmaker D.W. Griffith debuted *The Birth of a Nation*. It was the first film in history with a six-figure production budget, yet by selling out theaters at the unheard-of price of $2 per ticket—nearly $44 in current dollars—Griffith made a fortune. The movie brought the Lost Cause to cinematic life, with the Klan saving the day in the final reel, rescuing white families from a group of marauding blacks. Then in 1939, a new Lost Cause melodrama made an even bigger impact: David O. Selznick's *Gone with the Wind*. The story of plucky Scarlett O'Hara and the sad destruction of her "pretty world" of "Cavaliers and Cotton Fields called the Old South" is the top-grossing film of all time, adjusted for inflation, according to the website Box Office Mojo.

Both films begin in an antebellum South where all is peaceful and bright and trace the sad fall from paradise into a hellish postwar world of carpetbagging Northerners and rapacious, incompetent freed slaves. Such powerful cultural images were buttressed by the academic work of leading historians. At Columbia University, William A. Dunning established himself as the leading authority on the postwar South, and he brought up a generation of scholars with the belief that blacks were incapable of equality and that Reconstruction was a disastrous injustice.

Equally influential was University of Illinois historian James G. Randall, who towered among Lincoln scholars. Horrified by the senseless carnage of World War I, Randall saw it foreshadowed in the trenches and torched fields of the Civil War. The chief villains, in Randall's orthodoxy, were Northern abolitionists with their "reforming zeal."

Reigning over the study of slavery was Yale's U.B. Phillips, the son of slave owners. For decades he was the only scholar to undertake a systematic examination of the plantation economy, which, he argued, was a benign and civilizing force for African captives. He concluded that slavery was an unprofitable system that would have soon died out peacefully. That would have surprised the Southerners who in the 1850s certainly believed there was money to be made in slavery. In the decade before the war, per capita wealth grew more than twice as fast in the South as it did in the North, and the prices of slaves and land both rose by some 70%. If slavery was dying out, it sure was hard to tell.

Why It Matters

Historians began to break the grip of forgetfulness after World War II, as the civil rights movement restarted the march toward equality. In 1941, Franklin Roosevelt ordered equal treatment for "workers in defense industries or government." The next President, Harry Truman, desegregated the armed forces. The next one, Dwight Eisenhower, dispatched federal troops to enforce school desegregation in Arkansas. And so on, step by little step.

In 1947, the year Jackie Robinson broke baseball's color line, John Hope Franklin, a black historian then at Howard University, published *From Slavery to Freedom: A History of African Americans.* This runaway best seller revolutionized academic discussion of the black experience. The same year, Columbia's Allan Nevins published the first of eight volumes of *Ordeal of the Union,* which explored America's road to disaster in great depth and clarity.

The Dunning School lost its grip on Reconstruction when C. Vann Woodward of Johns Hopkins published *The Strange Career of Jim Crow* in 1955. The following year, Kenneth Stampp at Berkeley did the same to U.B. Phillips with *The Peculiar Institution,* which examined the slave system through the eyes of the slaves themselves for the first time.

With the centennial of the war approaching, a flood of outstanding Civil War history books hit shelves, and the half-century since then has been rich in scholarship. Robust controversies rage and always will, but the distortion and occluded memory that shaped the Lost Cause story is found now only on the academic fringe. What energy exists in the modern version comes from a clique of libertarians who view the Union cause as a fearsome example of authoritarian central government crushing individual dissent. Slave owners make odd libertarian heroes, but by keeping the focus narrowly on Big Government, this school uses the secession cause to dramatize issues of today. Outside academia, denial remains an irresistible temptation for some politicians. Virginia Governor Bob McDonnell last year issued a 400-word Confederate History Month proclamation without a single mention of slavery. "There were any number of aspects to that conflict between the states," McDonnell later explained. "Obviously it involved slavery, it involved other issues, but I focused on the ones that I thought were most significant for Virginia." (Barraged by criticism, he corrected the omission.)

And in popular culture, as University of Virginia historian Gary Gallagher writes, "The Lost Cause's Confederacy of gallant leaders and storied victories in defense of home ground retains enormous vitality." It shows up in movies like *Gods and Generals,* in commemorative paintings, decorative plates and battlefield re-enactments. By contrast, Gallagher searches in vain for a scene in any recent film that "captures the abiding devotion to Union that animated soldiers and civilians in the North."

Why does this matter? Because the Civil War gave us, to an unmatched degree, the nation we became—including all the good stuff. Had secession succeeded, it's unlikely that there could have been a stable, tranquil coexistence between an independent North and South. Slaves would have continued running away. The riches of the West would have been just as enticing. There never would have been the sort of roisterous hodgepodge of wide-open energy that America became. One of the blessings of being able to set up shop on a new continent was that Americans never had to be defined by clan or tribe or region. We're the people who order a Coke from Atlanta and some New England clam chowder at a diner in Las Vegas. The place where a boy from Mississippi goes to California to make a movie called *Blue Hawaii.* Secession was about making more borders. At its best, Americanism is about tearing them down.

To be blind to the reason the war happened is to build a sort of border of the mind, walling off an important truth. Slavery was not incidental to America's origins; it was central. There were slaves at Jamestown. In the 1600s, writes Yale's David Brion Davis, a towering figure among historians, slave labor was far more central to the making of New York than to the making of Virginia. As late as 1830, there were 2,254 slaves in New Jersey. Connecticut did not abolish slavery until 1848, a scant eight years before the fighting broke out in Kansas. Rhode Island dominated the American slave trade until it was outlawed in 1808. The cotton trade made Wall Street a global financial force. Slaves built the White House.

Furthermore, if slavery had spread to the West, the country would have found itself increasingly isolated in the world. Russia emancipated its serfs in 1861. The once sprawling slave system that had stretched from Canada to South America was by 1808 still vital only in Brazil, Cuba and the U.S. The first nation founded on the principle of liberty came dangerously close to being among the last slave economies on earth.

Two fallacies prop up the wall of forgetfulness. The first is that slavery somehow wasn't really that important—that it was a historical relic, unprofitable, dying out, or that all societies did it, or that the slaves were happy. But slavery was important, and not just to the 4 million men, women and children enslaved—a number equal to the population of Los Angeles today. And the fact that it ended is important too.

The second fallacy is that this was only the South's problem and that the North solved it. Not long ago, the New-York Historical Society mounted its largest-ever exhibition, titled "Slavery in New York." You can still visit the website and listen to public reactions. Over and over again, visitors repeat the same theme: as a teacher, as a college graduate, as a native New Yorker, "I knew absolutely nothing about this." As long as that belief persists, spoken or unspoken, Americans whose hearts lie with Dixie will understandably continue to defend their homes and honor against such Yankee arrogance.

Lincoln's words a few weeks before his death were often quoted after the war by those who wanted not just to forgive but also to forget: "With malice toward none, with charity for all." But those words drew their deepest power from the ones he spoke just before them: "Fondly do we hope, fervently do we pray, that this mighty scourge of war may speedily pass away. Yet, if God wills that it continue until all the wealth piled by the bondsman's 250 years of unrequited toil shall be sunk, and until every drop of blood drawn with the lash shall be paid by another drawn with the sword, as was said 3,000 years ago, so still it must be said 'the judgments of the Lord are true and righteous altogether.'"

In other words, the path to healing and mercy goes by way of honesty and humility. After 150 years, it's time to finish the journey.   [2011]

Understanding the Reading

1. Why is there a division among Americans as to what caused the Civil War?
2. How did the expansion into western territories relate to our division over slavery?
3. Why is it important to remember the causes of wars?

Suggestions for Responding

1. Watch D. W. Griffith's film *The Birth of a Nation*. Discuss his version of the Civil War and its aftermath. ✦

6

Every Good-Bye Ain't Gone

JAMES BALDWIN

I am writing this note just twenty-nine years after my first departure from America. It was raining—naturally. My mother had come downstairs, and stood silently, arms folded, on the stoop. My baby sister was upstairs, weeping. I got into the cab, waved, and drove away.

It may be impossible for anyone to tell the truth about his past. You drag your past with you everywhere, or it drags you. Therefore, the simplest thing for me to say concerning that first departure from America is that I had no choice. It was not the heroic departure of a prodigy. Time was to prove (and how!) that I was a prodigal son indeed, but, by the time the fatted calf came my way, intimacy with too many dubious hamburgers had caused me to lose my appetite. I *did* want the people I loved to know how much I loved them, especially that little girl weeping on the top floor of that tenement: I will say that. And my departure, which, especially in my own eyes, stank of betrayal, was my only means of proving, or redeeming, that love, my only hope. Or, in other words, I knew then that I was a writer, but did not know if I could last long enough to prove it. And, if I loved the people I loved, I also knew that they loved me, did not deserve and could scarcely afford the spectacle of the firstborn as a disaster. That seems a grandiose way of putting it, yet it is the only honest way for *me* to put it; and it is not really grandiose at all—it comes out of the life I saw all around me. The song says, *motherless children have a hard time!* And so do the fatherless, and the brotherless. The firstborn knows this first, and, therefore, the accident of being the firstborn is also a reality, and I took it very seriously.

For, in the years that I—we—were growing up in Harlem, Harlem was still, essentially, a southern community, but lately, and violently, driven north. The people had dragged the South with them, *in* them, to the northern ghetto, and one of the results of this was that all of the children belonged to all of the elders. If, for example, a grown-up, even a very young grown-up, caught me doing something I should not have been doing, blocks from my house, he, or she, would whip my behind and carry me, howling, to my house, to tell my mother or father why I had been whipped. Mama or Daddy would thank the person, and then whip my behind again. It is a hard way to learn, perhaps, but there are no easy ways, and so I learned that I was supposed to be an "example." That didn't make sense to me in the beginning—I hated what seemed to me to be an injustice—but it made sense to me later. We were *all* expected to be examples to each other. The eldest was expected to do his best to protect those behind him from being destroyed by the bloody discoveries the eldest had already made. The price for this was astronomical: that the eldest did not allow *himself* to be destroyed.

This was quite an assignment for a black, defenseless-looking high school graduate who—to remain within the confines of the mentionable—had had feet, fists, tables, clubs, and chairs bounced off his only head, and who, by the time of November 1949, trusted no one, and knew that he trusted no one, knew that this distrust was suicidal, and also knew that there was no question any longer of his *life* in America: his violent destruction could be taken as given; it was a matter of time. By the time I was twenty-two, I was a survivor—a survivor, furthermore, with murder in his heart.

A man with murder in his heart will murder, or be murdered—it comes to the same thing—and so I knew I had to leave. Somewhere else,

anywhere else, the question of my life might still be open, but in my own country that question was closed.

Well, I was lucky—the black people I grew up with would say I was blessed. Some things had happened to me because I was black, and some things had happened to me because I was me and I had to discover the demarcation line, if there was one. It seemed to me that such a demarcation line must certainly exist, but it was also beginning to be borne in on me that it was certainly not easy to find: and perhaps, indeed, when found, not to be trusted. How to perceive, define, a line nearly too thin for the naked eye, so mercurial, and so mighty. Only a really shattered, scotch-or martini-guzzling upward-mobility-struck house nigger could possibly deny the relentless tension of the black condition. Being black affected one's life span, insurance rates, blood pressure, lovers, children, every dangerous hour of every dangerous day. There was absolutely no way *not* to be black without ceasing to exist. But it frequently seemed that there was no way to be black, either, without ceasing to exist.

For one of the ways of being black is to accept what the world tells you about your mother and your father, your brother and your sister; and what that world tells you—in many ways from the language of the lawgiver to the language of the liberal—is that "your" people deserve, in effect, their fate. Your fate—"your" people's fate—involves being, forever, a little lower than these particular angels, angels who, nevertheless, are always ready to give you a helping hand.

Well, this is, after all, but another way of observing that it is exceedingly difficult for most of us to discard the assumptions of the society in which we were born, in which we live, to which we owe our identities; very difficult to defeat the trap of circumstance, which is, also, the web of safety; virtually impossible, if not completely impossible, to envision the future, except in those terms which we think we already know. Most of us are about as eager to be changed as we were to be born, and go through our changes in a similar state of shock.

Including this writer, of course, who was far, however, years ago, from being able to forgive himself for being so irretrievably human. The power of the social definition is that it becomes, fatally, one's own—but it took time, and much deep water, to make me see this. Rage and misery can be a source of comfort, simply because one has lived with rage and misery for so long.

But to accept this rage and misery as a source of comfort is to enter one of the vicious circles of hell. One does not, after all, forgive the world for this horror, nor can one forgive oneself. Because one cannot forgive oneself, one cannot forgive others, or, even, really, *see* others—one is always striking out at the wrong person, for only some other, poor, doomed innocent obviously, is likely to be in striking range. One's self-esteem begins to shrivel, one's hope for the future begins to crack. In reacting against what the world calls you, you endlessly validate its judgment.

I had not conceived, then, that I had only to study the hieroglyphic of my circumstances if I wished to decipher my inheritance. *Circumstances:* a rather heavy word, when you consider it, connecting, for me, by means of Ezekiel's *wheel in the middle of a wheel,* with the iron, inescapable truth of revolutions—we black folk say what goes around, comes around. Circumstances, furthermore, are complicated, simplified, and, ultimately, defined by the person's reaction to these circumstances—for no one, no matter how it may seem, simply *endures* his circumstances. If we are what our circumstances make us, we are, also, what we make of our circumstances. This is, perhaps, the key to history since *we* are history, and since the tension of which I am speaking is so silent and so private, with effects so unforeseeable, and so public.

In any case, the Americans' ladder is not Jacob's ladder, their pillow is not Jacob's pillow. Armed with this legacy, this testament, and this envelope which I had not yet opened, I went to France.

November 11, 1948: rain, fatigue, panic, the absolute certainty of being dashed to death on the vindictive tooth of the Eiffel Tower, which we circled, it seemed to me, for hours. I do not remember feeling the remotest exhilaration. I had a few "friends" in Paris, and $40 in my pocket, and expected a little less from my friends than I did from the $40. I was wrong, I must tell you at once, as to my friends, who were far more present than I would have dared allow myself to hope—my first lesson, perhaps,

in humility; perhaps the first opening of a certain door. For the people who were nice to me were very nice to me without, if you see what I mean, being *nice:* They forced me to recognize that they cared about me. This was a bewildering, a paralyzing revelation, and I know that I was not very graceful. The Bronx, Brooklyn, Texas, Princeton, and Alabama accents, stammered out a need and anguish like my own: If I were ever to grow up, ever, then I had to hear my accent in the accent of others, and to recognize that anguish was not a province which I had discovered only yesterday, alone. On the other hand, I was right about the $40, which melted in a day, and there I was, in Paris, on my ass.

My ass, mister, *mine:* and I was glad. In spite of everything—the cops, the concierges, the hotels, the alleys, the joints, eventually the hospital, finally the jail—I was glad. If the demarcation line existed, then I had to be somewhat close to it, for I refused to believe that I could be so abject as to blame my trials, those crises which I myself perpetually precipitated, on my color. Furthermore, I could not dare to see that the question of the demarcation line was a false question and that I could hide behind it, paralyzed, vindictive, and guilty, for the rest of my life.

It was not for this, however, that I had left a small girl crying on the top floor of a Harlem tenement.

There *was* a demarcation line, to be walked every hour of every day. The demarcation line was my apprehension of, and, therefore, my responsibility for, my own experience: the chilling vice versa of what I had made of my experience and what that experience had made of me. I will owe the French a debt forever, for example, only because, during one of my passionately insane barroom brawls, I suddenly realized that the Frenchman I was facing had not the remotest notion—and could not possibly have had the remotest notion—of the tension in my mind between *Orléans,* a French city, and *New Orleans,* where my father had been born, between *louis,* the coin, and *Louis,* the French king, for whom was named the state of Louisiana, the result of which celebrated purchase had been the death of so many black people. Neither did any African, as far as I could tell, at that moment of my own time and space, have any notion of this tension and torment. But what

I began to see was that, if they had no notion of *my* torment, I certainly had no notion of theirs, and that I was treating people exactly as I had been treated at home.

In order to keep the faith—climbing Jacob's ladder—I came home, to go to Little Rock and Charlotte, and so forth and so on, in 1957, and was based in America from 1957 to 1970.

I have been in and out of my country, in and out of various cauldrons, for a very long time, long enough to see the doctrine of white supremacy return, like a plague, to the continent which spawned it. This is not a bitter statement. It comes, to tell the truth, out of love, for I am thinking of the children. I watch—here, for example—French and Algerian children trying to become friends with each other, reacting to, but not yet understanding, the terrors of their parents, and very far indeed from having any notion of the terrors of the state. They have no way of knowing that the state is menace and shaken to the degree, precisely, that they, themselves, the presumed victims, or at least, the wards of the state, make manifest their identity—which is not what it might be, either for better or for worse, if they were still in Algeria. They cannot possibly know that they, ex-slave and ex-master, cannot be used as their fathers were used—that all identities, in short, are in question, are about to be made new.

Every good-bye ain't gone: human history reverberates with violent upheaveal, uprooting, arrival and departure, hello and good-bye. Yet, I am not certain that anyone ever leaves home. When "home" drops below the horizon, it rises in one's breast and acquires the overwhelming power of menaced love.

In my early years in Paris, I met and became friends with an elderly man who had left Germany in something like 1933 to become a hunted refugee because he had refused, in any way whatever, to be a part of the criminal Nazi state. I admired the man very much, and his pain was very vivid to me. God knows one couldn't quarrel with his reasons for leaving Germany, and yet his repudiation of his homeland was present in everything he said and did. The French landscape, which he loved as I did, could console, could even nearly reconcile: but it could not replace the landscape he carried in his heart. In the early

fifties his mother was dying and wanted to see her son one last time, and I took my friend to the railroad station. I never, never forgot that moment. I wondered if that was going to happen to me. I wanted to go home, I wanted to see *my* mother and my brothers and my sisters and my friends—but the novel wasn't finished (it seemed, indeed, that it would *never* be finished), and that was the only trophy I could carry home. All my love was in it, and the reason for my journey.

I suspect, though I certainly cannot prove it, that every life moves full circle—toward revelation: You begin to see, and even rejoice to see, what you always saw. You can even tell anguish to sit down, and shut up, you're busy right now—and anguish, as you should certainly know by now, ain't to go nowhere. It might go around the corner, on a particularly bright day, and there *are* those days: but anguish has your number, knows, to paraphrase the song, where you live. It's a difficult relationship, but mysteriously indispensable. It teaches you.

So, I *could* talk about the European panic, which takes so monotonous a form: but what is happening in Europe, now, to blacks, and to other, unprecedented niggers, has been happening for a very long time. Once I began to recover from my delirium, it was the first thing in Europe that I clearly saw: so it would be dishonest to pretend that this crisis, a global crisis, has anything to do with my motives or my movement now. I will say that my baby sister is a grown, married woman now, with an exceedingly swift and cunning son who has not the faintest intention of allowing me to forget that I'm his uncle: so, for me, for all of us, I believe, that dreadful day of November of' 48 is redeemed.

Neither do I want anyone to suppose that I think that the gem of the ocean has kept any of its promises, but my ancestors counseled me to *keep the faith:* and I promised, I vowed that I would. If I am a part of the American house, and I am, it is because my ancestors paid—*striving to make it my home*—so unimaginable a price: and I have seen some of the effects of that passion everywhere I have been, all over this world. The music is everywhere, resounds, no sounds: and tells me that now is the moment, for me, to return to the eye of the hurricane.   [1977]

Understanding the Reading

1. Why did the author write that his leaving his home and his country "stank of betrayal"?
2. What are some ways being black affected the author as a young man?
3. What does the title of this essay mean?

Suggestion for Responding

1. Research the Harlem Renaissance. ✦

7

The Loudest Voice

GRACE PALEY

There is a certain place where dumb-waiters boom, doors slam, dishes crash; every window is a mother's mouth bidding the street shut up, go skate somewhere else, come home. My voice is the loudest.

There, my own mother is still as full of breathing as me and the grocer stands up to speak to her. "Mrs. Abramowitz," he says, "people should not be afraid of their children."

"Ah, Mr. Bialik," my mother replies, "if you say to her or her father 'Ssh,' they say, 'In the grave it will be quiet.'"

"From Coney Island to the cemetery," says my papa. "It's the same subway; it's the same fare."

I am right next to the pickle barrel. My pinky is making tiny whirlpools in the brine. I stop a moment to announce: "Campbell's Tomato Soup. Campbell's Vegetable Beef Soup. Campbell's S-c-otch Broth . . ."

"Be quiet," the grocer says, "the labels are coming off."

"Please, Shirley, be a little quiet," my mother begs me.

In that place the whole street groans: Be quiet! Be quiet! but steals from the happy chorus of my inside self not a tittle or a jot.

There, too, but just around the corner, is a red brick building that has been old for many years. Every morning the children stand before it in double lines which must be straight. They are not insulted. They are waiting anyway.

I am usually among them. I am, in fact, the first, since I begin with "A."

One cold morning the monitor tapped me on the shoulder. "Go to Room 409, Shirley Abramowitz," he said. I did as I was told. I went in a hurry up a down staircase to Room 409, which contained sixth-graders. I had to wait at the desk without wiggling until Mr. Hilton, their teacher, had time to speak.

After five minutes he said, "Shirley?"

"What?" I whispered.

He said, "My! My! Shirley Abramowitz! They told me you had a particularly loud, clear voice and read with lots of expression. Could that be true?"

"Oh yes," I whispered.

"In that case, don't be silly; I might very well be your teacher someday. Speak up, speak up."

"Yes," I shouted.

"More like it," he said. "Now, Shirley, can you put a ribbon in your hair or a bobby pin? It's too messy."

"Yes!" I bawled.

"Now, now, calm down." He turned to the class. "Children, not a sound. Open at page 39. Read till 52. When you finish, start again." He looked me over once more. "Now, Shirley, you know, I suppose, that Christmas is coming. We are preparing a beautiful play. Most of the parts have been given out. But I still need a child with a strong voice, lots of stamina. Do you know what stamina is? You do? Smart kid. You know, I heard you read 'The Lord is my shepherd' in Assembly yesterday. I was very impressed. Wonderful delivery. Mrs. Jordan, your teacher, speaks highly of you. Now listen to me, Shirley Abramowitz, if you want to take the part and be in the play, repeat after me, 'I swear to work harder than I ever did before.'"

I looked to heaven and said at once, "Oh, I swear." I kissed my pinky and looked at God.

"That is an actor's life, my dear," he explained. "Like a soldier's, never tardy or disobedient to his general, the director. Everything," he said, "absolutely everything will depend on you."

That afternoon, all over the building, children scraped and scrubbed the turkeys and the sheaves of corn off the schoolroom windows. Goodbye Thanks giving. The next morning a monitor brought red paper and green paper from the office. We made new shapes and hung them on the walls and glued them to the doors.

The teachers became happier and happier. Their heads were ringing like the bells of childhood. My best friend Evie was prone to evil, but she did not get a single demerit for whispering. We learned "Holy Night" without an error. "How wonderful!" said Miss Glacé, the student teacher. "To think that some of you don't even speak the language!" We learned "Deck the Halls" and "Hark! The Herald Angels." . . . They weren't ashamed and we weren't embarrassed.

Oh, but when my mother heard about it all, she said to my father: "Misha, you don't know what's going on there. Cramer is the head of the Tickets Committee."

"Who?" asked my father. "Cramer? Oh yes, an active woman."

"Active? Active has to have a reason. Listen," she said sadly, "I'm surprised to see my neighbors making tra-la-la for Christmas."

My father couldn't think of what to say to that. Then he decided: "You're in America! Clara, you wanted to come here. In Palestine the Arabs would be eating you alive. Europe you had pogroms.[1] Argentina is full of Indians. Here you got Christmas. . . . Some joke, ha?"

"Very funny, Misha. What is becoming of you? If we came to a new country a long time ago to run away from tyrants, and instead we fall into a creeping pogrom, that our children learn a lot of lies, so what's the joke? Ach, Misha, your idealism is going away."

"So is your sense of humor."

"That I never had, but idealism you had a lot of."

"I'm the same Misha Abramovitch, I didn't change an iota. Ask anyone."

"Only ask me," says my mama, may she rest in peace. "I got the answer."

Meanwhile the neighbors had to think of what to say too.

Marty's father said: "You know, he has a very important part, my boy."

"Mine also," said Mr. Sauerfeld.

"Not my boy!" said Mrs. Klieg. "I said to him no. The answer is no. When I say no! I mean no!"

The rabbi's wife said, "It's disgusting!" But no one listened to her. Under the narrow sky of God's great wisdom she wore a strawberry-blond wig.

Every day was noisy and full of experience. I was Right-hand Man. Mr. Hilton said: "How could I get along without you, Shirley?"

He said: "Your mother and father ought to get down on their knees every night and thank God for giving them a child like you."

He also said: "You're absolutely a pleasure to work with, my dear, dear child."

Sometimes he said: "For God's sakes, what did I do with the script? Shirley! Shirley! Find it."

Then I answered quietly: "Here it is, Mr. Hilton."

Once in a while, when he was very tired, he would cry out: "Shirley, I'm just tired of screaming at those kids. Will you tell Ira Pushkov not to come in till Lester points to that star the second time?"

Then I roared: "Ira Pushkov, what's the matter with you? Dope! Mr. Hilton told you five times already, don't come in till Lester points to that star the second time."

"Ach, Clara," my father asked, "what does she do there till six o'clock she can't even put the plates on the table?"

"Christmas," said my mother coldly.

"Ho! Ho!" my father said. "Christmas. What's the harm? After all, history teaches everyone. We learn from reading this is a holiday from pagan times also, candles, lights, even Chanukah. So we learn it's not altogether Christian. So if they think it's a private holiday, they're only ignorant, not patriotic. What belongs to history, belongs to all men. You want to go back to the Middle Ages? Is it better to shave your head with a secondhand razor? Does it hurt Shirley to learn to speak up? It does not. So maybe someday she won't live between the kitchen and the shop. She's not a fool."

I thank you, Papa, for your kindness. It is true about me to this day. I am foolish but I am not a fool.

That night my father kissed me and said with great interest in my career, "Shirley, tomorrow's your big day. Congrats."

"Save it," my mother said. Then she shut all the windows in order to prevent tonsillitis.

In the morning it snowed. On the street corner a tree had been decorated for us by a kind city administration. In order to miss its chilly shadow our neighbors walked three blocks east to buy a loaf of bread. The butcher pulled down black window shades to keep the colored lights from shining on his chickens. Oh, not me. On the way to school, with both my hands I tossed it a kiss of tolerance. Poor thing, it was a stranger in Egypt.

I walked straight into the auditorium past the staring children. "Go ahead, Shirley!" said the monitors. Four boys, big for their age, had already started work as propmen and stagehands.

Mr. Hilton was very nervous. He was not even happy. Whatever he started to say ended in a sideward look of sadness. He sat slumped in the middle of the first row and asked me to help Miss Glacé. I did this, although she thought my voice too resonant and said, "Show-off!"

Parents began to arrive long before we were ready. They wanted to make a good impression. From among the yards of drapes I peeked out at the audience. I saw my embarrassed mother.

Ira, Lester, and Meyer were pasted to their beards by Miss Glacé. She almost forgot to thread the star on its wire, but I reminded her. I coughed a few times to clear my throat. Miss Glacé looked around and saw that everyone was in costume and in line waiting to play his part. She whispered, "All right. . . ." Then:

Jackie Sauerfeld, the prettiest boy in first grade, parted the curtains with his skinny elbow and in a high voice sang out:

"Parents dear
We are here
To make a Christmas play in time.
It we give
In narrative
And illustrate with pantomime."

He disappeared.

My voice burst immediately from the wings to the great shock of Ira, Lester, and Meyer, who were waiting for it but were surprised all the same.

"I remember, I remember, the house where I was born. . . ."

Miss Glacé yanked the curtain open and there it was, the house—an old hayloft, where Celia Kornbluh lay in the straw with Cindy Lou, her favorite doll. Ira, Lester, and Meyer moved slowly from the wings toward her, sometimes pointing to a moving star and sometimes ahead to Cindy Lou.

It was a long story and it was a sad story. I carefully pronounced all the words about my lonesome childhood, while little Eddie Braunstein wandered upstage and down with his shepherd's stick, looking for sheep. I brought up lonesomeness again, and not being understood at all except by some women everybody hated. Eddie was too small for that and Marty Groff took his place, wearing his father's prayer shawl. I announced twelve friends, and half the boys in the fourth grade gathered round Marty, who stood on an orange crate while my voice harangued. Sorrowful and loud, I declaimed about love and God and Man, but because of the terrible deceit of Abie Stock we came suddenly to a famous moment. Marty, whose remembering tongue I was, waited at the foot of the cross. He stared desperately at the audience. I groaned, "My God, my God, why hast thou forsaken me?" The soldiers who were sheiks grabbed poor Marty to pin him up to die, but he wrenched free, turned again to the audience, and spread his arms aloft to show despair and the end. I murmured at the top of my voice, "The rest is silence, but as everyone in this room, in this city—in this world—now knows, I shall have life eternal."

That night Mrs. Kornbluh visited our kitchen for a glass of tea.

"How's the virgin?" asked my father with a look of concern.

"For a man with a daughter, you got a fresh mouth, Abramovitch."

"Here," said my father kindly, "have some lemon, it'll sweeten your disposition."

They debated a little in Yiddish, then fell in a puddle of Russian and Polish. What I understood next was my father, who said, "Still and all, it was certainly a beautiful affair, you have to admit, introducing us to the beliefs of a different culture."

"Well, yes," said Mrs. Kornbluh. "The only thing . . . you know, Charlie Turner—that cute boy in Celia's class—a couple others? They got very small parts or no part at all. In very bad taste, it seemed to me. After all, it's their religion."

"Ach," explained my mother, "what could Mr. Hilton do? They got very small voices; after all, why should they holler? The English language they know from the beginning by heart. They're blond like angels. You think it's so important they should get in the play? Christmas . . . the whole piece of goods . . . they own it."

I listened and listened until I couldn't listen any more. Too sleepy, I climbed out of bed and kneeled. I made a little church of my hands and said, "Hear, O Israel . . ." Then I called out in Yiddish, "Please, good night, good night. Ssh." My father said, "Ssh yourself," and slammed the kitchen door.

I was happy. I fell asleep at once. I had prayed for everybody: my talking family, cousins far away, passersby, and all the lonesome Christians. I expected to be heard. My voice was certainly the loudest.   [1956]

Term

1. POGROM: An organized and often politically encouraged massacre or persecution of a minority group—in particular, one conducted against Jews.

Understanding the Reading

1. Characterize Shirley's family and neighbors.
2. What objections do the adults have to her part in the Christmas play?
3. Why do her parents allow her to participate?
4. What does she learn from this experience, and how does it change her?

Suggestions for Responding

1. Describe a situation in which you had to participate or at least confront a cultural activity that conflicted with or was alien to your own beliefs or values.
2. What does this story reveal about the lives and values of Jewish immigrants? ◆

8

To Be Hopi or American

POLINGAYSI QOYAWAYMA
(ELIZABETH Q. WHITE)

Like many converts to a new religion, Polingaysi was overly zealous. She was young, she was courageous, she was brash—brash enough to challenge her Hopi elders and the whole beautifully interwoven cultural pattern of Hopi life.

Had she at that time been able to do so, she would have abolished all the age-old rites, the kiva[1] rituals, the sprinkling of sacred cornmeal, and especially the making of *pahos,* or prayer sticks.

At the same time, tempering her radical approach, she had a deep and unsatisfied curiosity concerning the very things that aroused in her the strongest resentment. As she walked across the field one day after visiting her family at New Oraibi, she saw a *paho* thrust into the sand on a little hillock, its single eagle feather fluttering at the end of a short length of white cotton string.

Prayer sticks, either the long, wandlike ones with many feathers tied to them, or the short, sharpened sticks called *pahos,* are held in reverence by the Hopi people. For four days after the "planting" of a prayer, these sticks are thought to possess the essence of the offered prayer and to be very powerful and sacred. To disturb one before it has lost its power is to court disaster. Accident, even death, Polingaysi had been taught, might result.

Well known to her was the story of the white woman who took prayer sticks from a shrine, then fell and broke her leg. Behind this accident the Hopi people saw the work of the invisible forces. The spirits had resented her action and had tripped her, they were convinced.

As she bent to pull the *paho* from the sand, Polingaysi felt a wave of superstitious fear sweep over her. But she was a Christian now, she reminded herself, and need not fear the magic in a stick with a feather on it. Defiantly, she carried it home and challenged her father with it.

"What does this stick mean to you and to the Hopi people?" she asked with more arrogance than she realized. "To me, pah! It means nothing. It has no power. It's just a stick with a bit of cornhusk and a feather attached to it. Why do you, in this day and age, when you can have the message of the Bible, still have faith in sticks and feathers?"

Her father, true Hopi that he was, recoiled from the proffered *paho,* refusing to touch it. There was a worried look in his eyes.

"Must you know?" he asked.

"Of course, I must know," Polingaysi declared. "Why shouldn't I know?"

"Lay it on the table," her father said, "and I will tell you."

She placed the stick on the rough board table which she had goaded the little man into making, and the two of them bent over it.

"Do you see that blue-green, chipped-off place here at the top?" her father asked, pointing. "That is the face of the prayer stick. It represents mossy places, moisture. Now this below is the body of the prayer stick. A red color, as you can see, like our colored sand. That represents the earth. Moisture to the earth, then, is what the *paho* is for."

"A prayer for rain?"

"That, yes, and more. The stick carries a bundle on its back."

"The bit of cornhusk, bound with string? What is it for? What does it mean?"

"I don't know what is bound up in the cornhusk," her father said, "and I won't open it to find out. However, I think you might find there some grass seeds, a pinch of cornmeal, a pinch of pollen, and a drop of honey."

"But, why, why?" Polingaysi demanded impatiently. "What good does it do?"

The little Hopi man had been carving a Kachina doll[2] from the dried root of a cottonwood. He turned away and went back to his work, sitting down crosslegged on the floor and picking up his knife and the unfinished doll. Polingaysi stood looking down at him, waiting for his answer. He thought before he began to speak.

"The good it does depends on many things, my daughter. It depends most of all on the faith of the one who made the *paho*. If all those things I mentioned are inside the little bundle that it carries on its back, it would mean that the one making the *paho* planted it in Mother Earth as a prayer for a plentiful harvest, with moisture enough to help Earth produce full ears of corn, plump beans, sweet melons." He looked up at her and his small face was worried. "Surely you have not forgotten the meaning of the feather? Feathers represent the spirits that are in all things. This one represents the spirit that is in the prayer the *paho* offers up."

Polingaysi turned away and took the *paho* in her hands. About to tear open the cornhusk, she looked down to see her father's hands stilled and horror in his expression. Suddenly she could not open the *paho*'s treasure without his permission. She could not fly in the face of tradition to that extent, knowing it would offend his spirit, however silent he remained, however little he reproached her openly.

"May I open it?"

Her father bent his head, possibly questioning the propriety of such an action and fearing the harm it might do him and his daughter. After a moment of hesitation, he sighed, saying, "It seems well weathered. I think it is more than four days old. If so, its purpose has been served and the power has left it. Use your left hand."

Gently, in spite of her pretended scorn, Polingaysi opened the bit of wrapped cornhusk. It had been folded while still green into a tiny triangle. In this little pouch there was a bit of material about the size of a pea. Seeds, cornmeal, pollen, held together with honey, as her father had predicted.

"Can't you see there's nothing of value in here?" Polingaysi cried.

"Not to you," her father agreed. "Not to me. But to the one who made it in prayer."

She would have questioned him further, but he took his work and went outside, his face enigmatic.

"For pity's sake, Mother," Polingaysi burst out, turning to Sevenka who had been working quietly on a basket during the discussion, "does everything in the life of a Hopi have a hidden meaning? Why, for instance, should I use my left hand to open that thing?"

"It seems foolish to you because you are young and do not understand everything," her mother said patiently. "Perhaps you are foolish because you do not understand Hopi ways, though you are a Hopi. I will tell you about the left hand.

"The left hand is on the heart side of the body. It is the hand that moves most slowly. It selects, instead of grabbing as the right hand does. It is cleaner. It does not touch the mouth during the eating of food, nor does it clean the body after release of waste materials.

"Do you remember watching our medicine man—the Man With Eyes—at his work? In his healing rites and also in his religious ceremonies he uses the left hand, for those reasons I have just given you. The left hand, then, is the hand that is of the heart and the spirit, not of nature and the earth."

Polingaysi struggled to deny the beauty of the words her mother had spoken. She sought a scoffing answer, but found none. After a moment the older woman continued.

"One more thing I will tell you about the *pahos*. They must be kept free of the white man's ways if they are to have the full power of old times. That is why Hopi people do not sharpen them to a point with white man's steel blades, but grind them to sharpness on sandstone."

At that moment Polingaysi saw one of her mother's brothers passing the window. He knew nothing of the discussion and she had no desire to reopen it. With her left hand she placed the *paho* on the window sill.

"Polingaysi!" the old man cried, his face crinkling into a big smile of welcome. "It is a great treat to my spirit to see you after so long a time. We are always happy to see our child come home, even if she does make us sit at a wooden platform when we eat."

Polingaysi lost some of her contentiousness and laughed. He had always complained about sitting at the table, insisting that he could not keep his feet warm while he was eating unless he sat on them, Hopi-fashion. Her little grandmother had been completely mystified by the table, and though Polingaysi had patiently explained its use, the old lady had laboriously climbed up onto it, instead of seating herself on the wooden bench that served as a chair.

She looked at her uncle and thought of all the new ideas she had gleaned during her life among white people. The old man had no desire to share her knowledge. To him the old way was best. He asked little of life: enough food to keep the breath in his thin, worn old body, a little heat in the fireplace, a drink of water when he was dry.

It was she who was forever holding out her cup to be filled with knowledge.   [1964]

Terms

1. KIVA: An underground room used by Hopi men for ceremonies or councils.
2. KACHINA DOLL: A doll made of wood and decorated with paint, feathers, and other materials that represents various spirits to Native Americans in the Southwest.

Understanding the Reading

1. Why does Polingaysi respond to the *paho* with both fear and arrogance?
2. Explain what Polingaysi means when she asks, "does everything in the life of a Hopi have a hidden meaning?"
3. What does this selection tell you about "Hopi ways"?
4. Why would it be important that *pahos* "be kept free from white man's ways"?
5. What does the closing sentence mean?

Suggestions for Responding

1. Describe a generational conflict, especially one based on an ethnic tradition, between you and an older family member. What were the immediate and the long-term outcomes?
2. Both Paley and Qoyawayma describe the experience of assimilation. Some people feel this process was essential to creating a unified American society, whereas others believe that the costs, both the loss of cultural variety and the pain to individuals and families, were too high. Which position do you support? Why? ✦

9

People of Color Who Never Felt They Were Black

DARRYL FEARS

At her small apartment near the National Cathedral in Northwest Washington, Maria Martins quietly watched as an African American friend studied a picture of her mother. "Oh," the friend said, surprise in her voice. "Your mother is white."

She turned to Martins. "But you are black."

That came as news to Martins, a Brazilian who, for 30 years before immigrating to the

United States, looked in the mirror and saw a *morena*—a woman with caramel-colored skin that is nearly equated with whiteness in Brazil and some other Latin American countries. "I didn't realize I was black until I came here," she said.

That realization has come to hundreds of thousands of dark-complexioned immigrants to the United States from Brazil, Colombia, Panama and other Latin nations with sizable populations of African descent. Although most do not identify themselves as black, they are seen that way as soon as they set foot in North America.

Their reluctance to embrace this definition has left them feeling particularly isolated—shunned by African Americans who believe they are denying their blackness; by white Americans who profile them in stores or on highways; and by lighter-skinned Latinos whose images dominate Spanish-language television all over the world, even though a majority of Latin people have some African or Indian ancestry.

The pressure to accept not only a new language and culture, but also a new racial identity, is a burden some darker-skinned Latinos say they face every day.

"It's overwhelming," said Yvette Modestin, a dark-skinned native of Panama who works as an outreach coordinator in Boston. "There's not a day that I don't have to explain myself."

E. Francisco Lopez, a Venezuelan-born attorney in Washington, said he had not heard the term "minority" before coming to America.

"I didn't know what it meant. I didn't accept it because I thought it meant 'less than,'" said Martins, whose father is black. "'Where are you from?' they ask me. I say I'm from Brazil. They say, 'No, you are from Africa.' They make me feel like I am denying who I am."

Exactly who these immigrants are is almost impossible to divine from the 2000 Census. Latinos of African, mestizo and European descent—or any mixture of the three—found it hard to answer the question "What is your racial origin?"

Some of the nation's 35 million Latinos scribbled in the margins that they were Aztec or Mayan. A fraction said they were Indian. Nearly forty-eight percent described themselves as white, and only 2 percent as black. Fully 42 percent said they were "some other race."

BETWEEN BLACK AND WHITE

Race matters in Latin America, but it matters differently.

Most South American nations barely have a black presence. In Argentina, Chile, Peru and Bolivia, there are racial tensions, but mostly between indigenous Indians and white descendants of Europeans.

The black presence is stronger along the coasts of two nations that border the Caribbean Sea, Venezuela and Colombia—which included Panama in the 19th century—along with Brazil, which snakes along the Atlantic coast. In many ways, those nations have more in common racially with Puerto Rico, Cuba and the Dominican Republic than they do with the rest of South America.

This black presence is a legacy of slavery, just as it is in the United States. But the experience of race in the United States and in these Latin countries is separated by how slaves and their descendants were treated after slavery was abolished.

In the United States, custom drew a hard line between black and white, and Jim Crow rules kept the races separate. The color line hardened to the point that it was sanctioned in 1896 by the Supreme Court in its decision in *Plessy v. Ferguson,* which held that Homer Plessy, a white-complexioned Louisiana shoemaker, could not ride in the white section of a train because a single ancestor of his was black.

Thus Americans with any discernible African ancestry—whether they identified themselves as black or not—were thrust into one category. One consequence is that dark-complexioned and light-complexioned black people combined to campaign for equal rights, leading to the civil rights movement of the 1960s.

By contrast, the Latin countries with a sizable black presence had more various, and more fluid, experiences of race after slavery.

African slavery is as much a part of Brazil's history as it is of the United States's, said Sheila Walker, a visiting professor of anthropology at Spelman College in Atlanta and editor of the book "African Roots/American Cultures." Citing the census in Brazil, she said that nation has more people of African descent than any other in the world besides Nigeria, Africa's most populous country.

Brazil stands out in South America for that and other reasons. Unlike most nations there, its people speak Portuguese rather than Spanish, prompting a debate over whether Brazil is part of the Latino diaspora.

Brazilian slavery ended in 1889 by decree, with no civil war and no Jim Crow—and mixing between light- and dark-complexioned Indians, Europeans, Africans and mulattoes was common and, in many areas, encouraged. Although discrimination against dark-complexioned Brazilians was clear, class played almost as important a role as race.

In Colombia, said Luis Murillo, a black politician in exile from that country, light-complexioned descendants of Spanish conquistadors and Indians created the "mestizo" race, an ideology that held that all mixed-race people were the same. But it was an illusion, Murillo said: A pecking order "where white people were considered superior and darker people were considered inferior" pervaded Colombia.

Murillo said the problem exists throughout Latin American and Spanish-speaking Caribbean countries with noticeable black populations. White Latinos control the governments even in nations with dark-complexioned majorities, he said. And in nations ruled by military juntas and dictators, there are few protests, Murillo said.

In Cuba, a protest by Afro-Cubans led to the arming of the island's white citizens and, ultimately, the massacre of 3,000 to 6,000 black men, women and children in 1912, according to University of Michigan historian Frank Guridy, author of "Race and Politics in Cuba, 1933–34."

American-influenced Cuba was also home to the Ku Klux Klan Kubano and other anti-black groups before Fidel Castro's revolution. Now, Cuban racism still exists, some say, but black, mulatto and white people mix much more freely. Lopez, the Afro-Venezuelan lawyer, said, "Race doesn't affect us there the way it does here," he said. "It's more of a class thing."

Jose Neinstein, a native white Brazilian and executive director of the Brazilian-American Cultural Institute in Washington, boiled down to the simplest terms how his people are viewed. "In this country," he said, "if you are not quite white, then you are black." But in Brazil, he said, "If you are not quite black, then you are white."

The elite in Brazil, as in most Latin American nations, are educated and white. But many brown and black people also belong in that class. Generally, brown Brazilians, such as Martins, enjoy many privileges of the elite, but are disproportionately represented in Brazilian slums.

Someone with Sidney Poitier's deep chocolate complexion would be considered white if his hair were straight and he made a living in a profession. That might not seem so odd, Brazilians say, when you consider that the fair-complexioned actresses Rashida Jones of the television show "Boston Public" and Lena Horne are identified as black in the United States.

Neinstein remembered talking with a man of Poitier's complexion during a visit to Brazil. "We were discussing ethnicity," Neinstein said, "and I asked him, 'What do you think about this from your perspective as a black man?' He turned his head to me and said, 'I'm not black,'" Neinstein recalled. " . . . It simply paralyzed me. I couldn't ask another question."

By the same token, Neinstein said, he never perceived brown-complexioned people such as Maria Martins, who works at the cultural institute, as black. One day, when an African American custodian in his building referred to one of his brown-skinned secretaries as "the black lady," Neinstein was confused. "I never looked at that woman as black," he said. "It was quite a revelation to me."

Those perceptions come to the United States with the light- and dark-complexioned Latinos who carry them. But here, they collide with two contradictory forces: North American prejudice and African American pride. . . .   [2002]

Understanding the Reading

1. Why are some Latin Americans and Brazilians pressured to accept a different racial identity in the United States?
2. What is the reaction of many African Americans when Latin Americans are reluctant to identify as Black?
3. Why is the United States' view on race different from that of Brazil and many other Latin American countries?

Suggestions for Responding

1. Research the history of slavery in Brazil.
2. Research the Ku Klux Klan Kubano.
3. Listen to Brazilian music from Salvador, Bahia. ◆

10

Rosa Wakefield

John Langston Gwaltney

Florida-born, Miss Rosa Wakefield has known me practically all my life, and I have always thought of her as a worthy senior with so much dignity that the last thing she needs to think about is standing upon it. She is seventy-eight and hale and preeminently sound-minded. Her buttermilk pies and watermelon pork are as fine as they were when I was a fifth-grader puzzling with her over a text which asserted confidently that the Nigerian Hausa[1] were not black. I do not know anyone who has done more people more good with less noise than Miz Wakefield.

You understand that I am not an educated person. I was born with good sense and I read everything I can get to read. At least I know that I don't know very much. Now, if you still think I can help you, I'll be very glad to answer any question I can for you. I can't answer for nobody but myself. I will tell you what I think and why I happen to think that way. I was never the first person you heard when you came to my father's house or a party, but that never meant that I wasn't thinking as fast as some of these loud folks was talking.

Now, this first question is something I have thought about a great deal ever since I was a little girl. I think that I think more about anything I might think about than most people. That's because I was my father's oldest daughter and my mother died early, so I always had to think for more than one person. And that is a responsibility. It's bad enough when you make a mistake for one person, but when you make a mistake for more than one person—you know,

when you make a mistake that's going to hurt somebody who can't think for herself or hisself—then you really feel that more than you would if you had just hurt yourself. I always thought about that. My father and I sort of brought the others up. Now, I don't want to brag on myself, but I guess we didn't do but so bad. Now, the truth is that I think we did a good job.

But now, right there you have one of the big differences between blackfolks, or colored folks, or whatsoever you might call us, and whitefolks. We don't like to spell things out but so much. We know what we mean, like you knew what I meant. You know that I don't really mean that I think we did a pretty good job in raising all those children. You know that I mean that it was very hard to do so and we did it right.

White people are some writing folks! They will write! They write everything. Now, they do that because they don't trust each other. Also, they are the kind of people who think that you can think about everything, about whatever you are going to do, before you do that thing. Now, that's bad for them because you cannot do that without wings. I think that maybe you can't even do that *with* wings. They say that God's brightest angel fell. Now, ask yourself! Do you think God would have made this brightest angel if He knew that this angel was going to turn against Him? Now, it don't make one bit of sense to think that He would have done that. If He knew this brightest angel was going to ape up, what would He want to go and make this angel for? Now, if the Lord can be surprised, who are we to think that we can think about everything before it happens? All you can do is do what you know has got to be done as right as you know how to do that thing. Now, white people don't seem to know that.

I worked hard to put the others through school, and now they help me so the old lady can stir up a little sweet bread and talk to nice people like you. But, you see, there is hard work behind everything we do. You know that this sweet bread didn't make itself. I was telling you about my trips. You know that trip to Africa and that trip to Norway didn't pay for themselves! But, you see, if you eats these dinners and don't cook 'em, if you wears these clothes and don't buy or iron them, then you might start thinking that the good fairy or some spirit did all that. They asked a little white girl in this family I used to work for who made her cake at one of her little tea parties. She said she made it and then she hid her face and said the good fairies made it. Well, you are looking at that good fairy.

Blackfolks don't have no time to be thinking like that. If I thought like that, I'd burn cakes and scorch skirts. But when you don't have anything else to do, you can think like that. It's bad for your mind, though. See, if you think about what is really happening, you will know why these things are happening. When I get these cards on my birthday or Easter, I know that's because I sent my younger brother to school as clean as I could send him and made him get some sense into his head by seeing that he did what that teacher told him to do. They all send me a card on Mother's Day because they say that I was a mother to them. Now, they know that I am living all these other days, too, and they see to it that I don't want for anything I really need and a lot of things the old lady might just want. Rosa has washed her dishes and a lot of other folks' dishes for a long time, so she doesn't really need any machine to wash dishes, but she got one sitting right there in that kitchen! Now, Rosa didn't buy it and she didn't tell anybody to buy it, but it was bought. Now, my youngest brother is a professor too, but if he comes in here and sees something that has to be done, from washing dishes to scrubbing that floor, the next thing you know he just goes on and does it like anybody else. I never married, but any niece or nephew I got will come here if they *think* I need something and go wherever I want to send them.

Now, our children are more mannerable, but now so many of our children are trying to act like white children that it's hard to tell the difference just by the way they act these days. Some of these sorry things passing for young men and ladies that you see in the streets these days are enough to make you hang your head in shame! But so far, praise God, all our children have kept level heads and are doing just fine. In the summer we get together more and they tell me some things that are really hard to believe. I tell them to be nice to everybody that is nice to them and not to do every fool thing that they see being done. Little Rosa, my niece, brought a girl from Nigeria and a girl from Sweden. Now, that pleased me because I have read about those places and I have seen those countries and people there were nice to me, so I was glad to be nice to one of their girls.

We are revern' colored folks! We don't all have the same color skin, but we all have a strong family resemblance. My niece's mother is a German woman, and a finer lady you will never meet. But all you have to do is take one look at my niece and you will know that she is my niece. We all have a very strong family resemblance and we are a family that helps each other. If you know one of us, you know us all. We try to look out for each other. I told my brother about you and those mules and he said you looked just like a Wakefield. All you got to do to look just like a Wakefield is be black and do something good. But he's right this time—you do look a lot like us. You're quiet like we are, too. I guess in your work you have to be quiet because once you get us blackfolks talking, you won't get much of a chance to make much noise! But once a lady was out here, and she couldn't pay for her taxi because that driver had charged her way too much. We helped her and she swore that I looked just like her. Now, I'm a brown woman and this lady I'm telling you about looked as white as any white woman you will ever see. People like to claim kin with people they like. White people do that much more than we do, though. They can' stand the idea of anything good being black. If a black person does something good, they say he did that because of the white in him.

My father was sickly, but he worked hard all his life. He taught me and I tried to help teach the others. People have to go to school now, but they wouldn't have to do that if they would take up time with one another. I went to one college course to learn about the Negro. I'm sorry I did that now because all they did was to sit there and tell each other how they felt—I mean, how it felt to be black. Shoot! I have been feeling black all my life because I am not white! Now, what I wanted to know was not how they felt, because I already knew that; I wanted to know something about our great people and where we came from and how we kept on being folks all through slavery time.

My church and my folks got together and sent the old lady to Spain and Morocco. Everywhere I went I saw some of us. There was colored everywhere I set my foot. Now, I couldn't understand them, but I was looking at them and if I'm black, and we both know I am, there is nothing else in God's world for them to be but black too. There was all kinds of colors! Some of them were white like the people that call themselves white over here. Some of them looked mighty Wakefield. Now, I saw that in Spain and I saw that in Africa. In Morocco some of those people could have been your brother or mine. Some of them had kinky hair and some of them had straight hair and some had wavy hair. Some of them looked like Jews and Italians, but there was all kinds of folks. Most of those people looked like what we used to call munglas. I have read that the Moroccans are white and I know that Americans are supposed to be white, but it looks to me like they are just as mixed up as we are over here. Half of these whitefolks I see out here look like they are passing[2] to me. That's the same way it is in Cuba and Puerto Rico. I have seen those countries and I know that most of those people are colored, just like most of those people in Morocco. I'm telling you what I saw, not what somebody told me. A lot of these people from those foreign countries may not speak English, but you can look at them and see that they are Aun' Hagi's[3] children. A lot of them don't want to admit their color because they are afraid that these whitefolks over here would give them a hard time. Now, they are right about that.

I have been a cook and a maid and a housekeeper, and I have worked in hospitals. I still do every now and then, but I was in the hospital not long ago and I met this doctor that they said was an Arab. Well, he was darker than many people in my own family. I was proud to see one of the race better hisself. But, you know, that devil didn't want to hear a thing about his color! They had a lot of doctors from India and

Jordan working there too. Now, a lot of the colored people didn't want to have anything to do with them because they said if they will pass like that, maybe they are not really doctors, either. I know folks that pass, but these doctors were just plain fools about it! I know people who pass to get a job that they should be able to get anyway, but they don't try to act like them all the time. There was this young Iraqian doctor there and he was darker than me, but he sure did everything he could think of and then some to show how white he was supposed to be. I don't trust anybody who would deny their color like that. And if Rosa Wakefield can't put her trust in you, you will never get your hands on her blood pressure or her diabetes or anything else! [1980]

Terms

1. NIGERIAN HAUSA: Black people of Niger and northern Nigeria.
2. PASSING: A reference to light-skinned Blacks trying to "pass" as Whites.
3. AUNT HAGI: A reference to the biblical figure Hagar, the servant of Sarah and Abraham and mother of Abraham's son, Ishmael.

Understanding the Reading

1. What values does Rosa Wakefield hold?
2. What characteristics does she think differentiate "blackfolks" from "whitefolks"?
3. Explain her beliefs about racial identity.
4. What questions do you think Gwaltney posed to elicit Wakefield's responses?

Suggestions for Responding

1. What advice do you think Rosa Wakefield might give to any one of the preceding writers?
2. If you were collecting oral histories from your family or your community, what kinds of information would you want to focus on? In other words, what characteristics and values do you expect to identify? What questions would you ask to obtain that information? ✦

11

Are Doctors' Offices Places for Racial Profiling?

AHC Media, LLC

Are Race-Based Treatments Unethical?

Sally Satel, MD, is proud to be a racially profiling doctor.

The practicing psychiatrist and fellow at the Washington, DC-based conservative think tank The American Enterprise Institute says it's important for clinicians to consider racial and ethnic factors when making diagnostic and treatment decisions for patients.

"Certain diseases and treatment responses cluster by ethnicity," she wrote in the May 5 issue of *The New York Times Magazine*.[1] "Recognizing these patterns can help us diagnose disease more efficiently and prescribe medications more effectively. When it comes to practicing medicine, stereotyping often works."

For example, clinical research and her own personal experience have shown her that African-American patients metabolize antidepressants more slowly than Caucasian and Asian patients do. If this happens, levels of the medication in the body can build over time and lead to side effects, such as insomnia, nausea, and confusion. Therefore, Satel frequently starts her black patients at a lower dose of antidepressants.

Admittedly, not all black people metabolize these medications slowly—only an estimated 40% do. But the likelihood is significant enough that she feels she should take this into consideration, she tells *Medical Ethics Advisor*. "If you were wrong to start the patient at a lower dose, you can simply raise the dose later."

This is preferable to initiating drug therapy that might cause side effects that may lead an already vulnerable patient to stop taking the medication altogether.

Satel is not alone in her approach. Other doctors agree that they have long considered racial and ethnic background as factors in making decisions based on their experience with certain groups of patients.

Now, clinical studies are beginning to examine how members of different ethnic groups respond to standard treatment regimens and whether these groups may be at higher risk for certain types of diseases.

A report in the May issue of the journal *Clinical Infectious Diseases* indicates Hispanic immigrants are at higher risk for infections that do not usually occur in the U.S.-born population. A recent study in the journal *Hepatology* reported on the higher prevalence of gall-bladder disease among American Indians, and a study in the June issue of *The American Journal of Clinical Nutrition* proposed a need for different body-mass index cutoffs in different racial and ethnic groups.

A pair of particularly controversial studies published in the May 2001 issue of the *New England Journal of Medicine* highlighted differences in response to certain heart medications observed between African-American and Caucasian men.

The first study, by Exner and colleagues, found that the drug enalapril was more effective in treating left-ventricular dysfunction in white patients than in black patients.[2] Another study in the same issue concluded that the drug carvedilol was equally effective in treating chronic heart disease in both white and black patients.[3]

But some doctors and researchers are criticizing such studies, claiming that their focus on linking treatment responses and risk factors to specific racial and ethnic groups is misleading and scientifically dangerous.

Genetics, Not Race, Is the Key

"You have to bear in mind that, from a biological point of view, the definition of any race is arbitrary," says **Robert Schwartz**, MD, a deputy editor at the *New England Journal of Medicine,* who wrote an editorial commenting on the studies of racial differences in response to the heart medicines.

Genetic studies are showing what scientists have long believed—that there are no biologically distinct races of people, he says. Differences in response to treatment or risks for disease differ because of a person's genetic makeup.

People who are from one area of the world will tend to have similar genes and genetic mutations, he says. But, as world populations have intermingled it has become less likely that specific genetic mutations can be attributed to people of certain geographic origins.

"If you have an individual patient in your office, how do you know that patient has the gene that affects the metabolism of that drug?" Schwartz asks. "You can only guess. Just saying, 'Well, the patient is black and, therefore, I am not going to give him a beta-blocker' is, to me, not the way to practice medicine."

A recent study of the occurrence of genetic polymorphisms (gene mutations linked to specific traits) have found that of the five genes involved in metabolism, race was not an accurate predictor of the occurrence of the polymorphisms that made metabolism slower, he points out.

"The frequency of a polymorphism involving drug metabolism had the same frequency in Ethiopians as it did in Norwegians," he notes. "So that is why, from a biological point of view, we have to be very, very cautious."

The impetus behind many of these new studies is that for very many years, black people and members of other minority populations were not included in clinical research trials. So, information about effective treatments was largely determined by only studying one group of people, Schwartz admits.

But studies that now hope to remedy that situation risk making it worse by focusing on distinctions by racial groups or ethnic factors, which can lead to further stereotyping and stigmatization, he says.

The studies' real goal is to determine the environmental, cultural, and genetic factors that influence disease and response to treatment, so it would be better if researchers deliberately focused on these areas.

"Right now, we are on the edge of what many people are beginning to refer to as personalized therapy," he says. "You will be able to obtain accurate information on the likelihood of a response or no response from a single drop of blood, through DNA."

It's true that geographic ancestry and the currently identified racial groups are only rough markers for the genetic traits that may affect a person's response to treatment, but right now it is the best information available, and physicians would be remiss in ignoring it, argues Satel.

She does not advocate making a decision about a diagnosis or treatment based solely on a person's race or ethnicity, but says these factors, like so many others considered during a workup, must be considered.

"Diagnosing is a process of elimination," she explains. "You have to think of the likelihood of what is wrong, and you rule out with tests, typically. If that does not explain the pathology, you go on to the next potential diagnosis. The point is, you will get there eventually even if you do not know the person's race, but it is just a bit of information that might help you get there quicker."   [2002]

Notes

1. Satel S. I am a racially profiling doctor. *The New York Times Magazine*. May 5, 2002.
2. Exner DV, Dries DL, Domanski MJ, et al. Lesser response to angiostentin-converting enzyme inhibitor therapy in black as compared to white patients with left-ventricular dysfunction. *N Engl J Med* 2001; 344:1351–1357.
3. Yancy CW, Fowler MB, Colucci WS, et al. Race and the response to adrenergic blockade with carvedilol in patients with chronic heart failure. *N Engl J Med* 2001; 344:3558–3565.

Understanding the Reading

1. Why do some doctors think medical racial profiling is scientifically dangerous?
2. What is the difference between a person's race and a person's genetic makeup?
3. Why can geographic information about a person's ancestors be important when identifying and treating an illness?

Suggestions for Responding

1. Have a debate on the dangers or benefits of medical racial profiling, using this article and the preceding one by Satel.
2. Research your family's medical history; find out whether certain illnesses are more common in the part of the world from which your family came. ✦

12

In Search of Bruce Lee's Grave

SHANLON WU

It's Saturday morning in Seattle, and I am driving to visit Bruce Lee's grave.[1] I have been in the city for only a couple of weeks and so drive two blocks past the cemetery before realizing that I've passed it. I double back and turn through the large wrought-iron gate, past a sign that reads: "Open to 9 P.M. or dusk, whichever comes first."

It's a sprawling cemetery, with winding roads leading in all directions. I feel silly trying to find his grave with no guidance. I think that my search for his grave is similar to my search for Asian heroes in America.

I was born in 1959, an Asian-American in Westchester County, N.Y. During my childhood there were no Asian sports stars. On television, I can recall only that most pathetic of Asian characters, Hop Sing, the Cartwright family houseboy on "Bonanza."[2] But in my adolescence there was Bruce.

I was 14 years old when I first saw "Enter the Dragon," the granddaddy of martial-arts movies. Bruce had died suddenly at the age of 32 of cerebral edema, an excess of fluid in the brain, just weeks before the release of the film. Between the ages of 14 and 17, I saw "Enter the Dragon" 22 times before I stopped counting. During those years I collected Bruce Lee posters, putting them up at all angles in my bedroom. I took up Chinese martial arts and spent hours comparing my physique with his.

I learned all I could about Bruce: that he had married a Caucasian, Linda; that he had sparred with Kareem Abdul-Jabbar;[3] that he was a buddy of Steve McQueen and James Coburn, both of whom were his pallbearers.

My parents, who immigrated to America and had become professors at Hunter College, tolerated my behavior, but seemed puzzled at my admiration of an "entertainer." My father jokingly tried to compare my obsession with Bruce to his boyhood worship of Chinese folk-tale heroes.

"I read them just like you read American comic books," he said.

But my father's heroes could not be mine; they came from an ancient literary tradition, not comic books. He and my mother had grown up in a land where they belonged to the majority. I could not adopt their childhood and they were wise enough not to impose it upon me.

Although I never again experienced the kind of blind hero worship I felt for Bruce, my need to find heroes remained strong.

In college, I discovered the men of the 442d Regimental Combat Team, a United States Army all-Japanese unit in World War II. Allowed to fight only against Europeans, they suffered heavy casualties while their families were put in internment camps. Their motto was "Go for Broke."

I saw them as Asians in a Homeric epic, the protagonists of a Shakespearean tragedy; I knew no Eastern myths to infuse them with. They embodied my own need to prove myself in the Caucasian world. I imagined how their American-born flesh and muscle must have resembled mine: epicanthic folds[4] set in strong faces nourished on milk and beef. I thought how much they had proved where there was so little to prove.

After college, I competed as an amateur boxer in an attempt to find my self-image in the ring. It didn't work. My fighting was only an attempt to copy Bruce's movies. What I needed was instruction on how to live. I quit boxing after a year and went to law school.

I was an anomaly there: a would-be Asian litigator. I had always liked to argue and found I liked doing it in front of people even more. When I won the first-year moot court competition in law school, I asked an Asian classmate if he thought I was the first Asian to win. He laughed and told me I was probably the only Asian to even compete.

The law-firm interviewers always seemed surprised that I wanted to litigate.

"Aren't you interested in Pacific Rim trade?" they asked.

"My Chinese isn't good enough," I quipped.

My pat response seemed to please them. It certainly pleased me. I thought I'd found a place of my own—a place where the law would insulate me from the pressure of defining my Asian maleness. I sensed the possibility of merely being myself.

But the pressure reasserted itself. One morning, the year after graduating from law school,

I read the obituary of Gen. Minoru Genda—the man who planned the Pearl Harbor attack. I'd never heard of him and had assumed that whoever did that planning was long since dead. But the general had been alive all those years—rising at 4 every morning to do his exercises and retiring every night by 8. An advocate of animal rights, the obituary said.

I found myself drawn to the general's life despite his association with the Axis powers. He seemed a forthright, graceful man who died unhumbled. The same paper carried a front-page story about Congress's failure to pay the Japanese-American internees their promised reparation[5] money. The general, at least, had not died waiting for reparations.

I was surprised and frightened by my admiration for General Genda, by my still-strong hunger for images of powerful Asian men. That hunger was my vulnerability manifested, a reminder of my lack of place.

The hunger is eased this gray morning in Seattle. After asking directions from a policeman—Japanese—I easily locate Bruce's grave. The headstone is red granite with a small picture etched into it. The picture is very Hollywood—Bruce wears dark glasses—and I think the calligraphy looks a bit sloppy. Two tourists stop but leave quickly after glancing at me.

I realize I am crying. Bruce's grave seems very small in comparison to his place in my boyhood. So small in comparison to my need for heroes. Seeing his grave, I understand how large the hole in my life has been, and how desperately I'd sought to fill it.

I had sought an Asian hero to emulate. But none of my choices quite fit me. Their lives were defined through heroic tasks—they had villains to defeat and wars to fight—while my life seemed merely a struggle to define myself.

But now I see how that very struggle has defined me. I must be my own hero even as I learn to treasure those who have gone before.

I have had my powerful Asian male images: Bruce, the men of the 442d and General Genda; I may yet discover others. Their lives beckon like fireflies on a moonless night, and I know that they—like me—may have been flawed by foolhardiness and even cruelty. Still, their lives were real. They were not houseboys on "Bonanza."

[1990]

Terms

1. BRUCE LEE: A Chinese American movie star skilled in the martial arts.
2. *BONANZA:* A television series about a family of ranchers.
3. KAREEM ABDUL-JABBAR: A professional basketball star; Steve McQueen and James Coburn were White movie stars who played very physical roles.
4. EPICANTHIC FOLD: A fold of skin on the upper eyelid that tends to cover the inner corner of the eye.
5. REPARATION: Payment to Japanese Americans to compensate them for internment during World War II.

Understanding the Reading

1. Why couldn't Wu identify with his father's heroes?
2. What did the heroes Wu identified with have in common?
3. What does Wu mean when he says that the struggle for heroes "defined me"?

Suggestions for Responding

1. What "heroes" did you identify with as you grew up? Did they in any way influence your sense of your ethnic identity? If so, how? If not, why not?
2. Both Wu and Alvarez come to grips with their identity. Explain the similarities and differences in their experiences. ✦

13

American Dreamer

BHARATI MUKHERJEE

The United States exists as a sovereign nation; "America," in contrast, exists as a myth of democracy and equal opportunity to live by, or as an ideal goal to reach.

I am a naturalized U.S. citizen, which means that, unlike native-born citizens, I had to prove to the U.S. government that I merited citizenship. What I didn't have to disclose was that I desired "America," which to me is the stage for the drama of self-transformation.

I was born in Calcutta and first came to the United States—to Iowa City, to be precise—on a summer evening in 1961. I flew into a small airport surrounded by cornfields and pastures, ready to carry out the two commands my father had written out for me the night before I left Calcutta: Spend two years studying creative writing at the Iowa Writers' Workshop, then come back home and marry the bridegroom he selected for me from our caste and class.

In traditional Hindu families like ours, men provided and women were provided for. My father was a patriarch and I a pliant daughter. The neighborhood I'd grown up in was homogeneously Hindu, Bengali-speaking, and middle-class. I didn't expect myself to ever disobey or disappoint my father by setting my own goals and taking charge of my future.

When I landed in Iowa 35 years ago, I found myself in a society in which almost everyone was Christian, white, and moderately well-off. In the women's dormitory I lived in my first year, apart from six international graduate students (all of us were from Asia and considered "exotic"), the only non-Christian was Jewish, and the only non-white an African-American from Georgia. I didn't anticipate then, that over the next 35 years, the Iowa population would become so diverse that it would have 6,931 children from non-English-speaking homes registered as students in its schools, nor that Iowans would be in the grip of a cultural crisis in which resentment against immigrants, particularly refugees from Vietnam, Sudan, and Bosnia, as well as unskilled Spanish-speaking workers, would become politicized enough to cause the Immigration and Naturalization Service to open an "enforcement" office in Cedar Rapids in October for the tracking and deporting of undocumented aliens.

In Calcutta in the '50s, I heard no talk of "identity crisis"—communal or individual. The concept itself—of a person not knowing who he or she is—was unimaginable in our hierarchical, classification-obsessed society. One's identity was fixed, derived from religion, caste, patrimony, and mother tongue. A Hindu Indian's last name announced his or her forefathers'

caste and place of origin. A Mukherjee could *only* be a Brahmin from Bengal. Hindu tradition forbade intercaste, interlanguage, interethnic marriages. Bengali tradition even discouraged emigration: To remove oneself from Bengal was to dilute true culture.

Until the age of 8, I lived in a house crowded with 40 or 50 relatives. My identity was viscerally connected with ancestral soil and genealogy. I was who I was because I was Dr. Sudhir Lal Mukherjee's daughter, because I was a Hindu Brahmin, because I was Bengali-speaking, and because my *desh*—the Bengali word for homeland—was an East Bengal village called Faridpur.

The University of Iowa classroom was my first experience of coeducation. And after not too long, I fell in love with a fellow student named Clark Blaise, an American of Canadian origin, and impulsively married him during a lunch break in a lawyer's office above a coffee shop.

That act cut me off forever from the rules and ways of upper-middle-class life in Bengal, and hurled me into a New World life of scary improvisations and heady explorations. Until my lunch-break wedding, I had seen myself as an Indian foreign student who intended to return to India to live. The five-minute ceremony in the lawyer's office suddenly changed me into a transient with conflicting loyalties to two very different cultures.

The first 10 years into marriage, years spent mostly in my husband's native Canada, I thought of myself as an expatriate Bengali permanently stranded in North America because of destiny or desire. My first novel, *The Tiger's Daughter,* embodies the loneliness I felt but could not acknowledge, even to myself, as I negotiated the no-man's land between the country of my past and the continent of my present. Shaped by memory, textured with nostalgia for a class and culture I had abandoned, this novel quite naturally became an expression of the expatriate consciousness.

It took me a decade of painful introspection to put nostalgia in perspective and to make the transition from expatriate to immigrant. After a 14-year stay in Canada, I forced my husband and our two sons to relocate to the United States. But the transition from foreign student to

U.S. citizen, from detached onlooker to committed immigrant, has not been easy.

The years in Canada were particularly harsh. Canada is a country that officially, and proudly, resists cultural fusion. For all its rhetoric about a cultural "mosaic," Canada refuses to renovate its national self-image to include its changing complexion. It is a New World country with Old World concepts of a fixed, exclusivist national identity. Canadian official rhetoric designated me as one of the "visible minority" who, even though I spoke the Canadian languages of English and French, was straining "the absorptive capacity" of Canada. Canadians of color were routinely treated as "not real" Canadians. One example: In 1985 a terrorist bomb, planted in an Air-India jet on Canadian soil, blew up after leaving Montreal, killing 329 passengers, most of whom were Canadians of Indian origin. The prime minister of Canada at the time, Brian Mulroney, phoned the prime minister of India to offer Canada's condolences for India's loss.

Those years of race-related harassments in Canada politicized me and deepened my love of the ideals embedded in the American Bill of Rights. I don't forget that the architects of the Constitution and the Bill of Rights were white males and slaveholders. But through their declaration, they provided us with the enthusiasm for human rights, and the initial framework from which other empowerments could be conceived and enfranchised communities expanded.

I am a naturalized U.S. citizen and I take my American citizenship very seriously. I am not an economic refugee, nor am I a seeker of political asylum. I am a voluntary immigrant. I became a citizen by choice, not by simple accident of birth.

Yet these days, questions such as who is an American and what is American culture are being posed with belligerence, and being answered with violence. Scapegoating of immigrants has once again become the politicians' easy remedy for all that ails the nation. Hate speeches fill auditoriums for demagogues willing to profit from stirring up racial animosity. An April Gallup poll indicated that half of Americans would like to bar almost all legal immigration for the next five years.

The United States, like every sovereign nation, has a right to formulate its immigration policies. But in this decade of continual, large-scale diasporas,[1] it is imperative that we come to some agreement about who "we" are, and what our goals are for the nation, now that our community includes people of many races, ethnicities, languages, and religions.

The debate about American culture and American identity has to date been monopolized largely by Eurocentrists and ethnocentrists whose rhetoric has been flamboyantly divisive, pitting a phantom "us" against a demonized "them."

All countries view themselves by their ideals. Indians idealize the cultural continuum, the inherent value system of India, and are properly incensed when foreigners see nothing but poverty, intolerance, strife, and injustice. Americans see themselves as the embodiments of liberty, openness, and individualism, even as the world judges them for drugs, crime, violence, bigotry, militarism, and homelessness. I was in Singapore in 1994 when the American teenager Michael Fay was sentenced to caning for having spraypainted some cars. While I saw Fay's actions as those of an individual, and his sentence as too harsh, the overwhelming local sentiment was that vandalism was an "American" crime, and that flogging Fay would deter Singapore youths from becoming "Americanized."

Conversely, in 1994, in Tavares, Florida, the Lake County School Board announced its policy (since overturned) requiring middle school teachers to instruct their students that American culture, by which the board meant European-American culture, is inherently "superior to other foreign or historic cultures." The policy's misguided implication was that culture in the United States has not been affected by the American Indian, African-American, Latin-American, and Asian-American segments of the population. The sinister implication was that our national identity is so fragile that it can absorb diverse and immigrant cultures only by recontextualizing them as deficient.

Our nation is unique in human history in that the founding idea of "America" was in opposition to the tenet that a nation is a collection of like-looking, like-speaking, like-worshiping people. The primary criterion for nationhood in Europe is homogeneity of culture, race, and religion—which has contributed to blood-soaked balkanization in the former Yugoslavia and the former Soviet Union.

America's pioneering European ancestors gave us the easy homogeneity of their native countries for a new version of utopia. Now, in the 1990s, we have the exciting chance to follow that tradition and assist in the making of a new American culture that differs from both the enforced assimilation of a "melting pot" and the Canadian model of a multicultural "mosaic."

The multicultural mosaic implies a contiguity of fixed, self-sufficient, utterly distinct cultures. Multiculturalism, as it has been practiced in the United States in the past 10 years, implies the existence of a central culture, ringed by peripheral cultures. The fallout of official multiculturalism is the establishment of one culture as the norm and the rest as aberrations. At the same time, the multiculturalist emphasis on race- and ethnicity-based group identity leads to a lack of respect for individual differences within each group, and to vilification of those individuals who place the good of the nation above the interests of their particular racial or ethnic communities.

We must be alert to the dangers of an "us" vs. "them" mentality. In California, this mentality is manifesting itself as increased violence between minority, ethnic communities. The attack on Korean-American merchants in South Central Los Angeles in the wake of the Rodney King beating trial is only one recent example of the tragic side effects of this mentality. On the national level, the politicization of ethnic identities has encouraged the scapegoating of legal immigrants, who are blamed for economic and social problems brought about by flawed domestic and foreign policies.

We need to discourage the retention of cultural memory if the aim of that retention is cultural balkanization. We must think of American culture and nationhood as a constantly reforming, transmogrifying "we."

In this age of diasporas, one's biological identity may not be one's only identity. Erosions and accretions come with the act of emigration. The experience of cutting myself off from a biological homeland and settling in an adopted homeland that is not always welcoming to its dark-complexioned citizens has tested me as a person, and made me the writer I am today.

I choose to describe myself on my own terms, as an American rather than as an Asian-American. Why is it that hyphenation is imposed only on nonwhite Americans? Rejecting hyphenation is my refusal to categorize the cultural landscape into a center and its peripheries; it is to demand that the American nation deliver the promises of its dream and its Constitution to all its citizens equally.

My rejection of hyphenation has been misrepresented as race treachery by some India-born academics on U.S. campuses who have appointed themselves guardians of the "purity" of ethnic cultures. Many of them, though they reside permanently in the United States and participate in its economy, consistently denounce American ideals and institutions. They direct their rage at me because, by becoming a U.S. citizen and exercising my voting rights, I have invested in the present and not the past; because I have committed myself to help shape the future of my adopted homeland; and because I celebrate racial and cultural mongrelization.

What excites me is that as a nation we have not only the chance to retain those values we treasure from our original cultures but also the chance to acknowledge that the outer forms of those values are likely to change. Among Indian immigrants, I see a great deal of guilt about the inability to hang on to what they commonly term "pure culture." Parents express rage or despair at their U.S.-born children's forgetting of, or indifference to, some aspects of Indian culture. Of those parents I would ask: What is it we have lost if our children are acculturating into the culture in which we are living? Is it so terrible that our children are discovering or are inventing homelands for themselves?

Some first-generation Indo-Americans, embittered by racism and by unofficial "glass ceilings," construct a phantom identity, more-Indian-than-Indians-in-India, as a defense against marginalization. I ask: Why don't you get actively involved in fighting discrimination? Make your voice heard. Choose the forum most appropriate for you. If you are a citizen, let your vote count.

Reinvest your energy and resources into revitalizing your city's disadvantaged residents and neighborhoods. Know your constitutional rights, and when they are violated, use the agencies of redress the Constitution makes available to you. Expect change, and when it comes, deal with it!

As a writer, my literary agenda begins by acknowledging that America has transformed me. It does not end until I show that I (along with the hundreds of thousands of immigrants like me) am minute by minute transforming America. The transformation is a two-way process: It affects both the individual and the national-cultural identity.

Others who write stories of migration often talk of arrival at a new place as a loss, the loss of communal memory and the erosion of an original culture. I want to talk of arrival as gain.

[1997]

Term

1. DIASPORA: The geographical disbursement of a cultural people.

Understanding the Reading

1. What distinction does Mukherjee make between her American experience and "America"?
2. Compare and contrast Mukherjee's Indian background and her American experience.
3. What is the Canadian attitude toward people of color?
4. How do Indians and Americans see themselves, and how do foreigners see them?
5. How is America different from traditional nations?
6. What is Mukherjee's advice to immigrants to America?

Suggestion for Responding

1. Talk to an older family member about how his or her culture of origin has transformed American culture and how American culture has transformed him or her. Take good notes for use when you write your "identity" report. ✦

14

On the Other Side of the War: A Story

ELIZABETH GORDON

I. THE WAY WE CAME TO AMERICA

The way we came to America was this: My father, who was in the Army, made an overseas call to his mom and dad in West Virginia.

"Listen," he said, "I've decided to adopt this poor little Vietnamese baby and bring her to America. What do you think?"

Now, both Grandma and Grandpa were true hillbillies in their lineage, habits, and mental faculties—which means they were as broke, as stubborn, and as sharp as folks can be. Not that my father's story required much genius to be seen right through. A twenty-four-year-old enlisted man wanting to bring home some mysterious oriental infant? They hadn't brought him up *that* good.

"It's all right, Skip," they told him. "You can get married, if you love her, and bring 'em both. Bring 'em both on home."

II. NO ONE HAD EXPECTED

No one had expected anything like that to happen, least of all the people it happened to.

My father had been quite prepared to meet and marry a sweet girl with a name like Layuna or Ginny Lee. A girl who hailed from one of the good neighboring towns of Beckley or Rainelle. A girl with a daddy, like his, who liked to work on cars, who'd every once in a while hit the booze and start cursing about black lung. There'd been no Nguyen Ngoc Huong from Saigon in *his* crystal ball.

And my mother never dreamed she'd live in an aluminum house on wheels, or see shaved ice swirling down from the sky. Her kitchen window looked out onto a pasture of cows, who stood utterly still with the weather piling up around their legs. It was a difficult thing for her to understand.

So while my father was out climbing telephone poles for Ma Bell, my mother was in the trailer with me, crying and crying for the cows who had not a plank against the cold.

III. THINGS GOT MIXED UP

Things got mixed up sometimes between them. Though it was my father's unshakable belief that Common Sense prevailed in all circumstances, he seemed to forget that Common Sense is commonly rendered senseless whenever it crosses a few time zones.

For example, my mother would constantly confuse "hamburger" with "pancake," presumably because both were round, flat, and fried in a pan. So my father, after asking for his favorite breakfast, would soon smell the juicy aroma of sizzling ground beef coming from the kitchen. Other times, he'd find a stack of well-buttered flapjacks, along with a cold bottle of Coca-Cola, waiting for him at the dinner table.

One morning, before my father left for work, he asked my mother to make corn bread and pinto beans for supper. The result of this request was that my mother spent the remainder of the day peeling, one by one, an entire pound of pinto beans. How could she have known any better?

When my father returned home that night, he found her with ten sore fingers and a pot full of mush. He didn't know whether to laugh or cry, but he kissed her because there was nothing he could say.

IV. THE PHOTOGRAPH

The photograph, circa 1965, is somewhat unusual. In the background there is a row of neat, nearly identical frame houses. The street in front of the houses is spacious and clean, as wholesome and as decent as sunshine.

Up a little closer, there is a car. It's a two-tone Chevy with curvaceous fenders, gleaming as though it's just been washed and waxed by hand. The weather looks like Sunday.

In the foreground not unexpectedly, a woman with a small child. The woman is a wife because she wears a gold ring. She is also a mother because of the way she holds her child.

The woman has a slim, dainty figure. Her smile is wide and loose, as though she is close to laughter. Maybe her husband, who is taking her picture, is telling a joke or making a silly face. It seems quite natural that the photographer is the husband. Who else would it be?

But something in the photograph seems not quite right. Strangers often tilt their heads when looking at it, as if it is uncomfortable to view straight up and down. Possibly, it's the incomparable blackness of the woman's hair, or the way it seems forced into a wave it can barely hold. Or maybe it has something to do with the baby's eyes which, though blue, are shaped exactly like the woman's: round at the center, narrow at the corners, and heavy-lidded.

What are eyes like that doing among frame houses and a shiny Chevrolet? It seems a reasonable thing to ask.

V. WHEN I STARTED SCHOOL

When I started school there were numerous forms to be filled out. Some of the questions were so simple, I could have answered them myself.

The task belonged to my mother, though. She handled most of the questions with ease, and I liked to watch the way she filled all those boxes and blanks with her pretty handwriting.

There was one question, however, that gave my mother a lot of trouble. Even though it was multiple choice, none of the answers seemed to fit. She decided to ask my father what to do.

He didn't have an answer right away, and for some reason that made him angry. The problem was, I was supposed to be in a race, but he couldn't figure out which one.

Finally, he told my mother to put an "H" in that blank. "For *human* race," he said.

I didn't understand what that meant, back then. But it sounded like a good race to me.

[1989]

Understanding the Reading

1. Why do you think Skip initially announces that his plan was to adopt a Vietnamese baby? Were you surprised by his parents' response?

2. What do Gordon's mother's cooking errors illustrate about Americans' assumptions about our food?

3. Explain what Gordon is trying to show in her description of the photograph.

4. How do you think Gordon's parents should have filled out the school form?

Suggestions for Responding

1. If you have an old family photo that especially intrigues you, write a description of it and try to explain what it means to you.

2. If you have had occasion to eat the food of another culture, try to describe it and your reaction to it. ✦

15

Medicalization of Racial Features: Asian American Women and Cosmetic Surgery[1]

EUGENIA KAW

Throughout history and across cultures, humans have decorated, manipulated, and mutilated their bodies for religious reasons, for social prestige, and for beauty (Brain 1979). In the United States, within the last decade, permanent alteration of the body for aesthetic reasons has become increasingly common. By 1988, 2 million Americans, 87% of them female, had undergone cosmetic surgery, a figure that had tripled in two years (Wolf 1991:218). The cosmetic surgery industry, a $300 million per year industry, has been able to meet an increasingly wide variety of consumer demands. Now men, too, receive services ranging from the enlargement of calves and chests to the liposuction of cheeks and necks (Rosenthal 1991a). Most noticeably, the ethnic composition of consumers has changed so that in recent years there are more racial and ethnic minorities. In 1990, 20% of cosmetic surgery patients were Latinos, African Americans, and Asian Americans (Rosenthal 1991b). Not

surprisingly, within every racial group, women still constitute the overwhelming majority of cosmetic surgery patients, an indication that women are still expected to identify with their bodies in U.S. society today, just as they have across cultures throughout much of human history (Turner 1987:85).[2]

The types of cosmetic surgery sought by women in the United States are racially specific. Like most white women, Asian American women who undergo cosmetic surgery are motivated by the need to look their best as women. White women, however, usually opt for liposuction, breast augmentation, or wrinkle removal procedures, whereas Asian American women most often request "double-eyelid" surgery, whereby folds of skin are excised from across their upper eyelids to create a crease above each eye that makes the eyes look wider. Also frequently requested is surgical sculpting of the nose tip to create a more chiseled appearance, or the implantation of a silicone or cartilage bridge in the nose for a more prominent appearance. In 1990, national averages compiled by the American Society of Plastic and Reconstructive Surgeons show that liposuction, breast augmentation, and collagen injection were the most common surgical procedures among cosmetic patients, 80% of whom are white. Although national statistics on the types of cosmetic surgery most requested by Asian Americans specifically are not available, data from two of the doctors' offices in my study show that in 1990 eyelid surgery was the most common procedure undergone by Asian American patients (40% of all procedures on Asian Americans at one doctor's office, 46% at another), followed by nasal implants and nasal tip refinement procedures (15% at the first doctor's office, 23% at the second).[3] While the features that white women primarily seek to alter through cosmetic surgery (i.e., the breasts, fatty areas of the body, and facial wrinkles) do not correspond to conventional markers of racial identity, those featur~ that Asian American women primarily see~ alter (i.e., "small, narrow" eyes and a "flat"~ do correspond to such markers.[4]

My research focuses on the cu~ institutional forces that motivate A~ can women to alter surgically the~ eyes and noses. I argue that ~

women's decision to undergo cosmetic surgery is an attempt to escape persisting racial prejudice that correlates their stereotyped genetic physical features ("small, slanty" eyes and a "flat" nose) with negative behavioral characteristics, such as passivity, dullness, and a lack of sociability. With the authority of scientific rationality and technological efficiency, medicine is effective in perpetuating these racist notions. The medical system bolsters and benefits from the larger consumer-oriented society not only by maintaining the idea that beauty should be every woman's goal but also by promoting a beauty standard that requires that certain racial features of Asian American women be modified. Through the subtle and often unconscious manipulation of racial and gender ideologies, medicine, as a producer of norms, and the larger consumer society of which it is a part encourage Asian American women to mutilate their bodies to conform to an ethnocentric norm.

Social scientific analyses of ethnic relations should include a study of the body. As evident in my research, racial minorities may internalize a body image produced by the dominant culture's racial ideology and, because of it, begin to loathe, mutilate, and revise parts of their bodies. Bodily mutilation and adornment are symbolic mediums most directly and concretely concerned with the construction of the individual as social actor or cultural subject (Turner 1980). Yet social scientists have only recently focused on the body as a central component of social self-identity (Blacking 1977; Brain 1979; Daly 1978; Lock and Scheper-Hughes 1990; O'Neill 1985; Turner 1987). Moreover, social scientists, and sociocultural anthropologists in particular, have not yet explored the ways in which the body is central to the everyday experience of racial identity.

METHOD AND DESCRIPTION OF SUBJECTS

In this article I present findings of an ongoing ethnographic research project in the San Francisco Bay Area begun in April 1991. I draw on data from structured interviews with physicians and patients, medical literature and newspaper ʼrticles, and basic medical statistics. The sample ᶠ informants for this research is not random

in the strictly statistical sense since informants were difficult to locate. In the United States, both clients and their medical practitioners treat the decision to undergo cosmetic surgery as highly confidential, and practitioners do not reveal the names of patients without their consent. In an effort to generate a sample of Asian American woman informants, I posted fliers and placed advertisements in various local newspapers for a period of at least three months, but I received only one reply. I also asked doctors who had agreed to participate in my study to ask their Asian American patients if they would agree to be interviewed. The doctors reported that most of the patients preferred not to talk about their operations or about motivations leading up to the operation. Ultimately, I was able to conduct structured, open-ended interviews with eleven Asian American women, four of whom were referred to me by doctors in the study, six by mutual acquaintances, and one through an advertisement in a local newspaper. Nine have had cosmetic surgery of the eye or the nose; one recently considered a double-eyelid operation; one is considering a double-eyelid operation in the next few years. Nine of the women in the study live in the San Francisco Bay Area, and two in the Los Angeles area. Five had their operations from the doctors in my study, while four had theirs in Asia—two in Seoul, Korea, one in Beijing, China, and one in Taipei, Taiwan. Of the eleven women in the study, only two, who received their operations in China and in Taiwan, had not lived in the United States prior to their operations. The two who had surgery in Korea went there for their surgeries because the operations were cheaper there than in the United States and because they felt doctors in Korea are more "experienced" since these types of surgery are more common in Korea than in the United States.[5] The ages of the women in the study range from 18 to 71; one woman was only 15 at the time of her operation.

In addition to interviewing Asian American women, I conducted structured, open-ended interviews with five plastic surgeons, all of whom practice in the Bay Area. Of the eleven doctors I randomly selected from the phone book, five agreed to be interviewed.

Since the physicians in my study may not be representative of plastic surgeons, I reviewed the plastic surgery literature. To examine more carefully the medical discourse on the nose and eyelid surgeries of Asian American women, I examined several medical books and plastic surgery journals dating from the 1950s to 1990. I also reviewed several news releases and informational packets distributed by such national organizations as the American Society of Plastic and Reconstructive Surgeons, an organization that represents 97% of all physicians certified by the American Board of Plastic Surgery.

To examine popular notions of cosmetic surgery and, in particular, of how the phenomenon of Asian American women receiving double-eyelid and nose-bridge operations is viewed by the public and the media, I referenced relevant newspaper and magazine articles.

For statistical information, I obtained national data on cosmetic surgery from various societies for cosmetic surgeons, including the American Society of Plastic and Reconstructive Surgeons. Data on the specific types of surgery sought by different ethnic groups in the United States, including Asian Americans, are missing from the national statistics. At least one public relations coordinator told me that such data are quite unimportant to plastic surgeons. To compensate for this, I requested doctors in my study to provide me with data from their clinics. One doctor allowed me to review his patient files for basic statistical information. Another doctor allowed his office assistant to give me such information, provided that I paid his assistant for the time she had to work outside of normal work hours reviewing his patient files. Since cosmetic surgery is generally not covered by medical insurance, doctors often do not record their patients' medical information in their computers; therefore, most doctors told me that they have very little data on their cosmetic patients readily available.

MUTILATION OR A CELEBRATION OF THE BODY?

The decoration, ornamentation, and scarification of the body can be viewed from two perspectives. On the one hand, such practices can be seen as celebrations of the social and individual bodies, as expressions of belonging in society and an affirmation of oneness with the body

(Brain 1979; Scheper-Hughes and Lock 1991; Turner 1980). On the other hand, they can be viewed as acts of mutilation, that is, as expressions of alienation in society and a negation of the body induced by unequal power relationships (Bordo 1990; Daly 1978; O'Neill 1985).

Although it is at least possible to imagine race-modification surgery as a *rite de passage* or a bid for incorporation into the body and race norms of the "dominant" culture, my research findings lead me to reject this as a tenable hypothesis. Here I argue that the surgical alternation by many Asian American women of the shape of their eyes and nose is a potent form of self, body, and society alienation. Mutilation, according to *Webster's*, is the act of maiming, crippling, cutting up, or altering radically so as to damage seriously essential parts of the body. Although the women in my study do not view their cosmetic surgeries as acts of mutilation, an examination of the cultural and institutional forces that influence them to modify their bodies so radically reveals a rejection of their "given" bodies and feelings of marginality. On the one hand, they feel they are exercising their Americanness in their use of the freedom of individual choice. Some deny that they are conforming to any standard—feminine, Western, or otherwise—and others express the idea that they are, in fact, molding their own standards of beauty. Most agreed, however, that their decision to alter their features was primarily a result of their awareness that as women they are expected to look their best and that this meant, in a certain sense, less stereotypically Asian. Even those who stated that their decision to alter their features was personal, based on individual aesthetic preference, also expressed hope that their new appearance would help them in such matters as getting a date, securing a mate, or getting a better job.

For the women in my study, the decision to undergo cosmetic surgery was never purely or mainly for aesthetic purposes, but almost always for improving their social status as women who are racial minorities. Cosmetic surgery is a means by which they hope to acquire "symbolic capital" (Bourdieu 1984 [1979]) in the form of a look that holds more prestige. For example, "Jane," who underwent double-eyelid and nose-bridge procedures at the ages of 16 and 17, said that she thought she should get her surgeries "out of the way" at an early age since as a college student she has to think about careers ahead:

> Especially if you go into business, whatever, you kind of have to have a Western facial type and you have to have like their features and stature— you know, be tall and stuff. In a way you can see it is an investment in your future.

Such a quest for empowerment does not confront the cultural and institutional structures that are the real cause of the women's feelings of distress. Instead, this form of "body praxis" (Scheper-Hughes and Lock 1991) helps to entrench these structures by further confirming the undesirability of "stereotypical" Asian features. Therefore, the alteration by many Asian American women of their features is a "disciplinary" practice in the Foucauldian sense; it does not so much benignly transform them as it "normalizes" (i.e., qualifies, classifies, judges, and enforces complicity in) the subject (Foucault 1977). The normalization is a double encounter, conforming to patriarchal definitions of femininity and to Caucasian standards of beauty (Bordo 1990).

Gramsci anticipated Foucault in considering subjected peoples' complicity and participation in, as well as reproduction of their own domination in everyday practice. In examining such phenomena as Asian American women undergoing cosmetic surgery in the late 20th-century United States, however, one must emphasize, as Foucault does, how mechanisms of domination have become much more insidious, overlapping, and pervasive in everyday life as various forms of "expert" knowledge such as plastic surgery and surgeons have increasingly come to play the role of "traditional" intellectuals (Gramsci 1971) or direct agents of the bourgeois state (Scheper-Hughes 1992:171) in defining commonsense reality.

Particularly in Western, late capitalist societies (where the decoration, ornamentation, and scarification of the body have lost much meaning for the individual in the existential sense of "Which people do I belong to? What is the meaning of my life?" and have instead become commoditized by the media, corporations, and even medicine in the name of fashion), the normalizing elements of such practices as cosmetic surgery can become obscured. Rather than celebrations of the body,

they are mutilations of the body, resulting from a devaluation of the self and induced by historically determined relationships among social groups and between the individual and society.

INTERNALIZATION OF RACIAL AND GENDER STEREOTYPES

The Asian American women in my study are influenced by a gender ideology that states that beauty should be a primary goal of women. They are conscious that because they are women, they must conform to certain standards of beauty. "Elena," a 20-year-old Korean American said, "People in society, if they are attractive, are rewarded for their efforts . . . especially girls. If they look pretty and neat, they are paid more attention to. You can't deny that." "Annie," another Korean American who is 18 years old, remarked that as a young woman, her motivation to have cosmetic surgery was "to look better" and "not different from why [other women] put on makeup." In fact, all expressed the idea that cosmetic surgery was a means by which they could escape the task of having to put makeup on every day. As "Jo," a 28-year-old Japanese American who is thinking of enlarging the natural fold above her eyes, said, "I am still self-conscious about leaving the house without any makeup on, because I feel just really ugly without it. I feel like it's the mask that enables me to go outside." Beauty, more than character and intelligence, often signifies social and economic success for them as for other women in U.S. society (Lakoff and Scherr 1984; Wolf 1991).

The need to look their best as women motivates the Asian American women in my study to undergo cosmetic surgery, but the standard of beauty they try to achieve through surgery is motivated by a racial ideology that infers negative behavioral or intellectual characteristics from a group's genetic physical features. All of the women said that they are "proud to be Asian American" and that they "do not want to look white." But the standard of beauty they admire and strive for is a face with larger eyes and a more prominent nose. They all stated that an eyelid without a crease and a nose that does not project indicate a certain "sleepiness," "dullness," and "passivity" in a person's character. "Nellee," a 21-year-old Chinese American, said she seriously considered surgery for double eyelids in high school so that she could "avoid the stereotype of the 'Oriental bookworm'" who is "*dull* and doesn't know how to have fun." Elena, who had double-eyelid surgery two years ago from a doctor in my study, said, "When I look at Asians who have no folds and their eyes are slanted and closed, I think of how they would look better more *awake.*" "Carol," a 37-year-old Chinese American who had double-eyelid surgery seven years ago and "Ellen," a 40-year-old Chinese American who had double-eyelid surgery 20 years ago, both said that they wanted to give their eyes a "more spirited" look. "The drawback of Asian features is the puffy eyes," Ellen said. "Pam," a Chinese American aged 44, who had had double-eyelid surgery from another doctor in my study two months earlier, stated, "Yes. Of course. Bigger eyes look prettier. . . . Lots of Asians' eyes are so small they become little lines when the person laughs, making the person look *sleepy.*" Likewise, Annie, who had an implant placed on her nasal dorsum to build up her nose bridge at age 15, said:

> I guess I always wanted that *sharp* look—a look like you are smart. If you have a roundish kind of nose, it's like you don't know what's going on. If you have that sharp look, you know, with black eyebrows, a pointy nose, you look more *alert.* I always thought that was cool. [emphasis added]

Clearly, the Asian American women in my study seek cosmetic surgery for double eyelids and nose bridges because they associate the features considered characteristic of their race with negative traits.

These associations that Asian American women make between their features and personality characteristics stem directly from stereotypes created by the dominant culture in the United States and by Western culture in general, which historically has wielded the most power and hegemonic influence over the world. Asians are rarely portrayed in the U.S. popular media and then only in such roles as Charlie Chan, Suzie Wong, and "Lotus Blossom Babies" (a.k.a. China Doll, Geisha Girl, and shy Polynesian beauty). They are depicted as stereotypes with dull, passive, and nonsociable personalities

(Kim 1986; Tajima 1989). Subtle depictions by the media of individuals' minutest gestures in everyday social situations can socialize viewers to confirm certain hypotheses about their own natures (Goffman 1979). At present, the stereotypes of Asians as a "model minority" serve a similar purpose. In the model minority stereotype, the concepts of dullness, passivity, and stoicism are elaborated to refer to a person who is hardworking and technically skilled but desperately lacking in creativity and sociability (Takaki 1989:477).

Similar stereotypes of the stoic Asian also exist in East and Southeast Asia, and since many Asian Americans are immigrants or children of recent immigrants from Asia, they are likely to be influenced by these stereotypes as well. U.S. magazines and films have been increasingly available in many parts of Asia since World War II. Also, multinational corporations in Southeast Asian countries consider their work force of Asian women to be biologically suited for the most monotonous industrial labor because the "Oriental girl" is "diligent" and has "nimble fingers" and a "slow wit" (Ong 1987:151). Racial stereotypes of Asians as docile, passive, slow witted, and unemotional are internalized by many Asian American women, causing them to consider the facial features associated with these negative traits as defiling.

Undergoing cosmetic surgery, then, becomes a means by which the women can attempt to permanently acquire not only a feminine look considered more attractive by society, but also a certain set of racial features considered more prestigious. For them, the daily task of beautification entails creating the illusion of features they, as members of a racial minority, do not have. Nellee, who has not yet undergone double-eyelid surgery, said that at present she has to apply makeup every day "to give my eyes an illusion of a crease. When I don't wear makeup I feel my eyes are small." Likewise, Elena said that before her double-eyelid surgery she checked almost every morning in the mirror when she woke up to see if a fold had formed above her right eye to match the more prominent fold above her left eye: "[on certain mornings] it was like any other day when you wake up and don't feel so hot, you know. My eye had no definite folds, because when Asians sleep their folds change in and out—it's not definite." The enormous constraints the women in my study feel with regard to their Asian features are apparent in the meticulous detail with which they describe their discontent, as apparent in a quote from Jo who already has natural folds but wants to enlarge them: "I want to make an even bigger eyelid [fold] so that it doesn't look slanted. I think in Asian eyes this inside corner of the fold [she was drawing on my notebook] goes down too much."

The women expressed hope that the results of cosmetic surgery would win them better acceptance by society. Ellen said that she does not think her double-eyelid surgery "makes me look too different," but she nonetheless expressed the feeling that now her features will "make a better impression on people because I got rid of that sleepy look." She says that she will encourage her daughter, who is only 12 years old, to have double-eyelid surgery as she did, because "I think having less sleepy-looking eyes would help her in the future with getting jobs." The aesthetic results of surgery are not an end in themselves but rather a means for these women as racial minorities to attain better socioeconomic status. Clearly, their decisions to undergo cosmetic surgery do not stem from a celebration of their bodies.

MEDICALIZATION OF RACIAL FEATURES

Having already been influenced by the larger society's negative valuation of their natural, "given" features, Asian American women go to see plastic surgeons in half-hour consultation sessions. Once inside the clinic, they do not have to have the doctor's social and medical views "thrust" on them, since to a great extent, they, like their doctors, have already entered into a more general social consensus (Scheper-Hughes 1992:199). Nonetheless, the Western medical system is a most effective promoter of the racial stereotypes that influence Asian American women, since medical knowledge is legitimized by scientific rationality and technical efficiency, both of which hold prestige in the West and increasingly all over the world. Access to a scientific body of knowledge has given Western medicine considerable social power in defining

reality (Turner 1987:11). According to my Asian American informants who had undergone cosmetic surgery, their plastic surgeons used several medical terms to problematize the shape of their eyes so as to define it as a medical condition. For instance, many patients were told that they had "excess fat" on their eyelids and that it was "normal" for them to feel dissatisfied with the way they looked. "Lots of Asians have the same puffiness over their eyelid, and they often feel better about themselves after the operation," the doctors would assure their Asian American patients.

The doctors whom I interviewed shared a similar opinion of Asian facial features with many of the doctors of the patients in my study. Their descriptions of Asian features verged on ideological racism, as clearly seen in the following quote from "Dr. Smith."

> The social reasons [for Asian Americans to want double eyelids and nose bridges] are undoubtedly continued exposure to Western culture and the realization that the upper eyelid *without* a fold tends to give a *sleepy* appearance, and therefore a more *dull* look to the patient. Likewise, the *flat* nasal bridge and *lack of* nasal projection can signify *weakness* in one's personality and by *lack of* extension, a *lack of force* in one's character. [emphasis added]

By using words like "without," "lack of," "flat," "dull," and "sleepy" in his description of Asian features, Dr. Smith perpetuates the notion that Asian features are inadequate. Likewise, "Dr. Khoo" said that many Asians should have surgery for double eyelids since "the eye is the window to your soul and having a more open appearance makes you look a bit brighter, more inviting." "Dr. Gee" agreed:

> I would say 90% of people look better with double eyelids. It makes the eye look more spiritually alive. . . . With a single eyelid frequently they would have a little fat pad underneath [which] can half bury the eye and so the eye looks small and unenergetic.

Such powerful associations of Asian features with negative personality traits by physicians during consultations can become a medical affirmation of Asian American women's sense of disdain toward their own features.

Medical books and journals as early as the 1950s and as recent as 1990 abound with similar metaphors of abnormality in describing Asian features. The texts that were published before 1970 contain more explicit associations of Asian features with dullness and passivity. In an article published in 1954 in the *American Journal of Ophthalmology,* the author, a doctor in the Philippines armed forces, wrote the following about a Chinese man on whom he performed double-eyelid surgery:

> [He] was born with mere slits for his eyes. Everyone teased him about his eyes with the comment that as he looked constantly sleepy, so his business too was just as sleepy. For this reason, he underwent the plastic operation and, now that his eyes are wider, he has lost that sleepy look. His business, too, has, picked up. [Sayoc 1954:556]

The doctor clearly saw a causal link between the shape of his patient's eyes and his patient's intellectual and behavioral capacity to succeed in life. In 1964 a white American military surgeon who performed double-eyelid surgeries on Koreans in Korea during the American military occupation of that country wrote in the same journal: "The absence of the palpebral fold produces a passive expression which seems to epitomize the stoical and unemotional manner of the Oriental" (Millard 1964:647). Medical texts published after 1970 are more careful about associating Asian features with negative behavioral or intellectual characteristics, but they still describe Asian features with metaphors of inadequacy or excess. For instance, in the introductory chapter to a 1990 book devoted solely to medical techniques for cosmetic surgery of the Asian face, a white American plastic surgeon begins by cautioning his audience not to stereotype the physical traits of Asians.

> Westerners tend to have a stereotyped conception of the physical traits of Asians: yellow skin pigmentation . . . a flat face with high cheek bones; a broad, flat nose; and narrow slit-like eyes showing characteristic epicanthal folds. While this stereotype may loosely apply to the central Asian groups (i.e., Chinese, Koreans, and Japanese), the facial plastic surgeon should appreciate that considerable variation exists in all of these physical traits. [McCurdy 1990:1]

Yet, on the same page, he writes that the medicalization of Asian features is valid because Asians usually have eyes that are too narrow and a nose that is too flat.

> However, given an appreciation of the physical diversity of the Asian population, certain facial features do form a distinct basis for surgical intervention. . . . These facial features typically include the upper eyelid, characterized by an absent or poorly defined superior palpebral fold . . . and a small flattened nose with poor lobular definition. [McCurdy 1990:1]

Thus, in published texts, doctors write about Asians' eyes and noses as abnormal even when they are careful not to associate negative personality traits with these features. In the privacy of their clinics, they freely incorporate both metaphors of abnormality and the association of Asian features with negative characteristics into medical discourse, which has an enormous impact on the Asian American patients being served.

The doctors' scientific discourse is made more convincing by the seemingly objective manner in which they behave and present themselves in front of their patients in the clinical setting. They examine their patients as a technician diagnosing ways to improve a mechanical object. With a cotton swab, they help their patients to stretch and measure how high they might want their eyelids to be and show them in a mirror what could be done surgically to reduce the puffy look above their eyes. The doctors in my study also use slides and Polaroid pictures to come to an agreement with their patients on what the technical goals of the operation should be. The sterile appearance of their clinics, with white walls and plenty of medical instruments, as well as the symbolism of the doctor's white coat with its many positive connotations (e.g., purity, life, unaroused sexuality, superhuman power, and candor) reinforce in the patient the doctor's role as technician and thus his sense of objectivity (Blumhagen 1979). One of my informants, Elena, said that, sitting in front of her doctor in his office, she felt sure that she needed eyelid surgery: "[Dr. Smith] made quite an impression on me. I thought he was more than qualified—that he knew what he was talking about."

With its authority of scientific rationality and technical efficiency, medicine effectively "normalizes" not only the negative feelings of Asian American women about their features but also their ultimate decision to undergo cosmetic surgery. For example, "Dr. Jones" does not want to make her patients feel "strange" or "abnormal" for wanting cosmetic surgery. All the doctors in my study agreed that their role as doctor is to provide the best technical skills possible for whatever service their patients demand, not to question the motivation of their patients. Her goal, Dr. Jones said, is "like that of a psychiatrist in that I try to make patients feel better about themselves." She feels that surgeons have an advantage over psychiatrists in treating cosmetic surgery patients because "we . . . help someone to change the way they look . . . psychiatrists are always trying to figure out why a person wants to do what they want to do." By changing the patients' bodies the way they would like them, she feels she provides them with an immediate and concrete solution to their feelings of inadequacy.

Dr. Jones and the other doctors say that they only turn patients away when patients expect results that are technically impossible, given such factors as the thickness of the patient's skin and the bone structure. "I turn very few patients away," said Dr. Khoo. And "Dr. Kwan" notes

> I saw a young girl [awhile back] whose eyes were beautiful but she wanted a crease. . . . She was gorgeous! Wonderful! But somehow she didn't see it that way. But you know, I'm not going to tell a patient every standard I have of what's beautiful. If they want certain things and it's doable, and if it is consistent with a reasonable look in the end, then I don't stop them. I don't really discuss it with them.

Like the other doctors in my study, Dr. Kwan sees himself primarily as a technician whose main role is to correct his patient's features in a way that he thinks would best contribute to the patient's satisfaction. It does not bother him that he must expose an individual, whom he already sees as pretty and not in need of surgery, to an operation that is at least an hour long, entails the administering of local anesthesia with sedation, and involves the following risks: "bleeding," "hematoma," "hemorrhage," formation of a "gaping wound," "discoloration," scarring, and "asymmetry in lid folds" (Sayoc 1974:162–166). He finds no need to try to change his patients' minds. Likewise, Dr. Smith said of Asian American women who used to come to him to receive really large double eyelids: "I respect their ethnic background. I don't want to change them drastically." Yet he would not refuse them the surgery "as long as it was something I can accomplish. Provided I make them aware of what the appearance might be with the changes."

Though most of my Asian American woman informants who underwent cosmetic surgery recovered fully within six months to a year, with only a few minor scars from their surgery, they nonetheless affirmed that the psychologically traumatic aspect of the operation was something their doctors did not stress during consultation. Elena said of her double-eyelid surgery: "I thought it was a simple procedure. He [the doctor] should have known better. It took at least an hour and a half. . . . And no matter how minor the surgery was, I bruised! I was swollen." Likewise, Annie could remember well her fear during nose surgery. Under local anesthesia, she said that she was able to witness and hear some of the procedures.

> I closed my eyes. I didn't want to look. I didn't want to see like the knives or anything. I could hear the snapping of scissors and I was aware when they were putting that thing [implant] up my nose. I was kind of grossed out.

By focusing on technique and subordinating human emotions and motivations to technical ends, medicine is capable of normalizing Asian American women's decision to undergo cosmetic surgery.

MUTUAL REINFORCEMENT: MEDICINE AND THE CONSUMER-ORIENTED SOCIETY

The medical system bolsters and benefits from the larger consumer-oriented society by perpetuating the idea that beauty is central to women's sense of self and also by promoting a beauty standard for Asian American women that requires the alteration of features specific to Asian American racial identity. All of the doctors in my study stated that a "practical" benefit for Asian American women undergoing surgery to create or enlarge their eyelid folds is that they can put eye makeup on more appropriately. Dr. Gee said that after double-eyelid surgery it is "easier" for Asian American women to put makeup on because "they now have two instead of just one plane on which to apply makeup." Dr. Jones agreed that after eyelid surgery Asian American women "can do more dramatic things with eye makeup." The doctors imply that Asian American women cannot usually put on makeup adequately, and thus, they have not been able to look as beautiful as they can be with makeup. By promoting the idea that a beautiful woman is one who can put makeup on adequately, they further the idea that a woman's identity should be closely connected with her body and, particularly, with the representational problems of the self. By reinforcing the makeup industry, they buttress the cosmetic surgery industry of which they are a part. A double-eyelid surgery costs patients $1,000 to $3,000.

The medical system also bolsters and benefits from the larger consumer society by appealing to the values of American individualism and by individualizing the social problems of racial inequality. Dr. Smith remarked that so many Asian American women are now opting for cosmetic surgery procedures largely because of their newly gained rights as women and as racial minorities:

> Asians are more affluent than they were 15 years ago. They are more knowledgeable and Americanized, and their women are more liberated. I think in the past many Asian women were like Arab women. The men had their foot on top of them. Now Asian women do pretty much what they want to do. So if they want to do a surgery, they do it.

Such comments by doctors encourage Asian American women to believe that undergoing cosmetic surgery is merely a way of beautifying themselves and that it signifies their ability to exercise individual freedom.

Ignoring the fact that the Asian American women's decision to undergo cosmetic surgery has anything to do with the larger society's racial prejudice, the doctors state that their Asian American women patients come to cosmetic

surgeons to mold their own standards of beauty. The doctors point out that the specific width and shape the women want their creases to be or the specific shape of nose bridges they want are a matter of personal style and individual choices. Dr. Smith explains:

> We would like to individualize every procedure. There is no standard nose we stamp on everybody so that each patient's need is addressed individually. My goal is to make that individual very happy and very satisfied.

Dr. Kwan also remarked, "I think people recognize what's beautiful in their own way." In fact, the doctors point out that both they and their Asian American patients are increasingly getting more sophisticated about what the patients want. As evidence, they point to the fact that as early as a decade ago, doctors used to provide very wide creases to every Asian American patient who came for double eyelids, not knowing that not every Asian wanted to look exactly Caucasian. The doctors point out that today many Asian American cosmetic surgery patients explicitly request that their noses and eyelids not be made to look too Caucasian.

Recent plastic surgery literature echoes these doctors' observations. A 1991 press release from the American Academy of Cosmetic Surgery quotes a prominent member as saying, "The procedures they [minorities, including Asian Americans] seek are not so much to look 'western' but to refine their features to attain facial harmony." The double-eyelid surgery, he says, is to give Asian eyes "a more open appearance," not a Western look. Likewise, McCurdy points out in his book that double-eyelid procedures should vary in accordance with whether or not the patient actually requests a Western eyelid.

> In patients who desire a small "double eyelid," the incision is placed 6–7mm above the ciliary margin; in those patients desiring a medium-sized lid, the incision is placed 8mm above the ciliary margin; in patients who request westernization of the eyelid, the incision is placed 9–10mm above the ciliary margin. [McCurdy 1990:8]

Fifty percent of all Asians in the world do have a natural crease on their eyelids, and thus it can be argued that those Asians who undergo surgery for double eyelids are aiming for Asian looks, that they are not necessarily conforming to a Western standard. Yet, by focusing on technique, that is, by focusing on how many millimeters above the eyes their Asian American patients want their fold to be or how long across the eyelid they want their fold to be drawn, the doctors do not fully recognize that the trend in Asian American cosmetic surgery is still toward larger eyes and a more prominent nose. They ignore the fact that the very valuation attached to eyes with "a more open appearance" may be a consequence of society's racial prejudice. If the types of cosmetic surgery Asian Americans opt for are truly individual choices, one would expect to see a number of Asians who admire and desire eyes without a crease or a nose without a bridge. Yet the doctors can refer to no cases involving Asian Americans who wanted to get rid of their creases or who wanted to flatten their noses. Moreover, there are numerous cases of Asian Americans, such as many Southeast Asians, who already have a natural eyelid crease but feel the need to widen it even more for a less puffy appearance.[6] Clearly, there is a pattern in the requests of Asian American cosmetic surgery patients.

In saying that their Asian American women patients are merely exercising their freedom to choose a personal style or look, the doctors promote the idea that human beings have an infinite variety of needs that technology can endlessly fulfill, an idea at the heart of today's U.S. capitalism. As Susan Bordo explains, the United States has increasingly become a "plastic" culture, characterized by a "disdain for material limits, and intoxication with freedom, change, and self-determination" (Bordo 1990:654). She points out that many consumer products that could be considered derogatory to women and racial minorities are thought by the vast majority of Americans to be only some in an array of consumer choices to which every individual has a right. She explains:

> Any different self would do, it is implied. Closely connected to this is the construction of all cosmetic changes as the same: perms for white women, corn rows on Bo Derek, tanning, makeup, changing hair styles, blue contacts for black women. [Bordo 1990:659]

CONCLUSION

Cosmetic surgery on Asian American women for nose bridges and double eyelids is very much influenced by gender and racial ideologies. My research has shown that by the conscious or unconscious manipulation of gender and racial stereotypes, the American medical system, along with the larger consumer-oriented society of which it is a part, influences Asian American women to alter their features through surgery. With the authority of scientific rationality and technological efficiency, medicine is effectively able to maintain a gender ideology that validates women's monetary and time investment in beauty even if this means making their bodies vulnerable to harmful and risky procedures such as plastic surgery. Medicine is also able to perpetuate a racial ideology that states that Asian features signify "dullness," "passivity," and "lack of emotions" in the Asian person. The medicalization of racial features, which reinforces and normalizes Asian American women's feelings of inadequacy, as well as their decision to undergo cosmetic surgery, helps to bolster the consumer-oriented society of which medicine is a part and from which medicine benefits.

Given the authority with which fields of "expert" knowledge such as bio-medicine have come to define commonsense reality today, racism and sexism no longer need to rely primarily on physical coercion to legal authority. Racial stereotypes influence Asian American women to seek cosmetic surgery. Yet, through its highly specialized and validating forms of discourse and practices, medicine, along with a culture based on endless self-fashioning, is able to motivate women to view their feelings of inadequacy as individually motivated, as opposed to socially induced, phenomena, thereby effectively convincing them to participate in the production and reproduction of the larger structural inequalities that continue to oppress them.   [1993]

Notes

1. I would like to thank Nancy Scheper-Hughes, Aihwa Ong, and Cecilia de Mello for their help, insight, and inspiration from the inception of this research project.

This research was funded by the Edward H. Heller Endowment and a President's Undergraduate Fellowship, University of California, Berkeley.

Correspondence may be addressed to the author at 2226 Durant Avenue #302, Berkeley, CA 94704.

Reproduced by permission of the American Anthropological Association from Medical Anthropology Quarterly. 7(1): 74–89. Not for sale or further reproduction.

2. In a 1989 study of 80 men and women, men reported many more positive thoughts about their bodies than did women (Goleman 1991).

According to the American Society of Plastic Surgeons, 87% of all cosmetic surgery patients in 1990 were women. In my study, in one of the two doctors' offices from which I received statistical data on Asian American patients, 65% of Asian American cosmetic surgery patients in 1990 were women; in the other, 62%.

3. At the first doctor's office, the doctor's assistant examined every file from 1990. In all, 121 cosmetic procedures were performed, 81 on white patients, 20 on Asian American patients. Closely following national data, the most common procedure among white patients was liposuction (58% of all cosmetic surgeries performed on white patients).

The second doctor allowed me to survey his patient files. I examined the 1990 files for all patients with last names beginning with the letters A through L. Of these files, all the cosmetic patients were Asian American. Thus, I do not have data on white patients from this office.

It is important to note that at the first doctor's office, where data on white cosmetic surgery patients were available, the patients were older on average than the Asian American cosmetic surgery patients at the same clinic. Of the Asian American patients, 65% were in the age range of 19 to 34 years, compared with only 14.8% of whites. Only 20% of Asian American cosmetic surgery patients were in the age group of 35 to 64 years, however, compared with 80.2% of white cosmetic patients. All the other doctors in my study confirmed a similar trend in their practices. They stated that this trend results from

the tendency of whites to seek cosmetic procedures to remove fat and sagging skin that results from aging, in contrast to Asian Americans, who usually are not concerned with "correcting" signs of aging.

4. The shapes of eyes and noses of Asians are not meant in this article to be interpreted as categories that define an objective category of people called Asians. Categories of racial groups are arbitrarily defined by society. Likewise, the physical traits by which people are recognized as belonging to a racial group have been determined to be arbitrary (see Molnar 1983).

Also, I use the term "Asian American" to collectively name the women in this study who have undergone or are thinking about undergoing cosmetic surgery. Although I realize their ethnic diversity, people of Asian ancestry in the United States share similar experiences in that they are subject to many of the same racial stereotypes (see Takaki 1989).

5. Cosmetic surgery for double eyelids, nasal-tip refinement, and nose bridges is not limited to Asians in the United States. Asians in East and Southeast Asia have requested such surgeries since the early 1950s, when U.S. military forces began long-term occupations of such countries as Korea and the Philippines. (See Harahap 1982; Millard 1964; Sayoc 1954; and Kristof 1991.)

I do not mean to imply, however, that the situation within which Asian women develop a perspective on the value and meaning of their facial features is identical in Asia and the United States, where Asian women belong to a minority group. The situation in Asia would require further studies. My observations are limited to the United States.

6. Dr. Smith informed me that numerous Vietnamese, Thai, and Indonesian women come to him to widen their eyelid creases. I was allowed to see their before-and-after surgery photographs.

References

Blacking, John
1977 The Anthropology of the Body. London: Academic Press.

Blumhagen, Dan
1979 The Doctor's White Coat: The Image of the Physician in Modern America. Annals of Internal Medicine 91:111–116.

Bordo, Susan
1990 Material Girl: The Effacements of Postmodern Culture. Michigan Quarterly Review 29:635–676.

Bourdieu, Pierre
1984[1979] Distinction: A Social Critique of the Judgment of Taste. R. Nice, trans. Cambridge, MA: Harvard University Press.

Brain, Robert
1979 The Decorated Body. New York: Harper and Row.

Daly, Mary
1978 Gyn/ecology: The Metaethics of Radical Feminism. Boston: Beacon Press.

Foucault, Michel
1977[1975] Discipline and Punish: The Birth of the Prison. A. Sheridan, trans. New York: Vintage Books. (Original: Surveiller et punir: naissance de la prison.)

Goffman, Erving
1979 Gender Advertisement. Cambridge, MA: Harvard University Press.

Goleman, Daniel
1991 When Ugliness Is Only in the Patient's Eye, Body Image Can Reflect a Mental Disorder. New York Times 2 October:B9.

Gramsci, Antonio
1971 Selections from the Prison Notebooks of Antonio Gramsci. Q. Hoare and G. N. Smith, eds. New York: International.

Harahap, Marwali
1982 Oriental Cosmetic Blepharoplasty. In Cosmetic Surgery for Non-White Patients. Harold Pierce, ed. Pp. 79–97. New York: Grune and Stratton.

Kim, Elaine
1986 Asian Americans and American Popular Culture. In Dictionary of Asian American History. Hyung-Chan Kim, ed. Pp. 99–114. New York: Greenwood Press.

Kristof, Nicholas
1991 More Chinese Look "West." San Francisco Chronicle. 7 July: Sunday Punch 6.

Lakoff, Robin Tolmach, and Raquel L. Scherr
1984 Face Value: The Politics of Beauty. Boston, MA: Routledge and Kegan Paul.

Lock, Margaret, and Nancy Scheper-Hughes
1990 A Critical-Interpretive Approach in Medical Anthropology: Rituals and Routines of Discipline and Dissent. In Medical Anthropology: Contemporary Theory and Method. Thomas M. Johnson and Carolyn F. Sargent, eds. Pp. 47–72. New York: Praeger.

McCurdy, John A.
1990 Cosmetic Surgery of the Asian Face. New York: Thieme Medical Publications.

Millard, Ralph, Jr.
1964 The Oriental Eyelid and Its Surgical Revision. American Journal of Ophthalmology 57:646–649.

Molnar, Stephen
1983 Human Variation: Races, Types, and Ethnic Groups. Englewood Cliffs, NJ: Prentice-Hall.

O'Neill, John
1985 Five Bodies. Ithaca, NY: Cornell University Press.

Ong, Aihwa
1987 Spirits of Resistance and Capitalist Discipline: Factory Women in Malaysia. Albany: State University of New York Press.

Rosenthal, Elisabeth
1991a Cosmetic Surgeons Seek New Frontiers. New York Times 24 September:B5–B6.
1991b Ethnic Ideals: Rethinking Plastic Surgery. New York Times 25 September:B7.

Sayoc, B. T.
1954 Plastic Construction of the Superior Palpebral Fold. American Journal of Ophthalmology 38:556–559.
1974 Surgery of the Oriental Eyelid. Clinics in Plastic Surgery 1(1):157–171.

Scheper-Hughes, Nancy
1992 Death without Weeping. Berkeley: University of California Press.

Scheper-Hughes, Nancy, and Margaret M. Lock
1991 The Message in the Bottle: Illness and the Micropolitics of Resistance. Journal of Psychohistory 18:409–432.

Tajima, Renee E.
1989 Lotus Blossoms Don't Bleed: Images of Asian Women. In Making Waves: An Anthology of Writings by and about Asian American Women. Diane Yeh-Mei Wong, ed. Pp. 308–317. Boston, MA: Beacon Press.

Takaki, Ronald
1989 Strangers from a Different Shore. Boston, MA: Little Brown.

Turner, Bryan
1987 Medical Knowledge and Social Power.

London: Sage.

Turner, Terence

1980 The Social Skin. *In* Not Work Alone. J. Cherfas and R. Lewin, eds. Pp. 112–140. London: Temple Smith.

Wolf, Naomi

1991 The Beauty Myth: How Images of Beauty Are Used against Women. New York: William Morrow.

Understanding the Reading

1. What is the difference between the cosmetic surgery of these Asian American women and of Caucasian women?
2. Why does the author object to it?
3. What are the reasons these Asian American women give for getting cosmetic surgery?
4. What are the influences that encourage these women to undergo surgery?
5. What are the character traits they associate with their physical features?

Suggestions for Responding

1. Debate whether this is a mutilation or a celebration of the body and whether this is an "individual" choice or a socially pressured decision.
2. Discuss stereotypes of Asian males and females in the United States and whether these have changed lately, perhaps as a result of Hollywood.
3. Research and discuss male cosmetic surgery in the United States. ◆

16

Before the Great Gorge

CARLOS CUMPIÁN

She raised the oven's temperature,
he unpeeled the plump poultry
from its factory plastic wrap,
they chopped onion, garlic, celery,
poured teaspoons of salt and sage,
stirred together ground black pepper
green parsley, a moon of dry bread to expand
beneath steaming giblet broth, as the round

dining table sprouted silver knives, forks and spoons.
Back during Squanto's time, wild bird meat simmered
　with acorn stuffing
and hot honey pumpkin
　joined sweet yams in bright buttery optimism,
releasing great appetites among Pilgrims
　in the new Massachusetts' air.

No parade of football mascots' sportsbabble
had spread like unbelted American waistlines.
But even then, bald babies and tipsy husbands
took satisfied afternoon naps,
while tired women did all the work.

Squanto's great, great, great, great grandchildren
take Thanksgiving in stride, drink cokes, coffee or beer
after finishing tonight's meal made from reservation
　deer,
someone offers fat and meat scraps to backyard dogs,
　another clears
the table as three sisters talk about finding work
　before Christmas,
cars fill up to drive mothers, uncles, aunties and
　cousins home,
teenagers smoke cigarettes, their words cloud around
　school,
past due assignments, and basketball,
no one speaks of the dark Dutch
or English sailing ships that landed
on these shores long ago or pale-eyed captains
　conquering
a "savage-continent" for pagan crown and Christ.

What was Squanto's peoples' reward
　after more sullen travelers survived?
Warrior-proud Wampanogs or Algonquins
　did not serve them like some
brown-skinned waiters and waitresses,
　happy in Pocahontas feathers
with hands eager for jive-glass bead wampum tips,
or acting Tonto phonies, "You smart, Kemo sabe,"
after sharing a thousand-year-old tradition, then to
　be told,
"Thanks for the popcorn chief, now head West!"

[1996]

Understanding the Reading

1. Why does the poet describe the food of a modern Thanksgiving, followed by that of the seventeenth century?
2. What is different and what is similar between the celebrations?

3. Do the American Indians of today celebrate Thanksgiving in this poem?
4. What is the poet's view of this day?
5. What does the last paragraph mean?

Suggestions for Responding

1. Read about early colonial history and relationships with northeastern American Indian nations.
2. Research the contemporary legal battle between the Oneida Nation and New York State.
3. Research how much land owned by American Indian nations has been contaminated, used as a toxic waste dump by large commercial concerns. ◆

17

Race in a Genetic World

HARVARD MAGAZINE

"I am an African American," says Duana Fullwiley, "but in parts of Africa, I am white." To do fieldwork as a medical anthropologist in Senegal, she says, "I take a plane to France, a seven- to eight-hour ride. My race changes as I cross the Atlantic. There, I say, *'Je suis noire,'* and they say, 'Oh, okay—*métisse*—you are mixed.' Then I fly another six to seven hours to Senegal, and I am white. In the space of a day, I can change from African American, to *métisse,* to *tubaab* [Wolof for "white/European"]. This is not a joke, or something to laugh at, or to take lightly. It is the kind of social recognition that even two-year-olds who can barely speak understand. *'Tubaab,'* they say when they greet me."

Is race, then, purely a social construct? The fact that racial categories change from one society to another might suggest it is. But now, says Fullwiley, assistant professor of anthropology and of African and African American studies, genetic methods, with their precision and implied accuracy, are being used in the same way that physical appearance has historically been used: "to build—to literally *construct*—certain ideas about why race matters."

Genetic science has revolutionized biology and medicine, and even rewritten our understanding of human history. But the fact that human beings are 99.9 percent identical genetically, as Francis Collins and Craig Venter jointly announced at the White House on June 26, 2000, when the rough draft of the human genome was released, risks being lost, some scholars fear, in an emphasis on human genetic difference. Both in federally funded scientific research and in increasingly popular practice—such as ancestry testing, which often purports to prove or disprove membership in a particular race, group, or tribe—genetic testing has appeared to lend scientific credence to the idea that there is a biological basis for racial categories.

In fact, "There is no genetic basis for race," says Fullwiley, who has studied the ethical, legal, and social implications of the human genome project with sociologist Troy Duster at UC Berkeley. She sometimes quotes Richard Lewontin, now professor of biology and Agassiz professor of zoology emeritus, who said much the same thing in 1972, when he discovered that of all human genetic variation (which we now know to be just 0.1 percent of all genetic material), 85 percent occurs *within* geographically distinct groups, while 15 percent or less occurs *between* them. The issue today, Fullwiley says, is that many scientists are mining that 15 percent in search of human differences by continent.

Last October, Fullwiley and colleagues from 14 academic institutions around the country articulated some of their concerns about ancestry testing in *Science* magazine. More than half a million people have paid between $100 and $900 for such tests, and for some—those seeking to establish membership in a Native American tribe poised to open a lucrative casino, for example—the stakes can be high. Unfortunately, the *Science* authors noted, the tests have serious limitations.

Most tests focus on just two types of DNA: the paternally inherited Y sex chromosome that only men carry, and mitochondrial DNA, which is passed exclusively from mothers to their children. Scientists favor these markers with good reason: because only one parent can pass them to offspring, they are not subject to recombination, the reshuffling of genetic data that normally occurs in each generation. But they represent less than 1 percent of a subject's DNA, and each tells about only one ancestor per generation. Two generations back, a customer might learn about one of four grandparents; three generations back, about one of eight great-grandparents; and by 10 generations back (roughly 250 years ago), such genetic tests reference just one of the 1,024 ancestors in that generation. It doesn't take long to reach the point when, mathematically, a person's ancestors start to outnumber the sum total of all people who have ever lived.

Nor can genetic tests verify a person's race or ethnicity. Genes that affect skin pigmentation or blood proteins involved in malarial resistance, the authors note, may not measure direct and unique ancestry (for example, a founder effect), but reflect instead an evolutionary response to "shared environmental exposures." Furthermore, the tests are based on comparisons to databases of DNA from living populations, and are therefore vulnerable to "systematic bias" because of "incomplete geographic sampling" or the fact that "present-day patterns of residence are rarely identical to what existed in the past." One testing company even uses an underlying model that "reinforces the archaic racial view that four discrete 'parental' populations (Africans, Europeans, East Asians, and Native Americans) existed in the past" even though "there is little evidence that four biologically discrete groups of humans ever existed."

Recently, Fullwiley's concerns have centered on a new kind of genetic testing. For a substantial fee, companies such as 23 and Me will "tell you what your propensity is for hypertension, schizophrenia, breast cancer, lactose intolerance, and high or low IQ," she says. But the studies that have established links between genes and these outcomes are probabilistic, she says, and convey, like ancestry tests, what might be called a false precision. Except for known Mendelian traits or conditions (such as Huntington's disease) only a fraction of people with a gene variant linked to a disease actually become ill.

Lost in the discussion about genes, she fears, are "epigenetic" influences: factors that affect gene expression but are not part of one's genetic code, such as prenatal nutrition (which may influence rates of heart disease late in life). Such biosocial factors—environmental, cultural, and economic—can sometimes be more influential than genes. Fullwiley questions, for example, if the prevalence of diabetes among Native Americans on reservations, or of asthma among U.S. Latinos, is only genetic. Her research in Senegal has reinforced that doubt. Scientists have long searched for a genetic difference that would explain why many Senegalese experience a relatively mild form of sickle cell disease. Fullwiley's work suggests that many of them may instead be mitigating their symptoms with a widespread cultural practice: phytotherapy—the ingestion of roots from a plant that, preliminary studies suggest, triggers production of fetal hemoglobin, a blood-cell type that doesn't sickle. "When environmental history, or evolutionary history, gets reduced to racial or ethnic difference," she says, "that's a big mistake."

Not all genetics projects are so potentially divisive, however. In February, Spencer Wells, Ph.D. '94, a former Lewontin student, came to Harvard to tell a story of human connectedness. Wells, who heads the joint National Geographic Society–IBM nonprofit Genographic Project, spent an afternoon with student members of the Harvard Foundation, which represents 72 student organizations "from the Albanian Society to the Vietnamese Society," says director S. Allen Counter. Wells had previously invited the students to participate in the Genographic Project by sending in cheek swabs with their DNA for analysis. "The idea," says Counter, "was to show a diverse group of students how they connect to the rest of humanity."

Spencer Wells tells student volunteers of the Harvard Foundation about their deep ancestors' ancient migrations. Wells has created a human family tree that traces "the journey of man" (as he titled his 2002 book) in populating the entire planet from a homeland in Africa. The project has used linguistic and genetic studies to guide its sampling of indigenous populations from around the globe—many of them isolated and remote—and now has the world's largest and most representative anthropological database of human DNA.

At Harvard, a Pakistani-American student whose family had always told her they were originally from an area near the Arabian Sea had this confirmed by her DNA result. "Your family was part of the first migration out of Africa," noted Wells. "You share that with the Australian aborigines." An African-American student with ancestors from East Africa carried a genetic signature characteristic of that region. But an Asian-American student was surprised to find that she carried almost the same genetic markers as a Mexican-American student. Wells explained, "There is only one change, but you are fairly different because your lines diverged a long time ago. Still, you are part of the same branch of the tree": the Native Americans who populated the Western Hemisphere originally came from Asia.

The Genographic Project aims to tell people "where their ancestors were living as indigenous people" at different points in time, but can't, for example, tell most African Americans precisely where in Africa they are from because, Wells explains, "the database isn't quite there yet." Echoing Fullwiley's reservations about all such tests, he says he's "a bit concerned about some of the African-American DNA testing companies purporting to trace you back to your ancient tribe." Ancestry is actually *more* complex for the average African American, he says, not only because people in West Africa (where most of the slave trade occurred) have moved around a lot in the last 500 years, but also because "group composition within Africa has changed over time." Furthermore, because only a small number of humans survived the journey out of Africa some 50,000 years ago (and the slave trade on that continent was relatively localized), "there is more diversity *in* the average African village," Wells notes, "than there is outside of Africa combined."

When asked about the question of race, Wells's answer was unequivocal. "Racism is not only socially divisive, but also scientifically incorrect. We are all descendants of people who lived in Africa recently," he says. "We are all Africans

under the skin." The kinds of differences that people notice, such as skin pigmentation, limb length, or other adaptations are "basically surface features that have been selected for in the environment. When you peer beneath the surface at the underlying level of genetic variation, we are all much more similar than we appear to be. There are no clear, sharp delineations."

THE HUMAN FAMILY TREE

The movements of particular genetic markers—those from the male Y chromosome in blue, and those from maternally inherited mitochondrial DNA in orange—have been plotted on a map by the National Geographic Society–IBM Genographic Project to show the routes humans took as they moved out from an ancestral homeland in East Africa to populate the entire planet. For more information, visit www.nationalgeographic.com/genographic.

Fullwiley's own ethnographic research among genetic scientists suggests that much of current medical genetics may reinforce ideas of racial difference. Because certain diseases occur at higher frequencies in some populations (sickle cell anemia in blacks, Tay-Sachs disease in Jews of eastern European ancestry), they have become linked to the idea of race, even when the disease does not result from common ancestry. Sickle cell trait, for example, has arisen independently in several populations as an evolutionary response to malaria. The genetic change appeared first in India and then in Africa; it is also found in Greeks and Italians. But in the United States, Fullwiley says, sickle cell trait is very much linked to African-American racial identity through the history of medicine.

She says the potential for racialization of medical genetics has been institutionalized because "you can't get a grant from the NIH unless you recruit in racial groups, label people by census category, and then report back the data in terms of outcomes by racial type." The original intent—to counter the widespread use of the white male body as the working research norm—is "fine and good," she says, but there "ought to be some flexibility to these race categories, and some thinking about what they mean. This new construction of race . . . *is* socially inflected—but it is not *solely* a social construct because biology is front and center." ✦

18

Define "Real Indians"

KEVIN NOBLE MAILLARD

The intersection of race and citizenship in Indian Country never fails to create a tragicomedy of tribal politics. Whenever tribes are under attack about membership policies, the reliable Hail Mary is "sovereignty," even when it bears little relation to federal intrusion.

Natives safely ensconced as members are the first to step forward and defend obviously discriminatory actions, whether in a council meeting, a newspaper blog, or a T-shirt that says, "I'm a Real Indian." So very typically, "It's not about race; it's about sovereignty" and "outsiders don't understand" are the most common and ridiculous of arguments. Add in a healthy portion of Self-Determination and a generous serving of Tribal Autonomy, and there you have a typical recipe for Sovereignty Sauce.

At times, the Sauce is cooked in shady pots to defend even shadier behavior. When my own tribe went though this exact same issue 10 years ago, tribal council meetings took on state fair antics, with hooin', mooin' and hollerin' at Freedmen in attendance. Cries of "Go back to Africa!" followed Black Indians around town. Local papers quoted citizens saying, "We're trying to get the blacks out."

I wouldn't recommend tasting the new Sovereignty Sauce, though, because it's probably poisoned, and is nothing like the original. When deciding who would get to try it, they'll rig the election and pass a constitutional amendment. And likely fire anyone who doesn't agree. If you are black, there is a separate spoon for you to taste it. You don't deserve any Sauce because you were never entitled to taste it. And it's an acquired taste that you'll never understand. On second thought, the Sauce folks don't share so there will be more left for them. Why? Because they are Real Indians.

But Real Indians were created by Real White People. In the late 1800s, a group called "Friends of the Indian" convened annually at Lake Mohonk in upstate New York to address solutions to the "Indian problem." Their perceived solution was the General Allotment Act. Take away Native communal ownership and replace it with private possession. All adult citizens of the various Native nations would be given property, which was believed to have "civilizing influences." This happened in many tribes, including my own, the Seminole Nation.

But to give away all the land, federal officials had to answer the question: "Who is Indian?" White bureaucrats (not natives!) classified applicants of mixed Afro-Indian ancestry as Freedmen, while full-blood and mixed-blood white Indians became Citizens by Blood. Paradoxically, white European ancestry did not categorically threaten membership, but black ancestry was a likely trigger for Freedmen status.

The Holy Grail of "Indian Blood" comes from the federal government. This is the typical defense for self-determination. It is entirely true and valid that Indian nations retain the prerogative to determine membership as they choose, but in order for the argument to hold water, it should at least make some indigenous sense. Incongruously, the trumpet of 21st century sovereignty blows loudly from the extermination policies of dead white Victorians in upstate New York.   [2011]

Understanding the Reading

1. What is the central disagreement among tribal members in this article?
2. What is the General Allotment Act of 1887?
3. Who decided at that time which persons were legally Indian?

Suggestion for Responding

1. Research the historical relationship between African Americans and American Indians. ✦

SUGGESTIONS FOR RESPONDING TO PART I

1. Write a paper analyzing the racial and ethnic features of your identity. Consider your ancestral origins and how your heritage has influenced who you are today. Reflect on such factors as physical characteristics, language, religion, and family customs and traditions. Also, think about such expressive behaviors as dress, music, dance, family stories, holidays, and celebrations. These all may be markers of your ethnic heritage.

   If you think you have nothing to write about, remember that in the United States everyone has a racial and ethnic heritage. Whereas it is central to some people's identity, others may not be conscious of it at all. This is often because they are members of the dominant racial and ethnic culture, which assumes its values and traditions are "universal" or at least most significant or appropriate. If you belong to this group, look at yourself from the outside, from the perspective of another cultural system, several of which have been represented in these readings.

2. In response to the Gwaltney selection (Reading 10), you wrote questions you would ask if you were conducting an oral history interview. Singly or as a member of a group, evaluate those questions again. Then use them to interview an older person in your family or community.

   Many people find it helpful to write the questions on file cards, so they can be reorganized to adjust to the direction the interview takes. You may find some questions no longer relevant once the interview is underway; also, more important questions may occur to you on the spot. A tape recorder is useful, especially if you plan to prepare a word-for-word transcript, but always ask your informant for permission before you switch it on. Either with or without a recorder, it is important to take written notes (unless it makes your informant uncomfortable); in this way, you can highlight key pieces of information.

   Your final report could resemble Reading 10 (a verbatim transcription of the words of your informant), or it may be more interpretive. In either case, listen to the recording and reread your notes *several* times before you begin to write, and refer to them after you have completed your report to confirm its accuracy.

3. Your instructor may want you to make an oral presentation of your ethnicity analysis or your oral history. In this case, prepare *brief* notes, again on file cards. Try to talk naturally and not read word for word. Rehearse your presentation several times to be sure you stay within the required time limit. You will feel more comfortable in front of your class if you have rehearsed at least once before an audience (a friend or roommate, for example). If this isn't possible, try speaking to a wall mirror. Above all, relax. Try to look at your audience, even if it seems difficult, because their reactions will be encouraging. Remember, you are talking to friends.

4. After completing Part I, how would you answer the questions "Who is an American?" and "Is there an American culture?" Support your responses with evidence from the readings.

II
Gender and Sexual Identity

"Is it a girl or a boy?" This is inevitably the first question asked about a new baby. As we grow older, we identify ourselves and each other as boys or girls, as women or men. In American culture, gender is the most salient feature of one's identity. It shapes our attitudes, our behavior, our experiences, our beliefs about ourselves and about others. Gender is so central to our perception of social reality that we often are not even conscious of how it shapes our behavior and our social interactions.

We all know the traditional definitions of masculinity and femininity. A "real man" should be **masculine**—that is, he should be strong and mechanically oriented, ambitious and assertive, in control of his emotions, knowledgeable about the world, a good provider. A "real woman," in turn, should be **feminine**—that is, passive and domestic, nurturing and dependent, emotional, preoccupied with her appearance, and maternal. These gender-appropriate characteristics and behaviors affect many areas of our lives: physical and psychological aspects, occupational choices, interpersonal relations, and so on.

The basis for gender distinctions is not wholly clear as of now, and the "nature/nurture" debate—whether or to what degree gendered behavior is controlled by biology or by socialization—continues. Scientists are investigating the roles that hormones, genes, chromosomes, and other physical features play in

women's and men's psychological development, but these issues are complex and many are beyond the scope of this book.

We will concentrate on the view of many social scientists who study the diversity of appropriate or "natural" male and female behaviors in different cultures and other times. They see in this diversity strong evidence of the central role that culture plays in creating gender roles. As a result, they distinguish between **sex,** the biological "fact" of one's physiological and hormonal characteristics, and **gender,** the social categories that ascribe roles, appropriate behaviors, and personality traits to women and men. In this sense, male and female **sex roles** are differences in reproductive traits. The masculine and feminine behaviors are features of **gender roles.**

Social scientists believe that we learn our appropriate gender roles by a process called **socialization.** Gender roles are only one kind of role we learn. A **role** is any socially or culturally defined behavioral expectation that is presumed to apply to all individuals in the category. Socialization includes the many pressures, rewards, and punishments that compel us to conform to social expectations. These are deeply embedded in every aspect of our culture. Our treatment of infants and children, language, education, mass media, religion, laws, medical institutions and mental health systems, occupational

69

environments, intimate relationships—all teach and reinforce appropriate gender behaviors.

The first article in Part II (Reading 19) is about a U.S. soldier who reveals to his father on YouTube that he is gay. After seventeen years, the 'Don't Ask Don't Tell' policy of not allowing soldiers to be openly gay was struck down. Readings 20 and 21 look at how we are taught gender beliefs and behaviors. In Reading 20, Angela Phillips describes how parents and others begin to mold children into "appropriate" gender roles from birth—even when parents intend to raise them **androgynously,** having both female and male gender characteristics; she also considers the internal psychological factors that may influence gender learning. Ellen J. Reifler (Reading 21) writes about how adults (and children) make assumptions about gender in children and reinforce traditional expectations, even when the parents themselves may be trying to raise their children in a nonsexist way.

In Reading 22 Paula Gunn Allen speaks from her own experience about the value most Indian peoples attribute to women, despite distortions presented by the White mainstream.

Reading 23 considers male gender roles. Doug Cooper Thompson describes the male stereotype and analyzes what it costs men to conform to those expectations.

THIS PART ALSO SHEDS LIGHT ON THE DISTINCT AREAS THAT affect our sexual orientations. Tom Head gives us a short history of transgender rights in the United States in Reading 24. As the author of Reading 25, Jessica R. Stearns, writes: "first there is the anatomical sex of a person (M/F), second, the gender (M/F), then, third, sexual orientation (Hetero/Homosexual)." Although most people have all three segments the same and are heterosexual, there can be any combination. Most of us have been brought up to think only in terms of male and female. Both of these authors help us relearn this important piece of being human. Jessica R. Stearns, in "A Transsexual's Story," writes of her life, which began in 1940 as John Robert Stearns in rural Alabama. From her earliest memories, she remembers having the feeling of being a girl, but in the 1940s and 1950s there was very little known about transgendered people in this country. She joined the Air Force, became a pilot, and flew missions into Berlin and Vietnam. She eventually had very high security clearance but said, "If they had ever known!" Under great pressure from the military to conform to a particular masculine image, she married, became a father, and eventually flew for Continental Airlines. When she decided to go for the sex reassignment operation (strongly supported by her family and doctors), Continental Airlines fired her. Jessica sued and won. She made national headlines, was featured on the *Sally Jesse Raphael* show, and here writes her story for the first time.

Reading 26, by Anne Fausto-Sterling, "Two Sexes Are Not Enough," confronts us first with the information that the Western world has invested a great deal in the idea that there are only two sexes and, so, denies what biology does not: that intersexuals (those with a combination of male and female sexual organs) have always been around. Second, she asks us to question the ethics of "assigning" a sex by surgically altering a newborn. Fausto-Sterling suggests, instead, that we consider acknowledging what is already in nature: a five-sex system.

Readings 27 and 28 place us squarely in perhaps the most divisive topic in which the United States has been engaged in this millennium. Andrew Sullivan discusses why Americans should approve of gay marriage, and Ann Marie Nicolosi, in "When the Political Is Personal" (Reading 28), describes her coming out as a lesbian to her university students, and why.

The readings in this part should help us assess our own gender identity and give us fuller insight into the experiences of the opposite sex. A clearer sense of some of the consequences of traditional gender roles and gender expectations may encourage us to question just how "natural" traditional gender roles are. It will also help us consider whether or not we want to see changes in gender roles and sexual relationships and how to act on our decisions. Also, students and professors can discuss, debate, and pursue the implications of all the information within each essay. For example, when is sexual assignment surgery ethical, if ever? Do you think gay marriage will become a national right, as it has in other countries? Why or why not? Should gay couples adopt? Would you prefer to know if your professor were gay or lesbian, or should the professor maintain that distance? Are there differing circumstances?

What sorts of public policies would change if we acknowledged the existence of five sexes? Would an intersexed person be allowed to marry, and would it be to a man or to a woman? How would we organize the separation of sexes in prisons? Would they be eligible for a military draft?

Because of the complexity of sexuality, where external organs, internal organs, and our endocrine system all help sort out who we are and what makes us happy, there is a constant tension in our society when the jigsaw pieces do not fit the way we have been told they should. On June 26, 2003, the Supreme Court overruled a Texas sodomy law, legalizing gay sexual conduct. In dissent, Justice Antonin Scalia declared it a cultural war. On August 5, 2003, the Episcopal Church's first openly gay bishop was approved, the Reverend Gene Robinson of New Hampshire, and on November 18, 2003, Massachusetts' highest court ruled that gay couples have the right to marry. In contrast, in May 2007, before the end of the Iraq War, the *International Herald Tribune* reported that the Department of Defense was discharging linguists, including Arabic speakers, because they were gay. (Ten thousand have been discharged in the past decade because of sexual orientation.) In a time when national security was supposed to be top priority, and Arabic linguists were badly needed in Iraq and elsewhere, sexual orientation trumped the war on terrorism. There is a great deal of politics surrounding our sexuality these days, and the geographical fault lines show fairly clearly that the United States is split on subjects dealing with sexual identity. The repeal of the Don't Ask, Don't Tell policy in 2011 ended the mandate requiring military personnel who were not heterosexual to hide their sexual orientation. This change is a milestone in our country's history.

19

Soldier Tells Dad He's Gay on YouTube: With Expiration of "Don't Ask, Don't Tell," Military Members Come Out

MSNBC.COM STAFF AND NEWS SERVICE REPORTS

"Dad, I'm gay."

With those three emotion-drenched words, a 21-year-old U.S. soldier stationed in Germany reveals in a phone call to his father in Alabama what he had long kept secret but could now finally share with Tuesday's official repeal of the military's 17-year "Don't Ask, Don't Tell" policy.

The soldier, who goes by the online moniker "areyousurprised," captures himself on video telling his father something he says he's "known since forever" but was afraid to share. He posted the video to YouTube, and it quickly went viral. The soldier was among numerous U.S. military members who "came out" on Tuesday, guaranteed that they will no longer be punished or booted out of the service because of their sexual orientation.

The soldier doesn't give his name, and in previous YouTube videos chronicling his experience as a gay man in the military is careful not to show his face. But in the latest video, titled "Telling my dad that I am gay," he faces the camera directly, sitting in a room with a world map draped on a wall behind him. The Washington Post identified him as Randy Phillips and said the video was recorded with his web camera in his bedroom at Ramstein Air Base in Germany.

The soldier fidgets nervously as he tells viewers it's early Tuesday morning and he hasn't been able to sleep. He then calls home on his mobile phone. In the captivating five-minute conversation that follows, he reveals his sexual orientation to his father.

"Can I tell you something?" he asks.

"Yeah," the father replies.

"Will you love me, serious?"

"Yes," the father says.

"Dad, I'm gay."

The soldier explains that "I've known since forever" about his sexual orientation and has been aching to tell his family for a long time.

"I don't know when's the next time I would be able to see you. I didn't want to do it over the phone. I wanted to tell you in person, but uh . . . I didn't want you to find out in any other way." After a period of silence, the father says, "OK."

And then came the reassurance.

"Will you still love me?" the soldier asks.

"I still love you, son. Yes, I still love you," the father replies.

Viewers touched by the video posted multiple comments of praise and support. "You are the epitome of honestly, integrity, and your good southern manners show through as well. Congrats on being your true self, and thank you for your continued service to our nation," one person wrote, adding, "I am proud to call you a gay brother." "His father loves him unconditionally. How many times do you see this," another wrote.

Other service members also came out in dramatic ways, and said they're relieved to finally not have to hide their private lives from their straight colleagues while serving the country. Chief Warrant Officer Charlie Morgan, who serves with the New Hampshire National Guard, announced on MSNBC on Tuesday that she is a lesbian. "I have a 4-year-old daughter and in [a] civil union with a same-sex spouse for almost 11 years. I have not been able until today to actually share my family, my complete family," she said. "I'm (now) able to put on my desk our family photo and actually share my family with my colleagues that I deployed with."

More than 100 U.S. military members revealed their sexual orientations on Tuesday in the first publicly distributed issue of *OutServe Magazine*, according to Germany's Spiegel Online. Their photos are shown under an article titled "101 Faces of Courage." *OutServe* says there are approximately 70,000 currently serving military personnel stationed around the world who are lesbian, gay, transgender or bisexual.

Eddy Sweeney, an intelligence officer, and Jonathan Mills, a radio frequency transmissions technician, told Spiegel Online they came up with the idea of a publication for gay service members while they were both stationed at U.S. Air Force bases in Germany. "When you're stationed overseas, there are fewer Americans, so you don't have the luxury of making too many friends outside of the military community," Sweeney told Spiegel Online. "And when you meet someone in the military who happens to be gay and also happens to be stationed abroad, you form a kind of secret society."

U.S. Marine Maj. Darrel Choat, a Nebraska native, told NPR he knew he was gay when he signed up for the military 14 years ago. He said talk about other Marines threatening to leave the force over the acceptance of gays is nonsense. "When they say, 'Well, you know, I couldn't share a fighting position with a Marine that's gay,' or anything like that, I say, 'Wow. So gay Marines have that much power that they can totally disarm you and defeat you just by their simple presence? And you call yourself a Marine? Come on, dude. What's your problem? Get over it.'"

Choat told NPR he's planning to go to the Marine Corps ball in November, as he does every year—only this time, he'll bring a date. Dan Choi, the former Army lieutenant who was discharged from the military after coming out on "The Rachel Maddow Show" in March 2009, told Politico he will re-enlist after Tuesday's DADT repeal. Choi became an outspoken gay-rights activist after his discharge and wrote an open letter to President Barack Obama in which he criticized "Don't Ask, Don't Tell" as "a slap in the face" to him and his fellow soldiers. He told Politico he will meet with a military recruiter later this week to talk about joining the Army Reserves.

"Going back to the military will be a vindication," Choi told Politico. "[I'm] going back because I fought to go back. The seriousness of our claims was not just political theatre—it was really drawn from our lives. I sacrificed so much so I could go back."

In Vermont, Navy Lt. Gary Ross and his partner, Dan Swezy, celebrated the repeal of "Don't Ask, Don't Tell" by getting married. Vermont is among six states that recognize same-sex marriages, and the Arizona couple chose Duxbury's Moose Meadow Lodge, a log cabin bed-and-breakfast perched on a hillside about 15 miles northwest of Montpelier, for the site of their nuptials. The lodge says it hosted the state's first gay wedding in 2009.

Ross wore his dress uniform for the occasion. "I think it was a beautiful ceremony. The emotions really hit me . . . but it's finally official," Ross said.

Understanding the Reading

1. What was the Don't Ask Don't Tell Policy?
2. Why does the young man tell his father of his sexual orientation on the telephone?
3. What consequences does this policy change have for people's lives in the United States?

Suggestions for Responding

1. Bring a gay/lesbian/bi-sexual/transgender group into your classroom to discuss how this policy change affects everyone's lives in the United States.
2. Discuss generational , political, and religious divides on this policy change.

20

In the Beginning There Are Babies

ANGELA PHILLIPS

The making of a man starts from the moment of birth, or even before then, when the eye of the ultrasound scanner picks up the shadow that marks out a boy baby and Granny starts knitting in blue instead of pink. In many cultures the birth of a boy is overtly celebrated as a matter of more significance than that of a girl. A Pakistani friend told me that her husband had been considered very odd when he chose to celebrate the birth of a girl with the same show as he had the birth of his son.

Fathers in less traditional societies may not be able to make an overt display of their pleasure when they father a son, but surveys of fathers' behavior show that they still tend to take more interest in their male babies than in their female babies. They stay longer in the delivery room, handle them more, ask more questions about them, and stimulate them more. Girl babies are cuddled; boy babies are stimulated.

The research doesn't show nearly as much difference in the way mothers handle their different sex children as in the way fathers do after the first few weeks. To begin with, mothers tend to touch their daughters more than their sons—though they take care not to do so in the presence of their husbands—and they are also more likely to stimulate their daughters and to cuddle their sons, but after this early period the major difference lies in the fact that boys tend to be breast-fed for longer.

The similarity in the mothers' handling of boys and girls may lie in the fact that the physical demands of a small baby take up most of a mother's time. She doesn't differentiate her behavior because it is the baby who sets the pace of her care. A crying baby needs to be soothed no matter what its sex. Someone who only plays with a baby when it is clean, fed, and happy is more likely to initiate communication rather than simply responding to needs.

Nevertheless, while mothers may handle their small babies the same way, many express a very early sense of their sons as "different" and their daughters as extensions of themselves. One mother said to me: "I never expected to be the mother of sons. I don't know anything about boys." Another said: "My first sight of him was as very separate. My first thought was that he was very self-confident." I was reminded of my own first thoughts about my son that it wasn't me who knew how to feed him. He knew and showed me himself.

A newborn baby has no way of knowing that it is a separate being. As far as it is concerned, the body of its mother is an extension of its own body. When the baby cries this body is there. It is the difference between the person who mainly cares for the baby and other adults who come and go that helps the baby to understand both that people are separate creatures with their own boundaries and that people can leave—and come back.

The process of learning their separateness takes place between the ages of six months and eighteen months. At the same time the baby is also absorbing information about its gender. Indeed, some studies suggest that children as young as twelve months old can tell whether a strange child is male or female and will favor the child of the same sex. Most parents will testify that, once words come, they will very soon be used to divide and codify the world: big, little; boy, girl; man, woman.

For a girl, the road at first seems simple and straight. She realizes very early on that she is to become a woman. A woman is what her mother is. She is going to become a mother just like her own. She will be powerful, loving, and wise. Later she may come to understand that her father has a

greater power, out in the world; but in these first few years identification with the mother means that she is firmly rooted. She has already identified her future—she simply has to grow into it.

For a boy, the way ahead is not so simple. He learns that the person who leaves (if he has a resident father at all) is the person he is going to be like. He is not going to grow up to be like Mommy. For the girl, the moment of recognition is also a moment of power. For the boy, it is a moment of uncertainty. Even in families in which both parents go out to work, the mother is, almost always, the biggest and most important person in his universe, but he will never be like her. His destiny is to be different. He is going to grow up to be a man, and from the moment he discovers this difference the search is on to discover the elements of masculinity.

If his father is accessible he will provide him with a sense of what it is to be male. He will play rougher games, talk to him differently, offer him "appropriate" toys. However, in most families the father is rarely available, and in an increasing number of families he is not available at all. So the things that the father does are distant, remote, difficult. While a girl finds, in these early years, an easily available model of what it is to be female, her brother is floundering. In the first two years he is much the same as the girls he sees, but in order to be a boy he must define his difference from them. He starts looking for clues.

Research indicates that, even in the very first year of life, boys tend to be more exploratory, whereas girls are more "person-oriented." Yet these little explorers are also more anxious and more easily upset when the object of their exploration proves frustrating. Perhaps this little boy is searching for himself, for the person he is going to be, whereas the little girl stays close to Mother (or a female caregiver), the living model of her future. Indeed, it is the inherent difficulty of this search for masculinity that, according to psychoanalyst Robert Stoller, is the reason why there are so many more men than women who grow up biologically normal and yet feel themselves to belong to the opposite sex (transsexuals).

The first clues are the easy ones. He finds that he has a little thing at the front that makes him different from girls. Depending on the culture he comes from, quite a lot of fuss may be made of this little thing. It will be given a name, it may be played with while his diaper is being changed. It may be the object of interested comment. It is outside his body, easy to see, and, what is more, feels interesting.

Soon he will start picking up other clues. If there is a man around his house he will gravitate toward him. Fathers tend to play more with their sons than with their daughters and, when they do play, tend to play more physical rough-and-tumble games. For most boys the intervention of the father is an event. Most of the time he is not there. In his absence, his mother and the other women who care for him have to provide verbal evidence of what a man is. Marianne Grabrucker, in her diary of her daughter's first three years, noticed that mothers of boys were constantly referring to their "manliness":

> Whenever Martin has managed a little crap in the loo, it's praised as being just like a man's; if Martin has hurt himself and bleeds a little, it's described as being real man's blood; at mealtimes he's told to eat his food, just like a man, just like Daddy. . . . No one has ever told Aneli that she should eat up her food like a real woman.

Grabrucker sees this as part of the way in which a boy learns that men are more powerful. However, it could also be seen as one of the only ways in which mothers can present an image of the male to a boy who rarely sees his father. It isn't necessary to tell Aneli that she will grow up to be a real woman. Mommy is there and she can see her. A boy has to do much of his learning about men through what his mother says about them. His mother's view of men will become part of his own view—for good or ill.

When a female child is cared for wholly by a father rather than a mother, she too is likely to feel unsure of her gender role and need to be reminded that she will grow up to be a woman, "like Mommy." The few girls I know who have been brought up mainly by their fathers displayed very little interest in the homemaking games that occupy so much time for most other girls. Without the model of a mother to follow, housework games had little appeal. That is not what, in their eyes, Mommies do.

In families where both parents are equally involved in child care, gender difference in the behavior of children may still be quite marked, not because of what the parent is deliberately feeding in but because of what the child is looking for and adding to the sum of his or her own identity.

This father of two has a firm commitment to bringing up his children as equals. He works from home and has a high level of involvement with their day-to-day care. I asked him what games he plays with his children. He told me: "Football, Frisbee, kite flying, swimming, board and card games. Different only due to their ages." He then added: "But my daughter likes to play with the Playmobile [a construction set with people in it], while my son likes to construct complicated things with rope, wood and engines [real or imagined]. He liked cars best; she played with dolls from an early age."

Already these children seem to be selecting the characteristics that apply particularly to their same-gendered parents and practicing those with more diligence than the others. Of course, they are helped with their selecting by clues from elsewhere. Both these children have been cared for while their parents work. The alternative caregivers are female. Most of the other adults encountered during the first two years will have been female. The other male adults will have been, on the whole, fairly remote.

As soon as they start mixing regularly with other children, they will start picking up new clues. This same father says: "I remember my son playing with the toy stove and other homemaking things and being chased out by a girl who said boys weren't allowed in there. He was clearly shocked." A mother of three sons, who have mainly been cared for by their father, reported a similar experience:

> Claudio had two friends home from nursery and they played in my old doll's house. Claudio put the father doll in the kitchen and said, "Daddy's making dinner." His two male friends giggled and said, "Daddies don't make dinner." Claudio said, "Mine does," but he never played with the doll's house again.

In fact, boys have very little idea of what fathers actually do. Boys in a London primary school were asked: "What do fathers do which is different from mothers?" They answered: "Sit down a lot; laze about; smoke a pipe." Asked what fathers in the olden days might have done, one said: "They might have been challenging each other with duels and swords and stuff." Another suggested, "Pirates." When asked what fathers were for, two said: "To look after us." Another suggested: "To be sensible and don't rob banks and that." A third: "Helping you to live because they buy your clothes."

They were then asked what it would be like if the men had babies. One child said: "Maybe they might decide to give the women more difficult complicateder jobs, where you get more money and more sort of dangerous jobs like being a diver, which I don't think women are allowed to do." Another added, "Also being a police officer or a fire officer."

When my daughter and her friends play with boys, they always insist that the boys play "Daddies," which in this context always means getting bossed around or being sent out to "work"—whatever that means. Given their understanding of what their own fathers do, it isn't surprising that the boys quickly tire of such a role and ask to play the baby instead, where at least they can clown around.

So while most girls are industriously home-building with whatever they can lay their hands on, boys have no simple role to inhabit. Even those boys with no men in their lives will have picked up pretty early on the fact that men drive cars, trains, buses—and they will drive them too. Those with the coordination to do so may start making things (though boys often lag behind in the fine motor skills that would allow them to paint, draw, and color). Given encouragement, they will also dress up—though they soon work out that most dressing up includes dresses, which are intended for girls; men in our culture don't dress up, and boys have to make do with firemen's helmets while girls are swathing themselves in lace.

So just how can a three-year-old boy play out the fantasy of being a man? Is it any wonder that many of them are running around being loud and silly, trying to find a role to inhabit? In any given situation, small girls are more likely to be quietly getting on with something, learning to do something that their mother can do, while their male peers are still running around like mad things, as if trying to divine from the air a sense of what it is they would like to be getting on with. Perhaps this is one of the reasons why boys from as young as a year old appear to be naughtier than girls and are more often reprimanded.

However vague and imprecise the information about masculinity, there is no more dedicated detective than a small child in search of knowledge. Superheroes provide the most obvious and overt messages, just as folk and fairy tales have done in the past. If your son is behaving like Hulk Hogan, Superman, or Captain Planet, it is hardly surprising. These figures are very clearly identified as male. They are mostly involved in fighting and protecting other, more fragile (often female) people and they are also, clearly and unambiguously, *good*. . . .

LEARNING NOT TO BE GENTLE

What of the many boys who are not anxious, aggressive, and excitable? While most surveys confirm that boys are more likely than girls to be naughty and aggressive, they also show that the gender difference is not universal. In any group there are likely to be more aggressive boys than aggressive girls, but there will also be almost as many unaggressive boys as there are unaggressive girls. Gentleness is almost as often a male attribute as it is a female one, but it is not *labeled* as masculine behavior and it is not counted in surveys.

Between the ages of eighteen months and three years it is very common for both boys and girls to go through a phase in which they push, grab, and defend what they see as their own territory from others. Some children may take longer than others to learn how to control what is theirs and work out how to allow another child to "borrow" something without fearing that they will lose it forever. This behavior may be described as aggressive. Other children are so fearful that they never really manage to work out how they can hang on to what is theirs, nor do they learn how to lend. They feel perpetually at the mercy of more powerful forces.

Girls and boys may belong to either category. This is how one father described his son and daughter: "My son has been more dependent, more easily frightened and hurt, less communicative emotionally, and more likely to brood." A mother talked about her son's experience of starting nursery school: "He was desperately unhappy and I was desperately worried about him. He couldn't cope with the number of people and the range of options. He spent much of the time hiding under the table."

A third parent said: "I stopped going to my NCT [National Childbirth Trust mothers' group] after my second child because his brother, at three, was being victimized by the other boys."

These parents worry about their children's lack of assertiveness, and they may not be aware that many of the boys who spend their time running around and shouting, or losing their tempers and screaming, may also be demonstrating their anxiety. When John started nursery school at two and a half, he went into a small group of five children with one staff member. The day was well organized and he clearly felt safe and happy. After a few weeks, the staff decided that, since he was physically bigger than the other children and seemed more advanced in his play, he should join the older group of three- to five-year-olds. His behavior immediately deteriorated. He reacted to the bigger space, larger numbers, and less structured activity not by withdrawing but by running wildly around the room.

A child who is running wild and apparently out of control is far more likely to hurt someone else than a child who is sitting quietly building with Lego. This doesn't necessarily mean that he is aggressive, but it may well be seen that way. John, "promoted" because of his maturity, was now in danger of being labeled as a problem. In the preschool years boys are persistently scored as more aggressive than girls by researchers. The difference is more marked than at any other life stage.

The fact is that there is no socially sanctioned way in which boys can show their anxiety and ask for help. If they are rough and anxious they are seen as aggressive, but they are given precious little encouragement to show weakness. While girls are encouraged to seek help from adults, boys are expected to learn to cope. This encouragement may, again, not be explicit, but it is worth noting that girls and boys get different responses both to aggressive behavior and to defensive behavior.

Little girls quickly learn that by crying they will enlist adult help on their side. Crying is therefore a more effective defense than hitting back. It might be in the interests of boys to learn the same strategy, but too often crying in boys will elicit a very different and far less positive response.

In a study on the effects of divorce, researchers discovered that in all the family groups they studied: "Crying and distress in boys received less frequent and shorter periods of comforting and more ambivalent comforting than did distress signals from girls." By *ambivalent* the researchers meant responses such as "a hug, combined with: 'There, there! Boys don't cry.' Girls were far more likely to be given unqualified reassurance."

Because there are no models of gentle boys, these children may find that they also receive confusing messages about the way they should behave. Says Clarissa:

At four, Justin seems to get on better with girls. He loves singing and dancing and playing musical instruments and he also likes imaginary play, which is as much to do with things like going on holiday, going to a restaurant, or being Peter Pan and sprinkling people with pixie dust as it is with playing monsters.

I really do love him just as he is, but sometimes I feel slightly anxious. Are we making him too gentle, in a way which might open him to bullying later on? Are we overly soppy and affectionate with him, and might that make him different from the other boys? Should we toughen him up a bit? And that's really the dilemma. I am an avowed feminist. I want him to grow up to be gentle and kind. I want him to respect women as equals. But I also want him to hold his own in a world of men, and I don't want anyone, male or female, to regard him as a wimp. I keep thinking it's something of a battleground out there. But then I think, Would I even be asking these questions if Justin were a girl? I think not.
[1994]

Understanding the Reading

1. How do fathers and mothers tend to handle boy babies and girl babies differently?
2. What are the differences between girl infants and boy infants?
3. Infant boys are described as being more "exploratory" than infant girls are. What may be the cause?
4. How does being cared for by a father affect a female child?
5. What else, besides parents, influences gender behavior in small children?

6. How are boys affected by the relative unavailability of adult males in their lives?
7. What causes preschool boys to run wild and appear to be out of control?

Suggestions for Responding

1. If you know someone who has an infant, or if you can get permission to observe at a day-care center, watch the behaviors of a caregiver with girl infants and/or boy infants. Report on whether your observations conform with Phillips's analysis.
2. Watch parents of small children in some public place, like a park or mall, and note the differences between the males and females in their interactions with the little ones. ◆

21

Time Warp in the Toy Store

Ellen J. Reifler

Last week Linda went to the drive-up window at McDonald's and ordered a kid's meal for her daughter. "Is this for a boy or a girl?" asked the clerk. Annoyed, Linda turned to Shaina and translated.

"Do you want the Hot Wheels or the Barbie?"

"I want the car, Mommy."

How can this conversation be possible in 1994? Our children's world is littered with the sex role stereotypes we adults have tossed in the garbage.

It is 25 years since newspapers stopped categorizing their help-wanted sections by male and female. It is illegal to deny a job to someone on the basis of gender. But despite the resolve of many parents of the '70s, in the '90s there is still a firmly-entrenched time warp in the toy store. Girls play with dolls, tot-sized housewares, and make-up, reflecting the holy trinity of childcare, housework, and seduction. Boys play with cars, construction sets, and superheroes; that is, they operate vehicles, erect buildings, and rescue people.

OBSESSED BY GENDER

The rigid role-typing starts at birth. Try dressing a child in a gender-neutral way and see what happens. People are mortified when they guess the wrong sex. Once when I was out with my four-week-old son, who was dressed in yellow, an admiring grandma commented, "What a pretty girl." "Thanks, but he's a boy," I responded. Visibly embarrassed, she quickly countered, "What a big boy!"

Something similar happened after I gave birth to my daughter. Like all newborns, she bore a remarkable resemblance to Winston Churchill. However, the nurse felt socially obligated to comment on her girlish features. "Only little girls have such feminine eyebrows," I was told. In fact, she does have beautiful brows, which angle sharply down, just like her father's.

BEYOND PINK AND BLUE

Studies show that girls are handled, cuddled, and spoken to more than boys, and we have all observed that parents bounce and roughhouse more with their sons than with their daughters. By kindergarten, children have received thousands of hours of gender conditioning.

We also interpret their individual characteristics according to our preconceived notions, disregarding what doesn't fit. Watch a child playing quietly, building something in a sand box. Do you see a good girl playing quietly or a boy who is a budding engineer? Same sand box, only now the child has lost interest and is throwing sand. Is she manipulating for attention or is he acting out his natural aggressive instincts?

CULTURE COPS

Why? Why is a tantrum-throwing girl labeled manipulative and a tantrum-throwing boy called aggressive? Why is a clinging girl, who cries when Mommy leaves, seen as timid, while the same behavior in a boy is labeled oedipal? (Or, as one parent put it, "Little boys just have a thing about their mommies!")

Children can even become their own gender police. After all, one of the jobs of childhood is trying to figure out what it means to be a girl or a boy. My five-year-old daughter was told by another little girl, "You shouldn't watch Power Rangers, that's a boy's show." Clearly, my child could skip this show without missing out on a culturally enriching experience. But it does make me angry that someone is trying to stop her from identifying with superheroes. (Anyway, at least two of the five "Power Rangers" are women.)

What's going on here? It seems so easy for parents to accept, and even encourage, this sex-typing. And so hard to accept the obvious truth that children's personality traits and interests are not gender-based.

One reason may be a deeply-ingrained desire to perpetuate the family line. Parents may want their son to grow up to be the kind of father who willingly shares the childcare, but they fear that if he's too "sensitive" there may be no grandchildren at all.

But parental fears probably go deeper than this. Most of us didn't have kids to create a grandchildren factory. Besides, we're all aware of gay men and lesbians who joyfully had babies or adopted them and who are wonderful parents.

I believe that the real answer lies in our deeply rooted homophobia, grafted onto our cultural conditioning. Some of our best friends may be gay but most parents are dead set against such a fate for their own children. Partly, they fear the social stigma. Parents are not lulled by the veneer of acceptance found on TV talk shows. They know the world is harsher and harder on those who are different, and they want to protect their children from that reality. Add to this the fear of AIDS and you have a potent brew of paranoia. And parents' fears are not only for their children, but for themselves, too. What would it say about them if their children turned out to be gay? Deep-seated fears like these explain why so many people who believe in equal opportunity still want to preserve the illusion that boys and girls are intrinsically different. Unfortunately, the result is that these fears, unconscious or deliberate, limit their children's world.

A MODEST PROPOSAL

What do I suggest? Since I don't advocate censorship or toy burning, I don't want to ban "Barbie" or "GI Joe." What I would like to do is get rid of the artificial categories. When I walk into a toy store, I want the clerk to ask, "Do you want construction toys or dolls?" instead of "Is this for a boy or a girl?" Furthermore, if I were in charge, I would put the action figures on the same shelf as the Barbies. Yes, it will be a hundred years, if ever, before boys buy baby dolls in the same proportion as girls. So what? My point is, let's open up their universe and not limit it. Give girls more chances to build and to rescue and give boys more dolls to love.

I have seen one of my own children, at age four, play happily with a doll house and then 20 minutes later, stage a fight with toy soldiers. I can remember watching my son, at age six, play fight games with his favorite action figure (actually a boy doll but never described as such in TV ads) in the afternoon. At night, he made a bed out of a shoebox and lovingly tucked his action figure into it. Despite all the messages my six-year-old had been exposed to, he remained open to the whole range of "Let's pretend." Shouldn't we help that process? Life will place limits on our children all too soon. It's our responsibility to expand their world and let them find their own individual place in it.   [1994]

Understanding the Reading

1. What role do adults play in teaching children gender-appropriate behavior?
2. How is such behavior influenced by other children?
3. How does homophobia affect sex-typing?
4. What does Reifler recommend that we do to reduce or eliminate sex-typing?

Suggestions for Responding

1. Visit a toy store and observe how gender stereotypes affect its layout. Write a letter to the store manager, commenting on your observations and making any suggestions you feel might be appropriate.
2. Ask several people what they think about a preschool boy playing dress-up in female clothes and about a rough-and-tumble preschool girl. Report on their responses, especially on how their attitudes differ toward the boy and the girl. ✦

22

Where I Come From Is Like This

Paula Gunn Allen

I

Modern American Indian women, like their non-Indian sisters, are deeply engaged in the struggle to redefine themselves. In their struggle they must reconcile traditional tribal definitions of women with industrial and postindustrial non-Indian definitions. Yet while these definitions seem to be more or less mutually exclusive, Indian women must somehow harmonize and integrate both in their own lives.

An American Indian woman is primarily defined by her tribal identity. In her eyes, her destiny is necessarily that of her people, and her sense of herself as a woman is first and foremost prescribed by her tribe. The definitions of woman's roles are as diverse as tribal cultures in the Americas. In some she is devalued, in others she wields considerable power. In some she is a familial/clan adjunct, in some she is as close to autonomous as her economic circumstances and psychological traits permit. But in no tribal definitions is she perceived in the same way as are women in western industrial and postindustrial cultures.

In the west, few images of women form part of the cultural mythos, and these are largely sexually charged. Among Christians, the madonna is the female prototype, and she is portrayed as essentially passive: her contribution is simply that of birthing. Little else is attributed to her and she certainly possesses few of the characteristics that are attributed to mythic figures among Indian tribes. This image is countered (rather than balanced) by the witch-goddess/whore characteristics designed to reinforce cultural beliefs about women, as well as western adversarial and dualistic perceptions of reality.

The tribes see women variously, but they do not question the power of femininity. Sometimes they see women as fearful, sometimes peaceful, sometimes omnipotent and omniscient, but they never portray women as mindless, helpless, simple, or oppressed. And while the women in a given tribe, clan, or band may be all these things, the individual woman is provided with a variety of images of women from the interconnected supernatural, natural, and social worlds she lives in.

As a half-breed American Indian woman, I cast about in my mind for negative images of Indian women, and I find none that are directed to Indian women alone. The negative images I do have are of Indians in general and in fact are more often of males than of females. All these images come to me from non-Indian sources, and they are always balanced by a positive image. My ideas of womanhood, passed on largely by my mother and grandmothers, Laguna Pueblo women, are about practicality, strength, reasonableness, intelligence, wit, and competence. I also remember vividly the women who came to my father's store, the women who held me and sang to me, the women at Feast Day, at Grab Days, the women in the kitchen of my Cubero home, the women I grew up with; none of them appeared weak or helpless, none of them presented herself tentatively. I remember a certain reserve on those lovely brown faces; I remember the direct gaze of eyes framed by bright-colored shawls draped over their heads and cascading down their backs. I remember the clean cotton dresses and carefully pressed hand-embroidered aprons they always wore; I remember laughter and good food, especially the sweet bread and the oven bread they gave us. Nowhere in my mind is there a foolish woman, a dumb woman, a vain woman, or a plastic woman, though the Indian women I have known have shown a wide range of personal style and demeanor.

My memory includes the Navajo woman who was badly beaten by her Sioux husband; but I also remember that my grandmother abandoned her Sioux husband long ago. I recall the stories about the Laguna woman beaten regularly by her husband in the presence of her children so that the children would not believe in the strength and power of femininity. And I remember the women who drank, who got into fights with other women and with the men, and who often won those battles. I have memories of tired women, partying women, stubborn women, sullen women, amicable women, selfish women, shy women, and aggressive women. Most of all I remember the women who laugh and scold and sit uncomplaining in the long sun on feast days and who cook wonderful food on wood stoves, in beehive mud ovens, and over open fires outdoors.

Among the images of women that come to me from various tribes as well as my own are White Buffalo Woman, who came to the Lakota long ago and brought them the religion of the Sacred Pipe which they still practice; Tinotzin the goddess who came to Juan Diego to remind him that she still walked the hills of her people and sent him with her message, her demand and her proof to the Catholic bishop in the city nearby. And from Laguna I take the images of Yellow Woman, Coyote Woman, Grandmother Spider (Spider Old Woman), who brought the light, who gave us weaving and medicine, who gave us life. Among the Keres she is known as Thought Woman who created us all and who keeps us in creation even now. I remember Iyatiku, Earth Woman, Corn Woman, who guides and counsels the people to peace and who welcomes us home when we cast off this coil of flesh as huskers cast off the leaves that wrap the corn. I remember Iyatiku's sister, Sun Woman, who held metals and cattle, pigs and sheep, highways and engines and so many things in her bundle, who went away to the east saying that one day she would return.

II

Since the coming of the Anglo-Europeans beginning in the fifteenth century, the fragile web of identity that long held tribal people secure has gradually been weakened and torn. But the oral tradition has prevented the complete destruction of the web, the ultimate disruption of tribal ways. The oral tradition is vital; it heals itself and the tribal web by adapting to the flow of the present while never relinquishing its connection to the past. Its adaptability has always been required, as many generations have experienced. Certainly the modern American Indian woman bears slight resemblance to her forebears—at least on superficial examination— but she is still a tribal woman in her deepest

being. Her tribal sense of relationship to all that is continues to flourish. And though she is at times beset by her knowledge of the enormous gap between the life she lives and the life she was raised to live, and while she adapts her mind and being to the circumstances of her present life, she does so in tribal ways, mending the tears in the web of being from which she takes her existence as she goes.

My mother told me stories all the time, though I often did not recognize them as that. My mother told me stories about cooking and child-bearing; she told me stories about menstruation and pregnancy; she told me stories about gods and heroes, about fairies and elves, about goddesses and spirits; she told me stories about the land and the sky, about cats and dogs, about snakes and spiders; she told me stories about climbing trees and exploring the mesas; she told me stories about going to dances and getting married; she told me stories about dressing and undressing, about sleeping and waking; she told me stories about herself, about her mother, about her grandmother. She told me stories about grieving and laughing, about thinking and doing; she told me stories about school and about people; about darning and mending; she told me stories about turquoise and about gold; she told me European stories and Laguna stories; she told me Catholic stories and Presbyterian stories; she told me city stories and country stories; she told me political stories and religious stories. She told me stories about living and stories about dying. And in all of those stories she told me who I was, who I was supposed to be, whom I came from, and who would follow me. In this way she taught me the meaning of the words she said, that all life is a circle and everything has a place within it. That's what she said and what she showed me in the things she did and the way she lives.

Of course, through my formal, white, Christian education, I discovered that other people had stories of their own—about women, about Indians, about fact, about reality—and I was amazed by a number of startling suppositions that others made about tribal customs and beliefs. According to the un-Indian, non-Indian view, for instance, Indians barred menstruating women from ceremonies and indeed segregated them from the rest of the people, consigning them to some space specially designed for them. This showed that Indians considered menstruating women unclean and not fit to enjoy the company of decent (nonmenstruating) people, that is, men. I was surprised and confused to hear this because my mother had taught me that white people had strange attitudes toward menstruation: they thought something was bad about it, that it meant you were sick, cursed, sinful, and weak and that you had to be very careful during that time. She taught me that menstruation was a normal occurrence, that I could go swimming or hiking or whatever else I wanted to do during my period. She actively scorned women who took to their beds, who were incapacitated by cramps, who "got the blues."

As I struggled to reconcile these very contradictory interpretations of American Indians' traditional beliefs concerning menstruation, I realized that the menstrual taboos were about power, not about sin or filth. My conclusion was later borne out by some tribes' own explanations, which, as you may well imagine, came as quite a relief to me.

The truth of the matter as many Indians see it is that women who are at the peak of their fecundity are believed to possess power that throws male power totally out of kilter. They emit such force that, in their presence, any male-owned or -dominated ritual or sacred object cannot do its usual task. For instance, the Lakota say that a menstruating woman anywhere near a yuwipi man, who is a special sort of psychic, spirit-empowered healer, for a day or so before he is to do his ceremony will effectively disempower him. Conversely, among many, if not most, tribes, important ceremonies cannot be held without the presence of women. Sometimes the ritual woman who empowers the ceremony must be unmarried and virginal so that the power she channels is unalloyed, unweakened by sexual arousal and penetration by a male. Other ceremonies require tumescent women, others the presence of mature women who have borne children, and still others depend for empowerment on postmenopausal women. Women may be segregated from the company of the whole band or village on certain occasions, but on certain occasions men are also segregated. In short, each ritual depends on

a certain balance of power, and the positions of women within the phases of womanhood are used by tribal people to empower certain rites. This does not derive from a male-dominant view; it is not a ritual observance imposed on women by men. It derives from a tribal view of reality that distinguishes tribal people from feudal and industrial people.

Among the tribes, the occult power of women, inextricably bound to our hormonal life, is thought to be very great; many hold that we possess innately the blood-given power to kill—with a glance, with a step, or with a judicious mixing of menstrual blood into somebody's soup. Medicine women among the Pomo of California cannot practice until they are sufficiently mature; when they are immature, their power is diffuse and is likely to interfere with their practice until time and experience have it under control. So women of the tribes are not especially inclined to see themselves as poor helpless victims of male domination. Even in those tribes where something akin to male domination was present, women are perceived as powerful, socially, physically, and metaphysically. In times past, as in times present, women carried enormous burdens with aplomb. We were far indeed from the "weaker sex," the designation that white aristocratic sisters unhappily earned for us all.

I remember my mother moving furniture all over the house when she wanted it changed. She didn't wait for my father to come home and help—she just went ahead and moved the piano, a huge upright from the old days, the couch, the refrigerator. Nobody had told her she was too weak to do such things. In imitation of her, I would delight in loading trucks at my father's store with cases of pop or fifty-pound sacks of flour. Even when I was quite small I could do it, and it gave me a belief in my own physical strength that advancing middle age can't quite erase. My mother used to tell me about the Acoma Pueblo women she had seen as a child carrying huge ollas (water pots) on their heads as they wound their way up the tortuous stairwell carved into the face of the "Sky City" mesa, a feat I tried to imitate with books and tin buckets. ("Sky City" is the term used by the Chamber of Commerce for the mother village of Acoma, which is situated atop a high sandstone table mountain.) I was never very successful, but even the attempt reminded me that I was supposed to be strong and balanced to be a proper girl.

Of course, my mother's Laguna people are Keres Indian, reputed to be the last extreme mother-right people on earth. So it is no wonder that I got notably nonwhite notions about the natural strength and prowess of women. Indeed, it is only when I am trying to get non-Indian approval, recognition, or acknowledgment that my "weak sister" emotional and intellectual ploys get the better of my tribal woman's good sense. At such times I forget that I just moved the piano or just wrote a competent paper or just completed a financial transaction satisfactorily or have supported myself and my children for most of my adult life.

Nor is my contradictory behavior atypical. Most Indian women I know are in the same bicultural bind: we vacillate between being dependent and strong, self-reliant and powerless, strongly motivated and hopelessly insecure. We resolve the dilemma in various ways: some of us party all the time; some of us drink to excess; some of us travel and move around a lot; some of us land good jobs and then quit them; some of us engage in violent exchanges; some of us blow our brains out. We act in these destructive ways because we suffer from the societal conflicts caused by having to identify with two hopelessly opposed cultural definitions of women. Through this destructive dissonance we are unhappy prey to the self-disparagement common to, indeed demanded of, Indians living in the United States today. Our situation is caused by the exigencies of a history of invasion, conquest, and colonization whose searing marks are probably ineradicable. A popular bumper sticker on many Indian cars proclaims: "If You're Indian You're In," to which I always find myself adding under my breath, "Trouble."

III

No Indian can grow to any age without being informed that her people were "savages" who interfered with the march of progress pursued by respectable, loving, civilized white people. We are the villains of the scenario when we are mentioned at all. We are absent from much of white history except when we are calmly, rationally, succinctly, and systematically dehumanized. On the few occasions we are noticed in any way other than as howling, bloodthirsty beings, we are acclaimed for our noble quaintness. In this definition, we are exotic curios. Our ancient arts and customs are used to draw tourist money to state coffers, into the pocketbooks and bank accounts of scholars, and into support of the American-in-Disneyland promoters' dream.

As a Roman Catholic child I was treated to bloody tales of how the savage Indians martyred the hapless priests and missionaries who went among them in an attempt to lead them to the one true path. By the time I was through high school I had the idea that Indians were people who had benefited mightily from the advanced knowledge and superior morality of the Anglo-Europeans. At least I had, perforce, that idea to lay beside the other one that derived from my daily experience of Indian life, an idea less dehumanizing and more accurate because it came from my mother and the other Indian people who raised me. That idea was that Indians are a people who don't tell lies, who care for their children and their old people. You never see an Indian orphan, they said. You always know when you're old that someone will take care of you—one of your children will. Then they'd list the old folks who were being taken care of by this child or that. No child is ever considered illegitimate among the Indians, they said. If a girl gets pregnant, the baby is still part of the family, and the mother is too. That's what they said, and they showed me real people who lived according to those principles.

Of course the ravages of colonization have taken their toll; there are orphans in Indian country now, and abandoned, brutalized old folks; there are even illegitimate children, though the very concept still strikes me as absurd. There are battered children and neglected children, and there are battered wives and women who have been raped by Indian men. Proximity to the "civilizing" effects of white Christians has not improved the moral quality of life in Indian country, though each group, Indian and white, explains the situation differently. Nor is there much yet in the oral tradition that can enable us to adapt to these inhuman changes. But a force is growing in that direction, and it is helping Indian women reclaim their lives. Their power, their sense of direction and of self will soon be visible. It is the force of the women who speak and work and write, and it is formidable.

Through all the centuries of war and death and cultural and psychic destruction have endured the women who raise the children and tend the fires, who pass along the tales and the traditions, who weep and bury the dead, who are the dead, and who never forget. There are always the women, who make pots and weave baskets, who fashion clothes and cheer their children on at powwow, who make fry bread and piki bread, and corn soup and chili stew, who dance and sing and remember and hold within their hearts the dream of their ancient peoples—that one day the woman who thinks will speak to us again, and everywhere there will be peace. Meanwhile we tell the stories and write the books and trade tales of anger and woe and stories of fun and scandal and laugh over all manner of things that happen every day. We watch and we wait.

My great-grandmother told my mother: Never forget you are Indian. And my mother told me the same thing. This, then, is how I have gone about remembering, so that my children will remember too.   [1986, 1992]

Understanding the Reading

1. How do American Indian beliefs about womanhood differ from Western images?
2. What did Allen learn about being a woman from her mother, grandmother, and other women she grew up with?
3. How are women portrayed in tribal legends?
4. What did Allen learn from the stories she heard growing up?
5. How did White society distort tribal customs relating to women?
6. How do Indian women respond to living in a bicultural world?
7. How does the White society's representation of Indians differ from the Indian culture Allen knows?
8. What changes in Indian society has the dominant White society created?

Suggestions for Responding

1. Research and report on one or more Native American legends about women.
2. Allen says her mother told her stories that taught her who she is. Describe some of the stories you heard in your childhood that told you who you are. ◆

23

The Male Role Stereotype

DOUG COOPER THOMPSON

When you first consider that many men now feel that they are victims of sex role stereotyping, your natural response might be: "Are you kidding? Why should men feel discriminated against? Men have the best jobs; they are the corporation presidents and the political leaders. Everyone says, 'It's a man's world.' What do men have to be concerned about? What are their problems?"

It is obvious that men hold most of the influential and important positions in society, and it does seem that many men "have it made." The problem is that men pay a high cost for the ways they have been stereotyped and for the roles that they play.

To understand why many men and women are concerned, we need to take a look at the male role stereotype. Here is what men who conform to the stereotype must do.

CODE OF CONDUCT:
THE MALE ROLE STEREOTYPE

1. Act "Tough"

   Acting tough is a key element of the male role stereotype. Many boys and men feel that they have to show that they are strong and tough, that they can "take it" and "dish it out" as well. You've probably run into some boys and men who like to push people around, use their strength, and act tough. In a conflict, these males would never consider giving in, even when surrender or compromise would be the smartest or most compassionate course of action.

2. Hide Emotions

This aspect of the male role stereotype teaches males to suppress their emotions and to hide feelings of fear or sorrow or tenderness. Even as small children, they are warned not to be "crybabies." As grown men they show that they have learned this lesson well, and they become very efficient at holding back tears and keeping a "stiff upper lip."

3. Earn "Big Bucks"

Men are trained to be the primary source of income for the family. So men try to choose occupations that pay well, and then they stick with those jobs, even when they might prefer to try something else. Boys and men are taught that earning a good living is important. In fact, men are often evaluated not on how kind or compassionate or thoughtful they are, but rather on how much money they make.

4. Get the "Right" Kind of Job

If a boy decides to become a pilot, he will receive society's stamp of approval, for that is the right kind of a job for a man. But if a boy decides to become an airline steward, many people would think that quite strange. Boys can decide to be doctors, mechanics, or business executives, but if a boy wants to become a nurse, secretary, librarian, ballet dancer, or kindergarten teacher, he will have a tough time. His friends and relatives will probably try to talk him out of his decision, because it's just not part of the male role stereotype.

5. Compete—Intensely

Another aspect of the male role stereotype is to be super-competitive. This competitive drive is seen not only on athletic fields, but in school and later at work. This commitment to competition leads to still another part of the male stereotype: getting ahead of other people to become a winner.

6. Win—At Almost Any Cost

From the Little League baseball field to getting jobs that pay the most money, boys and men are taught to win at whatever they may try to do. They must work and strive and compete so that they can get ahead of other people, no matter how many personal, and even moral, sacrifices are made along the way to the winner's circle.

Those are some of the major features of the male stereotype. And certainly, some of them may not appear to be harmful. Yet when we look more closely, we find that many males who do "buy" the message of the male role stereotype end up paying a very high price for their conformity.

THE COST OF THE CODE: WHAT MEN GIVE UP

1. Men who become highly involved in competition and winning can lose their perspective and good judgment. Competition by itself is not necessarily bad, and we've all enjoyed some competitive activities. But when a man tries to fulfill the male stereotype, and compete and win at any cost, he runs into problems. You've probably seen sore losers (and even sore winners)—sure signs of overcommitment to competition. Real competitors have trouble making friends because they're always trying to go "one-up" on their friends. And when cooperation is needed, true-blue competitors have a difficult time cooperating.

   The next time you see hockey players hitting each other with their hockey sticks or politicians or businessmen willing to do almost anything for a Senate seat or a big deal, you know that you are seeing some of the problems of the male sex role stereotype: an overcommitment to competition and the need to win at any cost.

2. Hiding emotions can hurt. For one thing, hiding emotions confuses people as to what someone's real feelings are. Men who hide their emotions can be misunderstood by others who might see them as uncaring and insensitive. And men who are always suppressing their feelings may put themselves under heavy psychological stress. This pressure can be physically unhealthy as well.

3. The heavy emphasis that the male stereotype puts on earning big money also creates

problems. Some men choose careers they really do not like, just because the job pays well. Others choose a job which at first they like, only later to find out that they would rather do something else. But they stay with their jobs anyway, because they can't afford to earn less money.

In trying to earn as much as possible, many men work long hours and weekends. Some even take second jobs. When men do this, they begin to lead one-track lives—the track that leads to the office or business door. They drop outside interests and hobbies. They have less and less time to spend with their families. That's one reason why some fathers never really get to know their own children, even though they may love them very much.

4. Many men who are absorbed by competition, winning, and earning big bucks pay a terrible price in terms of their physical health. With the continual pressure to compete, be tough, earn money, with little time left for recreation and other interests, men find themselves much more likely than women to fall victim to serious disease. In fact, on the average, men die 8 years sooner than women. Loss of life is a high cost to pay for following the code of the male role stereotype.

5. Those boys and men who do not follow the male code of conduct may also find their lives more difficult because of this stereotype. For example, some boys choose to become nurses rather than doctors, kindergarten teachers rather than lawyers, artists rather than electricians. Social pressure can make it terribly difficult for males who enter these nonstereotyped careers. Other boys and men feel very uncomfortable with the continual pressure to compete and win.

And some boys do not want to hide their feelings in order to project an image of being strong and tough. These males may be gentle, compassionate, sensitive human beings who are puzzled with and troubled by the male role stereotype. When society stereotypes any group—by race, religion, or sex—it becomes difficult for individuals to break out of the stereotype and be themselves.   [1985]

Understanding the Reading

1. How are the six characteristics of the male role stereotype connected?
2. What characteristics does Cooper Thompson omit, and how do they relate to his six?
3. Explain the costs to men of conforming to this stereotype.
4. What other costs might the author have included?

Suggestions for Responding

1. Have masculine and/or feminine stereotypes undergone changes in recent years? If you think so, describe those changes and explain what has caused them. If not, explain why you think they have not changed.
2. Using Cooper Thompson's analysis as a model, analyze the "Code of Conduct" and the "Cost of the Code" of the female role stereotype. ◆

24

Transgender Rights in the United States: A Short History

TOM HEAD

There's nothing new about transgender and transsexual individuals—history is replete with examples, from the Indian hijras[1] to the Israeli sarisim (eunuchs) to the Roman emperor Elagabalus[2]—but there is something relatively new about transgender and transsexual rights, as a national movement in the United States.

1868

The Fourteenth Amendment to the U.S. Constitution is ratified. The equal protection and due process clauses in Section 1 would implicitly include transgender and transsexual persons, as well as any other identifiable group:

> No State shall make or enforce any law which shall abridge the privileges or immunities of citizens of the United States; nor shall any State deprive any person of life, liberty, or property, without due process of law; nor deny to any person within its jurisdiction the equal protection of the laws.

While the Supreme Court has not fully embraced the Amendment's implications for transgender rights, these clauses will presumably form the basis of future rulings.

1923

German physician Magnus Hirschfeld[3] coins the term "transsexual" in a published journal article titled "The Intersexual Constitution" ("Die intersexuelle Konstitution").

1949

San Francisco physician Harry Benjamin pioneers the use of hormone therapy[4] in the treatment of transsexual patients.

1959

Christine Jorgensen, a transwoman,[5] is denied a marriage license in New York on the basis of her birth gender. Her fiance, Howard Knox, was fired from his job when rumors of their attempt to marry became public.

1969

The Stonewall riots,[6] which arguably sparked the modern gay rights movement,[7] is led by a group that includes transwoman Sylvia Rivera.

1976

In *M.T. v. J.T.*, the Superior Court of New Jersey rules that transsexual persons may marry on the basis of their gender identity, regardless of their assigned gender.

1989

Ann Hopkins is denied a promotion on the basis that she is not, in the opinion of management, sufficiently feminine. She sues, and the U.S. Supreme Court rules that gender stereotyping can form the basis of a Title VII[8] sex-discrimination complaint; in the words of Justice Brennan, a plaintiff need only prove that "an employer who has allowed a discriminatory motive to play a part in an employment decision must prove by clear and convincing evidence that it would have made the same decision in the absence of discrimination, and that petitioner had not carried this burden."

1993

Minnesota becomes the first state to ban employment discrimination on the basis of perceived gender identity with the passage of the Minnesota Human Rights Act. In the same year, transman Brandon Teena is raped and murdered—an event that inspires the film *Boys Don't Cry* (1999), and prompts a national movement to incorporate anti-transgender hate crimes into future hate crime legislation.

1999

In *Littleton v. Prange*, the Texas Fourth Court of Appeals rejects the logic of New Jersey's *M.T. v. J.T.* (1976) and refuses to issue marriage licenses to opposite-sex couples in which one partner is transsexual.

2001

The Kansas Supreme Court refuses to allow transwoman J'Noel Gardiner to inherit her husband's property, on the basis that her non-assigned gender identity—and, therefore, her subsequent marriage to a man—was invalid.

2007

Gender identity protections are controversially stripped from the 2007 version of the Employment

Non-Discrimination Act,[9] but it fails anyway. Future versions of ENDA, beginning in 2009, include gender identity protections.

2009

The Matthew Shepard and James Byrd Jr. Hate Crimes Prevention Act,[10] signed by President Barack Obama, allows for federal investigation of bias-motivated crimes based on gender identity in cases where local law enforcement is unwilling to act. Later the same year, Obama issues an executive order banning the executive branch from discriminating on the basis of gender identity in employment decisions.

Notes

1. http://atheism.about.com/b/2006/05/28/
   gender-and-identity-just-male-and-female-book-notes-with-pleasure.htm
2. http://ancienthistory.about.com/cs/
   biocategory/a/elagabalus_2.htm
3. http://worldfilm.about.com/library/weekly/
   aafpr011503.htm
4. http://plasticsurgery.about.com/od/
   glossary/g/Hormone-Therapy.htm
5. http://civilliberty.about.com/od/
   gendersexuality/g/Transwoman-Transsexual-Woman.htm
6. http://manhattan.about.com/od/
   glbtscene/a/stonewallriots.htm
7. http://civilliberty.about.com/od/
   gendersexuality/tp/History-Gay-Rights-Movement.htm
8. http://careerplanning.about.com/od/
   federallawsus/a/civilrightsact.htm
9. http://gaylife.about.com/od/gayatwork/a/
   enda.htm
10. http://gaylife.about.com/od/hatecrimes/p/
    Matthewshepardjamesbyrdact.htm

Understanding the Reading

1. Who is Christine Jorgensen?
2. What is the Minnesota Human Rights Act?
3. What was the basis for disallowing J'Noel Gardiner's property inheritance in 2001?

Suggestion for Responding

1. Research transgender rights in other countries.

25

A Transsexual's Story

JESSICA R. STEARNS

What is a transsexual? For a great part of my life the term was little known. It was not even included in the dictionary. During the 1960's I could find no reference to the term in any dictionary or in any reference book in the public library. It was not until the late 1970's that Webster's included a definition. It was: *Transsexual:* 1. One predisposed to become a member of the opposite sex. 2. One whose sex has been changed externally by surgery and by hormone injections.

By the 1990's the term transsexual was becoming replaced by the more inclusive term Transgendered. This new term was meant to reduce the harsh narrow term of transsexual, and to include a broader group of people who may identify as transsexual but do not have the desire or means to undergo sex reassignment surgery, and may include cross dressers, transvestites and others who did not fit more restricted categories. The term continues to change with medical research, legal advances, and societal factors.

Though the term was first used by Dr. Harry Benjamin, author of the book "Transsexual Phenomenon," and came to public attention by the sex change of Christine Jorgenson in 1952, it seemed that it was such a provocative term that it was talked around, not used. I was 12 years old at the time of Christine's surgery. The impact on me was very powerful, it scared me. How could I be such a person, what would become of me if I was such a person? I was very troubled by this news. Some 51 years later I can remember the four photos published and most of the text of that Sunday Parade Magazine article. To even use the "T" word is difficult at best for a true transsexual.

What is a true transsexual? Dr. Benjamin developed a sexual orientation scale, one to six. On a scale of five a person was defined as wanting to be a member of the opposite sex, but not desiring to undergo surgery. A person rated as a six was a true transsexual who had to have surgery in order to have a chance of happiness and even survive. At first it was considered a mental disease thought curable by psychiatric treatment. One of the theories was that as a person got older the urge to change their sex would decrease. Perhaps the rate of suicide for older transsexuals helped discredit this theory.

Only in the past 15 years has the subject of transsexuality/transgender become a topic talked about through TV talk shows, news media, and progress has been made to legally protect the Transgender. Steps to protect the Transgender through the courts have met with great resistance. Only with great persistence, struggle, and dedicated legal help has any progress been made. The Gay/Lesbian community has had more success at getting anti-discrimination laws passed. The average attorney not only lacks training in handling a transgender case, but is unwilling for fear of being adversely labeled.

One more thing about sex/sexual orientation; first there is the anatomical sex of a person (M/F), second, the gender (M/F), then, third, sexual orientation (Hetero/Homosexual). These are distinct areas of a person's make-up. Of course they can occur in combinations with many variances. For most of the human population these three factors are the same, so that an individual only thinks in terms of male/female with no thoughts given to other factors. At a very early age, most say from their early memories, transsexuals identified with the opposite sex. However, the socialization process governs the process of growing up. A child rapidly learns to adapt to expectations of the sexual role in which they are born. The inner conflict of feeling that they were born in the wrong body is there from the start. It will never go away.

The desire to change sex is a matter of identity. Who am I? What am I? I feel like a girl, but I have a male body. The conflict is intense. This occurs at an age when the child can't understand why those feelings exist. Parents only desire a normal child. Even when they perceive that the behavior patterns are somewhat different, they will strive to reinforce what they perceive as normal behavior. This of course will only lead to greater conflict.

My story began on August 3rd, 1940. Born as John Robert Stearns in Birmingham, Alabama, I was the first grandchild to a family of farmers in Blount Co. My father, at the time, a traveling salesman from New York City, had been married to my mother only a year. My mother was 16 when married and had never been off the farm. I can't even recall if she finished high school. I know that we moved several times because I have photos of me as an infant in Jacksonville, FL. My sister was born in New Orleans, LA (no photos). My brother was born in Kansas City, MO. I do remember some events from when we lived in Little Rock, Arkansas. I also remember my father's brutality to my mother. I am the only one of the three of us to have any childhood memories of their being together. They were divorced when I was 3½ . My mother moved to Birmingham to find work. Most of the time that was at being a waitress. My grandparents had had six children; the first died in infancy, two had their own families, one was engaged to be married, the youngest was in high school and served as an older sibling, and my mother, who was struggling in Birmingham. Having to raise three more children was now a burden for my grandparents.

In 1946 my mother married a taxi driver who lived in Birmingham. Not only did he refuse to permit us to live with them, but also he was an alcoholic who was verbally and physically abusive to my mother. The task of our rearing fell upon my grandparents. We got to visit with our mother on rare occasions. Our grandparents were to become our sole caregivers for the next few years.

I can remember identifying with the female members of our family before I was four. I wanted to help my grandmother in the kitchen and about the house rather than be with the male members in the barns or fields. Our farm was typical of the time and area. Electricity had not been routed to our farm and the roads were unpaved. Mules were used to work the fields. Grandfather did have a 1935 Chevy truck; I still remember the WWII lend lease symbol on the doors. Everyone was expected to do all sorts of farm work. The day started by 5:00 AM and didn't stop until after dark. Almost every thing we ate was grown on our farm and processed by us. Work was long, hard and never ending. Still, the lessons I learned have always been of benefit. Just because a task was difficult, it had to be done and there was a certain satisfaction of doing it well. I learned to see a correlation between effort expended and rewards reaped.

Though I preferred helping my grandmother, all of us had assigned chores to accomplish day or night, every day, and without fail. Shirking was not tolerated and failure was severely punished. On the morning of my sixth birthday my grandfather called me into the living room. He told me that since I was getting to be a pretty big boy, he would only tell me to do something once. Then he gave me a small penknife, and wished me a happy birthday. I can still remember the few times he told me twice. Each time I wasn't able to sit for several hours. Grandfather was a stern disciplinarian and did not tolerate noncompliance. Still, I learned a lot from him that would help me cope with future trials.

During the summer my two female first cousins would travel by train to spend the summer with us. My oldest cousin Gail was only three months younger than me and very much a tomboy. We enjoyed playing with each other more than with the others. Many hours were spent exploring the wooded hollows on the farm and playing in the three streams that flowed through the farm. We climbed trees, built hay forts in the barn mow, picked blackberries, ate wild strawberries and persimmons that grew on the farm, and sometimes snitched a watermelon from a neighboring farm, though there were acres of them on our farm. My grandmother had stored boxes of her old clothes in one of the sheds on the farm. One day Kate and I found them, called the other children to join us and spent the afternoon dressing up. I not only found it fun, but suddenly felt that this was the proper clothing for me. When grandmother found out about this, she scolded us and told us not to do it any more. However, I would play dress up when I could do so without the fear of being caught. When I was seven, my grandmother actually punished me by making me wear one of my sister's dresses. I would hide behind the wood-burning stove in the kitchen, out of sight from prying eyes, and contentedly stay until called out and told to change into my boy clothing. No one knew that my punishment was actually very pleasing. I did not know why, except that somehow I really felt that I wanted to be a girl.

My early years were a mixture of very mixed feelings about myself. As a boy, my grandparents expected me to adhere to the male path. However, from the time that I was five until I was about 14 years old, my health was marginal. I easily caught colds, caught the whooping cough frequently, suffered from bronchitis, and other respiratory related ailments. My tonsils were removed at age six, but that didn't help much. The doctor at the country clinic told my grandparents that I'd probably not survive my childhood. To assist my health I was often restricted indoors. This I really didn't mind as I liked to help my grandmother and enjoyed being able to read any newspaper, magazine or book that I could get my hands on. Whenever I found an article about aviation I would read it over and over. On my very first day in school, my first grade teacher, Miss Haynes, asked us all to stand in turn and state what we wanted to be when we grew up. I was next to last and announced in a determined voice that I would grow up to be an airplane pilot. The spring before starting school I had seen two yellow Army Air Corps trainers fly low over the field we were working in, and knew at that instant what I wanted to be when I grew up; if I did.

I repeated 4th grade because of being very ill. I think that this prompted my grandparents into insisting that my father come for a visit from Brooklyn, NY to assess my health during the summer of 1950, as well as get to know his three children whom he hadn't seen in over six years. The visit was short but the financial help improved. New store-bought clothes were a treat to wear versus the home-made ones usually made from chicken feed sacks. Though we didn't have much, our status was the same as all the other farm families around us, so we didn't know different and accepted life as we knew it.

A decision was made to send my brother and me to visit my father in Brooklyn, NY during the summer of '51. Grandmother packed our cardboard suitcases, a box of food to last the 24-hour train trip from Birmingham to NYC. The conductors had been instructed to look after us. Our faces were glued to the windows viewing the changing countryside as the train rolled north. We arrived in NYC's Grand Central Station about 5:00 PM the next day, totally lost and not knowing where to look for our dad. The size of the station and throng of people was overwhelming. It seemed like an eternity before he found us, scared and close to tears. For us it was like arriving in a foreign country. We could hardly understand the language and our senses were on overload from the hustle and bustle of the big city. Occasional trips to Birmingham had not prepared us for this.

Dad worked in a hotel at Gramercy Park. My brother and I were left on our own at the apartment to read, play games and try to amuse ourselves. There was no TV or radio. We were top floor of a 5th floor walk up. The roof was used to hang laundry and it afforded us a bird's eye view of Brooklyn Heights. We started exploring the area using some of the high buildings as reference marks, just as I had learned to use tall trees or hills on the farm. Off we went to find and play in small city parks, or wander along the palisade overlooking the East River and docks. Within two weeks we wandered too far and became lost. Since I was the oldest the responsibility was mine and I knew that if we didn't get home before dad arrived, I would really be in trouble. At last I spotted a tall building that I recognized. It was a long walk home. Dad had called the police, but he saw us first, and had to call the police to say that we'd returned. I didn't sit down for a few hours.

Dad decided to keep us with him in Brooklyn. After finding a suitable apartment, we were enrolled in school. Me in the 5th grade and my brother in the 4th. Because of our very southern accent and lack of city smarts, we were the targets of neighborhood bullies. We learned to take a different route each time we went to school or any other destination. A classmate introduced me to his friends at a local church that had an after school program. Soon my brother and I were able to play in the gym. I became a member of the boy's choir when I found out that I'd be paid 15 cents for practice and 25 cents for Sunday service. That winter the church put on the play "Show Boat" and each of us had several parts. The cast was short of girls and I was talked into playing two scenes as a girl. I was embarrassed because of the teasing of the boys, but decided that I was brave enough to do it. Strangely, once I was dressed and made up, I secretly enjoyed it. I still have a photo taken of us girls and years later when a flight attendant friend saw it she couldn't pick me out from the other girls.

After a year in Brooklyn, my dad decided that we needed to move from the big city, but where? During the summer of '52 we visited all the towns and cities between NYC and Boston. He could not find work, so we backtracked and by late August found ourselves in Philadelphia. He was able to find work at a small hotel and a 5th floor-walkup apartment a few blocks away. This would be our home for the next few years. It was during the fall of '52 that the newspapers carried the sensational story of Christine Jorgenson. Its impact on me was profound. I felt scared. I didn't want to be like this person, but somehow I knew that I was. I couldn't tell anyone. There was no one to tell. If I told my dad, I was terribly afraid of his reaction. I had to keep my feelings a secret, no matter what. Besides, it would ruin my chances of becoming a pilot. It would ruin my life.

My sister joined us a year later. The apartment was just too small for four of us. Dad refused to get a larger one. During this time my sister and I became quite close, often playing together, or going to pretend shop for clothes, as we did not have money to buy any. I started running errands, bagging groceries, selling flowers for a street vendor, or anything I could do to earn money. I soon found that half of what I earned had to go to the household, then I could buy clothes for the three of us. As the oldest, I had to cook, clean house, shop for food, do laundry, and supervise my brother and sister.

The family situation began to deteriorate. Three of us were too much for my dad. My sister was literally shipped off to my grandparents, who by this time had sold the farm in Alabama and moved to Logansport, IN to be near their oldest son and his family, plus some cousins. I deeply missed my sister and being able to interact with her on a daily basis. For the rest of my teen years I would only see her for brief visits in Logansport.

It was becoming very clear to me that if I were to escape a life of hardships, then doing my best in school was imperative. I did well in the 6th grade, but upon entry to Jr. HS I still had a very heavy southern accent and was assigned to a remedial grade section. The first report period I received all A's, but I was made to wait to the next semester to be placed in the advanced section. I threw myself into my schoolwork. I avoided the rough and tumble activities of the boys while getting the two really smart girls to help me with English or any other area of study that I was weak in.

In 1953 I joined the Boy Scouts. I enjoyed outdoor activities because I had enjoyed the outdoors of the farm. Most of what was taught, I already knew. It was also a way for me to get out of the apartment one or two nights a week. The scoutmaster raised funds by collecting newspapers to sell at 2 cents per pound. Once a month three of us would make the rounds in his 1930's LaSalle, pack it full of newspapers, deliver them to the scrap dealer, and have enough to pay for a troop outing. He was everything my father wasn't, and I learned a lot from him.

Throughout my teen years I did very well in school, but was never comfortable socializing with boys. I did so at a level that helped me fit in so that I would not be harassed. In Jr. High I felt an attraction to some of the girls in my class but was too shy to get to know them well. Puberty had commenced and I felt uncomfortable with the male changes taking place. I did not look forward to shaving. It seemed that I wanted to live in a world that I could not enter. On weekends I went to the main library of Philadelphia to get any book that I could find on aviation and space. I also spent hours thumbing through books in the psychology section, but in those days there was nothing to explain what I felt I was going through. I needed knowledge, but it was not there.

One of my disappointments was not getting into Central HS for Boys. I needed to score 110 on the entrance exam. I scored 109.5. The school principal just told me that I didn't measure up. I desperately wanted to get into a four year high school and going to So. Philly HS where gangs were rampant was not in my plans. Fortunately, a friend told me of a small selective HS in the northwest section of the city that had both academics and agricultural tracks. The schedule called for doing three weeks of academics in two weeks, then spending a week learning agricultural subjects. Although it meant riding the bus for over two hours a day, I talked my father into letting me interview for a slot. The principal asked me to describe milking a cow. Well I knew, but my graphic description embarrassed his secretary, who was taking notes. I was admitted with no further questions.

The summer of '55 was spent at the school farm working in the barn, in the fields, and maintaining the school grounds. It was like being on the farm, but in the city at the same time. The school also provided contacts to local residents for students to mow grass and maintain yard work. A nearby family hired me to take care of their place. The dollar an hour would be used (after a 50% contribution to the household) to build up my bank account for future flying lessons. At the time I didn't know that this relationship would someday be my salvation. My routine was study, work and more work. Scouting and an occasional movie were my only recreation.

My relationship with my father was on the down slope. He could not be pleased. I determined to do the best that I could, as I now knew that my future depended solely on my efforts. I began to pay my brother to do some of my chores so that I would have more time for work and he would have his own money to spend. Dad was always bringing boxes of used clothing home for me to make repairs on; then he'd resell them. It was in this way that I accumulated a few female articles and wore them in secret. It was my only moments of being in tune with my identity. I was never sure if my brother ever found me out. He never said so.

For a couple of years I had been building model airplanes and rockets. Some flew and some didn't. When dad would get angry with me, he'd smash some of them. One day after he'd done just that, I told him that I would never build another model and that I would start taking flying lessons in a real airplane. I was almost 16 and had saved about $500.00 toward that goal. The weekend after my birthday I showed up at a flight school at the Philadelphia International Airport for my first lesson. When asked if my parents approved, I said that they didn't, but I had the money and knew what I wanted. On August 27th I came back and told them that I wasn't leaving until I had received a flight lesson. I'll never forget that 30-minute flight. I was at home in the air and now knew that my future would be in aviation. After each flight lesson, I would go over to the airport weather room, control tower and radar room. The men took me under their wings and taught me many valuable things about aviation. I became their mascot, and their knowledge filled me as water fills a sponge. On my sister's birthday, Oct. 27th, 1957, I passed my Private Pilot's flight test. However, storm clouds were on the horizon. I had also joined the Civil Air Patrol and loved every aspect of the program. I was the only cadet actually flying.

In the winter of '57, my father suddenly bought a farm in New Portland, Maine. It was a very small town, isolated, and 20 miles from the nearest high school located in another county. The four-room school that my brother and I were to attend was not even accredited and dad wouldn't pay for us to go to the school in Farmington. I could see that this was not going to work. In addition, dad had become very temperamental and physically abusive to us. He had a Jekyll & Hyde personality that was impossible to live with. One summer day, as I had just finished roofing the house, he started beating my brother. I came down from the roof to stop him. When he raised his fists at me, I blocked the blows and told him that he'd no longer hit us. He blew up, ordering us out of the house. We each packed a suitcase and walked a mile to our only friends' house. The couple agreed to let us stay in one of their three hunter's cabins. For two weeks I tried to find a way for us to get home to our grandparents. Living with mother was out of the question. I had fifteen dollars to my name. The local Red Cross refused to help. After two weeks, the couple took us to Portland, Maine. I bought bus tickets to Boston. We arrived there on a Monday evening just before the Traveler's Aid Society office closed. I had 50 cents left in my pocket.

The caseworker was in a state of disbelief after I told him our story. After he called my friends in New Portland he took us to a rooming house, gave us five dollars, and told us to be at his bus station office at 9:00 AM. We were assigned a new caseworker. For the next week, we lived on five dollars a day while it was determined who would take us and when we would leave. Finally, a week later we were given bus tickets to Birmingham and forty dollars for expenses. I did not really want to return to what I knew would be a life of hardship. We had to change buses in NYC so when we reached there I put my brother on the bus to Birmingham, gave him twenty dollars, and I took the one to

Philadelphia. I had twenty dollars, enough money to last me two or three days. My goal was to find a job, a place to live, and finish my last year of school.

As I spent the day downtown looking for work, not having any luck, I was walking along Broad St. when I heard my name called. It was my old boss who owned a Center City newsstand. After a brief talk, he agreed to sublease his news stand to me. That would provide the money to live on. Next I went to my school to see about enrolling. They were very happy to see me and agreed that if I could find a sponsor, there would be no tuition. As I walked back to the bus stop, I saw the people whose yard I had maintained for three years. After hearing my story, they gave me a room to live in and at the end of the first week invited me to stay with them on a permanent basis. I was to work off my room and board by doing chores and maintaining the yard. They arranged with my mother to have guardianship. Their three children had completed college, moved on, and were raising families of their own. Robert and Anne F . . . were the first people to treat me as a son, and take a real interest in my life, and goals. I thrived in this atmosphere. For a while I was able to sublimate all feminine desires.

It was during this year that I had to register for the draft. I knew that upon graduation from high school I would be called up unless I was accepted to college or was rated Four F, not fit. My final year of school went very well. Once again, I was flying, earning a good living, and competing for scholarships. In '59, scholarships were few and no college would let me work part time and go to school part time. I had scored very high on the Air Force Officer Qualifying Tests but was only selected for an alternate slot for the academy. The principal candidate decided to go to the Air Force Academy, so I lost out. Sure enough, I received my draft notice. I went to the AF recruiter and was selected for pilot training as a cadet. While awaiting orders I managed a small farm until my assignment came. That was not to be. The USAF decided that they had too many pilots, so the class was cancelled and the program shut down. I had to get into flying. I went back to the recruiter and was told that the Aviation Cadet Navigator program was still open. I signed up.

On June 20th, 1960 I reported to start training; little did I know of the challenges facing me. The month I started training the AF decided that they had too many navigators. The wash out rate was about 66% for my class. Bust one exam or flight check and you were done for. I learned to live one half day at a time. Somehow I got through the next ten months, and graduated as a Transport Navigator and was commissioned a Second Lieutenant. I was not an AF pilot, but at least I was flying, and becoming a pilot was very much a possibility. My first operational assignment was to Dover AFB, DE. Over the next five years I would see a great deal of the world.

The pay of a 2nd Lt. was just enough to survive on. Still, I was close enough to drive to Philadelphia and visit with my foster family and friends. I still had my old room. During this period I met a young lady and we began to date. I had dated occasionally but never cemented a relationship. Over the next four years we dated to the point that when I was 24 we actually thought of marriage. During this period, I gave her many gifts that I'd bought around the world, many of them of an intimate nature. I was also in a very confused state of mind about my own sexuality. I knew that I was not homosexual, but could not determine the source of my feelings. In private, I had acquired a limited female wardrobe. Dressed in these garments in private, I felt a sense of relief but also felt that I was committing a sin of sorts. I did not like the feeling. I often drove through Wilmington on the way to Philadelphia. I looked up a psychiatrist to try to find out what was going on with me. After three visits, he asked if I had ever had sex. Finding that I was still a virgin, he told me to go have sex and that after a dozen or so times, I'd give up my foolish notions when I found how good it was. I left there even more confused. I tried but it didn't work. My thoughts kept drifting back to the Christine Jorgenson case. I was scared and had no one to turn to.

When a transsexual gets up each morning and looks in the mirror, he/she sees a picture that doesn't match the mental image of who they want to be. As I grew older the disparity between mirror image and who I felt I was began to diverge. All around me I saw my friends getting married and fitting the societal image that I knew would probably not be mine. The current image of a military officer was a married one. My superiors would ask me about my prospects at least once a month. I had to develop a fantasy life to keep their curiosity at bay. All I wanted to do was fly and be left alone. Besides, if any of them suspected anything my career would be over in 24 hours. When I was not on a trip, I tried to get away from the base. In those days the world seemed to be in constant conflict and we pulled a lot of alert duty. Being in close contact with five other crewmembers for days at a time could lead to some very prying questions. I became very adept at revealing little and what I did say protected me.

I was in the Philippines when I received my promotion to Captain and orders to pilot training. My engagement had ended and I felt free to concentrate on my dream of becoming a jet pilot. I reported to Graig AFB in Selma, Al. to start class in June of 1966. By now, I was a seasoned officer and knew what to concentrate on so that I'd graduate in the top 10 and get a choice assignment. By now I had 3300 hours of navigator flight time and 300 hours as a civilian pilot. During the first week I took the final exams for most of the academic courses. Since I was a Captain I assisted with the administration of my classmates and did a lot of tutoring. Most of the students were 2nd Lieutenants and needed close supervision. Some would not survive the rigors of flight training. For me it was a time to excel, and I did.

As a single officer I was required to live on base, but I found a nice apartment in Selma and gave the phone number to my training officer. It rang at both locations so most never knew where I really lived. The privacy was essential at this time. I was cross-dressing frequently when in my apartment. I felt so relaxed and my concentration for study was much better. On nonflying weekends I would go visit relatives in north Alabama, take in a play in Birmingham, or drive down to the gulf coast for a weekend on the beach. Life was good. By now I had given up the thought of marriage, though the official pressure was still there. About six weeks into training a classmate talked me into going to a mixer dance in Montgomery. He was not familiar with the area and I was.

Little did I know that I would meet my future wife that evening. When we met it was the meeting of two lost souls who had been searching for each other for a long time, and had finally arrived at the same time in space. Still, I was uncertain about having a relationship that may lead to places in life I was afraid to go to. I had already faced serious danger in flight, had dealt with it, and survived. It was the emotional part of life that I was ill prepared for. To date, I had found very little information about the subject of transsexuality. I couldn't define it, let alone understand how and if it related to me, or how it would impact marriage.

As our relationship grew more intimate, I really began to feel that marriage was the solution. I purged my closet of all female things and with her on my arm at base social functions, basked in the warmth of having finally arrived. In five months my life consisted of flying and building a life with Beth. The way my superiors treated me now that I had a beautiful woman in my life gave me confidence that it would work. Little did I realize the deceptions that lay ahead. By January we made the decision to get married before I graduated. We were married at the base chapel with a few family members, friends, and some classmates present. To get a weekend off, I had flown two training flights daily for two weeks. We moved into a duplex near the base and set up housekeeping. While I was flying, she was getting to know the other wives and learn about AF life. We were only married ten days when a mid-air collision with a hawk almost did me in. Upon arriving home I stripped off a rather foul smelling flight suit, stuffed it into a trash bag, and went inside for a good stiff drink. It was her introduction to: flying can be dangerous. There would be many more close calls in the future.

Graduation day finally came. We said our goodbyes and headed off to my first operational assignment as a USAF pilot. I'd got my pick and chose to fly a C-141 Starlifter at Warner Robbins AFB, GA. Flying a heavy jet was a good way to move ahead in my career. We bought a small house in a nice neighborhood and got busy becoming part of the community. In 1967 the war in Viet Nam was really heating up. My turn to fly combat came sooner than I expected. Already, most of my flying in the C-141 was to Viet Nam,

hauling in supplies and often flying the wounded and bodies out. No one talked on the body bag flights. They still haunt me.

I started my training as a Forward Air Controller in late '68. FAC's flew light unarmed aircraft and controlled the air strikes by directing fighter aircraft to enemy targets. That's a nice way of saying that I killed people by telling the fighters where to drop the bombs. I arrived in Viet Nam in April of '69. What I didn't know was whether I could keep the bomb from going off inside me. I flew up to two times a day; three times when a battle was raging. The disparity of who I was and who I felt I should be was also raging. I even rationalized that it would be better to die a war hero, rather than live with the internal conflicts that raged within me. I guess that I did have a desire to live as I returned to base each day unscathed, though the army ground commanders were sure that my aircraft had taken hits.

At the nine-month point Beth and I met in Hawaii for a five day R & R. It was tough getting reacquainted but we did have a good visit. I made sure that she departed on her flight before I left on mine. I shall never forget the look of sorrow on her face at that time. Six weeks later I received a tape telling me that we were now expectant parents. This news encouraged me to be a little more cautious in my flying. After a year in the hell of Viet Nam and 381 combat missions, I got on the "Freedom Bird" and 18 hours later found myself in NJ exposed to an ungrateful nation.

For the next six years McGuire AFB would be our home. The flying continued to be a joy, but I knew that it would just be a matter of months before I would be tapped for a staff assignment. Our daughter was born in October and I was assigned to the training division at the same time. This permitted me to control my schedule to be able to be home most nights to help with the care of our little girl. Life seemed to be on track, except for . . .

The internal pressure continued to grow. Beth had suspected something was wrong after my return from Viet Nam. I finally screwed up the courage to tell her about how I felt. We came close to separating, but I promised to seek help so we decided not to do anything until we knew more. Besides we did have a very good life together and our love was sound. Our daughter was two and I really loved her. It took months of searching to find a doctor in Philadelphia who was experienced with transsexuals. What a disappointment! On the second visit he gave me an injection of testosterone saying: if this doesn't cure you in six months, then we'll reverse the hormones. On the drive home I felt so distraught that he might as well have injected me with arsenic. That night I walked the base golf course crying and screaming, "God—why me?"

I called every hospital and was told that the Pennsylvania Hospital had a doctor with the expertise that I needed. I made an appointment with him immediately. He gave me every test that was known, and after six sessions made his pronouncement. He said that I was a true transsexual but since I had been able to cope with military life for thirteen years, he believed as I got older the urge would decrease and therefore he would not recommend surgery. He referred me to a psychologist for group therapy. At the time this seemed a better course of action to me. Upon examination by the new doctor, group therapy was ruled out. Instead, he put me on a very low dose of hormone treatment to help me cope with the stress and inner conflicts. The new course of treatment enabled me to cope with the stress and help me delay decision time until I had more information. Simply stopping the hormones would reverse the treatment.

My spouse and I talked over the situation. We decided to remain together and live life as normally as possible. I made a promise to complete my AF career so that we would always have a modicum of income. I would also not do anything until our daughter had completed high school. We both began to get counseling so that we could keep open communications and cope with the high level of stress caused by my problem. From all outward appearances we were the model of a very normal military family.

In the spring of 1976, I obtained my last staff assignment. I was to be a liaison and training officer. My new assignment took us to the Sacramento area of California. Though stationed at Mather AFB, I worked over the six western states of our region. Once again I purged myself of my feminine wardrobe and tried to be a normal straight guy. Within a year I had failed. The hunt

for a new doctor began. Finally I found one nearby who was experienced. He felt that he should work with both of us to fully understand how we had coped and stayed together for so long. Once again I was put on a low dose of hormones, but not enough to cause any outward changes. I still had to pass my annual AF flight physicals.

My last four years passed quickly as I enjoyed my work, the flying, and our life in CA. I was retired from active duty at the end of June, 1980. Now I had to find a new career. Flying jobs were scarce. The airlines were not hiring and related fields were stagnant. I had taken the management exam for the major Bell Company and was hired to supervise an installation and repair crew of ten technicians. I mastered the technical aspects of the job in short order, but the other managers resented an outsider. It took three months for them to come around. During my three years with the company, I had three management jobs. However, I was hired just as deregulation had been ordained. The company went through several rounds of reorganization and lay offs. Two weeks shy of three years and tenure, my pink slip arrived. I decided that it was time to get back into the flying business.

Though I had flown four engine heavy jets in the Air Force, I did not have the required Airline Transport Pilot rating or Flight Engineer rating required for an interview. I went back to giving flight instruction and flying charter to hone my skills. One job I had was to deliver bank checks in the wee hours of the morning, bad weather or not. Many a young pilot has bought the farm doing this type of flying. As soon as I had the written exams and ATP flight check passed, my resumes went to all the airlines. In the spring of '84 I interviewed with People Express Airlines at Newark, NJ. Fortune was with me and I was to start training in August. The move back to NJ was a tough one. We managed to get almost everything into a large rental truck and the overflow into a trailer. We found a rental house near Princeton and settled in for the next phase of our lives.

While making the move, I decided to purge once more. Besides, I had left my doctor in CA and felt that for my and my family's sake I should try once again to be a real man.

Getting the household set up, getting settled in the community, and getting checked out as a Boeing 727 Flight Engineer kept me so busy that I didn't have time to think about gender problems. No matter how I tried to sublimate my feelings, like a cancer, they came back with a vengeance. By the spring of '85 I knew that I needed help. Again, the lack of information made it extremely difficult to find help. The doctor that I had gone to in Philadelphia had moved on. Through a medical listing I started blanket calling psychiatrists on the list, finally finding one in north NJ. My telephone interview with him was very unsatisfactory. It seemed that he was more interested in the weekly fee, which was very steep, than my well-being. The needle in the haystack search began once more. I went to the NYC Public Library to start the search. There I found an article written by Dr. Leo Wollman, who had been an associate of Dr. Harry Benjamin. A check of the telephone directories was next. No listing under medical, physicians, or doctors could be found. I checked the residential listings next. To my amazement his name and number was there, more so when I nervously dialed the number and he answered. My heart raced as I told him how I felt. Suddenly, he simply said: "Come to my office on Coney Island next week, we need to talk." Oh, how I looked forward to that.

It was a cold, rainy day as I drove to the office located in a nondescript building on Mermaid Avenue in the Coney Island section of Brooklyn. I had remembered it as a bustling place with a grand boardwalk, the Cyclone and Parachute Jump from '51. Now it was run down, bleak as the weather that day and I feared for my safety. Arriving at the office I signed in and took a seat among the very poor of the neighborhood. I really felt out of place, but I was as desperate as those around me. I was scheduled as the last patient, and as Dr. Wollman called me in, he told his nurse that she could go home. Just the two of us to deal with my future. Dr. Wollman pointed to a chair at the side of his desk for me to sit in. He then pulled his chair to a position directly in front of me with little distance between us. I briefly told him of my life and occupation. He cut me off and asked a question:

"Tell me, who are you?" I tried to answer in an indirect manner but once again he asked: "Who are you?" He looked me in the eyes. I knew that I had to answer directly. Finally, I stammered, I am a woman. He leaned back and then said: "And what are you going to do about that?" I stated that I was here to begin the process and needed his help. He said okay, but it's going to be very difficult and that he would make sure that I knew what faced me, and that there would be many tests.

I suddenly felt very much better and asked him what his medical training consisted of. He told me that he'd started as a general practitioner, and then became a gynecologist, then a surgeon, then an endocrinologist, and finally a psychiatrist, and had worked with many transsexual patients before retiring. He explained that he became bored, so he set up a community clinic for the poor, started treating transsexuals, and volunteered at a nearby military hospital. He called a local pharmacy to confirm that they had female hormones, wrote out a prescription and since my flying schedule changed each month, told me to call him for an appointment. It was snowing as I left, but to me it seemed like the spring of my life.

Throughout the next four years I would meet once a month on a Saturday at his home with a group of other transgendered people. One was post op, a couple were well along and no longer resembled their former selves, and the few others had been in the program a year or so. They immediately made me feel welcome and comfortable. Still, there was a lot that I didn't understand but my education had begun.

As I took the hormones, my body slowly began to change. One day I asked Dr. Wollman about it and he asked if I had experienced a short or long puberty. I said long. He then told me that as I changed, the male hormones would fight back and that I'd experience a long puberty once again. There was a war going on in my body. After an injection I would be nauseous and even have morning sickness for a while. So this is what women go through, I thought. It would take two to three years before my physical changes would become noticeable, and I didn't want to call undue notice to myself. By '88 my family doctor had picked up on my changed appearance during an annual physical and told me that he was requesting a mammogram. I told him what was going on and he said that that was my business, but it was his business to keep me healthy. The radiologist was taken aback, but I took the position that they only needed to know enough to accomplish what my doctor had ordered. It worked. Each year I also had to get a flight physical from an FAA Aero medical doctor. The medical certificate is necessary to exercise pilot privileges. Again, the doctor was surprised but wished me the best and issued the medical certificate. Both doctors demonstrated a compassion for my well-being that I would find lacking in most of society.

Throughout the period from '85, when I started taking hormones, to my decision point, the matter of my transsexuality weighed more heavily on the lives of my wife and daughter. Beth and I still enjoyed closeness, were affectionate and intimate, and really tried to effect, at least from outward appearances, a normal relationship. It was difficult for her to see that she was slowly losing her husband. We discussed how it would affect our relationship, the difficulties of my transition, legal and financial matters. It seemed that no matter how logically and methodically I continued, a disaster was in the making. In the AF, I had learned how to write operations plans. I did so now. My plan had sections for medical, legal, financial, logistics, etc. We would go over it from time to time and she asked a lot of "what if" questions. The unknown had to be thought of and dealt with. The plan was revised many times.

One of the most critical aspects facing me was that of money. I had monthly retirement income from the military, Beth worked full time, I made a good salary as an airline pilot, and I would have to—as I had done so far—pay the full expense of the surgery. Transsexual surgery is an elective procedure according to insurance companies. They won't pay for it. They ignore the suicide rate for TS victims. Though the FAA was the agency that finds a pilot fit and capable of flying, I anticipated that my company would probably fire me for some business or medical reason. The future was very uncertain. Flying was the one place I

truly felt at home and I would have to fight to stay there. At the same time I also knew that if I didn't achieve a union of body and psyche, I had no future. I squirreled away money as I could to fund the plan.

We had rented a house since we'd moved to NJ. We had to leave California at a time when the interest rates were 18% and we were forced to sell for the amount of the loans. All equity was lost. We started off in NJ at a time of rapidly increasing housing costs. My salary in the first four years was not enough to purchase a home, so we rented. By the spring of '89, our daughter was working and living with friends so we started house hunting. We found a nice townhouse nearby and bought it using my VA loan entitlement. Now we had the advantages of home ownership at a cost much less than renting. In the event I was fired, the mortgage was affordable.

During my daughter's last three years of high school, she became much more aware of my problem. Though she didn't talk directly to me about it, I knew that she had read my books on the subject that I had placed in the bookcases. She did start to ask her mom what was going on. I was in counseling when my wife sought counseling at our church. One of the priests, a woman, felt that something deeply troubled us. She made herself available and we both went to talk with her, singly and together. She also helped us find a psychologist for our daughter to talk to. At last we were able to express our innermost fears, concerns, and feelings with each other through the priest and doctor, and at times directly. In one session when my daughter was asked how she felt about my impending change, she replied, "I don't want to lose my father figure, but he's not happy and he deserves happiness, so I guess that I'll learn to accept him." Having her say this in front of me in the presence of her mother and the doctor brought tears to my eyes. Much debate had gone on between Beth and I about my future name. That was solved one day when my daughter arrived home from school. I was "dressed at the time" and didn't expect her home for another hour. She called up to the second floor where I was working on administrative matters in the office and announced that when she finished her snack, that she wanted to talk with me. Surprised, I told her to wait until I changed clothes. She said, don't bother—it doesn't matter. A short time later she came into the office and pulled up a chair. I asked what she wanted to talk about, but was not prepared for what was to follow.

When she was born we had a difficult time deciding on her first name. Two names were finalized but we couldn't seem to agree on which one. On the ninth day the head nurse gave us an ultimatum, decide today or it will be "Baby Girl." With that prompt, my choice won out. My daughter knew this so she said, "Since you got to name me I think it's only right for me to name you." I sat there stunned, then looked at her and said, "OK, what's it going to be?" "Jessica Page," she said. I had not tried Jessica and suddenly it seemed to fit. I told her that I liked the first name, but wanted to keep my initials of JRS. She told me that was okay and that we'd think of something. As she left, she turned and said: "Nice pumps—why don't I have some like that?" I told her to buy some if she wanted. Two weeks later she was wearing her pair. Though I knew that our troubles were far from over, this had given me hope that our relationship would survive. I am proud to have been named by my daughter.

The decision to undergo sex reassignment surgery must never be taken lightly and without thorough preparation. Once done, there is no going back. I did not know when I would arrive at my decision point. It happened the second Sunday of September '89. As my wife and I knelt in church to recite the Lord's prayer and as I said "thy will be done," I felt seized by only what I can say was the Holy Spirit, and instantly knew what had to be done. As we left the church, she suddenly turned to me and spoke: "You've made your decision." It was not a question, but a statement of fact. In reply, I simply said yes to her statement. We then went for brunch and only discussed the subject when we returned home.

The FAA had just completed the evaluations of the many exams required of me, and informed me by letter that I was cleared to proceed. Upon completion of surgery, I was to send the documents needed to obtain new pilot and medical certificates. I knew it would be different with the airline. I wrote a detailed letter explaining my situation, enclosed a copy of the FAA letter, and waited for the fireworks. I went to fly one early morning in November and as I tried to pull up the trip schedule in the computer, could not find it. When my Assistant Chief Pilot showed up two hours later he told me that I had been administratively grounded and he didn't know why. We stepped into his office, closed the door, and I told him why. We'd known each other in the AF and he told me that he'd always thought the best of my flying and staff work. He promised to do what he could do to help me but thought that the decision made at the highest level, by one of the most despised airline CEO's, would be impossible to overcome. Fortunately, we had a pilots' union and contract, but that would only enable me to go through the prescribed grievance process.

The company said that I was psychologically unsound, not fit to fly, would be a hazard in the cockpit, and passengers would not fly with me. The VP for Flight Operations ordered me to see the company drug abuse specialist and psychologist in LA. In early December my wife and I flew out to see Dr. GB. The company didn't know that he'd already helped several people like me and knew what was going on. He strongly recommended that I be returned to flying and be permitted to fly as a woman. The company rejected that idea, but I was returned to duty for a short time. In February of '90, the second letter came. I was fired. My fight had begun in earnest. Before I went to Viet Nam as a Forward Air Controller, I was fighter qualified. When a flight of fighters arrives over the target they set up a wheel formation so that when they roll off their high altitude perch, they can be most effective at striking from any direction. I now put myself in this mental mode of striking back. I needed help though; a tough, go-for-the-throat attorney who would not be afraid to take on a large corporation, and who would be understanding of my finances. I had read of a local attorney who liked to take on tough, unusual, and challenging cases. He had just beaten a large university in two cases. He sounded like the man for me. When I explained why I needed him, he was in a state of disbelief. He finally said okay, then looked at me and said that I would have to educate him. I paid his retainer and told him that on the next visit he would be seeing Jessica.

I had filed a discrimination complaint with the state and was quickly scheduled for a hearing. At the time my attorney was a little uncomfortable with me as a female, so for the hearing he asked that I appear in men's clothing. Mentally, I had made the switch to female and having to appear dressed as a man was very distressing to me. Of course the airline attorney and chief pilot jumped on that and tried to discredit me. He realized his mistake and quickly told them in very stern terms that it was he who was uncomfortable and that from then on he would treat me properly, as a woman. He apologized and the hearing was completed. As we walked from the room he put his arms around me, apologized again, and told me that the airline was going to be in for one hell of a fight. A couple of months later I was notified that the Division on Civil Rights had found for me, but that didn't mean that I could readily get my job back.

My date for surgery was set for August 28th, 1990 in Trinidad, Colorado. My sister, who was still uncertain about my decision, told me that she would be going with me. The hospital stay was scheduled for ten days and travel afterwards was going to be difficult and painful. Her car was a Lincoln Town car. The ride would prove to be very beneficial for me on the journey home. Her daughter lived in Topeka, Kansas, which was about halfway between Indianapolis and Trinidad, so we stopped there both ways. During '89 I had made the rounds of relatives and close friends to inform them of my plans. This came as a shock to most, but after the news sank in and they began to understand my feelings, most reacted with feelings of love and support. I don't recommend this as a way to find out who your real friends are, or who truly loves you, but you'll soon know. The level of love and support surprised me, and that helped to sustain me during some very dark hours. My sister and I spent a weekend at Colorado Springs. We felt like two sisters on vacation. The weather was perfect as we took the cog

rail train to the top of Pikes Peak, walked about the Garden of the Gods, shopped and dined in quaint restaurants.

About an hour from Trinidad my sister told me that it was OK with her if I changed my mind, that she'd love me just as much if I said no. My life was ahead, and as a woman. In my mind, there was no going back. Dr. Biber gave me my final exam on a Monday morning and I was admitted to the hospital that afternoon. Final checks were made, paperwork completed, and fees paid. I met all the staff involved and was given every chance to change my mind. For the first time in my life I felt totally at ease. All that I despised would soon be removed.

I was awakened at 6:30 AM Tuesday morning, rechecked and given a last chance to say no. By 7:00 I was in the operating room. Within seconds of being given a sedative I was asleep. I was told that the surgery took over four hours. When I awoke, numb as a log, the wall clock said 2:10 PM; Dr. Biber and the O.R. nurses were standing at the foot of my bed, with my blood on their scrubs, and smiling. Dr. Biber said to me: "Welcome to the world, Sleeping Beauty." Those words I'll never forget. I was truly born again. It would be a week before I was allowed out of bed. The pain was intense. I endured it, as I knew it would recede as my body healed. My sister came each morning and spent a lot of time with me and the other four new girls in our special section of the ward. Liz, Margaret and I bonded and to this day we consider ourselves sisters. My strength gradually returned, and on day eleven I was released into the world.

My sister did most of the driving on the return trip. The back seat of the town car was my bed. We spent two nights in Topeka with her daughter, and then drove on to Indianapolis. For two days I rested there before heading back to NJ in my car. I could go about one and a half hours between stops for rest and a change of bandages. When I arrived back in Princeton I truly felt that I had started over. Now I could focus on the legal fight ahead. Though my funds were low, I was getting unemployment, and earning some money from photography. In a short time I would find some part time work to pay for rent and living expenses. For now, I needed to concentrate on learning in months, what the normal female has years to learn. Fortunately, I had a lot of help from friends and family. Never once during my transition had I been challenged about who I was. That had given me a lot of confidence.

As the legal battle began, my airline filed for bankruptcy. Now I had to petition Federal Bankruptcy Court in Delaware in order to sue for reinstatement. More expense but I prevailed. After a lot of legal jousting, my case was taken by the Federal District Court in Trenton, NJ. No argument that the airline presented impressed the court. My case was put on a fast track, and we were kept busy with research, presentations, and legal arguments. At each hearing, the results favored me. Just before a trial was set to start, a summary court hearing was conducted. During the hearing, the judge suddenly ordered the airline attorney and mine to his chambers. He told the company that they would want to settle with me as they were going to lose. They were given thirty days to come to terms. I wrote out the terms and though they tried to weasel, I said to them: "Agree or I'll see you at trial." They gave in.

Almost two and a half years had passed since I'd been fired. I was excited about returning to the profession that I loved. I had made the national news twice and a level of public support had begun which gave me confidence that I could win. I had been on several TV and radio talk shows that helped me deal with public perception and questions about functioning and fitting in with society. Still, I knew that there would be many who didn't want me there, let alone fly with me. During a special interview with the company VP of Flight Operations, I told him that I was back to fly and do my job as a professional, not because they wanted me, but because a federal court had ordered it. If any pilot had a problem with who I was, it was their problem, not mine. Many of the pilots actively supported me, others had a wait-and-see attitude, while some tried to make my life miserable. On July 21st, 1992 I reported to training for requalification. It was good to be home.

Because I had beaten the company, stood up for my rights, and went after any pilot that harassed me, the flight attendants and gate agents were open about how they felt.

I'd become a folk hero of sorts. They warmly greeted me for each flight, made sure I had a bottle of water, made fresh coffee for me, and saved first class meals when possible. Many of the employees would let me know about the plots of those who wanted to embarrass or cause me problems. It took a while to get used to being stared at by pilots in the crew room. I knew that it would take some time to be accepted, but I earned it by conducting myself in a professional and friendly manner at all times. Those who crossed me learned that I knew how to use published pilot policies to stop harassment immediately. One of my captain friends told me one day that the word was "Don't mess with Jess."

Of over five thousand pilots, my company only had sixty-three female pilots in '93. It was rare to fly with another female, but a treat when it happened. I had upgraded to Captain before having an entire female crew. We had a lot of fun and it was amusing to see some of the passengers' expressions and hear their comments when they found out that the whole crew was female. When I flew to Mexico or South America airport employees, mostly male, reacted with surprise and amazement upon seeing a female Captain, especially one who wore a skirt instead of slacks. Some even whistled at me.

After I healed from surgery and had resumed as normal a life as I could, I started to become more social. I had to find out how I felt about men in a more intimate way. I was attractive enough that as I went about my daily routine I became aware of how others were looking at me. When I went to a dance it was as if I could read the minds of the men in the room. I knew exactly what they wanted. The question was, do I or how far do I let them go? I considered myself heterosexual before surgery, now how would I feel in the intimate company of men? I needed to find out. I had met a scientist at a church singles group and he always arranged to have me in the discussion group that he led and at the monthly dance would dance with me often. One Sunday he told me that he wanted to get to know me better. I invited him to dinner one cold winter evening when I had the house to myself. I discovered after dinner that his interests were more physical than intellectual. Now I'd been there in the past, but was I going to let him do to me what I knew he wanted? It was the situation every female finds herself in and has to decide—do I, or don't I? Well, I did and thus began my journey into the intimacy of being female. In a year I knew that I enjoyed being the object of men's desires.

How do men react when they find out that the woman they are attracted to turns out to have had that very different past? Those who are confident of their own sexuality have told me that since they only knew me as Jessica, it didn't matter. Others run immediately, while others become fearful of what their peers will think. I found that some men are very intimidated by a woman who has advanced education, highly developed technical skills, has coped with extreme danger, and has not had to ask a man to do it for her. My lady friends have done a reasonable job of teaching me, so that I don't scare off the prospective suitor. Of course, I could now write volumes about how women are treated at the local garage, hardware store, car dealership, etc. I won't, but I use that knowledge to my advantage.

In summary, I like to stress that no human chooses to be a transsexual. I feel that half of my life's energy was spent in coping with this. Statistics available in 1990 indicated that the population of transsexual people, both male and female, was about .0004%. Of that number only ten percent will achieve the goal of surgery. In a nation concerned about human health and well-being, we are left to fend for ourselves with little help. The situation has got somewhat better because some of us have been willing to educate, speak out, go to court (I was the first to win in a federal court), and insist that we deserve and have the right to happiness promised to all. Today one needs only to go to the World Wide Web to find support groups and resources for the transgendered. In the past few years, many local and state governments have passed antidiscrimination laws to help protect gays, lesbians, and transgendered people. Many companies have been in the lead as they value the employee and realize that disharmony in the work place affects profits.

When asked if I am happy, I can say without a doubt that I am. I have no regrets about having lived my life as I did. There's no going back, only forward with the total continuity of "freedom of identity."   [2003]

Understanding the Reading

1. What is a transsexual?
2. Do you think Jessica was born this way, or is it because of something in her background?
3. Describe her personality, as you see her.
4. In what different ways did she attempt to deal with her transsexuality throughout her life?
5. After her surgery, how did her employer react?
6. What was the legal outcome?

Suggestions for Responding

1. Research laws concerning transsexuality and report on them.
2. Find out what the U.S. Armed Forces' policy is toward transsexuals. What would have happened to her career had they known about her transsexuality?
3. Have a class discussion on why you think Jessica sought a career in flying, as traditionally it has been a very masculine arena. ◆

26

Two Sexes Are Not Enough

Anne Fausto-Sterling

In 1843 Levi Suydam, a 23-year-old resident of Salisbury, Connecticut, asked the town's board of selectmen to allow him to vote as a Whig in a hotly contested local election. The request raised a flurry of objections from the opposition party, for a reason that must be rare in the annals of American democracy: It was said that Suydam was "more female than male," and thus (since only men had the right to vote) should not be allowed to cast a ballot. The selectmen brought in a physician, one Dr. William Barry, to examine Suydam and settle the matter. Presumably, upon encountering a phallus and testicles, the good doctor declared the prospective voter male. With Suydam safely in their column, the Whigs won the election by a majority of one.

A few days later, however, Barry discovered that Suydam menstruated regularly and had a vaginal opening. Suydam had the narrow shoulders and broad hips characteristic of a female build, but occasionally "he" felt physical attractions to the "opposite" sex (by which "he" meant women). Furthermore, "his feminine propensities, such as fondness for gay colors, for pieces of calico, comparing and placing them together, and an aversion for bodily labor and an inability to perform the same, were remarked by many." (Note that this 19th-century doctor did not distinguish between "sex" and "gender." Thus he considered a fondness for piecing together swatches of calico just as telling as anatomy and physiology.) No one has yet discovered whether Suydam lost the right to vote. Whatever the outcome, the story conveys both the political weight our culture places on ascertaining a person's correct "sex" and the deep confusion that arises when it can't be easily determined.

European and American culture is deeply devoted to the idea that there are only two sexes. Even our language refuses other possibilities; thus to write about Levi Suydam I have had to invent conventions—s/he and h/er to denote individuals who are clearly neither/both male and female or who are, perhaps, both at once. Nor is the linguistic convenience an idle fancy. Whether one falls into the category of man or woman matters in concrete ways. For Suydam— and still today for women in some parts of the world—it meant the right to vote. It might mean being subject to the military draft and to various laws concerning the family and marriage. In many parts of the United States, for example, two individuals legally registered as men cannot have sexual relations without breaking antisodomy laws.[1]

But if the state and legal system has an interest in maintaining only two sexes, our collective biological bodies do not. While male and female stand on the extreme ends of a biological continuum, there are many other bodies, bodies such as Suydam's, that evidently mix together anatomical components conventionally attributed to both males and females. The implications of my argument for a sexual continuum are profound. If nature really offers us more than two sexes, then it follows that our current notions of masculinity and femininity are cultural conceits. Reconceptualizing the category of "sex" challenges cherished aspects of European and American social organization.

Indeed, we have begun to insist on the male-female dichotomy at increasingly early stages, making the two-sex system more deeply a part of how we imagine human life and giving it the appearance of being both inborn and natural. Nowadays, months before the child leaves the comfort of the womb, amniocentesis and ultrasound identify a fetus's sex. Parents can decorate the baby's room in gender-appropriate style, sports wallpaper—in blue—for the little boy, flowered designs—in pink—for the little girl. Researchers have nearly completed development of technology that can choose the sex of a child at the moment of fertilization. Moreover, modern surgical techniques help maintain the two-sex system. Today children who are born "either/or—neither/both"—a fairly common phenomenon—usually disappear from view because doctors "correct" them right away with surgery. In the past, however, intersexuals (or hermaphrodites, as they were called until recently), were culturally acknowledged.

Hermaphroditic Heresies

In 1993 I published a modest proposal suggesting that we replace our two-sex system with a five-sex one. In addition to males and females, I argued, we should also accept the categories herms (named after "true" hermaphrodites), merms (named after male "pseudohermaphrodites"), and ferms (named after female "pseudohermaphrodites").

[*Editor's note:* A "true" hermaphrodite bears an ovary and a testis, or a combined gonad called an ovo-testis. A "pseudohermaphrodite" has either an ovary or a testis, along with genitals from the "opposite" sex.] I'd intended to be provocative, but I had also been writing tongue in cheek and so was surprised by the extent of the controversy the article unleashed. Right-wing Christians somehow connected my idea of five sexes to the United Nations–sponsored Fourth World Conference on Women, to be held in Beijing two years later, apparently seeing some sort of global conspiracy at work. "It is maddening," says the text of a *New York Times* advertisement paid for by the Catholic League for Religious and Civil Rights, "to listen to discussions of 'five genders' when every sane person knows there are but two sexes, both of which are rooted in nature."

[Sexologist] John Money was also horrified by my article, although for different reasons. In a new edition of his guide for those who counsel intersexual children and their families, he wrote: "In the 1970's nurturists . . . became . . . 'social constructionists.' They align themselves against biology and medicine. . . . They consider all sex differences as artifacts of social construction. In cases of birth defects of the sex organs, they attack all medical and surgical interventions as unjustified meddling designed to force babies into fixed social molds of male and female. . . . One writer has gone even to the extreme of proposing that there are five sexes. . . ." (Fausto-Sterling).

Meanwhile, those battling against the constraints of our sex/gender system were delighted by the article. The science fiction writer Melissa Scott wrote a novel entitled *Shadow Man,* which includes nine types of sexual preference and several genders, including fems (people with testes, XY chromosomes, and some aspects of female genitalia), herms (people with ovaries and testes), and mems (people with XX chromosomes and some aspects of male genitalia). Others used the idea of five sexes as a starting point for their own multi-gendered theories.

Clearly I had struck a nerve. The fact that so many people could get riled up by my proposal to revamp our sex/gender system suggested that change (and resistance to it) might be in the offing. Indeed, a lot *has* changed since 1993, and

I like to think that my article was one important stimulus. Intersexuals have materialized before our very eyes, like beings beamed up onto the Starship Enterprise. They have become political organizers lobbying physicians and politicians to change treatment practices. More generally, the debate over our cultural conceptions of gender has escalated, and the boundaries separating masculine and feminine seem harder than ever to define. Some find the changes under way deeply disturbing; others find them liberating.

I, of course, am committed to challenging ideas about the male/female divide. In chorus with a growing organization of adult intersexuals, a small group of scholars, and a small but growing cadre of medical practitioners, I argue that medical management of intersexual births needs to change. *First,* let there be no unnecessary infant surgery (by *necessary* I mean to save the infant's life or significantly improve h/er physical well-being). *Second,* let physicians assign a provisional sex (male or female) to the infant (based on existing knowledge of the probability of a particular gender identity formation—penis size be damned!). *Third,* let the medical care team provide full information and long-term counseling to the parents and to the child. However well-intentioned, the methods for managing intersexuality, so entrenched since the 1950s, have done serious harm.   [1999]

Note

1. The antisodomy laws were overturned by the U.S. Supreme Court in June 2003.

Understanding the Reading

1. Why was there a question as to whether Levi Suydam should be allowed to vote?
2. What does the author mean when she says that biology has no interest in maintaining only two sexes?
3. What is "corrective" surgery for intersexuals and when is it done?
4. Do you think corrective surgery is ethical? If not, what is the alternative?
5. Why does the author suggest we change to a five-sex system?

Suggestions for Responding

1. What are the implications of changing to a five-sex system? Spend ten minutes outlining what would change, on a public policy level, interpersonal level, and psychological level.
2. Debate the ethics of assigning a sex through surgery, delaying surgery until after puberty, or not doing surgery at all. ✦

27

The Conservative Case for Gay Marriage

From the pages of

TIME

ANDREW SULLIVAN

A long time ago, the New Republic ran a contest to discover the most boring headline ever written. Entrants had to beat the following snoozer, which had inspired the event: WORTH-WHILE CANADIAN INITIATIVE. Little did the contest organizers realize that one day such a headline would be far from boring and, in its own small way, a social watershed.

Canada's federal government decided last week not to contest the rulings of three provincial courts that had all come to the conclusion that denying homosexuals the right to marry violated Canada's constitutional commitment to civic equality. What that means is that gay marriage has now arrived in the western hemisphere. And this isn't some euphemism. It isn't the quasi-marriage now celebrated in Vermont, whose "civil unions" approximate marriage but don't go by that name. It's just marriage—for all. Canada now follows the Netherlands and Belgium with full-fledged marital rights for gays and lesbians.

Could it happen in the U.S.? The next few weeks will give us many clues. The U.S. Supreme Court is due to rule any day now on whether it's legal for Texas and other states to prosecute sodomy among gays but not straights. More critical, Massachusetts' highest court is due to rule very soon on whether the denial of marriage to gays is illicit discrimination against a minority. If Massachusetts rules that it is,[1] then gay couples across America will be able to marry not only in Canada (where there are no residency or nationality requirements for marriage) but also in a bona fide American state. There will be a long process of litigation as various married couples try hard to keep their marriages legally intact from one state to another.

This move seems an eminently conservative one—in fact, almost an emblem of "compassionate conservatism." Conservatives have long rightly argued for the vital importance of the institution of marriage for fostering responsibility, commitment and the domestication of unruly men. Bringing gay men and women into this institution will surely change the gay subculture in subtle but profoundly conservative ways. When I grew up and realized I was gay, I had no concept of what my own future could be like. Like most other homosexuals, I grew up in a heterosexual family and tried to imagine how I too could one day be a full part of the family I loved. But I figured then that I had no such future. I could never have a marriage, never have a family, never be a full and equal part of the weddings and relationships and holidays that give families structure and meaning. When I looked forward, I saw nothing but emptiness and loneliness. No wonder it was hard to connect sex with love and commitment. No wonder it was hard to feel at home in what was, in fact, my home.

For today's generation of gay kids, all that changes. From the beginning, they will be able to see their future as part of family life—not in conflict with it. Their "coming out" will also allow them a "coming home." And as they date in adolescence and early adulthood, there will be some future anchor in their mind-set, some ultimate structure with which to give their relationships stability and social support. Many heterosexuals, I suspect, simply don't realize how big a deal this is. They have never doubted that one day they could marry the person they love. So they find it hard to conceive how deep a psychic and social wound the exclusion from marriage and family can be. But the polls suggest this is changing fast: the majority of people 30 and younger see gay marriage as inevitable and understandable. Many young straight couples simply don't see married gay peers next door as some sort of threat to their own lives. They can get along in peace.

As for religious objections, it's important to remember that the issue here is not religious. It's civil. Various religious groups can choose to endorse same-sex marriage or not as they see fit. Their freedom of conscience is as vital as gays' freedom to be treated equally under the civil law. And there's no real reason that the two cannot coexist. The Roman Catholic Church, for example, opposes remarriage after divorce. But it doesn't seek to make civil divorce and remarriage illegal for everyone. Similarly, churches can well decide this matter in their own time and on their own terms while allowing the government to be neutral between competing visions of the good life. We can live and let live.

And after all, isn't that what this really is about? We needn't all agree on the issue of homosexuality to believe that the government should treat every citizen alike. If that means living next door to someone of whom we disapprove, so be it. But disapproval needn't mean disrespect. And if the love of two people, committing themselves to each other exclusively for the rest of their lives, is not worthy of respect, then what is?   [2003]

Note

1. Massachusetts ruled in favor of gay marriages.

Understanding the Reading

1. What was the "worthwhile Canadian initiative"?
2. Why did Canada decide to extend the right of marriage to gay men and lesbian women?
3. How does the author argue that this is actually in line with conservatives' values?
4. Why is having the choice to marry or not important to gays and lesbians?

Suggestion for Responding

1. Since we are a nation of laws, get a copy of your state's constitution, study it, and discuss whether your state is in compliance with its written commitment on the matter of gay marriage or, in fact, is illegally discriminating. ✦

28

When the Political Is Personal

ANN MARIE NICOLOSI

Like many other colleges and universities across the nation, The College of New Jersey (TCNJ) has grappled with issues of diversity, tolerance, and, in the case of its GLBT [gay, lesbian, bisexual, transgendered] student body, staff and faculty, increased visibility. This essay is a narrative of personal conflict, and how a public exhibition of hate can stir up the most private inner struggles that are part of the GLBT experience and identity. . . .

Although I never hid the fact that I am a lesbian, I never publicly announced it in front of students either. I'm sure that some students knew, given the nature of campus grapevines, but most did not. When the decision was made to become more visible to the campus community, I had to take stock of my own unresolved feelings of shame, fear, and self-hate which I thought I had conquered years before. Suddenly, the memories and pictures of a lesbian teenager in the late 1970s who hid in the shadows surfaced. The name calling, sexual harassment, parental loathing, and physical violence of those years came to consciousness again. Would I return to my office one day to find "lezzie" spraypainted or chalked on my door as I had found on the door to my apartment when I was nineteen years old? Would some of my older colleagues look at me with the same disgust I had seen in my mother's eyes? Would I lose my credibility as a teacher if students only saw "the dyke from Women's and Gender Studies," which would provide further ammunition for those who deride the discipline, and perhaps deter budding feminist heterosexual women from joining our program for fear that someone might question their sexuality? And, what bothered me most was the possibility that I was afraid to give up the heterosexual privilege I enjoyed because of my ability to "pass" as a straight woman, and to experience what my butch sisters face everyday.

Yet, how could I not openly proclaim my lesbianism when my students were standing in front of their peers and teachers and doing so? How could I call myself an advisor or mentor to GUTS [former acronym for a support group for gays] and to the students, GLBT and straight, of the College if I were afraid to do what they were so bravely doing?

I decided I would start by coming out to my Gender and Popular Culture class. By a stroke of luck, we were in the midst of a section on GLBT representation in the media, and I had scheduled to show the film *The Celluloid Closet* for this class. I was quite nervous and felt my heart race and my palms sweat. I opened with a general discussion about what was happening on the campus with [some antigay] hate messages and the College's plans to respond to them. I told them that one of the ways to combat homophobia is with increased visibility, and that GLBT teachers were being encouraged to come out. "So, it starts here. Some of you might know this, most probably do not, but I suspect by this afternoon the entire school will know that I am a lesbian. I have never said this in a public forum, and I am quite nervous. But please feel free to ask me any questions—within reason—about what it's like to be gay in our society."

Well, I can honestly say that I never had their undivided attention as I did that morning. And being an opportunistic teacher, I seized the moment as an opening to discuss heterosexual privilege and homophobia and to speak to them openly as a person who lives as a homosexual in a heterosexual world. As we began our discussion, I noticed one of my lesbian students sitting quietly in the back of the room in tears. I saw in her eyes admiration and pride, and she gave me exactly what I needed to bolster my courage that rainy morning in March.

We began to discuss the concept of heterosexual privilege. My students had already read Peggy Macintosh's "Unpacking the Knapsack of White Privilege" so they were familiar with the concept of the systemic privilege of race as well as gender. But the privilege of sexuality is a bit more obscure; they needed to see how that privilege works. I used my partner, Marisa, and

myself as an example. And as I did so, I realized what a relief it was to speak about my partner as my colleagues spoke of their husbands and wives.

I created a scenario in which I was at a social function or cocktail party. Invariably, someone will ask me if I am married or have a boyfriend. If I had heterosexual privilege, my answer would be automatic, said without thinking. But because I do not have that privilege, I must assess the situation in about ten seconds and make a decision how to handle the situation. I must determine if I am safe or not. If I feel safe, I can then say I'm not married, I'm gay and I have a partner. If not, I can either play the pronoun game, or I can deny the existence of the woman with whom I've chosen to share my life. I then asked the students to imagine if their parents (if they are still together and if they are heterosexual) had to deny the existence of one another, would they be able to do it? How would it change their lives if they had to? Would it put a strain on the relationship if they had to hide it?

It ended up being the most productive class I have ever taught. I think that my willingness to be vulnerable enabled the students to open up to each other about their own homophobia. The result was an honest dialogue among students who were grappling with the complex ways in which our world uses not only gender but also sexuality to organize and maintain privilege and hierarchical structures.

Having the ability to speak freely in front of my students was a liberating experience. Yes, I am sure that there are those who refer to me as "the dyke from Women's and Gender Studies," but my misgivings about being totally out and public were ill-founded. My trepidation has now been replaced with a sense that I can give my GLBT students something I never had: a positive, out and proud—and public—role model.

But I am also under no delusions. Despite the success of the teach-in and all the other activities that took place in response to the hate that plagued our community, I know that momentum fades and there is a tendency to backslide into complacency. It is easy and it is comfortable.

There needs to be a sustained effort on the part of administration, faculty, and staff to make sure that issues of racism, sexism, heterosexism, and homophobia have a prominent place in the curriculum and in the mission of the institution. On our campus, as I'm sure on many others, Women's Studies and Gender Studies programs, along with African American and Ethnic Studies programs, lead the way in keeping these topics in the forefront of academic inquiry. We must also have visible support for our GLBT students. As those of us who are queer know, the coming out process can be frightening, painful, and risky. It is essential that we provide, as Edward Stiles' group did, a haven for students struggling with their identity and coming to terms with their sexuality.

The phrase "silence equals death," which became popular during the early years of the AIDS crisis, is as applicable in the academy as it is in the streets and the halls of Congress. Certainly there remains the threat of physical violence against GLBT communities in our institutions, but a more pervasive threat is the emotional death and damage to the psyche that homophobia causes. Being closeted, no matter how comfortable or personally advantageous, assists in upholding the systemic oppression that queer people across the world live under. How can we expect our GLBT children to have the emotional and psychological health necessary to face their lives under this system if we ourselves are afraid to provide the role models they need to do so? How can we instill in them the courage of their convictions if we ourselves lack the courage of our own?   [2002]

References

Agostini, A. (2001, April 10). College should pander to majority [Letter to the editor]. *The Signal,* p. 9.

Burtnik, M., & D'Agnolo, M. (2001, September 11). Alleged victim arrested after deluding campus. *The Signal,* p. 3.

Houston, B. (2001, April 17). Do days off matter? [Letter to the editor]. *The Signal,* p. 9.

McIntosh, P. (2001). Unpacking the invisible knapsack. In P. Rothenberg (Ed.), *Race, Class and Gender in the United States* (pp. 143–152). New York: Worth Publishers.

Pharr, S. (2001). Homophobia as a weapon of sexism. In P. Rothenberg (Ed.), *Race, Class and Gender in the United States* (pp. 143–152). New York: Worth Publishers.

Rogers, M. (2001, April 3). Chalking was pointless [Letter to the editor]. *The Signal,* p. 9.

Sullivan, K. (2001, April 10). Anti-chalking letter misdirected [Letter to the editor]. *The Signal,* p. 9.

Understanding the Reading

1. What does GLBT mean?
2. What moved the author to tell her students that she is a lesbian?
3. Why was she so afraid?
4. What actually happened in the class once she had revealed her secret?
5. Why does Nicolosi consider being "closeted" an extreme threat against GLBT communities?

Suggestions for Responding

1. Compare U.S. attitudes toward lesbians as opposed to those toward gay men. Watch the media and talk with family and friends.
2. If you know someone who is homophobic, strategically plan to challenge his or her fears, perhaps moving your friend toward change. (This is sometimes done by bringing people together, friends whom you have in common but who have never met each other.) ✦

SUGGESTIONS FOR RESPONDING TO PART II

1. The readings in this part have examined both traditional and changing gender and sexual roles in our society. As the introduction suggested, our socialization into gender-appropriate behavior is complex and both subtle and overt. Consider how you learned to behave appropriately in terms of your gender. Think back to your earliest memories. When were you first aware of being male or female? How did your placement in your family (first-born, only child, etc.) affect your family's expectations about you as a girl or a boy? If you have siblings of the other sex, were they treated differently than you or held to different standards of behavior? At various points in your life, you were probably quite self-consciously masculine or feminine. Can you explain those moments? Also, your attitudes toward your femininity or masculinity have probably undergone changes; record these changes and try to figure out what triggered them. After you have reflected on these matters, write an autobiography of your gender development.

2. The importance of gender and sexuality in our society can scarcely be overstated. Whether we accept or reject all the social mandates of our assigned gender role, we cannot escape its influence. However, try to imagine that you were born a different sex. How would your life have been different, and what would you be like today? Think about specific moments in your life when the switch would have been especially important—from your earliest childhood through adolescence into adulthood. Consider how it would influence and alter your expectations for your own future. Write an autobiography of this imaginary you.

3. Describe your versions of the female stereotype and of the male stereotype. Then describe your ideal woman and your ideal man. Analyze the differences between the two pairs and explain what this reveals about stereotypes and reality.

4. Many of the selections in Part II focus on the difficulties of traditional femininity or masculinity, yet most of us are quite content to be who we are. Write an essay about why you like being the sex you are. You probably want to look at both its advantages and rewards and the disadvantages and difficulties of another sex.

5. The selections in this section can be disturbing and confusing, for some of us have been brought up with the straightforward understanding that there are clear-cut divisions between males and females. To confront the information that sometimes the borders are blurry, and that as members of a society we must acknowledge that fact in personal relations and public policy, can be challenging. For some the knowledge is a great relief. Begin researching on the Internet to see what recent information is available about transsexual, transgendered, gay, lesbian, bisexual, and intersexual individuals.

6. Today there are many support groups for members of these communities, as opposed to thirty or forty years ago. Do more Internet research and discuss in class or with friends how such organized groups help or hurt our society.

7. Discover the roles or consequences other cultures offer for being a member of the transsexual, transgendered, gay, lesbian, bisexual, or intersexual communities. Several cultures are changing their official stances as a response to world opinion on human rights demands, or as a means of "having it under control." (See Iran's policy of paying for sex-change operations.)

III

Economics and the American Dream

THE AMERICAN DREAM! WE ALL KNOW WHAT THAT means—a good job with plenty of opportunity for advancement, a good family, a nice house with at least one car (probably two) in the driveway, plenty of good food and frequent dining out with enough money left over for the kids' education at good schools, a few luxuries, and an annual vacation. Each of us can add specific details—appliances, electronic games, and so on—but we would probably agree on the general features of the dream.

This dream arrived on our shores with the early Puritans, who held to the doctrine that God rewarded virtue with earthly wealth; to them, economic success was a way to glorify God. Thus, the **Protestant work ethic** became a core principle of American culture. This ethic is the belief in the importance of hard work and productivity and the corresponding faith that this behavior will be rewarded appropriately. In the eighteenth century, national icon Benjamin Franklin and his "Poor Richard's" maxims advocating frugality, initiative, industry, diligence, honesty, and prudence secularized and popularized the doctrine. Franklin personified the ethic, both for his contemporaries and for succeeding generations, right up to today.

Franklin also represents another facet of the American dream: the ideal of the **self-made man** (who, of course, adheres to the Protestant work ethic). The self-made man has appeared throughout this country's history. In the nineteenth

century, Horatio Alger made a fortune with his popular fictional heroes who rose "from rags to riches" by "luck and pluck and hard work." One of the most admired American presidents is the log-cabin-born, rail-splitting Abraham Lincoln, another self-made man. Recent presidents also tend to flaunt their humble beginnings, from grocer's son Richard Nixon to peanut farmer Jimmy Carter to alcoholic's son Ronald Reagan. George Bush Sr. prefers to be seen as an oil-field wildcatter rather than as a privileged Yale graduate, and Bill Clinton focuses on the single-parent family of his early childhood. George W. Bush, despite his family wealth, places himself as an anti-elitist, with a folksy way of speaking, shown frequently on his Texas ranch, doing manual labor. Barack Obama, our first African American president, identifies with both his black and white family members, and like Clinton was raised by his mother. One might say that in America if you are self-made, you have "made it," and in the twenty-first century that certainly includes women.

The myth of the American dream, based as it is on the assumption that opportunities are boundless and that success depends solely on one's character, has a flip side that makes the dream more like a nightmare for many Americans. If individuals are responsible for their own success, they must also be responsible for their own failure and, therefore, deserving of their fate. Even in the beginning of the twenty-first century, we still hold to these myths, which conceal the realities of class distinctions. We like to think of the United States as a **classless society;** we don't even like to talk about class, except to claim that we all belong to the middle class. This thinking makes it possible for us to ignore the problems created by inequitable economic distribution.

The disparity between the wealthiest and the poorest members of society is, in fact, extensive; while 21 percent of U.S. children lived in poverty in 2011, the richest 1 percent controlled 40 percent of the nation's wealth. In 2011 there were 15 million children living below the poverty line in the United States, according to the National Center for Children in Poverty. Yet there is resistance to changing the system because we have faith in **upward mobility,** the possibility that we will someday strike it rich ourselves—the good old American dream.

Janet Zandy's essay (Reading 29) is an analysis of what class is—more than the amount of money one has, class is also defined by economic privilege and power and access to resources. Zandy suggests five ways we can use to see and understand class and our own class positions. She also points out how the dominant class controls knowledge, especially historical knowledge, and has distorted our understanding of our national past. She closes with student responses to her argument when she presented it as a lecture. The next selection speaks to the issue of upward mobility. In Reading 30 Sallie Bingham describes the disadvantages of being a woman in a very wealthy family. She argues that such women are suppressed and controlled to serve the interests of the family wealth, to which they have only indirect access.

Upward mobility may create its own difficulties. On the other hand, some people learn to cope with the stresses. Author bell hooks (Reading 31) attended and now teaches at "elite" universities, embracing a lifestyle that differs from the one she experienced growing up as part of a poor, rural, Black family. Although her decision to be part of a different world caused tension between her and her mother, she has managed to turn her "outsider" status in her professional life into an asset. In Reading 32, growing up in poverty that he hated, Randall Williams was ashamed to take friends to his house.

Part III ends with the experiences of people who are homeless. In Reading 33, Peter Swet's interview with Gerald Winterlin helps us see that homeless people are hardworking Americans who just happen to fall between the cracks and that they want to pull themselves back up. In Reading 34, Jackie Spinks describes his experiences as he lived in his old van and ate junk food and in a mission soup kitchen; he details the psychological and physical impact of this lifestyle.

Although the myth of a classless, middle-class America is an appealing concept, the readings in Part III reveal that it is a myth and not an accurate description of our nation. It masks many cruel realities that are embedded in our economic system. In addition, our faith in the American dream and its underlying principles of hard work and self-reliance allow us to ignore the problems of those who are ill-served by the system and even to *blame those victims* for their plight. On the other hand, upward mobility, while possible, exacts a considerable toll on those who are forced to choose between the behavior patterns, beliefs, values, and even family and friends of their original world and the chance to "move up," to enter a culture that is both alien and alienating. Thus, in many senses, class in our "classless" society is problematic.

29

Decloaking Class: Why Class Identity and Consciousness Count

JANET ZANDY

To be sure, class is one of those "where do you begin?" subjects. It is a kind of ghost issue, there but not there. Often it is named as part of a cluster of multicultural concerns, but then it seems to disappear, eclipsed by other identities. This is understandable because class is so complex and so mystified, especially in a country as large and diverse as the United States. I use the word "decloaking" in my title not only because I love Star Trek, but because the term fits the process of revealing what is clearly there, but cloaked and hidden. To reveal class involves crossing several time zones, of simultaneously having a sense of the past, the present, and the future.

Also, it involves seeing class as both personal and public, a kind of inheritance we carry with us as individuals and as a country. In other words, class is too important to ignore. I wish I could offer you a neat package of class information that would be psychologically comforting and intellectually satisfying. But, frankly, that would be about as real as a hologram on a holodeck. Instead, I want to speak out of my own experience, and to leave you with more questions than answers.

CLASS IDENTITY

How many of you are first generation college students or college graduates? How many of you have grandparents who do not have college degrees? How many think that working class and middle class are essentially the same thing? How many of you are uncomfortable with these questions?

Questions about class identity seem to evoke feelings and responses that are different from questions about other identities. If I asked, how many of you are from Italian or Irish ancestry, Caribbean, or Asian, there would probably be little hesitation in your response. But class identity is not so evident. Students

may be from significantly different economic circumstances—in terms of whether you need to work to stay in school or whether you have significant loans to repay after graduation or whether someone else is paying your tuition—but those differences are not apparent. And except for the styles of dress of different majors, you can't tell class difference by appearance.

Even bringing up the issue of class seems vaguely impolite, even un-American. People respond by saying: "I don't care about class identity; I treat everyone the same. What does it matter what class you come from, we are all equal."

The truth is class does count. It shapes our lives and intersects with race, ethnicity, gender, and geography in profound ways. What is class? I offer this as a working definition: Class is an experience of shared economic circumstances and shared social and cultural practices in relation to positions of power. Unlike caste (slavery), there is some mobility between classes. That is, it is possible to be born poor and acquire great wealth. (But, not likely.) Conversely, it is possible to keep a sense of one's original class identity as one moves into different economic circumstances. What needs to be understood is that although class identity is shaped by income and wealth, money is only a part of the story. It is what economic privilege can purchase in terms of access and power that really marks class difference.

Each of us is born into a family with a particular class identity and class history—sometimes it is a mixed or hybrid identity—but almost always it is part of a network of other relationships—to other families in a community, to work and jobs, and to institutions. For example, if you are born into a family that owns lands and buildings, a family that has access to the best lawyers and doctors, and has sent generations of sons (and more recently daughters) to boarding schools and then on to Yale or Dartmouth or Harvard then you have a different class history than someone whose parents may own one small house, whose grandparents had to drop out of school to go to work, who does not have easy access to lawyers and doctors, not to mention judges and lobbyists, and whose parents work long hours at a job site they do not own or control, performing labor that may be physically exhausting and even dangerous. It is conceivable that the sons and daughters from both families might even call themselves "middle class," but in terms of power, autonomy, and opportunity, they clearly are not the same.

How do we measure class? Well, it is the academic way to begin with data, definitions, and statistics. To be sure, we have plenty of statistics—most of which [come] from government sources. Even a cursory look at wealth distribution reveals the reality of the economic landscape. At the top, is a tiny, tiny percent of people who control and own an enormous amount of wealth. (And that wealth has increased dramatically in the last 15 years.) At the bottom, are the official poor (whose numbers are growing, about 32 million—about 60 percent of those people are working poor—that is, that have jobs but don't make enough to support their families). And between the rich and the growing number of poor are the middle and working classes. This is where the classification gets blurred. Although there are about twice as many working class people as middle class (about 50 percent to 20 percent), there is a media and political tendency to avoid the term working class and to lump anyone who isn't either very rich or very poor into the amorphous middle (sometimes called "working middle"). I think it is important to unpack the differences between the working class and middle class. To perceive these differences you need to go beyond definitions of a middle salary and look at the nature of work: the degree of autonomy a job has, who is managed, who is the manager; the physicality of work, working-class jobs tend to be harder on the human body, are sometimes even dangerous; the degree of control or ownership one has over one's own labor; and differences of status, options, expectations, language, education, and culture.

Both the middle class and the working class have experienced change: there are fewer well paying, blue-collar jobs, more low-paying white and pink collar jobs. There are fewer independent middle class storekeepers and farmers and more professionals and managers. What both the middle class and the working class have in common is a downward economic pull. The middle class is losing autonomy and security, and the working class is getting poorer as union jobs decline. Both groups are experiencing the economic frustration of being on a no-fat economic diet

of little or no income gain in the last decade. On the other hand, the number of people reporting incomes of more than a half million increased in the same decade 985 percent. When class resentments surface, those in positions of power encourage a criticism aimed downward—at the poor—increasingly the scapegoats for people's economic frustrations—and not upward at the rich. This is perhaps a truer reflection of who owns and controls the media than it is of which class is really oppressing another.

But numbers and definitions are not sufficient to decloak class. We need to understand better the everyday class experiences of ordinary people and we need to ask what is missing or distorted in our own notions about class. I'd like to suggest some ways to break down and think about this large concept:

First, think across generations. Consider how class identity changes or stays the same from one generation to the next. For example, your class experience may be different from your parents and significantly different from your grandparents, but, on the other hand, there may be common values, attitudes, ways of using language that continue from generation to generation. That is the cultural aspect of class. Also, if you look across generations, you can see how tools and technology may have changed—bank clerks use computers instead of adding machines—but the structure of power relationships remains fairly consistent.

Second, consider the concept of relationship as a key to understanding class. That is, class is most visible in juxtaposition or in relationship to something else. You begin to know your class identity when you cross class borders and see your own circumstances through someone else's eyes. For some of you these insights come through community service. For others, class difference was evident when you left home or on your first day in college when you notice what kind of stuff students bring with them. But tangible material differences are only a part of class relationships. There are other relational questions—especially in discerning differences between the middle and working class: For example, in order to advance in the world (and what that means is not always clear), do you need to leave your home and community or can you develop within it? What are the expectations of your family? Are you encouraged to get a secure job with a future and a pension, or are you encouraged to experiment, take a year off, and find yourself? When you went to school as a child, was the language that the school teachers used in first grade familiar to you? Or was it different from the language that you heard at home? And I am referring to the dialects of spoken English, not just other languages. The middle class child does not have to switch language patterns at home and at school; the working class child often does. Also, class difference can be seen in the relationship one has to community. Do you feel alone or do you feel that you are part of a network of people and traditions? These are questions that pull us closer to understanding class as a lived experience and not just an academic category.

Third, consider the intersections between class identity and other identities, especially race and ethnicity. I think that the issue of multiculturalism would be complicated in a positive way if class is factored in. That is, it would be a very healthy thing for working-class people of all different backgrounds to know each other's work history. This would mean also that this huge category of whiteness would have to be broken down and understood in relation to issues of power. This does not mean that there is no such thing as white skin privilege; rather, it means that all whites do not have the same degree of privilege. And, of course, in terms of gender issues, all men do not have the same degree of power.

Fourth, if you want to understand class look at how work is constructed. There are careers, there is work, and there are jobs. Each [is] nuanced differently. Most of us are so busy either preparing for future work or struggling to sustain what we have, that there isn't much time to step back and look at how our work is managed or how it fits into a larger social context. Also, how often do we see the working conditions of other people? How aware are we of the production process behind the goods we consume? It is a fact that most people on this planet do not own or control their own labor, but must sell it in order to survive. And few of them can afford to give their own children the toys and clothes they are assembling for other markets. How work is shaped, who controls and defines it, whether it is scarce or plentiful are all class relational questions.

Fifth, consider the meaning of class consciousness. Consciousness is an awareness, an opening. Class consciousness is an awareness of mutual interests and desires. We are all bombarded with messages coaxing us to identify our interests with those at the economic top. The usual model for this kind of consciousness is the ladder—climbing in an individualistic and competitive way, higher and higher rung by rung. But there are other models. Another is the web; that is, we see ourselves as having a place in a complex network of mutually interrelated positions, and that our individual well being depends on the well being of the group—including the least privileged. This is closer to a model that you find among native peoples and it is closer to the model of a working-class consciousness. It is a sense that survival depends on helping each other out, on a sense of mutuality, not exclusion. Success—if the word is used at all—lies with collective well being not merely with individual achievement—a sense of pushing everything up with us as we rise.

How Class Is Cloaked

Let me begin with a small incident that happened several years ago at an academic conference I attended. These conferences are usually in big hotels in big cities. The usual routine is to get up early and begin attending sessions on different topics in hot crowded hotel rooms. On this occasion, I am standing in the hotel lobby and another English professor makes small talk with me. He asks, "What is your field?" I answer, "American working-class literature." After a significant pause, he replies, "Oh, I didn't know there was a working class anymore." I suggest to him that there still is a working class as I glance around the hotel lobby to see people clearing tables, carrying food, cleaning ashtrays, washing windows, setting up chairs, etc. The room hummed with human activity, but it wasn't visible. These individual workers blurred into the deep background of academic humanism.

It seems to me that this small event is telling of a larger pattern in American culture. It is a problem of seeing—an "unequal distribution of visibility." It works on two levels: people are literally invisible to each other, but also their intelligence and experience are devalued. Sometimes the working class—the class that holds everything up—has to literally punch through in order to be seen.

Part of the problem of visibility is a problem of knowledge—how knowledge is constructed, layer after layer, generation after generation. Working-class people have not had much say about how school knowledge is constructed. Textbooks, curricula, course design were developed by other class interests—initially by an elite intelligentsia or more recently driven by business and corporate needs. The formation of knowledge has not included the subjectivities and experiences and histories of working people in any significant way.

Why is this omission important to understand? It means that the point of view of the majority of people—living today and in the history of the country—has not been included in the big history story—the story that gets delivered to school kids at a very young age. Perhaps it has changed since I was a student or since my children were young, but I noticed that what is taught—who won what battle and who was President at the time—doesn't seem to have a lot of connection or relevance to the lives of ordinary people. What seems to be remembered, is not a rich and dense, conflicted and complex U.S. history, but a kind of Disney-like nostalgic history. Youngsters learn about someone called Betsy Ross sweetly sewing the American flag, but nothing about the noisy, sweaty history of textile work. Or they learn about George Washington chopping down the cherry tree and not telling a lie, but not about the unsafe history of the logging industry or how many lies were told to acquire Indian land. These simplistic little stories have amazing endurance in people's memories and reference points. Indeed, children seem to be protected from serious American history.

And serious American history is violent. It is not safe; it makes people uncomfortable. Class difference and class struggle were—from the very beginning—part of the story. Recent labor and social historians often use words like "hidden," "forgotten," "untold" to tell this other story. Some of this untold story is now part of the history curriculum—but it wasn't when I was a student. I had to learn for myself how to see the point of view in the historical story, how to adjust my angle of vision to look from the bottom up instead of the top down. This adjustment in perspective makes relationships more visible: for instance, in a world of finite resources, if a small group of people own and control vast amounts, it is likely that a large group of people will have very little—no matter how hard they work. And it makes it easier to see how this imbalance is maintained by coaxing people to identify with the very forces that oppress their own kin.

When it comes to the history of class disparity there is a great deal to uncover. At the very beginning of the new nation, Alexander Hamilton advised George Washington to give to the "rich and well born . . . a distinct permanent share in the government." And he did. The very first Congress provided money for bankers to set up a national bank and manufacturers were subsidized in the form of tariffs. In the 1850s state governments gave railroad speculators 25 million acres of public land, free of charge! The first transcontinental railroad was built with government land and money.

When the story is told from the top down, we learn about the feat of building the railroad, how it opened new frontiers and provided jobs. We may not hear that 10,000 Chinese and 3,000 Irish got the opportunity to earn about $1 a day; and die by the hundreds building those *railroads*. And how those very same Chinese workers were hounded and driven out after the job was done. And how none of the workers who built the railroad could claim ownership or even a free ride.

Today, information highways have replaced railroads, but government benefits for businesses and corporations continue. And I am speaking of huge corporate entities, not small businesses or middle class family owned companies. One reason the national debt is so enormous is because of the shifting of the tax burden from corporations to individuals. In the 1950s, corporate share of federal income tax collected was 39 percent, in the 1980s it was 17 percent. By 1991 it was down to 9.2 percent, while the corporate share of state and local taxes stayed about what it was in 1965. This is trickle down economics. But I haven't seen any new cars or fur coats trickle down lately; have you?

But this is only one side of the story. What role did ordinary working people play in shaping their own economic lives? This history, what some historians call "the other civil war," is a record of resistance and endurance in the face of great odds. It seems unfair to the majority of Americans not to know it. To know, for instance, that people fought back. From time to time ordinary citizens—because of unsafe working conditions, long hours, and unlivable wages—would spontaneously refuse to work. The railroad strike of 1877, sometimes called the "great uprising of 1877," was the first national strike in United States history. Within two weeks the strike which began among the railroad workers in Martinsburg, West Virginia (triggered because of five years of wage cuts for workers on the Baltimore & Ohio line) spread through four states—Pennsylvania, Ohio, Indiana and Missouri. It was a general, national strike that included mill workers, miners, laborers, and steel workers; 100,000 workers were on strike at the same time. But they were defeated when federal troops were sent in and, at the end, 100 people were dead. This was neither the first nor the last general strike: between the years 1881–1885 there were 500 strikes a year. In 1886 there were 1,400 strikes, involving 500,000 workers. In 1934 there was a general strike in San Francisco and 130,000 workers went out. That same year, 325,000 textile workers in the South struck.

What is troubling to learn is that so many strikes were lost because the National Guard or the army were employed by business and government against working people. Workers were literally outgunned in battles with soldiers who came from the same working class backgrounds. One brief example. In 1913 in Ludlow, Colorado miners went on strike because of low wages and dangerous working conditions against the Rockefeller owned Colorado Fuel & Iron Corporation. The miners were evicted from their company-owned shacks and set up tents near the coal fields during the cold winter of 1913–14. The National Guard was called; the miners and their families, waving American flags, thought the soldiers were there to protect them. They didn't know that the Rockefellers were paying the salaries of the soldiers. On April 20, 1914 the National Guard began a machine gun attack on the tents. Women and children dug pits beneath the tents to escape the gunfire. The Guard then set fire to the tents. The next day the charred

bodies of eleven children and two women were found. That became known as the Ludlow Massacre. One miner said, "Well, they value their mules more."

Seeing history from the bottom up illuminates other issues in American culture, some surprisingly current. For example, when you look at differences within the working class as a whole, you see a pattern on the part of the owners to pit one ethnic or racial group or gender against another in competition for scarce jobs. It is a strategy of divide and conquer—of terracing skills—so that one race or ethnic group comes to understand that they cannot advance beyond a certain level because they are Hispanic or Hungarian or Italian or women. But even deeper than this, and crucial to our coping with racial tensions today, is how the category of "whiteness" is used to block class awareness. What happens is that the white working class comes to think of its interests in terms of race difference rather than class oppositions. The insecurities that white workers feel about their own status—and the tensions between the ideology of equality and the reality of economic inequality—is displaced by a psychological wage of whiteness, a wage of false superiority because they are white. And so they would compensate for their feelings of class alienation by defining themselves against blackness.

This is just a sliver of American history told from the perspective of working people. It is not history as a sporting event—who won and who lost. I like to imagine what it would mean if this workers' history were embedded in people's consciousness today. What if labor history were half as well known as entertainment trivia? What if the Ludlow massacre were as familiar to school children as sightings of Elvis?

But generally I suspect that most people don't know this history or understand these power relationships. The media does not focus on ordinary people pooling their resources and overcoming differences of language and culture to engage in common struggle. Instead, we have distractions—sports, sensational murder stories (sometimes sports and murder are combined), race and gender antagonisms, and false promises. Instead of examples of how collective effort can change conditions, we have an almost religious reverence for a single leader. Instead of narratives of worker consciousness we have narratives of minuscule possibility—stories of winning, stardom, and lucky breaks. Practice every day, wear these sneakers, and you will make it to the NBA. Right. Play LOTTO and you'll make it big. Hey, you never know. Indeed, you never know. There's a lot of talk about "empowerment" these days, but it doesn't appear to me that ordinary people feel particularly powerful.

TODAY'S VIRTUAL WORK REALITY

Now why should people who are just beginning their careers pay any attention to this history? What are the connections, if any, between individual achievement and communal well being? I want to share with you a bit of student writing that caused me to think about these questions. This was something a student of mine wrote in her journal in December 1988. You may remember that this particular December a bomb exploded on Pam Am Flight 103 over Lockerbie, Scotland. Two hundred and seventy people were killed, including a number of upstate New York students who were on the way home for the holidays after a semester abroad. In response to this event, this RIT student wrote, "From 31,000 feet they had no chance to save themselves. Thirty-eight students, thirty-eight fewer people competing for jobs."

I have to ask myself why this student reacted to the explosion of a packed airplane in terms of job competition. I wonder whether she was completely unique in her reaction or she voiced something that others think, but may not write down. I don't know. I wonder, though, if she reflects the experience of growing up with a different set of historical circumstances and more rigid economic opportunities. Has she gotten the message that life is a game based on scarcity, and the rules say that if someone else loses, I may win.

In a number of ways the rules have changed. Middle class families are getting new and disturbing labels—they are being called the fear of falling class or the anxious class. Part of it is uncertainty about the future. There are no guarantees—no one can say what tomorrow's cutting edge will be or where the jobs will be in ten, even five years from now, or whether

there will be any employment continuity in a project-driven work environment. It may be hard to believe that your parents' generation was once on the cutting edge too but now many of them are being downsized (I understand the current term is "rightsized") out. The cutting up of the work force is a class issue. What are the implications for family or community if workers are disposed of like so many Bic razors? This uncertainty is coupled with the reality of enormous college debt faced by graduating college students and their families. My generation—the 60s generation—were in some ways luckier. We had greater access to grants and scholarships rather than loans and second mortgages. And so there were many working-class kids like myself who had full scholarships to get educations their parents could never afford to give them. Also, twenty years earlier, over two million service men and women of the generation of the 1940s were able to take advantage of Public Law 346, commonly known as the G.I. Bill. Free education and a subsistence allowance to any eligible veteran. It was an enormous leap, a great opportunity to become engineers, educators, judges, lawyers and get degrees from Princeton, Yale, and Stanford via the G.I. Bill.

Today we have what some are calling job virtual reality (now the job exists, now it doesn't). We have a lot of interesting technology. And a great deal of pressure to be technically prepared to face this changing world. But, there doesn't seem to be a lot of time—unless students do it for themselves—to consider how the pleasures of engineering or the writing of an elegant computer program or the crafting of a beautiful table—how the work we enjoy doing—relates to a larger community of people. We don't have time to ask how technology conforms to existing power relationships. The computer scientist Richard Stallman asserts that "the greatest scarcity in the United States is not technical innovation, but rather the willingness to work together for the public good. It makes no sense [he says] to encourage the former at the expense of the latter."

By speaking about history tonight I was reminding myself and others whose shoulders we stand on as we climb. The theologian Dorothee Soelle says we need alternative visions to see what she describes as "work [that] is communal, not only in the space of a given community but also in time, as the shared memory of what we have received from the past that accompanies us into the future."

I realize that we academics in liberal arts tend to frustrate students by delivering a lot of critical information but not offering any solutions. But of course you know that the solutions are not simple because the issues are so complex. Frankly, I would be skeptical of anyone who offers simplistic answers to complex questions. Maybe the better way to go—if we are going to salvage a sense of community—is to figure out the right questions, especially in relation to issues of power and class.

Using Class Difference Personally and Collectively

Since I was the first woman in my family to earn a college degree, I was driven to take in knowledge as hard and fast as I could, but not to think very critically about it. Along the way, I sensed a distance, sometimes even a rupture, between the lived experience of my working-class family and what I learned in school. In myriad subtle and not so subtle ways, I was taught in school not to value nor to see the dignity and worth of my own heritage. The message that I received as a young woman wanting to be an educated person was my working class identity had to be discarded—like a dark and heavy coat—at the university door. Getting clear about that identity was a long and complicated process. Claiming that identity as crucial to who I am and the work that I want to do in the world was at once liberating and reconciling. My work is sustained because of a sense of kinship and responsibility to my beginnings—not despite them. This is not about survivor's guilt, nor is it about romanticizing economic hardship; there's nothing romantic about not having enough money. Rather, it is trusting what you know even if it is not part of officially sanctioned knowledge. I realized that I could write, research, and act out of my own sense of class difference. And that what I needed to do was to use my resources and privileges to provide a space for some of this history and culture that was so frequently ignored or even despised. And the work had to be collective, not just my own story.

In *Calling Home* I wanted to create a book that would prove that working-class women have created their own written literary culture, that an aesthetic sense is shaped by class but does not belong to one class. I also wanted to show that the experiences of working class women were not the same as those of working class men or of middle class women. Without any lofty expectations of what might happen, I began collecting writing by working class women and putting it into shoe boxes and then bigger boxes, and finally filing two file drawers. I shaped the material around the interplay of different and linked voices—I, we, and they. And finally—ten years later—I mustered the courage to send it out. No one was more surprised than I was when two prestigious university presses competed for this book. To produce it, I used the tools that I learned in the academy, but the writing itself is grounded outside the academy in the work lives of people like my parents.

In this second book, *Liberating Memory: Our Work and Our Working-Class Consciousness,* I wanted to show how this effort of linking working-class lived experience to cultural work was not unique to me. I wanted to make visible how other working class people like myself managed to use their class experiences in culturally productive ways. I asked for memory, not nostalgia. That is, not a sugar-coated celebration of the past, a self-congratulating, "look how far I've come," but rather a painful reconstruction of class experiences and loss, a way of using grief to tell a larger story. These essays written by photographers and painters and academics and secretaries and musicians and social activists all begin with a biographical record: I was born at this time and in this place and this is the work that my parents and my grandparents did. All of the writers grew up with the uncertain economic rhythms of working class life. Their parents' work included: seamstress, short order cook, chemical factory worker, auto line worker, welder, rubber plant worker, bookkeeper, tenant farmer, truck driver, riveter, millwright, domestic, and housewife. All the writers bring the knowledge of physical labor either personally or through the lives of their parents into the current work that they do. This is a knowledge of the body that is not easily articulated and not often part of bourgeois intellectual circles. All of the contributors oppose the dehumanization of workers—of turning human beings who do not own and control their own labor into things. They all see risk taking as necessary for their cultural work—not because they are more heroic than anyone else—but because it is strategically necessary in order to accomplish democratic change. All of the contributors know what it feels like to be cut out of the action, even though they are of the majority class, the working class. And they all love learning and books.

I'll finish with this short excerpt from the introduction to *Liberating Memory* that describes an episode of class consciousness among working people. It takes place on April 28, Workers Memorial Day.

> For the last five years, hundreds of communities across the country have held memorial services on this day to remember dead and injured workers. In Rochester we meet late in the afternoon on a windy knoll in Highland Park. The setting is landscaped with junipers and white and yellow daffodils. Nested in the grass is a small memorial plaque inscribed with Mother Jones' feisty injunction to "Pray for the dead, but fight like hell for the living."
>
> The event is organized by the local labor council. Dignitaries, public officials, politicians, and the media often show up—though how many depends on whether or not it is an election year. The crowd is mostly a mixture of activists, union leaders, and working people. Some are retired; some were able to get off early from work. We do not necessarily know each other, but faces are familiar and recognizable year after year. We hold red carnations and carry names of fallen workers. We are working class people who have come to honor our own.
>
> The ceremony begins. After the speeches, the display of public language, comes the remembrance. One by one we walk to the podium and read the name of a worker who has died or been injured in the Rochester area, and we place a carnation on the memorial. Sometimes people use this moment at the podium to remember special friends, co-workers, heroes of the labor movement. This year Cesar Chavez was remembered along with the three women social service workers who were gunned down in their offices. One by one, the names are read, and the blood-red carnations accumulate on the memorial.
>
> The reading of the names opens us to each other. Not just the names, but the experience of unsafe work behind the names. A shift occurs. We are no longer an assemblage of strangers, but a community who share a special knowledge about work and struggle. Two local men died this year. In accidents that didn't have to happen. One was digging a tunnel, laying the foundation for a new Taco Bell. Perhaps because of the heavy spring rains, or because of inadequate shoring, the earth gave way, and he was buried alive. The other was a young carpenter. He was injured on the job and died within a week. There were many blue carpenter's union caps this year, the man's family was there, his wife and two young sons. The look on the wife's face was familiar—the flat stare of shock. It is the body's way of absorbing the knowledge of loss. Then shock wears off and grief permeates the body.
>
> Grief is physical. On this chilly April afternoon we share communal grief. It is a particular kind of knowledge—of the body at risk because of the conditions of work, of swift and sudden economic uncertainty. How to live with this knowledge is a personal question. How to put this knowledge to good use is a public and cultural question. That is the question I want to leave with you.

William: I actually took the opportunity to watch the video of this lecture twice, taking several days to think about the topic between viewing. I enjoyed the lecture very much. I could quickly identify with the awareness that I do not come from the same class background as many of my friends or even my peers in the workplaces. I come from a working class family and am experiencing many changes as I prepare to graduate. It's a sobering feeling to realize that in a few weeks I will begin the first job of my career with a starting salary higher than my father ever made in his life, working overtime and supporting a family of four. Class does matter. It affects who I believe I am and what I believe I'm capable of.

While there were many provocative points to the lecture, I really felt strongly about the teachings of other class perspectives in the classroom. As I recall the history lessons I was taught in both elementary and high school, I remember covering essentially the same material year after year. "The Great Roman Empire fell when . . . The Renaissance started in this country . . . The cause of World War was . . ." The stories were lifeless and had nothing to do with me. . . . I liked very much hearing the quote about having a sense of community in time, and I think that's a very important issue that is not being addressed in our educational system.

Gaetana: I understood what you meant by having to work even harder in school because you were the first to attend college . . . with my family it is the same. I was the first to go to school and I had so much pressure on me it seemed all the time to do well and not smear the family name. I wonder how many students could actually relate to that? My parents were not educated. I even was almost held back from first grade because I could not speak English well just Italian. So I have had to work at everything 100 percent all alone since I could not lean on my parents to help me with my academic career. Even today my dad makes me laugh because he insists on weekends I have to come home since I don't have school . . . he thinks that on weekends, breaks, or even after school you have no homework to do.

Charles: The central theme of Decloaking Class was the problems faced by people in this world against the stigma of class and the struggles to not only recognize it but to see class for what it is. . . . Being a 29 year old full-time student and worker, class identification is more noticeable to me now than ever before. I see it everywhere I go, in school, at work, and even places I go to eat. . . . The sad fact is that I've experienced it firsthand, I lived in the inner-city growing up and when friends of mine learned that, it was enlightening how their attitudes toward me changed. The one incident that Professor Zandy referenced which was especially poignant to me was the Ludlow incident of April 20, 1914. I have taken many history classes during school and I never recall hearing of this before this lecture. To me this is a perfect example of class invisibility.

Michael: Professor Zandy's examples of the working class being erased, distorted and omitted from history stand out the most to me. For me, and most every one else attending the lecture, it was the first time I had ever heard about the Ludlow Massacre, the National Strikes

otherwise known as the Great Uprising of 1877, or the treatment of the Chinese who built the railroad. I think that many of my high school history teachers were good at what they did, but now when I look back on it I realize they often spent a lot of time on the important characters in history such as George Washington and Abe Lincoln. They often spent little time, if any, on the working class. I can remember learning all about the wealthy Rockefeller, Morgan, and Carnegie families, but very little about the workers they used to gain their wealth.

Jennifer: Being a college student, you get used to everyone being pretty much like yourself— poor. You usually don't have much spending money to speak of, chances are you live in a hole in the wall, whether it's on or off campus, and it's expected that you'll be especially broke around the first of the month. For us, there is very little class distinction. But growing up, I felt that my family was definitely part of the lower-working class. All you had to do was walk by our house to see that. It never occurred to me that my parents might be ashamed of the way we lived. I just figured, one day I'll get out of this. No big deal. I never thought about my parents never getting out of it, never being able to keep the Joneses in sight, let alone keep up with them. I didn't think about the fact that while I'll probably eventually have a better life than them, they'll die that way. I don't want them to die ashamed. I'm scared that my Dad already has.

Your lecture was the first time I had ever heard of Workers Memorial Day or the Ludlow massacre. It's very frightening to think that huge numbers of Americans will go through life totally ignorant of what goes on in our society, of how small a percentage of people control such enormous amounts of power and wealth. The majority of us fall into the category of working and lower classes. Do the majority of us feel desolate and ashamed? Your point about invisibility is something I see every day here at school. I was so glad to hear it mentioned. Maybe that is the first step. Maybe decloaking class and teaching people that because they are struggling doesn't mean they have to be ashamed is possible. My father said he wanted me to have a better life than he did. I now wish I had told him that I hoped I was half as good a person as he was, instead of telling him that someday I'd buy him the Cadillac he always wanted.

Mike: Professor Zandy, in your lecture "Decloaking Class: Why Class Identity and Consciousness Count" you have raised very important, but not easy to talk about issues. I would like to talk about wealth distribution. In three months I will be graduating from RIT as a Financial Manager and I am worried. My professors gave me knowledge and ability to comprehend complex economic and financial problems. I excelled at it, and I have my grades and letters of recommendation to show my future employers. I, probably, should be happy, go out, get a job, make a pot of money and live happily ever after. However, I am worried. I will always remember what [my professor] said in his Corporate Finance course. He said that our knowledge is a very powerful "sword," and our decisions will affect other people's lives, and that we need to be careful in how we make our decisions. That's why I am worried.

Before coming to the United States, I thought that there are no classes. Six years taught me a lot. In my opinion, people are judged by who they are more often than not. If you are born to a wealthy family your chances of becoming poor are almost nil, but if you are born in a ghetto your chances of becoming rich are almost nil. We always hear that if you work hard you will eventually succeed. I find it difficult to believe.

Distribution of wealth in the society plays an important role in how we live our lives, what values we value, how we communicate with each other. How could the richest country in the world have so many poor and homeless people? Believe me, being born in the former Soviet Union, I am not a socialist. However, I am for social justice.

United States remains a land of opportunity, although I wish this opportunity was available for everyone.   [1996]

Understanding the Reading

1. What does Zandy mean when she calls class a "ghost issue"?
2. How does Zandy define class?
3. What are the differences between the working class and the middle class?

4. How does power factor into our understanding of class?
5. What impact does class have on the construction of knowledge?
6. Explain the role of government in the strikes of the late nineteenth and early twentieth centuries.
7. In what ways have the rules changed today since earlier generations (the 1960s and the 1940s)?
8. What did Zandy want her books to accomplish?
9. Explain the purpose and impact of the Workers Memorial Day ceremony.

Suggestions for Responding

1. Write a paper responding to Zandy's questions in the first paragraph of the "Class Identity" section.
2. Research and report on one of the labor strikes Zandy mentions.
3. Write your response to the Zandy selection—what you learned and how you now feel about the working class. ✦

30
The Truth About Growing Up Rich

SALLIE BINGHAM

Very few people think of rich women as being "highly vulnerable." We are usually portrayed as grasping and powerful, like Joan Collins's character in the television miniseries "Sins." Yet in reality, most rich women are invisible; we are the faces that appear behind well-known men, floating up to the surface infrequently, palely; the big contributors, often anonymous, to approved charities, or the organizers of fund-raising events. Rich women have been so well rewarded by an unjust system that we have lost our voices; we are captives, as poor women are captives, of a system that deprives us of our identities.

Growing up a daughter in a very rich family placed me in this special position. It was important to avoid all displays of pride; what made me unusual, after all, was not really my own. I hadn't earned it. It had been given to me, willy-nilly, along with a set of commandments, largely unspoken, that enforced my solitariness:

- Always set a good example.
- Do not condescend to those who have less.
- Never ask the price of anything.
- Avoid being conspicuous in any way.

These commandments were backed by fear. Rich women are always vulnerable to criticism; we do not share the justifications of the men who actually made the money. We neither toil, nor do we spin, yet we have access to a wide range of material comforts. But here there is a delicate line. The jewels must not be too big, nor the furs too obvious.

Often in a rich family the jewels are inherited, obscuring, with their flash and dazzle, the ambivalent feelings of the women who first wore them. In my family, attention was focused on a pair of engagement rings, one made of diamonds, the other of sapphires, which had belonged to our grandmothers. When the time came to divide the rings, my two older brothers, then adolescents, were allowed to choose. Knowing nothing about the value of jewels, but liking the color of the sapphires, the eldest chose it for his eventual bride; the younger brother took possession, by default, of the much more valuable diamonds.

Both those rings were conspicuous, which broke a cardinal tenet of my childhood. It was a rule I had broken before. All bright children are naturally conspicuous; they talk in loud voices and move about in unhampered ways. But when the whole world is watching for a mistake, this natural exuberance must be curbed. And when the child in question is a girl, the curbing is especially intense: as a sexual object, she represents the family's peculiar vulnerability to outsiders, predators—husbands. The little rich girl must learn to sit with her legs firmly crossed and her skirt prudently down at the same time she is learning to modulate both the tone of her voice and the color of her opinions. The result is paleness.

Her models are pale as well. The hard-driving ancestor who made the fortune is not a good choice for his retiring granddaughter. Yet her female relatives, because of their learned conformity, offer little color or originality to the small girl; their rebellions are invisible, their opinions matched to the opinions of their male counterparts. The most sympathetic woman may be a maid or nurse, but her educational and social limitations restrict her effectiveness as a model. This, in turn, can lead to a split between love and admiration: the cozy, uneducated nurse is loved; the remote, perfect mother is admired. How can one satisfactory role be forged out of two contradictions?

The little rich girl realizes, with a chill, that she must treat the women around her differently. When I was a very small child, I kissed my nurse and the servants when I felt like it; as I grew older, I realized that such displays embarrassed them. As a very small child, I pitied my nurse because she had to work so hard, tending five children; a little later, I realized that such pity was inappropriate. The love doesn't change, but the little girl must look elsewhere for someone to imitate.

Obeying all the rules can never be enough, however. No amount of proper behavior can place a rich woman on comfortable terms with a world where there is so much poverty and suffering. She will always be suspect in a democracy, either as a decoration for a tyrant or a parasite with little feeling for women struggling to survive.

Another obligation is added to the role of the third- or fourth-generation heiress, whose male relatives have led lives nearly as protected as her own. From private boarding school and Ivy League college, these men return to the family fold and a lifetime career managing assets or running the family business. The harsh bustle and hard knocks of independent life have been avoided, at some cost. Yet since these sheltered individuals are men, they are expected to play roles of some importance in society, as executives or politicians, donors or secret political kingmakers. Unused to stress and criticism, they must be protected if they are to survive; here, the rich woman's role as peacemaker becomes crucial.

Most women are expected to balance demands for equity with a special sensitivity to human needs. We are asked to value compassion more than fairness, understanding more than critical judgment. Since family fortunes and family businesses usually descend to male heirs, this protective duty becomes essential to the maintenance of the whole structure. If the inheriting males are revealed as vulnerable and uncertain, the whole enterprise is likely to fall. And so the role of rich women becomes, essentially, that of buttressing rich men.

From this buttressing and sheltering springs an intolerance for conflict, for the harsh give-and-take that characterizes most families. A silken silence prevails, a nearly superhuman attempt to agree on every issue. This is the example provided for the children, who are at the same time secretly or openly competing for affection and favor. Emotional inhibition does not really quell raging emotional needs, which are seldom satisfied in families that value appearances highly. And since there can be no open conflict, no channels are carved out for carrying off animosity. Everything must go underground. This is a recipe for an explosion.

Explosions don't wreck most families. At worst, they cause hurt feelings and temporary alienation. But where there are no channels for the resolution of conflict, an explosion leaves nothing but desolation behind it. No one knows how to proceed.

In addition, explosions in rich families may cause a widespread tremor. Employees may be laid off, elaborate households may be dismembered because of a purely personal falling-out. The rich family supports a large number of dependents: domestics, poor relations, down-at-heel friends, the managers of charitable foundations and their grantees, enormous business ventures with their scaled layers of managers and employees, and a huge retinue of legal and financial advisers. All these people tremble when the family that supports them disagrees. This is a strong inducement to contrived peace.

But to preserve a contrived peace, some people will be permanently silenced. And since the point of view of women is generally less acceptable than the point of view of men, it will be women, in rich families, who are silenced for the sake of peace.

This leads to a good deal of distance between the women in such families. Young girls, like young boys, usually express some degree of rebellion. However, there is no way to express such a rebellion inside such a family without causing the tinkling of crystal chandeliers, which sounds too much like tears. And so the rebellious girl will never find an ally to moderate or encourage her in mother, sister, grandmother, or aunt.

They have subscribed to a system that supports them in comfort, and so the system cannot be questioned. The rebel must learn silence or leave.

Rich families shed, in each generation, their most passionate and outspoken members. In the shedding, the family loses the possibility of renewal, of change. Safety is gained, but a safety that is rigid and judgmental. And the price, for the mothers, is terrible: to sacrifice their brightest, most articulate children to the dynasty.

So around the main fire of the wealthy family one usually sees the little winking campfires of the cast-out relatives. Lacking in skills, these relatives may spend their lives on the fringes of poverty, dependent on an occasional check from home. Often they retain emotional ties with the main fire, strengthened by unresolved conflicts; but they will never thrive either within its glow or in outer darkness. Some of these cast-out souls are women.

For no matter how well paid we are for our compliance, in the end, we do not inherit equally. Most rich families work on the English system and favor male heirs. There's an assumption that the women will marry well and be taken care of for life; there's an assumption that the men will do the work of the world, or of the family, and should be adequately compensated for it. When the will is read, the women inherit houses, furniture, and jewels; the men inherit cash, stocks, and securities. Yet the same commandments that rule out conspicuous behavior prevent rich women from fighting for their inheritance. Instead, we learn early to accept, to be grateful for what we are given. The slave mentality abounds in the palaces of the rich, even when the slave is decked in precious attire. We are dependent, after all, on the fickle goodwill of those who will never proclaim us their heirs.

What a fruitless arrangement this is for families, as well as for the society as a whole, may be seen in the absence of wealthy women from positions of power and influence. Without strong women models and allies, we sink into silence. Bribed by material comfort, stifled by guilt, we are not strong leaders, strong mothers, or strong friends. We are alone. And often, we are lost.

For what personal ethic can transcend, or transform, the ethic of the men in our lives? What sense of self-justification can grow out of a sheltered, private, silenced life?

A fine sense of decorum often prevents us from cherishing friendships with women, friendships that are often untidy, provocative, and intimate. The same sense of decorum makes us hesitate to join groups that may also contain unruly elements. Our good looks and fine clothes are separating devices as well; our smooth, sophisticated deportment doesn't encourage intimacies. And so the most envied women in this country today are probably the loneliest, the least effective, the most angry and forlorn. Yet we have everything. How do we dare to complain?

"Everything" is largely material. It's the charge cards, the jewelry, the clothes. We are not taught skills, self-discipline, or self-nurturing; we are left, by and large, to fend for ourselves inside prohibitions that discourage us from experimenting. And if we are unable to persuade or force our daughters to follow our example, we will lose them, in the end. And in the end, we may find ourselves totally dependent on our male relatives, for friendship, status, affection, a role in life—and financial support. Such total dependence breeds self-distrust, bitterness, and fear.

It doesn't have to be this way. But in order to change, the women in a rich family must realize that its covenants are simply self-perpetuating prejudices: a prejudging of events and individuals so that no untoward thought or action will upset the family's ethic, which is, first and foremost, to preserve the status quo.

Young girls growing up isolated by wealth must find their allies, whether inside or outside the family. They must get themselves educated and prepared for careers, not at the Eastern establishments that are geared to perpetuating male leadership, but at schools and colleges that are sympathetic to the special fears and vulnerabilities of women. And they must rid themselves of their guilt and their compulsion to smooth the way for the heirs.

This is a large bill. But the releasing of energy and hope, for this small group of wealthy women, would have results, in the country at large, far out of proportion to our numbers. What a difference it would make, for example, if rich women contributed their wealth to the causes that benefit poor women rather than to the sanitized, elitist cultural organizations favored by their fathers, brothers, and financial advisers.

What a difference it would make to women running for political office if they could draw on the massive resources of rich women, as men political candidates have drawn on the rich for generations.

What a difference it would make if wealthy women, who hire so many professionals, made sure those professionals were women lawyers, doctors, bankers, and advisers.

What a difference it would make to women as a whole if we, who are so misperceived, became visible, actively involved in working out our destiny.

Wealthy men have always influenced the course of this nation's history. Wealthy women have, at best, worked behind the scenes. We share our loneliness, our sense of helplessness, and our alienation from the male establishment with all our sisters. Out of our loneliness and alienation, we can learn to transform the world around us, with a passion for equality that we learned, at close hand, from observing the passionate inequalities practiced by wealthy families.   [1986]

Understanding the Reading

1. What does Bingham mean when she says rich women are captives?
2. What is the responsibility of a rich woman to her family, especially to its males?
3. Why is conflict especially difficult in rich families?
4. Why are rich women "silenced" and lonely?
5. What effects would changing the lives of rich women have on society?

Suggestions for Responding

1. Most of us dream that being rich would make us happy; however, as Bingham points out, wealth has disadvantages. What drawbacks, beyond those she describes, do you think you might face if you were a female or a male member of a very wealthy family?
2. Can you think of any advantages a working class life would have over? ♦

31

Keeping Close to Home: Class and Education

bell hooks

We are both awake in the almost dark of 5 A.M. Everyone else is sound asleep. Mama asks the usual questions. Telling me to look around, make sure I have everything, scolding me because I am uncertain about the actual time the bus arrives. By 5:30 we are waiting outside the closed station. Alone together, we have a chance to really talk. Mama begins. Angry with her children, especially the ones who whisper behind her back, she says bitterly, "Your childhood could not have been that bad. You were fed and clothed. You did not have to do without—that's more than a lot of folks have and I just can't stand the way y'all go on." The hurt in her voice saddens me. I have always wanted to protect mama from hurt, to ease her burdens. Now I am part of what troubles. Confronting me, she says accusingly, "It's not just the other children. You talk too much about the past. You don't just listen." And I do talk. Worse, I write about it.

Mama has always come to each of her children seeking different responses. With me she expresses the disappointment, hurt, and anger of betrayal: anger that her children are so critical, that we can't even have the sense to like the presents she sends. She says, "From now on there will be no presents. I'll just stick some money in a little envelope the way the rest of you do. Nobody wants criticism. Everybody can criticize me but I am supposed to say nothing." When I try to talk, my voice sounds like a twelve year old. When I try to talk, she speaks louder, interrupting me, even though she has said repeatedly, "Explain it to me, this talk about the past." I struggle to return to my thirty-five year old self so that she will know by the sound of my voice that we are two women talking together. It is only when I state firmly in my very adult voice, "Mama, you are not listening," that she becomes quiet. She waits. Now that I have her attention, I fear that my explanations will be lame, inadequate. "Mama," I begin, "people usually go to therapy because they feel hurt inside, because they have pain that will not stop, like a wound that continually breaks open, that does not heal. And often these hurts, that pain has to do with things that have happened in the past, sometimes in childhood, often in childhood, or things that we believe happened." She wants to know, "What hurts, what hurts are you talking about?" "Mom, I can't answer that. I can't speak for all of us, the hurts are different for everybody. But the point is you try to make the hurt better, to heal it, by understanding how it came to be. And I know you feel mad when we say something happened or hurt that you don't remember being that way, but the past isn't like that, we don't have the same memory of it. We remember things differently. You know that. And sometimes folk feel hurt about stuff and you just don't know or didn't realize it, and they need to talk about it. Surely you understand the need to talk about it."

Our conversation is interrupted by the sight of my uncle walking across the park toward us. We stop to watch him. He is on his way to work dressed in a familiar blue suit. They look alike, these two who rarely discuss the past. This interruption makes me think about life in a small town. You always see someone you know. Interruptions, intrusions are part of daily life. Privacy is difficult to maintain. We leave our private space in the car to greet him. After the hug and kiss he has given me every year since I was born, they talk about the day's funerals. In the distance the bus approaches. He walks away knowing that they will see each other later. Just before I board the bus I turn, staring into my mother's face. I am momentarily back in time, seeing myself eighteen years ago, at this same bus stop, staring into my mother's face, continually turning back, waving farewell as I returned to college—that experience which first took me away from our town, from family. Departing was as painful then as it is now. Each movement away makes return harder. Each separation intensifies distance, both physical and emotional.

To a southern black girl from a working-class background who had never been on a city bus, who had never stepped on an escalator, who had never travelled by plane, leaving the comfortable confines of a small town Kentucky life to attend Stanford University was not just frightening; it was utterly painful. My parents had not been delighted that I had been accepted and adamantly opposed my going so far from home. At the time, I did not see their opposition as an expression of their fear that they would lose me forever. Like many working-class folks, they feared what college education might do to their children's minds even as they unenthusiastically acknowledged its importance. They did not understand why I could not attend a college nearby, an all-black college. To them, any college would do. I would graduate, become a school teacher, make a decent living and a good marriage. And even though they reluctantly and skeptically supported my educational endeavors, they also subjected them to constant harsh and bitter critique. It is difficult for me to talk about my parents and their impact on me because they have always felt wary, ambivalent, mistrusting of my intellectual aspirations even as they have been caring and supportive. I want to speak about these contradictions because sorting through them, seeking resolution and reconciliation has been important to me both as it affects my development as a writer, my effort to be fully self-realized, and my longing to remain close to the family and community that provided the groundwork for much of my thinking, writing, and being.

Studying at Stanford, I began to think seriously about class differences. To be materially underprivileged at a university where most folks (with the exception of workers) are materially privileged provokes such thought. Class differences were boundaries no one wanted to face or talk about. It was easier to downplay them, to act as though we were all from privileged backgrounds, to work around them, to confront them privately in the solitude of one's room, or to pretend that just being chosen to study at such an institution meant that those of us who did not come from privilege were already in transition toward privilege. To not long for such transition marked one as rebellious, as unlikely to succeed. It was a kind of treason not to believe that it was better to be identified with the world of material privilege than with the world of the working class, the poor. No wonder our working-class parents from poor backgrounds feared our

entry into such a world, intuiting perhaps that we might learn to be ashamed of where we had come from, that we might never return home, or come back only to lord it over them.

Though I hung with students who were supposedly radical and chic, we did not discuss class. I talked to no one about the sources of my shame, how it hurt me to witness the contempt shown the brown-skinned Filipina maids who cleaned our rooms, or later my concern about the $100 a month I paid for a room off-campus which was more than half of what my parents paid for rent. I talked to no one about my efforts to save money, to send a little something home. Yet these class realities separated me from fellow students. We were moving in different directions. I did not intend to forget my class background or alter my class allegiance. And even though I received an education designed to provide me with a bourgeois sensibility, passive acquiescence was not my only option. I knew that I could resist. I could rebel. I could shape the direction and focus of the various forms of knowledge available to me. Even though I sometimes envied and longed for greater material advantages (particularly at vacation times when I would be one of few if any students remaining in the dormitory because there was no money for travel), I did not share the sensibility and values of my peers. That was important—class was not just about money; it was about values which showed and determined behavior. While I often needed more money, I never needed a new set of beliefs and values. For example, I was profoundly shocked and disturbed when peers would talk about their parents without respect, or would even say that they hated their parents. This was especially troubling to me when it seemed that these parents were caring and concerned. It was often explained to me that such hatred was "healthy and normal." To my white, middle-class California roommate, I explained the way we were taught to value our parents and their care, to understand that they were not obligated to give us care. She would always shake her head, laughing all the while, and say, "Missy, you will learn that it's different here, that we think differently." She was right. Soon, I lived alone, like the one Mormon student who kept to himself as he made a concentrated effort to remain true to his religious beliefs and values. Later in graduate school I found that classmates believed "lower class" people had no beliefs and values. I was silent in such discussions, disgusted by their ignorance.

Carol Stack's anthropological study, *All Our Kin,* was one of the first books I read which confirmed my experiential understanding that within black culture (especially among the working class and poor, particularly in southern states), a value system emerged that was counterhegemonic, that challenged notions of individualism and private property so important to the maintenance of white-supremacist, capitalist patriarchy. Black folk created in marginal spaces a world of community and collectivity where resources were shared. In the preface to *Feminist Theory: from margin to center,* I talked about how the point of difference, this marginality can be the space for the formation of an oppositional world view. That world view must be articulated, named if it is to provide a sustained blueprint for change. Unfortunately, there has existed no consistent framework for such naming. Consequently both the experience of this difference and documentation of it (when it occurs) gradually lose presence and meaning.

Much of what Stack documented about the "culture of poverty," for example, would not describe interactions among most black poor today irrespective of geographical setting. Since the black people she described did not acknowledge (if they recognized it in theoretical terms) the oppositional value of their world view, apparently seeing it more as a survival strategy determined less by conscious efforts to oppose oppressive race and class biases than by circumstance, they did not attempt to establish a framework to transmit their beliefs and values from generation to generation. When circumstances changed, values altered. Efforts to assimilate the values and beliefs of privileged white people, presented through media like television, undermine and destroy potential structures of opposition.

Increasingly, young black people are encouraged by the dominant culture (and by those black people who internalize the values of this hegemony) to believe that assimilation is the only possible way to survive, to succeed. Without the framework of an organized civil rights or black resistance struggle, individual and collective efforts at black liberation that focus on the primacy of self-definition and self-determination often go unrecognized. It is crucial that those among us who resist and rebel, who survive and succeed, speak openly and honestly about our lives and the nature of our personal struggles, the means by which we resolve and reconcile contradictions. This is no easy task. Within the educational institutions where we learn to develop and strengthen our writing and analytical skills, we also learn to think, write, and talk in a manner that shifts attention away from personal experience. Yet if we are to reach our people and all people, if we are to remain connected (especially those of us whose familial backgrounds are poor and working-class), we must understand that the telling of one's personal story provides a meaningful example, a way for folks to identify and connect.

Combining personal with critical analysis and theoretical perspectives can engage listeners who might otherwise feel estranged, alienated. To speak simply with language that is accessible to as many folks as possible is also important. Speaking about one's personal experience or speaking with simple language is often considered by academics and/or intellectuals (irrespective of their political inclinations) to be a sign of intellectual weakness or even antiintellectualism. Lately, when I speak, I do not stand in place—reading my paper, making little or no eye contact with audiences— but instead make eye contact, talk extemporaneously, digress, and address the audience directly. I have been told that people assume I am not prepared, that I am anti-intellectual, unprofessional (a concept that has everything to do with class as it determines actions and behavior), or that I am reinforcing the stereotype of black people as nontheoretical and gutsy.

Such criticism was raised recently by fellow feminist scholars after a talk I gave at Northwestern University at a conference on "Gender, Culture, Politics" to an audience that was mainly students and academics. I deliberately chose to speak in a very basic way, thinking especially about the few community folks who had come to hear me. Weeks later, Kum-Kum Sangari, a fellow participant who had shared with me what was said when I was no longer present, and I engaged in quite rigorous critical dialogue about the way my presentation had been perceived primarily by privileged white female academics. She was concerned that I not mask my knowledge of theory, that I not appear anti-intellectual. Her critique compelled me to articulate concerns that I am often silent about with colleagues. I spoke about class allegiance and revolutionary commitments, explaining that it was disturbing to me that intellectual radicals who speak about transforming society, ending the domination of race, sex, class, cannot break with behavior patterns that reinforce and perpetuate domination, or continue to use as their sole reference point how we might be or are perceived by those who dominate, whether or not we gain their acceptance and approval.

This is a primary contradiction which raises the issue of whether or not the academic setting is a place where one can be truly radical or subversive. Concurrently, the use of a language and style of presentation that alienates most folks who are not also academically trained reinforces the notion that the academic world is separate from real life, that everyday world where we constantly adjust our language and behavior to meet diverse needs. The academic setting is separate only when we work to make it so. It is a false dichotomy which suggests that academics and/ or intellectuals can only speak to one another, that we cannot hope to speak with the masses. What is true is that we make choices, that we choose our audiences, that we choose voices to hear and voices to silence. If I do not speak in a language that can be understood, then there is little chance for dialogue. This issue of language and behavior is a central contradiction all radical intellectuals, particularly those who are members of oppressed groups, must continually confront and work to resolve. One of the clear and present dangers that exist when we move outside our class of origin, our collective ethnic experience, and enter hierarchical institutions which daily reinforce domination by race, sex, and class, is that we gradually assume a mind-set similar to those who dominate and oppress, that we lose critical consciousness because it is not reinforced or affirmed by the environment. We must be ever vigilant. It is important that we know who we are speaking to, who we most want to hear us, who we most long to move, motivate, and touch with our words.

When I first came to New Haven to teach at Yale, I was truly surprised by the marked class divisions between black folks—students and professors—who identify with Yale and those black folks who work at Yale or in surrounding communities. Style of dress and self-presentation are most often the central markers of one's position. I soon learned that the black folks who spoke on the street were likely to be part of the black community and those who carefully shifted their glance were likely to be associated with Yale. Walking with a black female colleague one day, I spoke to practically every black person in sight (a gesture which reflects my upbringing), an action which disturbed my companion. Since I addressed black folk who were clearly not associated with Yale, she wanted to know whether or not I knew them. That was funny to me. "Of course not," I answered. Yet when I thought about it seriously, I realized that in a deep way, *I* knew them for they, and not my companion or most of my colleagues at Yale, resemble my family. Later that year, in a black women's support group I started for undergraduates, students from poor backgrounds spoke about the shame they sometimes feel when faced with the reality of their connection to working-class and poor black people. One student confessed that her father is a street person, addicted to drugs, someone who begs from passersby. She, like other Yale students, turns away from street people often, sometimes showing anger or contempt; she hasn't wanted anyone to know that she was related to this kind of person. She struggles with this, wanting to find a way to acknowledge and affirm this reality, to claim this connection. The group asked me and one another what we do to remain connected, to honor the bonds we have with working-class and poor people even as our class experience alters.

Maintaining connections with family and community across class boundaries demands more than just summary recall of where one's roots are, where one comes from. It requires knowing, naming, and being ever-mindful of those aspects of one's past that have enabled and do enable one's self-development in the present, that sustain and support, that enrich. One must also honestly confront barriers that do exist, aspects of that past that do diminish. My parents' ambivalence about my love for reading led to intense conflict. They (especially my mother) would work to ensure that I had access to books, but would threaten to burn the books or throw them away if I did not conform to other expectations. Or they would insist that reading too much would drive me insane. Their ambivalence nurtured in me a like uncertainty about the value and significance of intellectual endeavor which took years for me to unlearn. While this aspect of our class reality was one that wounded and diminished, their vigilant insistence that being smart did not make me a "better" or "superior" person (which often got on my nerves because I think I wanted to have that sense that it did indeed set me apart, make me better) made a profound impression. From them I learned to value and respect various skills and talents folk might have, not just to value people who read books and talk about ideas. They and my grandparents might say about somebody, "Now he don't read nor write a lick, but he can tell a story," or as my grandmother would say, "call out the hell in words."

Empty romanticization of poor or working-class backgrounds undermines the possibility of true connection. Such connection is based on understanding difference in experience and perspective and working to mediate and negotiate these terrains. Language is a crucial issue for folk whose movement outside the boundaries of poor and working-class backgrounds changes the nature and direction of their speech. Coming to Stanford with my own version of a Kentucky accent, which I think of always as a strong sound quite different from Tennessee or Georgia speech, I learned to speak differently while maintaining the speech of my region, the sound of my family and community. This was of course much easier to keep up when I returned home to stay often. In recent years, I have endeavored to use various speaking styles in the classroom as a teacher and find it disconcerts those who feel that the use of a particular patois excludes them as listeners, even if there is translation into the usual, acceptable mode of speech. Learning to listen to different voices, hearing different speech challenges the notion that we must all assimilate—share a single, similar talk—in educational institutions. Language reflects the culture from which we emerge. To deny ourselves daily use of speech patterns that are common and familiar, that embody the unique and distinctive aspect of our self is one of the ways we become estranged and alienated from our past. It is important for us to have as many languages on hand as we can

know or learn. It is important for those of us who are black, who speak in particular patois as well as standard English to express ourselves in both ways.

Often I tell students from poor and working-class backgrounds that if you believe what you have learned and are learning in schools and universities separates you from your past, this is precisely what will happen. It is important to stand firm in the conviction that nothing can truly separate us from our pasts when we nurture and cherish that connection. An important strategy for maintaining contact is ongoing acknowledgement of the primacy of one's past, of one's background, affirming the reality that such bonds are not severed automatically solely because one enters a new environment or moves toward a different class experience.

Again, I do not wish to romanticize this effort, to dismiss the reality of conflict and contradiction. During my time at Stanford, I did go through a period of more than a year when I did not return home. That period was one where I felt that it was simply too difficult to mesh my profoundly disparate realities. Critical reflection about the choice I was making, particularly about why I felt a choice had to be made, pulled me through this difficult time. Luckily I recognized that the insistence on choosing between the world of family and community and the new world of privileged white people and privileged ways of knowing was imposed upon me by the outside. It is as though a mythical contract had been signed somewhere which demanded of us black folks that once we entered these spheres we would immediately give up all vestiges of our underprivileged past. It was my responsibility to formulate a way of being that would allow me to participate fully in my new environment while integrating and maintaining aspects of the old.

One of the most tragic manifestations of the pressure black people feel to assimilate is expressed in the internalization of racist perspectives. I was shocked and saddened when I first heard black professors at Stanford downgrade and express contempt for black students, expecting us to do poorly, refusing to establish nurturing bonds. At every university I have attended as a student or worked at as a teacher, I have heard similar attitudes expressed with little or no understanding of factors that might prevent brilliant black students from performing to their full capability. Within universities, there are few educational and social spaces where students who wish to affirm positive ties to ethnicity—to blackness, to working-class backgrounds—can receive affirmation and support. Ideologically, the message is clear—assimilation is the way to gain acceptance and approval from those in power.

Many white people enthusiastically supported Richard Rodriguez's vehement contention in his autobiography, *Hunger of Memory,* that attempts to maintain ties with his Chicano background impeded his progress, that he had to sever ties with community and kin to succeed at Stanford and in the larger world, that family language, in his case Spanish, had to be made secondary or discarded. If the terms of success as defined by the standards of ruling groups within white-supremacist, capitalist patriarchy are the only standards that exist, then assimilation is indeed necessary. But they are not. Even in the face of powerful structures of domination, it remains possible for each of us, especially those of us who are members of oppressed and/or exploited groups as well as those radical visionaries who may have race, class, and sex privilege, to define and determine alternative standards, to decide on the nature and extent of compromise. Standards by which one's success is measured, whether student or professor, are quite different for those of us who wish to resist reinforcing the domination of race, sex, and class, who work to maintain and strengthen our ties with the oppressed, with those who lack material privilege, with our families who are poor and working-class.

When I wrote my first book, *Ain't I A Woman: black women and feminism,* the issue of class and its relationship to who one's reading audience might be came up for me around my decision not to use footnotes, for which I have been sharply criticized. I told people that my concern was that footnotes set class boundaries for readers, determining who a book is for. I was shocked that many academic folks scoffed at this idea. I shared that I went into working-class black communities as well as talked with family and friends to survey whether or not they ever read books with footnotes and found that they did not. A few did not

know what they were, but most folks saw them as indicating that a book was for college-educated people. These responses influenced my decision. When some of my more radical, college-educated friends freaked out about the absence of footnotes, I seriously questioned how we could ever imagine revolutionary transformation of society if such a small shift in direction could be viewed as threatening. Of course, many folks warned that the absence of footnotes would make the work less credible in academic circles. This information also highlighted the way in which class informs our choices. Certainly I did feel that choosing to use simple language, absence of footnotes, etc. would mean I was jeopardizing the possibility of being taken seriously in academic circles but then this was a political matter and a political decision. It utterly delights me that this has proven not to be the case and that the book is read by many academics as well as by people who are not college-educated.

Always our first response when we are motivated to conform or compromise within structures that reinforce domination must be to engage in critical reflection. Only by challenging ourselves to push against oppressive boundaries do we make the radical alternative possible, expanding the realm and scope of critical inquiry. Unless we share radical strategies, ways of rethinking and revisioning with students, with kin and community, with a larger audience, we risk perpetuating the stereotype that we succeed because we are the exception, different from the rest of our people. Since I left home and entered college, I am often asked, usually by white people, if my sisters and brothers are also high achievers. At the root of this question is the longing for reinforcement of the belief in "the exception" which enables race, sex, and class biases to remain intact. I am careful to separate what it means to be exceptional from a notion of "the exception."

Frequently I hear smart black folks, from poor and working-class backgrounds, stressing their frustration that at times family and community do not recognize that they are exceptional. Absence of positive affirmation clearly diminishes the longing to excel in academic endeavors. Yet it is important to distinguish between the absence of basic positive affirmation and the longing for continued reinforcement that we are special. Usually liberal white folks will willingly offer continual reinforcement of us as exceptions— as special. This can be both patronizing and very seductive. Since we often work in situations where we are isolated from other black folks, we can easily begin to feel that encouragement from white people is the primary or only source of support and recognition. Given the internalization of racism, it is easy to view this support as more validating and legitimizing than similar support from black people. Still, nothing takes the place of being valued and appreciated by one's own, by one's family and community. We share a mutual and reciprocal responsibility for affirming one another's successes. Sometimes we have to talk to our folks about the fact that we need their ongoing support and affirmation, that it is unique and special to us. In some cases we may never receive desired recognition and acknowledgement of specific achievements from kin. Rather than seeing this as a basis for estrangement, for severing connection, it is useful to explore other sources of nourishment and support.

I do not know that my mother's mother ever acknowledged my college education except to ask me once, "How can you live so far away from your people?" Yet she gave me sources of affirmation and nourishment, sharing the legacy of her quilt-making, of family history, of her incredible way with words. Recently, when our father retired after more than thirty years of work as a janitor, I wanted to pay tribute to this experience, to identify links between his work and my own as writer and teacher. Reflecting on our family past, I recalled ways he had been an impressive example of diligence and hard work, approaching tasks with a seriousness of concentration I work to mirror and develop, with a discipline I struggle to maintain. Sharing these thoughts with him keeps us connected, nurtures our respect for each other, maintaining a space, however large or small, where we can talk.

Open, honest communication is the most important way we maintain relationships with kin and community as our class experience and backgrounds change. It is as vital as the sharing of resources. Often financial assistance is given in circumstances where there is no meaningful contact.

However helpful, this can also be an expression of estrangement and alienation. Communication between black folks from various experiences of material privilege was much easier when we were all in segregated communities sharing common experiences in relation to social institutions. Without this grounding, we must work to maintain ties, connection. We must assume greater responsibility for making and maintaining contact, connections that can shape our intellectual visions and inform our radical commitments.

The most powerful resource any of us can have as we study and teach in university settings is full understanding and appreciation of the richness, beauty, and primacy of our familial and community backgrounds. Maintaining awareness of class differences, nurturing ties with the poor and working-class people who are our most intimate kin, our comrades in struggle, transforms and enriches our intellectual experience. Education as the practice of freedom becomes not a force which fragments or separates, but one that brings us closer, expanding our definitions of home and community.   [1989]

Understanding the Reading

1. Explain the conflict between hooks and her mother.
2. In what ways did hooks's working-class realities separate her from her fellow students at Stanford?
3. As a member of the Black working class, what cultural values are important to hooks?
4. Why is hooks perceived to be anti-intellectual?
5. Why were hooks's parents ambivalent about her reading?
6. Explain the author's attitude about language and academic practices (like footnotes).
7. Why does hooks believe it is important to retain the values of the class she was born into?

Suggestions for Responding

1. Do you agree with hooks that it is important to retain the values of one's origins? Why or why not?
2. Why do you think hooks was able to survive and thrive by her move into the middle class? ◆

32

Daddy Tucked the Blanket

RANDALL WILLIAMS

About the time I turned 16, my folks began to wonder why I didn't stay home anymore. I always had an excuse for them, but what I didn't say was that I had found my freedom and I was getting out.

I went through four years of high school in semirural Alabama and became active in clubs and sports; I made a lot of friends and became a regular guy, if you know what I mean. But one thing was irregular about me: I managed those four years without ever having a friend visit at my house.

I was ashamed of where I lived. I had been ashamed for as long as I had been conscious of class.

We had a big family. There were several of us sleeping in one room, but that's not so bad if you get along, and we always did. As you get older, though, it gets worse.

Being poor is a humiliating experience for a young person trying hard to be accepted. Even now—several years removed—it is hard to talk about. And I resent the weakness of these words to make you feel what it was really like.

We lived in a lot of old houses. We moved a lot because we were always looking for something just a little better than what we had. You have to understand that my folks worked harder than most people. My mother was always at home, but for her that was a full-time job—and no fun, either. But my father worked his head off from the time I can remember in construction and shops. It was hard, physical work.

I tell you this to show that we weren't shiftless. No matter how much money Daddy made, we never made much progress up the social ladder. I got out thanks to a college scholarship and because I was a little more articulate than the average.

I have seen my Daddy wrap copper wire through the soles of his boots to keep them together in the wintertime. He couldn't buy new boots because he had used the money for food and shoes for us. We lived like hell, but we went to school well-clothed and with a full stomach.

It really is hell to live in a house that was in bad shape 10 years before you moved in. And a big family puts a lot of wear and tear on a new house, too, so you can imagine how one goes downhill if it is teetering when you move in. But we lived in houses that were sweltering in summer and freezing in winter. I woke up every morning for a year and a half with plaster on my face where it had fallen out of the ceiling during the night.

This wasn't during the Depression; this was in the late 60's and early 70's.

When we boys got old enough to learn trades in school, we would try to fix up the old houses we lived in. But have you ever tried to paint a wall that crumbled when the roller went across it? And bright paint emphasized the holes in the wall. You end up more frustrated than when you began, especially when you know that at best you might come up with only enough money to improve one of the six rooms in the house. And we might move out soon after, anyway.

The same goes for keeping a house like that clean. If you have a house full of kids and the house is deteriorating, you'll never keep it clean. Daddy used to yell at Mama about that, but she couldn't do anything. I think Daddy knew it inside, but he had to have an outlet for his rage somewhere, and at least yelling isn't as bad as hitting, which they never did to each other.

But you have a kitchen which has no counter space and no hot water, and you will have dirty dishes stacked up. That sounds like an excuse, but try it. You'll go mad from the sheer sense of futility. It's the same thing in a house with no closets. You can't keep clothes clean and rooms in order if they have to be stacked up with things.

Living in a bad house is generally worse on girls. For one thing, they traditionally help their mother with the housework. We boys could get outside and work in the field or cut wood or even play ball and forget about living conditions. The sky was still pretty.

But the girls got the pressure, and as they got older it became worse. Would they accept dates knowing they had to "receive" the young man in a dirty hallway with broken windows, peeling wallpaper and a cracked ceiling? You have to live it to understand it, but it creates a shame which drives the soul of a young person inward.

I'm thankful none of us ever blamed our parents for this, because it would have crippled our relationships. As it worked out, only the relationship between our parents was damaged. And I think the harshness which they expressed to each other was just an outlet to get rid of their anger at the trap their lives were in. It ruined their marriage because they had no one to yell at but each other. I knew other families where the kids got the abuse, but we were too much loved for that.

Once I was about 16 and Mama and Daddy had had a particularly violent argument about the washing machine, which had broken down. Daddy was on the back porch—that's where the only water faucet was—trying to fix it and Mama had a washtub out there washing school clothes for the next day and they were screaming at each other.

Later that night everyone was in bed and I heard Daddy get up from the couch where he was reading. I looked out from my bed across the hall into their room. He was standing right over Mama and she was already asleep. He pulled the blanket up and tucked it around her shoulders and just stood there and tears were dropping off his cheeks and I thought I could faintly hear them splashing against the linoleum rug.

Now they're divorced.

I had courses in college where housing was discussed, but the sociologists never put enough emphasis on the impact living in substandard housing has on a person's psyche. Especially children's.

Small children have a hard time understanding poverty. They want the same things children from more affluent families have. They want the same things they see advertised on television, and they don't understand why they can't have them.

Other children can be incredibly cruel. I was in elementary school in Georgia—and this is interesting because it is the only thing I remember about that particular school—when I was about eight or nine.

After Christmas vacation had ended, my teacher made each student describe all his or her Christmas presents. I became more and more uncomfortable as the privilege passed around the room toward me. Other children were reciting the names of the dolls they had been given, the kinds of bicycles and the grandeur of their games and toys. Some had lists which seemed to go on and on for hours.

It took me only a few seconds to tell the class that I had gotten for Christmas a belt and a pair of gloves. And then I was laughed at—because I cried—by a roomful of children and a teacher. I never forgave them, and that night I made my mother cry when I told her about it.

In retrospect, I am grateful for that moment, but I remember wanting to die at the time.[1975]

Understanding the Reading

1. How did Williams feel about his life as a child? Why?
2. Why did Williams's parents fight?
3. How did Williams's parents really feel about each other?
4. What impact do peers and the media have on impoverished children?

Suggestions for Responding

1. Write a short essay describing why you think Williams's parents finally divorced.
2. Research how problems of poverty and homelessness are solved in other modern industrial nations. How do their rates of poverty compare to ours? ✦

33

"We're Not Bums"

PETER SWET

For more than three years, Gerald Winterlin, now in his 40s, was one of the estimated 3 million homeless Americans. Forced by joblessness to live in his car or abandoned buildings, he had to cope with a sense of hopelessness and despair that could, and occasionally did, destroy others like himself.

Now he lives in a warm, modest apartment near the University of Iowa, where he's a scholarship student working on his degree in accounting and maintaining a 3.9 average. I traveled to Iowa to speak with him, hoping to understand how this bright, well-spoken, typical-seeming American could ever have hit such a deep low in his life. Just as important, I wanted to know how he fought his way back.

On the first of two long nights we would spend talking together, the burly Winterlin sat at his kitchen table and recalled an incident that still haunts him.

"I was on the cashier's line at a supermarket," he began, "behind this young, healthy-looking black woman. When her groceries were rung up, she pulled out a bunch of food stamps. I said, 'Hey, get a job. I'm tired of having money taken from my paycheck for people like you!' I expected a sharp answer, but instead she looked embarrassed and said, 'There's nothing I'd like better than a job, but nobody will give me one.' 'Bull,' I shot back, then turned away. Twenty years later, I'd love to find that lady and tell her I'm sorry. Little did I realize that what happened to her could happen to anyone. It happened to me."

Winterlin was born in an area known as the Quad Cities, encompassing Davenport and Bettendorf on the Iowa side of the Mississippi River, with Rock Island and Moline on the Illinois side. One of four children of a tool-and-die man, he graduated from Bettendorf High and eventually began work at the International Harvester plant. "I worked there about eight years," he said, "till '82, after the farm recession hit. Quad Cities is a world center for manufacturing farm equipment, and over 18,000 people, including me, were laid off."

"At first we figured the government would help," he said, adjusting his large framed glasses. "Hell, they bailed out Chrysler, right? But, instead, weeks turned into months with no work. With only two or three weeks of unemployment left, my demands dropped real fast, from $15 an hour to begging to sweep floors—anything. One day I just picked up the phone book and started with the A's. I made a list of every company I applied to. The final number was 380, and I remember realizing that what few jobs there were went to younger people. Still, I'd go out all day looking."

Winterlin heaved a deep sigh and glanced out the window at the cold Iowa night. "I kept thinking there'd be a tomorrow. Late one night, I finally said, 'Well, Gerry, this is it. No tomorrow.' I packed what I hadn't already sold or pawned and walked out. I never planned on living in my car for long," he added, "but then, no one *plans* to be homeless."

What about his family—couldn't they help? "They'd have probably taken me in," he said, "but people who ask that don't understand how impossible it is to say, 'Hey, folks, here I am in my late 30s, such a pathetic loser I can't even take care of myself.' Besides, my old man had lost his own job after 25 years, just six months shy of a full pension."

I asked about welfare, and Winterlin laughed. "Don't get me started on that," he said. "Welfare is the fast route to nowhere. They give you everything except what you need—a job. Some people have no option, like women with kids, but guys like me who want just enough to get started again would rather freeze than fall into a system that gives you a roof but robs you of hope. You trade your individualism and spirit for survival, and for some of us that's not a fair trade. Homeless people are proud people too."

For months, Winterlin lived in his '60 Mercury with rags stuck in the rust holes. Finally, the car died, and he was forced to find shelter wherever he could. "Somehow I made it from day to day," he said. "I tried to look as good as I could, to keep clean. Sometimes I did odd jobs, but never enough to put a roof over my head. I kept trying, but before I knew it, three years of my life were gone."

"Unless you've been there, you can't understand the loneliness, the misery, the humiliation, the self-disgust at what you've been reduced to," Winterlin continued. "I knew guys who just couldn't take it anymore and did themselves in. We're talking big, proud men, not junkies or drunks. They killed themselves, but I say they died of broken hearts because they couldn't handle the way people look at you, the loss of self-respect."

We both fell silent for a moment, then I asked how he had managed to persevere. "When times got darkest," Winterlin answered, "when thoughts of death and feelings of hatred began to overwhelm me, I thought of the people in my life who have known how to give, not just take. One of them was Linda, the girl I should have married. I wish I could name all the others, but the good people know who they are. It's for them that I wanted to succeed."

"Anyway," he added, "I read about something called the Dislocated Workers Program, which was designed to help people from old, dying industries become trained in new technologies. They put me into Scott Community College in the Quad Cities. I got straight A's. Everything looked great, then the program was cut back after six months. I almost fell apart, but because my grades were so good a woman named Mary Teague took the time to care, to help me piece together enough funding to keep going."

I noted the framed scholarship certificates displayed proudly on the wall, and Winterlin smiled, putting a hand up to conceal the spaces where he'd once been forced to pull his own teeth. "No big secret to that," he laughed. "Just plain hard work." He studies 50 hours a week, besides attending classes and working 20 hours at a part-time job. He has no friends, he admitted, and spends weekends alone. "I know it wasn't my fault, but when you're homeless you lose so much self-respect, you stay away from people." I asked if he felt his fellow Americans understood the homeless problem.

"The thing most people *don't* understand," he replied, "is that most of the folks you see huddled in doorways in Eastern cities or living in parks in Santa Monica or begging for a roof right here in America's Heartland aren't there by *choice*. I didn't ask to lose my job. None of us did. We're not bums," he said pointedly, his voice rising. "We're good, hardworking Americans who happened to fall between the cracks."

How does he see his future? He hopes that, after receiving his degree, "at least one person out there will say, 'Hey, I hire a person by what he's got, not by his age or where he has been.'" He added, "I've got to prove I can be part of society again, that Gerald Winterlin and the millions of other homeless out there really do count. There are just five words I'm determined to leave behind me—words that no one can ever, ever take away from me. The words are 'Gerald Winterlin, summa cum laude.'"   [1990]

Understanding the Reading

1. What beliefs underlie Winterlin's confrontation with the woman in the supermarket?
2. How did Winterlin initially respond to unemployment?
3. Why didn't he turn to his family for help or go on welfare?
4. Why do some homeless men commit suicide?
5. Why may Winterlin escape his homelessness permanently? What obstacles does he face?

Suggestions for Responding

1. Winterlin says that the welfare system "robs you of hope." In what ways does Gore's story illustrate this point?
2. Imagine that you, like Winterlin, were suddenly made homeless due to unemployment. Describe the difficulties you would face, especially the obstacles to pulling yourself out of it on your own. ✦

34

Poverty or at Home in a Car

JACKIE SPINKS

For seven months, my home has been my 1973 Dodge van. Life in a car is similar to life in a garbage can: trash filled, cramped, and with a smell to die from. Before that, I lived in a shed. I live here because I was kicked out of the shed.

Guys, suited in black worsted, the authority clothes of caliphs-in-waiting, circle around me; avoiding eye contact.

Sometimes I wonder what's going through their minds when they see me? Do they ever wonder what's going through mine? Or do they give a damn? Or maybe they assume I don't have a mind? Or are they thinking, "Bum! Loser! What's the matter with you? There's work out there. It isn't a recession. You corks think you're too good to work. So okay, be a stiff, but why do I have to support you, and why do you dirty up nice streets? Where's your pride? Where's your work ethic?"

Yeah, I pretty much know them. But they don't know me from marmalade. So here's to making my acquaintance.

I'm one of those seedy guys at the bottom of America's class system, who knows that he's going to stay there. I'm not taken in by that "rags to riches" hooey our teachers, parents, media, in fact, the whole culture, fed us. I am 40-years old, and have not earned more than $20,000 in my entire life, which means I've lived on less than $100 a month, for the past 20 years. So I know, after all this time, I'm not going anywhere.

Before I go on I'd better forewarn you: I'm not a curator of America's art of scrimping, a chronicler of poverty's abasements, or a bemoaner of its inequality. I'm just a down-and-outer trying to puzzle out my life, figure out how guys like me get where they are, especially when they don't have the excuse of alcohol or dope for their downward spiral.

I sold my Yamaha for $100 and bought this beater I'm living in for $75. Pretty lucky break. I got it for $75 because the interior was gutted, the windows broken, the roof rusted through. It was ready for the compactor, so nobody bid on it at the city auction. Thus, I have a home—my first in a long time.

I tinkered with it and got it moving. The reverse gear needs money to fix, so I can only go forward. The back brakes are bad (more money) and I worry driving, because of the brakes. So I don't drive it far. Besides, I have to hang onto my space, where my car's parked. But every once in a while I take a spin around the block just to keep my beater alive, as who knows when the local Praetorians will hustle me off. They'll give me a ticket for something, probably driving without registration. The constabulary knows and hates me. Not only am I an outcast, but being only five and a half feet tall, I'm an easy nab.

Mostly I stay where I am. What's important is keeping my corner. Three other guys have found my spot and are now parked near me. If I move my car, they'll grab it, as it is the best space, so I protect my claim. It's particularly valuable to me, as it's the only place where I can move forward and don't need to go into reverse.

It's a challenge, living in a crouched position in my van: minus toilet, water, telephone, electricity, and privacy. But the toughest part is the temperature: 95 degrees in the summer and freezing in winter.

I eat at the mission. Before I forced myself to check out the place (I was afraid of it), I lived on stuff like vanilla wafers, nachos, half-eaten pizzas, or sandwiches I found lying around.

Why the mission spooked me was, first, it was strange; and second, a lot of beefy guys with nothing to lose hung around the entrance. I had no weapon, no back-up, and there's always some guy hankering to beat up a little guy. On the one hand, poverty makes brutes, but on the other hand, people are poor because they're basically passive. Telling myself they all just want to be somebody and have you recognize it, I stiffened my mettle.

Nevertheless, just to avoid trouble, I smiled. I'm the kind of guy who smiles a lot, tells jokes, shows he's a regular guy. But I confess the adrenaline was pumping, and a rigid smile was shellacked on my face when I ambled cool, but not cocky, into the mission. It smelled like fat frying, a good smell, and the eating space was big—a high-ceilinged room with about 80 guys and 2 women sitting at long tables.

A lot of the guys were Mexican farmworkers, all talking in Spanish. They had serious faces. A couple years back, I climbed on a field bus and for about two weeks, picked strawberries. Those people were fast, about four times as fast as me. A little girl about 10 picked faster than I ever could—if I lived to be 100. I watched her to figure out her method. She'd kind of hold the bush and pull three or four berries at one reach. And did it with miniature fingers, that didn't crush the berries—such ingenuity wasted on a berry bush. She said she wanted a house and three kids when she grew up.

The food at the mission will never disturb McDonald's, but it fills me up and that's what counts. For instance, on my first day, they gave us two choices: bean soup or venison soup. We have a lot of deer hunters in this part of the country and most of them dislike venison, so the mission gets a lot of venison.

Most of the guys chose venison soup, but I chose bean soup. I'm a vegetarian, more by necessity than by conviction, but I think going without meat is a good idea. Besides, I have a soft spot for deer.

The mission, also, gets a lot of good pastries, the kind you buy at a bakery, usually about a week old. I eat a lot of doughnuts. You can take them with you when you leave. Sometimes we have ripe bananas. Sometimes we even have salad.

Often the food at the mission is spoiled, but nobody reports it, as it's better to be sick than risk closure. The bathroom, which is next to the kitchen, has been without toilet paper or paper towels for months. Four of the six toilets don't flush and nobody mops or uses cleanser, so you can figure it's a shopping mall of microbes, but nobody expects Trump Towers. Often I puke. Once, I did it for two days, but as one guy said, "How do you know it was the food at the mission. It could have been the flu."

Illness is for the rich. The poor that try to join that club, get two minutes and a swift heave-ho. It's been 20 years since I've been to a doctor. A few weeks back, I drove a guy with a severed finger to emergency, and sat with some mothers, who said they'd been waiting three hours. The mothers held their sick kids and scolded the others.

Many of the guys at the mission are here illegally. Nervous. Worried about trouble, too. Like me. And they're dirty. Like me. I can't speak Spanish, maybe a few words like "por favor, como esta, adios, and gracias." Wish I knew more. A big regret—flunking Spanish in high school. Their English is better than my Spanish, but still hard to understand. So mostly we just smile at one another.

My little forays into conversation with mission Saxons usually consist of mutual brag-a-thons. You'd think we'd all just dumped our portfolios with our brokers and decided to do a little slumming. And, if not that, we all have ships that will be tooting in, around the bend, any minute.

According to all of us displaced whites (I gas along with the best), we just need a little capital to get started. Some of the guys have pretty good ideas. One guy, a wood carver, thought he'd make Sasquash dolls and sell them at local fairs and bazaars. Another guy built a toilet for car dwellers, but fearing theft of his idea, was cagey in explaining how it operated. I listened up on that one. Then his paranoia took over, and he clammed up. Another had an idea for paper blankets.

It's all just talk. Nobody will ever do anything. To build up our self-esteem, we peg ourselves as 20th century pariahs, like frontier sheep farmers. We perceive ourselves as urban pioneers staking our claims, front runners of things to come. We carve out places, on the street, protect our turf, think of ourselves as prototypes of those guys who straggled over the Cascades without a penny to their names: sometimes desperate, often lonely, frequently surviving by their wits. They were giants. Stoics. Squatters like us. Our heroes. Deep in all of us, we mourn not having been born in the 18th century. Because we believe (probably incorrectly), that then poverty was a clean and honorable estate, not just wacko actions and fantasizing, like it is today.

How does a homeless, jobless, middle-aged man occupy his day? Well, first off, I sleep. Besides sleeping I post myself in the library. I arrive at opening time, ten in the morning, and stay most of the day. It's cool in there. Air conditioned. But temperature is only a minor reason I like the library. The main reason is the people. The people are quiet. No one bothers me or tells me to move on.

I read everything: religion, carpentry, mechanics, electrical, police training, political, biographies, nutrition, baseball novels, and a lot of gun, boat, news, and alternate press magazines. Sometimes I walk along the docks, examine the boats, imagine stowing away on a Russian cargo ship.

I scrutinize, with the eye of a tourist: buildings, factories, guys working—and I especially like to study bees. When I've exhausted looking, I sit in my car and read.

How do I live? Well, I use a can for my bowels and dump my loo near some pole beans and tomatoes in a garden nearby. I expected big beans and red, ripe tomatoes in that spot, but to my surprise they're limping along. One of my fellow car-dwelling aficionados said, "Living on the streets, you probably got toxic crap." I do my "miss congeniality" smile, but don't think it's funny. I don't think he meant it to be funny. I used recycled newspaper for toilet paper.

I mosey up to the college about once a month and sneak a shower in the college gym. I'm careful to use it when it's empty, shower as quickly as possible, just in case I get caught.

Probably the biggest problem for guys like me is water. I'm always looking for water. Every chance I get, I fill up a jug I carry everywhere in my backpack and haul it back to my Dodge.

And that's strictly for drinking—not to wash hands, face, dishes, or clothes.

Apart from begging, the thing about poor people that riles rich people the most is our grime. Cleanliness is identified with goodness in America. It's next to Godliness. Dirt is evil. I think we're supposed to clean up and pretend we're real. I don't oppose cleanliness. It's that cleanliness for someone living in a car is a labyrinthine ordeal.

First, to wash and dry two loads of clothes—it costs about $5.00 total. Plus, you need a way to get to the laundry; plus, you need soap; plus, you need something to wear while you're washing the clothes.

But now and then a car-dwelling paisano does spiff up. Once cleaned up, he isn't too bad. I wonder why I've been going on ad nauseam about cleanliness and appearance? I just have some insecurity there. But then, so when aren't we insecure?

As for work, in my 20s when hope bloomed, I choo-chooed along, the little engine that could—but not anymore. Now, it's "tote that barge, lift that bail, wish to hell I could land in jail." I've worked for bosses that were drill sergeants with little concern about their oxen's safety, who expected it to plow away at minimum pay. I got chemical burns on my hands that ate away chunks of the flesh, burns that still eat my fingers ten years later. I have no hope for anything better than a grinding $4.60 an hour.

A guy at the mission said, "I'd rather be poor than work. Why should I help make the rich richer?"

I'm anxious all the time. Until I found the mission, I worried constantly about where my next meal was coming from; I was anxious about my future; anxious about people. But mostly I was anxious that if—by some remote possibility I landed a decent job—that after so many years of non-work, with its absence of punctuality, drive, and concentration, I would fail again.

Hey, I sound like the mother of all bellyachers, bitching about contaminated food, cleanliness, jobs, pisspots, anxiety. I forget the other class has troubles, too; that they whip themselves, unmercifully, if some friend gains on them. That if their cash flow falls from ten million to two million, they worry they're finished and stumble home,

get swacked, and feel like they'll never be a real player.

I heard some social worker-type talk about homelessness being a new deviant career. Sure am glad I have a career at last. Deviant or otherwise. Is homelessness better than being male, white, 40, and working at McDonalds? Yeah, I guess so, but then, Hell, McDonalds wouldn't hire a bum like me—even if he did have nice teeth.

The inner awareness I live with and fight every day is that I'm nothing. To get rid of this feeling, I'd like to try Prozac. But two bucks for a pill, without a buzz. Then again, maybe I'm lucky. At some later date, they'd probably discover Prozac caused some kink, like edema of the brain, or elephantiasis, or more likely, an old stand-by like high blood pressure or cancer. They always find some pea to stick in our comfort zone. So I sleep Prozacless.

Because I sleep a lot, the books I've read label me depressed. I question that, as I've never contemplated suicide; but maybe I am depressed and don't know it. Or maybe I sleep because I'm bored. About the only truism about poverty in America in the 1990s is that it's one giant yawn.

Maybe that's what depression is—nothing to do. Rutsville. And doing the rut alone, at ebb tide, and feeling it's all your fault. That everything's your fault. Feeling something's wrong with you because you would rather be poor than be under the foot of a master. So who wants to think. Better to sleep.

About our depression, whenever you channel onto a poor person's wave, male or female, what you discover is that—underneath the defenses, they're thinking, "There's something haywire with me. I'm worse than second-rate, I'm rotten. I can't do anything right. Nobody will ever hire a creep like me for any job that has a future. I'll never do anything that's even slightly smart."

To illustrate, a guy at the mission, came out from lunch and found the side of his Kawasaki dented. A few minutes before he'd been chair of the brag-a-thon. Now, you'd expect the guy to say, "I'm gonna kill the bastard who did this." But no, all this poor jerk could do was stare and mutter, "It's all my fault. I can't do anything right."

We all walked away, but it hit close. We understood.

In contrast to Americans, who place so much emphasis on individualism, people from other countries don't blame themselves. A Hindu cab driver, so black that he felt forced to reiterate three times, to our inquiring minds, that he was Caucasian, told us about an experience he had here. He was sitting in a park and noticed several Americans going over to a marble protrusion, bending over it, and when water gushed out, drinking. Being thirsty, he went over to the protrusion, bent over it, but no water came out. He bent over it several times, still no water. Finally, he walked away, telling himself even the water over here in America is prejudiced.

Now that's what we considered an intelligent response, the kind we wish we could make.

It's like the world has a negative image of us, so we absorb that image, make it ours, and agree with the world, that, yes, because we aren't successes, we're slime.

Yeah, we're lazy. The dictionary definition of lazy is slow moving, resistant to exertion, slothful. And gadzooks, the perfect definition of depression.

Those active, employed people, who run around doing this and that, who talk briskly, walk with that high-stepping gait, who complain about having too much on their calendar, who, after a quick handshake, dash off to another appointment, are as strange to us as a bidet. We watch, and wonder, and shuffle off, when we're around them. I guess they don't understand us either; the passive, the depressed, the underclass. Yet, we all share the same boat and it's gaining water. And maybe we know it better than they do.

Whatever. So, I sleep about 11 or 12 hours a day. Wish it were the sleep of the frazzled or anesthetized, but it's a half awake sleep. When awake I contemplate ways to make our world better. On good days, I dream of a revolution in concept. On bad days I decide, "Blow 'er up. Start over."

As I lie here, watching the rain drip alongside the car window, I forage around for something positive to say about poverty. What I come up with is freedom. Yeah, I have freedom—no worry about stocks or kids or lovers. I click around the idea of freedom for a while and finally decide, next to a high IQ, freedom is the most over-rated quality any sociologist ever extolled.   [1996]

Understanding the Reading

1. Describe Spinks's life in his van.
2. What does he think about eating at the mission?
3. How do Saxons at the mission talk? Why?
4. How does Spinks occupy his day? Why?
5. How does he take care of his sanitary needs?
6. How do poor people respond to negative occurrences in their lives?

Suggestions for Responding

1. Write a paper explaining why you do or do not believe in the "rags to riches" proposition.
2. Imagine you were homeless and describe how you would cope with that situation. ✦

SUGGESTIONS FOR RESPONDING TO PART III

1. Most of the writers in Part III discuss in one way or another how family values and attitudes, language, leisure activities, manners, dress, possessions, and education influence and reflect socioeconomic class. Describe how your socioeconomic class was reflected in such features during your own childhood and youth. Since socioeconomic class is strongly influenced by race and ethnicity, some of your considerations may overlap.

Careful thinking should help you sort out the economic factors and come to a fuller understanding of another of the complex factors that shape your identity.

2. If you no longer live in the socioeconomic class into which you were born, consider how and why the change took place. In what ways have you retained the influences of your earlier class experience? What characteristics, behaviors, and values of that class have you

rejected, either consciously or unconsciously? Evaluate the strengths of both classes.

3. In recent years, homelessness has become a severe problem throughout the country. Research the manifestations of homelessness in your region. What are the estimated number and proportion of homeless people? What demographic categories—such as gender, age, racial and ethnic groupings—do they represent? To what causes can your local homelessness problem be attributed? What programs, both governmental and private sector ones, exist to assist homeless people? What additional services are needed?

SUGGESTIONS FOR RESPONDING TO IDENTITY

Apply the concepts you have explored in "Identity" to write an autobiographical report about how your present identity has been shaped by your race and ethnicity, your gender, and your economic class.

Power in its simplest sense means the ability to do, act, think, and behave as we like, to have control over our own lives. Because we are members of society as well as individuals, however, there are substantial restrictions on our ability to exercise this kind of personal power. Society influences who we are, what we can do, how we act, what we believe or think about, and—central to our purposes here—how we interact with others.

Most interpersonal relationships reflect the relative power of the individuals involved, and the individual with the greater power can exercise greater control. We derive power from our capacity to distribute rewards or punishment, from being liked or admired, or from our position of authority or expertise. If, for example, John is more in love with Shelby than she with him, she can exercise power over him, deciding where they go for dinner or how often they go out. She can reward him with her company or punish him by refusing to see him. Similarly, you may proofread a paper more carefully for a professor you like than for one whose lectures you find boring. Physicians and plumbers have power over their clients who need their expert services. However, not all social power differentials are determined by or are under the control of the individual.

Our society is organized **hierarchically;** that is, it is structured according to rank and authority, and power is distributed unevenly within this hierarchy. Moreover, membership in a particular group, in and of itself, tends either to enhance or to reduce one's power because some groups of people have more power and others have less. Access to power and our place in the social hierarchy both depend on a number of variable factors, including gender, race, sexual orientation, socioeconomic class, age, and religion.

In our society, men generally have more power than women, White people more power than people of color, heterosexuals more than homosexuals, wealthy people more than workers, and so on. The intersection of these hierarchies confers the greatest social power on the group at the "top" of each scale: White heterosexual men *as a group*. Their power relative to other groups both rests on and reflects their greater wealth, more prestigious positions, and greater access to information and education. Thus, even though individual men may be relatively powerless (a gardener employed by a wealthy widow, for instance), *as a group* White, heterosexual men are better able to control their own lives, to influence and control others, and to act in their own interests.

People who have established power under any social system find it beneficial to retain that system and maintain the status quo. The interests and needs of members of less powerful social groups are not relevant to their goals. In fact, within any social system, mechanisms operate to **marginalize,** confine to the edges of society, and subordinate its less powerful members. This is often accomplished by projecting stereotypes onto others.

A **stereotype** is a set of assumptions and beliefs about the physical, behavioral, and psychological characteristics assigned to a particular group or class of people. If we know that someone belongs to a given group, we make other suppositions about that person by attributing to him or her those qualities and characteristics we associate with that group. Stereotypes exist for every class of people imaginable; they can be based on such identifiers as age, education, profession, regional origin, economic status, family role, interests, sexual orientation, and disability. Stereotypes assigned by gender, race and ethnicity, and socioeconomic class, however, are the ones most deeply embedded in our culture, and the ones that we examine in the "Power" division.

Even though we may not like to admit that we stereotype people, we all do it. Stereotyping makes it easier to function in a world filled with unknowns. We use the oversimplified and exaggerated generalizations of stereotypes to filter and interpret the complexities of reality. They provide us with an easy way to both respond to and interact with this often confusing world; they also provide a simplified way to structure our social relationships.

The trouble with stereotypes, however, is that the filter also blocks our perceptions. If we see people in terms of the standardized pictures we project onto a group to which they belong, we don't see or interact with them as individuals. Worse still, we usually block and deny any characteristics that don't fit our preconceived ideas. The word *stereotype* originally referred to the solid metal plate of type used in printing. This origin reveals the truth about stereotypes: Not only are they rigid and inflexible, but they also perpetuate unchanging images.

Although some stereotypes may seem harmless enough, in general, stereotyping is hardly a benign process. This is made clear by the fact that none of us likes to be pigeonholed. We actively resist seeing ourselves and those with whom we are intimate in stereotypic ways; we insist on our individuality. We apply stereotypes only to others—to those who are unknown to us or who are different from us. And herein lies the rub.

Because difference often makes us uneasy and because we tend to fear the unknown, our collective characterizations of "others" incorporate many undesirable or less valued traits or behaviors. This provides the basis for prejudice against members of those groups. Without knowledge of specific individuals or examination of how they present themselves, we make adverse judgments about them. We come to believe in their inferiority based solely on such traits as race, ethnicity, sex, class, age, disability, or sexual orientation. It is, in fact, a way of denying the inner life of that individual.

In "Power," we look at what happens when these **prejudices,** belief in the inferiority of people because of their membership in a certain group, are acted on. **Discrimination** is behavior that disadvantages one group in relation to another group and maintains and perpetuates conditions of inequality. In our culture, it is practiced most often against women, minority men, lesbians and gay men, and poor people. Both individuals and organizations can discriminate, either consciously or unconsciously, and discrimination can be **institutionalized,** built into the system. **Institutionalized discrimination** includes those policies, procedures, decisions, habits, and acts that overlook, ignore, or subjugate members of certain groups or that maintain control by one group of people over another group—lighter-skinned people over darker-skinned individuals or groups, men over women, heterosexuals over homosexuals, rich over poor. Such discrimination creates obstacles and barriers for its targets and provides unfair privileges for its beneficiaries.

In Part IV, "Power and Racism," we examine the experience of racism, discrimination against and subordination of a person or group because of color. Part V, "Power and Sexism," takes a comparable look at discrimination against men and women in our society and the corollary mistreatment of lesbians and gays. We also focus on the power of the federal government, as they argue about women's rights in cases of violence within domestic relations. In Part VI, "Power and Classism," we consider the impact of socioeconomic class in the United States, focusing on the forces that cause economic inequities and poverty. Part VII, "Race, Class, and Gender after 9/11 and Post-Katrina," shows a time of crisis in the United States that crystallizes many of the ideas that we are exploring in this text.

We like to think of America as a place of liberty, equality, and justice for all, but, as the readings in "Power" document, this ideal has yet to be realized. Racism, sexism, and classism, as we will see, are intertwined and augment and reinforce one another. Moreover, they are not simply problems for minorities, women, and people who are economically disadvantaged; they are, as a bumper sticker declares, "a social disease." The more fully each of us understands these problems, the closer we all will be to finding a cure.

IV
Power and Racism

RACISM IS NOT SIMPLY A BLACK AND WHITE ISSUE; IT IS the subordination of any person or group because of skin color or other distinctive physical characteristics. As discussed in the introduction to Part I, racial identity is not as fixed and immutable as we think. It is a **social construct**—a classification based on social values—that could be said to exist only in the eye of the beholder. At one point or another, many different peoples have been considered to be racial groups—Jews, Irish, Italians, Poles, Latinas, Latinos, Native Americans, Asian Americans, and African Americans—and have been subjected to racist treatment.

With few exceptions, Americans agree that racism is a bad thing, but there is less consensus about precisely what racism is or how it actually operates. The U.S. Commission on Civil Rights identifies two levels of racism. The first, **overt racism,** is the use of color and other visible characteristics related to color as subordinating factors. The roots of overt racism lie in our national history: the institution of slavery, the belief in the "manifest destiny" of European Americans to rule the entire North American continent, and the sense of America as a Christian nation, to name just three.

These beliefs provided the basis for and justification of racially discriminatory laws, social institutions, behavior patterns, language, cultural viewpoints, and thought patterns. Even after the Civil War and the abolition of slavery, new

segregationist laws and practices, known as **Jim Crow,** extended overt racism against African Americans into the middle of the twentieth century. Shifting federal policies—such as removals, termination of tribal status, Indian boarding schools—greatly harmed much of the Native American culture and population. Exclusionary immigration laws and **restrictive covenants,** excluding members of certain groups from living in specified areas, limited the opportunities of Jews and Asian Americans.

The civil rights movement of the 1950s and 1960s awakened most White Americans to the evils of overt racism. However, this change of attitude by itself has been inadequate to address the residual racial inequities that survive in the second level of racism, indirect institutional subordination. More subtle, often invisible, **institutionalized racism** does not explicitly use color as the subordinating mechanism. Instead, decisions are based on such other factors as skill level, residential location, income, and education—factors that appear to be racially neutral and reasonably related to the activities and privileges concerned.

In reality, however, such practices continue to produce racist inequities because they fail to take into account the problems created by a 300-year history of overt racist practices. For example, having a parent with insufficient job training is likely to mean that a child will grow up poor and attend poor schools, without access to sufficient job training, leading to another generation of deprivation and poverty. In this way, no matter how unintentionally, a wide variety of policies, procedures, decisions, habits, attitudes, actions, and institutional structures perpetuate racism—the subordination and subjugation of people of color.

Part IV examines the behavioral extension of racial prejudice: racial discrimination. One can be **prejudiced,** believing in the inferiority of certain kinds of individuals based on their membership in a certain group, but not **discriminate,** not act on those beliefs. As stated earlier, discrimination is individual, organizational, or structural behavior that disadvantages one group in relation to another group and that maintains and perpetuates conditions of inequality for members of the disadvantaged group.

Reading 35, "The 2000 Presidential Election in Black and White" by Frank Louis Rusciano, discusses how Blacks and Whites in America perceive the 2000 presidential election differently. The results raise questions about the legitimacy of the election, the courts, and the political system as a whole. Reading 36 brings us to an analysis done by the Pew Research Center on blacks' observations about black progress since President Obama has been elected. In Reading 37, the U.S. Commission on Civil Rights reports on immigration policies, codified in a series of racial exclusion orders beginning with the 1882 Chinese Exclusion Act, which was extended to 1924 to Japanese, Koreans, Burmese, Malayans, Polynesians, Tahitians, and New Zealanders. Unfortunately, as the report makes clear, these were not the only immigration laws enacted for racist purposes. Reading 38 by Barbara Franz brings us up to date with immigration laws since 1980. The following two articles (Readings 39 and 40) explore the impact of immigration raids on children and the increasing hate violence towards Hispanic immigrants.

Next, Reshma Baig (Reading 41) brings us into the world of a second grader, recently immigrated, and attending school in Queens, New York. More currently, in Reading 42 Gloria Yamato writes of the various expressions of racism she has had to endure, but she also provides some concrete suggestions for steps that individuals, both Whites who want to be allies of people of color and people of color who are working through internalized racism, can take to combat racism. Then, Peggy McIntosh (Reading 43) looks at the other side of the coin as she examines the invisible privileges that light-skinned people enjoy simply because of their skin color, and she recommends the extension of those positive advantages to all people.

Readings 44, 45, 46, and 47 consider racist treatment to which Native Americans have been and continue to be subjected. As Michael Dorris reports, the federal government has consistently initiated policies that regulate and restrict Native Americans, despite legal treaties between the Indian nations and the U.S. government. Even today, Native Americans face continued encroachments on their rights. In "Urban Indians," by Roberta Fiske-Rusciano, we learn of the history of the U.S. government's attempt to speed up the process of assimilation of American Indians, by enticing them to leave their communities and relocate to large U.S. cities. Although relocation of the 1950s was a failure, Indians from many tribal nations have found a place, permanently or seasonally, in America's largest cities, often forming large communities of kin.

Carol Lee Sanchez (Reading 46) shows how, over the past 150 years, novels, movies, and even children's games have negated the humanity of American Indians. She also offers five actions non-Indians can take to counteract the stereotypes—to everyone's benefit. On a subtler level, as Ward Churchill argues in Reading 47, the exploitation of Indian names, images, and symbols by mainstream society is racist and degrading and should be eliminated.

In Reading 48 Robert Cherry reviews the various theories that historians have offered to explain one manifestation of religion-based racism: the widespread anti-Semitism of the late nineteenth and early twentieth centuries.

Next, Elizabeth Martinez (Reading 49) passionately argues for our country to acknowledge that many groups besides African Americans are subjected to overt racism, especially, she says, Latinos. Since the population will be 32 percent Latino, Asian/Pacific American, and Native American by the year 2050, we need greater knowledge of, understanding of, and openness to learning about all ethnic groups if we are to work together as a society and live in harmony.

Most of us know the shameful episode in our national history when 40,000 Japanese aliens and 70,000 Japanese American citizens were evacuated from the entire West Coast to inland relocation camps during World War II. John Hersey's detailed narrative (Reading 50) makes clear the racism implicit in that policy. As Asian Americans understand, even being assigned a positive stereotype is damaging; in Reading 51 Robert Daseler demonstrates how the 30-year-old claim that they are the "model minority" is destructive to Asian Americans, as well as to other minority groups, which are compared with them.

Reading 52, by Benjamin Quarles, considers anti-Black racism in the latter part of the nineteenth century. After the Civil War, the abolition of slavery, and the enfranchisement of African American males, the dominant segment of society used a variety of tactics to continue the oppression of the former slaves. Well into the twentieth century, African Americans were subjected to random acts of violence intended to intimidate them and to enforce their "Jim Crow" inferiority.

Next, Greg Palast and Martin Luther King III, in "Jim Crow Revived in Cyberspace" (Reading 53), discuss the computerized purges of voter rolls as a threat to minority voters. In Reading 54 Earl Ofari Hutchinson reviews how sociologists, theologians, journalists, and other intellectual leaders purportedly "proved" the inferiority of the Negro race, especially its males.

Teenager Emmett Till was one of more than 40 people murdered between 1955 and 1968 in Mississippi and Alabama by White terrorists who wanted to "set an example" to Blacks and civil rights workers. As the Southern Poverty Law Center reports in Reading 55, Till was murdered and mutilated because he "thought he was as good as any White man."

Today, overt racism may be generally unacceptable, but David K. Shipler (Reading 56) describes how echoes of racist beliefs remain current in our society and result in the subtle racism that continues to disadvantage Black citizens. In Reading 57 Robert Anthony Watts describes similar experiences that Blacks are perpetually subjected to, regardless of their achievements.

Racism continues to exist in our society because the subordination of people of color benefits those who do the subordinating. These psychological, economic, and political benefits will be reduced if racism is eliminated. However, the social costs of excluding a substantial proportion of our population from full participation in society—contributing to as well as benefiting from its bounty—are immense. Hearing the voices of those subjected to racism gives us fuller and more sympathetic insight into the problem. Even those of us who personally reject overt racism still need to work to loosen its less visible institutionalized tentacles.

35

The 2000 Presidential Election in Black and White

Frank Louis Rusciano

"We really don't have a racial problem in this country any more. We're all getting along better. Things aren't like they used to be."

Unfortunately, we have deluded ourselves to believe everything is okay now. And then when things happen like the Rodney King uprising in L.A. or the O.J. trial, suddenly this sort of ugly sore that is the foundation of our country surfaces. And we do our best and want immediately to try to ignore it and hope it goes away, because everything's better now and there isn't discrimination like there used to be . . . [but then something happens] and brings this ugly sore, this boil that exists right to the surface and we really don't want to deal with it. [We say] Johnny Cochran played the race card, and I ask, "What deck did he deal this card from? It was a deck that was stacked by White America." . . . We do have a problem still with the way we make our decisions in this country and how they are based upon race. And we don't want to talk about it, and I want to talk about it, and I think that the more we talk about it, the better.

—Michael Moore, in a speech at Rider University, 1999

The different perceptions of the 2000 presidential election among blacks and whites underscore the racial divisions in our society. Beyond the documented irregularities of racial imbalances in the counting of votes, and beyond the "urban legends" about young blacks being held by police until the polls closed or campus voter registrations being ignored, there was fertile ground for the racial divisions in the United States to grow and be revealed.

There are three levels upon which we can see these divisions in American politics. The first level deals with support for a public official, which may increase or decrease due to their actions. Their popularity may be affected, but the legitimacy of their governance is never questioned. The second level deals with support for the administration or what we call "the regime." These attitudes are deeper and more important, as they deal with whether citizens feel the public official's governance is "legitimate"—i.e., whether he or she deserves support or obedience. The third level deals with support for the political system; these attitudes are the most crucial for a polity, since they reflect whether citizens consider our political institutions worthy, regardless of who happens to be occupying political office at any given time. Variations in support on the first level are commonplace in American politics; variations on the second level can be problematic for an administration, particularly at election time; variations on the third level may herald a crisis of legitimacy in the making.

The strange circumstances of the 2000 presidential election caused disruptions on all of these levels—and on all of these levels, the disruptions were greater within the black community than in the white community. On the first level, we may look at responses to the statement that "the country is more deeply divided on issues than in the past several years." Nearly 80% of blacks agreed, as compared with a little more than 60% of whites. The difference is not solely attributable to black Americans' overwhelming support for Al Gore, either. Even though George W. Bush received a lower percentage of the African American vote than Ronald Reagan did in 1980, this difference is not explained by partisanship; only 65% of white Democrats agreed with this statement.

This pattern is repeated with reference to the statement that "George W. Bush will not work hard to represent the interests of black Americans"; 70% of African Americans expressed this sentiment, compared with 28% of white Americans, and just over 50% of white Democrats. Finally, reactions to the election results also reflected the same pattern. African Americans were more likely to feel "bitter," "cheated" and "angry" about the election results than either white Americans or white Democrats.

Similar responses result when one moves to the next level of analysis, regarding questions of leadership and legitimacy. When asked if they believed George W. Bush "stole the election," a full 50% of African Americans agreed, as compared with only 14% of white Americans, and only 25% of white Democrats. Not surprisingly, this finding corresponds to responses on authority—40% of black Americans stated they "did not consider George W. Bush the legitimate President"; only 14% of whites, and 26% of white Democrats, gave this answer.

Finally, numerous measures suggest that this dissatisfaction carries over into basic questions about the operations of the electoral and political systems:

- African Americans were more likely to believe there was "Fraud involved" in the Florida voting; 64% expressed this opinion, as compared with 26% of whites, and 39% of white Democrats.
- African Americans were most likely to "believe that the system of voting in the United States discriminates against some people"; 76% expressed this opinion, as compared with 39% of whites, and 42% of white Democrats.
- African Americans were most likely to "have very little confidence in the way votes are cast and counted in the United States"; 51% expressed this opinion, as compared with 32% of white Americans, and 44% of white Democrats.
- African Americans were most likely to feel "the way votes are cast and counted in the United States needs major overhaul"; 43% expressed this view, as compared with 27% of white Americans, and 32% of white Democrats.
- African Americans were most likely to believe "permanent harm has been done to the United States by the election"; 68% expressed this view, as compared with 37% of white Americans, and 42% of white Democrats.

What is perhaps most disturbing about these results is that in most cases, even up to the critical systemic level, a majority of African Americans express a loss of faith in the system, while a majority of white Americans disagree. Further, this result cannot be explained just as sour grapes over the outcome of the election; there are similar, and significant, gaps in the perceptions of black Americans and white *Democrats,* both of whom overwhelmingly supported Al Gore in the 2000 race.

Why, then, do we find such differences in perception between black and white Americans? Part of the answer lies in the particular types of irregularities and inequalities that occurred in this election. As William Chafee, dean of Arts and Sciences at Duke University notes, "votes in predominantly black precincts were invalidated at a rate four to five times as great as was the case in white counties." Also, the dilapidated voting machines which were most likely to undercount ballots were three times more likely to be located in majority black districts. No doubt these two findings are at least somewhat related—African American votes were more likely to be undercounted because the black population was, in many cases, concentrated in poorer areas with malfunctioning voting equipment. Hence, one may argue, the differences were a matter of unfortunate happenstance, and not intentional discrimination. The black criticism of the system thus seems less justified.

The problem with this argument is that the principle of "equal protection" in the Fourteenth Amendment would seem to extend to these circumstances. Certainly, equal protection would appear to mandate a careful recount of these votes to make sure that social class did not combine with race to disenfranchise voters. After all, the reason why the poll tax was eliminated by constitutional amendment was to ensure that political equality did not depend upon one's economic resources.

Further, the Voting Rights Act would seem to support intervention to ensure the votes were counted. As noted in an editorial in *The New York Times* on December 12, 2000:

> The Voting Rights Act, enacted originally to rule out literacy tests and other efforts to keep blacks from the polls, *does not require evidence of conspiracy to keep minority voters away from the polls*. Instead, the law was designed to protect minority voters whenever they confront more difficulties than whites in trying to cast their votes. [emphasis added]

In effect, whether the disenfranchisement was intentional or not is irrelevant; all that matters is the result. If differential opportunities for casting or counting ballots exist, the Voting Rights Act and the equal protection clause are valid reasons for demanding legal relief. Why, then, were these votes not recounted?

The answer lies, in part, in the peculiar way in which the Supreme Court in 2000 had applied the equal protection clause with regard to race, even in the most important cases. As an editorial in *Time* magazine noted on December 18, 2000:

> The [Court has] not previously been receptive to pleas of unequal treatment in other areas, even when the most important rights are at stake. In *McCleskey v. Kemp,* for example, a black man on death row showed that capital punishment is administered without uniform standards from one jurisdiction to the next and is more often applied to blacks than whites for the same crime. But [the Court] held that this did not violate the Constitution.

The denial of equal protection would, in and of itself, be galling to African Americans in the 2000 election as it was in the *McCleskey* case. But here, the Court added insult to injury by invoking the equal protection clause as a *justification for stopping the vote count.* Its reasoning ran that without similar standards for hand counting votes, the equal protection clause barred any recounts in this fashion. Put another way, different standards for putting African Americans to death were not evidence of a violation of equal protection, but different standards that would allow black votes to be counted were a violation. It is no wonder distraught civil rights advocates were quoted in *Time* as pointing out "the irony that the conservative Justices, long reluctant to apply the [equal protection] law's protections to minorities, were eager to cite its protections when the victim was a wealthy white Ivy League political candidate." Indeed, the justices were even cautious to limit this decision explicitly to the case at hand, stating that their use of the equal protection clause was not a precedent, and was "limited to the present circumstances."

One would be naïve to assume that the particular manner in which the Court decided this case had nothing to do with black discontent about the outcome of the election. Certainly, critiques of this decision have been many and varied. Some have invoked the words of former chief justice Robert Jackson, who, in a case from a previous Court, wrote in a blistering dissent, "We are not final because we are infallible, but we are infallible because we are final." The problem here is that Court decisions are never final, first because their decisions form precedents for subsequent judgments, and second because the Court will continue to make decisions for a nation that looks to it as a fair and conscientious arbiter of the Constitution. For the Supreme Court, as with any political institution, our faith in its infallibility is based upon our acceptance of its decisions. And here African Americans have been offered little upon which to base this faith.

Upon this point, William H. Chafe of Duke University offers a cogent analysis:

> Was there an issue of "equal protection" in this election? It would seem so. Only it was not the one the Court identified. The smoldering ember in this election dispute is the likelihood that minority voters in 2000—as in 1876—will once again see themselves as the primary victims of an election they view as stolen. Probably not by coincidence, the dissenting justices in this case invoked the language of "disenfranchisement," and pointed to the degree that this ruling, like the *Dred Scott* decision, represented a "self-inflicted" wound for the Supreme Court.

The *Dred Scott* decision, as many no doubt remember, stated in 1857 that because slaves were property, a slave brought into a free territory was still a slave. By effectively eliminating the distinction between slave and free states, this decision made inevitable the Civil War, by proving Abraham Lincoln's statement that "A House divided against itself cannot stand for long; we cannot remain half-slave and half-free."

This is not to say, of course, that we are on the verge of another civil war due to this ruling. But the Court's decision in *Bush v. Gore* does indicate that it is no longer the institution invoked by Martin Luther King Jr. when he spoke of the highest court in the land as synonymous with the highest law of the land and the Constitution. No longer is the Court "the conscience of the nation," but rather an institution dedicated to "expediency" and "avoiding confusion" in making this decision.

However, such despair may not be justified. The Court does not have the last word as long as its legitimacy rests upon the acceptance of its citizens—especially when those citizens are a prominent minority like African Americans. The aftermath of the 2000 presidential election gave Americans something that was lacking in the presidential campaign, something that was sorely needed, but curiously absent. Listening to the commentary on this campaign as it occurred, it seemed as though we were facing the "Seinfeld" election—an election about nothing, in a time of peace and prosperity when our only concerns were our own self-centeredness. The aftermath of the campaign brought forth to us issues of equal protection for all Americans that belie this description, though. Now, in its aftermath, the election can be made to mean something of principle, by opening a debate about "equal protection" and why we all need it—not just the African Americans who question the legitimacy of a system that apportions it to the privileged.

Elections matter, not the least because they are the citizens' main line of defense for our common principles. One of our founding principles was restated in the Fourteenth Amendment, which extended the goals of the Declaration of Independence constitutionally to all Americans, regardless of race. Our capacity to elevate our institutions to positions of respect based upon their decisions ultimately rests upon our ability to reexamine and fulfill the meaning of equality. We may then begin to bridge the gap between black and white perceptions of our system that resulted from the perversion of this principle.   [2008]

Understanding the Reading

1. Describe the three levels of government legitimacy used in this article that measure the divisions in American politics.
2. What were the serious differences in public perception between Black and White voters in the 2000 presidential election?
3. What are the reasons for and consequences of these differences?

Suggestion for Responding

1. Have a class discussion about its perception of the legitimacy of U.S. presidential elections, U.S. courts, and the political system as a whole. ✦

36

Blacks Upbeat about Black Progress, Prospects: A Year after Obama's Election

PEW RESEARCH CENTER

Despite the state of the economy, blacks' assessments about the state of black progress in America have improved more dramatically during the past two years than at any time in the past quarter century, according to a comprehensive new nationwide Pew Research Center survey on race.

Barack Obama's election as the nation's first black president appears to be the spur for this sharp rise in optimism among African Americans. It may also be reflected in an upbeat set of black views on a range of other matters, including race relations, local community satisfaction and expectations for future black progress.

In each of these realms, the perceptions of blacks have changed for the better over the past two years, despite a deep recession and jobless recovery that have hit blacks especially hard.

The telephone survey was conducted from Oct. 28 to Nov. 30, 2009 among a nationally representative sample of 2,884 adults, including 812 blacks.

In some topic areas, the survey finds little change in black opinions. For example, four decades after the turmoil, triumphs and tragedies of the Civil Rights era, most blacks still doubt the basic racial fairness of American society. More than eight-in-ten blacks—compared with just over a third of whites—say the country needs to make more changes to ensure that blacks have equal rights with whites. Blacks also continue to lag behind whites in their satisfaction with their lives and local communities, and most remain skeptical that the police treat blacks and whites equally.

However, in the teeth of what may be the deepest recession since the Great Depression, nearly twice as many blacks now (39%) as in 2007 (20%) say that the "situation of black people in this country" is better than it was five years earlier, and this more positive view is apparent among blacks of all age groups and income levels. Looking ahead, blacks are even more upbeat. More than half (53%) say that life for blacks in the future will be better than it is now, while just 10% say it will be worse. In 2007,

A Sharp Spike in Blacks' Sense of Progress

% of blacks who say blacks are better/ worse off now than five years ago

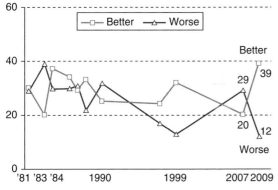

Note: Blacks include only non-Hispanic blacks. "Same" and "Don't know" responses not shown. Q20.

BLACKS MORE UPBEST ON MANY FRONTS % OF BLACKS WHO SAY . . .	2007	2009	change
	%	%	
Blacks are better off than five years ago	20	39	+19
Black-white standard of living gap is smaller than 10 years ago	41	56	+14
The future for blacks will be better	44	53	+9
They are "very satisfied" with local community	36	44	+8
Blacks and whites get along "very well" or "pretty well"	69	76	+7

Note: Blacks include only non-Hispanic blacks. Q20, Q21F1, Q54, Q1a & Q17c.

44% said things would be better for blacks in the future, while 21% said they would be worse.

A majority of blacks (54%) also report that Obama's barrier-breaking election has improved race relations in America; just 7% say it has made race relations worse. Whites, too, see progress on this front, though by much smaller margins. A plurality of whites (45%) say Obama's election has made no difference to race relations, while about a third (32%) say it has made things better and 15% say it has made race relations worse.

For both races, these appraisals are not as effusive as the expectations expressed immediately after the November 2008 election, when nearly half of white voters (48%) and three-quarters of black voters (74%) said they expected to see race relations improve during Obama's presidency.

As for Obama himself, one year into his presidency, his personal favorability rating runs well ahead of public support for his policies, though both have declined in the course of a year marked by highly partisan battles over his policy agenda. His support is higher among blacks than whites, but there is little to suggest that negative opinions about Obama among whites have been driven mostly by race. For example, only a small share of whites (13%) say Obama has been paying too much attention to the concerns of blacks.

And while whites who score low on an index of racial liberalism have much more negative views of Obama than do other whites, it is also the case that many whites with an unfavorable opinion of the president have more liberal racial views.[1]

MOST SEE A BLACK-WHITE CONVERGENCE ON VALUES, LIVING STANDARDS

In what may be some of the most intriguing findings of this survey, most blacks join with most whites in saying that the two racial groups have grown more alike in the past decade, both in their standard of living and their core values.

Seven-in-ten whites (70%) and six-in-ten blacks (60%) say that the values held by blacks and whites have become more similar in the past 10 years. Similarly, a majority of blacks (56%) and nearly two-thirds of whites (65%) say the standard of living gap between whites and blacks has narrowed in the past decade.

Compared with 2007, whites have changed little in either perception. But more blacks now say that the values of blacks and whites have become more similar (from 54% then to 60%

BLACKS AND WHITES SEE A RACIAL CONVERGENCE IN PAST DECADE		
	Whites	*Blacks*
In past ten years, have values of blacks and whites become more . . .		
	%	%
Similar	70	60
Different	1B	34
No change (vol,)	2	2
Don't know	9	3
Number of respondents	1447	812
In past ten years, Standard of living gap between blacks and whites has grown . . .		
	%	%
Wider	16	33
Narrower	65	56
No change (vol,)	8	5
Don't know	11	6
Number of respondents	734	418

Note: Whites include only non-Hispanic whites, Blacks include only non-Hispanic blacks. Q28 & Q22F2.

BLACK HOUSEHOLD INCOME AS A PERCENTAGE OF WHITE HOUSEHOLD INCOME	
Year	*(%)*
2008	61.8
2000	64.8
1989	61.5
1979	61.2
1969	56.7

Note: Whites include only non-Hispanic whites, Blacks include only non-Hispanic blacks.

today) and that the standard of living gap has narrowed (41% then, 56% now).

The changing views about the size of the black-white economic gap are all the more notable because they run counter to underlying economic realities. According to a widely-used indicator of a group's standard of living—median household income—blacks in this country have lost ground to whites since 2000, after having spent the previous three decades narrowing the gap (For details see page 62 in the full report).

BLACKS AND DISCRIMINATION: NO LONGER THE BIGGEST TARGET?

Blacks and whites continue to have very different views about the pervasiveness of discrimination against African Americans. Some 43% of blacks now say there is a lot of anti-black discrimination, about the same as in 2001. Among whites, just 13% see a lot of anti-black bias now, down from 20% in 2001.

Moreover, among whites some 21% say that Hispanics face a lot of discrimination. As a result, Hispanics have not only passed blacks as the nation's biggest minority group, they are also now seen by slightly more Americans as frequent targets of discrimination (23% vs. 18% for African Americans). This was not the case in 2001.

Fewer Americans see a lot of discrimination against three of four other demographic groups tested in this question: women (13%), whites (10%) and Asian-Americans (8%).

Which Group Faces Discrimination?

% saying that that each racial/ethnic group is discriminated against "a lot" in society today

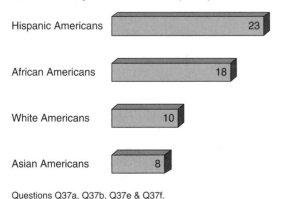

Questions Q37a, Q37b, Q37e & Q37f.

But many Americans see a lot of discrimination against another group tested: gays and lesbians. Nearly half (45%) of all Americans (and 55% of all blacks) say they face a lot of discrimination.

These findings are in sync with surveys taken over the last decade that show the public perceives substantial bias against gays and lesbians.[2]

Overall, blacks are much more inclined than whites to see discrimination against all groups tested, except whites.

The survey finds other sizable black-white racial gaps in perceptions of bias. As noted earlier, blacks are much more likely than whites to say that the police do not treat blacks the same as whites.

Has the Country Done Enough to Give Blacks Equal Rights with Whites?

% saying...

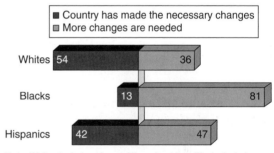

Note: Whites include only non-Hispanic whites. Blacks include only non-Hispanic blacks. Hispanics are of any race. "Don't know" and "neither/both" responses not shown, Q10.

They are also much more likely to say the country needs to continue to make changes to ensure blacks have equal rights with whites. Fully eight-in-ten blacks (81%) say so, compared with just over a third (36%) of whites.

But on a related question, a majority of blacks (52%) now say that blacks who cannot get ahead in this country are mainly responsible for their own situation, whereas only about a third (34%) say that racial discrimination is the main reason. Fifteen years ago, most blacks held the opposite view. Multiple surveys taken since 1994 show that this shift in blacks' perceptions has occurred in fits and starts over time, and that the change pre-dates the election of Obama.

Blacks' View of Why Many Blacks Don't Get Ahead

% of blacks saying...

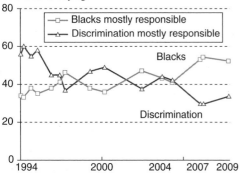

Note: In surveys in 2005 and earlier, blacks include Hispanic blacks, in the 2007 and later surveys, blacks include only non-Hispanic blacks,

Question wording: Which of these statements comes closer to your own views—even if neither is exactly right. Racial discrimination is the main reason why many black people can't get ahead these days, OR, Blacks who can't get ahead in this country are mostly responsible for their own condition, Q38.

Do You Think of Obama as Black or Mixed Race?

% saying...

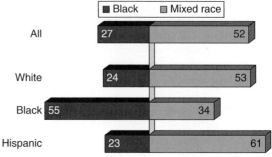

Note: Whites include only non-Hispanic whites. Blacks include only non-Hispanic blacks. Hispanics are of any race. "Don't know" and "both/neither" responses not shown.

Question wording: Do you mostly think of Obama as a black person or mostly as a person of mixed race? Q63.

RACIAL IDENTITY: DO THE OLD CATEGORIES STILL WORK?

From slavery to segregation to the civil rights era, the terms "black" and "white" have generally been regarded in this country as mutually exclusive. The simplicity of that classification scheme has served to obscure the racial mixing that has always been a part of the national tapestry.

It is not clear if the nation's racial lexicon will one day grow more nuanced. But several findings from this new Pew Research survey demonstrate that, at the very least, the old categories are hard-pressed to describe America's new demographic realities—and that public opinion has begun to take notice.

A particularly vivid challenge to the old categories comes from the bloodlines of the man who now lives in the White House—the son of an African father from Kenya and a Caucasian mother from Kansas.

Racially speaking, who is Barack Obama?

It depends on whom you ask. Offered a choice, most blacks (55%) say Obama is black, while about a third (34%) say he is mixed race. Among whites, the pattern is reversed. Most (53%) say he is mixed race, while just a quarter (24%) say he is black. Hispanics are even more inclined than whites to see him as mixed race; 61% do so.

There are only minor sub-group differences by age, education or income on this question. So race is the overriding factor that divides public opinion on the question of Obama's racial identity. But even within racial groups, there is considerable disagreement—witness the fact that only a bare majority of both blacks and whites agree among themselves.

Nor is Obama the only source of semantic confusion on the racial classification front. In this survey, when respondents were asked to state what race they are (black; white; Asian; some other race) and told they could choose as many categories as they wished, just 1% chose to identify with more than one category.[3] However, later in the same survey, when respondents were asked explicitly if they consider themselves to be of mixed race—fully one-in-six (16%) said they did, including 20% of blacks, 8% of whites and 37% of Hispanics.

In short, responses to racial identity questions vary widely depending on wording and context—a sign that the old classification scheme may be losing some of its descriptive power in a country that is rapidly growing more racially and ethnically diverse, and that is experiencing, from a small base, a sharp rise in interracial marriage. As of 2008, 8.1% of marriages in this country were between spouses of a different race, up from 3.2% in 1980, according to U.S. Census Bureau figures.[4]

INTERRACIAL MARRIAGE

Once a social and legal taboo in this country, interracial marriage is now widely accepted by Americans of all racial groups. In the Pew Research survey, about two-thirds of whites (64%) say they would be fine with a member of their family marrying a black person; an additional 27% say they would be bothered but would accept it.

Among blacks, eight-in-ten (80%) say it would be fine with them if a family member were to marry a white person, and another 16% say they would be bothered but would accept it. Just 6% of whites and 3% of blacks say they could not accept a black-white interracial marriage in their family.

Within both races, degrees of acceptance are higher among younger respondents than older ones.

Since 2001, acceptance of black-white interracial marriage has risen slightly among whites. It is still the case that more blacks than whites approve, but the black-white gap on this question has fallen from 31 percentage points in 2001 to 16 percentage points in 2009.

The survey finds that most Americans also are ready to accept intermarriage in their family if the new spouse is Hispanic or Asian. But there is one new spouse that most Americans would have trouble accepting into their families: someone who does not believe in God. Seven-in-ten people who are affiliated with a religion say they either would not accept such as marriage (27%) or be bothered before coming to accept it (42%).

OBAMA AND RACE

An overwhelming share of blacks—95%—have a favorable opinion of President Obama. This number has remained in the stratosphere among blacks throughout his first year in office. Among whites, however, Obama has seen his popularity ratings decline significantly—from a high of 76% just before he was inaugurated to 56% in the current survey. (Even so, Obama's personal favorability ratings continue to run ahead of public approval for his policies; his December Pew Research Center job approval rating among whites was 39% approve and 48% disapprove).

Marriage Across Racial and Ethnic Lines

% saying they will ___ if a member of the family were to marry...

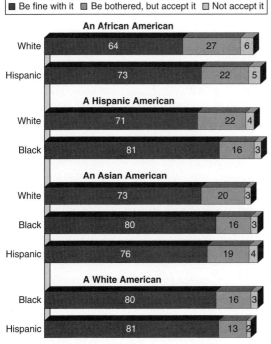

Note: Whites include only non-Hispanic whites. Blacks include only non-Hispanic blacks. Hispanics are of any race. "Don't know" responses not shown. Q50a, Q50b, Q50c &Q50d.

Opinion of Obama, by Race, 2007–2009

% who have a favorable opinion of Barack Obama

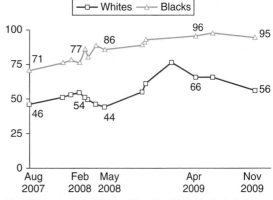

Note: Whites include only non-Hispanic whites. Blacks include only non-Hispanic blacks. Q5a.

Paralleling the near-unanimous black support for Obama is the near unanimous view among blacks that he shares the values and interests of black people; 61% of blacks say he shares "a lot" of values and interests with blacks and an additional 31% say he shares "some." These numbers are up from 2007 when, during the early stages of the Democratic nomination contest, some questioned whether the then long-shot candidate was "black enough." In a Pew Research survey taken in the fall of 2007, 42% of blacks said he shared "a lot" of the values and interests of black people, while an additional 33% said he shared "some."

The new survey finds that a year into Obama's presidency, few Americans of any race believe he has been favoring his black constituents over other groups. Just 13% of both whites and Hispanics and 1% of blacks say he is paying too much attention to the concerns of blacks.

A small share of all three groups (10% of whites and Hispanics, 13% of blacks) take the opposite view; that he is paying *too little* attention to the concerns of blacks. A majority of whites (57%) and Hispanics (60%), as well as 80% of blacks say he is paying the right amount of attention to blacks.

The survey findings suggest that blacks are disinclined to press race-based claims on Obama. The share who say the nation's first African-American president is paying too little attention to blacks is not as large as the share of blacks who say he is paying too little attention to the concerns of other groups, including labor unions (23%) and seniors (22%).

Both whites and Hispanics have more group-based complaints about Obama than blacks do. Fully 42% of Hispanics say he isn't paying enough attention to the concerns of Hispanics. And 22% of whites say he isn't paying enough attention to the concerns of whites.

There are also sharp racial and ethnic differences in perceptions about whether people who oppose Obama's policies are motivated to a significant degree by race. More than half of blacks (52%) say this, compared with 29% of Hispanics and just 17% of whites.

The survey also finds a striking shift in black opinions about Obama's principal opponent for the Democratic presidential nomination, Hillary

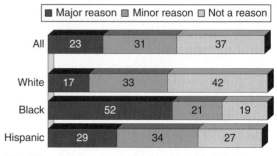

Is Race a Factor in Opposition to Obama's Policies?
% saying his race is a...

Legend: ■ Major reason ▨ Minor reason ☐ Not a reason

	Major reason	Minor reason	Not a reason
All	23	31	37
White	17	33	42
Black	52	21	19
Hispanic	29	34	27

Note: Whites include only non-Hispanic whites, Blacks include only non-Hispanic blacks. Hispanics are of any race. "Don't know" responses not shown. Q64.

Clinton. Going back to her years in the 1990s as First Lady, blacks have always held Clinton in very high regard, but her ratings plummeted in the spring of 2008, at the height of her political battle with Obama. At that time, about six-in-10 blacks viewed her favorably, down from about eight-in-ten at the beginning of 2008. However, she has since made up all that lost ground— and more. Her current favorability rating among blacks is 93%, virtually identical to that of Obama.

PROBLEMS IN BLACK COMMUNITIES AND FAMILIES

Blacks have long trailed whites in their level of satisfaction with their communities. This is still the case now, but the black-white gap on this question has narrowed in the past two years.

Overall, 44% of blacks say they are very satisfied with their local community as a place to live, compared with 52% of Hispanics and 64% of whites. Two years ago, just 36% of blacks were very satisfied with their community. During the same period, there was no substantial shift in community satisfaction among the other groups.

In response to a question about the problems facing black families, a majority of blacks rate not enough jobs (79%), drugs and alcoholism (74%), crime (67%) and poor public education (56%) as big problems.

Most blacks (61%) say churches are helping "a lot" to tackle these problems. But blacks are less impressed by the problem-solving role being played by community organizations (47%)

Problems Facing Black Families Today

% of blacks saying each is a big problem...

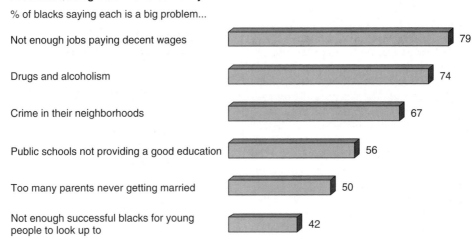

Not enough jobs paying decent wages — 79

Drugs and alcoholism — 74

Crime in their neighborhoods — 67

Public schools not providing a good education — 56

Too many parents never getting married — 50

Not enough successful blacks for young people to look up to — 42

Note: Blacks include only non-Hispanic blacks. Q43a–f.

Who is Helping Black Families?

% of blacks saying that each "helps a lot"

Churches — 61

Community organizations — 47

Black people themselves — 39

Government — 27

Note: Blacks include only non-Hispanic blacks. Q44a–d.

say they help a lot), black people themselves (39%) and the government (26%).

BLACKS, WHITES AND THE ECONOMY

When it comes to employment rates, blacks have been hit harder than whites by the recession and so-far jobless recovery. But when it comes to perceptions about the economy, the opposite is true: whites have turned sharply negative since the recession began, while black perceptions (starting from a more downbeat base) have held steady. For example, the

Whites, Blacks and the Recession: A Difference in Perspective

% saying national economy is excellent/good

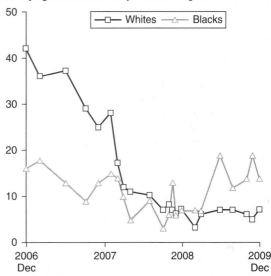

Note: Whites include only non-Hispanic whites. Blacks include only non-Hispanic blacks. Data from Pew Research Center for the People & the Press surveys.

share of whites who rate the national economy as excellent or good has plummeted from 42% in late 2006 to just 7% in late 2009. During this same period, black assessments barely budged—from 16% in December 2006 to 14% three years later.

The contrast is even more dramatic in perceptions about one's personal finances. The share of whites who rate their personal financial situation as excellent or good has declined during this period from 52% to 35%, while the share of blacks who rate their personal finances as excellent or good has changed very little (32% in late 2009, 27% in late 2006).   [2010]

Notes

1. The index of racial liberalism is based on three questions: perceptions of discrimination against blacks, acceptance of a family member's marriage to an African American, and perceptions of whether the U.S. has made all of the changes needed to ensure equal rights for blacks For details, see page 48 in the full report.
2. See, e.g., surveys by the National Conference for Community and Justice, January 2000 and January 2005.
3. Starting in 2000, the U.S. Census for the first time allowed people to identify with two or more races; 2.4% of the population did so in that decennial Census.
4. These figures include marriages between spouses of different races (white, black, Asian, Native American) and ethnicities (Hispanic and non-Hispanic).

Understanding the Reading

1. Why are black Americans generally optimistic in spite of the state of the economy in 2009?
2. Which two other demographic groups do whites and blacks agree face a lot of discrimination?
3. Describe the difference in perceptions between whites and blacks concerning the health of the economy and their own personal finances.

Suggestion for Responding

1. Choose two survey questions that interest you from this article and conduct your own campus poll. ✦

37

Historical Discrimination in the Immigration Laws

U.S. COMMISSION ON CIVIL RIGHTS

THE EARLY YEARS

During the formative years of this country's growth, immigration was encouraged with little restraint. Any restrictions on immigration in the 1700s were the result of selection standards established by each colonial settlement. The only Federal regulation of immigration in this period lasted only 2 years and came from the Alien Act of 1798, which gave the President the authority to expel aliens who posed a threat to national security.

Immigrants from northern and western Europe began to trickle into the country as a result of the faltering economic conditions within their own countries. In Germany, unfavorable economic prospects in industry and trade, combined with political unrest, drove many of its nationals to seek opportunities to ply their trades here. In Ireland, the problems of the economy, compounded by several successive potato crop failures in the 1840s, sent thousands of Irish to seaports where ships bound for the United States were docked. For other European nationals, the emigration from their native countries received impetus not only from adverse economic conditions at home but also from favorable stories of free land and good wages in America.

THE NATIVIST MOVEMENTS

As a result of the large numbers of Catholics who emigrated from Europe, a nativist movement began in the 1830s. It advocated immigration restriction to prevent further arrivals of Catholics into this country. Anti-Catholicism was a very popular theme, and many Catholics and Catholic institutions suffered violent attacks from nativist sympathizers. The movement, however, did not gain great political strength and its goal of curbing immigration did not materialize.

Immigrants in the mid-19th century did not come only from northern and western Europe. In China, political unrest and the decline in agricultural productivity spawned the immigration of Chinese to American shores. The numbers of Chinese immigrants steadily increased after the so-called Opium War, due not only to the Chinese economy, but also to the widespread stories of available employment, good wages, and the discovery of gold at Sutter's Mill,[1] which filtered in through arrivals from the Western nations.

The nativist movement of the 1830s resurfaced in the late 1840s and developed into a political party, the Know-Nothing Party.[2] Its western adherents added an anti-Chinese theme to the eastern anti-Catholic sentiment. But once again, the nativist movement, while acquiring local political strength, failed in its attempts to enact legislation curbing immigration. On the local level, however, the cry of "America for Americans" often led to discriminatory state statutes that penalized certain racially identifiable groups. As an example, California adopted licensing statutes for foreign miners and fishermen, which were almost exclusively enforced against Chinese.

In the mid-1850s, the Know-Nothing Party lost steam as a result of a division over the question of slavery, the most important issue of that time. The nativist movement and antiforeign sentiment receded because of the slavery issue and the Civil War. It maintained this secondary role until the Panic of 1873 struck.

CHINESE EXCLUSION

The depression economy of the 1870s was blamed on aliens who were accused of driving wages to a substandard level as well as taking away jobs that "belonged" to white Americans. While the economic charges were not totally without basis, reality shows that most aliens did not compete with white labor for "desirable" white jobs. Instead, aliens usually were relegated to the most menial employment.

The primary target was the Chinese, whose high racial visibility, coupled with cultural dissimilarity and lack of political power, made them more than an adequate scapegoat for the economic problems of the 1870s. Newspapers adopted the exhortations of labor leaders, blaming the Chinese for the economic plight of the working class. Workers released their frustrations and anger on the Chinese, particularly in the West. Finally, politicians succumbed to the growing cry for exclusion of Chinese.

Congress responded by passing the Chinese Exclusion Act of 1882. That act suspended immigration of Chinese laborers for 10 years, except for those who were in the country on November 17, 1880. Those who were not lawfully entitled to reside in the United States were subject to deportation. Chinese immigrants were also prohibited from obtaining United States citizenship after the effective date of the act.

The 1882 act was amended in 1884 to cover all subjects of China and Chinese who resided in any other foreign country. Then in 1888, another act was enacted that extended the suspension of immigration for all Chinese except Chinese officials, merchants, students, teachers, and travelers for pleasure. Supplemental legislation to that act also prohibited Chinese laborers from reentering the country, as provided for in the 1882 act, unless they reentered prior to the effective date of the legislation.

Senator Matthew C. Butler of South Carolina summed up the congressional efforts to exclude Chinese by stating:

> [I]t seems to me that this whole Chinese business has been a matter of political advantage, and we have not been governed by that deliberation which it would seem to me the gravity of the question requires. In other words, there is a very important Presidential election pending. One House of Congress passes an act driving these poor devils into the Pacific Ocean, and the other House comes up and says, "Yes, we will drive them further into the Pacific Ocean, notwithstanding the treaties between the two governments."

Nevertheless, the Chinese exclusion law was extended in 1892 and 1902, and in 1904 it was extended indefinitely.

Although challenged by American residents of Chinese ancestry, the provisions of these exclusion acts were usually upheld by judicial decisions. For example, the 1892 act mandated that Chinese laborers obtain certificates of residency within 1 year after the passage of the act or face deportation. In order to obtain the certificate the testimony of one credible white witness was required to establish that the Chinese laborer was an American resident prior to the passage of the act. That requirement was upheld by the United States Supreme Court in *Fong Yue Ting v. United States.*

LITERACY TESTS AND THE ASIATIC BARRED ZONE

The racial nature of immigration laws clearly manifested itself in further restrictions on prospective immigrants who were either from Asian countries or of Asian descent. In addition to extending the statutory life of the Chinese exclusion law, the 1902 act also applied that law to American territorial possessions, thereby prohibiting not only the immigration of noncitizen Chinese laborers from "such island territory to the mainland territory," but also "from one portion of the island territory of the United States to another portion of said island territory." Soon after, Japanese were restricted from free immigration to the United States by the "Gentleman's Agreement"[3] negotiated between the respective governments in 1907. Additional evidence would be provided by the prohibition of immigration from countries in the Asia-Pacific Triangle as established by the Immigration Act of 1917.

During this period, congressional attempts were also made to prevent blacks from immigrating to this country. In 1915 an amendment to exclude "all members of the African or black race" from admission to the United States was introduced in the Senate during its deliberations on a proposed immigration bill. The Senate approved the amendment on a 29 to 25 vote, but it was later defeated in the House by a 253 to 74 vote, after intensive lobbying by the NAACP.[4]

In 1917 Congress codified existing immigration laws in the Immigration Act of that year. That act retained all the prior grounds for inadmissibility and added illiterates to the list of those ineligible to immigrate, as a response to the influx of immigrants from southern and eastern Europe. Because of a fear that American standards would be lowered by these new immigrants who were believed to be racially "unassimilable" and illiterate,

any alien who was over 16 and could not read was excluded. The other important feature of this statute was the creation of the Asia-Pacific Triangle, an Asiatic barred zone, designed to exclude Asians completely from immigration to the United States. The only exemptions from the zone were from an area that included Persia and parts of Afghanistan and Russia.

The 1917 immigration law reflected the movement of American immigration policy toward the curbing of free immigration. Free immigration, particularly from nations that were culturally dissimilar to the northern and western European background of most Americans, was popularly believed to be the root of both the economic problems and the social problems confronting this country.

THE NATIONAL ORIGINS QUOTA SYSTEM

Four years later, Congress created a temporary quota law that limited the number of aliens of any nationality who could immigrate to 3 percent of the United States residents of that nationality living in the country in 1910. The total annual immigration allowable in any one year was set at 350,000. Western Hemisphere aliens were exempt from the quota if their country of origin was an independent nation and the alien had resided there at least 1 year.

The clear intent of the 1921 quota law was to confine immigration as much as possible to western and northern European stock. As the minority report noted:

> The obvious purpose of this discrimination is the adoption of an unfounded anthropological theory that the nations which are favored are the progeny of fictitious and hitherto unsuspected Nordic ancestors, while those discriminated against are not classified as belonging to that mythical ancestral stock. No scientific evidence worthy of consideration was introduced to substantiate this pseudoscientific proposition. It is pure fiction and the creation of a journalistic imagination. . . .
>
> The majority report insinuates that some of those who have come from foreign countries are nonassimilable or slow of assimilation. No facts are offered in support of such a statement. The preponderance of testimony adduced before the committee is to the contrary.

Notwithstanding these objections, Congress made the temporary quota a permanent one with the enactment of the 1924 National Origins Act. A ceiling of 150,000 immigrants per year was imposed. Quotas for each nationality group were 2 percent of the total members of that nationality residing in the United States according to the 1890 census. Again, Western Hemisphere aliens were exempt from the quotas (thus, classified as "nonquota" immigrants). Any prospective immigrant was required to obtain a sponsor in this country and to obtain a visa from an American consulate office abroad. Entering the country without a visa and in violation of the law subjected the entrant to deportation without regard to the time of entry (no statute of limitation). Another provision, prohibiting the immigration of aliens ineligible for citizenship, completely closed the door on Japanese immigration, since the Supreme Court had ruled that Japanese were ineligible to become naturalized citizens. Prior to the 1924 act, Japanese immigration had been subjected to "voluntary" restraint by the Gentleman's Agreement negotiated between the Japanese Government and President Theodore Roosevelt.

In addition to its expressed discriminatory provisions, the 1924 law was also criticized as discriminatory against blacks in general and against black West Indians in particular.

THE MEXICAN "REPATRIATION" CAMPAIGN

Although Mexican Americans have a long history of residence within present United States territory, Mexican immigration to this country is of relatively recent vintage. Mexican citizens began immigrating to this country in significant numbers after 1909 because of economic conditions as well as the violence and political upheaval of the Mexican Revolution. These refugees were welcomed by Americans, for they helped to alleviate the labor shortage caused by the First World War. The spirit of acceptance lasted only a short time, however.

Spurred by the economic distress of the Great Depression, federal immigration officials expelled hundreds of thousands of persons of Mexican descent from this country through increased Border Patrol raids and other immigration

law enforcement techniques. To mollify public objection to the mass expulsions, this program was called the "repatriation" campaign. Approximately 500,000 persons were "repatriated" to Mexico, with more than half of them being United States citizens.

EROSION OF CERTAIN DISCRIMINATORY BARRIERS

Prior to the next recodification of the immigration laws, there were several congressional enactments that cut away at the discriminatory barriers established by the national origins system. In 1943 the Chinese Exclusion Act was repealed, allowing a quota of 105 Chinese to immigrate annually to this country and declaring Chinese eligible for naturalization. The War Brides Act of 1945 permitted the immigration of 118,000 spouses and children of military servicemen. In 1946 Congress enacted legislation granting eligibility for naturalization to Filipinos and to races indigenous to India. A Presidential proclamation in that same year increased the Filipino quota from 50 to 100. In 1948 the Displaced Persons Act provided for the entry of approximately 400,000 refugees from Germany, Italy, and Austria (an additional 214,000 refugees were later admitted to the United States).

THE McCARRAN-WALTER ACT OF 1952

The McCarran-Walter Act of 1952, the basic law in effect today, codified the immigration laws under a single statute. It established three principles for immigration policy:

1. the reunification of families,
2. the protection of the domestic labor force, and
3. the immigration of persons with needed skills.

However, it retained the concept of the national origins system, as well as unrestricted immigration from the Western Hemisphere. An important provision of the statute removed the bar to immigration and citizenship for races that had been denied those privileges prior to that time. Asian countries, nevertheless, were still discriminated against, for prospective immigrants whose ancestry was one-half of any Far Eastern race were chargeable to minimal quotas for that nation, regardless of the birthplace of the immigrant.

"OPERATION WETBACK"

Soon after the repatriation campaign of the 1930s, the United States entered the Second World War. Mobilization for the war effort produced a labor shortage that resulted in a shift in American attitudes toward immigration from Mexico. Once again Mexican nationals were welcomed with open arms. However, this "open arms" policy was just as short lived as before.

In the 1950s many Americans were alarmed by the number of immigrants from Mexico. As a result, then United States Attorney General Herbert Brownell, Jr., launched "Operation Wetback," to expel Mexicans from this country. Among those caught up in the expulsion campaign were American citizens of Mexican descent who were forced to leave the country of their birth. To ensure the effectiveness of the expulsion process, many of those apprehended were denied a hearing to assert their constitutional rights and to present evidence that would have prevented their deportation. More than 1 million persons of Mexican descent were expelled from this country in 1954 at the height of "Operation Wetback."

THE 1965 AMENDMENTS

The national origins immigration quota system generated opposition from the time of its inception, condemned for its attempts to maintain the existing racial composition of the United States. Finally, in 1965, amendments to the McCarran-Walter Act abolished the national origins system as well as the Asiatic barred zone. Nevertheless, numerical restrictions were still imposed to limit annual immigration. The Eastern Hemisphere was subject to an overall limitation of 170,000 and a limit of 20,000 per country. Further, colonial territories were limited to 1 percent of the total available to the mother country (later raised to 3 percent or 600 immigrants in the 1976 amendments). The Western Hemisphere, for the first time, was subject to an overall limitation of 120,000 annually, although no individual

per-country limits were imposed. In place of the national origins system, Congress created a seven category preference system giving immigration priority to relatives of United States residents and immigrants with needed talents or skills. The 20,000 limitation per country and the colonial limitations, as well as the preference for relatives of Americans preferred under the former selections process, have been referred to by critics as "the last vestiges of the national origins system" because they perpetuate the racial discrimination produced by the national origins system.

RESTRICTING MEXICAN IMMIGRATION

After 1965 the economic conditions in the United States changed. With the economic crunch felt by many Americans, the cry for more restrictive immigration laws resurfaced. The difference from the 19th century situation is that the brunt of the attacks is now focused on Mexicans, not Chinese. High "guesstimates" of the number of undocumented Mexican aliens entering the United States, many of which originated from Immigration and Naturalization Service sources, have been the subject of press coverage.

As a partial response to the demand for "stemming the tide" of Mexican immigration, Congress amended the Immigration and Nationality Act in 1976, imposing the seven category preference system and the 20,000 numerical limitation per country on Western Hemisphere nations. Legal immigration from Mexico, which had been more than 40,000 people per year, with a waiting list 2 years long, was thus cut by over 50 percent.

RECENT REVISIONS OF THE IMMIGRANT QUOTA SYSTEM*

Although the annual per-country limitations have remained intact, Congress did amend the Immigration and Nationality Act in 1978 to eliminate the hemispheric quotas of 170,000 for Eastern Hemisphere countries and 120,000 for Western Hemisphere countries. Those hemispheric ceilings were replaced with an overall annual worldwide ceiling of 290,000.

In 1980 the immigrant quota system was further revised by the enactment of the Refugee Act. In addition to broadening the definition of refugee, that statute eliminated the seventh preference[5] visa category by establishing a separate worldwide ceiling for refugee admissions to this country. It also reduced the annual worldwide ceiling for the remaining six preference categories to 270,000 visas, and it increased the number of visas allocated to the second preference[6] to 26 percent. [1980]

Terms

1. SUTTER'S MILL: The site where gold was discovered in 1848, precipitating the California gold rush.
2. KNOW-NOTHING PARTY: A political movement in the mid-nineteenth century that was antagonistic to Catholics and immigrants.
3. GENTLEMAN'S AGREEMENT: The 1908 treaty between Japan and the United States to restrict, but not eliminate altogether, the issuance of passports allowing Japanese immigration to the United States, except that wives could enter, including "picture brides," who were married by proxy.
4. NAACP: National Association for the Advancement of Colored People.
5. SEVENTH PREFERENCE: Refugee status.
6. SECOND PREFERENCE: Spouses and unmarried children of U.S. citizens.

Understanding the Reading

1. What were the nativist movement and the Know-Nothing Party?
2. Explain the Chinese exclusion laws.
3. Explain the national origins quota system.
4. What was Operation Wetback?

---

* After the terrorist attacks on 9/11/01, the Immigration and Naturalization Service was folded into the Department of Homeland Security, whose main priority is to protect the country against attacks and to gather intelligence. The broad liberties given to the federal government by the Patriot Act have frightened many immigrants, who are afraid of being targeted, and have slowed down all immigration procedures.

5. How do the 1965 amendments perpetuate racial discrimination?

Suggestions for Responding

1. Explain what current immigration policy is and why you think it is good and/or bad.
2. Research and report on one law or policy that was mentioned in the article. ◆

38

Immigration Laws since 1980: The Closing Door

BARBARA FRANZ

Since the 1980s, both refugee and immigration status are becoming harder to attain in the United States. Refugee protection in the United States has changed from a Cold War foreign policy tool to a policy of refugee deterrence and institutionalized exclusion. Increasingly, refugees and displaced people must remain close to or in regions of civil or environmental distress. Often states have chosen to repatriate displaced populations to their areas of origin after the initial civil or environmental misery has receded. These patterns of exclusion are reflected in the 1996 Welfare and Illegal Immigration Reform and Immigration Control Acts.

Undocumented immigration has become a key issue in the U.S. immigration debate. Laws such as the 1986 IRCA [Immigration Reform and Control Act] and the 1990 Immigration Act, state-based referenda such as Proposition 187, the post 9/11 Department of Homeland Security (DHS) and Immigration and Customs Enforcement (ICE) schemes to deport thousands of illegal immigrants, and the current guest worker debate sought to officially limit entry and exclude "unwanted" clandestine newcomers. Even though entire industries could not survive without the labor of undocumented immigrants in the U.S., it appears Congress will soon pass another potentially highly ineffective legislation aiming to curb illegal immigration.

However, because clandestine immigration is a matter of labor surplus in underdeveloped regions and of labor demand in the prosperous regions of the world, little will change in the migration patterns of immigrants.

THE IMMIGRATION REFORM AND CONTROL ACT OF 1986

Legal immigration and refugee admissions remained a minor problem during the 1970s and 1980s. What concerned the U.S. public and government rather was the great number of undocumented immigrants. The increased number of illegal entrants at the Mexican-American border led to the creation of the Select Commission on Immigration and Refugee Policy (SCIRP) in 1978, which received increased public attention with the influx of 125,000 Cuban and 10,000 Haitian "boat people" by 1980. In its report, SCIRP called for deterring illegal immigration through better border enforcement and through civil and possibly criminal penalties on employers who knowingly hired unauthorized immigrants. Some proposals from the commission became part of a major congressional effort to amend the Immigration and Nationality Act in the 1980s and a new legislative assault was mounted that included for the first time in U.S. history employer sanctions.[1]

Although employer sanctions were at the heart of the Simpson-Mazzoli bill, it also provided for a new version of the existing H-2 visa program, which allowed for the admittance of aliens for temporary jobs. The bill was supported by *The New York Times,* which declared it was "not nativist, not racist, not mean" but "a rare piece of legislation, a responsible immigration bill" that at the same time was "tough, fair, and humane." There was, however, also widespread opposition to the bill. Hispanic political activists attacked it as discriminatory. Organized labor turned against the House version because the temporary worker program was seen as threatening American's jobs. Many conservatives rejected it because it meant the legalization of large numbers of people who would swell the population and burden social service programs. Growers and industrial employers of illegal workers bitterly rejected the concept of sanctions directed against them. The bill passed in either the Senate or the House over a number of Congresses but never in both at the same time. After ten years, in October 1986, the bill, which then included a compromise that satisfied the growers, won final approval in Congress.[2]

It was in a context of contradictory economic and political pressures that the U.S. Congress enacted this bill named Immigration Reform and Control Act of 1986 (IRCA). The three fundamental components of IRCA: (1) its legalization provision allowed undocumented immigrants who had been in the U.S. on an illegal basis since before January 1, 1982, to apply for legal residence. (2) Sanctions made it illegal for an employer to knowingly hire undocumented workers. (3) The Special Agricultural Workers provision allowed certain undocumented workers in the agricultural sector to apply for legalization and provided for the admission of additional farm workers in times of farm labor shortages. Overall the IRCA's most significant consequence was the legalization of millions of undocumented farm migrants who for years have survived on the black market. However, employer sanctions—IRCA's political centerpiece—have had little concrete impact. The most comprehensive study of their effect on illegal border crossings concludes that the initial reduction in apprehensions was less a product of employer sanctions than a predictable consequence of the IRCA's legalization provisions (by 1990, the IRCA had legalized close to 3 million immigrants). Observing the political decision-making process of IRCA were watchful voluntary organizations such as the Federation for American Immigration Reform (FAIR), the American Immigration Control Foundation (AICR), and the Center for Immigration Studies, all trying to create a "Nation of Americans." Not only have these voluntary organizations been instrumental in perpetuating the anti-immigrant sentiment that swept the nation through such projects as "Light the Border" or Proposition 187 in 1994, they also have commissioned studies on the economic impact of immigration and financed opinion polls that reflect a growing public resentment of illegal immigration.[3]

The IRCA remains an outstanding example of U.S. ambivalent legislation and regulatory practices of immigration. In response to widespread public pressure to curtail the flow of illegal immigration across the U.S.-Mexican border, the act included, for the first time, employer sanctions that made hiring undocumented workers punishable and illegal. However, the employer sanctions were largely symbolic. Not only did the law include provisions like the Special Agricultural Worker and Replenishment Agricultural Worker, which made it possible for farmers and growers to employ temporary Mexican workers, it also included an "affirmative defense clause that protects employers from prosecution as long as they request documentation from workers, regardless of the validity of the documents presented." IRCA was a response to the general public's demand for restricted movement of illegal immigration across the southern border, thus acting against the interests of agricultural and industrial employers; it also, however, paid attention to the latter's lobbying for light sanctions that would not disrupt their business.[4]

THE IMMIGRATION ACT OF 1990

The Immigration Act of 1990 constituted a major revision of the 1952 Immigration and Nationality Act. Its primary focus was the numerical limits and preference system regulating permanent legal immigration. The legal immigration changes included an increase in total immigration under an overall flexible cap, an increase in annual employment-based immigration from 54,000 to 140,000, and a permanent provision for the admission of "diversity immigrants" from underrepresented countries. The new system provided for a permanent annual level of approximately 700,000 during fiscal years 1992 through 1994. Besides legal immigration, the eight-title act dealt with many other aspects of immigration law ranging from nonimmigrants to criminal aliens to naturalization. The act established the three-track preference system for family-sponsored, employment-based, and diversity immigrants. Additionally, the act significantly amended the work-related nonimmigrant categories for temporary admission.

The 1990 legislation also addressed a series of other issues. For example, it provided undocumented Salvadorans with temporary protected status for a limited period of time; it also amended the Immigration and Nationality Act to authorize the Attorney General to grant temporary protected status to nationals of designated countries subject to armed conflict or natural disasters. As a response to criticism of employer sanctions, the act expanded the anti-discrimination provisions of the IRCA, and increased the penalties for unlawful discrimination. It significantly revised the political and ideological grounds for exclusion and deportation which had been controversial since their enactment in 1952.[5]

LOS INDOCUMENTADOS AND PROPOSITION 187

The traditional issue of tension in U.S. immigration politics—undocumented migrants—however, did not go away after the passage of IRCA in 1986. Moreover, with Proposition 187 Californian nativism fueled a backlash against illegal workers which spread over the entire U.S. The debate over Proposition 187 was the dominant feature of the 1994 election in California, but it spread to several other states and received national attention. While commentators agreed that many immigrants came to California to find jobs, backers of Proposition 187 felt that free public education, health care, and additional welfare benefits served as magnets for illegal immigrants and drained the state budget (with education costs alone estimated by some at close to $2 billion in the early 1990s, and $7.7 billion in 2006). A series of federal court rulings declared most of the proposition's major sections to be unconstitutional. Underlying most of the rulings was the argument that California was attempting to regulate immigration, a responsibility that solely belonged to the federal government.[6]

Supporters of Proposition 187 expressed basic nativist fears when referring to it as the SOS initiative—"Save Our State." The *Los Angeles Times* cited one Republican congressman who stated that "if this doesn't pass, the flood of illegal immigrants will turn into a tidal wave, and a huge neon sign will be lit up above the state of California that reads 'Come and get it.'" Opponents of the measure were able to diminish its impact through the courts. But the Proposition 187 movement spread to other states, and brought to light deep-seated feelings held by many Americans about immigration and refugee issues which influenced the congressional debate on immigration and welfare legislation. Opposition to immigration was frequently articulated as a stance against the erosion of "American" values and the disintegration of national unity.[7]

THE WELFARE REFORM ACT OF 1996 AND THE ILLEGAL IMMIGRATION REFORM AND IMMIGRATION RESPONSIBILITY ACT

Nativist fears and patriotic subjects also influenced congressional debates over the passage of the U.S. 1996 Illegal Immigration Reform and Immigration Responsibility Act (IIRIRA). IIRIRA derived at least in part from the influx of Haitians into the U.S. The so-called Haitian crisis was perhaps the biggest U.S. refugee dilemma in the 1990s. Washington began to forcibly return Haitian refugees [without a hearing]. This forced return of more than 40,000 Haitian refugees in and after 1991 was soundly criticized for violating national and international prohibitions against *refoulement* [forced return] and selectively discriminating against Haitians. The U.S. government's treatment of Haitians contrasts sharply with that accorded to Cubans, who for years have journeyed to the U.S. to escape Fidel Castro's communism. While Haitians have been routinely sent back, Cubans have been automatically allowed into the U.S.[8]

The 1996 IIRIRA ushered in the era of enforcement-dominated immigration policy. Because the law mandated the detention of certain immigrants and asylum seekers, the INS detained (prior to September 11, 2001) more than 200,000 immigrants and refugees annually at more than 900 sites, the majority of which were county and local jails. The chair of the American Bar Association's Immigration Pro Bono Development and Bar Activation Project, Llewelyn G.

Pritchard, argued in February 2001 that "immigration detainees have become the fastest growing segment of the incarcerated population in the United States." Even prior to the terrorist attacks of September 11, 2001, the INS budgeted approximately one billion dollars for refugee and immigration detention and removal.[9]

In addition, the 1996 Welfare Reform Act severely limited welfare aid for legal immigrants and the IIRIRA signaled a more coordinated attempt by the government to stop the flow of illegal immigration. Undocumented migrants became ineligible for most federal or state PA programs, in particular supplemental SSI, AFDC, Medicaid, and food stamps. In addition, the IIRIRA provided for 1,000 new border guards and 300 new INS agents each year through 2002 to strengthen border controls and to investigate unlawful hiring and the smuggling of illegal immigrants. Moreover, a 14-mile triple fence was to be constructed along parts of the border near San Diego, California. Penalties for fraud or the misuse of identification documents were increased. While the Border Patrol might not have been successful in keeping all the illegal migrants out, it has established a pattern of social control and generalized mode of surveillance in the border regions, if not throughout the country.[10]

The 1996 immigration and welfare reform also included several provisions to limit legal immigration or make it more difficult for potential asylum seekers to enter the country. Those who sponsored legal immigrants needed to earn now more than 125 percent of the poverty level to ensure that new arrivals would not need welfare assistance. Asylum seekers have to prove a "credible fear of persecution" at an initial meeting with an INS officer. The final bill provided for a review hearing within seven days before an immigration judge, with no appeals of the judge's decision possible. Moreover, those ordered to leave would be held in mandatory detention until departure, and anyone entering the country without proper documentation would be subject to deportation. Many observers agree that the 1996 expedited removal clause led to arbitrary decisions and possible violations of international guidelines. These policies present special problems for immigrants and refugees from Latin America and the Caribbean.[11]

Several governors who originally supported the 1996 IIRIRA's more restrictive measures later voiced concerns, especially when it appeared that their state might suffer the loss of federal revenue in programs for legal immigrants. Then-Republican presidential candidate Patrick Buchanan, cited in the *Los Angeles Times,* tied immigrants to declining living standards, the widening income gap, the evils of free trade, high crime rates, declining property values, and the general sense that communities were veering out of control.[12]

Along the same lines FAIR, one of the strongest advocates of cuts in legal immigration, stated that

> near-record levels of immigration are deforming the nation's character. The inexorable influx . . . could have dire long-term consequences: overpopulation, rampant bilingualism, reduced job opportunities for native-born, and demographic shifts that could result in dangerous ethnic separatism.[13]

As a consequence the 1996 legislation greatly expanded the grounds on which noncitizens (including legal permanent residents) could be deported. The act essentially gives the police a blank check to trigger the deportation of any suspected immigrant.

THE POST-9/11 REACTION

The attacks of September 11 provided the political decision makers in the U.S. with greater justification to increase the securitization of immigration policies. The mainstream public supported and often collaborated with these measures after September 11, 2001, because of the widespread misperception that the terrorists involved in the attacks arrived on immigration visas. Following this logic, immigration policies needed to be restructured to "close the loopholes" through which terrorists entered the U.S. In reality, all but one of the terrorists had entered the U.S. legally on temporary tourist visas with entry permits for six months, and only one held an F-1 student visa. Only one of the hijackers was in the U.S. prior to July 2001 and not one of the hijackers had immigration status. Nevertheless, the attacks legitimized a number of large-scale immigration searches and expulsions that began late in 2001 and denied the newcomers' constitutional rights, such as due process and fair trial rights.[14]

The U.S. government quickly created a new cabinet-level department and engaged in large administrative restructuring. In January 2003, the Department of Homeland Security (DHS) was established to centralize and coordinate strategic functions within the federal government to "synchronize policy and structure on the U.S. 'war against terrorism'." The Immigration and Naturalization Service (INS) immigration enforcement and service components have been separated from each other in the DHS. According to the National Network for Immigrant and Refugee Rights (NNIRR), all immigration matters are now "overwhelmingly dominated by so-called 'national security' concerns." Two pieces of legislation, passed shortly after September 11, 2001, the USA PATRIOT Act (in October 2001) and the Enhanced Border Security and Visa Entry Reform Act (May 2002), both amplified the powers of agencies such as the FBI and DHS and authorized significant increases in personnel and technology for border enforcement. The U.S. moreover accelerated its pursuit of bilateral deportation and repatriation agreements with countries that had previously refused to take deportees, such as Cambodia and Nigeria. With Canada the U.S. signed a safe-third country agreement in 2002.[15]

The consequences of these legislative acts and a number of interagency operations were disastrous for particular immigrant communities in the U.S. The crackdown on suspected terrorists within U.S. territory soon degenerated into witch hunts for immigrants accused of criminal offenses or whose records simply indicated processing irregularities. It is well known that thousands of immigrants were detained and deported without access to legal representation in the aftermath of the September 11 attacks. In June 2003, the U.S. Justice Department's Office of the Inspector General (OIG) released a 239-page report outlining the FBI-led terrorism investigations following the attacks. The report criticized the treatment of 762 Arab and Muslim immigrants, documenting how detainees were beaten, kept from contacting lawyers and family members, and jailed for months under an official "no bond policy." The FBI and INS cooperated to detain immigrants by labeling the detainees "of interest" to the terrorism investigations, violating their due process rights, even when there were no grounds for suspicion.[16]

Many people who have been arrested during the investigation of September 11, 2001, attacks were charged with immigration violations, such as visa discrepancies. The detainees were frequently portrayed as possible "sleeper" terrorists by the mainstream media, but little was known initially about their actual treatment and accusations. Some were held for months in solitary confinement. Others suffered physical and psychological torture—some were beaten by INS guards, kept in cold cells and refused blankets, and others received no *halal* food (which conforms to specific dietary laws) or toilet paper for weeks. One detainee died of a heart attack while imprisoned. Moreover, as a result of frequent raids of stores, kiosks, and stands in the following year dozens of foreigners, mostly from Pakistan, were detained or questioned and more than 500 detainees were eventually deported, but none of those rounded up has been charged with terrorism.[17]

Soon the investigations' focus shifted entirely from security concerns to immigration-related issues. With the start of the "Absconder Apprehension Initiative," "fugitive apprehension teams" invaded and searched homes throughout the U.S. for persons with outstanding deportation orders. A January 25, 2002, memorandum from the Deputy Attorney General to the INS (now USCIS), FBI, U.S. Marshals Service, and U.S. Attorneys discusses guidelines for implementing the initiative. The purpose of the initiative was to "locate, apprehend, interview and deport . . . 'absconders'." The memo defines "absconders" as "aliens who, though subject to a final order of removal [deportation], have failed to surrender for removal or to otherwise comply with the order." The INS estimated there were approximately 314,000 such absconders in the U.S. At this point the officials were no longer engaged in terrorist or national security investigations; instead, the operation shifted to cracking down on immigration violators. Other initiatives emerged to crack down on illegal immigrants.

For example, the Immigration and Customs Enforcement's (ICE) Detention and Removal Operations (DRO) cites as its purpose promoting public safety and national security by deporting all removable aliens through the enforcement of immigration laws. Since March 1, 2003, ICE's DRO division has removed "more than 52,684 criminal aliens

and an additional 40,802 non-criminal aliens." In 2003 DRO detained more than 230,000 immigrants and refugees. ICE's DRO has also created more than 18 fugitive absconder teams across the nation whose mission is to seek out the more than 80,000 criminal absconders and 320,000 non-criminal absconders over the next six years. In 2005, DRO created a "Most Wanted" list of "criminal aliens" to solicit public assistance in locating the worst criminal immigrant and refugee fugitives.[18]

The new procedures that the INS developed to regulate immigration (Expedited Removal of Aliens, Detention and Removal of Aliens, Conduct of Removal Proceedings), the USA PATRIOT Act, and the ongoing ICE's DRO do not significantly affect the nation's security, but they do add to the insecurity of certain migrant and foreign groups in the country. This is particularly true for millions of undocumented immigrants who have arrived from mostly Latin American countries seeking jobs to escape poverty.

NEW PROPOSALS FOR IMMIGRATION REFORM: GUEST WORKERS

Presently, approximately 11 million unauthorized migrants live in the United States. In June 2005 the Pew Hispanic Center report "Unauthorized Migrants: Numbers and Characteristics" put that number at 10.3 million. An estimated 57 percent of these men, women, and children come from Mexico, 24 percent from other Latin American countries, and the rest from other parts of the world. These immigrants have a major effect on America's health, educational, social service, and legal systems. Many observers have repeatedly argued that the immigration system needs "fixing." However, the last major reworking of U.S. immigration law in 1986 took 14 years of discussion, plus 5 years of congressional negotiation.[19]

President George W. Bush's immigration reform plan includes a program that allows employers to hire temporary guest workers. Those guest workers, either migrating from outside of the United States or already residing in the country, legally or illegally, could work within U.S. territory for up to 6 years, after which they would have to return to their countries of origin. Americans—presumably legal permanent residents and citizens—would have first choice in the proposed preferential ranking system, after which Mexican and other migrants would be eligible for employment in the U.S. with temporary visas. These new temporary visas would legalize some of the estimated 11 million clandestine residents, who would then be eligible for legal employment and short-term residence in the U.S. The visas would be valid for 3 years, renewable for another three. Incentives would be provided for guest workers to return home after their visas expired, in the form of Social Security accounts earned through wages in the U.S. but disbursed in the countries of origin. While purporting to allow the market to dictate the need for workers, Bush's plan neither addresses the specific sectors in need of temporary workers nor provides specific protections for these workers.[20]

A more comprehensive alternative to the Bush plan passed the Senate in May 2006. Sponsored by Senators Edward Kennedy and John McCain, the Secure America and Orderly Immigration Act (S. 1033) provides for more realistic enforcement measures, stronger border security, help for matching U.S. employers with foreign workers, and a way for a substantial segment of the immigrants who currently reside in the country illegally to work toward lawful residency. The McCain-Kennedy bill would allow both legal and illegal immigrants to apply for temporary worker visas. Unlike Bush's bill, this legislation would allow a substantial segment of the clandestine immigrants currently in the country to stay and pursue permanent resident status.[21]

The bill proposes a three-tiered scheme: The first tier would encompass illegal immigrants who have been in the country 5 years or longer, allowing them to stay and apply for permanent residence (the Green Card), provided they pay back taxes, learn English, and have no serious criminal records. The second tier would include illegal immigrants who have been in the U.S. 2 to 5 years. They would eventually have to return to a point of entry in Mexico or Canada and apply for lawful entry and guest worker status, which could allow for their immediate return. The third tier would consist of the roughly 2 million immigrants who have been in the country illegally for less than 2 years; they would be

ordered to return to their countries of origin. The bill has practical problems such as the difficulty of clandestine immigrants to prove their 5-year residence within the country and the logistical nightmare of apprehending and deporting 2 million people. It also has other shortcomings— for example, it calls for a 370-mile fence along the Mexican border, thousands of National Guard troops to support border agents, aerial surveillance, road construction to aid border patrols, and other border security measures. In contrast to Bush's proposal, however, the bill recognizes that large-scale, permanent immigration is both inevitable and desirable.[22]

The Senate's plan juxtaposes a proposal supported by the chair of the Judiciary Committee James Sensenbrenner, called the Border Protection, Antiterrorism, and Illegal Immigration Control Act (H.R. 4437) which passed the House of Representatives in December 2005. The bill defines immigration strictly as a problem of unauthorized entrants and responds by strengthening existing enforcement tools. It includes the effective organization of border security agencies, detention and removal of aliens, employment eligibility verifications, and the construction of fencing and security improvements on the southern border from the Pacific Ocean to the Gulf of Mexico. The bill does not consider changes to the basic structure of the legal migration system but it makes unlawful presence in the United States, which is currently a civil offense, a felony.[23]

According to the U.S. Committee for Refugees and Immigrants (USCRI), the largest network of non-profit legal immigration service providers, the act would criminalize unlawful entry into the U.S. and thus potentially render refugees ineligible to claim asylum after entering U.S. territory. USCRI also emphasizes that the criminalization of unlawful presence will separate family members with varying residence status, eliminate or at least reduce even further judicial review of contested immigration cases, including those of refugees and asylum seekers, and require detention of all persons in expedited removal procedures without exception. By contrast, the current law stipulates that "unaccompanied children are not to be put in expedited removal and cannot be detained by DHS [Department of Homeland Security] longer than 3 days."[24] If signed into law the act will also require all employers to verify that both citizens and non-citizens are eligible to work in the U.S. before they can be hired.[25]

Several other obscure proposals are circulating in Washington, D.C. For example, the Republican representative of Virginia, Virgil Goode, has proposed that a fence be built along the U.S.-Mexican border that will cost between $5 and $7 million and will be an extension of the existing 10-foot-high steel wall demarcating the California–Mexican border at San Diego, built by Army Reserves from 180,000 metal sheets.[26]

Even though the McCain-Kennedy bill passed the Senate with a 62 to 36 bipartisan majority and has powerful supporters, including the U.S. Chamber of Commerce and, of late, the president himself, conservative House representatives have warned that it will not pass the conference committee without being substantially altered. Given the realities of today's immigration debate, hard-line Republicans will likely insist on jettisoning the citizenship provisions of the Senate bill but will retain its guest worker program. It can be expected that the compromise bill will at best introduce a new guest worker program with regularized residence periods for temporary migrants because any provision leading to citizenship will be considered an amnesty, which is strongly opposed by the right wing of the Republican Party. However, the stalemate continued—immigration reform did not pass. Over the next decades, ineffective legislation might indeed weaken the coalition that currently intends to restructure U.S. immigration until eventually anti-immigrant demagogues have enough power to take drastic steps.[27]

Conclusion

America's "Golden Door" is slowly closing for refugees and immigrants alike. The 1986 IRCA attempted to regulate the country's increasing number of illegal immigrants. While allowing millions of mostly agricultural workers to legalize their status the IRCA's political focus, employer sanctions, had few concrete consequences for the planters and farmers. In part responding to mounting xenophobic pressures, the IRCA remains a noteworthy piece of legislation because of its ambivalent character and its rather successful balancing of farming and industrial interests with the general public's stipulation for restrictions on the movements of undocumented immigration across the southern border. The 1990 Immigration Reform Act changed legal immigration by including an overall cap, an increase in the annual employment-based immigration, and a provision for the admission of immigrants from underrepresented countries.

The 1996 IIRIRA increased the enforcement component of immigration law by mandating the detention of certain immigrants and asylees. It also included an expedited removal clause for asylees whose claims of persecution in their countries of origin were not deemed credible by the INS officer. The act also enlarged the border personnel and initiated the triple fence along the California border. The 1996 Welfare Reform Act strictly reduced public assistance for legal immigrants. By the mid-1990s, not only undocumented immigrants but also more documented immigrants and asylees were forced to live under increased governmental surveillance and scrutiny, often while making ends meet in the lowest economic strata with no or very limited public assistance.

After the September 11, 2001, terrorist attacks, these developments multiplied. The USA PATRIOT Act and the Enhanced Border Security and Visa Entry Reform Act and institutions such as ICE of the newly formed DHS, for all practical purposes did away with due process rights of many Arab-looking immigrants who had the misfortune of being arrested in the aftermath of the September 11 attacks. Many of the operations and procedures that initially were designed to make the U.S. safe from terrorists soon deteriorated into witch hunts for certain immigrants and contributed less to the security of the country than the insecurity and anxiety of immigrants.

The proposed legislation in 2006 attempts solutions: from turning illegal immigrants into guest workers, to deploying thousands of National Guard troops to the southern border and to building a 10-foot-high steel wall. Almost all of these proposals misunderstand undocumented immigration as a border control and regulation problem, while in reality it is an issue of supply and demand. As long as Mexico and other Latin American countries have a surplus of labor (exacerbated by the North American Free Trade Agreement's (NAFTA) agricultural policies that have plunged hundreds of thousands of Mexican farmers into severe economic hardship), and the United States a surplus of manual seasonal and/or low-wage jobs, immigrants from the global South will find ways to enter the country. The oscillation of American immigration policies, focusing either on regulating immigrants and refugees or limiting access to the country and/or its services for clandestine immigrants during the past 35 years, has led to at times a severe limiting of civil and human rights of certain newcomer groups. There have been periodic witch hunts among immigrant populations and an understanding of permanent social control in the cities and neighborhoods where immigrants subsist. Immigrants remain the victims of America's ambivalent and inconsistent policies.   [2008]

Notes

1. Barbara Franz, "Refugees in Flux: The Resettlement of Bosnian Refugees in Austria and the United States, 1992–2000" (Syracuse University, 2001): 314; David Bennett, *The Party of Fear: From Nativist Movements to the New Right in American History* (Chapel Hill: The University of North Carolina Press, 1988), 366.
2. Franz (2001): 315; Bennett: pp. 371–73.
3. Kitty Calavita, "U.S. Immigration and Policy Responses: The Limits of Legislation." In *Controlling Immigration: A Global Perspective,* edited by Wayne Cornelius, Philip Martin, and James Hollified (Palo Alto, CA: Stanford University Press, 1994), 55–82; Keith Crane, Beth Ash, Joanna Zorn Heilbrunn, and Danielle Cullinane, *Effect of Employer Sanctions on the Flow of Undocumented Immigrants to the United States* (Lanham, Md.: University Press of America, 1990); Franz (2001): 315–16.
4. Kitty Calavita, *Inside the State: The Bracero Program, Immigration, and the I.N.S.* (New York: Routledge, 1992), pp. 8, 169; Ali Behdad, "Nationalism and Immigration to the United States," *Diaspora* 6, no.2 (Fall 1997): 155–78; Franz (2001): 317.
5. Franz (2001): 318.
6. Patrick McDonnell summarized the claims of Proposition 187 for the *Los Angeles Times*. The proposition called for the following changes regarding illegal immigrants: prohibiting of enrollment in all public schools; requirement of parents or guardians of all school children to show legal residence; obligatory reporting by school administrators of suspected illegal immigrants; denial of nonemergency public health care, including pre-natal and post-natal services, to those who could not prove legal status; cutoff of many state programs dealing with troubled youth, the elderly, the blind and others with special needs; requirement of law enforcement agencies to cooperate fully with INS officials; and increased penalties for the sale and use of fraudulent documents. Patrick McDonnell, "Proposition 187 turns up heat in US immigration debate," *Los Angeles Times,* August 10, 1994; Michael McBride, "Migrants and Asylum Seekers: Policy Responses in the United States to Immigrants and Refugees from Central America and the Caribbean," *International Migration* 37, no. 1 (1999): 298.
7. Congressman cited in Martin Miller, "Proposition 187: fund-raiser by supporters draws 100 in Orange County," *Los Angeles Times,* October 29, 1994, A24; Ali Behdad, "Nationalism and Immigration to the United States," *Diaspora* 6 (no. 2)(1997):174; Franz (2001): 318–19.
8. Barbara Franz, "Immigration und nationale Sicherheit in der EU und den USA: Die Demontage des *Flüchtlingsrechts,*" *AWR Bulletin: Quarterly on Refugee Problems,* Nos. 3–4 (2004): 58–71.
9. In 1996, Congress passed the Anti-terrorism and Effective Death Penalty Act (AEDPA). Combined with IIRIRA, this law made it virtually impossible for a lawful permanent resident who had committed a crime to remain in the United States. Under IIRIRA, most immigrants subject to deportation for crimes also became subject to mandatory detention for 90 days following the issuance of a final removal order. IIRIRA permits the INS to detain immigrants for a period beyond 90 days. This gave rise to the population of detainees known as "lifers" because the INS interpreted the law to allow indefinite detention. According to INS regulations, published in December 2000, the detainee

has the burden of convincing the INS that she poses no "danger to public safety or a flight risk" in order to be considered for release. If the INS does not believe that the detainee has offered convincing evidence, detention can continue indefinitely. The regulations prohibit appeal of a denial of release to the Board of Immigration Appeals. USCR, "Ashcroft Responds to Supreme Court Ruling Against Indefinite Detention," Worldwide Refugee Information: http://www.refugees.org/world/articles/ashcroft_rr01_7.htm (downloaded on March 7, 2004); Llewelyn G. Pritchard, "The INS Issues Detention Standards Governing the Treatment of Detained Immigrants and Asylum Seekers," USCR: http://www.refugees.org/world/articles/developments_rr01_02.cfm (downloaded on March 4, 2004).

10. Robert Pear, "G.O.P governors seek to restore immigrant aid," *The New York Times,* January 25, 1997, 1; Robert Pear, "Panel urges that immigration become further Americanized," *The New York Times,* October 1, 1997, A20; Mirta Ojito, "Painful choices for immigrants in US illegally," *The New York Times,* September 25, 1997, 1; Behdad, "Nationalism and Immigration": 174.

11. Pear, "Panel urges": A20; McBride, "Migrants and Asylum Seekers": 299, Franz (2001): 320–21.

12. McBride, "Migrants and Asylum Seekers": 299; Patrick McDonnell, "California: immigration hot button awaits GOP candidate," *Los Angeles Times,* March 2, 1996, A10; Franz (2001): 322.

13. FAIR cited in: Patrick McDonnell, "Activists see dire immigration threat," *Los Angeles Times,* August 11, 1996, A3.

14. Federation for American Immigration Reform (FAIR), "Identity and Immigration Status of 9/11 Terrorists," http://www.fairus.org/ImmigrationIssueCenters/ImmigrationIssueCenters.cfm?ID=1205&c=14 (downloaded on March 5, 2004).

15. Heba Nimr, *Human Rights and Human Security at Risk: The Consequences of Placing Immigration Enforcement and Services in the Department of Homeland Security* (National Network for Immigrant and Refugee Rights, September 2003), 1.

16. David Caruso, "FBI Agents Raid Immigrants' Stores," *The Washington Post,* July 9, 2002, http://www.washingtonpost.com/wp-dyn/articles/A42205-2002Jul9.html (downloaded on July 12, 2002).

17. Anne-Marie Cusac, "Ill-Treatment on Our Shores," *The Progressive* (March 2002): 24–28; Barbara Franz, "American Patriotism and Nativist Fears After September 11: A Historical Perspective," *AWR Bulletin: Quarterly on Refugee Problems,* No. 1–2, (2003), also accessible at: http://www.braumueller.at/service/downloads/, pp. 10–11.

18. There is no additional information available on these deported persons. Immigration and Customs Enforcement, "Selected one-year accomplishments of ICE," http://www.ice.gov/text/news/newsrel/articles/oneyearFS_030304.htm (downloaded on March 7, 2004); Barbara Franz, *Uprooted and Unwanted: Bosnian Refugees in Austria and the United States* (College Station: Texas A&M University Press).

19. Catholic Online, "Getting Immigration Reform Right," *St. Anthony's Messenger,* March 6, 2006, http://www.catholic.org/views/views_news.php?id=18988&pid=0; Barbara Franz, "Fortress America? Efforts in Fence Building, Controlling Migration, and the Creation of a New Managed Migration System," *IMIS Beiträge,* no. 30 (2006): 28–29.

20. Franz (2006): 29; P. Donnelly, "The Anti-Assimilation President: Democrats Need a Values-Based Alternative to Bush Immigration Initiative," 2004, The Immigration Portal, http://www.ilw.com/articles/2004,0121-donnelly.shtm (downloaded on April 1, 2006).

21. Franz (2006): 30.

22. Ibid.:31.

23. Ibid.: 29.

24. Ibid.

25. Ibid: 30; U.S. Committee for Refugees and Immigrants (USCR), "House Votes to Toughen Laws on Immigration," 2005, http://www.refugees.org/newsroomsub.aspx?id=1455 (downloaded on December 20, 2005).

26. "Resident Evil", *The New Republic,* December 19, 2005, p. 7; Franz (2006): 30.

27. J. Rutenberg, "Border Fight Divides G.O.P.," *The New York Times,* May 26, 2006, http://www.nytimes.com/2006/05/26/washington/26assess.html?pagewanted=1&_r&th&emc=th; Mark Rosenblum, "'Comprehensive' Legislation vs.

Fundamental Reform: The Limits of Current Immigration Proposals," *Migration Policy Institute Policy Brief* (January 2006): 13.

Terms

1. *REFOULEMENT:* Forced to return to a country from which one has fled because of fear of bodily harm.
2. XENOPHOBIC: Highly fearful of anyone of foreign origin.

Understanding the Reading

1. Why do U.S. employees continue to hire undocumented immigrants?
2. What are the controversies surrounding the H-2 visa?
3. What is Proposition 187?
4. Describe the different treatment accorded Cuban refugees as opposed to Haitian refugees to the United States.
5. What actions did the U.S. government take that collapsed the categories of "immigrant" and "terrorist"?

Suggestions for Responding

1. Research the "Protocol Relating to the Status of Refugees," which was signed by the United States in 1967. Forced return, or *refoulement,* is in direct defiance of our signed principles. Discuss this in class.
2. Design your own solution to controversial U.S. immigration policies, or offer a partial solution. ✦

39

The Impact of Immigration Raids on Children

RANDY CAPPS AND ROSA MARIA CASTANEDA

On March 6, 2007, several hundred federal immigration agents raided Michael Bianco Inc., a military contractor in New Bedford, Massachusetts.

Michael Bianco, which made U.S. military backpacks, had been under investigation for employing unauthorized immigrants and operating a sweatshop. U.S. Immigration and Customs Enforcement (ICE) officers questioned every employee about citizenship and immigration status, and arrested 361 workers for being in the country illegally and lacking work authorization. Within weeks, the plant's owner had reopened in Puerto Rico. Most of the arrested workers, however, remained in federal detention for months.

Later that spring, researchers from the Urban Institute, a nonprofit, nonpartisan research organization, visited New Bedford and two other large raid sites—Greeley, Colorado, and Grand Island, Nebraska—to talk to arrested immigrants, family members, and others in the community.[1] The research focused on the raids' short-term impacts on families with children.

Altogether, more than 900 adults were arrested, including parents of over 500 children, two-thirds of whom were U.S. citizens. In New Bedford, most of those arrested were Central Americans. Comprising the largest group were Guatemala's Maya Kiche people, many of whom had fled poverty and civil unrest. In some cases, those arrested were single parents, and almost three-quarters of the children were age five or under.

IMPACTS ON CHILDREN

The children experienced a variety of challenges, including separation from parents, economic hardship, isolation, and social stigma.

Family Separation

Most of those arrested came from two-parent homes, which are a particular strength of the Latino immigrant community. Many were detained a long time, so their children went from living with two parents to living with one. With many immigrants in detention six months after the raids, the remaining parents often had difficulty coping. For example, some spouses lacked access to or familiarity with bank accounts or other financial resources.

About 60 of the New Bedford immigrants were released the same day because they were single parents or had very young or sick children. Others were held for days or weeks. The Massachusetts Department of Social Services sent three dozen social workers to Texas—where many detainees were moved after their arrest. They obtained the release of 21 parents, many of whom had not divulged that they had children for fear that the children could be taken away or deported. Many children felt abandoned and could not understand why a parent had simply "disappeared."

Economic Hardship

Many families lost the adult with the better job, and household incomes plunged. In New Bedford, the Michael Bianco jobs only paid between $7 and $9 per hour, and some were part-time. But the other two sites' meat-packing jobs paid more than $10 per hour, were full- or overtime unionized jobs, and offered full benefits.

For a while, extended families and informal networks helped provide child care and economic support, keeping the majority of children from living alone without supervision or becoming homeless. Other than three adolescents who were themselves arrested at the New Bedford work site, no children wound up in foster care.

Most families also received some form of community assistance lasting three or four months. Some families lost their homes or crowded in with other families. Utilities were temporarily cut off for some, and often there wasn't enough money for food.

Fear and Isolation

The raids created a climate of fear, especially in Grand Island, where follow-up raids continued for over a week. Researchers spoke to families who hid in their homes for days or weeks. Many were fearful of seeking help—even at trusted locations such as churches. Some would not open the doors for people who brought food baskets and other assistance.

Social Stigma

The remaining parents and caregivers struggled to explain to children what had happened. It was especially difficult for younger children to under-

stand. One child said that his parent was "arrested for working." Some older children, mostly high school students, went to the work sites and saw their parents taken away in handcuffs. Children also had to deal with signs of increased community hostility, especially in Greeley.

The separation, economic hardship, fear, isolation, and stigma led to children showing more aggressive behavior, changes in sleep patterns and appetites, mood swings, and prolonged bouts of crying. Mental health professionals that the researchers interviewed spoke of elevated stress in children, signs of depression, and even suicidal thoughts. (The researchers were unable to interview a random sample of parents and could not document the prevalence of mental health effects.)

COMMUNITY RESPONSES

All three communities initiated intensive and broad response efforts to assist immigrant families after the raids. The relief was especially well organized in New Bedford, where the Massachusetts Immigration and Refugee Advocacy (MIRA) coalition led an effort to bring together state and local government officials, representatives from the Honduran and Maya Kiche communities, faith leaders, foundations, and others to plan the effort. Local foundations and individual philanthropists raised significant funds, and aid was distributed to families for rent, housing, food assistance, clothing, and other necessities.

Public health and social service agencies also helped, but their roles varied substantially across the three sites. The New Bedford city government was particularly supportive of families in need, and social workers from the Massachusetts Department of Social Services worked to link parents with children and distribute relief. Public assistance through welfare programs and food stamps, however, was limited to U.S. citizens and legal residents. Most adults did not qualify, and many families were afraid to apply even if they did qualify.

Churches emerged as central distribution points for relief because immigrant families trusted them. In all three sites, public agencies and nonprofit service providers stationed their staff at churches. Religious and community leaders also went door-to-door to provide assistance, although some families were afraid to open their doors even to them.

How Can We Improve?

The study offers a preliminary view of the immigration raids' impacts on children. It covers three of the largest raids ever conducted by ICE, but there have been more than 10,000 work-site arrests—and other arrests in homes and on streets—over the past several years.[2] With about 12 million unauthorized immigrants in the country and more than 5 million children with at least one unauthorized parent, more families with children are at risk of raids and their consequences.[3]

The research report offered recommendations for the way in which raids are conducted, and ICE issued guidelines in November 2007 addressing many of the recommendations. One recommendation was to grant arrestees access to lawyers, consular officials, social workers, and other intermediaries to inquire about children. Another was to allow easier communication between arrested parents and children by improving telephone access and not moving parents out of the states in which they were arrested. Single parents and parents with very young children (nursing mothers, for instance) should be released on the same day of the arrest, as early in the day as possible.

There were also recommendations for state and local governments and the private sector. In all three cases, schools did an excellent job of ensuring that children did not return to empty homes, and the Grand Island School District developed a particularly successful model. State and local governments would be wise to develop similar plans, and a centralized planning and coordinating body—such as the group set up by MIRA in New Bedford—could help ensure efficient service delivery. Further, the report suggested that trusted religious institutions should be used as assistance and outreach centers and that a national clearinghouse should be established to share information.

Many immigrant parents may eventually face the choice of leaving their children in the United States or taking them to an uncertain future in another country. Families themselves need to prepare. Both parents should have access to bank accounts and other financial assets. They need to gather their documents and their

children's, and make sure that children who are U.S. citizens have passports in case they have to leave the country after a parent's arrest.

Even if all the recommendations are followed, however, children could still face harm from the arrest, detention, and deportation of their parents. So far there is no hard evidence on the longer-term impacts. Researchers from the Urban Institute plan to return to New Bedford and other communities to investigate the longer-term impacts of work-site raids and other types of enforcement actions on immigrants' children.   2008

Notes

1. See *Paying the Price: The Impact of Immigration Raids on America's Children,* published in October 2007 with support from the Annie E. Casey Foundation and posted on the Internet sites of the National Council of La Raza (www.nclr.org) and the Urban Institute (www.urban.org). NCLR supported the research with funding from the Atlantic Foundation.
2. U.S. Immigration and Customs Enforcement, "Work Site Enforcement Overview" (Washington DC: U.S. Department of Homeland Security, August 2007), http://www.ice.gov/pi/news/factsheets/work site.htm.
3. Jeffrey S. Passel, *The Size and Characteristics of the Unauthorized Migrant Population in the U.S.: Estimates Based on the March 2005 Current Population Survey* (Washington, DC: Pew Hispanic Center, 2006).

Understanding the Reading

1. What are the consequences for owners who hire undocumented workers and are discovered?
2. What happens to the workers and their families when they are discovered?
3. What are the specific effects on children in this situation?
4. How have communities responded to the crises that have come from immigration raids?

Suggestion for Responding

1. Ask for community work at one of your local service organizations that deal especially with undocumented people. ◆

40

The State of Hate: Escalating Hate Violence Against Immigrants

THE LEADERSHIP CONFERENCE EDUCATION FUND

The increase in hate crimes directed against Hispanics for the fourth consecutive year is particularly noteworthy and worrisome because the number of hate crimes committed against other racial, ethnic, and religious groups has over the same period shown either no increase or a decrease.

The increase in violence against Hispanics correlates closely with the increasingly heated debate over comprehensive immigration reform and an escalation in the level of anti-immigrant vitriol on radio, television, and the Internet. While reasonable people can and will disagree about the parameters of comprehensive immigration reform, in some instances, the commentary about immigration reform has not been reasonable; it has been inflammatory. Warned an April 2009 assessment from the Office of Intelligence and Analysis at the U.S. Department of Homeland Security (DHS), "in some cases, anti-immigration or strident pro-enforcement fervor has been directed against specific groups and has the potential to turn violent."

This toxic environment, in which hateful rhetoric targets immigrants while the number of hate crimes against Hispanics and others perceived to be immigrants steadily increases, has caused a heightened sense of fear in communities around the country.

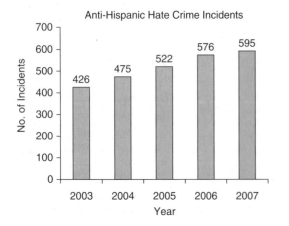

Anti-Hispanic Hate Crime Incidents

THE ROLE OF EXTREMIST ANTI-IMMIGRATION GROUPS

Some groups opposing immigration reform, such as the Federation for American Immigration Reform (FAIR), the Center for Immigration Studies (CIS), and NumbersUSA, have portrayed immigrants as responsible for numerous societal ills, often using stereotypes and outright bigotry. While these groups, and other similar organizations, have strived to position themselves as legitimate, mainstream advocates against illegal immigration in America, a closer look at the public record reveals that some of these organizations have disturbing links to or relationships with extremists in the anti-immigration movement. These seemingly "legitimate" advocates against illegal immigration are frequently quoted in the mainstream media, have been called to testify before Congress, and often hold meetings with lawmakers and other public figures. This is one of the most disturbing developments of the past few years: the legitimization and mainstreaming of virulently anti-immigrant rhetoric that veers dangerously close to—and too often crosses the line beyond civil discourse over contentious immigration policy issues.

The Leadership Conference on Civil Rights, the Anti-Defamation League, the Southern Poverty Law Center (SPLC), the National Council of La Raza (NCLR), and the Mexican American Legal Defense and Educational Fund (MALDEF) have become increasingly concerned about the virulent anti-immigrant and anti-Latino rhetoric employed by a handful of groups and coalitions that have tried to position themselves as legitimate, mainstream advocates against illegal immigration in America. Recently, SPLC published *The Nativist Lobby: Three Faces of Intolerance,*[1] which investigated three of these groups and found: Three Washington, D.C.-based immigration-restriction organizations stand at the nexus of the American nativist movement: the Federation for American Immigration Reform (FAIR), the Center for Immigration Studies (CIS), and NumbersUSA. Although on the surface they appear quite different—the first, the country's best-known anti-immigrant lobbying group; the second, an "independent" think tank; and the third, a powerful grassroots organizer—they are fruits of the same poisonous tree.

FAIR, CIS and NumbersUSA are all part of a network of restrictionist organizations conceived and created by John Tanton, the "puppeteer" of the nativist movement and a man with deep racist roots. Tanton has for decades been at the heart of the white nationalist scene. He has met with leading white supremacists, promoted anti-Semitic ideas, and associated closely with the leaders of a eugenicist foundation once described by a leading newspaper as a "neo-Nazi organization." He has made a series of racist statements about Latinos and worried that they were out-breeding whites. At one point, he wrote candidly that to maintain American culture, "a European-American majority" is required.

FAIR, which Tanton founded and where he remains on the board, has been listed as a hate group by the Southern Poverty Law Center. Among the reasons are its acceptance of $1.2 million from the Pioneer Fund, a group founded to promote the genes of white colonials that funds studies of race, intelligence and genetics. FAIR has also hired as key officials men who also joined white supremacist groups. It has board members who regularly write for hate publications. It promotes racist conspiracy theories about Latinos. And it has produced television programming featuring white nationalists.

CIS was conceived by Tanton and began life as a program of FAIR. CIS presents itself as a scholarly think tank that produces serious immigration studies meant to serve "the broad national interest." But the reality is that CIS has never found any aspect of immigration that it liked, and it has frequently manipulated data to achieve the results it seeks. Its executive director last fall posted an item on the conservative National Review Online website about Washington Mutual, a bank that had earlier issued a press release about its inclusion on a list of "Business Diversity Elites" compiled by *Hispanic Business* magazine. Over a copy of the bank's press release, the CIS leader posted a headline—"Cause and Effect?"—that suggested a link between the bank's opening its ranks to Latinos and its subsequent collapse.

Like CIS, NumbersUSA bills itself as an organization that operates on its own and rejects racism completely. In fact, NumbersUSA was for the first five years of its existence a program of U.S. Inc., a foundation run by Tanton to fund numerous nativist groups, and its leader was an employee of that foundation for a decade. He helped edit Tanton's racist journal, *The Social Contract*, and was personally introduced by Tanton to a leader of the Pioneer Fund. He also edited a book by Tanton and another Tanton employee that was banned by Canadian border officials as hate literature and on one occasion spoke to the Council of Conservative Citizens, a hate group which has called blacks "a retrograde species of humanity."

Together, FAIR, CIS and NumbersUSA form the core of the nativist lobby in America. In 2007, they were key players in derailing bipartisan, comprehensive immigration reform that had been expected by many observers to pass. Today, these organizations are frequently treated as if they were legitimate, mainstream commentators on immigration. But the truth is that they were all conceived and birthed by a man who sees America under threat by nonwhite immigrants. And they have never strayed far from their roots.[2]

The Infiltration of Mainstream Media

The increasing number of shrill anti-immigration reform commentaries from high-profile national media personalities, including CNN's Lou Dobbs and Talk Show Network's *The Savage Nation* host Michael Savage, correlates closely with the increase in hate crimes against Hispanics. There is a direct connection between the tenor of this rhetoric and the daily lives of immigrants, and many fear that the unintended consequence of media celebrities vilifying immigrants will be an atmosphere in which some people will act on these demonizing screeds, violently targeting immigrants and those perceived to be immigrants.

The frequent appearance of extremist groups such as FAIR on mainstream media programs and even at congressional hearings is extremely worrisome. After reviewing FAIR's virulent rhetoric, SPLC found: None of this—or any other material evidencing the bigotry and racism that courses through the group—seems to have affected FAIR's media standing. In 2008, the group was quoted in mainstream media outlets nearly 500 times. FAIR staff have been featured several times on CNN's *Lou Dobbs Tonight*, along with countless appearances on other television news shows. Dobbs even ran his radio program from a FAIR event in Washington, D.C. this past September. And, perhaps most remarkably of all, FAIR has been taken seriously by Congress, claiming on its home page that it has been asked to testify on immigration bills "more than any other organization in America."[3]

As Alex Nogales, president and CEO of the National Hispanic Media Coalition (NHMC) has noted, "We are very respectful of the First Amendment and free speech, but the hateful rhetoric, particularly against the immigrant minority communities, espoused by irresponsible TV and radio talk show hosts on American airwaves needs to be addressed." NHMC has undertaken a study to quantify hate speech in commercial radio, petitioned the Federal Communications Commission (FCC) to open an inquiry into hate speech on the nation's airwaves, and requested that the National Telecommunications and Information Administration (NTIA) update its 1993 report, *The Role of Telecommunications in Hate Crime.*[4] In that report, NTIA found "deeply troubling" examples where "telecommunications has been used to advocate or encourage the commission of hate crimes." But the report concluded that "the extent to which such messages (of hate) actually lead to the commission of crimes is unclear."[5]

On July 5, 2007, Michael Savage suggested America would be a better place if students staging a hunger strike in the hope of securing immigration reform legislation starved to death:

> SAVAGE: Then there's the story of college students who are fasting out here in the Bay Area. They're illegal aliens and they want green cards simply because they're students. I don't understand what—how this two and two adds up. I would say, let them fast until they starve to death, then that solves the problem. Because then we won't have a problem about giving them green cards because they're illegal aliens; they don't belong here to begin with. They broke into the country; they're criminals.[6]

Like Savage, Lou Dobbs has also stated on his CNN show, *Lou Dobbs Tonight*, "illegal aliens are criminals" (*Lou Dobbs Tonight* transcript, 4/6/05). As NCLR has pointed out, illegal immigrants are not considered criminals under current U.S. law. NCLR has chronicled many

of Lou Dobbs's other comments made on CNN about immigrants and immigration reform:

• Dobbs has used the term "anchor babies" to refer to the U.S.-born children of undocumented immigrants, suggesting inaccurately that having a U.S. citizen child is a means of acquiring legal immigration status or being protected from deportation (*Lou Dobbs Tonight* transcript, 3/31/05).

• Dobbs refers frequently to illegal aliens from Mexico into the United States as the "invasion" and as an "army of invaders" (*Lou Dobbs Tonight* transcript, 3/31/06). One of his reporters referred to a visit from Mexico's then-President Vicente Fox as a "Mexican military incursion."

• Dobbs linked illegal aliens to a host of diseases including tuberculosis, malaria, and leprosy. In 2005, a reporter on the show claimed that there had been 7,000 new cases of leprosy in the previous three years (*Lou Dobbs Tonight* transcript, 4/14/05). This claim has been disputed by the Centers for Disease Control and Prevention.[7] To date, and despite protests to the contrary, Dobbs has never acknowledged the error on his show.

• Dobbs has featured several stories on *Lou Dobbs Tonight* concerning the "reconquest" of the American Southwest. In one 2005 segment, a map purportedly showing "Aztlan" was provided to the show by the Council of Conservative Citizens, a prominent White supremacist organization (*Lou Dobbs Tonight* transcript, 5/23/06).

• Dobbs has also been a cheerleader for the Minuteman Project. He devoted extensive coverage to the Minuteman's first action in 2005, calling the group a "remarkable success." Minuteman leaders were frequent guests on *Lou Dobbs Tonight*, and on one occasion Dobbs wished one "all the success in the world."[8]

• Dobbs featured on *Lou Dobbs Tonight* the late Madeline Cosman as a "medical expert" in a discussion of the diseases that illegal aliens are bringing into the country. Ms. Cosman was not a medical doctor, but a prominent anti-immigrant activist who stated that

Mexican immigrants were prone to molesting children (*Lou Dobbs Tonight* transcript, 6/8/05).

- As noted above, the Council of Conservative Citizens, one of the most well-known White supremacist groups in the country, was featured as a "source" in a 2006 segment on the show.[9]

On May 2, 2007, Dobbs held a special "Broken Borders" town hall meeting edition of *Lou Dobbs Tonight* in Hazleton, Pennsylvania to spotlight that town's passage of its "Illegal Immigrant Relief Act." This town ordinance sought to suspend the business permits and licenses of employers who hired "unlawful workers" or landlords who rented to illegal aliens. During the show, Dobbs praised the town: "Hazleton, the community, is leading the battle against illegal immigration, stepping in where the federal government has simply failed to perform its duty." The website of the *Lou Dobbs Tonight* show solicited contributions for the town's "legal defense fund" after a lawsuit filed by MALDEF and the American Civil Liberties Union (ACLU) prevented the law from taking effect.[10]

Fourteen months later, 20 miles from Hazleton in Shenandoah, Pennsylvania, Luis Ramirez, a 25-year-old Mexican and father of two, was murdered because of his ethnicity in a brutal beating allegedly by four current and former high school football players. The teenagers reportedly yelled, "This is Shenandoah, this is America, go back to Mexico," as well as ethnic slurs. They then repeatedly punched Ramirez, knocking him to the ground, and then kicked him multiple times in the head. As Ramirez lay unconscious, convulsing and foaming at the mouth, one of the assailants reportedly yelled "Tell your fucking Mexican friends to get the fuck out of Shenandoah or you'll be fucking laying next to them."

On May 1, 2009, a jury convicted two teens of simple assault, a misdemeanor, acquitting them of the most serious charges brought against them, including murder, aggravated assault, and ethnic intimidation. A third teen faces counts of aggravated assault and ethnic intimidation in juvenile court, while a fourth pleaded guilty in federal court to violating Ramirez's civil rights in exchange for charges of third-degree murder,

aggravated assault, and related counts against him being dropped.

Shenandoah had been considering an ordinance similar to Hazelton's but held off after the ACLU and MALDEF lawsuit blocked it from taking effect. Still, the Hazelton ordinance caused considerable tension between the town's Hispanic and white communities, which had formerly enjoyed peaceful relations. "They (the Hispanic community) just didn't feel comfortable then," said Flor Gomez, whose family runs a Mexican restaurant in Shenandoah. As *The New York Times* reported, "Many people believe the debate fueled by Hazleton's actions helped create the environment that led to Mr. Ramirez's death."

"Clearly there were a lot of factors here," said Gladys Limón, a lawyer for MALDEF. "But I do believe that the inflammatory rhetoric in the immigration debate does have a correlation with increased violence against Latinos."[11]   [2009]

Notes

1. Heidi Beirich, *The Nativist Lobby: Three Faces of Intolerance* (pdf), ed. Mark Potok, Southern Poverty Law Center, February 2009.
2. Mark Potok, Southern Poverty Law Center website, "The Nativist Lobby: Three Faces of Intolerance," February 2009.
3. Beirich, *The Nativist Lobby: Three Faces of Intolerance*, 9.
4. Summary: FCC Petition for Inquiry on Hate Speech in Media (pdf).
5. U.S. Dept. of Commerce, National Telecommunications and Information Administration, *The Role of Telecommunications in Hate Crime*, December 1993, i.
6. County Fair Blog, Media Matters for America, "Savage on Immigrant Students' Hunger Strike..." July 6, 2007.
7. New U.S. Reported Hansen's Disease (Leprosy) Cases by Year, 1976/2006, U.S. Department of Health and Human Services Health Resources and Service Administration.
8. Additional information on the Minuteman Project.
9. WeCanStopTheHate.org, National Council of La Raza, "Journalists as Anti-immigrant Activists," n.d.
10. County Fair Blog, Media Matters for America, "Hosting Segment from Hazleton, Pa., Dobbs

Did Not Acknowledge Fundraising for the Embattled Town," May 9, 2007.

11. Sean D. Hamill, "Mexican's Death Bares a Town's Ethnic Tension," *New York Times*, August 5, 2008. John J. Moser, "1st-, 2nd-Degree Murder Charges Tossed in Death of Ramirez," *The Morning Call,* August 19, 2008.

Understanding the Reading

1. What does this article suggest is the reason for the increase in hate crimes against Hispanics for the fourth year in a row?
2. Give an example of an extremist group in the U.S. that uses hate speech against Hispanics in the mainstream media.
3. How does this hate speech affect our society?

Suggestion for Responding

1. Have a class discussion on our right to free speech and free press, balanced with the existence of hate speech that possibly incites some people to violence.

41

2-205

RESHMA BAIG

Mrs. Silverstein was my second grade teacher. She was the blue haired queen of the second floor. The green eyeshadowed matron of innocent six-year-olds poised on the precipice of a new world. Every night of my second grade life hinged on the fear that I would have to take my seat in row 2 seat 2 and watch the frosted pink lips of my large hipped teacher mouth out phrases, words, numbers and dates in scary slow motion so that those new to *"our* country" could understand.

For a child who had recently immigrated from a country where primary schools were *always* built on ground level, a child who hadn't had enough time to learn to trust her environment, life was scary enough without having to trudge

back to a room guarded by the gaze of a woman who announced freely that doom resided in the dense blood of her red marker pen.

Every morning, I faced the prospect of returning to a room full of felt numbers, flag pledging and bathroom visits in pairs.

The maze of hallways on the second floor of PS 20 were purely frightening. At any turn, you could find yourself face to face with another pair of disoriented second graders who, like you and your "bathroom buddy," had found themselves lost while using the pass. If you were truly unlucky, you would find yourself at the mercy of tall third or fourth graders who called you a "baby bumper" before they knocked you into a wall. If there existed the fate of something worse, it could probably have been traced back to the confines of room 2-205. This was the place where the fears of my six-year-old mind began *and* ended.

Every night after I finished my homework, when the reality of returning to room 2-205 crept up in my mind, the fear would start again. That was one thing I had no control over.

The things that I did have control over were sheets of crisp, lined paper, sharpened pencils and tightly-bound black and white notebooks. All these things brought me joy, and when I found a pink eraser on my father's desk one day, it just made everything magical. If I made a mistake, it rubbed clean off. Just blow on the paper a little and everything could be scrubbed brand new. Then the paper was clean and ready. With the pink eraser, there was always a second chance for straight etched *T's,* swirling *S's* and rapid *O's.*

After the last page of homework, just after Mary and Dick took the last skip around their yard, the fear planted itself in my head. I was knotted in sweaty sleep until the morning. I smelled the classroom in my dreams and felt the swift pummel of Mrs. Silverstein's fist on my desk if any spelling errors should arise.

In the morning I washed my face with hard splashes of cold water. Like a soldier, I thought. I would freeze the skin on my face and deal with the agony of the day.

Mum'i would always be smiling and issuing advice for the day as I wiped the sleep from my eyes at 7:15 A.M. She sweetly hollered as she peeked at me from the kitchen, "Zafran, fix that collar and put some socks on! Come here so I can pin the hair away from your face. Zafran! Remember to say Bismillah before you eat."

While I ate my corn flakes, she came over to kiss the side of my head, say three prayers and then blow softly on my face. The wooly nubs of her cardigan brushed my cheek, embracing me in the scent of sandalwood: the perfume of safety and strong women who promised to raise even stronger daughters.

My mother was the sixth child in a family of seven. She was named after a constellation of seven stars, moved with my father to three countries and spoke five languages. While cooking four dishes at a time, she could still find the time to comb my hair, slide in two hair pins and find the missing plastic sheep from the Fisher-Price Farm Family.

She was all these things as well as a woman of beauty and kindness who always packed the tomatoes separately, so the bread would not get mushy. She was the doctor of lunch distress who cured the morning blahs by wrapping toffee and cake in floral paper napkins. They would be waiting in the corner of my lunch box providing five minutes of sweet relief in a lunchroom sagging from the misery and stench of cold bologna and spilt milk.

After leaving my mother's gentle hands, I had to find the strength to battle the Dragon Lady of room 2-205. Mum'i didn't know that dragons awaited me in PS 20. I never told her.

"School is good for little girls. You both should be thankful that you have a school to go to," was what Mum'i said in her melodious voice before she kissed Sugrah and [me] . . . goodbye at All Grades morning line-up in the school yard.

Morning line-up was first call to the lunch-box army. The portly assistant principal, Mr. Kaufman, blew his whistle to signal ranks of three and a half foot soldiers, outfitted in Garanimals and Health-Tex separates, to march slowly, methodically to their designated rooms. Each infantry followed a bouffant haired drill sergeant armed with a pocket book and silver necklace of twenty-nine keys. Clanging keys dangled over hearts pierced like

a sieve to mark thirty-four long years with short people of many requests.

After following Mrs. Silverstein's double-knit hem to the confines of room 2-205, there would be another line-up to deposit lunch box, coat and school-bag inside the closet. The closet was opened by a willowy sixth grade monitor, named Lisa, who was assigned to Mrs. Silverstein for the year. Among her other duties were to get a "sugar no [cream]" coffee for our teacher from the teachers' lounge and bring us down to lunch.

Lisa always did the same thing after lunch. She led our class into the middle of the school yard and separated us into dodgeball teams. Even if we didn't want to play dodgeball, we were forced to comply. Lisa was taller than any of us, and she was **the monitor.** She even had a green and yellow badge that said Service Squad. What Lisa wanted, Lisa got. As she swung her waist-length blond hair to the side, and adjusted the cuffs on her hip-hugging bell-bottoms, she stuck a wad of gum on the back of her hand and pointed to the yellow line on the ground. That meant we had to line up while she separated us into specific teams. If there was a protester or two, a couple of kids who questioned their team assignment, they were immediately served a red demerit card and forced to stand with their faces against the chain-link fence until the end of recess.

Lisa, with her polished skills of sorting (probably acquired by way of South Africa or Mississippi), always divided the two teams according to the Lisa Principle. According to this principle, all the cutesy boys and pretty girls were placed on Team A. And all the non-white and recently immigrated children were placed on Team B. If anyone on Team B touched Lisa at any point during the game, she would squeal "Yuck, foreigner cooties." This would incite Team A members to follow her lead in stereo.

Lisa made sure there was no horsing around while we hung our coats on metal hooks which protruded like gunmetal question marks from the recesses of the closet. Mrs. Silverstein put her in charge while she went to her personal closet at the back of the room to change her shoes. This happened every day like clockwork. Third graders who had her last year told stories about her closet at lunch time. Mrs. Silverstein's closet became the last frontier, a place of mystery and unmentionable amazement, a Pandora's box of secrets which entranced the observer with a sharp whiff of Ben-Gay ointment.

The students who were on the back of the closet hang-up line always peered inside Mrs. Silverstein's closet to see which shoes would be stalking up the aisles for the day. Inside her closet lay a neat shelf of shoes, a mirror and a large photograph of her with . . . three happy looking kids who looked just like her.

As she locked her closet with one of the twenty-nine keys around her neck, Mrs. Silverstein placed the day's pair next to her neat desk by the window. She carefully sat down, adjusted the pleats of her skirt, briskly reprimanded her aching knees and then slipped off the rubber soled shoes to reveal stubby, soft pink toes that looked like a family of hard boiled eggs.

For an old lady who spent most of her time with those who hadn't even mastered the skill of fine motor coordination, Mrs. Silverstein was still very particular with the shape, style and color of her shoes. There were always little bows or large rhinestones on the back of brightly colored, well polished pumps.

The shoes designated the day's turn of events. Open toes meant art in the afternoon. Double straps meant some sorry child would be called to the board for a math problem which would inevitably result in the wrong answer. Stacked black heels always meant a child would vomit after a spelling test; but red high heels were a flag in the wind. Red heels were cause for celebration. They signaled that at the end of the day one lucky row would get to pick prizes from the Scholastic Books grab bag.

There was no need for fortunes resting on the tiny faces of tea leaves. We, the crayon bearing masses of 2-205, always received the daily horoscope, squished and screaming, from inside Mrs. Silverstein's pumps.

After gongs signaling the end of first hour, the class was led down to the music room for recorder lessons. Recorders, fake plastic flutes for the safety-scissors population, were dependable, easy and generous with immediate gratification. They gave us meaning even though we were pinched if we played the wrong note.

Going down to the music room always meant being greeted by a bob-haired teacher named Mrs. Heleno. A woman who never seemed to blink and perpetually picked lint off her clingy Quiana wrap-dresses. She was the type of teacher whose sharply outlined lips gave credence to the rumor that there were people on this planet who actually did eat children for breakfast.

The rumors were there, but the worst we were forced to endure was maybe a nasty pinch or two if we were off-key for "Three Blind Mice."

Mrs. Heleno was a woman for whom music was something pathological. It was a thing that consumed oneself—a thing to suffer for and make others suffer for as well. Before each lesson, she would clear her throat and with an air of pride deliver Words Of Meaning in her lilting First Lady of MGM via the Sorbonne accent.

"I used to play weez zah London Symphony and seeng weez zah Paris Opera. But ven I came to zees country, I decided I vaz going to help leetle cheeldren. You too can become great person of museek like your teejher."

We couldn't disappoint a woman of such experience and passion. We were going to play those saliva sprayed recorders, and we were going to play them well.

"Cheeldren, if you punish the museek, then you, too, must be punished."

If we played incorrectly, we were pinched. Some of us wore our tiny black and blues like battle scars. We had suffered for the music, and for Mrs. Heleno, that was noble suffering, indeed.

The end of recorder lessons would be followed with American Folk Songs Unit Four. We had graduated from "She'll Be Coming Around The Mountain" to the epic "This Land is Your Land."

It was only during the squeaky voiced singing of these songs that America would come alive. It was only during these songs that my classmates and I actually sang at the top of our lungs. The fear of the day would somehow dissolve for a three minute reverie of redwood forests, purple mountains and darling Clementine.

We looked at one another, backs straight, hands locked at our waists and smiled. We looked at Mrs. Heleno's bob swaying, her fingers pounding with furious intensity at her Board of Education piano and felt that things were not all that bad after all. Our voices, within the wood floored music room of a public elementary school in Queens, sang high. For that moment, our lungs were strengthened with something small and mighty that mattered.

It was usually at this point that Mrs. Silverstein showed up. Her shoes announced her arrival. She stood nodding her head and smiling. Smiling? Smiling at us with a face glowing under a fresh dusting of powder. She stood, feet firmly stationed nine inches apart, batting ancient eyelashes covered in the tar of mascara petrified since 1953. The weight on her lids alone could have most certainly caused blindness. Yet, she saw us clear enough to put a smile on her face. She looked at us with surprised doe eyes full of hope and expectation. As though she had accidentally come upon twenty-four of her best friends while purchasing discounted nylons in the hosiery section of Gertz department store on Roosevelt Avenue.

When we finished our song, Mrs. Silverstein clapped along with all of us. She even joined Mrs. Heleno in a flurry of "Bravos."

As she walked to the front of the room, she tapped me and each person in row five on the shoulder. "Very nice, children. Very nice."

She smelled like Ponds cold cream and when she came closer, I saw that her hands and arms were covered with light brown spots. Spots which moved with the sudden shift of the fragile skeleton they clung to. Spots just like my Nan'na's.

She could be somebody's grandma I thought. And if she could be somebody's grandma, she most certainly was somebody's mother. I pictured her powdered face next to her grandchild's. I pictured her putting a warm plate of eggs and toast in front of her children.

A six year old philosophized about teachers actually being people and having real families. That a teacher could have a life outside of class 2-205 and sit with an actual family outside the red brick walls of PS 20 was something truly bizarre.

Second graders should be the nation's philosopher laureates. Their experience in the world at the bright old age of six or seven proves that even the most primitive of philosophies arises from the Original Truth. Namely, that human suffering always occurs as a result of mean teachers and cheap parents. And if a teacher could actually be nice, then there was always room to celebrate and abrogate the Original Truth—even if it was only half-way.

While Mrs. Silverstein and Mrs. Heleno exchanged gossip and class behavior notes before the twin gongs signaling third hour, I thought about my Nan'na who always took her chai in a garden of wild grass and jasmine three oceans away. A Nan'na whose name meant leader of women. An aging spirit who rose before dawn for her morning prayers and counted tasbee beads with fingers embroidered in black henna.

With all her fiery breath, expert frigidity and favoritism, Mrs. Silverstein was only human after all. Had I been born in Queens to an American family named Silverstein, I could very well be calling her grandma and speaking with a weird American accent to some cousin named David.

Although the thought had a frightening ring to it, it actually comforted me in a way. I still hated her for making me feel the seizing fear each night but now she was no longer a dragon lady. She was different. She was human and had spots on her hands just like my Nan'na.   [1998]

Understanding the Reading

1. What was so frightening about Zafran's second-grade teacher?
2. Compare her mother with her teacher.
3. What is the Lisa Principle?
4. Why do the children notice Mrs. Silverstein's shoes?
5. Describe Mrs. Heleno's method of teaching music.
6. What made Zafran realize that her teacher was "only human after all"?

Suggestions for Responding

1. Find out something about the author's native country—Tanzania, East Africa.
2. Zafran drew strength from her knowledge and memories of her mother and grandmother, who helped her understand her world. Do you have one person from whom you draw strength? ✦

42

Something About the Subject Makes It Hard to Name

GLORIA YAMATO

Racism—simple enough in structure, yet difficult to eliminate. Racism—pervasive in the U.S. culture to the point that it deeply affects all the local town folk and spills over, negatively influencing the fortunes of folk around the world. Racism is pervasive to the point that we take many of its manifestations for granted, believing "that's life." Many believe that racism can be dealt with effectively in one hellifying workshop, or one hour-long heated discussion. Many actually believe this monster, racism, that has had at least a few hundred years to take root, grow, invade our space and develop subtle variations . . . this mind-funk that distorts thought and action, can be merely wished away. I've run into folks who really think that we can beat this devil, kick this habit, be healed of this disease in a snap. In a sincere blink of a well-intentioned eye, presto—poof—racism disappears. "I've dealt with my racism . . . (envision a laying on of hands) . . . Hallelujah! Now I can go to the beach." Well, fine. Go to the beach. In fact, why don't we all go to the beach and continue to work on the sucker over there? Cuz you can't even shave a little piece off this thing called racism in a day, or a weekend, or a workshop.

When I speak of *oppression,* I'm talking about the systematic, institutionalized mistreatment of one group of people by another for whatever reason. The oppressors are purported to have an innate ability to access economic resources, information, respect, etc., while the oppressed are believed to have a corresponding negative innate ability. The flip side of oppression is *internalized oppression.* Members of the target group are emotionally, physically, and spiritually battered to the point that they begin to actually believe that their oppression is deserved, is their lot in life, is natural and right, and that it doesn't even exist. The oppression begins to feel comfortable, familiar enough that when mean ol' Massa lay down de whip, we got's to pick up and whack ourselves and each other. Like a virus, it's hard to beat racism, because by the time you come up with a cure, it's mutated to a "new cure-resistant" form. One shot just won't get it. Racism must be attacked from many angles.

The forms of racism that I pick up on these days are (1) aware/blatant racism, (2) aware/covert racism, (3) unaware/unintentional racism, and (4) unaware/self-righteous racism. I can't say that I prefer any one form of racism over the others, because they all look like an itch needing a scratch. I've heard it said (and understandably so) that the aware/blatant form of racism is preferable if one must suffer it. Outright racists will, without apology or confusion, tell us that because of our color we don't appeal to them. If we so choose, we can attempt to get the hell out of their way before we get the sweat knocked out of us. Growing up, aware/covert racism is what I heard many of my elders bemoaning "up north," after having escaped the overt racism "down south." Apartments were suddenly no longer vacant or rents were outrageously high, when black, brown, red, or yellow persons went to inquire about them. Job vacancies were suddenly filled, or we were fired for very vague reasons. It still happens, though the perpetrators really take care to cover their tracks these days. They don't want to get gummed to death or slobbered on by the toothless laws that supposedly protect us from such inequities.

Unaware/unintentional racism drives usually tranquil white liberals wild when they get called on it, and confirms the suspicions of many people of color who feel that white folks are just plain crazy. It has led white people to believe that it's just fine to ask if they can touch my hair (while reaching). They then exclaim over how soft it is, how it does not scratch their hand. It has led whites to assume that bending over backwards and speaking to me in high-pitched (terrified), condescending tones would make up for all the racist wrongs that distort our lives. This type of racism had led whites right to my doorstep, talking 'bout, "We're sorry/we love you and want to make things right," which is fine, and further, "We're gonna give you the opportunity to fix it while we sleep. Just tell us what you need. 'Bye!!"—which *ain't* fine. With the best of intentions, the best of educations, and the greatest generosity of heart, whites, operating on the misinformation fed to them from day one, will behave in ways that are racist, will perpetuate racism by being "nice" the way we're taught to be nice. You can just "nice" somebody to death with naïveté and lack of awareness of privilege. Then there's guilt and the desire to end racism and how the two get all tangled up to the point that people, morbidly fascinated with their guilt, are immobilized. Rather than deal with ending racism, they sit and ponder their guilt and hope nobody notices how awful they are. Meanwhile, racism picks up momentum and keeps on keepin' on.

Now, the newest form of racism that I'm hip to is unaware/self-righteous racism. The "good wife" racist attempts to shame Blacks into being blacker, scorns Japanese-Americans who don't speak Japanese, and knows more about the Chicano/a community than the folks who make up the community. They assign themselves as the "good whites," as opposed to the "bad whites," and are often so busy telling people of color what the issues in the Black, Asian, Indian, Latino/a communities should be that they don't have time to deal with their errant sisters and brothers in the white community. Which means that people of color are still left to deal with what the "good whites" don't want to . . . racism.

Internalized racism is what really gets in my way as a Black woman. It influences the way I see or don't see myself, limits what I expect of myself or others like me. It results in my acceptance of mistreatment, leads me to believe that being treated with less than absolute respect, at least this once, is to be expected because I am Black, because I am not white. Because I am (*you fill in the color*), you think, "Life is going to be hard." The fact is life may be hard, but the color of your skin is not the cause of the hardship. The color of your skin may be used as an excuse to mistreat you, but there is no reason or logic involved in the mistreatment. If it seems that your color is the reason; if it seems that your ethnic heritage is the cause of the woe, it's because you've been deliberately beaten down by agents of a greedy system until you swallowed the garbage. That is the internalization of racism.

Racism is the systematic, institutionalized mistreatment of one group of people by another based on racial heritage. Like every other oppression, racism can be internalized. People of color come to believe misinformation about their particular ethnic group and thus believe that their mistreatment is justified. With that basic vocabulary, let's take a look at how the whole thing works together. Meet "the Ism Family," racism, classism, ageism, adultism, elitism, sexism, heterosexism, physicalism, etc. All these ism's are systematic, that is, not only are these parasites feeding off our lives, they are also dependent on one another for foundation. Racism is supported and reinforced by classism, which is given a foothold and a boost by adultism, which also feeds sexism, which is validated by heterosexism, and so it goes on. You cannot have the "ism" functioning without first effectively installing its flip-side, the internalized version of the ism. Like twins, as one particular form of the ism grows in potency, there is a corresponding increasing in its internalized form within the population. Before oppression becomes a specific ism like racism, usually all hell breaks loose. War. People fight attempts to enslave them, or to subvert their will, or to take what they consider theirs, whether that is territory or dignity. It's true that the various elements of racism, while repugnant, would not be able to do very much damage, but for one generally overlooked key piece: power/privilege.

While in one sense we all have power we have to look at the fact that, in our society, people are stratified into various classes and some of these classes have more privilege than others. The owning class has enough power and privilege to not have to give a good whinney what the rest of the folks have on their minds. The power and privilege of the owning class provides the ability to pay off enough of the working class and offer that paid-off group, the middle class, just enough privilege to make it agreeable to do various and sundry oppressive things to other working-class and outright disenfranchised folk, keeping the lid on explosive inequities, at least for a minute. If you're at the bottom of this heap, and you believe the line that says you're there because that's all you're worth, it is at least some small solace to believe that there are others more worthless than you, because of their gender, race, sexual preference . . . whatever. The specific form of power that runs the show here is the power to intimidate. The power to take away the most lives the quickest, and back it up with legal and "divine" sanction, is the very bottom line. It makes the difference between who's holding the racism end of the stick and who's getting beat with it (or beating others as vulnerable as they are) on the internalized racism end of the stick. What I am saying is, while people of color are welcome to tear up their own neighborhoods and each other, everybody knows that you cannot do that to white folks without hell to pay. People of color can be prejudiced against one another and whites, but do not have an ice-cube's chance in hell of passing laws that will get whites sent to relocation camps "for their own protection and the security of the nation." People who have not thought about or refuse to acknowledge this imbalance of power/privilege often want to talk about the racism of people of color. But then that is one of the ways racism is able to continue to function. You look for someone to blame and you blame the victim, who will nine times out of ten accept the blame out of habit.

So, what can we do? Acknowledge racism for a start, even though and especially when we've struggled to be kind and fair, or struggled to rise above it all. It is hard to acknowledge the fact that racism circumscribes and pervades our lives. Racism must be dealt with on two levels, personal and societal, emotional and institutional. It is possible—and most effective—to do both at the same time. We must reclaim whatever delight we have lost in our own ethnic heritage or heritages. This so-called melting pot has only succeeded in turning us into fast food-gobbling "generics" (as in generic "white folks" who were once Irish, Polish, Russian, English, etc. and "black folks," who were once Ashanti, Bambara, Baule, Yoruba, etc.). Find or create safe places to actually *feel* what we've been forced to repress each time we were a victim of, witness to or perpetrator of racism, so that we do not continue, like puppets, to act out the past in the present and future. Challenge oppression. Take a stand against it. When you are aware of something oppressive going down, stop the show. At least call it. We become so numbed to racism that we don't even think twice about it, unless it's immediately life-threatening.

Whites who want to be allies to people of color: You can educate yourselves via research and observation rather than rigidly, arrogantly relying solely on interrogating people of color. Do not expect that people of color should teach you how to behave non-oppressively. Do not give in to the pull to be lazy. Think, hard. Do not blame people of color for your frustration about racism, but do appreciate the fact that people of color will often help you get in touch with that frustration. Assume that your effort to be a good friend is appreciated, but don't expect or accept gratitude from people of color. Work on racism for your sake, not "their" sake. Assume that you are needed and capable of being a good ally. Know that you'll make mistakes and commit yourself to correcting them and continuing on as an ally, no matter what. Don't give up.

People of color, working through internalized racism: Remember always that you and others like you are completely worthy of respect, completely capable of achieving whatever you take a notion to do. Remember that the term "people of color" refers to a variety of ethnic and cultural backgrounds. These various groups have been oppressed in a variety of ways. Educate yourself about the ways different peoples have been oppressed and how they've resisted that oppression. Expect and insist that whites are capable of being good allies against racism. Don't give up. Resist the pull to give out the "people of color seal of approval" to aspiring white allies. A moment of appreciation is fine, but more than that tends to be less than helpful. Celebrate yourself. Celebrate yourself. Celebrate the inevitable end of racism.   [1988]

Understanding the Reading

1. Explain oppression and internalized oppression.
2. Explain the four forms of racism Yamato describes.
3. How does internalized racism work?
4. How do power and privilege reinforce "the Ism Family"?
5. What steps does Yamato suggest need to be taken to combat racism?

Suggestions for Responding

1. Describe an incident in which you were a victim of, witness to, or perpetrator of racism; then, analyze what feelings you were forced to repress.
2. What power and privileges do you enjoy as a result of your race, class, age, gender, sexual orientation, and so forth? ✦

43

White Privilege: Unpacking the Invisible Knapsack

Peggy McIntosh

Through work to bring materials from Women's Studies into the rest of the curriculum, I have often noticed men's unwillingness to grant that they are over-privileged, even though they may grant that women are disadvantaged. They may say they will work to improve women's status, in the society, the university, or the curriculum, but they can't or won't support the idea of lessening men's. Denials which amount to taboos surround the subject of advantages which men gain from women's disadvantages. These denials protect male privilege from being fully acknowledged, lessened or ended.

Thinking through unacknowledged male privilege as a phenomenon, I realized that since hierarchies in our society are interlocking, there was most likely a phenomenon of white privilege which was similarly denied and protected. As a white person, I realized I had been taught about racism as something which puts others at a disadvantage, but had been taught not to see one of its corollary aspects, white privilege, which puts me at an advantage.

I think whites are carefully taught not to recognize white privilege, as males are taught not to recognize male privilege. So I have begun in an untutored way to ask what it is like to have white privilege. I have come to see white privilege as an invisible package of unearned assets which I can count on cashing in each day, but about which I was "meant" to remain oblivious. White privilege is like an invisible weightless knapsack of special provisions, maps, passports, codebooks, visas, clothes, tools and blank checks.

Describing white privilege makes one newly accountable. As we in Women's Studies work to reveal male privilege and ask men to give up some of their power, so one who writes about having white privilege must ask, "Having described it, what will I do to lessen or end it?"

After I realized the extent to which men work from a base of unacknowledged privilege, I understood that much of their oppressiveness was unconscious. Then I remembered the frequent charges from women of color that white women whom they encounter are oppressive. I began to understand why we are justly seen as oppressive, even when we don't see ourselves that way. I began to count the ways in which I enjoy unearned skin privilege and have been conditioned into oblivion about its existence.

My schooling gave me no training in seeing myself as an oppressor, as an unfairly advantaged person, or as a participant in a damaged culture. I was taught to see myself as an individual whose moral state depended on her individual moral will. My schooling followed the pattern my colleague Elizabeth Minnich has pointed out: whites are taught to think of their lives as morally neutral, normative, and average, and also ideal, so that when we work to benefit others, this is seen as work which will allow "them" to be more like "us."

I decided to try to work on myself at least by identifying some of the daily effects of white privilege in my life. I have chosen those conditions which I think in my case *attach somewhat more to skin-color privilege* than to class, religion, ethnic status, or geographical location, though of course all these other factors are intricately intertwined. As far as I can see, my African American co-workers, friends and acquaintances with whom I come into daily or frequent contact in this particular time, place, and line of work cannot count on most of these conditions.

1. I can if I wish arrange to be in the company of people of my race most of the time.
2. If I should need to move, I can be pretty sure of renting or purchasing housing in an area which I can afford and in which I would want to live.
3. I can be pretty sure that my neighbors in such a location will be neutral or pleasant to me.
4. I can go shopping alone most of the time, pretty well assured that I will not be followed or harassed.
5. I can turn on the television or open to the front page of the paper and see people of my race widely represented.
6. When I am told about our national heritage or about "civilization," I am shown that people of my color made it what it is.

7. I can be sure that my children will be given curricular materials that testify to the existence of their race.

8. If I want to, I can be pretty sure of finding a publisher for this piece on white privilege.

9. I can go into a music shop and count on finding the music of my race represented, into a supermarket and find the staple foods which fit with my cultural traditions, into a hairdresser's shop and find someone who can cut my hair.

10. Whether I use checks, credit cards, or cash, I can count on my skin color not to work against the appearance of financial reliability.

11. I can arrange to protect my children most of the time from people who might not like them.

12. I can swear, or dress in second hand clothes, or not answer letters, without having people attribute these choices to the bad morals, the poverty, or the illiteracy of my race.

13. I can speak in public to a powerful male group without putting my race on trial.

14. I can do well in a challenging situation without being called a credit to my race.

15. I am never asked to speak for all the people of my racial group.

16. I can remain oblivious of the language and customs of persons of color who constitute the world's majority without feeling in my culture any penalty for such oblivion.

17. I can criticize our government and talk about how much I fear its policies and behavior without being seen as a cultural outsider.

18. I can be pretty sure that if I ask to talk to "the person in charge," I will be facing a person of my race.

19. If a traffic cop pulls me over or if the IRS audits my tax return, I can be sure I haven't been singled out because of my race.

20. I can easily buy posters, postcards, picture books, greeting cards, dolls, toys, and children's magazines featuring people of my race.

21. I can go home from most meetings of organizations I belong to feeling somewhat tied in, rather than isolated, out-of-place, outnumbered, unheard, held at a distance, or feared.

22. I can take a job with an affirmative action employer without having co-workers on the job suspect that I got it because of race.

23. I can choose public accommodation without fearing that people of my race cannot get in or will be mistreated in the places I have chosen.

24. I can be sure that if I need legal or medical help, my race will not work against me.

25. If my day, week, or year is going badly, I need not ask of each negative episode or situation whether it has racial overtones.

26. I can choose blemish cover or bandages in "flesh" color and have them more or less match my skin.

I repeatedly forgot each of the realizations on this list until I wrote it down. For me white privilege has turned out to be an elusive and fugitive subject. The pressure to avoid it is great, for in facing it I must give up the myth of meritocracy. If these things are true, this is not such a free country; one's life is not what one makes it; many doors open for certain people through no virtues of their own.

In unpacking this invisible knapsack of white privilege, I have listed conditions of daily experience which I once took for granted. Nor did I think of any of these perquisites as bad for the holder. I now think that we need a more finely differentiated taxonomy of privilege, for some of these varieties are only what one would want for everyone in a just society, and others give licence to be ignorant, oblivious, arrogant and destructive.

I see a pattern running through the matrix of white privilege, a pattern of assumptions which were passed on to me as a white person. There was one main piece of cultural turf; it was my own turf, and I was among those who could control the turf. *My skin color was an asset for any move I was educated to want to make.* I could think of myself as belonging in major ways, and of making social systems work for me. I could freely disparage, fear, neglect, or be oblivious to anything outside of the dominant cultural forms. Being of the main culture, I could also criticize it fairly freely.

In proportion as my racial group was being made confident, comfortable, and oblivious, other groups were likely being made inconfident, uncomfortable, and alienated. Whiteness protected me from many kinds of hostility, distress, and violence, which I was being subtly trained to visit in turn upon people of color.

For this reason, the word "privilege" now seems to me misleading. We usually think of privilege as being a favored state, whether earned or conferred by birth or luck. Yet some of the conditions I have described here work to systematically overempower certain groups. Such privilege simply *confers dominance* because of one's race or sex.

I want, then, to distinguish between earned strength and unearned power conferred systematically. Power from unearned privilege can look like strength when it is in fact permission to escape or to dominate. But not all of the privileges on my list are inevitably damaging. Some, like the expectation that neighbors will be decent to you, or that your race will not count against you in court, should be the norm in a just society. Others, like the privilege to ignore less powerful people, distort the humanity of the holders as well as the ignored groups.

We might at least start by distinguishing between positive advantages which we can work to spread, and negative types of advantages which unless rejected will always reinforce our present hierarchies. For example, the feeling that one belongs within the human circle, as Native Americans say, should not be seen as privilege for a few. Ideally it is an *unearned entitlement.* At present, since only a few have it, it is an *unearned advantage* for them. This paper results from a process of coming to see that some of the power which I originally saw as attendant on being a human being in the U.S. consisted [of] *unearned advantage* and *conferred dominance.*

I have met very few men who are truly distressed about systemic, unearned male advantage and conferred dominance. And so one question for me and others like me is whether we will be like them, or whether we will get truly distressed, even outraged, about unearned race advantage and conferred dominance and if so, what we will do to lessen them. In any case, we need to do more work in identifying how they actually affect our daily lives. Many, perhaps most, of our white students in the U.S. think that racism doesn't affect them because they are not people of color; they do not see "whiteness" as a racial identity. In addition, since race and sex are not the only

advantaging systems at work, we need similarly to examine the daily experience of having age advantage, or ethnic advantage, or physical ability, or advantage related to nationality, religion, or sexual orientation.

Difficulties and dangers surrounding the task of finding parallels are many. Since racism, sexism, and heterosexism are not the same, the advantaging associated with them should not be seen as the same. In addition, it is hard to disentangle aspects of unearned advantage which rest more on social class, economic class, race, religion, sex and ethnic identity than on other factors. Still, all of the oppressions are interlocking, as the Combahee River Collective[1] Statement of 1977 continues to remind us eloquently.

One factor seems clear about all of the interlocking oppressions. They take both active forms which we can see and embedded forms which as a member of the dominant group one is taught not to see. In my class and place, I did not see myself as a racist because I was taught to recognize racism only in individual acts of meanness by members of my group, never in invisible systems conferring unsought racial dominance on my group from birth.

Disapproving of the systems won't be enough to change them. I was taught to think that racism could end if white individuals changed their attitudes. [But] a "white" skin in the United States opens many doors for whites whether or not we approve of the way dominance has been conferred on us. Individual acts can palliate, but cannot end, these problems.

To redesign social systems we need first to acknowledge their colossal unseen dimensions. The silences and denials surrounding privilege are the key political tool here. They keep the thinking about equality or equity incomplete, protecting unearned advantage and conferred dominance by making these taboo subjects. Most talk by whites about equal opportunity seems to me now to be about equal opportunity to try to get into a position of dominance while denying that *systems* of dominance exist.

It seems to me that obliviousness about white advantage, like obliviousness about male advantage, is kept strongly inculturated in the United States so as to maintain the myth of meritocracy, the myth that democratic choice is equally available to all. Keeping most people unaware that freedom of confident action is there for just a small number of people props up those in power, and serves to keep power in the hands of the same groups that have most of it already.

Though systemic change takes many decades, there are pressing questions for me and I imagine for some others like me if we raise our daily consciousness on the perquisites of being light-skinned. What will we do with such knowledge? As we know from watching men, it is an open question whether we will choose to use unearned advantage to weaken hidden systems of advantage, and whether we will use any of our arbitrarily-awarded power to try to reconstruct power systems on a broader base.   [1989]

Term

1. COMBAHEE RIVER COLLECTIVE: A group of Black feminist women in Boston from 1974 to 1980.

Understanding the Reading

1. Why is it important to consider the concept of being overprivileged as well as the concept of being disadvantaged?
2. Explain what each of the conditions that arise from White privilege reveals about our cultural values.
3. Why are these privileges important?
4. What does McIntosh mean when she says she must give up the "myth of meritocracy"?
5. Which White privileges "give licence to be ignorant, oblivious, arrogant and destructive"?
6. What assumptions underlie White privilege?
7. What connections does McIntosh make among privilege, power, and dominance?
8. How is Whiteness a racial identity?

Suggestion for Responding

1. What did you learn from McIntosh's analysis of racism and White privilege, and what did you begin to think about after reading it? What additional privileges can you add to McIntosh's list? What will you do with such knowledge?   ◆

44

Native Americans vs. the U.S. Government

MICHAEL DORRIS

The turn of the twentieth century was an unhappy time for the Native people of America. Their total population was at its lowest ebb, the vast majority of their land had been taken away, their religions were outlawed, their children removed from home and incarcerated in hostile institutions where it was deemed a crime to so much as speak in one's own language. In 1900 few Native Americans were citizens and as a group they constituted the poorest, unhealthiest, and least likely to survive—much less succeed—population in all of the United States. And yet they not only survived, but they survived as a culturally intact group of peoples; against all odds, tribes maintained their languages and wisdom, guarded their art and music and literature, and for the most part, chose to continue to be Indians rather than assimilate and disappear.

The United States government, however, continued to advocate a melting-pot policy, and in 1924 Congress passed the Curtis Act, which conferred American citizenship on all native-born Indians. In many areas, such a change in status did not mean automatic access to the ballot box, however, and Native "citizens" remained disenfranchised "persons under guardianship" in Arizona and New Mexico until 1948.

Nevertheless, citizenship did, in the minds of some congressmen and others, abrogate the rights to special status which were guaranteed through treaty. Questions like "How can we have treaties with our own citizens?" (with its correlative answer: "We can't, therefore throw out the treaties and open up the land!!") should have been asked and answered before any such act was passed. *If* it had been made clear that United States citizenship meant abandonment of Native American identity, and *if* the opinion of Native American people had been solicited, it is improbable that even a significant minority of Indian people would have opted for it in 1924.

In effect, the Curtis Act was tantamount to the American government deciding to celebrate the Bicentennial in 1976 by unilaterally declaring all inhabitants of the Western Hemisphere "American citizens" and then immediately forcing any (former) Brazilian, Canadian, or Venezuelan engaging in international trade to comply with United States tariff restrictions and oil prices. Such an expanded Monroe Doctrine precludes all argument. The American experiment with instant naturalization is not unique: The Portuguese tried it in Angola, the Belgians in Zaire, and the French in Algeria—but somehow most Africans apparently never *felt* like Europeans. Most Native Americans didn't either, but by the twentieth century they lacked the population or resources to successfully dispute the denial of their sovereignty.

Four years later, a blue-ribbon congressional committee chaired by Lewis Meriam issued a report on conditions in Indian country. Its aim was to assess the effects of the Dawes[1] and Curtis acts and to inform the government of the progress these pieces of legislation had made possible for Native American people. The situation on reservations in 1928, however, yielded little in the way of optimistic forecast. Since 1887 conditions had universally worsened: The educational level was in most cases lower, the poverty greater, the death rate higher (and for younger people) than at any time previous to the enactment of the "benevolent" policies. Federal enforcement of the misguided and totally unjust severalty laws[2] was, in effect, cultural genocide.

In 1934 President Roosevelt appointed the anthropologist John Collier as Commissioner of Indian Affairs. Unlike too many of his predecessors in office, Collier actually knew something of at least one Native society (Pueblo) and had long opposed the Allotment policy[3] both for its inhumanity and its naiveté. His major achievement was to assist in the development and passage of the Indian Reorganization Act (the Wheeler-Howard Act), a policy which sought to undo most of the provisions of the Dawes Act and begin to remedy the disasters recounted in the Meriam Report of 1928.

Almost half a century, however, was a long time, and it was beyond realistic possibility that either the land base or the cultural, educational, and economic health of Native American societies could be restored as they were in 1880.

The Wheeler-Howard Act aimed to revive the traditional "bilateral, contractual relationship between the government and the tribes." Commissioner Collier emphasized the Native American right to a kind of self-determination and banned any further allotment of tribal land. The Indian Reorganization Act further authorized severely limited appropriations to purchase new holdings and reclaim certain lost property; it also established a federal loan policy for Native groups and reaffirmed the concept of self-government on reservations.

Many tribes opposed this legislation, however, on the basis of the restrictions and regulations it placed on the participating tribes. The act, for instance, prohibited any individual transfer of tribal land without governmental approval, and it required that all tribal governments conform to a single political system based on majority rule. No tribe was eligible for a single benefit of the act unless it agreed to it *in toto,* and therefore its acceptance necessarily became widespread.

The period following the Collier administration and extending into the early 1950's was one in which many Americans seemed to forget about Indians and assumed that *at last* "they" had finally vanished as predicted. The national interest was focused on World War II and the Korean War, and domestic treaties seemed a thing of the far-distant past.

After one of these "dormant cycles," the public and its government usually seem particularly piqued and frustrated to discover that Native Americans are still very much alive and intact. Once again in the 1950's, as in the 1880's, the presumptuous and thoroughly invalid assumption was made that if Indians had not chosen to disappear into the melting pot, something sinister was to blame. It seems never to have occurred to those in power that Crows or Yakimas, for instance, simply preferred being Crows or Yakimas!

As usual, the federal government, liberal "friends of the Indian," and rural land developers concluded that special status, and the reservation system in particular, were somehow retarding Native assimilation, and therefore it was decided, once again, to breach all legal precepts of international and United States law and unilaterally break treaty agreements. It was further concluded that if some Native Americans insisted that they didn't want to change their relationship with the government, they simply didn't know what was good for them. The rivers were still running, the grass was still growing, but the promises made by the American government and written to apply in perpetuity could not exist for even a century without twice being violated.

A committee was therefore appointed to divide, like Gaul,[4] all reservations into three parts: the "prosperous," the "marginal," and the "poor." Even with this license, only a handful of tribes could be found to fit, by any stretch of the imagination, into the first category, and these were marked for quick termination. The implications of this policy are clear: Apparently Congress regarded reservations as transitory steps between "primitive" and "modern" society. As soon as a group achieved a margin of success (according to the ethnocentric standards of American culture), a reservation ceased to have a rationale for existence. This self-serving attitude totally ignores both the political circumstances which brought about the reservation system in the first place (e.g., aboriginal right of title), and the legal treaties and sanctions which supposedly protected it.

Two of the most economically self-sustaining tribes, the Klamath in Oregon and the Menominee in Wisconsin, were located in timberland areas and operated logging industries. The government exerted tremendous pressure, employing levers of doubtful legal and ethical practice, and the manipulation of misunderstanding, to force these tribes to submit to termination. Whether this consent was ever actually granted in either case is a debatable point, but it is clear that neither group, had it sufficiently understood the policy, would have agreed.

Termination meant the absolute cessation, in exchange for a monetary settlement, of any special treaty arrangements or status which existed between the tribe and its members and the United States government. Upon termination, the Menominees would be expected, in legal effect, to cease being Indians and to somehow turn themselves into Wisconsonians overnight. On a date set by the government, the dependent, sovereign Menominee Nation, hundreds of years old, would become simply another county within the state.

Historical retrospect clearly shows that in all cases the termination policy was even more ill-conceived and socially disruptive than the Allotment policy had been before it—and just as illegal. The net effects of termination were the loss of large amounts of valuable land by the tribes involved, plus an enormous psychological blow to thousands of Indian people. The fallacy of the policy was patently obvious so quickly that it was suspended shortly after implementation, sparing other tribes similar losses. To date, one of the victimized tribes, the Menominee, has, through persistent and valiant efforts of a group of its members, managed to be reestablished as a reservation in 1973. But as a direct result of termination, the new Menominee lands were much smaller and poorer than the reservation had been before 1953.

Subsequent government policies aimed at assimilating the Native American were more subtle. Among these were the urban relocation programs, often hastily conceived and poorly managed attempts to induce Native Americans to migrate to cities. A substantial percentage of the participants in these programs eventually returned, frustrated and cynical, to their reservations.   [1975]

Term

1. DAWES ACT: The federal law that abolished tribal organizations and allotted 160 acres to the head of each family.
2. SEVERALTY LAWS: Laws mandating that land must be held by individuals rather than in common by the whole group.
3. ALLOTMENT POLICY: The distribution of reservation land under the Dawes Act and the opening of undistributed land to Whites.
4. GAUL: An ancient name for what are now France and Belgium. Julius Caesar opened his history with the statement "All Gaul is divided into three parts."

Understanding the Reading

1. What effect did the Curtis Act have on Native Americans?
2. What were conditions like on reservations in 1928?
3. What were the benefits and restrictions of the Indian Reorganization Act?
4. What was "termination," and what were its effects?

1. Dorris presents the analogy of the U.S. government unilaterally declaring all inhabitants of the Western Hemisphere to be American citizens. Suppose this actually happened and write about how you would respond personally if you were a citizen of one of the annexed countries.
2. Research one of the governmental policies Dorris mentions; explain what it was supposed to do and what it actually did. ✦

45

Urban Indians

ROBERTA FISKE-RUSCIANO

The term "urban Indians" is problematic for most non-Native Americans. Whether thinking of Native Americans brings forth positive, negative, or neutral images, most non-natives do not imagine natives as members of an urban, technological society, and this lack of urban image has led to a blindness regarding the presence and needs of Native Americans in the cities. Identification of the urban Native American has therefore been one of the central problems surrounding government policy-making regarding American Indians since the early 1960's.

RELOCATION AND MIGRATION

All members of a federally recognized tribe in the United States, according to the U.S. Constitution, are due certain benefits and services, by right of their heritage. This unique legal relationship with the U.S. government was never meant to end once an individual moved to a metropolitan area, but in effect that is what has happened. In the mid-1950's, the Bureau of Indian Affairs (BIA), in accord with Congress, began the Voluntary Relocation Program. BIA officers on each reservation were instructed to "sell" the idea of city living to likely candidates. Individuals, and sometimes families, were given a one-way ticket to the chosen city, where housing and employment awaited,

all arranged by the BIA. Subsistence money was guaranteed for six weeks, after which these newest immigrants were on their own. It was informally known as a "sink-or-swim policy." As anthropologist Sol Tax noted twenty years after relocation, however, "Indians don't sink or swim, they float."

Most Indians who arrived in the city under the relocation program left as soon as they got a good look at their new way of life. Many of the jobs were unskilled, and Native Americans found they were able to afford only the worst housing available in the city. Under these conditions, transition to city dwelling was, for many, impossible. Yet the BIA did not recognize the shortcomings of its multimillion-dollar program and continued to relocate as many Native Americans as possible. Noticing that many of their clients were returning to their reservations, the BIA began relocating people as far away from their reservations as could be managed, to make it as difficult as possible to return. Part of the plan was to terminate the reservations eventually. Authors Watt Spade and Willard Walker illustrate one Indian view of this phase of the relocation program. They wrote of overhearing two Indian men humorously discussing the government's wanting to land a man on the moon. It could be done, one man said, but nobody knew how to get the man home again after he landed on the moon. All the government had to do, he said, was put an Indian in the rocket ship and tell him he was being relocated: "Then, after he got to the moon, that Indian would find his own way home again and the government wouldn't have to figure that part out at all." The Voluntary Relocation Program was a failure according to its own goals. This program was based on the prejudiced notion that Native American culture and life-ways will, and should, disappear. The BIA and the U.S. Congress of the 1950's counted on America's cities to speed that process.

Most Native Americans presently living in urban areas did not arrive through the relocation program but migrated independently, usually looking for employment, and settled near relatives or friends from their reservation or hometown. Many are permanent residents, but an approximately equal number are transient—relocating within the city, going from city to city, or spending part of the year in the city and part on the reservation. There is no known "typical" pattern of migration; tribal nations, families, and individuals differ according to their needs. A family may live in the city during the winter so the children can stay in school, then leave for the reservation in the summer. Construction workers are often busy in the cities during the warm months and leave in the winter. The powwow season and harvests also draw many urban Native Americans back to the reservations. Jeanne Guillemin points out in *Urban Renegades* (1975) that the young Micmac women of Boston often prefer to return to their kin in the Canadian Maritime Provinces when it is time to give birth. There they receive the physical, emotional, and spiritual support they need and avoid the frightening aspects of the city, such as its clinics and hospitals. The frequent moving to and from the reservation and within the city is one factor in the urban Native American's invisibility or elusiveness.

Urban Indian Identity

Another factor until recently has been their reluctance to identify themselves as Native Americans to non-Native Americans in the city. In 1976 the director of the American Indian Health Service in Chicago illustrated this problem with an anecdote. A young man had been playing baseball and had been hit hard by the bat. When he was taken to the emergency room, he removed all his turquoise beads, giving them to a friend to keep for him, and stuffed his long braids inside his baseball cap; he said, "Now the receptionist will think I'm a Mexican." His friend said they frequently try to pass as Mexicans in order to be treated better. The urban Native Americans' attempts to remain unidentified, coupled with the tremendous mobility of individuals and families, has made it impossible in past years for the U.S. Census to come close to an accurate count in the cities. In the 1990 U.S. Census, however, there was a huge increase in people identifying themselves as Native Americans, Eskimos, and Aleuts. As the increase cannot be completely explained by actual population growth, there is much speculation regarding what has made so many more Native Americans willing to be identified. Some cynical observers insist that the motive must be

monetary: to obtain funds and services that are due Native Americans under the law. One thing that scholars studying Native American culture have learned over the decades, however, is that Native Americans usually cannot be coaxed to take a particular course of action because of the promise of money. Most Native Americans living in cities do not receive federal funds or services of any kind, because of distrust of Indian or non-Indian agencies and a preference for finding survival strategies among one another.

In the past, most sociological studies have focused on the atypical urban Native American—the one most visible, "lying in the gutter," cut off from kin. It is important to learn how most urban Native Americans (neither the upper middle-class professionals nor the indigent) have found their way in this foreign environment, maintaining strong kin relationships and networks and not necessarily assimilating. Native Americans have arrived in cities all over the United States for many reasons; work opportunities and education are the most commonly cited. Guillemin states another very important reason in her chapter "The City as Adventure." For the Micmac of Canada, she points out, going to Boston is seen as extending one's tribal boundaries. While trying to survive in this environment, the young Micmac learn much about coping with conditions as they meet them in the South End, a settling ground for immigrants from all over the world. Their risk-taking and networking are important parts of a young urban Native American's education. Flexibility is seen as one key to their tribal nation's survival. While it is often assumed that cities temper and neutralize (if not actually melt) the unique cultures of their residents, in this case a native people is claiming the city as their own and using it for their own purposes—to strengthen themselves as members of an Indian nation as well as to survive and enjoy themselves. Some cities, such as Chicago, operate high-quality schools for Native American children as further insurance against their losing precious traditions and ways of thinking.

Gambling as Urban Legacy

One clear consequence of Native Americans learning to deal with the bureaucratic state has been the

TEN LARGEST PLACES IN TOTAL POPULATION AND IN AMERICAN INDIAN AND ALASKA NATIVE POPULATION: 2000
(For information on confidentiality protection, nonsampling error, and definitions, see www. census. gov/ prod/cen2000/doc/sf1. pdf)

Place	Total Population		American Indian and Alaska Native Alone		American Indian and Alaska Native Alone or in Combination		Percent of Total Population	
---	---	---	---	---	---	---	American Indian and Alaska Native Alone	American Indian and Alaska Native Alone or in Combination
	Rank	Number	Rank	Number	Rank	Number		
New York, NY	1	8,008,278	1	41,289	1	87,241	0.5	1.1
Los Angeles, CA	2	3,694,820	2	29,412	2	53,092	0.8	1.4
Chicago, IL	3	2,896,016	9	10,290	8	20,898	0.4	0.7
Houston, TX	4	1,953,631	11	8,568	10	15,743	0.4	0.8
Philadelphia, PA	5	1,517,550	24	4,073	21	10,835	0.3	0.7
Phoenix, AZ	6	1,321,045	3	26,696	3	35,093	2.0	2.7
San Diego, CA	7	1,223,400	13	7,543	9	16,178	0.6	1.3
Dallas, TX	8	1,188,580	18	6,472	18	11,334	0.5	1.0
San Antonio, TX	9	1,144,646	10	9,584	12	15,224	0.8	1.3
Detroit, MI	10	951,270	40	3,140	25	8,907	0.3	0.9
Oklahoma, OK	29	506,132	6	17,743	5	29,001	3.5	5.7
Tucson, AZ	30	486,699	8	11,038	11	15,358	2.3	3.2
Albuquerque, NM	35	448,607	7	17,444	7	22,047	3.9	4.9
Tulsa, OK	43	393,049	5	18,551	4	30,227	4.7	7.7
Anchorage, AK	65	260,283	4	18,941	6	26,995	7.3	10.4

Source: U.S. Census Bureau, Census 2000 Summary File 1.

success stories of Indian nations using the existing laws to repair damages done to their nations, such as bringing an economic base to their reservation. One example comes from the small Pequot Nation in Ledyard, Connecticut. In response to a 1988 ruling holding that federal law allows recognized Indian tribes to have gambling on reservations if the state in which they live allows some sort of gambling off the reservation, the Pequots set up a large gambling center, the Foxwoods Resort and Casino. The gambling question affects reservations all over the country; from California to New Jersey, Native Americans are debating the serious question of what effects the presence of casinos would have on their reservations. Many are now in operation. Although most reservation casinos are not located in large metropolitan areas, the situation clearly involves the bringing of some aspects of the city (in concentrated doses) to the reservation. Although various forms of gambling have existed traditionally among many Native American nations, the dangers and problems that seem to surround non-Native American casino centers worry many people. It has been predicted that the Pequots will become millionaires, for example; whether this will help the Pequots to strengthen their nation or will pull it apart at the seams is an unanswered question. Many of the same questions that have concerned native peoples for generations—about the quality of life left for their people—continue to worry them, whether they be on an impoverished reservation, in a large city, or on a reservation that has made casino gambling the economic base of its people's lives. Certainly the revenues are benefiting many people now, Indian and non-Indian alike.

It is impossible to predict accurately what the long-term effects of such changes will be, but it is likely that current and future generations of Native Americans will be able to draw upon the resilience typical of Indian peoples. They will remain strong and independent as a group while balancing the need to protect their traditions with the need to accept, even embrace, change.   [1995, 2012]

References

Fiske, Roberta. "Native American Artists in Chicago." In *A Report on the Chicago Ethnic Arts Project*. Washington, D.C.: Library of Congress, American Folklife Center, 1978.

Guillemin, Jeanne. *Urban Renegades*. New York: Columbia University Press, 1975.

Johnson, Kirk. "Seeking Lost Culture at a Pow-wow: Pequots Draw Ritual Dancers Across U.S. with Rich Prizes." *The New York Times*, September 19, 1993, 52.

Kaufman, Michael T. "A James Bond with $100 Tries out a Tribal Casino." *The New York Times*, March 18, 1994, C1.

Lurie, Nancy. "The Contemporary American Indian Scene." In *North American Indians in Historical Perspective*, edited by Eleanor Burke Leacock and Nancy Lurie. New York: Random House, 1971.

Spade, Watt, and Willard Walker. "Relocation." In *The Way: An Anthology of American Indian Life*, edited by Shirley Hill Witt and Stan Steiner. New York: Alfred A. Knopf, 1972.

Understanding the Reading

1. What was the purpose of the Voluntary Relocation Program?
2. Why was it a failure?
3. Why do Native Americans go to cities to live?
4. Why have they been reluctant, until recently, to be identified as Indians in urban areas?
5. What is one survival strategy they have learned, as a result of dealing with the bureaucratic state?

Suggestions for Responding

1. Research which American Indians live nearest to you. How do they make a living?
2. Look for data on the general health and other socioeconomic markers of Indians in any U.S. urban area. ◆

46

Sex, Class, and Race Intersections: Visions of Women of Color

CAROL LEE SANCHEZ

> "As I understand it," said the American Indian [to one of the Puritan fathers], "you propose to civilize me."
> "Exactly."
> "You want to get me out of the habit of idleness and teach me to work."
> "That is the idea."
> "And then lead me to simplify my methods and invent things to make my work lighter."
> "Yes."
> "And after that I'll become ambitious to get rich so that I won't have to work at all."
> "Naturally."
> "Well what's the use of taking such a roundabout way of getting just where I started from? I don't have to work now."
>
> —[American jokelore]

To identify Indian is to identify with an invisible or vanished people; it is to identify with a set of basic assumptions and beliefs held by *all* who are not Indian about the indigenous peoples of the Americas. Even among the Spanish-speaking Mestizos or mezclados,[1] there is a strong preference to "disappear" their Indian blood, to disassociate from their Indian beginnings. To be Indian is to be considered "colorful," spiritual, connected to the earth, simplistic, and disappointing if not dressed in buckskin and feathers;

shocking if a city-dweller and even more shocking if an educator or other type of professional. That's the positive side.

On the negative side, to be Indian is to be thought of as primitive, alcoholic, ignorant (as in "Dumb Indian"), better off dead (as in "the only good Indian is a dead Indian" or "I didn't know there was any of you folks still left"), unskilled, non-competitive, immoral, pagan or heathen, untrustworthy (as in "Indian-giver") and frightening. To be Indian is to be the primary model that is used to promote racism in this country.

How can that happen, you ask? Bad press. One hundred and fifty years of the most consistently vicious press imaginable. Newspapers, dime novels, textbooks and fifty years of visual media have portrayed and continue to portray Indians as savage, blood-thirsty, immoral, inhuman people. When there's a touch of social consciousness attached, you will find the once "blood-thirsty," "white-killer savage" portrayed as a pitiful drunk, a loser, an outcast or a mixblood not welcomed by, or trusted by, either race. For fifty years, children in this country have been raised to kill Indians mentally, subconsciously through the visual media, until it is an automatic reflex. That shocks you? Then I have made my point.

Let me quote from Helen Hunt Jackson's book, *A Century of Dishonor,* from the introduction written by Bishop H. B. Whipple of Minnesota, who charged that

> the American people have accepted as truth the teachings that the Indians were a degraded, brutal race of savages, who it was the will of God should perish at the approach of civilization. If they do not say with our Puritan fathers that these are the Hittites[2] who are to be driven out before the saints of the Lord, they do accept the teaching that manifest destiny[3] will drive the Indians from the earth. The inexorable has no tears or pity at the cries of anguish of the doomed race.

This race still struggles to stay alive. Tribe by Tribe, pockets of Indian people here and there. One million two hundred thousand people who identify as Indians—raised and socialized as Indian—as of the 1980 census, yet Cowboys and Indians is still played every day by children all over America of every creed, color, and nationality. Well—it's harmless, isn't it? Just kids playing kill Indians. It's all history. But it's still happening every day, and costumes are sold and the cheap western is still rolling out of Hollywood, the old shoot-'em-up westerns playing on afternoon kid shows, late night T.V. Would you allow your children to play Nazis and Jews? Blacks and KKKs? Complete with costume? Yes! It is a horrifying thought, but in thinking about it you can see how easy it is to dismiss an entire race of people as barbaric and savage, and how almost impossible it is, after this has been inculcated in you, to relate to an Indian or a group of Indians today. For example, how many famous Indians do you know offhand? Certainly the great warrior chiefs come to mind first, and of course the three most famous Indian "Princesses"—Pocahontas, Sacajawea and La Malinche. Did you get past ten? Can you name at least five Indian women you know personally or have heard about? That's just counting on one hand, folks.

As Indians, we have endured. We are still here. We have survived everything that European "civilization" has imposed on us. There are approximately 130 different Indian languages still spoken in North America of the some 300 spoken at contact; 180 different Tribes incorporated and recognized by the Federal Government of the approximately 280 that once existed, with an additional 15 to 25 unrecognized Tribes that are lumped together on a reservation with other Tribes. We still have Women's Societies and there are at least 30 active women-centered Mother-Rite Cultures[4] existing and practicing their everyday life in that manner, on this continent.

We have been displaced, relocated, removed, terminated, educated, acculturated and in our hearts and minds we will always "go back to the blanket"[5] as long as we are still connected to our families, our Tribes and our land.

The Indian Way is a different way. It is a respectful way. The basic teachings in every Tribe that exists today as a Tribe in the western hemisphere are based on respect for all the things our Mother gave us. If we neglect her or anger her, she will make our lives very difficult and we always know that we have a hardship on ourselves and on our children. We are raised to be cautious and concerned for the *future* of our people, and that is how we raise our children—because *they* are *our* future. Your "civilization" has made all of us very sick and has made our mother earth sick and out of balance. Your kind of thinking and education has brought the whole world to the brink of total disaster, whereas the thinking and education among my people forbids the practice of almost everything Euro-Americans, in particular, value.

Those of you who are socialists and marxists have an ideology, but where in this country do you live communally on a common land base from generation to generation? Indians, who have a way of life instead of an ideology, do live on communal lands and don't accumulate anything—for the sake of accumulation.

Radicals look at reservation Indians and get very upset about their poverty conditions. But poverty to us is not the same thing as poverty is to you. Our poverty is that we can't be who we are. We can't hunt or fish or grow our food because our basic resources and the right to use them in traditional ways are denied us. In order to live well, we must be able to provide for ourselves in such a way that we can continue living as we always have. We still don't believe in being slaves to the "domineering" culture systems. Consequently, we are accused of many things based on those standards and values that make no sense to us.

You want us to act like you, to be like you so that we will be more acceptable, more likeable. You should try to be more like us regarding communal co-existence; respect and care for all living things and for the earth, the waters, and the atmosphere; respect for human dignity and the right to be who they are.

During the 1930s, '40s and '50s, relocation programs caused many Indians to become lost in the big cities of the United States and there were many casualties from alcoholism, vagrancy and petty crime. Most Indians were/ are jailed for assault and battery in barroom brawls because the spiritual and psychological violation of Indian people trying to live in the dominant (domineering) culture generally forces us to numb ourselves as frequently as possible. That is difficult, if not impossible, for you to understand. White science studies dead things and creates poisonous substances to kill and maim the creatures as well as the humans. You call that progress. Indians call it insanity. Our science studies living things; how they interact and how they maintain a balanced existence. Your science disregards—even denies— the spirit world: ours believes in it and remains connected to it. We fast, pray to our ancestors, call on them when we dance and it rains—at Laguna, at Acoma, at Hopi—still, today. We fight among ourselves, we have border disputes, we struggle to exist in a modern context with our lands full of timber, uranium, coal, oil, gasoline, precious metals and semi-precious stones; full—because we are taught to take only what we need and not because we are too ignorant to know what to do with all those resources. We are caught in the bind between private corporations and the government—"our guardian"— because they/you want all those resources. "Indians certainly don't need them"—and your people will do *anything* to get their hands on our mineral-rich lands. They will legislate, stir up internal conflicts, cause inter-Tribal conflicts, dangle huge amounts of monies as compensation for perpetual contracts and promise lifetime economic security. If we object, or sue to protect our lands, these suits will be held in litigation for fifteen to twenty years with "white" interests benefiting in the interim. Some of us give up and sell out, but there are many of us learning to hold out and many many more of us going back to the old ways of thinking, because we see that our ancestors were right and that the old ways were better ways. So, more Indians are going "back to the blanket," back to "Indian time," with less stress, fewer dominant (domineering) culture activities and occupations. Modern Indians are recreating Indian ways once again. All this leads to my vision as an Indian woman. It is my hope:

1. that you—all you non-Indians—study and learn about our systems of thought and internal social and scientific practices, leaving your Patriarchal Anthropology and History textbooks, academic training and methodologies at home or in the closet on a dusty shelf.

2. that your faculties, conference organizers, community organizers stop giving lip service to including a "Native American" for this or that with the appended phrase: "if we only knew one!" Go find one. There are hundreds of resource lists or Indian-run agencies,

hundreds of Indian women in organizations all over the country—active and available with valuable contributions to make.

3. that you will strongly discourage or STOP the publication of any and all articles *about* Indians *written by non-Indians,* and publish work written by Indians about ourselves—whether you agree with us, approve of us or not.

4. that you will *stop colonizing us* and reinterpreting *our* experience.

5. that you will *listen* to us and *learn* from us. We carry ancient traditions that are thousands of years old. We are modern and wear clothes like yours and handle all the trappings of your "civilization" as well as ours; maintain your Christianity as well as our ancient religions, and we are still connected to our ancestors, and our land base. You are the foreigners as long as you continue to believe in the progress that destroys our Mother.

You are not taught to respect our perfected cultures or our scientific achievements which have just recently been re-evaluated by your social scientists and "deemed worthy" of respect. Again, let me re-state that 150 years of bad press will certainly make it extremely difficult for most white people to accept these "primitive" achievements without immediately attempting to connect them to aliens from outer space, Egyptians, Vikings, Asians and whatever sophisticated "others" you have been educated to acknowledge as those who showed the "New World" peoples "The Way." Interestingly, the only continents that were ever "discovered" (historically) where people already lived are North and South America. Who discovered Europe? Who discovered Africa? Who discovered Asia? Trade routes, yes—continents, no. Manifest Destiny will continue to reign as long as we teach our children that Columbus "discovered" America. Even this "fact" is untrue. He actually discovered an island in the Caribbean and *failed* to discover Cathay!

When we consistently make ourselves aware of these "historical facts" that are presented by the Conqueror—the White Man—only then can all of us benefit from cultural traditions that are ten to thirty thousand years old. It is time for us to *share* the best of all our traditions and cultures, all over the world; and it is our duty and responsibility as the women of the world to make this positive contribution in any and every way we can, or we will ultimately become losers, as the Native Race of this hemisphere lost some four hundred years ago.   [1988]

Terms

1. Mestizos or Mezclados: The Latin American name for the offspring of a Native American and a Spaniard.

2. Hittites: Ancient non-Black peoples of Asia Minor and Syria.

3. Manifest destiny: A nineteenth-century belief that White people had the duty and right to control and develop the entire North American continent.

4. Mother-Rite Cultures: Societies in which motherhood is the central kinship bond and women are highly valued and have considerable influence.

5. "Go back to the blanket": A phrase used by missionaries and White educators referring to "educated" Indian children who rejected White "civilized" values and returned to their native culture.

Understanding the Reading

1. What are the positive and negative stereotypes of American Indians?

2. What does Sanchez mean when she says, "Children of this country have been raised to kill Indians"?

3. How does Sanchez characterize the Indian way?

4. Why do you think Sanchez objects to "articles about Indians written by non-Indians"?

5. What point is Sanchez making by her list of hopes?

Suggestions for Responding

1. Name and identify all the Native Americans you can think of. What does your list show you?

2. Write a summary of what you learned and thought about Indians when you were a child. Analyze how this correlates with Sanchez's assertions about cultural stereotypes of Indians. ✦

47

Crimes Against Humanity

Ward Churchill

During the past couple of seasons, there has been an increasing wave of controversy regarding the names of professional sports teams like the Atlanta "Braves," Cleveland "Indians," Washington "Redskins," and Kansas City "Chiefs." The issue extends to the names of college teams like Florida State University "Seminoles," University of Illinois "Fighting Illini," and so on, right on down to high school outfits like the Lamar (Colorado) "Savages." Also involved have been team adoption of "mascots," replete with feathers, buckskins, beads, spears and "warpaint" (some fans have opted to adorn themselves in the same fashion), and nifty little "pep" gestures like the "Indian Chant" and "Tomahawk Chop."

A substantial number of American Indians have protested that use of native names, images and symbols as sports team mascots and the like is, by definition, a virulently racist practice. Given the historical relationship between Indians and non-Indians during what has been called the "Conquest of America," American Indian Movement leader (and American Indian Anti-Defamation Council founder) Russell Means has compared the practice to contemporary Germans naming their soccer teams the "Jews," "Hebrews," and "Yids," while adorning their uniforms with grotesque caricatures of Jewish faces taken from the Nazis' anti-Semitic propaganda of the 1930s. Numerous demonstrations have occurred in conjunction with games—most notably during the November 15, 1992 match-up between the Chiefs and Redskins in Kansas City—by angry Indians and their supporters.

In response, a number of players—especially African Americans and other minority athletes—have been trotted out by professional team owners like Ted Turner, as well as university and public school officials, to announce that they mean not to insult but to honor native people. They have been joined by the television networks and most major newspapers, all of which have editorialized that Indian discomfort with the situation is "no big deal," insisting that the whole thing is just "good, clean fun." The country needs more such fun, they've argued, and "a few disgruntled Native Americans" have no right to undermine the nation's enjoyment of its leisure time by complaining. This is especially the case, some have argued, "in hard times like these." It has even been contended that Indian outrage at being systematically degraded—rather than the degradation itself—creates "a serious barrier to the sort of intergroup communication so necessary in a multicultural society such as ours."

Okay, let's communicate. We are frankly dubious that those advancing such positions really believe their own rhetoric, but, just for the sake of argument, let's accept the premise that they are sincere. If what they say is true, then isn't it time we spread such "inoffensiveness" and "good cheer" around among *all* groups so that *everybody* can participate *equally* in fostering the round of national laughs they call for? Sure it is—the country can't have too much fun or "intergroup involvement"—so the more, the merrier. Simple consistency demands that anyone who thinks the Tomahawk Chop is a swell pastime must be just as hearty in their endorsement of the following ideas—by the logic used to defend the defamation of American Indians— [to] help us all really start yukking it up.

First, as a counterpart to the Redskins, we need an NFL team called "Niggers" to honor Afro-Americans. Half-time festivities for fans might include a simulated stewing of the opposing coach in a large pot while players and cheerleaders dance around it, garbed in leopard skins and wearing fake bones in their noses. This concept obviously goes along with the kind of gaiety attending the Chop, but also with the actions of the Kansas City Chiefs, whose team members—prominently including black team members—lately appeared on a poster looking "fierce" and "savage" by way of wearing Indian regalia. Just a bit of harmless "morale boosting," says the Chiefs' front office. You bet.

So that the newly-formed Niggers sports club won't end up too out of sync while expressing the "spirit" and "identity" of Afro-Americans in the above fashion, a baseball franchise—let's call this one the "Sambos"—should be formed. How about a basketball team called the "Spearchuckers"? A hockey team called the "Jungle Bunnies"? Maybe the "essence" of these teams could be depicted by images of tiny black faces adorned with huge pairs of lips. The players could appear on TV every week or so gnawing on chicken legs and spitting watermelon seeds at one another. Catchy, eh? Well, there's "nothing to be upset about," according to those who love wearing "war bonnets" to the Super Bowl or having "Chief Illiniwik" dance around the sports arenas of Urbana, Illinois.

And why stop there? There are plenty of other groups to include. "Hispanics"? They can be "represented" by the Galveston "Greasers" and San Diego "Spics," at least until the Wisconsin "Wetbacks" and Baltimore "Beaners" get off the ground. Asian Americans? How about the "Slopes," "Dinks," "Gooks," and "Zipperheads"? Owners of the latter teams might get their logo ideas from editorial page cartoons printed in the nation's newspapers during World War II: slant-eyes, buck teeth, big glasses, but nothing racially insulting or derogatory, according to the editors and artists involved at the time. Indeed, this Second World War–vintage stuff can be seen as just another barrel of laughs, at least by what current editors say are their "local standards" concerning American Indians.

Let's see. Who's been left out? Teams like the Kansas City "Kikes," Hanover "Honkies," San Leandro "Shylocks," Daytona "Dagos," and Pittsburgh "Polacks" will fill a certain social void among white folk. Have a religious belief? Let's all go for the gusto and gear up the Milwaukee "Mackerel Snappers" and Hollywood "Holy Rollers." The Fighting Irish of Notre Dame can be rechristened the "Drunken Irish" or "Papist Pigs." Issues of gender and sexual preference can be addressed through creation of teams like the St. Louis "Sluts," Boston "Bimbos," Detroit "Dykes," and the Fresno "Fags." How about the Gainesville "Gimps" and Richmond "Retards," so the physically and mentally impaired won't be excluded from our fun and games?

Now, don't go getting "overly sensitive" out there. None of this is demeaning or insulting, at least not when it's being done to Indians. Just ask the folks who are doing it, or their apologists like Andy Rooney in the national media. They'll tell you—as in fact they *have* been telling you—that there's been no harm done, regardless of what their victims think, feel, or say. The situation is exactly the same as when those with precisely the same mentality used to

insist that Step 'n' Fetchit was okay, or Rochester on the Jack Benny Show, or Amos and Andy, Charlie Chan, the Frito Bandito, or any of the other cutesy symbols making up the lexicon of American racism. Have we communicated yet?

Let's get just a little bit real here. The notion of "fun" embodied in rituals like the Tomahawk Chop must be understood for what it is. There's not a single non-Indian example used above which can be considered socially acceptable in even the most marginal sense. The reasons are obvious enough. So why is it different where American Indians are concerned? One can only conclude that, in contrast to the other groups at issue, Indians are (falsely) perceived as being too few, and therefore too weak, to defend themselves effectively against racist and otherwise offensive behavior.

Fortunately, there are some glimmers of hope. A few teams and their fans have gotten the message and have responded appropriately. Stanford University, which opted to drop the name "Indians" from Stanford, has experienced no resulting dropoff in attendance. Meanwhile, the local newspaper in Portland, Oregon, recently decided its long-standing editorial policy prohibiting use of racial epithets should include derogatory team names. The Redskins, for instance, are now referred to as "the Washington team," and will continue to be described in this way until the franchise adopts an inoffensive moniker (newspaper sales in Portland have suffered no decline as a result).

Such examples are to be applauded and encouraged. They stand as figurative beacons in the night, proving beyond all doubt that it is quite possible to indulge in the pleasure of athletics without accepting blatant racism into the bargain.

On October 16, 1946, a man named Julius Streicher mounted the steps of a gallows. Moments later he was dead, the sentence of an international tribunal composed of representatives of the United States, France, Great Britain, and the Soviet Union having been imposed. Streicher's body was then cremated, and—so horrendous were his crimes thought to have been—his ashes dumped into an unspecified German river so that "no one should ever know a particular place to go for reasons of mourning his memory."

Julius Streicher had been convicted at Nuremberg, Germany, of what were termed "Crimes Against Humanity." The lead prosecutor in his case—Justice Robert Jackson of the United States Supreme Court—had not argued that the defendant had killed anyone, nor that he had personally committed any especially violent act. Nor was it contended that Streicher had held any particularly important position in the German government during the period in which the so-called Third Reich had exterminated some 6,000,000 Jews, as well as several million Gypsies, Poles, Slavs, homosexuals, and other untermenschen (subhumans).

The sole offense for which the accused was ordered put to death was in having served as publisher/editor of a Bavarian tabloid entitled *Der Stürmer* during the early-to-mid 1930s, years before the Nazi genocide actually began. In this capacity, he had penned a long series of virulently anti-Semitic editorials and "news" stories, usually accompanied by cartoons and other images graphically depicting Jews in extraordinarily derogatory fashion. This, the prosecution asserted, had done much to "dehumanize" the targets of his distortion in the mind of the German public. In turn, such dehumanization had made it possible—or at least easier—for average Germans to later indulge in the outright liquidation of Jewish "vermin." The tribunal agreed, holding that Streicher was therefore complicit in genocide and deserving of death by hanging.

During his remarks to the Nuremberg tribunal, Justice Jackson observed that, in implementing its sentences, the participating powers were morally and legally binding themselves to adhere forever after to the same standards of conduct that were being applied to Streicher and the other Nazi leaders. In the alternative, he said, the victorious allies would have committed "pure murder" at Nuremberg—no different in substance from that carried out by those they presumed to judge—rather than establishing the "permanent benchmark for justice" which was intended.

Yet in the United States of Robert Jackson, the indigenous American Indian population had already been reduced, in a process which is ongoing to this day, from perhaps 12.5 million in the year 1500 to fewer than 250,000 by the beginning of the 20th century. This was accomplished, according to official sources, "largely through the cruelty of [Euro-American] settlers," and an informal but clear governmental policy which had made it an articulated goal to "exterminate these red vermin," or at least whole segments of them.

Bounties had been placed on the scalps of Indians—any Indians—in places as diverse as Georgia, Kentucky, Texas, the Dakotas, Oregon, and California, and had been maintained until resident Indian populations were decimated or disappeared altogether. Entire peoples such as the Cherokee had been reduced to half their size through a policy of forced removal from their homelands east of the Mississippi River to what were then considered less preferable areas in the West.

Others, such as the Navajo, suffered the same fate while under military guard for years on end. The United States Army had also perpetrated a long series of wholesale massacres of Indians at places like Horsehoe Bend, Bear River, Sand Creek, the Washita River, the Marias River, Camp Robinson, and Wounded Knee.

Through it all, hundreds of popular novels—each competing with the next to make Indians appear more grotesque, menacing, and inhuman—were sold in the tens of millions of copies in the U.S. Plainly, the Euro-American public was being conditioned to see Indians in such a way as to allow their eradication to continue. And continue it did until the Manifest Destiny[1] of the U.S.—a direct precursor to what Hitler would subsequently call Lebensraumpolitik (the politics of living space)—was consummated.

By 1900, the national project of "clearing" Native Americans from their land and replacing them with "superior" Anglo-American settlers was complete; the indigenous population had been reduced by as much as 98 percent while approximately 97.5 percent of their original territory had "passed" to the invaders. The survivors had been concentrated, out of sight and mind of the public, on scattered "reservations," all of them under the self-assigned "plenary" (full) power of the federal government. There was, of course, no Nuremberg-style tribunal passing judgment on those who had fostered such circumstances in North America. No U.S. official or private citizen was ever imprisoned—never mind hanged—for implementing or propagandizing what had been done. Nor had the process of genocide afflicting Indians been completed. Instead, it merely changed form.

Between the 1880s and the 1980s, nearly half of all Native American children were coercively transferred from their own families, communities, and cultures to those of the conquering society. This was done through compulsory attendance at remote boarding schools, often hundreds of miles from their homes, where native children were kept for years on end while being systematically "deculturated" (indoctrinated to think and act in the manner of Euro Americans rather than as Indians). It was also accomplished through a pervasive foster home and adoption program—including "blind" adoptions, where children would be permanently denied information as to who they were/are and where they'd come from—placing native youths in non-Indian homes.

The express purpose of all this was to facilitate a U.S. governmental policy to bring about the "assimilation" (dissolution) of indigenous societies. In other words, Indian cultures as such were to be caused to disappear. Such policy objectives are directly contrary to the United Nations 1948 Convention on Punishment and Prevention of the Crime of Genocide, an element of international law arising from the Nuremberg proceedings. The forced "transfer of the children" of a targeted "racial, ethnical, or religious group" is explicitly prohibited as a genocidal activity under the Convention's second article.

Article II of the Genocide Convention also expressly prohibits involuntary sterilization as a means of "preventing births among" a targeted population. Yet, in 1975, it was conceded by the U.S. government that its Indian Health Service (IHS), then a subpart of the Bureau of Indian Affairs (BIA), was even then conducting a secret program of involuntary sterilization that had affected approximately 40 percent of all Indian women. The program was allegedly discontinued, and the IHS was transferred to the Public Health Service, but no one was punished. In 1990, it came out that the IHS was inoculating Inuit children in Alaska with Hepatitis-B vaccine. The vaccine had already been banned by the World Health Organization as having a demonstrated correlation with the HIV-Syndrome which is itself correlated to AIDS. As this is

written, a "field test" of Hepatitis-A vaccine, also HIV-correlated, is being conducted on Indian reservations in the northern plains region.

The Genocide Convention makes it a "crime against humanity" to create conditions leading to the destruction of an identifiable human group, as such. Yet the BIA has utilized the government's plenary prerogatives to negotiate mineral leases "on behalf of" Indian peoples, paying a fraction of standard royalty rates. The result has been "super profits" for a number of preferred U.S. corporations. Meanwhile, Indians, whose reservations ironically turned out to be in some of the most mineral-rich areas of North America, which makes us, the nominally wealthiest segment of the continent's population, live in dire poverty.

By the government's own data in the mid-1980s, Indians received the lowest annual and lifetime per capita incomes of any aggregate population group in the United States. Concomitantly, we suffer the highest rate of infant mortality, death by exposure and malnutrition, disease, and the like. Under such circumstances, alcoholism and other escapist forms of substance abuse are endemic in the Indian community, a situation which leads both to a general physical debilitation of the population and a catastrophic accident rate. Teen suicide among Indians is several times the national average.

The average life expectancy of a reservation-based Native American man is barely 45 years; women can expect to live less than three years longer.

Such itemizations could be continued at great length, including matters like the radioactive contamination of large portions of contemporary Indian Country, the forced relocation of traditional Navajos, and so on. But the point should be made: Genocide, as defined in international law, is a continuing fact of day-to-day life (and death) for North America's native peoples. Yet there has been—and is—only the barest flicker of public concern about, or even consciousness of, this reality. Absent any serious expression of public outrage, no one is punished and the process continues.

A salient reason for public acquiescence before the ongoing holocaust in Native North America has been a continuation of the popular legacy, often through more effective media.

Since 1925, Hollywood has released more than 2,000 films, many of them rerun frequently on television, portraying Indians as strange, perverted, ridiculous, and often dangerous things of the past. Moreover, we are habitually presented to mass audiences one-dimensionally, devoid of recognizable human motivations and emotions; Indians thus serve as props, little more. We have thus been thoroughly and systematically dehumanized.

Nor is this the extent of it. Everywhere, we are used as logos, as mascots, as jokes: "Big Chief" writing tablets, "Red Man" chewing tobacco, "Winnebago" campers, "Navajo" and "Cherokee" and "Pontiac" and "Cadillac" pickups and automobiles. There are the Cleveland "Indians," the Kansas City "Chiefs," the Atlanta "Braves," and the Washington "Redskins" professional sports teams—not to mention those in thousands of colleges, high schools, and elementary schools across the country—each with their own degrading caricatures and parodies of Indians and/or things Indian. Pop fiction continues in the same vein, including an unending stream of New Age manuals purporting to expose the inner works of indigenous spirituality in everything from pseudo-philosophical to do-it-yourself styles. Blond yuppies from Beverly Hills amble about the country claiming to be reincarnated 17th century Cheyenne Ushamans ready to perform previously secret ceremonies.

In effect, a concerted, sustained, and in some ways accelerating effort has gone into making Indians unreal. It is thus of obvious importance that the American public begin to think about the implications of such things the next time they witness a gaggle of face-painted and war-bonneted buffoons doing the "Tomahawk Chop" at a baseball or football game. It is necessary that they think about the implications of the grade-school teacher adorning their child in turkey feathers to commemorate Thanksgiving. Think about the significance of John Wayne or Charlton Heston killing a dozen "savages" with a single bullet the next time a western comes on TV. Think about why Land-o-Lakes finds it appropriate to market its butter with the stereotyped image of an "Indian princess" on the wrapper. Think about what it means when non-Indian academics profess—as they often do—to "know more about Indians than Indians do themselves." Think about the significance of charlatans like Carlos Castaneda and Jamake Highwater and Mary Summer Rain and Lynn Andrews churning out "Indian" best-sellers, one after the other, while Indians typically can't get into print.

Think about the real situation of American Indians. Think about Julius Streicher. Remember Justice Jackson's admonition. Understand that the treatment of Indians in American popular culture is not "cute" or "amusing" or just "good, clean fun."

Know that it causes real pain and real suffering to real people. Know that it threatens our very survival. And know that this is just as much a crime against humanity as anything the Nazis ever did. It is likely that the indigenous people of the United States will never demand that those guilty of such criminal activity be punished for their deeds. But the least we have the right to expect—indeed, to demand—is that such practices finally be brought to a halt.   [1993]

Terms

1. MANIFEST DESTINY: A nineteenth-century belief that White people had the duty and right to control and develop the entire North American continent.

Understanding the Reading

1. Why do American Indians object to the use of Indian names, images, and symbols?
2. How has such usage been justified by non-Indians?
3. How does Churchill expose the racism and degradation of this practice?
4. How is this practice beginning to change?
5. Why was Julius Streicher executed after World War II?
6. What caused the dramatic decline in the Native American population?
7. What happened to Native American children between the 1880s and the 1980s?
8. What is the U.N. Genocide Convention, and how has it been violated in the United States?
9. What are the conditions of life in the Indian community?
10. How have Indians been portrayed in the mass media?

Suggestions for Responding

1. Write a short essay explaining why you think American Indians have been singled out by the sports industry.
2. Write a letter to the editor of your local newspaper stating your position on the exploitation of Native American images. ◆

48

Anti-Semitism in the United States

ROBERT CHERRY

From most accounts, it appears that anti-Semitism was most intense during the period 1877 to 1927, from the time Joseph Seligman was refused admittance to the Grand Hotel in Saratoga, New York, until Henry Ford publicly apologized for anti-Semitic articles in his Dearborn Press.[1] Prior to this period, there were examples of anti-Semitism, beginning with the reluctance of Peter Stuyvesant to allow the first group of Jews to enter New York in 1654. Anti-Semitism also was part of the Know Nothing party's[2] anti-immigration campaign in the 1850s and General Grant's policies during the Civil War. However, anti-Semitism became widespread only during the latter part of the nineteenth century.

Oscar Handlin and Richard Hofstadter identify anti-Semitism with the short-lived agrarian Populist movement[3] of the 1890s. They contend that the Populists associated traditional Jewish stereotypes with the evils faced by the yeomanry. Increasingly forced into debt peonage, the yeomanry demanded elimination of the gold standard. However, President Cleveland pursued a scheme with the Rothschild banking empire[4] to protect the gold standard. This led many Populists to attack Jews for what they perceived as Jewish control of world finance. Also, the yeomanry often divided society into those who engaged in productive labor and those who did not. Typically, Jews in rural areas were identified with nonproductive labor—that is, they were commercial and financial middlemen who gained income from the work of others.

Other historians claim that early twentieth century anti-Semitism was associated with xenophobic fears fueled by mass immigration. Later Jewish immigrants tended to be poorer, less skilled, and less urbanized than the Jews who had emigrated from Germany during the 1850s. They were considered a dangerous criminal element. In 1908 New York City's police commissioner Theodore Bingham suggested that half of all criminals were Jews. The 1910 report of the Dillingham commission claimed that large numbers of Jews scattered throughout the United States seduced and kept girls in prostitution and that many were petty thieves, pickpockets, and gamblers. The report stated, "Jews comprise the largest proportion of alien prisoners under sentence for offenses against chastity."

During this era, Jews were not pictured simply as petty criminals. The stereotypic Jewish businessman was one who manipulated laws and engaged in white-collar crimes, especially insurance fraud. [Michael N.] Dobkowski gives numerous examples of how these stereotypes became part of the popular culture. In describing a Jewish businessman, *Puck,* a popular New York City humor magazine, noted that "despite hard times, he has had two failures and three fires." It claimed, "There is only one thing [their] race hates more than pork—asbestos." So pervasive were these images that the Anti-Defamation League (ADL)[5] in 1913 noted, "Whenever a theatre producer wishes to depict a betrayer of the public trust, a white slaver or other criminal, the actor is directed to present himself as a Jew." Indeed, for more than fifty years, *Roget's Thesaurus* included the word *Jew* as a synonym for usurer, cheat, extortioner, and schemer.

Some historians, including John Higham, believe that anti-Semitism was more significant among the elite than among either the rural yeomanry or middle-class xenophobic nativists. Higham notes that the patrician class, typified by Henry and Brooks Adams, realized that the industrialization process was transforming the United States into a materialistic, pragmatic society that had less concern for tradition and culture than previously. This transformation, which meant the end of patrician hegemony over political and economic affairs, was thought to be the result of Jewish influence.

According to Higham, the patrician class believed that Jewish commercial values undermined basic American traditions. While most became defeatist, some, including Henry Cabot Lodge and John J. Chapman, attempted to reduce Jewish influence. In 1896 Lodge proposed legislation requiring immigrants to be literate in the language of their country of origin rather than in another language. Since most Polish and Russian Jews were literate in Yiddish but not in Polish or Russian, this would have made them ineligible for immigration. Lodge's legislative proposal was defeated, and Jewish immigration continued. Chapman was an active urban reformer who did not have anti-Semitic values until the time of World War I. Dobkowski contends that his inability to reform urban society led him to agree with Henry Adams that the reason for urban decay was growing Jewish influence.

Dobkowski documents how progressive muckrakers,[6] including George Kibbe Turner, Jacob Riis, and Emily Balch, echoed many of the charges against Jews made by the patrician class. Lamenting the decay of cities, Turner considered Jewish immigrants to be at the "core of this festering human cancer." Riis believed that the lack of social values among Jewish immigrants was overwhelming urban society. He thought that recent Jewish immigrants believed that "money is God. Life itself is of little value compared with even the leanest bank account." Even Balch, a leading defender of social welfare reforms, accepted negative Jewish stereotypes.

Liberal sociologist E. A. Ross believed that Jewish immigrants were cunning in their ability to use their wit to undermine business ethics and to commercialize professions and journalism. He claimed that attempts to exclude Jews from professional associations and social clubs had nothing to do with discrimination; instead they reflected a strong desire not to associate with individuals from an immoral culture. Tom Watson, a former Populist and later KKK leader, used Ross's writings to justify his organization's anti-Semitism.

These examples of anti-Semitic views sometimes provide the basis for contentions that Jews faced discrimination similar to that of other groups. Thomas Sowell implies this when he states, "Anti-Semitism in the United States assumed growing and unprecedented proportions in the last quarter of the nineteenth century with the mass arrival of eastern European Jews. . . . [H]elp wanted ads began to specify 'Christian,' as they had once specified 'Protestant' to exclude the Irish."

This is an incorrect assessment. During the last quarter of the nineteenth century, the United States adopted a reservation program for American Indians, an exclusionary policy for Orientals, Jim Crow laws for blacks, and an anti-immigration movement to harass Italian and Polish newcomers. In contrast, before World War I, Jewish immigrants faced few anti-Semitic barriers to their advancement. For example, in 1910 it was estimated that only 0.3 percent of employment advertisements specified Christians and no colleges had adopted restrictive entrance policies.

Only after World War I and the Bolshevik Revolution when xenophobic fears peaked did anti-Semitic restrictions become significant. Zosa Szakowski documents the vigorous attack on Jews during the anti-immigrant Palmer raids[7] in 1919. In 1920, 10 percent of employment ads specified Christians, rising to 13.3 percent by 1926. [Stephen] Steinberg summarizes the restrictive entrance policies many prestigious universities, including Columbia and Harvard, adopted at that time to reduce Jewish enrollment.

At about this time, Henry Ford began publishing anti-Semitic tracts in his Dearborn Press. Like Ross, Ford was a Progressive. He supported Wilson,[8] social legislation, antilynching laws, and urban reforms. Unlike Ross, Ford had nothing but praise for the ordinary Jewish businessman, and he could count Jews among his personal friends. However, Ford thought that industrialists were at the mercy of financial institutions controlled by international Jewry.

Adopting a similar perspective, Robert La Follette introduced a petition to Congress in 1923 assigning responsibility for World War I to Jewish international bankers. This petition also asserted that Wilson, Lloyd George, Clemenceau, and Orlando[9]—the officials in charge of negotiating the peace treaty at Versailles—were surrounded by Jewish advisors.

World's Work and other liberal publications also complained that Jews were not 100 percent

American. They not only identified Jews with draft dodgers and war profiteers, but also complained that Jews, though taking advantage of the opportunities given by democracy, had not taken "the one essential act of a democratic society. . . . They are not willing to lose their identity." By the end of the decade, however, after immigration restrictions laws had been passed and the anticommunist hysteria had subsided, anti-Semitism again subsided to a minimum level.   [1989]

Terms

1. DEARBORN PRESS: The publisher of the very conservative, anti-Semitic magazine the *Dearborn Independent*.
2. KNOW NOTHING PARTY: A political movement in the mid-nineteenth century that was antagonistic to Catholics and immigrants.
3. POPULIST MOVEMENT: A political movement advocating the rights of the common people.
4. ROTHSCHILD BANKING EMPIRE: An international financial empire created by a Jewish banking dynasty during the first half of the nineteenth century.
5. ANTI-DEFAMATION LEAGUE (ADL): A Jewish civil rights organization.
6. MUCKRAKERS: Investigative reporters who focused on corruption.
7. PALMER RAIDS: Raids authorized by Attorney General A. Mitchell Palmer, who zealously enforced the Espionage Act of 1917 to suppress antiwar and socialist publications.
8. WILSON: Woodrow Wilson, Democratic president of the United States, 1913–1921.
9. LLOYD GEORGE, CLEMENCEAU, AND ORLANDO: David Lloyd George, British prime minister, 1916–1922; Georges Clemenceau, French premier, 1906–1909, 1917; Vittorio Emanuele Orlando, Italian prime minister, 1917–1919.

Understanding the Reading

1. Explain why the Populists attacked Jews.
2. What stereotypes were assigned to Jews in the early part of the twentieth century?
3. Why were the elites anti-Semitic?
4. What other justifications have been given to rationalize anti-Semitism?

Suggestions for Responding

1. Describe the Jewish stereotype that underlies the various beliefs Cherry discusses, and explain its inconsistencies.
2. Do you agree with the claim by *World's Work* that losing one's identity is "the one essential act of a democratic society"? Why or why not? ✦

49

Seeing More Than Black and White

ELIZABETH MARTINEZ

A certain relish seems irresistible to this Latina as the mass media [have] been compelled to sit up, look south of the border, and take notice. Probably the Chiapas[1] uprising and Mexico's recent political turmoil have won us no more than a brief day in the sun. Or even less: liberal Ted Koppel still hadn't noticed the historic assassination of presidential candidate Colosio three days afterward. But it's been sweet, anyway.

When Kissinger[2] said years ago "nothing important ever happens in the south," he articulated a contemptuous indifference toward Latin America, its people and their culture which has long dominated U.S. institutions and attitudes. Mexico may be great for a vacation and some people like burritos but the usual image of Latin America combines incompetence with absurdity in loud colors. My parents, both Spanish teachers, endured decades of being told kids were better off learning French.

U.S. political culture is not only Anglo-dominated but also embraces an exceptionally stubborn national self-centeredness, with no global vision other than relations of domination. The U.S. refuses to see itself as one nation sitting on a continent with 20 others all speaking languages other than English and having the right not to be dominated.

Such arrogant indifference extends to Latinos within the U.S. The mass media complain, "people can't relate to Hispanics"—or Asians, they say. Such arrogant indifference has played an important role in invisibilizing La Raza[3] (except where we become a serious nuisance or a handy scapegoat). It is one reason the U.S. harbors an exclusively white-on-Black concept of racism. It is one barrier to new thinking about racism which is crucial today. There are others.

In a society as thoroughly and violently racialized as the United States, White-Black relations have defined racism for centuries. Today the composition and culture of the U.S. are changing rapidly. We need to consider seriously whether we can afford to maintain an exclusively white/Black model of racism when the population will be 32 percent Latino, Asian/Pacific American and Native American—in short, neither Black nor white—by the year 2050. We are challenged to recognize that multi-colored racism is mushrooming, and then strategize how to resist it. We are challenged to move beyond a dualism comprised of two white supremacist inventions: Blackness and Whiteness.

At stake in those challenges is building a united anti-racist force strong enough to resist contemporary racist strategies of divide-and-conquer. Strong enough, in the long run, to help defeat racism itself. Doesn't an exclusively Black/white model of racism discourage the perception of common interests among people of color and thus impede a solidarity that can challenge white supremacy? Doesn't it encourage the isolation of African Americans from potential allies? Doesn't it advise all people of color to spend too much energy understanding our lives in relation to Whiteness, and thus freeze us in a defensive, often self-destructive mode?

For a Latina to talk about recognizing the multi-colored varieties of racism is not, and should not be, yet another round in the Oppression Olympics. We don't need more competition among different social groupings for that "Most Oppressed" gold. We don't need more comparisons of suffering between women and Blacks, the disabled and the gay, Latino teenagers and white seniors, or whatever. We don't need more surveys like the recent much publicized Harris Poll showing that different peoples of color are prejudiced toward each other—a poll patently designed to demonstrate that us coloreds are no better than white folk. (The survey never asked people about positive attitudes.)

Rather, we need greater knowledge, understanding, and openness to learning about each other's histories and present needs as a basis for working together. Nothing could seem more urgent in an era when increasing impoverishment encourages a self-imposed separatism among people of color as a desperate attempt at community survival. Nothing could seem more important as we search for new social change strategies in a time of ideological confusion.

My call to rethink concepts of racism in the U.S. today is being sounded elsewhere. Among academics, liberal foundation administrators, and activist-intellectuals, you can hear talk of the need for a new "racial paradigm" or model. But new thinking seems to proceed in fits and starts, as if dogged by a fear of stepping on toes, of feeling threatened, or of losing one's base. With a few notable exceptions, even our progressive scholars of color do not make the leap from perfunctorily saluting a vague multi-culturalism to serious analysis. We seem to have made little progress, if any, since Bob Blauner's 1972 book *Racial Oppression in America.* Recognizing the limits of the white-Black axis, Blauner critiqued White America's ignorance of and indifference to the Chicano/a's experience with racism.

Real opposition to new paradigms also exists. There are academics scrambling for one flavor of ethnic studies funds versus another. There are politicians who cultivate distrust of others to keep their own communities loyal. When we hear, for example, of Black/Latino friction, dismay should be quickly followed by investigation. In cities like Los Angeles and New York, it may turn out that political figures scrapping for patronage and payola have played a narrow nationalist game, whipping up economic anxiety and generating resentment that sets communities against each other.

So the goal here, in speaking about moving beyond a bi-polar concept of racism, is to build stronger unity against white supremacy. The goal is to see our similarities of experience and needs. If that goal sounds naive, think about the hundreds of organizations formed by grassroots women of different colors coming together in recent years. Their growth is one of today's most energetic motions and it spans all ages. Think about the multicultural environmental justice movement. Think about the coalitions to save schools. Small rainbows of our own making are there, to brighten a long road through hellish times.

It is in such practice, through daily struggle together, that we are most likely to find the road to greater solidarity against a common enemy. But we also need a will to find it and ideas about where, including some new theory.

Until very recently, Latino invisibility—like that of Native Americans and Asian/Pacific Americans—has been close to absolute in U.S. seats of power, major institutions, and the non-Latino public mind. Having lived on both the East and West Coasts for long periods, I feel qualified to pronounce: an especially myopic view of Latinos prevails in the East. This, despite such data as a 24.4 percent Latino population of New York City alone in 1991, or the fact that in 1990 more Puerto Ricans were killed by New York police under suspicious circumstances than any other ethnic group. Latino populations are growing rapidly in many eastern cities and the rural South, yet remain invisible or stigmatized—usually both.

Eastern blinders persist. I've even heard that the need for a new racial paradigm is dismissed in New York as a California hangup. A black Puerto Rican friend in New York, when we talked about experiences of racism common to Black and brown, said, "People here don't see Border Patrol brutality against Mexicans as a form of police repression," despite the fact that the Border Patrol is the largest and most uncontrolled police force in the U.S. It would seem that an old ignorance has combined with new immigrant bashing to sustain divisions today.

While the East (and most of the Midwest) usually remains myopic, the West Coast has barely begun to move away from its own denial. Less than two years ago in San Francisco, a city almost half Latino or Asian/Pacific American, a leading daily newspaper could publish a major series on contemporary racial issues and follow the exclusively Black-white paradigm. Although millions of TV viewers saw massive Latino participation in the April 1992 Los Angeles uprising, which included 18 out of 50 deaths and the majority of arrests, the mass media and most people labeled that event "a Black riot."

If the West Coast has more recognition of those who are neither Black nor white, it is mostly out of fear about the proximate demise of its white majority. A second, closely related reason is the relentless campaign by California Gov. Pete Wilson to scapegoat immigrants for economic problems and pass racist, unconstitutional laws attacking their health, education, and children's future. Wilson has almost single-handedly made the word "immigrant" mean Mexican or other Latino (and sometimes Asian). Who thinks of all the people coming from the former Soviet Union and other countries? The absolute racism of this has too often been successfully masked by reactionary anti-immigrant groups like FAIR blaming immigrants for the staggering African-American unemployment rate.

Wilson's immigrant bashing is likely to provide a model for other parts of the country. The five states with the highest immigration rates—California, Florida, New York, Illinois and Texas—all have a Governor up for re-election in 1994. Wilson tactics won't appear in every campaign but some of the five states will surely see intensified awareness and stigmatization of Latinos as well as Asian/Pacific Islanders.

As this suggests, what has been a regional issue mostly limited to western states is becoming a national issue. If you thought Latinos were just Mexicans down at the border, wake up—they are all over North Carolina, Pennsylvania and 8th Avenue Manhattan now. A qualitative change is taking place. With the broader geographic spread of Latinos and Asian/Pacific Islanders has come a nationalization of racist practices and attitudes that were once regional. The west goes east, we could say.

Like the monster Hydra, racism is growing some ugly new heads. We will have to look at them closely.

A bi-polar model of racism—racism as white on Black—has never really been accurate. Looking for the roots of racism in the U.S. we can begin with the genocide against American Indians which made possible the U.S. land base, crucial to white settlement and early capitalist growth. Soon came the massive enslavement of African people which facilitated that growth. As slave labor became economically critical, "blackness" became ideologically critical; it provided the very source of "whiteness" and the heart of racism. Franz Fanon would write, "colour is the most outward manifestation of race."

If Native Americans had been a crucial labor force during those same centuries, living and working in the white man's sphere, our racist ideology might have evolved differently. "The tawny," as Ben Franklin dubbed them, might have defined the opposite of what he called "the lovely white." But with Indians decimated and survivors moved to distant concentration camps, they became unlikely candidates for this function. Similarly, Mexicans were concentrated in the distant West; elsewhere Anglo fear of them or need for control was rare. They also did not provide the foundation for a definition of whiteness.

Some anti-racist left activists have put forth the idea that only African Americans experience racism as such and that the suffering of other people of color results from national minority rather than racial oppression. From this viewpoint, the exclusively white/Black model for racism is correct. Latinos, then, experience exploitation and repression for reasons of culture and nationality—not for their "race." (It should go without saying in Z^4 that while racism is an all-too-real social fact, race has no scientific basis.)

Does the distinction hold? This and other theoretical questions call for more analysis and more expertise than one article can offer. In the meantime, let's try out the idea that Latinos do suffer for their nationality and culture, especially language. They became part of the U.S. through the 1846–48 war on Mexico and thus a foreign population to be colonized. But as they were reduced to cheap or semi-slave labor, they quickly came to suffer for their "race"— meaning, as non-whites. In the Southwest of a super-racialized nation, the broad parallelism of race and class embraced Mexicans ferociously.

The bridge here might be a definition of racism as "the reduction of the cultural to the biological," in the words of French scholar Christian Delacampagne now working in Egypt. Or: "racism exists wherever it is claimed that a given social status is explained by a given natural characteristic." We know that line: Mexicans are just naturally lazy and have too many children, so they're poor and exploited.

The discrimination, oppression and hatred experienced by Native Americans, Mexicans, Asian/Pacific Islanders, and Arab Americans are forms of racism. Speaking only of Latinos, we have seen in California and the Southwest, especially along the border, almost 150 years of relentless repression which today includes Central Americans among its targets. That history reveals hundreds of lynchings between 1847 and 1935, the use of counter-insurgency armed forces beginning with the Texas Rangers, random torture and murder by Anglo ranchers, forced labor, rape by border lawmen, and the prevailing Anglo belief that a Mexican life doesn't equal a dog's in value.

But wait. If color is so key to racial definition, as Fanon and others say, perhaps people of Mexican background experience racism less than national minority oppression because they are not dark enough as a group. For White America, shades of skin color are crucial to defining worth. The influence of those shades has also been internalized by communities of color. Many Latinos can and often want to pass for whites; therefore White America may see them as less threatening than darker sisters and brothers.

Here we confront more of the complexity around us today, with questions like: What about the usually poor, very dark Mexican or Central American of strong Indian or African heritage? (Yes, folks, 200–300,000 Africans were brought to Mexico as slaves, which is far, far more than the Spaniards who came.) And what about the effects of accented speech or foreign name, characteristics that may instantly subvert "passing"?

What about those cases where a Mexican-American is never accepted, no matter how light-skinned, well-dressed or well-spoken? A Chicano lawyer friend coming home from a professional conference in suit, tie and briefcase found himself on a bus near San Diego that was suddenly stopped by the Border Patrol. An agent came on board and made a beeline through the all-white rows of passengers direct to my friend. "Your papers." The agent didn't believe Jose was coming from a U.S. conference and took him off the bus to await proof. Jose was lucky; too many Chicanos and Mexicans end up killed.

In a land where the national identity is white, having the "wrong" nationality becomes grounds for racist abuse. Who would draw a sharp line between today's national minority oppression in the form of immigrant-bashing and racism?

None of this aims to equate the African American and Latino experiences; that isn't necessary even if it were accurate. Many reasons exist for the persistence of the white/Black paradigm of racism; they include numbers, history, and the psychology of whiteness. In particular they include centuries of slave revolts, a Civil War, and an ongoing resistance to racism that cracked this society wide open while the world watched. Nor has the misery imposed on Black people lessened in recent years. New thinking about racism can and should keep this experience at the center.

The exclusively white/Black concept of race and racism in the U.S. rests on a western, Protestant form of dualism woven into both race and gender relations from earliest times. In the dualist universe there is only black and white. A disdain, indeed fear, of mixture haunts the Yankee soul; there is no room for any kind of multi-faceted identity, any hybridism.

As a people, La Raza combines three sets of roots—indigenous, European and African— all in widely varying degrees. In short we represent a profoundly un-American concept: *mestizaje* (pronounced mess-tee-zah-hey), the mixing of peoples and emergence of new peoples. A highly racialized society like this one cannot deal with or allow room for *mestizaje*. It has never learned to do much more than hiss "miscegenation!" Or, like that Alabama high school principal who recently denied the right of a mixed-blood pupil to attend the prom to say: "your parents made a mistake." Apparently we, all the millions of La Raza, are just that—a mistake.

Mexicans in the U.S. also defy the either-or, dualistic mind in that, on the one hand, we are a colonized people displaced from the ancestral homeland with roots in the present-day U.S. that go back centuries. Those ancestors didn't cross the border; the border crossed them. At the same time many of us have come to the U.S. more recently as "immigrants" seeking work.

The complexity of Raza baffles and frustrates most Anglos; they want to put one neat label on us. It baffles many Latinos too, who often end up categorizing themselves racially as "Other" for lack of anything better. For that matter, the term "Latino" which I use here is a monumental simplification; it refers to 20-plus nationalities and a wide range of classes.

But we need to grapple with the complexity, for there is more to come. If anything, this nation will see more *mestizaje* in the future, embracing innumerable ethnic combinations. What will be its effects? Only one thing seems certain: "white" shall cease to be the national identity.

A glimpse at the next century tells us how much we need to look beyond the white/Black model of race relations and racism. White/Black are real poles, central to the history of U.S. racism. We can neither ignore them nor stop there. But our effectiveness in fighting racism depends on seeing the changes taking place, trying to perceive the contours of the future. From the time of the Greeks to the present, racism around the world has had certain commonalties but no permanently fixed character. It is evolving again today, and we'd best labor to read the new faces of this Hydra-headed monster. Remember, for every head that Hydra lost it grew two more.

Sometimes the problem seems so clear. Last year I showed slides of Chicano history to an Oakland high school class with 47 African Americans and three Latino students. The images included lynchings and police beatings of Mexicans and other Latinos, and many years of resistance. At the end one Black student asked, "Seems like we have had a lot of experiences in common—so why can't Blacks and Mexicans get along better?" No answers, but there was the first step: asking the question.   [1994]

Terms

1. CHIAPAS: A southeastern Mexican state where peasant uprisings have occurred.
2. KISSINGER: Former U.S. secretary of state Henry Kissinger.
3. LA RAZA: Spanish for "the people."
4. Z: The magazine where this article originally appeared.

Understanding the Reading

1. How is political culture in the United States self-centered?
2. Why do we need to see that racism is not simply a Black–White matter?
3. What opposition is there to the growing new paradigms of racism?
4. What examples of coalition building does Martinez identify?
5. How do attitudes toward Latinos and Asian/Pacific Islanders differ on the East Coast and the West Coast and why?
6. According to Martinez, how do Latinos suffer from racism?
7. Why, according to Martinez, is it difficult for Americans to see beyond dualistic thinking and to accept multifaceted complexity?

Suggestion for Responding

1. Write a short paper agreeing or disagreeing with Martinez's thesis that racism is not just a Black and White issue. ◆

50

Behind Barbed Wire

JOHN HERSEY

On March 31, 1942, there appeared on notice boards in certain communities on the Western Seaboard of the United States a number of broadsides bearing the ominous title, "Civilian Exclusion Orders." These bulletins warned all residents of Japanese descent that they were going to have to move out of their homes. No mention was made of where they would have to go. One member of each family was directed to report for instructions at neighboring control stations.

The Japanese attack on Pearl Harbor had taken place a little less than four months earlier. These Exclusion Orders cast a wide net. There were about 125,000 persons of Japanese ancestry scattered along the coastal tier of states then, and 7 out of 10 of them, having been born there, were full-fledged citizens of the United States; yet no distinction between alien and native was made

among those summoned to control stations. The United States had declared war on Germany and Italy, as well as Japan, but no German or Italian enemy aliens, to say nothing of German-Americans or Italian-Americans, were subjected to these blanket Exclusion Orders. Only "Japanese aliens and non-aliens," as the official euphemism put it.

Each person who responded to the summons had to register the names of all family members and was told to show up at a certain time and place, a few days later, with all of them, bringing along only such baggage as they could carry by hand—for a trip to a destination unknown. Names had become numbers.

"Henry went to the control station to register the family," wrote a Japanese-American woman years later. "He came home with 20 tags, all numbered 10710, tags to be attached to each piece of baggage, and one to hang from our coat lapels. From then on, we were known as Family No. 10710." "I lost my identity," another woman would assert, describing the replacement of her name by a number. "I lost my privacy and dignity."

There followed a period of devastating uncertainty and anxiety. "We were given eight days to liquidate our possessions," one of the evacuees testified at an investigation by the Department of Justice many years later. The time allowed varied from place to place. "We had about two weeks," another recalled, "to do something. Either lease the property or sell everything." Another: "While in Modesto, the final notice for evacuation came with a four-day notice." Under the circumstances, the evacuees had to dispose of their businesses, their homes and their personal possessions at panic prices to hostile buyers.

"It is difficult," one man would later testify, "to describe the feeling of despair and humiliation experienced by all of us as we watched the Caucasians coming to look over our possessions and offering such nominal amounts, knowing we had no recourse but to accept whatever they were offering because we did not know what the future held for us." One woman sold a 37-room hotel for $300. A man who owned a pickup truck, and had just bought a set of new tires and a new battery for $125, asked only that amount of a prospective buyer. "The man 'bought' our pickup for $25." One homeowner, in despair, wanted to burn his house down. "I went to the storage shed to get the gasoline tank and pour the gasoline on my house, but my wife . . . said don't do it, maybe somebody can use this house; we are civilized people, not savages."

By far the greatest number of Nisei—the term for first-generation Japanese-Americans that came to be used as the generic word for all ethnic Japanese living in America—were in agriculture, growing fruit, vegetables, nursery plants and specialty crops. They had worked wonders in the soil. They owned about one-fiftieth of the arable land in the three Pacific Coast states, and what they had made of their farms is suggested by the fact that the average value per acre of all farms in the three states in 1940 was roughly $38, while an acre on a Nisei farm was worth, on average, $280.

But now the farmers had to clear out in a matter of days. The Mother's Day crop of flowers, the richest harvest of the year, was about to be gathered; it had to be abandoned. An owner of one of the largest nurseries in southern California, unable to dispose of his stock, gave it all to the Veterans Hospital adjoining his land. A strawberry grower asked for a deferral of his evacuation summons for a few days, so he could harvest his crop. Denied the permission, he bitterly plowed the berries under. The next day, the Federal Bureau of Investigation charged him with an act of sabotage and put him in jail.

Assured by authorities that they could store property and reclaim it after the war, many put their chattels in impromptu warehouses—homes and garages and outbuildings—only to have the stored goods, before long, vandalized or stolen. Some leased their property but never received rents. Some were cheated by their tenants, who sold the property as if it were their own.

On the day of departure, evacuees found themselves herded into groups of about 500, mostly at railroad and bus stations. They wore their numbered tags and carried hand-baggage containing possessions that they had packed in fear and perplexity, not knowing where they were going. They embarked on buses and trains. Some trains had blacked-out windows. Uniformed guards carrying weapons patrolled the cars. "To this day," one woman recalled long afterward, "I can remember vividly the plight of the elderly, some on stretchers, orphans herded onto the

train by caretakers, and especially a young couple with four preschool children.

"The mother had two frightened toddlers hanging on to her coat. In her arms, she carried two crying babies. The father had diapers and other baby paraphernalia strapped to his back. In his hands he struggled with duffel bag and suitcase."

Each group was unloaded, after its trip, at one of 16 assembly centers, most of which were located at fairgrounds and racetracks. There seeing barbed wire and searchlights, and under the guard of guns, these "aliens and non-aliens" were forced to realize that all among them—even those who had sons or brothers in the United States Army—were considered to be dangerous people. At the entrance to the Tanforan Assembly Center, one man later remembered, "stood two lines of troops with rifles and fixed bayonets pointed at the evacuees as they walked between the soldiers to the prison compound. Overwhelmed with bitterness and blind with rage, I screamed every obscenity I knew at the armed guards, daring them to shoot me." Most evacuees were silent, dazed. Many wept.

A typical assembly center was at the Santa Anita race track. Each family was allotted a space in the horse stalls of about 200 square feet, furnished with cots, blankets and pillows; the evacuees had to make their own pallets, filling mattress shells with straw. There were three large mess halls, in which 2,000 people at a time stood in line with tin plates and cups, to be served mass-cooked food that cost an average of 39 cents per person per day—rough fare, usually overcooked, such as brined liver, which, one testified, "would bounce if dropped."

"We lined up," another later wrote, "for mail, for checks, for meals, for showers, for washrooms, for laundry tubs, for toilets. . . . " Medical care, under jurisdiction of the Public Health Service, was provided by evacuee doctors and nurses who were recruited to serve their fellow inmates in an improvised clinic, supplied at first with nothing more than mineral oil, iodine, aspirin, sulfa ointment, Kaopectate and alcohol. Toilets were communal, without compartments. The evacuees bathed in what had been horse showers, with a partition between the men's and the women's section. When the women complained that men were climbing the partition and looking at them, a camp official responded, "Are you sure you women are not climbing the walls to look at the men?"

Toward the end of May 1942, evacuees began to be transferred from these temporary assembly centers to 13 permanent concentration camps—generally called by the more decorous name of "relocation centers"—where they would be held prisoner until several months before the end of the war. By Nov. 1, some 106,770 internees had been put behind barbed wire in six western states and Arkansas.

Thus began the bitterest national shame of the Second World War for the sweet land of liberty: the mass incarceration, on racial grounds alone, on false evidence of military necessity, and in contempt of their supposedly inalienable rights, of an entire class of American citizens—along with others who were not citizens in the country of their choice only because that country had long denied people of their race the right to naturalize. (A 1924 federal law had cut off all Japanese immigration and naturalization; it was not rescinded until 1952.)

"My mother, two sisters, niece, nephew, and I left" by train, one recalled in later years. "Father joined us later. Brother left earlier by bus. We took whatever we could carry. So much we left behind, but the most valuable thing I lost was my freedom."

The Manzanar camp was quickly built in the desert country of east-central California. Its second director, a humane and farsighted man named Ralph Merritt, realized that history ought to have some testimony of what its victims had managed to salvage from an unprecedented American social crime. He had seen the consummate artistry of photographs taken in nearby Yosemite National Park by a friend of his, Ansel Adams, and he invited the great photographer to come to the camp to capture its woes and its marvels on film.

"Moved," Adams would later write, "by the human story unfolding in the encirclement of desert and mountains, and by the wish to identify my photography . . . with the tragic momentum of the times, I came to Manzanar with my cameras in the fall of 1943."

Adams' photographs restore energy to the sorry record—and remind us that this very word

"record" in its ancient origins meant "to bring back the heart."

But first it seems appropriate to re-engage the mind, for the stories of Manzanar and the other camps raise grave questions for the American polity: Could such a thing occur again? How did this slippage in the most precious traditions of a free country come about?

The Japanese attack on Pearl Harbor on Dec. 7, 1941, threw the American psyche into a state of shock. Despite four years' demonstration of the skill and dispatch—and cruelty—of the Japanese invasion of China, American military commanders in the Philippines and elsewhere had issued boastful statements, over and over again, about how quickly the "Japs," as they were scornfully called, would be wiped out if they dared attack American installations.

Then suddenly, within hours, the United States Pacific Fleet was crippled at anchor. Most of the United States air arm in the Philippines was wrecked on the ground. American pride dissolved overnight into American rage and hysteria—and nowhere so disastrously as on the country's Western shores.

President Franklin D. Roosevelt promptly proclaimed, and Congress voted, a state of war against Japan, and within days the other Axis powers, Germany and Italy, also became belligerents. The President issued orders that classified nationals of those countries as enemy aliens. These orders gave responsibility for carrying out certain restrictions against enemy aliens of all three countries to Attorney General Francis Biddle and the Department of Justice. Biddle was given authority to establish prohibited zones, from which enemy aliens could be moved at will; to seize as contraband any weapons and other articles as required for national security; to freeze enemy aliens' funds, and to intern any of them who might be deemed dangerous. These were perfectly normal wartime precautions against enemy aliens only, for which there had been statutory precedent under President Woodrow Wilson in the First World War.

With great speed and efficiency, beginning on the very night of the attack, the Justice Department arrested certain marked enemy aliens of all three belligerent nations. Within three days, 857 Germans, 147 Italians and 1,291 Japanese (367 of them on the Hawaiian Islands, 924 on the continent) had been rounded up.

On the night of Dec. 8, when Pearl Harbor jitters were at their highest pitch, San Francisco suffered a false alarm of an air incursion. Military and/or naval radio trackers reported that enemy aircraft were soaring in over the Bay Area and later that they had turned back to sea without attacking. Planes of the Second Interceptor Command took off from Portland, Ore., and searched as far as 600 miles offshore for a nonexistent Japanese aircraft carrier, from which the enemy planes were assumed to have been launched. At the first alarm, sirens sounded a warning, and San Francisco was supposed to be blacked out at once. But skyscrapers blazed, neon lights winked at hundreds of night spots, and Alcatraz was like a heap of sparkling diamonds in the bay.

Enter, the next morning, to center stage, a military figure in a high state of excitation. As commanding officer of the Fourth Army and Western Defense Command, Lieut. Gen. John L. DeWitt was charged with making sure that there would be no Pearl Harbors on the West Coast. That morning, a meeting at City Hall was called with Mayor Angelo Rossi and 200 of the city's civic leaders, and as *Life* magazine would put it, DeWitt "almost split with rage."

"You people," he said to them, "do not seem to realize we are at war. So get this: Last night there were planes over this community. They were enemy planes. I mean Japanese planes. And they were tracked out to sea. You think it was a hoax? It is damned nonsense for sensible people to think that the Army and Navy would practice such a hoax on San Francisco."

He shouted that it might have been "a good thing" if some bombs *had* been dropped. "It might have awakened some of the fools in this community who refuse to realize that this is a war."

On the night of this "air attack," one of DeWitt's subordinates, Maj. Gen. Joseph W. Stilwell, later to be the famous "Vinegar Joe" of the doomed campaigns in Burma and China, wrote in pencil in a dime-store notebook that he used as a diary, "Fourth Army"—obviously meaning its headquarters—"kind of jittery." Two nights later, DeWitt and his staff, hearing that there was to be an armed uprising of 20,000 Nisei in the San Francisco area, whipped up a plan to put all

of them in military custody. The plan fortunately was aborted by the local F.B.I.[1] chief of station, Nat Pieper, who told the Army that the "reliable source" for their news of the uprising was a flake whom Pieper had once employed and had had to dismiss because of his "wild imaginings."

Next, on Dec. 13, came "reliable information" that an enemy attack on Los Angeles was imminent, and DeWitt's staff drafted a general alarm that would have advised all civilians to leave the city. Fortunately, it was never broadcast. That night, General Stilwell wrote in his notebook that General DeWitt was a "jackass."

The first week of the war brought news of one setback after another. The Japanese struck at Midway, Wake, the Philippines, Hong Kong, the Malay Peninsula and Thailand. On Dec. 13, they captured Guam. The American dream of invulnerability had suddenly been replaced by a feeling that the Japanese could do just about anything they wanted to do—including landing at any point along DeWitt's vast coastal command.

Two days after Pearl Harbor, Navy Secretary Frank Knox went to Hawaii to try to find out what had gone wrong there. On Dec. 15, he returned to the mainland from his scouting trip and called a press conference at which he said, "I think the most effective fifth-column work[2] of the entire war was done in Hawaii, with the possible exception of Norway." He carried back to Washington this report of treachery by resident Japanese, "both from the shores and from the sampans," and his absurdly impracticable recommendation that all those with Japanese blood be evacuated from Oahu.

His charges were quickly denied, in confidential reports, by J. Edgar Hoover of the F.B.I.; by John Franklin Carter, a journalist whom Roosevelt had enlisted to give him intelligence reports; and, after a few days, by Lieut. Gen. Delos C. Emmons, the newly appointed commanding officer in the Hawaiian Islands. But Frank Knox's statement was never denied by the Government—which, from Pearl Harbor to V-J Day, would record not a single case of sabotage by a Japanese alien or a Japanese-American worse than the plowing under of strawberries.

In 1943, when General DeWitt would submit to the Secretary of War his "Final Report" on the removal of the Japanese from the West Coast, one of its first assertions would be: "The evacuation was impelled by military necessity." DeWitt wrote, "There were hundreds of reports nightly of signal lights visible from the coast, and of intercepts of unidentified radio transmissions."

Hoover scornfully ridiculed the "hysteria and lack of judgment" of DeWitt's Military Intelligence Division. An official of the Federal Communications Commission reported on the question of radio intercepts: "I have never seen an organization that was so hopeless to cope with radio intelligence requirements. . . . The personnel is unskilled and untrained. . . . As a matter of fact, the Army air stations have been reported by the Signal Corps station as Jap enemy stations."

DeWitt urged random spot raids on homes of ethnic Japanese to seize "subversive" weapons and cameras. Attorney General Biddle stipulated that raiders should follow the constitutional requirement of finding probable cause for arrest, but DeWitt argued that being of Japanese descent was in itself probable cause. He insisted on searches without warrants, even of the homes of citizens. Yet the Justice Department concluded from F.B.I. reports: "We have not found a single machine gun, nor have we found any gun in any circumstances indicating that it was to be used in a manner helpful to our enemies. We have not found a camera which we have reason to believe was for use in espionage."

When it came right down to it, the mere fact of having Japanese blood and skin was, to DeWitt, enough basis for suspicion. When he wrote in his "Final Report" of the way the ethnic Japanese population was scattered through his Defense Command, he used the military term "deployed"—"in excess of 115,000 persons deployed along the Pacific Coast"—as if these people, these farmers and merchants and house servants, had been posted by plan, poised for attack.

Testifying before a Congressional subcommittee, DeWitt would say, as if this alone proved the military necessity he was trying to assert, "A Jap is a Jap."

The news from the Pacific after the first shock of Pearl Harbor grew worse and worse, and nerves in the Presidio[3] tightened. On Dec. 24 and 25, 1941, the Japanese took Wake Island and Hong Kong. On Dec. 27, Manila fell, and United States forces retreated to the Bataan Peninsula.

On Dec. 19, DeWitt urged on the War Department "that action be initiated at the earliest practicable date to collect all alien subjects 14 years of age and over, of enemy nations and remove them" to inland places, where they should be kept "under restraint after removal." This recommendation covered only aliens—Germans and Italians as well as Japanese.

Toward the end of the month, according to Roger Daniels, who has written two authoritative books on the evacuation, DeWitt began talking by phone—outside the normal chain of command, without telling his superiors—with an officer he knew in Washington, Maj. Gen. Allen W. Gullion. Gullion was Provost Marshal General, the Army's top law enforcement officer. Since the fall of France in June 1940, he had been concerning himself with the question of how the military could acquire legal control over civilians in wartime—in case there should be a domestic fifth column—and DeWitt, evidently stung by the ridicule of his alarms by civilian agencies like the F.B.I. and the F.C.C.,[4] was much attracted by Gullion's views.

Gullion had the chief of his Aliens Division, Major Karl R. Bendetsen, draft a memorandum proposing that the President "place in the hands of the Secretary of War the right to take over aliens when he thought it was necessary."

In one of their turn-of-the-year conferences, Bendetsen outlined to DeWitt plans for surveillance and control of West Coast Nisei; if the Justice Department wouldn't do the job, Bendetsen told DeWitt, then it would be up to the Army— really, to the two of them—to do it. According to notes taken at the session, DeWitt went along with Bendetsen, saying that he had "little confidence that the enemy aliens are law-abiding or loyal in any sense of the word. Some of them, yes; many, no. Particularly the Japanese. I have no confidence in their loyalty whatsoever."

In organizations like the Native Sons of the Golden West and the American Legion, clamor for the incarceration of all Nisei was growing. Congressman Leland Ford of Los Angeles argued for their removal with a most peculiar logic. On Jan. 16, he wrote to Secretary of War Henry L. Stimson a formal recommendation "that all Japanese, whether citizens or not, be placed in inland concentration camps. As justification for this, I submit that if an American-born Japanese, who is a citizen, is really patriotic and wishes to make his contribution to the safety and welfare of this country, right here is his opportunity to do so. . . . Millions of other native-born citizens are willing to lay down their lives, which is a far greater sacrifice, of course, than being placed in a concentration camp."

There were, in fact, lots of patriotic Nisei. Many of them were fiercely and showily patriotic precisely because so many "real Americans" doubted their fidelity. Some had joined together in the Japanese-American Citizens League, which did all it could to flaunt its members' loyalty. Their idealistic creed, adopted before Pearl Harbor, said, "Although some individuals may discriminate against me, I shall never become bitter or lose faith, for I know that such persons are not representative of the majority of American people."

Nisei in many cities and towns helped with civil defense. Furthermore, many young Nisei volunteered for the Army. (In Italy and France, the Japanese-American 442d Combat Regimental Team would turn out to be one of the most decorated units in the entire United States Army—with seven Presidential Distinguished Unit Citations, one Congressional Medal of Honor, 47 Distinguished Service Crosses, 350 Silver Stars, 810 Bronze Stars and more than 3,600 Purple Hearts. President Truman, attaching a Presidential Distinguished Unit Citation to the regimental colors, would say, "You fought not only the enemy, but you fought prejudice. . . . ")

DeWitt's anxieties, however, flowered more and more, and they soon bore fruit. On Jan. 21, 1942, he recommended to Secretary Stimson the establishment of 86 "prohibited zones" in California, from which all "enemy" aliens would be removed, as well as a handful of larger "restricted zones," where they would be kept under close surveillance.

On Jan. 25, persuaded by DeWitt's reports of danger, Stimson recommended to Biddle that these zones be established. Since this request touched only enemy aliens, and meant moving them in most cases for very short distances, Biddle acceded.

At the beginning of February, voices raised on the West Coast against Japanese-Americans became more and more shrill. The Los Angeles Times took up the cry that Japanese citizens were just as much enemies as Japanese aliens: "A viper is nonetheless a viper wherever the egg is hatched—so a Japanese-American, born of Japanese parents, grows up to be a Japanese, not an American." California's liberal Governor, Culbert L. Olson, who had earlier taken the position that Japanese-Americans should continue in wartime to enjoy their constitutional rights, reversed himself in a radio address. Evidently on information from DeWitt, he said: "It is known that there are Japanese residents of California who have sought to aid the Japanese enemy by way of communicating information, or have shown indications of preparation for fifth column activities." He hinted that there might have to be large-scale removals.

Biddle wanted to issue a press release jointly with the Army, designed to calm public fears on the West Coast about sabotage and espionage, and on Feb. 4, he, Assistant Attorney General James Rowe Jr., J. Edgar Hoover, Stimson, McCloy, Gullion and Bendetsen met to discuss it. Gullion later described this encounter:

"[The Justice officials] said there is too much hysteria about this thing; said these Western Congressmen are just nuts about it and the people getting hysterical and there is no evidence whatsoever of any reason for disturbing citizens, and the Department of Justice—Rowe started it and Biddle finished it—the Department of Justice will [have] nothing whatsoever to do with any interference with citizens, whether they are Japanese or not. They made me a little sore, and I said, well listen, Mr. Biddle, do you mean to tell me that if the Army, the men on the ground, determine it is a military necessity to move citizens, Jap citizens, that you won't help me? He didn't give a direct answer, he said the Department of Justice would be through if we interfered with citizens and writ of habeas corpus,[5] etc."

When DeWitt, on Feb. 9, asked for the establishment of much larger prohibited zones in Washington, Oregon and Arizona, Biddle refused to go along. "Your [recommendations] of prohibited areas . . . include the cities of Portland, Seattle, and Tacoma," he wrote, "and therefore contemplate a mass evacuation of many thousands. . . . No reasons were given for this mass evacuation. . . . The Department of Justice is not physically equipped to carry out any mass evacuation."

If there were to be any question of evacuating citizens, the Attorney General wanted no part of it—yet in washing his hands of this eventuality, he now conceded that the Army might justify doing this as a "military necessity. . . . Such action, therefore, should in my opinion, be taken by the War Department and not by the Department of Justice."

Two days later, Stimson went over Biddle's head to Roosevelt. Unable to fit an appointment into a busy day, the President talked with Stimson on the phone. The Secretary told Roosevelt that the Justice Department was dragging its feet and asked if he would authorize the Army to move American citizens of Japanese ancestry as well as aliens away from sensitive areas. Further, he asked whether the President would favor evacuating more than 100,000 from the entire West Coast; 70,000 living in major urban areas; or small numbers living around critical zones, such as aircraft factories, "even though that would be more complicated and tension-producing than total evacuation."

Right after Stimson hung up, Assistant Secretary John J. McCloy jubilantly called Bendetsen in San Francisco to say that the President had declined to make a specific decision about numbers himself but had decided to cut out the Justice Department and had given the Army "*carte blanche*[6] to do what we want to." Roosevelt's only urging was to "be reasonable as you can."

The very next day—so promptly as to suggest that there had been some orchestration—the most influential newspaper pundit in the country, Walter Lippmann, in a column entitled "The Fifth Column on the Coast," [laid] out the basis for advocating the removal of citizens as well as aliens. "The Pacific Coast," he wrote, "is in imminent danger of a combined attack from within and without. . . . It is a fact that the Japanese Navy has been reconnoitering the coast more or less continuously. . . . There is an assumption [in Washington] that a citizen may not be interfered with unless he has committed an overt act. . . . The Pacific Coast is officially a combat zone. Some part of it may at any moment be a battlefield. And nobody ought to be on a battlefield who has no good reason for being there. There is plenty of room elsewhere for him to exercise his rights."

The day after the Lippmann article, the entire Pacific Coast Congressional delegation signed and delivered to Roosevelt a resolution urging "the immediate evacuation of all persons of Japanese lineage and all others, aliens and citizens alike, whose presence shall be deemed dangerous or inimical to the defense of the United States from . . . the entire strategic areas of the states of California, Oregon, and Washington, and the Territory of Alaska."

On Feb. 14, freed by Roosevelt's green light to the Army, doubtless encouraged by Lippmann and by the vociferousness of the West Coast press and West Coast Congressmen, DeWitt finally submitted to Stimson his recommendation for "Evacuation of Japanese and Other Subversive Persons From the Pacific Coast," to be carried out by his command. In justifying the "military necessity" of such an action, DeWitt wrote that ". . . along the vital Pacific Coast over 112,000 potential enemies, of Japanese extraction, are at large today. There are indications that these are organized and ready for concerted action at a favorable opportunity. The very fact that no sabotage has taken place to date is a disturbing and confirming indication that such action will be taken."

Here was logic worthy of "Animal Farm":[7] Proof that all ethnic Japanese were "ready for concerted action" lay in their not having taken it yet.

On Feb. 17, Biddle, in a letter to the President, made a last-ditch protest. "My last advice from the War Department," he wrote, "is that there is no evidence of imminent attack and from the F.B.I. that there is no evidence of planned sabotage."

The protest came too late. By this time, the Attorney General—whose voice had been absolutely solo in reminding those in power of central values in the Bill of Rights—was not only ignored; he was brutally vilified. Congressman Leland Ford told later of a call to Biddle:

"I gave them 24 hours' notice that unless they would issue a mass evacuation notice I would drag the whole matter out on the floor of the House and of the Senate and give the bastards everything we could with both barrels. I told them they had given us the runaround long enough . . . and that if they would not take immediate action, we would clear the goddamned office out in one sweep. . . . "

On the day Biddle transmitted his final protest to Roosevelt, Stimson convened a meeting with War Department aides to plan a Presidential order enabling a mass evacuation under Army supervision. Gullion was sent off to draft it.

That evening, McCloy, Gullion and Bendetsen went to Biddle's house, and Gullion read his draft aloud to the Attorney General. The order was to be sweeping and open-ended. Basing the President's right as Commander in Chief to issue it on a war powers act that dated back to the First World War, it authorized "the Secretary of War, and the military commanders whom he may from time to time designate . . . to prescribe military areas . . . from which any or all persons may be excluded, and with respect to which, the right of any person to enter, remain in, or leave shall be subject to whatever restriction the Secretary of War or the appropriate military commander may impose in his discretion."

On Feb. 19, 1942, Roosevelt set his signature to Executive Order No. 9066, "Authorizing the Secretary of War to Prescribe Military Areas."

The next day, Secretary Stimson formally appointed DeWitt "the military commander to carry out the duties and responsibilities" under Executive Order 9066. He specified that DeWitt should not bother to remove persons of Italian descent. There was widespread affection for Italian-Americans. The Mayor of San Francisco was one, and the baseball stars Joe and Dom DiMaggio, whose parents were aliens, were among the most popular idols in the country. "I don't care so much about the Italians," Biddle later quoted Roosevelt as having said in his cavalier way. "They are a lot of opera singers. . . . "

Stimson took a slightly harder line on German aliens, though he never authorized evacuating German-Americans. Instructions to DeWitt were that German aliens who were "bona fide refugees" should be given "special consideration." In any case, the F.B.I. had long since taken into custody German aliens who had been marked as potentially subversive.

As to ethnic Japanese, the message was clear. Classes 1 and 2 of those who were to be moved out were "Japanese Aliens" and "American Citizens of Japanese Lineage." A sharp racist line had been drawn.

Congress had set up a Select Committee to investigate the need for what it euphemistically called "National Defense Migration." Testifying in San Francisco on Feb. 21, Earl Warren, then Attorney General of California, echoed DeWitt's amazing "proof" of trouble to come. "Unfortunately [many] are of the opinion that because

we have had no sabotage and no fifth column activities in this State . . . that none have been planned for us," Warren said. "But I take the view that this is the most ominous sign in our whole situation. It convinces me more than perhaps any other factor that the sabotage we are to get, the fifth column activities we are to get, are timed just like Pearl Harbor was timed and just like the invasion of France, and of Denmark, and of Norway, and all of those other countries."

Two evenings later, almost as if designed to make irrational fears like these seem plausible, a Japanese submarine, the I-17, having recently returned to the coastal waters, fired about 25 five-and-a-half-inch shells at some oil storage tanks on an otherwise empty hillside west of Santa Barbara. There were no casualties. But was this a prelude to an invasion?

The next night, the Army detected nonexistent enemy airplanes over Los Angeles, and at 2:25 A.M., an antiaircraft battery opened fire. Other gun crews, hearing the explosions, began firing, and within a couple of hours, 1,430 three-inch shells had gone off above the city. Their fragments rained down, causing a fair amount of damage to automobiles. It took quite a while before this happening could be given the joking title it came finally to bear: "The Battle of Los Angeles." At the time, it reinforced the public's panic.

On Feb. 27, the Cabinet in Washington met to discuss how the evacuations should be carried out. Bendetsen had been arguing that the Army should not bear the burden of administering the removals because, as he said in a phone call to the State Department, the Army's job was "to kill Japanese, not to save Japanese." And indeed, the Cabinet did decide that day that the "resettlement" should be handled by a new civilian agency, which would eventually be called the War Relocation Authority. Milton S. Eisenhower, an official of the Department of Agriculture, brother of the popular general who would one day be elected President, was put in charge of it. The Army would round up the evacuees and move them to temporary collection centers, and then the civilian W.R.A. would settle and hold them for the duration of the war in permanent camps.

On March 2, DeWitt established as Military Area No. 1—the field of hottest imaginary danger—the entire western halves of Washington, Oregon and California, and the southern half of Arizona. Presumably somewhat cooler was Military Area No. 2, comprising the remainder of the four states.

DeWitt did not yet, however, issue any orders for actual removals, because in Washington, Gullion had realized that there was no law on the books that made a civilian's disobedience of a military command a crime, so there was no way for DeWitt to force anyone to move. Gullion's office therefore went to work drawing up a statute—something absolutely new in American legal history—that would invent such a crime. DeWitt urged that imprisonment be mandatory, and that the crime be classified as a felony because, he argued, "you have a greater liberty to enforce a felony than you have to enforce a misdemeanor, *viz,* You can shoot a man to prevent the commission of a felony."

On March 9, Stimson submitted to Congress the proposed legislation, which would subject any civilian who flouted a military order in a military area to a year in jail and a fine of $5,000. Only one person in either House rose in debate to challenge the measure: the archconservative Senator Robert A. Taft of Ohio, who would be known in later years as "Mr. Republican." This bill, he said, was "the 'sloppiest' criminal law I have ever read or seen anywhere."

When it came to a vote, not a single member of either House voted against the bill, which was signed into law by Roosevelt on March 21. The way was cleared. On March 31, 1942, with the posting of Civilian Exclusion Orders, the cruel capture of the ethnic Japanese was set in motion.

By early 1943, McCloy and others in the War Department and Army had clearly seen that "military necessity" could no longer, by the wildest imagining, justify keeping loyal American citizens of Japanese ancestry—or loyal aliens—away from the West Coast in "pens." DeWitt was horrified, but the War Department had had enough of his obsessive fears and complaints. He was relieved of his Western Defense Command that fall.

In the spring of 1944, the War Department finally urged the President to dissolve the camps. Others, however, urged caution. "The question appears to be largely a political one," wrote Under Secretary of State Edward Stettinius Jr., in a memo to the President. Roosevelt would be running for a fourth term in November. The evacuees would have to wait.

At the first Cabinet meeting after Roosevelt's re-election, it was decided that all evacuees who passed loyalty reviews could, at last, go home.

They went home to a bitter freedom. It took more than a year to empty all the camps. Given train fare and $25, the evacuees returned to the coast, many to learn that their goods had been stolen or sold; their land had been seized for unpaid taxes; strangers had taken possession of their homes. Jobs were plentiful, but not for the returning detainees, who met with notices: "No Japs Wanted." Housing was hard to find; whole families moved into single rooms.

One man, who had a brother still overseas with the 442d Regimental Combat Team, would testify that his mother "finally had enough money for a down payment on a house. We purchased the house in 1946 and tried to move in, only to find two Caucasian men sitting on the front steps with a court injunction prohibiting us from moving in because of a restrictive covenant.[8] If we moved in, we would be subject to a $1,000 fine and/or one year in the County Jail."

One ordeal had ended; another had begun.

[1988]

Terms

1. F.B.I.: Federal Bureau of Investigation.
2. FIFTH-COLUMN WORK: Secret subversive activities aiding an invading enemy.
3. THE PRESIDIO: The U.S. Army base in San Francisco that served as DeWitt's headquarters.
4. F.C.C.: FEDERAL COMMUNICATIONS COMMISSION.
5. WRIT OF HABEAS CORPUS: An order to release or bring a prisoner before a court.
6. *CARTE BLANCHE:* Full discretionary power.
7. "ANIMAL FARM": A satirical novel by George Orwell with the climactic slogan "All animals are equal, but some animals are more equal than others."
8. RESTRICTIVE COVENANT: A law prohibiting certain ethnic groups from residing in a given area.

Understanding the Reading

1. What were the Civilian Exclusion Orders?
2. What was the economic impact of the orders?
3. In what ways were the Japanese Americans treated like criminals?

4. What were conditions like at the Assembly Centers?
5. What was Lieutenant General DeWitt's response to the supposed San Francisco fly-over by Japanese planes?
6. What was the single case of sabotage by a Japanese American?
7. What were some of the problems with the Military Intelligence Division?
8. What were some of the most bizarre justifications offered in support of the evacuation?
9. What was the 442d Combat Regimental Team, and what was its service record like?
10. What triggered the "Battle of Los Angeles"?
11. Why did evacuation have to wait for Congress to act?
12. What problems did Japanese Americans face after they left the camps?

Suggestions for Responding

1. Hersey raises the question of whether such an incident as the relocation program could occur again. How would you answer him?
2. Imagine you were a Japanese American attending a West Coast university at the time of the evacuation order. How would you have reacted?
3. Explain DeWitt's role in the evacuation. ✦

51

Asian Americans Battle "Model Minority" Stereotype

Robert Daseler

For decades, Asian Americans have borne the peculiar burden of being the "model minority." Their signal success, especially in technical and scientific fields, has resulted in their being viewed more favorably than other American minorities, who supposedly lack their initiative.

The idea that Asians can serve as a model for other minorities seems to have originated in the 1960s, during the heyday of the civil rights movement. In a 1966 *New York Times Magazine* article, Berkeley sociologist William Petersen wrote: "By any criterion of good citizenship that we choose, the Japanese Americans are better than any other group in our society, including native-born whites. They have established this remarkable record, moreover, by their own almost totally unaided effort."

Later in the article, Petersen, having further elaborated the accomplishments of Japanese Americans, made the invidious comparison to other minorities: "This is not true (or, at best, less true) of such 'non-whites' as Negroes, Indians, Mexicans, Chinese, and Filipinos."

Despite the fact that Petersen included Chinese and Filipinos on his list of less successful minorities, the idea spread that Asians generally work hard, send their children to college, rise rapidly in American society, and are "by any criterion of good citizenship that we choose" better than, for example, African Americans, Latinos, and Native Americans.

Although Petersen did not explicitly state that other minorities ought to emulate Japanese Americans or other Asian Americans, the notion of Asians as a model minority acquired a certain popular acceptance in the 1970s and 1980s.

According to . . . Ruth Gim, a Pomona College psychologist whose family emigrated to this country from Korea in 1970, the "model minority" tag stereotypes Asians, denying their many social, psychological, and financial difficulties and falsifying the actual record of their assimilation into American culture.

In Gim's view, the model minority image is dangerous to Asian Americans because it results in the denial of their actual needs, it imposes a set of expectations for Asian Americans that they do not create for themselves ("Someone else is prescribing to us what we should be"), and it biases their relations with other minorities.

Gim also believes that there was an implicit message behind the development of the myth of the model minority: "It was sending a message to the other minorities, saying, 'Why can't you be like them?' It was trying to use one minority group to send a message to another minority group." Many Asian Americans came quite naturally to resent the dubious distinction of being hailed as models for other minorities.

A study, released by UCLA in May, pointed out that Asian Americans are just as likely to be impoverished and disadvantaged as they are to be economically successful. According to Paul Ong, editor of the report, "It's been an uphill battle to get decision-makers and the population overall to realize that the Asian Pacific American population is a diverse one." The UCLA study paints a picture of a rapidly growing population (the 1990 Census said the nation's Asian and Pacific Islander population totaled 7,273,662, more than double the 1980 total) whose veneer of success camouflages some disturbing struggles.

At a series of luncheons sponsored by Pomona's Asian American Resource Center during the spring semester, Gim, who directs the center, and other speakers examined the myth, trying to understand its origins, the reasons for its widespread acceptance (even among many Asian Americans), and its dangers.

PROMOTING SUPER-ACHIEVERS

Gim, who teaches courses in Asian American studies and psychology at Pomona, was the lead-off speaker in the series. Promoting Asians as super-achievers was, in effect, a tactic that conservatives could use to undercut criticism of mainstream culture by dissidents within the minority communities, Gim said.

In fact, Petersen, in his 1966 piece, emphasized the point that discrimination against Japanese Americans had been, if anything, more virulent than discrimination against other minorities. The implication of the Petersen article was clear: if other minorities did not prosper, it was because they were not as industrious or as determined as the Japanese.

By holding up Asian Americans as a model for other minorities, mainstream culture could, in effect, deny that racial prejudice was to blame for unemployment and poverty among African Americans, Latinos, and others. Drawing attention to the success of thousands of Asian Americans was, in other words, an indirect way of placing the blame for racial inequality upon the minorities themselves, rather than the dominant culture.

Gim believes that embedded in the model minority myth was an assumption of cultural determinism: that Asian cultures are superior to other cultures, and for that reason, Asians tend to rise to the top of whatever culture they enter. She asserts that this presumption of Asian superiority is actually harmful for Asian Americans, especially those who are not academic superstars.

Gim also notes, ironically, that the model minority portrayal of Asian Americans is in stark contrast to the "Yellow Peril" image of them promulgated earlier in the century.

In the years prior to World War II, the prevailing view of Asians was represented by the figure of Charlie Chan, the movie detective who outwitted (usually Irish) policemen to solve crimes. Chan was an icon of the "inscrutable" Oriental: astute, mysterious, and ultimately risible. (Although he possessed a good vocabulary, his grammar was defective.)

Gim points out that many Asian Americans have internalized the "model minority" image, resulting in a narrowing of their social horizons. They know they are expected to enter technical and scientific fields—mathematics, engineering, medicine, economics—but not the humanities. Asian American students who do *not* do well in math or technical subjects often feel that they have not lived up to the expectations they have inherited. Asian American students do not have the freedom to be mediocre.

Furthermore, those who want to study history, sociology, or art often feel they are stepping over an invisible line between what is and is not an appropriate career path.

Contrary to the myth of invulnerability, Asian American students have a significantly higher rate of major depression and diagnosed schizophrenia than European Americans. "The superficial view seems to support the model minority image," Gim says, "but when you dig deeper, you find that cultural factors influence the underutilization of psychological services by Asian American students."

Moreover, the severity of psychiatric problems reported by Asian American students belies the image of them as programmed automatons.

The pressure on these students is coming not only from the culture, of course, but primarily from their families, who often steer the students into traditional and lucrative professions.

The concluding speaker in the series, Linus Yamane, as assistant professor of economics at Pitzer College, further debunked the myth by noting that, while the average family income of Asian Americans, $42,250, is higher than that for

European Americans, $36,920, the proportion of Asian Americans living below the poverty line is much higher than for European Americans.

Yamane also pointed out that Asian American families tend to be larger than families of European Americans, somewhat vitiating their higher average income.

Yamane drew a complex picture of Asians in the United States, saying that poverty rates for Chinese, Japanese, and Korean families are lower than for European Americans, while poverty rates for Filipino and Native American families are higher.

Yamane also argued that discrimination against Asians in the work force varies with their ethnic background. Japanese and Korean males are found to do as well as European American males with comparable education, but Chinese and Filipino males do less well, and Native American men earn about 30 percent less, on the average, than European American males with comparable education.

MANAGEMENT GLASS CEILING

Yamane believes that there is a "glass ceiling" for Asian Americans in management. Studies appear to show that, while Asian Americans rise rapidly in the lower ranks of organizations, they are excluded from higher managerial positions.

Between Gim and Yamane came three other speakers. One of these was David Yoo, a historian at Claremont McKenna College, whose specialty is ethnicity, immigration, and race. Yoo characterized the model minority view of Asian Americans as just the latest wrinkle in the evolution of the stereotype of Asians in America.

Proclaiming Asian Americans to be a model minority "works against the true notion of a multicultural America," Yoo says. "It reinforces a racial hierarchy, which is kept intact if you can pit one minority against another."

Yoo believes that embracing Asians as exemplary gives people an excuse not to ask more fundamental questions about race and inequality.

While debunking the model-minority image as a myth, Gim, Yamane, and Yoo agree that there is some truth to the characterization of Asian Americans as high achievers. The proportion of Asian American students at highly

selective colleges and universities is itself an indicator that at least a few ethnic groups within the Asian American community place high status on education, discipline, and intellectual distinction.

In March, homosexuality in the Asian Pacific Islander communities was discussed by Eric Reyes, a member of the Asian Pacific AIDS Intervention Team in Los Angeles, and Alice Y. Hom, a doctoral candidate in history at The Claremont Graduate School; and Jack Ling, a psychologist and environmental consultant, spoke on the subject of Asian American gangs. Reyes, Hom, and Ling highlighted aspects of the Asian American experience that conflict with the model-minority stereotype.

The number of Asian American students at The Claremont Colleges and in the University of California system does not signify that the story of Asian Americans is one of unalloyed success and social advance. Stereotyping, a pervasive sense of being suspended between two strong cultures, high stress levels, and a concern about loss of identity also are elements in the story.

Asian American students tend, for the most part, to associate with one another, and sometimes this leads to resentment by European American students, who view the Asians as cliquish and unfriendly.

A Pomona sophomore, who asked that his name not be mentioned, is a good example of the Asian American student who has taken the traditional path toward a career. With a double major in chemistry and Chinese, he is conforming, at least for the moment, to his father's expectation that he should become a doctor.

"He has one thing in mind," this young man says of his father, who was raised in Taiwan. "He thinks medicine is the best way to go."

A graduate of a prep school at which there was "a substantial" number of Asian students, the young man associated primarily with other Asian students in high school. At Pomona College, too, he associates with other Asians more than with Caucasian students. "Just for some reason, a lot of the people I know happen to be Asian," he says. He thinks that Koreans tend to be more cliquish than other Asians, though.

This sophomore learned about the model minority myth when he took Ruth Gim's "Asian American Perspectives" class as a freshman.

"You can apply it to some people," he says, "but I don't think you can apply it to Asians as a whole. Asians do work hard and try to do well in school. I think the model-minority myth could be applied to a lot of my friends, but a lot of my Caucasian friends would fit the myth, too, if they were Asians."

A recent graduate, who also asked for anonymity, chose a nontraditional major for a student whose parents were born, as the sophomore's were, in Taiwan. She majored in sociology and Women's Studies, and in her senior thesis, she compared the cultural sensitivity of two centers for battered women: one mainstream, the other for Pacific Islanders and Asians.

Except for her social sciences major, she believes that "I do fall into what people would call a model-minority category." That is, she works hard, attends a prestigious college, and will pursue graduate studies. She also acknowledges the generational linguistic and class privileges that have allowed her to achieve these goals.

She is troubled by the stereotype, however, "I think it's very dangerous," she says. "It creates suspicion between groups, and it prevents us from forming coalitions in our similar struggle."

She says that majoring in sociology and Women's Studies wasn't something she planned. "I could barely do the natural sciences," she admits. So she switched into a field in which she had an interest . . . and could excel.

She graduated from a high school in Cerritos, California, in which the Asian Pacific Islander enrollment was 75 percent.

"It was the most comfortable social environment I was ever in or that I expect I ever will be in," she says. "It was difficult adjusting to Pomona, where suddenly I was the minority. I was not a part of the dominant culture."

Although being in the majority was pleasant, she now believes that "she would have benefited more from high school if there had been a greater diversity of students, particularly more African American and Latino students."

She took a course from Gim, who helped her put the Asian American experience in perspective. "It really allowed me to see the Asian American contributions to American history," she says.

Growing up in Riverside and Orange counties, Gim found that there were two ways for her to compensate for being a minority: "I made sure I did better academically [than other students]. I don't think I really was smarter than other kids, but I made sure I worked harder. The other defense mechanism was that I dressed well."

Gim hopes that the increasing number of Asian American courses will help Asian American students find their own identity in a dominantly European American culture, without having to rely upon stereotypes imposed either by that culture or by their own minority culture.

"I am more American than most Americans walking around," Gim asserts. "I really believe that. I don't think most people realize what it is to be an American. I believe I have a better understanding and appreciation of what it means to be an American because of my bicultural background."   [1994]

Understanding the Reading

1. What led to the development of the myth that Asian Americans are a "model minority"?
2. Why is this image dangerous for Asian Americans?
3. What is the reality of life in the United States for Asian/Pacific Americans?
4. What impact has the model-minority image of Asian Americans had on other minorities?
5. How has it affected Asian Americans themselves?
6. How are Asian Americans affected by the "glass ceiling"?
7. How do Asian American students tend to behave in college?
8. How do college classes in Asian American studies affect Asian American students?

Suggestions for Responding

1. Think about Hersey's description of Japanese Americans during World War II and write an explanation of why you think their image has changed so much in the past sixty years.
2. Write a short essay explaining how your life has been affected by a stereotype that others have applied to you. ◆

52

"Jim Crow" Law

BENJAMIN QUARLES

If the Conservatives in the South were aided by the do-nothing policy of the Republican party, they were abetted in a more positive way by the Supreme Court. This high tribunal consistently interpreted the Fourteenth and Fifteenth Amendments[1] in such a way as to weaken their protection of the Negro.

A variety of considerations moved the Court in its handling of the war amendments and the acts of Congress relating to the Negro. Rightly concerned with maintaining a proper balance between the power of the national government and those of the states, the Court tended to restrict federal powers which it felt were excessive. Moreover, the Courts of the nineteenth century did not regard the purely human factor as crucial as the assumed first principles of the law: the letter of the law took precedence over its spirit. And, finally, the men of the Supreme Court could not escape the influence of public opinion on matters of race and color; for all their apparent Olympian aloofness, the justices were subject to the all-pervasive temper of the times.

In a series of cases, the Court set up four basic principles that worked in the interests of the southern whites. To begin with, it decreed that the war amendments applied only to actions taken by states or their agents, and not to private parties. Hence if a private individual or group kept a Negro from voting, the latter had no recourse in the federal courts. Another principle related to the emphasis on appearance rather than reality: if a state law were not plainly discriminatory, the Court would not attempt to ascertain whether it was being applied alike to black and white. A third principle was that of holding the state's police power paramount and therefore more important than the rights given to the individual under the Fourteenth Amendment. The state's police power—its inherent right to protect the public health, safety, or morals—of necessity had to be broad. At any rate, the Court obligingly found that state "Jim Crow" laws were a valid exercise of this power. Finally, the Court favored the white southerner in its ruling that there was a substantial difference between "race discrimination" and "race distinction," the latter not being contrary to the Constitution.

The two most publicized of the Court's decisions affecting Negroes were the Civil Rights Cases of 1883 and *Plessy v. Ferguson,* thirteen years later. The former related to the Civil Rights Act of 1875, a measure which sought to secure equal rights for all citizens at hotels, theaters, and other places of public amusement. It also stipulated that no person should be disqualified to sit on juries because of race. This bill had been strongly supported by Negroes, James T. Rapier of Alabama, in a speech in Congress, having called attention to the fact that there was "not an inn between Washington and Montgomery, a distance of more than a thousand miles, that will accommodate me to a bed or meal."

The Civil Rights Act remained on the books for only eight years before the Court struck it down. Negroes were up in arms, holding a series of indignation meetings, heaping ridicule and invective on the Court, and offering it lessons in constitutional law. Anxious to soften the blow to its colored population, many nonsouthern states, numbering eighteen by 1900, passed state civil rights bills. But the national legislature was not destined to pass another such measure until seventy-five years after the Court's adverse ruling in 1883.

After the Court's action in the Civil Rights Cases, no one should have been unprepared for the *Plessy* decision. The high-water mark of the constitutional sanction of state "Jim Crow" laws, this decision in 1896 upheld a Louisiana law calling for separate railroad accommodations for white and colored passengers. Revealing something of the popular belief in white superiority, the Court ruled that laws were "powerless to eradicate racial instincts or to abolish distinctions based upon physical differences." In his dissenting opinion, Justice John Marshall Harlan pointed out that the "Constitution is color-blind, and neither knows nor tolerates classes among citizens." He ventured the opinion that "the judgment this day rendered will, in time, prove to be quite as pernicious as the decision made by this tribunal in the *Dred Scott Case*."[2] Prophetic words, but in 1896, Justice Harlan's was a lone voice. "*Plessy* was bad law: it was not supported by precedent," writes Barton J. Bernstein. But it remained the law of the land for over half a century.

The Court's rulings encouraged the white South to launch a final bloodless offensive to relegate the Negro to his proper political and social sphere. Regarding voting, the white South felt that the time was ripe to exclude the Negro legally, that it could adopt better and more permanent techniques of disfranchisement than those of intimidation and violence.

Mississippi was the first state to employ the new devices. In 1890 her constitution established three conditions for voting: a residence requirement, the payment of a poll tax, and the ability to read or to interpret a section of the state constitution. Five years later South Carolina adopted these same requirements, adding to them a list of crimes—such as larceny, which had a high incidence among Negroes—which disfranchised the offender. Another requirement southern states found useful was the good-character test: an applicant seeking to become a voter had to produce a responsible witness to vouch for his worth and standing. In many states, tricky registration procedures were legalized, giving local registers broad powers to thwart the Negro applicant. "White primary" laws were passed, asserting that the Democratic party was a voluntary association of citizens and could therefore limit voting as it pleased in party elections.

So sweeping and effective were these measures to disfranchise the Negro that they caught in their dragnet a number of whites, particularly the poor and illiterate. Hence some southern states hastened to pass "grandfather clauses," bestowing the franchise upon those whose grandfathers had voted. This measure added to the total number of voters, but all the persons on whom it bestowed the vote were white, since no Negro's grandfather had voted or been eligible to vote. (Such measures were declared unconstitutional in 1915.)

The white South's grim determination to keep the Negro voteless was strengthened by a half-hearted, unsuccessful attempt by Congress in 1890 to pass a "Force Bill," which would enforce the section of the Fourteenth Amendment stipulating that if a state denied the suffrage to its adult population, its representation in the House would be proportionally reduced. The South was more angered than alarmed by the "Force Bill," but it aroused her spirit of defiance and thus fanned her zeal for Negro disfranchisement.

More than any other factor, the white South's determination to totally separate the Negro from the ballot stemmed from the Populist revolt. Populism was the outgrowth of an effort by the American farmer to improve his lot. Believing that both major political parties were the creatures of business interests in the North, the aroused farmers formed a People's Party.

In the South the leaders of the agrarian crusade—Tom Watson, for example—sought Negro support, holding that the poor white man and the poor colored man were in the same economic strait jacket. Seeking cooperation across the color line, many southern Populists appealed to the remaining Negroes who could vote and tried to obtain the vote for those Negroes from whom it had been wrested. Taking alarm, many of the businessmen and planters decided to fight fire with fire. They, too, sought the Negro vote, opening their pursestrings for barbecues and entertainment, and for the services of Negro spellbinders. Where Populism was successful at the polls, as in North Carolina, Negroes were placed in such offices as alderman, magistrate, deputy sheriff, and collector of the port. But this reemergence of the Negro voter and officeholder as a power to be reckoned with during the mid-nineties was shortlived.

Reviving the cry of "Negro domination," defeated or ambitious politicians charged that the Populists were taking the South back to the days of the carpetbagger. The Populists were stigmatized as the lineal descendants of the Loyal Leaguers. Such charges spelled doom, for in the South no political accusation was more fatal than that of being the party of the Negro. Although the reform measures championed by the Populists were directly aimed to benefit the poor white farmer, he tended to forget everything else whenever someone shouted Negro, and the white South closed ranks, determined to eliminate the agrarians. Populism's failure in the South stemmed in large measure from its attempt to bridge the color line.

To Negroes the aftermath of the Populist revolt was particularly galling. Seeking a scapegoat, many of the party's former leaders turned on the Negro, blaming him for its downfall. Moreover, the growing political influence of the poor whites and their pronounced anti-Negro bias led to the widespread adoption of "Jim Crow" legislation. To bolster their own self-esteem, the lower-class whites insisted on their social superiority to the Negro, and even such titles as "Hon." or "Mr." for the exceptional Negro were abandoned. In most southern states this sentiment received more formal expression in the laws requiring that Negroes be segregated at inns, hotels, restaurants, theaters, and on public carriers. And, as was to be expected, those who advocated "Jim Crow" measures had no trouble in convincing themselves that segregation was in the Negro's own best interests—indeed, that it upheld a status that he himself wanted.   [1969]

Terms

1. FOURTEENTH AND FIFTEENTH AMENDMENTS: Post–Civil War constitutional amendments; the Fourteenth guaranteed due process and equal protection, and the Fifteenth granted Negro male suffrage.
2. DRED SCOTT CASE: The Supreme Court ruled in 1857 that the federal government was obligated to protect the ownership rights of slaveholders, even in the "free" states, thus effectively legalizing slavery throughout the country, even though many states had banned it.

Understanding the Reading

1. Why did the Supreme Court's decisions weaken the protection of Blacks guaranteed by the Fourteenth and Fifteenth Amendments?
2. Explain the four basic principles the Supreme Court established that favored the interests of southern Whites.
3. What was the Civil Rights Act of 1875?
4. Explain the *Plessy v. Ferguson* decision.
5. How did southern states stop Blacks from voting?
6. Why did the Populists court the Black vote, and why did they then turn against Blacks?

Suggestions for Responding

1. Why do you think the Supreme Court didn't protect the rights of African Americans at the end of the nineteenth and beginning of the twentieth centuries?
2. Research the *Plessy v. Ferguson* decision and explain its impact on African Americans for the subsequent sixty years. ✦

53

Jim Crow Revived in Cyberspace

GREG PALAST AND MARTIN LUTHER KING III

Birmingham, Ala.—Astonishingly, and sadly, four decades after the Rev. Martin Luther King Jr. marched in Birmingham, we must ask again, "Do African-Americans have the unimpeded right to vote in the United States?"

In 1963, Dr. King's determined and courageous band faced water hoses and police attack dogs to call attention to the thicket of Jim Crow laws—including poll taxes and so-called "literacy" tests—that stood in the way of black Americans' right to have their ballots cast and counted.

Today, there is a new and real threat to minority voters, this time from cyberspace: computerized purges of voter rolls.

The menace first appeared in Florida in the November 2000 presidential election. While the media chased butterfly ballots and hanging chads, a much more sinister and devastating attack on voting rights went almost undetected.

In the two years before the elections, the Florida secretary of state's office quietly ordered the removal of 94,000 voters from the registries. Supposedly, these were convicted felons who may not vote in Florida. Instead, the overwhelming majority were innocent of any crime—and just over half were black or Hispanic.

We are not guessing about the race of the disenfranchised: A voter's color is listed next to his or her name in most Southern states. (Ironically, this racial ID is required by the Voting Rights Act of 1965, a King legacy.)

How did mass expulsion of legal voters occur?

At the heart of the ethnic purge of voting rights was the creation of a central voter file for Florida placed in the hands of an elected, and therefore partisan, official. Computerization and a 1998 "reform" law meant to prevent voter fraud allowed for a politically and racially biased purge of thousands of registered voters on the flimsiest of grounds.

Voters whose name, birth date and gender loosely matched that of a felon anywhere in America were targeted for removal. And so one Thomas Butler (of several in Florida) was tagged because a "Thomas Butler Cooper Jr." of Ohio was convicted of a crime. The legacy of slavery—commonality of black names—aided the racial bias of the "scrub list."

Florida was the first state to create, computerize and purge lists of allegedly "ineligible" voters. Meant as a reform, in the hands of partisan officials it became a weapon of mass voting rights destruction. (The fact that Mr. Cooper's conviction date is shown on state files as "1/30/2007" underscores other dangers of computerizing our democracy.)

You'd think that Congress and President Bush would run from imitating Florida's disastrous system. Astonishingly, Congress adopted the absurdly named "Help America Vote Act," which requires every state to replicate Florida's system of centralized, computerized voter files before the 2004 election.

The controls on the 50 secretaries of state are few—and the temptation to purge voters of the opposition party enormous. African-Americans, whose vote concentrates in one party, are an easy and obvious target.

The act also lays a minefield of other impediments to black voters: an effective rollback of the easy voter registration methods of the Motor Voter Act; new identification requirements at polling stations; and perilous incentives for fault-prone and fraud-susceptible touch-screen voting machines.

No, we are not rehashing the who-really-won fight from the 2000 presidential election. But we have no intention of "getting over it." We are moving on, but on to a new nationwide call and petition drive to restore and protect the rights of all Americans and monitor the implementation of frighteningly ill-conceived new state and federal voting "reform" laws.

Four decades ago, the opposition to the civil right to vote was easy to identify: night riders wearing white sheets and burning crosses. Today, the threat comes from partisan politicians wearing pinstripe suits and clutching laptops.

Jim Crow has moved into cyberspace—harder to detect, craftier in operation, shifting shape into the electronic guardian of a new electoral segregation.   [2003]

Understanding the Reading

1. What does the title "Jim Crow Revived in Cyberspace" mean?
2. How exactly were minority voters targeted in this example?
3. How has Congress reacted to this allegation, since the 2000 election?

Suggestions for Responding

1. Make a list of ways minorities have been nonviolently disenfranchised in the United States throughout history.
2. Have a class discussion on how the possibility of computer fraud and improprieties could be eliminated from future U.S. elections. ✦

54

The Negro a Beast . . . or in the Image of God?

EARL OFARI HUTCHINSON

I wish Rodney King[1] would read Charles Carroll's *The Negro a Beast or in the Image of God*. He might understand why many white folks said rotten things about him. This is what I mean. In November 1992, King spoke to about seventy-five students at Tustin High School in the mostly white southern California suburban bedroom community of Orange County. This was King's first major public appearance in nearly a year. King, being a modest unassuming man, had purposely kept a low profile.

It didn't help. People still bad-mouthed him. They called him a doper, an alcoholic and a violence-prone ex-convict. Many openly grumbled that King himself had provoked the cops. Some even smirked and whispered that he deserved the ass-whipping. In the Simi Valley trial of the four LAPD[2] cops who beat King, defense attorneys in a bravura performance used this sneaky racism to their advantage and got them off. One unnamed juror said of King, "He was obviously a dangerous person, massive size and threatening actions."

King and his attorney Milton Grimes were fed up with this kind of talk. They figured that high school students would be sympathetic. King, himself a high school dropout, would benignly tell the kids to stay in school. They hoped this would improve his image.

It didn't. The following day, angry readers deluged the *Los Angeles Times* with calls objecting to school officials letting "a dangerous parolee" on a high school campus. The Tustin High School principal felt the heat, back-pedaled fast and claimed it was all a mistake. Sounding properly indignant, he agreed that King was not a suitable "role model."

II

He was "dangerous," of "massive size," "threatening," and "a poor role model." Remember those words as I turn back the pages of history a century and more. Carroll said that and much more about black men in his grotesque little book published in 1900. Reading the passages of his book even without the filter of America's hideous racial past, one might have reason to laugh.

Carroll, however, was dead serious. His book was not published by the Ku Klux Klan in rural Mississippi or Alabama, but by the American Book and Bible House in St. Louis. The book was a brisk seller. Carroll argued that the black man was left out of human creation and was a subspecies of the animal world.

Carroll was not a quack. He did not make any of this up. He considered himself a man of pure science. He based his "theory" on the meticulous research of Alexander Winchell, a distinguished professor of geology and paleontology at the University of Michigan. When the evidence got a little skimpy in some places, Carroll retreated into scripture. He swore that God warned that since creation the world's troubles began when human beings let the Negro "beast" mingle among them.

Carroll had his critics. Georgia theologian W. S. Armstead was indignant that he would dare bring the word of God into this. By calling black men beasts, he felt Carroll was letting them off the hook. Armstead said the black man was a cunning, calculating degenerate who followed his "murderous heart" and brutally "waylaid" white women.

Armstead didn't have much chance against learned men like Carroll and Winchell. They were Northerners and for nearly a half century they had beaten the South to the punch every time when it came to propagating myths about black bestiality.

George Fitzhugh, a Virginia newspaperman, sometime planter and always articulate defender of slavery, was delighted to find that his Northern brethren were very receptive to his views. In 1854, Fitzhugh, in *Sociology for the South,* wrote that "slavery rescued blacks from idolatry and cannibalism, and every brutal vice and crime that can disgrace humanity."

Fitzhugh took his act on the road and headed North. He quickly discovered that many influential power brokers thought that his *Sociology for the South* should be the sociology for the North. Many leading newspapermen quoted him. Businessmen wined and dined him. Some Northern congressman snipped quotes from his writings and placed them into the *Congressional Globe* (later *Record*).

During the Civil War, dozens of Northern newspaper editors and politicians were livid because Old Abe and his Republican political cronies had the audacity to shed white blood to free black savages. At every turn, they raised the bloody flag and tried to sabotage the war effort.

III

The Civil War ended legal slavery, but it did not put the old planters entirely out of business. They still had one big trump card to play: The Black Scare. They played it hard by convincing whites, North and South, that blacks were out to get land, power and white women. Soon men in white sheets silhouetted the night sky with their fiery crosses. Their terror campaign to whip the black beasts back in line was a smashing success.

Reconstruction[3] was dead. The abolitionists who had pricked the conscience of the nation were too old and tired to care anymore. The ranks of the Radicals in Congress were thinning by the hour. And, Northern whites were dead set against risking their necks to fight for the rights of men who they didn't really believe were men.

Meantime, the learned men of the North like Carroll were busy mangling science to shape the image of the black man as criminal, sex crazed, violent and degenerate. Dr. Frank Hoffman, in 1896, backed Carroll to the hilt. Hoffman like Carroll was not a Southerner. In fact, he was not a Northerner. In fact, he was not even an American. Hoffman, writing from Germany, declared that there was such an "immense amount of immorality and crime" among black men it had to be part of their "race traits and tendencies."

The message to worried whites: sit back, relax and let nature take its course. All those decadent black men would soon die out from their own "inferior organs and constitutional weaknesses." Hoffman's wise words were rushed into print by the prestigious American Economic Association (AEA).

Another learned Northerner, Walter F. Wilcox, chief statistician for the U.S. Census Bureau, thought the good doctor had the right ZEITGEIST.[4] Three years later with the blessing of the American Social Science Association, Wilcox pinned up his charts, juggled figures and solemnly predicted that blacks were "several times" more likely to commit crime than whites. He wasn't finished. The next year he told the social scientists that Hoffman was right. Blacks were doomed to go the way of the Dodo Bird and Dinosaur because of "disease, vice and profound discouragement."

The American Economic Association was on a fast track to get the official words of its scholars out to the public. They rushed Historian Paul Tillinghast's paper on "The Negro in Africa and America" into print. Tillinghast agreed with the other scholars. He cautioned them not to forget that blacks were "seriously handicapped by the inherited conditions" they brought with them from savage Africa.

Around the same time, Dr. G. Stanley Hall was determined not to be outdone by the AEA. The president of the American Psychological Association and founder of the *American Journal of Psychology* thought his fellow academics were putting too much emphasis on "race traits."

As a clinician, he believed there were murky forces at work in the black psyche. According to his diagnosis, the black man's "disthesis, both psychic and physical is erethic, volatile, changeable, prone to transcoidal, intensely emotional and even epileptoid states." Buried somewhere between the "erethic" and "transcoidal" gibberish was a hopeless dimwit. The public should be on the alert.

A soon to be president didn't dispute this. In 1901, [Princeton] University Professor Woodrow Wilson in the *Atlantic Monthly* asked what could one really expect of individuals who were really little more than a "host of dusky children," "insolent and aggressive, sick of work, covetous of pleasure."

The line-up of highbrow intellectual magazines that endorsed this gobbledygook read like a roll call of academia. They included *Popular Science Monthly, The Annals of the American Academy of Political and Social Science, Medicine* and the *North American Review.* They all chimed in with volumes of heady research papers, articles and scholarly opinions that "proved" blacks were hopelessly inferior, crime- and violence-prone defectives from which society had to be protected.

IV

Since art does imitate life, it was only a matter of time before this pap crept into the literature. At first, Northern and Southern novelists did not lay it on too thick. The blacks in their stories were mostly grinning, buck-dancing, lazy, slightly larcenous darkies. As the scientists kept up their drumbeat warnings about the black menace, the novelists soon turned vicious. Upton Sinclair had impeccable credentials as a Socialist crusader. Still, in his popular muckraking novel, *The Jungle,* published in 1905, Sinclair was appalled that white girls working in Chicago's hellish stockyards rubbed shoulders "with big black buck Negroes with daggers in their boots."

This was too tame for Thomas Nelson Page. He wasn't a man of subtlety when it came to racial matters. But, first, he had to lay the proper groundwork. In an essay, *The Negro: The Southerner's Problem,* he warned that the old time darkies were dying off and that the "new issue" was "lazy, thrift-less, intemperate, insolent, dishonest and without the most rudimentary elements of morality." In his novel, *Red Rock,* he continued to warn of the dangers of the black peril.

Thomas Dixon, Jr., wasn't satisfied with this. Page only talked about the "new issue" Negro. Dixon set out to vanquish him. In his big, sprawling novel, *The Clansman,* published in 1905, Dixon described him as "half child, half animal, the sport of impulse, whim and conceit . . . a being who left to his will, roams at night and sleeps in the day, whose speech knows no word of love, whose passions once aroused, are as the fury of the tiger." It sent collective chills up the spines of much of white America. Bolt the doors. Turn out the lights. Praise the Lord and pass the ammunition. The black beast was coming. In *The Clansman,* Dixon had the right men to defend society and (white womanhood) from this creature, the Ku Klux Klan.

Dixon knew he was on to something big. When *The Clansman* was adapted for the stage, it brought down theater houses everywhere. Audiences were delirious. They had to see the KKK destroy the black beasts. Soon Broadway's great white way picked up on Dixon and made him the toast of New York. *Theater IV,* the trendy magazine of the *haute art* crowd, gave him a free platform to explain "Why I Wrote *The Clansman.*" Dixon swore that he wasn't a bigot [and] that it was based on "historical authenticity." *The New York Evening Post* was impressed. It praised him for tackling "a question of tremendously vital importance."

Filmmaker D. W. Griffith wanted Americans to know just how important it was. A decade later, he turned *The Clansman* into *Birth of a Nation.* He brushed off vehement protests from the NAACP[5] and black leaders that it was all a lie. He could afford to. By then cash registers were jingling everywhere as the film smashed house records nationally. When the film hit the White House, an ecstatic Woodrow Wilson exclaimed, "It's like writing history with lightning." Griffith wasn't the only filmmaker who sniffed dollars and glory in foisting the black brute's criminal image on the public. Between 1910–1911, these gems graced the screen, *Rastus in Zululand, Rastus and Chicken, Pickaninnies and Watermelon* and *Chicken Thief.*

NOTE: *I always thought it appropriate that these parts were played by white actors in messy cream black face. I knew then who the real toms, coons, mulattos, mammies and bucks were.*

By then, there were many whites who didn't need to read Dixon's novel, or see Griffith's film to know what to do with the "half child, half animal." The year *The Clansman* was published, more than one black person was lynched, burned, shot or mutilated every week in America. The year Griffith's film debuted the weekly lynch toll was still the same.

The NAACP's W. E. B. DuBois bitterly called lynching America's "exciting form of sport." Page was undaunted. He chalked lynching up to the "determination to put an end to the ravishing of their women by an inferior race."

NOTE: *Many people still think that black men were lynched because they committed rape. They weren't. In most cases, they weren't even accused of rape. Even then, the apologists for "the sport" knew this. . . .*

V

Politicians, being politicians, seemed to feel that if the public believed that black men were inherent rapists, then why spoil it with the truth. So, when Teddy Roosevelt rose to address Congress in 1906, lynching was very much on his mind. He sternly lectured that "The greatest existing cause of lynching is the perpetration, especially by black men, of the hideous crime of rape."

The old Rough Rider didn't want anyone to get the idea that he was condoning lynching, [for] after all, it would look a little odd for the man sworn to uphold the law to applaud those who broke it. He obligingly denounced the "lawbreakers." But Teddy had made his point. The *Cincinnati Inquirer* in 1911 railed against black men for committing the "unspeakable crime" and bragged that "the mob is the highest testimony to the civilization and enlightenment and moral character of the people."

The *Inquirer* was not a lone voice. The press, always on the lookout for a sensational story, read the public mood. In the crimson days before the doughboys of World War I marched off to save the world for democracy, the press milked the black beast angle for all it was worth. The *New York Times, Chicago Tribune, Boston Evening Transcript, San Francisco Examiner, Atlantic Monthly* and *Harpers* heisted the lingo from the academics and had great fun ridiculing, lampooning, butchering and assailing black men in articles and cartoons. They were "brutes," "savages," "imbeciles," "moral degenerates," and always "lazy, lazy, lazy." *Century Magazine* claimed it overheard this exchange between two blacks:

Uncle Rastus: "Now dat you daddy too ole to work, why don yah get a job?
Young Rastus: "No! indeed ain't going to have folks say everybody works but father 'bout mah family."

Remember Uncle Rastus was a good ole darkie. The young one, well. . . .

The San Francisco Examiner had a word about him and his ilk. In a cartoon a menacing-looking darkie shouts: "Don't be bumping into me, white man. I'se tough, Remembah the Civil War is over I'se tough."

Between World Wars I and II, a few liberals and radicals hoped that the press and the public would knock off the crude stuff and start down the path of racial enlightenment. Black editors knew better. They were still fighting tough battles to get the white press to stop stereotyping black men. Whenever a crime was committed, if a black was involved or suspected, newspapers almost always mentioned it. In case some were slow to make the connection, they would plaster a black face across the page.

NOTE: Black folks, as always, tried to find some humor in the situation. They joked that if a black ever wanted to get the white press to write about them, commit a crime and make sure the victim was white.

The defeat of Hitler and America's ascension to superpowerdom ushered in the American Century. This was supposed to be the era [when] American military might and economic muscle would bring permanent prosperity and freedom to the world. It would be an era when the winds of racial change would end segregation and race hate forever.

For a short while it seemed that blacks might get a little breathing space. The civil rights movement pricked the consciences of many whites. Congress, the White House and the Courts, with varying degrees of enthusiasm, finally relented and eliminated legal segregation. But, with the death of Martin Luther King, Jr., and Malcolm X, the collapse of the civil rights movement, political repression and the self-destruction of black power radicalism, young blacks were organizationally adrift.

Recession and economic shrinkage began to wreak havoc on the black poor. Many whites once again began to use terms about black men that sounded faintly reminiscent of the by-gone days, "law and order," "welfare cheats," "crime in the streets," "subculture of violence," "subculture of poverty," "culturally deprived" and "lack of family values."

By the end of the Reagan years, the language got rougher. The press now routinely tossed around terms like "crime prone," "war zone," "gang infested," "crack plagued," "drug turfs," "drug zombies," "violence scarred," "ghetto outcasts" and "ghetto poverty syndrome." Some, in the press, let it all hang out and called black criminals "scum," "leeches" and "losers." Their pictures routinely began to appear on the front pages, and for some strange reason they were all mostly black males.

NOTE:. Why drag up what happened a century ago? Americans don't believe any of this anymore. On October 31, 1993, two students at Yosemite High School in Oakhurst, a community just south of San Francisco, showed up at the school's Halloween party in Ku Klux Klan costumes. A third student wore black face.

The two students proceeded to stage a mock lynching of the "black." The three self-appointed white Knights may not have known any better. But what about school officials, parents and the other students? The three won prizes for their costumes. Students said it was "cool, like original." The principal took no disciplinary action against them. That's why!   [1994]

Terms

1. RODNEY KING: A Black man whose beating by Los Angeles police officers was caught on videotape.
2. LAPD: Los Angeles Police Department.
3. RECONSTRUCTION: The period after the Civil War (1865–1877) during which the states of the Southern Confederacy were controlled by the federal government and forced to reorganize their political and social institutions as a prerequisite to full readmission to the Union.
4. ZEITGEIST: German word meaning "spirit of the times."
5. NAACP: National Association for the Advancement of Colored People, a civil rights organization.

Understanding the Reading

1. Explain the purpose of and reaction to Rodney King's appearance at a mostly White high school.
2. What was Charles Carroll's theory about race?
3. Why did W. S. Armstead object to Carroll's book?
4. What was the response to George Fitzhugh's book?
5. What was "The Black Scare"?
6. What arguments were put forward to show that African Americans were doomed?
7. What was *The Clansman* about, and what impact did it have?
8. How did the press of the late nineteenth century treat Black men?
9. Why is late-nineteenth-century racism relevant today?

Suggestions for Responding

1. Try to view the film *Birth of a Nation* and describe your reactions to it.
2. Write a short essay responding to Hutchinson's closing anecdote about the Oakhurst high school Halloween party. ✦

55

Emmett Louis Till, 1941–1955

SOUTHERN POVERTY LAW CENTER

Mamie Till was a devoted, well-educated mother who taught her son that a person's worth did not depend on the color of his or her skin. Nevertheless, when she put 14-year-old Emmett on a train bound for Mississippi in the summer of 1955, she warned him: "If you have to get down on your knees and bow when a white person goes past, do it willingly."

It was not in Emmett Till to bow down. Raised in a working-class section of Chicago, he was bold and self-assured. He didn't understand the timid attitude of his Southern cousins toward whites. He even tried to impress them by showing them a photo of some white Chicago youths, claiming the girl in the picture was his girlfriend.

One day he took the photo out of his wallet and showed it to a group of boys standing outside a country store in Money, Mississippi. The boys dared him to speak to a white woman in the store. Emmett walked in confidently, bought some candy from Carolyn Bryant, the wife of the store owner, and said "Bye baby" on his way out.

Within hours, nearly everyone in town had heard at least one version of the incident. Some said Emmett had asked Mrs. Bryant for a date; others said he whistled at her. Whatever the details were, Roy Bryant was outraged that a black youth had been disrespectful to his wife. That weekend, Bryant and his half-brother J. W. Milam went looking for Till. They came to the cotton field shack that belonged to Mose Wright, a 64-year-old farmer and grandfather of Emmett Till's cousin. Bryant demanded to see "the boy that did the talking." Wright reluctantly got Till out of bed. As the white men took Emmett Till away, they told Wright not to cause any trouble or he'd "never live to be 65."

A magazine writer later paid Milam to describe what happened that night. Milam said he and Bryant beat Emmett Till, shot him in the head, wired a 75-pound cotton gin fan to his neck and dumped his body in the Tallahatchie River.

When asked why he did it, Milam responded: "Well, what else could I do? He thought he was as good as any white man."

So the World Could See

Till's body was found three days later—a bullet in the skull, one eye gouged out and the head crushed in on one side. The face was unrecognizable. Mose Wright knew it was Till only because of a signet ring that remained on one finger. The ring had belonged to Emmett's father Louis, who had died ten years earlier, and bore his initials L.T.

Mamie Till demanded the body of her son be sent back to Chicago. Then she ordered an open-casket funeral so the world could see what had been done to Emmett. *Jet* magazine published a picture of the horribly disfigured corpse. Thousands viewed the body and attended the funeral.

All over the country, blacks and sympathetic whites were horrified by the killing. Thousands of people sent money to the NAACP[1] to support its legal efforts on behalf of black victims.

In the meantime, J. W. Milam and Roy Bryant faced murder charges. They admitted they kidnapped and beat Emmett Till, but claimed they left him alive. Ignoring nationwide criticism, white Mississippians raised $10,000 to pay the legal expenses for Milam and Bryant. Five white local lawyers volunteered to represent them at the murder trial.

Mose Wright risked his life to testify against the men. In a courtroom filled with reporters and white spectators, the frail black farmer stood and identified Bryant and Milam as the men who took Emmett away.

Wright's act of courage didn't convince the all-white jury. After deliberating just over an hour, the jury returned a verdict of not guilty.

The murder of Emmett Till was the spark that set the civil rights movement on fire. For those who would become leaders of that movement, the martyred 14-year-old was a symbol of the struggle for equality.

"The Emmett Till case shook the foundations of Mississippi," said Myrlie Evers, widow of civil rights leader Medgar Evers, " . . . because it said even a child was not safe from racism and bigotry and death."

NAACP Executive Director Roy Wilkins said white Mississippians "had to prove they were superior . . . by taking away a 14-year-old boy."

Fred Shuttlesworth, who eight years later would lead the fight for integration in Birmingham, said, "The fact that Emmett Till, a young black man, could be found floating down the river in Mississippi just set in concrete the determination of the people to move forward . . . only God can know how many Negroes have come up missing, dead and killed under this system with which we live."   [1989]

Term

1. NAACP: National Association for the Advancement of Colored People.

Understanding the Reading

1. What did Emmett Till do to provoke the White Southerners?
2. What did Bryant and Milam do to Till?
3. What were the charges and the verdict against Bryant and Milam?
4. Nationally, what effect did Till's death produce, and why?

Suggestion for Responding

1. Write a short essay explaining why an incident like this could or could not happen today; support your position with some specific examples. ♦

56

Subtle vs. Overt Racism

David K. Shipler

In Washington recently, after a panel discussion on race, a black attorney approached me with the following story. He had just headed a project for a federal agency. Midway through the work, one of his subordinates, a white woman, had confided to several other whites that she could not bear to take orders from a black person.

The whites, one of whom had been regarded by the black attorney as a friend, said nothing to him about her remark. Not until months later, toward the end of the project, did the friend finally inform him of the white woman's bias, and he then realized that the woman had been quietly sabotaging the work. The Federal agency dismissed her.

Incidents like this pockmark the surface of America, but they're rarely visible. Usually, whites camouflage their prejudices more deftly and are seldom fired for them. Here, however, the contradictory contours of the country's racial landscape were in plain view. On the one hand, a black man had risen to be the boss, and the white woman lost her job for acting out her bigotry—testimony to the anti-racism that has evolved since the civil rights movement.

But hidden roots of racial prejudice and tension were revealed: The white woman said what many whites feel but do not say—that blacks in authority make them uncomfortable. And many whites, like the black attorney's friend, are paralyzed into silence by others' expressions of racism. Where was the white friend's loyalty to the black boss? Had the friendship survived? I asked the black man. "We're working on it," he said.

COMPLICATIONS

The United States now finds itself in an era of race relations more complex than in the days of legal segregation. Bigotry then was blatant, so entrenched that it could be shattered ultimately only by the conscience of the country and the hammer of the law. Today, when explicit discrimination is prohibited and blatant racism is no longer fashionable in most circles, much prejudice has gone underground. It may have diminished in some quarters, but it is far from extinct. Like a virus searching for a congenial host, it mutates until it finds expression in a belief, a statement, or a form of behavior that seems acceptable.

The camouflage around such racism does not make it benign. It can still damage life opportunities. Take the durable, potent stereotype of blacks as unintelligent and lazy.

In 1990, when the National Opinion Research Center at the University of Chicago asked a representative sample of Americans to evaluate various racial and ethnic groups, blacks ended up at the bottom. Most of those surveyed across the country labeled blacks as less intelligent than whites (53 percent); lazier than whites (62 percent); and more likely than whites to prefer being on welfare than being self-supporting (78 percent).

Much of this prejudice is no more than a thought, of course. To inhibit the translation of biased thoughts into discriminatory actions, American society has built a superstructure of laws, regulations, ethics and programs that include affirmative action and diversity training. Still, images manage to contaminate behavior, often subtly and ambiguously.

It happens in the Air Force, explained Edward Rice, a black B-52 pilot who was a lieutenant colonel and a White House Fellow when I met him several years ago. I asked him why, despite the military's exemplary record of opening doors to minorities, only about 300 of nearly 15,000 pilots in the Air Force were black. This shapes careers, since key commands are barred to Air Force officers who are not pilots. Why do many blacks wash out of flight school?

Rice offered a theory. In the cockpit with a black trainee, a white flight instructor must make split-second decisions about when to take control of the aircraft. If he thinks the trainee is flying dangerously, he will grab the stick. If in the back of the instructor's mind there lurks that age-old, widely held suspicion that blacks are less intelligent and less capable, perhaps he will move just a little more quickly to take control from a black trainee than from a white. And if he does that repeatedly, Rice noted, the black will not advance to the next level of training.

Consider another example. A white couple in northern California adopted a biracial girl as an infant. Their two biological children, both boys, were close in age, so all three youngsters attended the same high school at around the same time. When the white boys fell behind in class, notes and calls came home from teachers. But when the biracial girl had academic problems, there were no notes or calls. She looked black and hung out with black friends, and her parents concluded that the teachers had written her off.

Those teachers did not wear white hoods and stand in the schoolhouse door. They came from the mainstream of white America, where the images of blacks as less capable run strongly just beneath the surface of polite behavior. Even in the finest integrated schools across the country, I found black youngsters, pushed hard by their parents, who complained that white teachers made insufficient demands on them, assumed that they would be satisfied with less than A's, and discouraged them from taking honors courses or applying to top colleges.

ECHOES OF THE PAST

Decoding such encrypted racism is an uncertain art that requires a sense of history—the history of racial stereotyping in America—and a capacity to listen and observe how frequently the present echoes the past.

Many institutions that look integrated, for example, are often segregated within, for integration has largely meant the mere physical mixing of people of various races, not the sharing of power and the blending into an integral whole. Therefore, blacks who enter mostly white institutions often feel like invited guests—and not always very welcome guests—who are there at the pleasure of the whites. Rarely do the blacks attain ownership, authority, or the standing to set agendas. They are confronted by glass walls that whites often do not see.

A black man worked for IBM for three years before learning that every evening a happy hour was taking place in a nearby bar. Only white men from the office were involved—no women, no minorities. Had it been strictly social it would have been merely offensive. But it was also professionally damaging, for business was being done over drinks, plans were being designed, connections made. Excluded from that network, the black man was excluded from opportunity for advancement, and he left the job.

This is a common experience among blacks and women who have integrated the workplace, and it raises questions about possible remedies. Two come to mind: affirmative action and diversity training.

Assume that the white men at the happy hour are not extreme racists, do not decide deliberately to exclude blacks and don't think about the implications of their gatherings at the bar. They go to the bar with people with whom they are most comfortable, and the most comfortable are people like themselves.

If an affirmative action plan were in place, promotions into management would be monitored by race and gender, and the marginalization of minorities and women—whether intentional or not—would become a matter of concern.

Just calling attention to the problem could be enough to make the white men conscious of the need to consider the black man for promotion. They might even reflect on how to bring him into the loop. Beyond that, diversity workshops, where office dynamics are discussed and minority employees can be heard, would highlight the happy hour as a tool of exclusion.

The difficulty is that one has to perceive the problem to embrace the solutions. If you think that racism isn't harmful unless it wears sheets or burns crosses or bars blacks from motels and restaurants, you will support only the crudest anti-discrimination laws and not the more refined methods of affirmative action and diversity training. If you recognize how subtle racism can be, the subtler tools seem appropriate.

One of the great divides in the country is between those Americans who see only blatant racism and those who see the subtle forms as well. It is such a fundamental disagreement that it has shaped much of the current debate over affirmative action.

Opponents of affirmative action believe that prejudice and discrimination have diminished enough to have leveled the playing field for non-whites. The argument holds that affirmative action introduces unfairness and demeans non-whites by suggesting that they could not succeed without it.

FEELING BRANDED

Every solution, however, creates at least one new problem, and affirmative action is no exception. It is designed in principle to require that the best candidates be recruited from groups that have suffered discrimination. Nothing in the concept calls for the acceptance of unqualified people. Yet some managers have been so skittish about lawsuits or so eager to prove themselves non-racist that they have pushed certain black employees into jobs where they have foundered. That has played to the age-old stereotype of blacks as less competent than whites.

Many blacks complain about being branded with an assumption that without affirmative action they would not be in this college or on that construction crew or in that corporate office. Occasionally that reinforces self-doubt. A few black students at Princeton told me that when papers came due and exam time approached, they wondered if they really belonged at such a demanding school.

But it is wise to remember that these doubts—and even blacks' self-doubts—have existed for generations, since long before desegregation and affirmative action. The assumption that blacks were less able was a major reason that affirmative action was needed to overcome the obstacles to admitting, hiring and promoting them.

The old stereotype of blacks as unintelligent and lazy remains a constant as the remedy changes, and the constant hangs itself on whatever hook happens to be available. Before, it was said that blacks were unqualified and therefore weren't hired. Now, the argument goes, blacks are unqualified but are hired because they're black—same belief, different outcome.

If we have to choose—and apparently we do—it is the outcome that matters more than the belief. Would the black student rather be at Princeton and be thought less competent, or be thought less competent and *not* be at Princeton? Before affirmative action, Princeton and other top colleges admitted precious few blacks.

Another key criticism of affirmative action holds that it works against more qualified whites. Here again, the assumption is that whites are more qualified than blacks. Polls and focus groups have found that while most whites think that under affirmative action less qualified blacks are hired and promoted over more qualified whites, most blacks think that *without* affirmative action, less qualified *whites* are hired and promoted over more qualified *blacks*. Both sides want fairness, but each has a different notion of how to achieve it.

Surveys show that few whites can cite personal experience to justify their fears. With the total black population at just 13 percent, and a smaller percentage of blacks in a position to compete for jobs covered by affirmative action, the chance of edging out a more qualified white is slim. Moreover, even when a white person thinks he has been passed over for a less qualified black, he may be wrong. Some supervisors admit that they have told whites whom they didn't want to hire or promote, "I'd love to take you, but I've got to take a black—you know how it is." It's easier than telling the applicant that he doesn't measure up.

THE BOTTOM LINE

Paradoxically, just as affirmative action is being chipped away by the courts, legislators, and by voters in referendums, it is putting down deeper roots in colleges, corporations and government agencies. In many places, institutional ethics have evolved to the point where an all-white workforce or management team is automatically seen as inadequate and a diverse staff is seen as beneficial. The rationale has shifted from altruism to pragmatism, from high-minded compassion to bottom-line competition.

Business, for example, looks at the demographics of its potential employees and of its customers and reasons that it must diversify racially to profit. Colleges look at the world for which they're preparing students and conclude that a homogeneously white setting does not provide the best education. It may be sad, but morality is less potent than self-interest.

For the last 20 years, the military has managed race relations by emphasizing behavior, not beliefs. "You can think anything you want—that's your business," the military says to its members. "But what you do is our business. If you act in ways that deny opportunity on the basis of race, you interfere with the cohesiveness of the unit, and it becomes the concern of the service."

As practical as this is, it is a bit of a false dichotomy. Thoughts and actions interact with each other, cause each other, reinforce each other. And to assess behavior across racial lines, you have to keep coming back to beliefs as a reference point. It is not an institution's role to enforce certain beliefs on its students or employees, but in addressing racial dynamics the entrenched stereotypes need to be kept in mind. They illuminate and explain the actions.

Getting at the stereotypes requires some acknowledgement that whites benefit from racial prejudice, even as society suffers as a whole. Few white Americans reflect on the unseen privileges they possess or the greater sense of worth they acquire from their white skin. In addition to creating the traditional alignments of power in America, negative beliefs about blacks tend to enhance whites' self-esteem.

If blacks are less intelligent, in whites' belief, then it follows that whites are more intelligent. If blacks are lazier, whites are harder working. If blacks would prefer to live on welfare, then whites would prefer to be self-supporting. If blacks are more violent, whites are less violent—and the source of violence can be kept at a safe distance.

Many conservatives these days urge us to make an "optimistic" assessment of the racial situation. At the same time, they refuse to see the pernicious racism that persists. That blindness does not justify optimism. Legitimate optimism comes from facing the problems squarely and working to overcome the insidious subtleties of bigotry that still abide in the land.   [1998]

Understanding the Reading

1. What is the point of the Black attorney's story about the White woman employee?
2. Why didn't the Black attorney's White friend tell him about the woman's bias?
3. Why does Edward Rice think so few Air Force pilots are Black?
4. Why is it significant that the Black IBM male employee wasn't included in the happy hour?
5. How does Shipler evaluate affirmative action programs and why?
6. Why do many colleges, businesses, and government agencies apply affirmative action even when they are not legally bound to?

Suggestions for Responding

1. Write a letter to Shipler, adding support for or arguing against his thesis about racism.
2. Do you think affirmative action is a good or bad policy? Why? Be specific. ✦

57
Blacks Feel Indignities

ROBERT ANTHONY WATTS

Joe Reed grew up in the birthplace of the civil rights movement, hearing haunting stories from his relatives about the horrors of segregation.

But when Reed considers the impact of racism on his life, his mind moves north from Montgomery, Ala., to the corridors of power of Congress, where he began working as a legislative aide this year.

Reed repeatedly was stopped by lobbyists sponsoring receptions and asked to produce identification, while white aides walked in without question. Sometimes, he was turned away, told the gatherings were restricted to members of Congress, then learned later that was a lie.

"It makes you angry," says Reed, who is 23. "It makes you feel second class. No matter how far you go, no matter how well-dressed you are, you're still black."

For many black Americans, these kinds of snubs and slights are common experiences in restaurants, stores and social settings.

Usually subtle and almost never involving slurs, the incidents are far less obvious than Jim Crow laws that prevailed in the South three decades ago.

But still, many blacks say, such behavior is jarring, leads to simmering anger and widens the racial divide in America. They say they rarely share the slights with white friends and co-workers, fearing they'll be considered overly sensitive.

• • •

In one of the most notable examples, some blacks contend they were given poor or no service at restaurants run by the Denny's chain and asked to pre-pay for their meals.

Six black Secret Service agents filed suit against the chain in May, alleging that they were waited on, then ignored and not served, while white agents sitting nearby in the Annapolis, Md., outlet received prompt service.

The agents' lawsuit came on the heels of a similar suit filed by 32 blacks in California against Denny's, which has signed a nondiscrimination settlement in which it admitted no wrongdoing. The chain did, however, say it would stop certain practices, such as asking customers in some restaurants to pre-pay.

Dr. Carl Bell, a Chicago psychiatrist known for his work on racism, says such behavior is called "micro-insults" or "micro-aggressions." The experiences can be particularly frustrating for blacks, he says, because they are so personal and subjective.

"How do you prove that someone jumped in line in front of you?" Bell said. "You go into a store and look at a suit, the guy takes you to the cheapest suits in the store. How can you prove racial bias in that? It's not hard evidence. . . . White people can blow you off and say, 'No, you're just touchy.' And you walk away feeling, maybe I was."

But in Reed's case, one of his white colleagues, Ken Mullinax, also noticed the difference in treatment on Capitol Hill. Both men worked for U.S. Rep. Earl Hilliard, an Alabama Democract, before Reed left to start law school at the University of Pittsburgh.

"It's weird," said Mullinax, who often was the lone white among Hilliard aides attending the receptions. "We all go together, and every time, they let me walk right in."

But black aides "are always stopped and questioned," he said. "It has happened so many times now, I can't think it's anything else but a black-white issue."

Reed said snubs continued in the receptions, where lobbyists seemed reluctant to shake his hand, uninterested in what he has to say and more attentive to white aides.

"Sometimes you almost want to cry, but you start to believe it sometimes," he said. "You start to feel like, 'Is there really something wrong with me?'"

• • •

Many blacks—especially those who grew up under segregation—say such modern-day insults, even subtle ones, are jolting because they occur at moments when they feel they have escaped the burden of race.

"As bad as segregation is, the rules are clear," said Melvin Sikes, a retired black psychologist in Austin, Texas, who still is angry over an experience three years ago with a cab driver. "If you are prepared to be hit—even if you are hit—you know how to absorb it. This, you don't know how to deal with."

Sikes and his wife, Zeta, say their 1990 anniversary weekend was ruined when a cab driver bypassed them and picked up a white couple.

After returning from a wonderful celebration aboard a dinner train in nearby San Antonio, the couple had walked to the street to hail a cab. A white couple came up behind them, Sikes said, and agreed to wait for a second cab.

But when the first cab arrived and Sikes reached to open the door for his wife, the cab rolled past, he said, pulling up to the white couple, who, after a short exchange with the driver, climbed inside.

"Had it been 20 years ago, it wouldn't have bothered me, because that was the story of my life," said Mrs. Sikes, 75, who grew up at a time when blacks couldn't vote in Texas. "But in 1990, I certainly didn't expect that."

Unable to forget the experience, the couple cut short a planned stay out of town and returned home.

• • •

Michael Thurmond, a lawyer and former chairman of the Black Caucus in the Georgia Legislature, remembers the sting of leaving an elegant reception for lawmakers at the Ritz-Carlton hotel in Atlanta last year and being asked by an elderly white woman, and then her husband, to retrieve their car.

Thurmond, dressed in a $250 tailor-made blazer, white shirt and silk tie, was standing by the hotel door waiting for his car when the wife approached him. Thurmond says he politely told her he was not an employee.

But when her husband asked moments later, Thurmond angrily snapped at the man, who stammered an apology and nervously walked away.

"I was really ticked," Thurmond said. "Here I am being entertained upstairs as chairman of the black caucus with all these business people trying to shake your hand, and you come downstairs and get mistaken for a parking attendant." [1993]

Understanding the Reading

1. How was legislative aide John Reed treated in Congress?
2. How did Denny's treat six Black Secret Service agents?
3. What is a "micro-insult" or "micro-aggression"?
4. How did Ken Mullinax react to the treatment of his Black colleague?
5. What indignity did Melvin Sikes experience?

6. Describe Michael Thurmond's experience at an Atlanta hotel.

Suggestions for Responding

1. How do you think Blacks should respond to "micro-insults"?
2. Compare and contrast the incidents described here with those Cofer describes in "The Myth of the Latin Woman: I Just Met a Girl Named Maria." ◆

SUGGESTIONS FOR RESPONDING TO PART IV

1. Research and report on a specific example of racism in American history, such as the Cherokee removal and the Trail of Tears, anti-Semitic quotas in admission to colleges such as Harvard in the 1920s, restrictive covenants, the "scientific" studies that "proved" racial inferiority on the basis of such characteristics as brain size and physique, or the treatment of Mexican citizens under the treaty of Guadalupe Hidalgo.

2. Investigate a minority "first," such as baseball player Jackie Robinson; athlete James Thorpe; Harriet Tubman, the "Moses" of the Underground Railroad; Virginia governor Eugene Wilder; Arctic explorer Matthew Henson; Rosa Parks, the woman whose arrest prompted the Montgomery bus boycott; Olympic athlete Jesse Owens; Olympic gold medalist Kristi Yamaguchi; Supreme Court justice Thurgood Marshall; tennis champion Arthur Ashe; heavyweight boxing champion Joe Lewis; poet Phillis Wheatley; Jean Baptiste Point du Sable, founder of Chicago; Nobel peace prize winner Ralph Bunche; congressional representatives Hiram Fong and Daniel Inouye; Academy Award winner Sidney Poitier; Springfield, Ohio, mayor Robert C. Henry; Senator Edward Brooke; Dr. Daniel Hale Williams, the physician who performed the first open-heart surgery; President Barack Obama; or any of the many others. Report on their achievements, and focus on the racial barriers they faced and overcame.

3. Imagine you are a member of a different race, and write an autobiography in which you analyze the impact that your new race has on your opportunities and accomplishments.

4. Research how the stereotype of one racial or ethnic group in America evolved—for example, the image of Native Americans as noble savages evolving into the drunken Indian or the inscrutable Chinese into the model minority. Analyze how historical contexts influenced the various characterizations and how each variation benefited the dominant culture.

5. In American society, it is almost impossible not to be affected in some way by racism. Write a critical analysis of a manifestation of your own racism.

Power and Sexism

SCARCELY MORE THAN A GENERATION AGO, TRADItional gender roles were accepted as natural, normal, even inevitable. Men were expected to be strong, unemotional, aggressive, competitive, and devoted to concerns of the outside world; women were to be gentle, emotional, passive, nurturing, and devoted to home and family. Those who violated these norms were labeled deviant. A man whose eyes appeared to moisten in public was immediately perceived as less than fully qualified to be U.S. president. An ambitious middle-class woman who wanted more than a domestic role was declared by psychiatrists to be suffering from a psychological personality disorder.

The word *sexism* did not exist until approximately fifty years ago. In the early 1960s, everyone assumed that women had the same rights and opportunities that men had and that they were content with their domestic role, caring for their homes and families. Magazines, movies, television, school textbooks, church leaders, politicians—everyone, everywhere, including most women—extolled the virtues of the traditional division of labor: man the breadwinner and woman the homemaker.

However, economic reality was already making this ideal more and more difficult for White, middle-class women to maintain. Increasingly, they had to work outside the home, but working women were also expected to continue to serve as wife and mother. In the workplace, however, they were restricted in the kinds of jobs they could get. Newspapers printed ads under separate "Help Wanted—Male" and "Help Wanted—Female" listings, shunting even women with college degrees, for example, into secretarial rather than professional positions. Paying less for women's work was considered natural because men were regarded as the family breadwinners.

In 1963, Betty Friedan published *The Feminine Mystique,* in which she investigated the unhappiness and malaise that haunted the well-educated suburban homemaker. Suddenly, everybody began talking about the "woman problem." Women organized **consciousness-raising groups,** where they shared their experiences as women. Simple as this sounds, this sharing almost immediately altered the way people saw the gendered social system. Problems previously regarded as personal were revealed to be part of a larger web of social limitations that society imposed on women simply because of their sex.

The value of women and a women-centered perspective and the advocacy of social, political, and economic equality for both women and men became the widely accepted and widely debated platform of modern **feminism.** Scrutinizing every facet of society through a feminist lens revealed that fundamental gender inequality was (and still is) embedded in the

241

entire social system. The system was exposed as **patriarchal,** meaning that it is hierarchical and that its structures of power, value, and culture are **androcentric;** that is, they are male-centered and male-dominated. Every aspect of society—employment, education, religion, media, law, economic arrangements, and even the family—reinforced and maintained men's social superiority and women's social inferiority and subordination.

As soon as feminist analysis exposed the inherent inequities of this system, women organized to change it. Equating the position of all women with that of Blacks, they coined the term *sexism* to emphasize the correspondence between racism and the discriminatory treatment to which women were subjected. **Sexism** is the subordination of an individual man or woman or a group of men or women and the assumption of the superiority of an individual woman or man or a group of women or men, based solely on sex. Like racism, sexism is reflected in both individual and institutional acts, decisions, habits, procedures, and policies that neglect, overlook, exploit, subjugate, or maintain the subordination of an individual man or woman or all men or women.

Feminist activism throughout the past forty years has changed society dramatically. Textbooks from basal readers to medical volumes are scrupulously edited to eliminate blatant sexism and gender stereotyping. Women today have access to higher education and professional training, and they are represented in nearly every occupation from carpentry and mining to the clergy and the securities market. Men are more likely to share housework and child-care responsibilities. Advertisements present women taking business trips (other than to the supermarket) and climbing telephone poles.

These changes have led many of us to believe that women in the United States have come closer to achieving equality with men than most other women in the world. In fact, however, when it comes to women's nonagricultural wage as a percentage of men's, the United States ranks behind thirty other countries—including Hungary, Tanzania, Vietnam, Jordan, Zambia, and most of western Europe. In 2010, American women earned 77.4 percent of what men earned, even when the comparisons were adjusted for education and experience. (This is two cents higher than in 1995. If we stay at this rate of change, we will see women on par with men in 138 years.)

We begin with *The American Prospect's* "Citizenship and Violence" (Reading 58), focusing upon the tension of some states with the power of the federal government as it is deliberated whether violence against women within a relationship falls under civil rights or the privacy due to "domestic relations."

In Reading 59 of Part V, Jackson Katz and Sut Jhally explain that professional wrestling's greatest threat is not that it teaches violence but that it presents a "multiplexed model for success." As Martha Burk and Kirsten Shaw show in Reading 60, movies, advertising, television, and music all exploit and degrade women, making gender-specific violence seem acceptable.

As the gay marriage debate gets louder, Andrew Sullivan, a gay Catholic, writes in "Losing a Church, Keeping the Faith" (Reading 61) about his reaction when a gay couple, who have sung in the choir for twenty-five and thirty-two years, are told they may no longer be part of the choir. Students can decide whether this is a decision made according to theological doctrine or is a political one.

One of the most serious problems women and men face in the workplace is **sexual harassment,** which is unwanted, unsolicited, and nonreciprocated sexual behavior or attention. The testimony by Anita Hill before the Senate Judiciary Committee finally brought this issue fully into the public awareness. She contested the qualifications of Clarence Thomas to serve on the United States Supreme Court, charging that he had sexually harassed her when she worked for him at the Equal Employment Opportunity Commission. In Reading 62, she shares her understanding of the impact such harassment has had on the women who responded to her presentation.

Sexist attitudes and beliefs and homophobia continue to be challenged on many fronts. Barbara Trees (Reading 63) describes how women trying to break into the building trades still have to endure extreme sexual harassment and humiliation simply to keep their jobs.

Violence is the use of physical force to control the behavior of another person, to compel him or her to follow a certain course of action or enforced inaction, to coerce him or her into acting or thinking in whatever way the person with power dictates, and to leave the victim with no alternative except compliance. In other words, violence—physical, verbal, emotional, and sexual —is used to enforce the dominance of the perpetrator and the subordination of the victim.

Readings 64 and 65 address the issues of battery, what is often referred to as *domestic violence* or *spousal abuse*. Spouse beating is the most common and least reported crime in this country, afflicting men and women of all races and classes. According to FBI statistics, a woman is beaten by her husband or partner every eighteen seconds. As Mariah Burton Nelson reports, wife beating seems almost built in to sports culture, which uses the degradation of women to affirm the masculinity of its participants. Furthermore, battery is not confined to marital relationships. Nancy Worcester reports on violence against adolescent women and its effects on the victims, particularly on their self-esteem; Worcester insists that society must recognize this problem and work to rectify it.

In "Why Doesn't She Just Leave?" (Reading 66) Clarethia Ellerbe brings us face-to-face with specific methods of controlling a woman in an intimate relationship, with and without the threat of physical violence. The author first interviews an aunt, who had been in a physically violent marriage for almost forty years. Next, she interviews a man who straightforwardly explains his methods of being a "controller": "I start by building her ego . . . send her flowers. . . . She now opens up. . . . I listen to every word she has to say. . . . This is my opportunity to find out which of her girlfriends or family members has the strongest influence on her. . . . I start planning how to eliminate that person from her circle. . . ." It is an unforgettable window into the insidiousness of emotional and psychological abuse.

The threat of **rape,** of being forced to have sex without consent is a real threat for men and women, but especially for women. A woman is raped every six minutes, and one out of every three women will be raped in her lifetime. Notwithstanding the frequency with which this crime occurs, rape victims are still treated with skepticism, even by friends and family. If a rape survivor decides to press charges against

his or her attacker and the case goes to trial, the defense may try to introduce the plaintiff's behavior into the proceedings and may well claim that he or she enticed the assailant or that he or she wanted or enjoyed it.

Readings 67, 68, and 69 address this issue. One of the most important points James A. Doyle makes is that rape is an act of dominance, not sex; he explains why, despite general recognition of this fact, society tends to **blame the victim,** accusing him or her of being somehow responsible for what was done. Doyle also examines how **pornography,** some of which links violence against women with sexuality, contributes to the degradation of women. In Reading 68, Kathleen Hirsch analyzes fraternity gang rape; she sees it as the effort of young men to establish their heterosexual identity and to create male bonds at the expense of women. She also contends that the tendency of universities to protect the perpetrators more than the victim silences women— the victim herself *and* all women on campus. On a lighter note, the anonymous sketch "'The Rape' of Mr. Smith" (Reading 69) tellingly exposes the injustice of our societal attitudes toward and treatment of rape victims.

Concluding Part V, Readings 70 and 71 look at diminishing rights for women in 2007. Allison Stevens's essay analyzes the Bush administration's Supreme Court and its effects on the health of women, while Linda Chavez-Thompson and Gabriela Lemus break down the gender wage gap according to ethnic groups in "Erosion of Unions Hurts Women, Particularly Latinas."

Today, it is not fashionable to express racist and, to a lesser extent, sexist attitudes. Although racism and sexism may have become less visible recently, both remain well entrenched in our culture and within ourselves. They continue to distort our perceptions of one another and to impair our interpersonal behavior. They constrict the educational, economic, social, and cultural opportunities of people of color, women, and gay men and lesbians. Bad as this situation is, even worse has been the use of law and violence to oppress some groups and to serve the interests of others. We shall watch carefully to see what effects the Obama administration will have as we enter a phase of our history that sharply contrasts with the previous administration.

58

Citizenship and Violence

THE AMERICAN PROSPECT

Why, when the issue is violence against women, do some people talk about sex? While some violence directed at women is sexualized, calling it "sex" softens the brutality, implicates the victim as possibly an inciter or a participant, and offers the perpetrator the justification of lust.

Think also about the phrase "domestic violence." True, a good deal of violence against women does occur inside houses, but the coziness assumed to reside within the "domestic" stands in contrast to the cruelty of violence imposed by someone so close.

Linking violence against women to sex and domestic life illustrates more than a problem of rhetoric; it demonstrates the ongoing effects of laws that have treated women unequally. For centuries, state laws wove notions of sex and domesticity into a fabric of toleration of violence against women. And now that federal law is trying to protect women from the residue of that discrimination, objectors are arguing that federal remedies are unconstitutional—because violence against women is about sex and the home, which they say are state, not federal, concerns.

Two centuries ago, husbands had the prerogative of beating their wives. One century ago, state courts constructed rules about the sanctity of the home, thereby justifying under a rubric of privacy a reluctance to interfere when men beat or raped their wives. Indeed, up until about 10 years ago, under the United States military code, a man could not be convicted of the rape of his wife because the code defined rape as "the act of sexual intercourse with a female not his wife, by force and without her permission."

In short, the law decided which harms against women were tolerable. And even when those exemptions no longer exist, police, prosecutors, juries, and judges continue to be influenced by the long-standing assumption that women do not have rights of bodily integrity equal to those of men.

But law is not static. Particularly when civil rights are at issue, Congress has often enabled groups that have suffered discrimination under state laws to turn to federal courts for protection.

Recall that after the Civil War, some states did not allow African Americans to marry. When Congress considered federal remedies, some opponents responded that marriage was a matter of "domestic relations"—outside the purview of Congress. Congress concluded otherwise; federal civil rights law guaranteed newly freed slaves the right to marry.

In the early part of the twentieth century, labor's opponents argued that employment relations were personal relations, a matter for state, not federal, governance; but Congress began to pass labor laws, including legislation protecting the right of workers to unionize.

These federal laws now seem unremarkable. Yet in a case currently before the U.S. Supreme Court, opponents of the Violence Against Women Act (VAWA), passed by Congress in 1994, are once again raising the familiar themes of personal relations and states' rights.

Congress enacted VAWA after four years of hearings and many revisions; it crafted a multi-faceted statute that provides substantial funding to state, tribal, and local programs to combat violence against women. VAWA also authorizes federal criminal prosecutions in limited circumstances, for example, if a person crosses state lines to harm an intimate partner already protected by a permanent state court order. And VAWA includes a new civil rights remedy for victims of gender-based violence akin to the remedy already on the books for race discrimination: VAWA lets plaintiffs sue assailants for damages, in either state or federal court, upon proof that a crime of violence was motivated by "animus based on gender."

Now at issue before the Supreme Court is the constitutionality of this one aspect of VAWA, the civil remedy. Thus far, most of the federal judges who have considered it have upheld it. However, one federal appellate court, the Fourth Circuit, thought otherwise, holding that neither the Constitution's Commerce Clause nor the 14th Amendment enabled Congress to create federal court remedies for victims of gender-based violence. . . .

The Fourth Circuit's view that VAWA harms states' rights is not shared by many representatives of state government. When the legislation was pending, the attorneys general of 38 states told Congress that VAWA's civil rights provisions would be a useful supplement to—not a displacement of—state remedies. At the time, few laws in the United States still expressly exculpated men who had attacked their wives. But many prosecutors worried that the residue of both legal and social attitudes about violence against women results in systematically less protection for women victims of violence than for men.

States did more than worry. In the 1980s and 1990s, the chief justices of more than half the states commissioned task forces to explore the treatment of women in their courts. What they learned was powerful and disheartening. Connecticut's task force concluded, for example, that "women are treated differently from men in the justice system, and because of it, many suffer from unfairness." From states as different as California, Georgia, Maryland, Minnesota, and Kentucky, reports came that women victims of violence faced special hurdles—their claims of injury were often discounted, their testimony often disbelieved.

The record of systemic discrimination was before Congress when it enacted VAWA. And that record explains why, in 1999, the National Association of Attorneys General supported the reauthorization of VAWA and 36 states signed onto a brief filed in the current Supreme Court case, urging that the civil rights remedy be upheld. (Only one state—Alabama—argued for invalidation.)

Power is surely at stake here, but not only how to allocate it between state and federal governments. Also at issue is the Supreme Court's ability to override congressional enactments. Will the Court now ignore congressional fact-finding and substitute its own? Will it change its current interpretation of the Commerce Clause and cut back on Congress's power to legislate in this sphere?

To understand why the Court should not, first focus on the Fourth Circuit's argument that violence against women is about sex, crimes, family life, and the home, and that states have exclusive dominion here. That claim is untrue, and as policy it would be unwise.

Federal law oversees state criminal law and family law in a variety of contexts. States cannot, for example, enforce criminal laws discriminatorily, nor can they forbid interracial marriage. Outside the domain of civil rights, many other federal laws define and structure relations that could be termed "domestic"—like welfare law (requiring

beneficiaries to work, so that children need to be in child care programs), the Equal Retirement Income Security Act (creating marital property rights in pensions), or tax law (defining economic obligations by reference to marital status).

The point is not that Congress has taken over state law, but rather that state and federal governance—overlapping, often cooperative—is the norm in virtually all fields of human endeavor in the United States, family life and criminal law included.

Second, focus on Congress's powers over interstate commerce. Since the 1930s, the Constitution has been understood as permitting Congress to regulate not only commercial transactions themselves but activities substantially related to commerce. Since the 1960s, the Constitution has been understood as permitting Congress to remove obstacles to engaging in commerce—especially discriminatory obstacles. Before enacting VAWA, Congress heard testimony from both business executives and individuals detailing not only that violence has an economic effect on the GDP, but that violence against women limits women's full participation as economic actors. Congress learned both that women were beaten to prevent them from going to work and that the threat of violence restricted women's employment options.

At the time, VAWA's opponents predicted its civil rights remedy would open the floodgates to lawsuits having little or nothing to do with commerce. Yet to date, only about 50 decisions have been reported under the civil rights remedy, and of those, more than 40 percent involved allegations of attacks in commercial or educational settings. Indeed, the case before the Supreme Court involves a young woman allegedly raped by two students at her college, one of whom explained publicly that he liked to "get girls drunk and fuck the shit out of them."

Third, consider Congress's power to enforce the 14th Amendment, forbidding states to deny equal protection of the laws. Opponents of VAWA argue that violence inflicted by individuals is a private act, not state action. But state laws have failed to protect women's physical security equally with men's. State prosecutors have told Congress that inequality continues. Congress can therefore fashion proportionate remedies, as it has done before to protect blacks from racially motivated violence.

VAWA, in other words, is an ordinary exercise of congressional powers, executed in a "federalism-friendly" fashion to provide complementary means of rights enforcement. Its opponents want to identify women with the home, focus on violence in bedrooms, and confine a woman's remedies to whatever is available in the locality in which she finds herself. What they fail to understand is that the federal government has an obligation to secure women's physical safety and to protect women's rights to participate in the national economy free from the threat of targeted violence. VAWA is not about sex, and it is not about a family any of us would want to be in; citizenship in the nation is what is at stake.   [2001]

Understanding the Reading

1. Give two examples in U.S. history where states have fought with the federal government over jurisdiction concerning "domestic relations."
2. How does violence against women affect our country's economy?
3. Give at least two arguments of supporters of the Violence Against Women Act that explain why this act is constitutional.

Suggestion for Responding

1. Research your state's laws that pertain to violence against women. ◆

59

Manhood on the Mat

Jackson Katz and Sut Jhally

As professional wrestling explodes in popularity, cultural analysts are struggling to catch up to its significance for society. The traditional ways of seeing it—for example, as a morality play of good vs. evil—have been transcended, as wrestling has morphed into perhaps the ultimate expression of the entertainment industry's new, multiplexed model for success.

Vince McMahon, head of the World Wrestling Federation, describes it as "contemporary sports entertainment which treats 'professional wrestling' as an action/adventure soap opera. With the sexuality of '90210,' the subject matter of 'NYPD Blue,' the athleticism of the Olympics, combined with reality-based story lines, the WWF presents a hybrid of almost all forms of entertainment and sports combined in one show." Add to that the fertile brew of traditional advertising, product merchandising, and frequent pay-per-view special events and the result is revenue in the tens of millions of dollars, not to mention a forceful new strain of sports entertainment.

But understanding pro wrestling's immense popularity, especially with (white) men and boys, requires viewing it in the broader context of shifting gender relations.

The accomplishments of social movements such as feminism, as well as the shift to a postindustrial, high-tech era of automated production and e-commerce, have challenged the culture to construct new definitions of masculinity. In the new social, cultural, and employment context, there is less emphasis on characteristics such as strength and physicality that, in an earlier age, not only clearly defined men and women in very different ways, but made masculinity dominant.

In threatened response, many men have retreated into the safe and cartoonish masculinity of a more primal gender order, a world typified by the wildly popular program "WWF Smackdown!" where size, strength, and brutality are rewarded. In wrestling's contemporary incarnation, it's not who wins and loses that matters, but how the game is played. And the way the game is played in the WWF and its companion league, World Championship Wrestling, or WCW, reinforces the prime directive—might makes right, with extreme violence defining how power is exercised.

In the past, discussions about wrestling's effects on "real world" violence have typically centered on the behavioral effects of exposure to it. Does it cause imitative violence?

But that misses the point. For the question is not, "Are children imitating the violence they see?" but "Are children learning that taunting, ridiculing, and bullying define masculinity?"

We know from decades of research that depictions of violence in the entertainment media create a cultural climate in which such behavior is accepted as a normal, even appropriate, response to various problems.

We can see this process of normalization clearly in pro wrestling, where intimidation, humiliation, control, and verbal aggression (toward men as well as women) is the way that "real men" prevail. Manhood is equated explicitly with the ability to settle scores, defend one's honor, and win respect and compliance through force of conquest.

Already, this definition of manhood is at the root of much interpersonal violence in our society. For example, abusive men use force (or the threat of it) in an attempt to exercise power and control in their relationships with women. While there is no causal relationship between pro wrestling and male violence, it is clear that the wrestling subculture contributes to a larger cultural environment that teaches boys and men that manhood is about achieving power and control.

Real (or simulated) physical violence actually comprises a small percentage of the length of a pro wrestling telecast. Most of the time is devoted to setting up the narratives, and to verbal confrontation and bullying. In wrestling video games, each combatant not only has signature moves, but also verbal taunts that can be directed against either an opponent or the crowd. The object of the game is to see who can be the most effective bully.

It is a lesson that resonates all too clearly in our schools: A recent survey of 6,000 children in grades 4 to 6 found that about 1 in 10 said they were bullied one or more times a week, and 1 in 5 admitted to being bullies themselves. And we know from the 1990s' series of school shootings that, all too often, guns become the great equalizer for boys who have been bullied, ridiculed, and verbally taunted.

The hyper-masculine wrestling subculture is also deeply infused with homophobic anxiety. Macho posturing and insults ("wimps," and other worse epithets) can barely mask the fear of feminization that is always present in the homoerotic entanglement of male bodies. (The most popular of the trademark taunts by the wrestler X-Pac involves a thrusting of the crotch, accompanied by a sexual vulgarity, and his signature move of humiliation is to back his opponent into a corner and "ride" his face.)

As the enactment of gender has moved to center stage in wrestling narratives, so have women become much more central to the plot lines. In the days of Hulk Hogan and the Macho Man, women were essentially restricted to a couple of sexualized figures. But now, there are many stereotypically hyper-sexualized female characters, especially in the WWF.

More frequently male wrestlers have "girl-friends" who accompany them to the ring. And every week, in one of the most overtly racist and sexist characterizations on contemporary television, the Godfather, an over-the-top stereotype of a hustling pimp (and one of the few important black figures in the WWF) leads out his "ho train" of scantily-clad white women to the leering and jeering crowds.

As female sexuality is increasingly used in the scripts, the line between the bimbo/prostitute sidekick and the female wrestlers is eroding. A recent WWF women's champion is Miss Kitty, a former hyper-sexualized sidekick, who during one pay-per-view event removed her top. And the big contests for female wrestlers often involve mud or chocolate baths, or the "evening dress" contest (where you lose by having your dress ripped from your body).

The few exceptions, such as Chyna, a wrestler in her own right (who, with The Rock, graced last week's [Feb. 7, 2000] Newsweek magazine cover) emerge from another place in heterosexual male fantasy, the Amazon warrior—tall, muscular, lithe, and buxom.

While ambiguity about proper gender assignments may be the contemporary norm, in the mock-violent world of professional wrestling, masculinity and femininity are clearly defined. And while pro wrestling shares many of the values sometimes associated with elements of the political far right (among them patriarchy, opposition to homosexuality, and respect for hierarchy), many conservatives have condemned its vulgarity and sexuality.

This criticism (much of it egged on by master promoters like McMahon) fuels the erroneous belief of some youngsters that somehow the WWF and WCW are alternative and rebellious. However, one of the great insights of cultural studies is that adherence to a conservative and repressive gender order can appear powerful and liberating—or rebellious—even as it assigns greater suffering to those deemed less powerful in the social order.

Some people will argue that analyzing the social impact of wrestling is a useless exercise because, after all, it's only play acting, right? But to those who still believe that there is no connection between popular culture and broader social and political issues, that an analysis of wrestling has nothing to teach us about where our culture is heading, we have two words of caution: Jesse Ventura.   [2000]

Understanding the Reading

1. If teaching violence isn't the main problem with professional wrestling, then what is, according to the authors?
2. Why do men, especially, like this kind of entertainment, according to the authors?
3. How is masculinity defined within the world of professional wrestling?
4. How might the lessons of bullying be threatening to us as a society?

Suggestions for Responding

1. Watch a tape of WWF or WCW as a class; debate its messages versus its entertainment value.
2. Research the political views of Jesse Ventura—professional wrestler and former governor of Minnesota. ◆

60

How the Entertainment Industry Degrades Women

MARTHA BURK AND KIRSTEN SHAW

When 1992 draws to a close, how will media watchers remember it? As the year TV gave us a single mother who became the target of a phony "family values" crusade by the Republican party? Or the year when police and the "decent people" recruited by politicians shook their fists at the Time-Warner Corporation to get the anti-police song "Cop Killer" taken off the market?

Presumably few will notice that 1992 was the year in which neither politicians nor the public raised so much as an eyebrow about a song on the same album, entitled "KKK Bitch," that described the sodomizing of a Klansman's daughter. Nor did many protest the thousands of images of violence against women in movies, on TV, in advertising, and in music. 1992 will pass without remark as yet another year in which women were demeaned, degraded, and abused in the mass media.

The very survival of American women is being threatened by an epidemic of gender-specific violence that is legitimized and glamorized every day in the media while politicians and the public sit back and enjoy, even pay to see it. Battery is now the single largest cause of injury to women in America—more common than auto accidents, muggings, and rapes combined. You wouldn't know it from the media images pushed on society and the silent acceptance coming back in answer.

A woman is more likely to be killed by her husband or boyfriend than by anyone else. A woman is raped every five minutes. Yet popular movies such as *Basic Instinct,* opening with a gratuitous date-rape; *Batman Returns,* a "children's" movie depicting a woman thrown from a skyscraper by her boss; or *Unforgiven,* where a woman is knifed repeatedly in the face, trade on images of women as the passive victims of rape, murder, and abuse.

This epidemic of violence against women has evoked only complacency that is shored up by the background noise of media images telling us it is acceptable.

"Gangster rap" has been roundly criticized for its promotion of violence against the police. Yet "bitches" and "ho's" are the only female characters it portrays. Women are objectified as sex objects and scorned as manipulators who must be controlled with a fist or a weapon: "If I have to go get a gun you girls will learn." N.W.A.'s recently released Niggaz4life album includes graphic lyrics boasting about the abuse, rape, and murder of women.

Opponents of Ice-T's "Cop Killer" worried that its malicious anti-police message demoralized officers working in an already hostile environment. Women live every day in a hostile world, though there has been no demonstration of concern about the malice continually expressed against them.

Gangster rap, of course, is only guilty of graphically depicting the messages that more mainstream media send out regularly—that women must be kept in their place through violence, and that they deserve and even enjoy being abused.

"Her body's beautiful so I'm thinkin' rape / Shouldn't have had her curtains open so that's her fate." Such a rhyme is not really shocking in the context of an industry where one of every eight Hollywood movies depicts a rape theme. And it's not a modern phenomenon—in the classic *Gone with the Wind* Scarlett O'Hara is all smiles the morning after she is raped by her own husband.

Slasher movies, popular with teenagers, rely almost exclusively on the torture and murder of women for their plots. The same basic theme is churned out every year in sequels of *Halloween, Friday the 13th,* and *Nightmare on Elm Street:* young women are slaughtered one by one by an anonymous killer (typically cheered by the audience) who in the end escapes or is reborn. The murder and mutilation is broken only with a smattering of scenes of women undressing and engaging in sexual activity. The viewer is led to believe they got what they deserved.

Directors like Brian DePalma and David Lynch, hailed as artistic geniuses, derive an "aesthetic effect" from graphic images of torture, mutilation, and murder of females. Lynch's television series "Twin Peaks" featured abuse of most of its women characters, and a glamorous rape scene embellished his movie *Wild at Heart.*

Television embraces its share of violent themes as well, with women in "jep" (jeopardy) a common element. Sex and violence are the core of MTV fare, with 18 instances of aggression each hour and women's bodies the most common decorative element. Rivaling in frequency the image of woman as victim is that of woman as sex object. Popular series like "Married . . . with Children" get their laughs from the die-hard portrait of woman as empty-headed sex fiend. The devaluation of women through this kind of objectification lays the necessary groundwork for their exploitation and abuse.

Madison Avenue capitalizes on degrading images of women to sell everything from beer to blue jeans. Advertisements featuring sex, implied domination, and sometimes explicit bondage appear as often in women's magazines as those aimed at men. From roadside billboards to prime time television, gratuitous bikini-clad beauties ornamenting product slogans sustain society's perception of women as secondary, decorative, and expendable. The September issue of *Vogue* featured a full color picture of a woman with a bare, bruised back dressed in a red formal gown against the backdrop of a dungeon complete with chains.

The connection between viewing an act of violence and committing one has been dismissed as ludicrous by supporters of unregulated corporate free speech. While there is more to violence than mere imitation, psychologists have demonstrated an association time and time again. When a person continually sees dehumanization and physical abuse glamorized and legitimized through television, movies, music, and magazines, it is hard to imagine how that message could fail to be internalized and sometimes acted on.

Studies on children have shown that aggressive behavior increases after viewing aggression on television, even in cartoons. This violence, combined with the ever-present images of the victimization of women, is also sending powerful messages about inappropriate sex role behavior.

Adults are prone to the influence of media violence and victimization as well. Studies show that men watching movies depicting violence against women become progressively more callous toward the humanity of the victims and the reality of their suffering. Other research has shown that after viewing these films men are more inclined to believe that women want to be raped and actually enjoy the pain.

Trainers in the armed forces harden men for combat by desensitizing them to the sounds of screaming and the humanity of their enemies. In the same way, the profusion of images of violence and degradation of women make men (and even young boys) more callous toward women and more insensitive to their humanity.

And women are not immune to the messages. While men are learning to regard women with contempt and use force to deal with them, women are learning to expect and accept the abuse as their due.

Assumptions about women are formed at an early age. A now famous survey of Rhode Island youngsters found that at least half the boys and almost as many girls thought it was okay for a man to force a woman to kiss him if he had spent at least $15 on her. Rap fans in D.C. schools interviewed by the *Washington Post* this year expressed similar opinions. "Women get what they deserve," one eleven-year-old commented.

Last summer politicians were stumbling all over each other to express their concern that children were being harmed by the images and language of "cop killer" music, since kids are unable to see it as metaphor and are likely to take it at face value. They should be equally concerned by the portrayals of women that the majority of children see daily in the mass media.

If politicians wish to concern themselves with whether "cop killer" music is offensive and soapbox on "family values," they need to look at what those values are. Are females valued equally?

Women must hold media corporations accountable. Women are 52% of the population, and despite our low pay compared to men, we have considerable economic clout. If a few picketing police officers could force Time-Warner to stop selling violence against the police, imagine what a few million women could do if we decided to fight back with economic boycotts of companies that debase us for the bottom line.

Women did not let the openly misogynist treatment of Anita Hill[1] or the anti-feminist rhetoric of the Republican convention pass without comment. Neither should we ignore the daily barrage of anti-woman images that are pushed as entertainment. [These are] images that influence both adults and children, male and female. These are the more subtle tools of indoctrination, and ultimately the more devastating.   [1992]

Term

1. ANITA HILL: Hill testified before the Senate Judiciary Committee against the nomination of Clarence Thomas for the Supreme Court.

Understanding the Reading

1. What is the impact of the images of violence against women in the mass media?
2. How are women portrayed in "gangster rap," and how does that image compare with portrayals in the mainstream media and slasher movies?

3. Is there a connection between violent images and behavior?

Suggestions for Responding

1. Explain why you think politicians are concerned about "cop killer" music but are silent about the portrayal of women in popular media.
2. "Family values" is a popular political theme these days. What do you think this term means? Do you think it should be a political concern? Why or why not? ◆

61

Losing a Church, Keeping the Faith

ANDREW SULLIVAN

Last week, something quite banal happened at St. Benedict's Church in the Bronx. A gay couple were told they could no longer sing in the choir. Their sin was to have gotten a civil marriage license in Canada. One man had sung in the choir for 32 years; the other had joined the church 25 years ago. Both had received certificates from the church commending them for "noteworthy participation." But their marriage had gained publicity; it was even announced in The New York Times. This "scandal" led to their expulsion. The archbishop's spokesman explained that the priest had "an obligation" to exclude them.

In the grand scheme of things, this is a very small event. But it is a vivid example of why this 2002 has made the once difficult lives of gay Catholics close to impossible. The church has gone beyond its doctrinal opposition to emotional or sexual relationships between gay men and lesbians to an outspoken and increasingly shrill campaign against them. Gay relationships were described by the Vatican earlier this year as "evil." Gay couples who bring up children were described as committing the equivalent of "violence" against their own offspring. Gay men are being deterred from applying to seminaries and may soon be declared unfit for the priesthood, even though they commit to celibacy.

The American Catholic church has endorsed a constitutional amendment that would strip gay couples of any civil benefits of any kind in the United States.

For the first time in my own life, I find myself unable to go to Mass. During the most heated bouts of rhetoric coming from the Vatican this summer, I felt tears of grief and anger welling up where once I had been able to contain them. Faith beyond resentment began to seem unreachable.

For some, the answer is as easy as it always has been. Leave, they say. The gay world looks at gay Catholics with a mixture of contempt and pity. The Catholic world looks at us as if we want to destroy an institution we simply want to belong to. So why not leave? In some ways, I suppose, I have. What was for almost 40 years a weekly church habit dried up this past year to close to nothing. Every time I walked into a church or close to one, the anger and hurt overwhelmed me. It was as if a dam of intellectual resistance to emotional distress finally burst.

But there was no comfort in this, no relief, no resolution. There is no ultimate meaning for me outside the Gospels, however hard I try to imagine it; no true solace but the Eucharist; no divine love outside of Christ and the church he guides. In that sense, I have not left the church because I cannot leave the church, no more than I can leave my family. Like many other gay Catholics, I love this church; for me, there is and never will be any other. But I realize I cannot participate in it any longer either. It would be an act of dishonesty to enable an institution that is now a major force for the obliteration of gay lives and loves; that covered up for so long the sexual abuse of children but uses the word "evil" for two gay people wanting to commit to each other for life.

I know what I am inside. I do not believe that my orientation is on a par with others' lapses into lust when they also have an option for sexual and emotional life that is blessed and celebrated by the church. I do not believe I am intrinsically sick or disordered, as the hierarchy teaches, although I am a sinner in many, many ways. I do not believe that the gift of human sexuality is always and everywhere evil outside of procreation. (Many heterosexual Catholics, of course, agree with me, but they can hide and pass in ways that gay Catholics cannot.)

I believe that denying gay people any outlet for their deepest emotional needs is wrong. I think it slowly destroys people, hollows them out, alienates them finally from their very selves.

But I must also finally concede that this will not change as a matter of doctrine. That doctrine—never elaborated by Jesus—was constructed when gay people as we understand them today were not known to exist; but its authority will not change just because gay people now have the courage to explain who they are and how they feel. In fact, it seems as if the emergence of gay people into the light of the world has only intensified the church's resistance. That shift in the last few years from passive silence to active hostility is what makes the Vatican's current stance so distressing. Terrified of their own knowledge of the wide presence of closeted gay men in the priesthood, concerned that the sexual doctrines required of heterosexuals are under threat, the hierarchy has decided to draw the line at homosexuals. We have become the unwilling instruments of their need to reassert control.

In an appeal to the growing fundamentalism of the developing world, this is a shrewd strategy. In the global context, gays are easily expendable. But it is also a strikingly inhumane one. The current pope is obviously a deep and holy man; but that makes his hostility even more painful. He will send emissaries to terrorists, he will meet with a man who tried to assassinate him. But he has not and will not meet with openly gay Catholics. They are, to him, beneath dialogue. His message is unmistakable. Gay people are the last of the untouchables. We can exist in the church only by silence, by bearing false witness to who we are.

I was once more hopeful. I saw within the church's doctrines room for a humane view of homosexuality, a genuinely Catholic approach to including all nonprocreative people—the old, the infertile, the gay—in God's church. But I can see now that the dialogue is finally shutting down.

Perhaps a new pope will change things. But the odds are that hostility will get even worse. I revere those who can keep up the struggle within the channels of the church. I respect those who have left. But I am somewhere in between now.

There are moments in a spiritual life when the heart simply breaks. Some time in the last year, mine did. I can only pray that in some distant future, some other gay people not yet born will be able to come back to the church, to sing in the choir, and know that the only true scandal in the world is the scandal of God's love for his creation, all of it, all of us, in a church that may one day, finally, become home to us all.   [2003]

Understanding the Reading

1. Why was the gay couple expelled from the church choir, after so many decades of service?
2. What kind of a change in response does this signal for the Catholic Church?
3. What was Sullivan's reaction?
4. Why can he not leave the Church?
5. What is the one way, according to the author, a gay Catholic can exist in the Church?

Suggestions for Responding

1. If you belong to a faith, what is your religion's official stance toward homosexuality? How does that translate into practice? What do you believe? Are there any elements of your faith with which you disagree?
2. Many churches and synagogues within the United States are dividing over the issue of homosexuality. Research these discussions, find out which churches and synagogues are involved, and determine whether they have resolved anything.
3. Research Islam's and Hinduism's stances toward homosexuality. ◆

62

Sexual Harassment: The Nature of the Beast

ANITA HILL

The response to my Senate Judiciary Committee testimony[1] has been at once heartwarming and heart-wrenching. In learning that I am not alone in experiencing harassment, I am also learning that there are far too many women who have experienced a range of inexcusable and illegal activities—from sexist jokes to sexual assault—on the job.

My reaction has been to try to learn more. As an educator, I always begin to study an issue by examining the scientific data—the articles, the books, the studies. Perhaps the most compelling lesson is in the stories told by the women who have written to me. I have learned much; I am continuing to learn; I have yet ten times as much to explore. I want to share some of this with you.

"The Nature of the Beast" describes the existence of sexual harassment, which is alive and well. [It is] a harmful, dangerous thing that can confront a woman at any time.

What we know about harassment, sizing up the beast:

Sexual harassment is pervasive . . .

1. It occurs today at an alarming rate. Statistics show that anywhere from 42 to 90 percent of women will experience some form of harassment during their employed lives. At least one percent experience sexual assault. But the statistics do not fully tell the story of the anguish of women who have been told in various ways on the first day of a job that sexual favors are expected. [Nor do they tell] the story of women who were sexually assaulted by men with whom they continued to work.
2. It has been occurring for years. In letters to me, women tell of incidents that occurred 50 years ago when they were first entering the workplace, incidents they have been unable to speak of for that entire period.
3. Harassment crosses lines of race and class. In some ways, it is a creature that practices "equal opportunity" where women are concerned. In other ways it exhibits predictable prejudices and reflects stereotypical myths held by our society.

We know that harassment all too often goes unreported for a variety of reasons . . .

1. Unwillingness (for good reason) to deal with the expected consequences;
2. Self-blame;
3. Threats of blackmail by coworkers or employers;
4. What it boils down to in many cases is a sense of powerlessness that we experience in the workplace, and our acceptance of a certain level of inability to control our careers and

professional destinies. This sense of power-lessness is particularly troubling when one observes the research that says individuals with graduate education experience more harassment than do persons with less than a high school diploma. The message: when you try to obtain power through education, the beast harassment responds by striking more often and more vehemently.

That harassment is treated like a woman's "dirty secret" is well known. We also know what happens when we "tell." We know that when harassment is reported the common reaction is disbelief or worse . . .

1. Women who "tell" lose their jobs. A typical response told of in the letters to me was: I not only lost my job for reporting harass-ment, but I was accused of stealing and charges were brought against me.
2. Women who "tell" become emotionally wasted. One writer noted that "it was fully eight months after the suit was conducted that I began to see myself as alive again."
3. Women who "tell" are not always supported by other women. Perhaps the most disheart-ening stories I have received are of moth-ers not believing daughters. In my kindest moments I believe that this reaction only represents attempts to distance ourselves from the pain of the harassment experience. The internal response is: "It didn't happen to me. This couldn't happen to me. In order to believe that I am protected, I must believe that it didn't happen to her." The external response is: "What did you do to provoke that kind of behavior?" Yet at the same time that I have been advised of hurtful and unpro-ductive reactions, I have also heard stories of mothers and daughters sharing their experi-ences. In some cases the sharing allows for a closer bonding. In others a slight but cogni-zable mending of a previously damaged rela-tionship occurs.

What we are learning about harassment requires recognizing this beast when we encoun-ter it, and more. It requires looking the beast in the eye.

We are learning painfully that simply hav-ing laws against harassment on the books is not enough. The law, as it was conceived, was to provide a shield of protection for us. Yet that shield is failing us: many fear reporting, others feel it would do no good. The result is that less than 5 percent of women victims file claims of harassment. Moreover, the law focuses on quid pro quo,[2] but a recent New York *Times* article quoting psychologist Dr. Louise Fitzgerald says that this makes up considerably less than 5 per-cent of the cases. The law needs to be more responsive to the reality of our experiences.

As we are learning, enforcing the law alone won't terminate the problem. What we are seek-ing is equality of treatment in the workplace. Equality requires an expansion of our attitudes toward workers. Sexual harassment denies our treatment as equals and replaces it with treat-ment of women as objects of ego or power grat-ification. Dr. John Gottman, a psychologist at the University of Washington, notes that sexual harassment is more about fear than about sex.

Yet research suggests two troublesome responses exhibited by workers and by courts. Both respond by . . .

1. Downplaying the seriousness of the behav-ior (seeing it as normal sexual attraction between people) or commenting on the sen-sitivity of the victim.
2. Exaggerating the ease with which victims are expected to handle the behavior. But my let-ters tell me that unwanted advances do not cease—and that the message was power, not genuine interest.

We are learning that many women are angry. The reasons for the anger are various and per-haps all too obvious . . .

1. We are angry because this awful thing called harassment exists in terribly harsh, ugly, demeaning, and even debilitating ways. Many believe it is criminal and should be punished as such. It is a form of violence against women as well as a form of economic coercion, and our experiences suggest that it won't just go away.
2. We are angry because for a brief moment we believed that if the law allowed for women to be hired in the workplace, and if we worked hard for our educations and on the job, equal-ity would be achieved. We believed we would be respected as equals. Now we are realizing

this is not true. We have been betrayed. The reality is that this powerful beast is used to perpetuate a sense of inequality, to keep women in their place notwithstanding our increasing presence in the workplace.

What we have yet to explore about harassment is vast. It is what will enable us to slay the beast.

Research is helpful, appreciated, and I hope will be required reading for all legislators. Yet research has what I see as one shortcoming: it focuses on our reaction to harassment, not on the harasser. How we enlighten men who are currently in the workplace about behavior that is beneath our (and their) dignity is the challenge of the future. Research shows that men tend to have a narrower definition of what constitutes harassment than do women. How do we expand their body of knowledge? How do we raise a generation of men who won't need to be reeducated as adults? We must explore these issues, and research efforts can assist us.

What are the broader effects of harassment on women and the world? Has sexual harassment left us unempowered? Has our potential in the workplace been greatly damaged by this beast? Has this form of economic coercion worked? If so, how do we begin to reverse its effects? We must begin to use what we know to move to the next step: what we will do about it.

How do we capture our rage and turn it into positive energy? Through the power of women working together, whether it be in the political arena, or in the context of a lawsuit, or in community service. This issue goes well beyond partisan politics. Making the workplace a safer, more productive place for ourselves and our daughters should be on the agenda for each of us. It is something we can do for ourselves. It is a tribute, as well, to our mothers—and indeed a contribution we can make to the entire population.

I wish that I could take each of you on the journey that I've been on during all these weeks since the hearing. I wish that every one of you could experience the heartache and the triumphs of each of those who have shared with me their experiences. I leave you with but a brief glimpse of what I've seen. I hope it is enough to encourage you to begin—or continue and persist with—your own exploration. And thank you.   [1992]

Terms

1. SENATE JUDICIARY COMMITTEE TESTIMONY: Anita Hill testified against the nomination of Clarence Thomas to the Supreme Court on the grounds that he sexually harassed her when she worked for him at the Equal Employment Opportunity Commission.
2. QUID PRO QUO: The demand for sexual favors in exchange for employment, job retention, promotion, a salary increase, and so on.

Understanding the Reading

1. How pervasive is sexual harassment?
2. Why don't women report sexual harassment?
3. What are the frequent responses to reported harassment?
4. Why are women angry about harassment?
5. What is the drawback to research on harassment?
6. What are the broader effects of harassment?

Suggestions for Responding

1. Hill asks what we will do about sexual harassment. How would you answer her question?
2. Have you, or has someone you know, experienced or been witness to sexual harassment? Describe the incident, including the victim's response and what you now think the response should have been.
3. Investigate and report on the antiharassment policies and procedures on your campus. ♦

63

Like a Smack in the Face: Pornography in the Trades

BARBARA TREES

I want to tell you a bit about myself and construction work because most people who don't work in construction have no idea what it's like. I am a carpenter in New York City. I applied to the Carpenters' Union in 1978 and began my four-year apprenticeship in 1980. I am college educated and was thirty years old at the time. There were maybe ten women—tops—and 20,000 men in the union at the time.

I wanted to be a carpenter because it was daring, well paid, and out of the mainstream. I thought women merely had to prove we could do the work and then many more women would join us.

It made perfect sense to see the building trades as a great opportunity for women to achieve equality with men. Jobs were available, and the apprenticeships were open to people with limited educations. But, in spite of the possibilities, this field has not really opened up for women. And the mistreatment of women in construction is a horror story which has not been adequately told.

A woman who is sent to a job at a construction site can usually expect to be the only one on a crew of hundreds of men. For the first five or six years I went through the motions of fitting in. I guess we all did, we "first women." It was so very important to get along. The job sites were dirty and dangerous and the work was hard; we all got the difficult jobs, not the "tit" jobs, as easy work is called. The men we were supposed to learn the trade from usually had no intention of teaching us. They thought it was the most preposterous thing that women actually wanted to do this work.

These men found ways to push us out, and they were *not* nice about it. They were scary and belligerent and did not want "girls" around (the lone woman on a job or crew is always called "the girl"). The atmosphere was and is horrible. There is filthy language. There is total contempt for women and wives. The men piss and shit out in the open and on the floor instead of in toilets. Women are given the worst jobs to do, made to work alone at a job two or three men would do, and laid off first without cause. There are no changing facilities or bathrooms with locks for women. The men use binoculars to look for women in nearby buildings, and when they spot one in a bathroom or undressed, they yell, "There's one, there's one!" In addition to all this harassment, physical violence is common. I know of several women who were hit or punched by fellow construction workers, and nothing was done about it.

Pornography is commonplace on construction jobs. You see it in the locker rooms; on drinking fountains, on and inside lunch boxes, on and inside toolboxes, on tools, on walls in management, union, and other offices. It is often posted on job sites or on half-constructed buildings. I found it humiliating. I began to avoid areas where I found it and tore it down when I saw it. After that, it had a funny way of showing up where I was working or walking—just one little dirty picture, like a smack in the face—and nobody around to take the credit. The men feel they have an absolute right to display these pictures. It is very risky to complain about pornography in the construction industry. You can get harassed. You can get hurt. You can get fired, and once fired, you have no recourse. The contractor does not have to say why you were fired. The union stewards don't want to hear about it. There is no grievance procedure. I was fired from a job after politely asking a foreman to remove a beaver shot from our shanty, but only found out a year later that that was why I was fired. But losing your job is not the only threat. The mafia, some of whom deal in prostitution and pornography, lurk everywhere. Most of us who are activists have nightmares about construction workers chopping our doors down to get into our homes. We fear for our lives.

Many women in the trades try to ignore the pornography, but I could not do that and survive. I had listened to filthy woman-hating "jokes," had coworkers "accidentally" touch my breasts or ass, and put up with the idea of women as funny—the mere mention of breasts or anything about women's bodies bringing smirks. I just couldn't take it anymore.

So I got sick, quite seriously sick, and stayed out of work for two years. For women, this is not an uncommon reaction to these pressures in the nontraditional work world. But during the time I was ill, I thought about the situation, and when I went back I vowed that I would practice pro-woman self-defense. It worked. It gave me a sense of entitlement—to dignity, to the job, to fight for the women in my union as if we are the most important people on earth. It meant that I refused to listen to men bad-mouthing women, that I took these "jokes" and remarks for the insults they were, and that I responded accordingly.

In 1989, I founded New York Tradeswomen, a support group for women in the building trades. We formed a Women Carpenters Committee in the New York City District Council. I was appointed a shop steward in my local union in 1990, the first woman in my 2,000-member local to hold this position. As a steward, the union representative for the carpenters on a particular job site, I've battled pornography for the last three years. The union office gave me the protection to fight it and not be fired. But I still have problems. I've had long pornographic phone messages placed on my answering machine from men who boasted of being in my local. I've had a contractor tell me to go fuck myself when I asked him to remove the pornography from the trailer where, as a steward, I had to go to call my union. I told a teamster that I wouldn't hang a door in his shanty until he removed a nude picture. Later he chases me around waving a nude picture, yelling, "This is beautiful, this is good!" Once a pornographic picture showed up on the cooler. I saw it and took off my hard hat and bashed the closest guy to me over the head with it and said, "Is that yours?!" He may not even have put it there, but I didn't care, I was so mad. When I asked a tin knocker to simply turn his large toolbox, which was covered with beaver shots, away from the door so that I wouldn't have to see them, he accused me of being ridiculous and said that I should know better, that these pictures are everywhere, that this is the way it is in the construction industry, that I had to fit in, and that I would be to blame if he got fired over something so "minor." After I complained to union officials, this same guy followed me, glaring, to the subway.

I thought that women could change these job sites, but so far we haven't. There aren't enough of us, and the men are picking us off, one by one, both the weak and the strong. Using pornography and other forms of sexual harassment, men have successfully kept women out of construction in any significant numbers. Now that the recession has hit, we are devastated.   [1994]

Understanding the Reading

1. Why did Trees want to become a carpenter?
2. How are women in construction mistreated?
3. What was Trees's response to the harassment she endured?

Suggestion for Responding

1. Interview a woman you know who works in a traditionally male field about her experience of sexual harassment and pornography on the job. ◆

64

Bad Sports

Mariah Burton Nelson

O. J. Simpson is not alone.

The baseball star Darryl Strawberry has admitted beating his wife and pointing a gun in her face.

John Daly, the golfer, was arrested at his home after allegedly hurling his wife against a wall, pulling her hair and trashing the house. He pleaded guilty to a misdemeanor harassment charge and was placed on two years' probation with the stipulation that he complete a domestic violence treatment program.

The basketball star Moses Malone was accused by his wife of physical and verbal brutality, including death threats. He insisted he never hit her or threatened to kill her but admitted having "moved her out of the way."

Wimp Sanderson resigned as the men's basketball coach at the University of Alabama in 1992 after his secretary, Nancy Watts, filed a sex discrimination complaint against him. Ms. Watts, with whom he had had a longtime affair, alleged that he hit her as part of a continuing pattern of physical and sexual abuse, and was awarded $275,000 in a settlement. Mr. Sanderson claimed in court documents that Ms. Watts got her black eye by colliding with his outstretched hand.

Juanita Leonard testified in divorce court in 1991 that her husband, Sugar Ray Leonard, often punched her, threw her around and harassed her "physically and mentally in front of the children." He threatened to kill himself with a gun, she said. He threw lamps and broke mirrors.

The boxer denied none of this. At a press conference, he admitted having struck his wife with his fists. Yet he justified the behavior by saying that he and Juanita "fought, argued" and "grabbed each other," but that it "was in our house, between us."

Spectators also get into the spirit of things. Boston Celtics fans have hung banners saying they like to beat rival teams almost as much as they like to "beat our wives."

"I'm going to go home and beat my wife," Coach Joe Paterno of Penn State once said at a press conference after his football team lost to the University of Texas. Later he defended the statement as "just part of the sports culture, locker room talk, harmless, a joke that did not mean anything."

What is this "harmless" sports culture?

Whether hockey fights, football tackles or baseball brawls, intentionally hurtful acts are portrayed as natural—for men. Society's concept of violence is inextricably interwoven with its concept of expected, condoned male behavior. Boys are given boxing gloves as toys; girls and women who try to join wrestling or football teams are often ridiculed, sexually harassed or simply barred from taking part.

Most of the women whom male players see are not coaches or other athletes. They are the short-skirted cheerleaders and the university "hostesses" who escort them around campus during the recruiting process. The locker room is not a place to brag about your wife's or girlfriend's accomplishments. It is a place where men discuss women's bodies in graphic sexual terms, where they boast about "scoring" and joke about beating women.

In *The Hundred Yard Lie,* Rick Telander, a reporter for *Sports Illustrated,* writes that he has heard so much degrading talk of women in the locker room he's sure that "the macho attitudes promoted by coaches contribute (perhaps unwittingly) to the athlete's problems in relating to women."

Sexist comments can get men fired in some circles. But in sports, a world where sexism is a badge of honor, it is a common ground, a familiar language.

Timothy Jon Curry, an Ohio State sociologist who employed researchers to record locker-room conversations over several months, found that talk of women as objects took the form of loud performances for other men. Talk about ongoing relationships with women, on the other hand,

took place only in hushed tones, often behind rows of lockers, and was subject to ridicule. "This ridicule tells the athlete that he is getting too close to femaleness, because he is taking relatedness seriously," he writes. "'Real men' do not do that."

A former college football star who spoke to me only on the condition that he not be named said of Mr. Curry's research: "That's right on target. We never talked about respecting women." This man, who later signed with the Philadelphia Eagles, recalls college teammates making crude boasts about sexual conquests. His college teammates hosted "pig parties." The man who brought the ugliest date would win a trophy. This football star says he learned to respect women from his mother and three athletic sisters, and did not attend the parties. But he would laugh at his teammates' jokes, which he now regrets.

"I remember the first time they showed the trophy, in the locker room," he says. "I was a 17-year-old freshman in a room full of upperclassmen. It was boisterous, raunchy, there was screaming and yelling. I laughed along. Men are extremely cliquish. I didn't want to be left out."

When quarterback Timm Rosenbach of the Phoenix Cardinals quit pro football after the 1992 season, he told Ira Berkow of *The New York Times:* "I thought I was turning into some kind of animal. You go through a week getting yourself up for a game by hating the other team, the other players. You're so mean and hateful, you want to kill somebody. Football's so aggressive. Things get done by force. And then you come home, you're supposed to turn it off? 'Oh, here's your lovin' daddy.' It's not that easy. It was like I was an idiot. I felt programmed. I had become a machine."

O. J. Simpson, who pleaded not guilty to charges of murdering his former wife and her friend, was programmed. He was, like all of us, a product of a culture that allows more than two million women each year to be beaten by husbands or boyfriends. About 1,400 women a year die at the hands of these "lovers." He was also part of a football culture that taught him to equate masculinity with violence.

Our society reveres athletes regardless of their behavior off the field. Even after he pleaded no contest to beating his wife on New Year's Day 1989, Mr. Simpson continued to work for Hertz and NBC, and to be described by fans and in the media as a "great guy" and an "American hero." When he was chased by police cars along the Los Angeles freeways, commuters stopped their cars to wave to him and chant, "Go, O. J., go!" They acted as if nothing—not wife-beating, not alleged murder—mattered, as if star athletes should be able to do exactly as they please.

Which is what they will continue to do until we stop glorifying them and stop training them to hate women.   [1994]

Understanding the Reading

1. How do the sports figures mentioned here rationalize their violence against the women in their lives?
2. What factors lead to and reinforce such male violence?
3. What did Timothy Jon Curry's research show?

Suggestions for Responding

1. Why do you think so many professional sports figures are involved in domestic violence?
2. Imagine that your favorite sports figure has just been convicted of sexual violence. Write him or her a letter expressing your feelings about the conviction. ✦

65

A More Hidden Crime: Adolescent Battered Women

NANCY WORCESTER

Domestic violence has often been referred to as our nation's most hidden crime. However, after 15 years of activism and the establishment of more than 1000 battered women's shelter programs around the country, the battered women's movement has made many people and community services aware of the fact that huge numbers of women are entrapped in relationships of ongoing abuse of power, control, and physical coercion. The FBI estimates that a woman is battered every 15–18 seconds in this country and that approximately one of

every three women experiences some physical violence in her long-term relationship(s). The pervasiveness of the violence may be best represented by the statement that one of every five women probably experiences five or more serious battering incidents each year.

Just as there is finally a public consciousness of the magnitude of the problem of women being battered, we are discovering an even more hidden, perhaps even more prevalent crime—violence against adolescent women. It turns out that most of the understanding of the dynamics of power and control in intimate relationships gained from the battered women's movement applies as much to adolescent women in dating relationships as it does to adult women. Tragically, the ramifications of violence for younger women are often exaggerated by a number of factors, but there are far fewer resources and options available to adolescent than adult women who are trying to end the violence in their lives.

Working to prevent violence in young people's lives must be a high priority for any of us committed to creating a better world for the next generation and to helping young women maximize on their full potential. The isolation and lowered self-esteem which are so often a *consequence* of violence will have exaggerated ramifications for a young woman if they cause her to limit or eliminate skill-building, career options, or educational opportunities which could affect the rest of her life. (It is important to emphasize that the isolation, lowered self-esteem, and unhealthy coping mechanisms which are often observed in abused women are predictable *consequences* of violence and are not the *cause* of the violence. Confusing a consequence of violence with a cause can lead to dangerous, victim-blaming misunderstandings of the violence.)

If a woman is experiencing violence in her dating relationship(s), it will almost certainly be related to many other issues in her life. Anyone working with adolescents will benefit from seeing the connections between violence and the issues they already address. Why she is not always able to show up for study group, why she "had to go" to a concert instead of studying the night before an important exam, why she is no longer best friends with "the nice girl who seemed to have such a positive influence on her," or why she "suddenly" started dressing in a way which always *or* never shows off her figure may be explained by knowing that a young woman is in a relationship where someone else is taking control over almost all aspects of her life. Health educators need to recognize that many women are beaten up if they try to insist that male partners wear a condom or abstain from sexual activity. Because battering so often starts or accelerates during pregnancy and because sexual assault and other forms of violence are so intimately connected, anyone who works with adolescent pregnancy or sexual assault issues needs to be aware of the connections.

Ironically, many women learn about motherhood and battering at exactly the same time. Retrospective studies show that 25% of battered women experienced their first physical abuse during a pregnancy and that 40–60% of battered women were abused during a pregnancy or during pregnancies. The consequences are a much higher rate of miscarriage, stillbirth, premature delivery, and low birth weight infants in battered than non-battered women. The problem may be even more exaggerated in pregnant teens. A study looking specifically at physical abuse during teen pregnancy found that 26% of pregnant teens reported they were involved with a man who physically hurt them and 40–60% said that the battering had begun or escalated since their boyfriends knew they were pregnant. This study also provides an urgent reminder that services are not addressing the issue of violence for adolescent women: 65% of pregnant teens had not talked to *anyone* about the abuse.

Looking at the continuum of violence issues (The Power and Control and Equity Wheels by the Duluth Domestic Abuse Intervention Project and the Continuum of Family Violence Chart from Village to Village, by the Alaska Dept. of Public Safety are particularly useful), it becomes apparent how a range of forms of violence—physical, verbal, emotional, and sexual—are used by abusers to dominate their partners. The more subtle forms of sexual violence (unwanted touching, sexual name calling, unfaithfulness or threat of unfaithfulness, saying "no one else will ever love you," false accusations) are clearly emotionally as well as sexually controlling. These need to be identified as "violence issues" which are related to, and can escalate into, unwanted sex, unprotected sex, hurtful sex, and other forms of sexual assault. Sexual violence is often the expression of violence which is the most painful for a woman to discuss. Emotional abuse is almost always present if there are other forms of abuse in a relationship but a clever abuser may achieve sufficient control by emotional abuse without ever resorting to other forms. Women consistently say that emotional abuse is the hardest form to identify (Is this really happening? Is this abuse? Am I making too much of this?) but recognize it as the form of abuse which has the most impact on their lives and their view of themselves. Many women who have been in life-threatening situations say, "The physical battering was nothing compared to the daily emotional abuse." Helping young women see the interconnectedness of verbal, emotional, physical, and sexual power and control issues may be the most useful information in empowering them to end *all* forms of violence in their lives.

By the time adolescents start experimenting with their own dating relationships, they have been bombarded with messages that violence against women is tolerated and even encouraged and that dominance, aggression, and abuse of power and control are appropriate masculine behaviors which are rewarded by society. Today's young people have been exposed to a tolerance and perpetuation of male violence which is unique to this generation. They grew up in the era when the average child was watching 24 hours of television a week with children's programming averaging 15.5 violent acts per hour. By the time they reach 18, the average US adolescent has witnessed approximately 26,000 murders, in their own homes, via the TV screen.

The role of television in sex-role socialization and the perpetuation of male violence has been grossly exaggerated for today's young people because changes in federal regulations, in the early 1980s, allowed the sale of toys directly connected to TV shows, removed regulations limiting the amount of advertising allowed on children's programming, and ruled that product-based shows were legal. The result was a totally new integration of the TV and toy industries. By 1986 all of the ten best selling toys had shows connected with them and by 1988, 80% of children's TV programming was produced by toy companies. Parallel marketing promoted definitions of masculinity and femininity as clearly defined as the distinct lines of boys' toys vs. girls' toys. Because of the new integration of TV and toys, today's young people did not learn to explore their own creativity or imagination in healthy ways but instead learned to "act out their scripts" as dominant and competitive or caring, helpless, and concentrating on appearance, either as GI Joe or Ghostbusters vs. Barbie or My Little Pony.

With electronic video games, an even newer and unstudied phenomenon, young people get to act out and be rewarded for playing their violent roles. The direct participation in "performing" the violence of video games is predicted to magnify whatever effect more passive TV viewing has on one's acceptance or perpetuation of violence. In a violence promoting and accepting culture, it is not surprising to find that most video games are very violent (a sampling of 120 machines in three arcades in Madison, Wisconsin, found that more than 70 involved either hand-to-hand combat or shooting to kill enemies) and that the most popular games in an arcade are the most violent.

Consequently, *unlearning* the tolerance of violence and *learning* how to achieve violence-free, equal relationships are skills which are now as crucial to *teach* young people as reading, writing, math, and the use of computers. The way people learn, in their earliest experimentation, to be in intimate relationships can set the pattern for what they expect in future relationships. It is a time when the highest standards should be set! Adolescents need to see models of healthy, equal, violence-free relationships, in order to aim for that in their own lives, and *to be able to model that for their peers.*

At this stage, many teens do not have the knowledge or skills to prevent or react against violence in their own lives or in their friends' lives. In fact, exactly the opposite is much more likely. Many young women have said that even when they have told friends they were being hurt by their boyfriends, the response was that they were lucky to have boyfriends. There is enormous peer pressure not to break up. Many teens regard violence as a normal part of dating and have no idea they deserve better. Extreme possessiveness, jealousy, dominance, and not being "allowed" to break up get wrongly identified as desirable, positive signs of caring, love, and commitment,

rather than strong warning signs that they are in an unhealthy, potentially dangerous relationship.

Figuring out what to expect in relationships may be particularly confusing for anyone who grew up in a home where there was violence. Many young men only see abusing males (in reality *and* in the media) as role models. Many young women who told their mothers about being hurt by their boyfriends have heard, "you have to learn to take the bad and the good in a relationship to make it work."

Many teens who have grown up in violent homes face the difficulty of trying to figure out how they want to be in their own young adult relationships while they are still learning (or not learning) to cope with being affected by the violence with which they grew up. The battered women's movement has very effectively identified that when a woman is battered, her children are almost always affected by the violence. Seventy-five percent of women who are battered in this country have children living at home. Children in homes where domestic violence occurs are physically abused or seriously neglected at a rate 1500% higher than the national average in the general population. Even witnessing domestic violence can have a tremendous impact on young people and may result in symptoms very similar to those seen in people who have been abused. Helping these young people learn healthy relationship skills can be particularly challenging as many teens do not recognize the impact the violence in their homes has had on them and many teens do not want to talk about witnessing or experiencing abuse.

Particularly crucial to how we help young people learn relationship skills *and* acknowledge that violence in their lives may have already influenced their attitudes and behaviors is how we address the impact of the "intergenerational transmission of violence." There is a confusing body of work which examines how the cycle of violence can be passed on through the generations. We now know the old "dad beats mom, mom beats the children, and the children beat the pets" picture was much too simplistic and inaccurate. Increasingly, it is being shown that the person beating mom may also be the one beating the children and protecting the mother is often the best way to protect the children. Although research is inconsistent in documenting the rates of intergenerational transmission of violence, there is a consistent trend which shows that boys who witness domestic violence as children are more likely to batter their female partners as adults than are men from non-violent homes.

How we use this information can be a key factor in determining whether we help break the intergenerational transmission of violence or actually contribute to its perpetuation. Too much of the literature deals with this pattern as if it were inevitable. Central to breaking the pattern is addressing and researching a different set of questions. If 30% of boys who witness violence become abusers, the question must be asked, "What can we learn from the 70% who witness violence but do not become abusers?" What factors help young people who have witnessed violence learn to resist violent behavior? Young people from violent homes who have experienced the ugliness of violence and have learned to value non-violent relationships can be exactly the people most committed to breaking the cycle of violence and can be incredibly effective peer leaders.

Most important, young people must *never* learn that violence is inevitable. Many dating violence resources (including some of the materials I highly recommend on other aspects) include information on the intergenerational transmission of violence without making it clear that the cycle can be broken. Information on warning signs of potential abusers almost always includes "boys who grew up in violent homes." What does it feel like to see that information if you are a young man who witnessed violence at home? We must make certain that none of our materials or our messages ever contribute towards a young man feeling that he is destined to be violent.

Studies on dating violence consistently show that many teens in violent relationships have not talked to *any* adults about the violence in their lives. We need to start identifying the barriers which have made us so ineffective on this issue and acknowledge that we are only starting to have the language and tools for opening a dialogue on dating violence.

The good news is that a wide range of excellent resources, curricula, and videos have been produced on dating violence issues and violence-free relationships in recent years. It's a very exciting stage to be working on this issue because no one needs to "start from scratch." However, work needs to be done to make the excellent resources and services available to, and appropriate for, many more teens. Few of the resources address the issue in a way that has any meaning for lesbian, gay, or bisexual teens or for young people of color. Many of the materials seem to have the underlying assumption that children grow up in homes where there is one male and one female adult. Special issues for teens with disabilities need to be addressed because of both the high rate of sexual assault of people with disabilities and the complexities of dating which arise from the myth that people with disabilities are "asexual." The obsession with body image and a very narrow definition of attractiveness can also be particularly cruel and abusive in adolescence.

"You deserve to be treated with respect."

"You are not alone if someone is hurting you. There are excellent resources to help you end the violence in your life."

These messages which we have been giving adult battered women for the last 15 years are now the same messages we have to give to much younger women.   [1993]

Understanding the Reading

1. Describe the magnitude of battery against women.
2. How do young women react to violence in their dating relationships?
3. What is the relationship between pregnancy and battering, especially for adolescent women?
4. What forms does this violence take?
5. What makes emotional abuse difficult to deal with?
6. What is the influence of television on sex role behaviors and violence in relationships?
7. Why may video games increase violent relationships?
8. Why is it important for young people to learn to have violence-free, equal relationships?
9. What impact does growing up in a violent home have on children?
10. What have studies shown about the intergenerational transmission of violence?
11. What can be done to reduce or eliminate dating violence?
12. In addition to young people from traditional, middle-class families, what other groups of adolescents need to be addressed?

Suggestions for Responding

1. What factors do you think may help young people who have witnessed violence learn to resist becoming violent themselves?
2. After watching Saturday morning television, write a description of the violent episodes you witnessed, and try to analyze what effect viewing this violence would have on young children. ◆

66

Why Doesn't She Just Leave?

CLARETHIA ELLERBE

On the first night of a university course I was taking, "Gender, War and Peace," the class viewed a film called "Speak Truth to Power." Rita Moreno was one of the actors reading the testimony of a Russian woman who had created a hotline for abused women. After the film, the class discussed the film's contents, but spoke very little on the subject of domestic violence. This made me wonder whether the topic was taboo, or just something that people do not feel comfortable discussing. Or, is it something that society is not aware of, or feels that it only happens in a certain part of society?

Before viewing this film I had never really given domestic violence much consideration. As I sat there listening to Rita Moreno, a celebrity reading the words of a woman fighting domestic violence, it made me want to do some research on how deeply it cuts. From my research, I learned that when people hear the words "domestic violence," they often think of the physical aspect of it, such as pushing, shoving, hitting, twisting arms, punching, choking and slapping. While the abuser and the victim are in the relationship, they are not willing to admit to themselves or anyone else that they are in an abusive relationship. A co-worker once told me that her husband could beat her the night before and she could wear a one-piece bathing suit the next day, and you, as the observer, could not detect her bruises. I asked her how he was

able to accomplish this. She had no answer, but her statement did make me wonder about the abuser's view of domestic violence. Observing relationships of some of my family and friends, I decided to ask the ones that appeared to be in abusive relationships, or have been in the past.

INTERVIEW I

The following story is told me by my aunt, who was in an abusive marriage for almost forty years. "At the age of 16, I met my husband, and I enjoyed a wonderful, romantic courtship with him. Then people began to make comments, like: 'Why would a pretty girl like you get married to an ugly duckling'; that is when my problems started. The comments led him to thoughts of jealousy, verbal and mental abuse, and eventually physical abuse."

"It got to the point where he painted our windows black and did not allow me and the children to visit with relatives or friends. I had choke marks on my neck, and wore these bruises as if they were some kind of trophy. Along with my bruises, I received cuts, wounds and black eyes. My head was banged against the walls, doors, the floor, and the refrigerator, and during all this time I thought he loved me. When people used to ask me about the beatings I was taking from my husband, I would say: 'If a man doesn't beat you every now and then, he doesn't love you.' I strongly believed that all his hitting was about him loving me, and teaching me the right way to go in life. It makes me laugh when I tell someone that my husband was going to teach me the right things to do. I have asked myself a thousand times, 'What could my husband have taught me, as dumb as he was?' I'm glad that my husband didn't love me to death! But it would be nice if one day he came to me and asked me to forgive him."

INTERVIEW II

Joe is a friend of the family, and we grew up in the same town. He likes to call himself a controller. This is his story about his method for control. Joe says: "When I first meet someone who I want to be in my life, I start by building her ego, you know, like telling her things I know women like to hear. I tell her how beautiful she is, and I might add something like how lucky I am to have found her. Women love it when a man talks like that to them, especially when the guy tells them that they are a cut above all the common Janes."

"After the first few dates I send her flowers or some other token gift. You know, not an expensive gift, but just something to make her feel good about herself. By now, she is thanking her lucky stars that she finally met the man of her dreams. I know how women like to brag to their girlfriends about meeting the man of their dreams. Soon I have her all happy and excited about the start of her ideal relationship with her ideal man. She now opens up and begins to talk freely about what she wants. I listen to every word she has to say. She talks about her girlfriends, as well as her family, at this stage of the game. This is my opportunity to find out which of her girlfriends or family members has the strongest influence in her life."

"After I learn the name of the strongest person in her life, I start planning how to eliminate that person from her circle of friends. Because I know that this person is strong, I know that this person will not let me treat her friend in an unkind way. I know that she will come between me and my woman, once she sees me trying to mistreat her friend. Women have something called 'sisterhood', and once they get this sisterhood working there is nothing in the world that a man can do to break this bond. I am not strong enough to break that bond; it is a bond that will take me out of life so fast I wouldn't know what hit me. We men are afraid of the sisterhood bond; women don't really know how powerful that sisterhood is. We men keep you women fighting amongst yourselves, so you guys cannot form that strong bond."

"But once I eliminate her strongest friend, it is easy to keep her away from her other friends, co-workers, as well as interfering family members. I am now in control. My strategy is to control her completely and make her totally dependent on me, to the point where she cannot make her own decisions without first asking me, which also includes when and where to go to the bathroom. Feeling powerful and feeling the need for more

control, I begin to downplay all her achievements she made before she met me. It doesn't matter if she had a better job than me, or if she owns her own home, or has a car and I don't. I am constantly telling her that if it weren't for me she would have nothing. I am the one who makes her look good in the eyes of her friends, her co-workers, and family. I make her look respectable in the neighborhood, as well as to her female friends and family. I make her feel like all of her friends are jealous of her good man."

While doing this research I learned that an abused person's perceptions are altered by the abuse, and that domestic violence has nothing to do with conflict resolution. It has a purpose of its own. That purpose is to establish a relationship of power over and control of the partner. [2003]

References

Aunt "Jane," personal communication, 2003

Domestic Abuse & Sexual Assault Intervention Services (www.dasi.org)

Domestic Violence Statistical Summary (www.fultonpd.com/stats.htm)

Dr. Susan Forward and Joan Torres (1987). *Men Who Hate Women & the Women Who Love Them*

"Joe," personal communication, 2003

MSN Learning and Research—Domestic Violence http://encarta.msn.com/encnet/refpages/RefArticle.aspx?refid=762529482

Understanding the Reading

1. What kinds of abuse are featured in this essay?
2. Why did the author's aunt stay with her husband for so long?
3. How does Joe control women?
4. Why does Joe control women?
5. What is his greatest obstacle?

Suggestions for Responding

1. Interview someone who was in an abusive relationship (without asking why he or she stood for it).
2. Share stories in the class of people you have known who were in abusive relationships.
3. Invite a representative from a women's shelter to speak to the class. ◆

67

Rape and Sexual Assault

JAMES A. DOYLE

Few words strike as much terror in a person's heart as rape. Few human acts are so fraught with misinformation and misconception as rape. Few other acts so degrade a human being as rape. And few other acts show the imbalance of power between men and women and men's quest for domination over women as rape does.

Rape is first and foremost an act of *violence,* an attempted or completed sexual assault instigated by one or more persons against another human being. The historical roots of rape run deep in the patriarchal tradition of male violence toward women. Rape, to be understood, must not be seen as simply a violent sexual act of a few lunatics or pathologically disordered persons, but rather a violent sexual act performed by many and reinforced by the dominant patriarchal values coming to the fore in their most twisted and disturbing forms in our culture. A few cultures may be less prone to violent sexual acts between males and females, but ours and most others are definitely "rape-prone" cultures. No discussion of power and its imbalance between women and men would be complete without a discussion of rape.

. . . We will first take up the issue of rape as an act of dominance (not sex) and of power (not pathology) that is ingrained in the very fiber of the male's gender role. Next we will attempt to put the statistics of rape in perspective by trying to give some scope to the enormity of the act of rape in the everyday lives of many women and some men. And then, we will note the rising concern and some of the actions taken among feminists and nonfeminists alike over the issue of rape as a social phenomenon of epidemic proportions and not merely an isolated criminal act affecting a few.

RAPE AND POWER

Throughout most of this century those who influenced what others thought about rape saw it as a "victim-precipitated phenomenon." Sigmund Freud, in his study of the female personality, theorized that the female was more "masochistic" than the male and that rape—either in fantasy or in fact—was the one sexual act wherein the female acted out her masochism to the utmost. However, such nonsense was soon dismissed by the psychiatric and psychological communities who began to speculate that rape was the result of a disordered or aberrant sexual impulse within a certain small group of men. Today, however, rape—whether the victim is female or male—is seen as an act of power or dominance of one person over another. Recently, some social scientists have noted that rape is one of the most terrifying means used by men to dominate other men inside and outside of prison. To focus on rape as a power or dominance act we need only analyze how rape is used in prison:

> Rape in prison is rarely a sexual act, but one of violence, politics and an acting out of power roles. "Most of your homosexual rapes [are] a macho thing," says Col. Walter Pence, the Chief of Security here at the Louisiana State Penitentiary at Angola. "It's basically one guy saying to another: 'I'm a better man than you and I'm gonna turn you out ["turn you out" is prison slang for rape] to prove it.' I've investigated about a hundred cases personally, and I've not seen one that's just an act of passion. It's definitely a macho/power thing among the inmates."

A prime ingredient in rape is the element of aggression that is so deeply embedded in the male's gender role. For many men, aggression is one of the major ways of proving their masculinity and manhood, especially among those men who feel some sense of powerlessness in their lives. The male-as-dominant or male-as-aggressor is a theme so central to many men's self-concept that it literally carries over into their sexual lives. Sex, in fact, may be the one area where the average man can still prove his masculinity when few other areas can be found for him to prove himself manly or in control, or the dominant one in a relationship. Diana Russell addresses this issue when she declares that rape is not the act of a disturbed male, but rather an act of an overconforming male. She writes:

Rape is not so much a deviant act as an over-conforming act. Rape may be understood as an extreme acting-out of qualities that are regarded as super masculine in this and many other societies: aggression, force, power, strength, toughness, dominance, competitiveness. To win, to be superior, to be successful, to conquer—all demonstrate masculinity to those who subscribe to common cultural notions of masculinity, i.e., the *masculine mystique*. And it would be surprising if these notions of masculinity did not find expression in men's sexual behavior. Indeed, sex may be the arena where these notions of masculinity are most intensely played out, particularly by men who feel powerless in the rest of their lives, and hence, whose masculinity is threatened by this sense of powerlessness.

The fusion of aggression and sexuality for many men can be seen when we examine the area of sexual arousal as stimulated by graphic scenes of rape. Initially, researchers found that convicted rapists were more sexually aroused by depictions of violent sexuality than were men who had not raped. Thus it was thought that rapists must have a very low threshold for sexual arousal, and that the least little provocation would set off a male rapist (e.g., a woman who would assertively say "no" to sexual advances or even put up a fight was enough to trigger off a rapist, or so it was thought). In more recent studies, however, when men who had never raped were exposed to depictions of sexual assault, they reported a heightened sexual arousal from such scenes and an increase in their rape fantasies. Another disquieting note is that when nonrapist males were shown depictions of sexual assault, they reported the possibility that they would even consider using force themselves in their sexual relations. The research appears to suggest that most men (i.e., rapists and nonrapists) find violence a stimulant to heighten or arouse their sexual feelings. There is evidence that seems to indicate that males in general find sexuality related at some level to an expression of aggression, and in turn aggression heightens their sexual fantasies or actual sexual behaviors.

In summary, we can say that sexual assault or rape is first and foremost an act of sexual violence that to some degree draws upon the sexual fantasies of the rapist; it is linked to the rapist's need to show superiority and dominance over another.

THE PROBLEM OF NUMBERS

Rape is one of the most underreported of all serious crimes in the United States and in other countries as well. When we try to get a true picture of the enormity of its incidence, we find the issue complicated by the lack of reliable rape statistics. The crime of rape presents some uniquely confounding problems.

One problem we encounter is the simple fact that many, if not most, rape victims simply refuse to come forward and report to the authorities incidents of sexual violence. For many rape victims, a sense of shame or guilt or self-blame about their role in the rape assaults may be enough to prevent them from coming forward and pressing charges. Those who do press charges, however, are apt to meet with questions, accusations, and other degrading and humiliating experiences by the very authorities that are sworn to uphold the laws of society that make the rape of a person a serious felony.

Another problem is that when rape victims do press charges against their assailants, their life histories, especially sexual activities, are dragged before the public. In many instances, the public seems willing to blame the victim for the assault rather than the rapist. The reason for such an attribution of guilt to the victim rather than to the assailant seems to lie in the fact that many people have a tendency to blame others for their misfortunes, as if the world we live in was and is a "just world" where bad things happen only to those who somehow bring on or somehow deserve the consequences of their acts. Consequently, a likely result of such a "just world" orientation is that more often than not, the defenders of rapists will try to show that the rape victims acted in such a manner as to infer their complicity in the sexual assaults or that they "had it coming" because of their actions. We find such a courtroom tactic used by many defense attorneys, and it was one that apparently did not work in the much publicized 1984 New Bedford, Massachusetts, gang-rape case. There the rape-victim's motives for stopping at a bar were questioned and inferences were made impugning her behavior while in the bar. For example, during the trial, it was pointed out that the rape victim had talked with several of the accused rapists before the gang rape occurred. (If the mere act of talking is sufficient cause in some people's minds for a group of men to rape a woman, then we indeed have a twisted view of the causes of rape.) Thus, with all the barriers preventing the victims of sexual assault from coming forward, it is no wonder that rape continues to be one of the most underreported crimes. Even so, the Federal Bureau of Investigation reported that in the decade between 1967 and 1977 the number of reported rapes doubled in the United States. [I have] noted that:

> During 1977 alone, over 63,000 cases of rape were reported by the FBI. The most shocking feature of these statistics is that rape is considered by many experts in crime statistics to be one of the *least* reported violent crimes. The best available estimates suggest that for every one reported rape case there are anywhere from three to ten unreported cases. The conservative estimate of three means that over a quarter of a million women were forcibly raped in the United States in 1977!

While we have no absolute statistics for the total number of completed or attempted rapes committed annually in North America, we can estimate the probability of a woman being the victim of sexual assault during her lifetime. Allan Johnson estimated that "Nationally, a *conservative* estimate is that, under current conditions, 20–30 percent of girls now twelve years old will suffer a violent sexual attack during the remainder of their lives." Even with this estimate, however, we should keep in mind that this percentage excludes females under twelve, married women, and male rape victims. The enormity of the incidence of rape becomes even more staggering when we note that untold numbers of children under twelve are often the victims of sexual assault, as well as the many cases of male rape both inside and outside of prison.

RAPE AS A SOCIAL CONCERN

Due to the mounting concern over women's rights heralded by the reemergent women's movement, sexual assaults and their debilitating consequences for the victims have become one of the more pressing central issues of the 1970s and 1980s. Consequently, many social scientists have turned their attention toward understanding the dynamics of rapists and their motives, the institutional and cultural factors promoting rape, and of course, the various factors affecting the assault on rape victims and their reactions.

To combat the growing number of rapes, more and more people are beginning to think in terms of prevention and not only of ways to deal with the debilitating aftermath of sexual assault. Many different ways have been suggested to stop the growing wave of sexual assaults in our society.

Two such preventive approaches commonly thought of are, first, a "restrictive approach" that focuses on women changing their life-styles (e.g., not going out alone or not talking to strangers), and second, an "assertive approach" that suggests that women learn martial arts in order to fight back if assaulted. Both of these approaches have, however, some drawbacks. The restrictive approach, asking women to change their pattern of living, is an affront to women. Do we ask merchants to stop keeping money in their cash registers to prevent robberies? Why then should women change, for example, their dress or their social habits? The assertive approach has one possible value: the demise of the myth of the "defenseless woman." However, one problem with this approach is that many times in order to coerce a victim a rapist uses a deadly weapon, which totally nullifies any preventive action or force a victim may take to ward off an assailant.

Along with teaching young children and women to skillfully defend themselves, it seems that a broader based attack against sexual assaults should be taken against the social and institutional factors that promote sexual violence in our society. Two additional areas should be addressed if we are to see a reduction and, hopefully, an elimination in sexual assaults in our society. First, we need to examine the male's gender role with its prescriptive aggressive element, especially aggression against women. Aggression and violence are still seen by many as an integral part of the male's gender role. One way to reduce sexual assault in our society would be to redefine the male gender role, incorporating nonaggressive or nonviolent elements rather than aggressiveness. Of course, many people would object to such a major change in the male role, fearing that our country would fall prey to its national enemies who may wish to attack a nation of nonaggressive men.

Another controversial change that would reduce the number of sexual assaults is an open attack on hard-core and violence-oriented pornography and the multi-million dollar business that supports it. First of all, we should dismiss the notion that only males find sexually explicit materials arousing. Research has found that men *as well as* women find various kinds of erotic material sexually stimulating. However, the pornography industry has mainly directed its sales to a male audience. Although some erotic material does not focus on violent sexual aggression, a large proportion of the male-oriented pornography that is sold in stores across our country portrays the female as the victim of physical and sexual assault.

Researchers Neil Malamuth and Edward Donnerstein have found that exposure to violent pornography generally increases sexual arousal as well as negative attitudes toward women and favorable attitudes toward sexual assault. Thus one possible way to reduce the sexual violence in our society against women would be to eliminate such material. However, those who oppose such a plan immediately bring up the issue of a person's First Amendment rights, which guarantee freedom of speech; such opposition, however, misinterprets the Constitution and its intent.

Would society be as accepting if various media presented graphic anti-Semitic portrayals of Jews being shoved into gas chambers or American Indians being shot for sport for their land? And yet many people support the multi-million dollar industry that shows women assaulted and maimed for the sake of sexual stimulation.

If our society is to rectify the age-old problem of unequal power between females and males, we need to challenge many of our behaviors, our attitudes, and our social institutions that continue to cast women in an inferior role. Until that day, the problem of inequality between the genders is everyone's concern.   [1985]

Understanding the Reading

1. How does rape reflect patriarchal values?
2. How have theories about rape changed during the past 100 years, and how is it viewed today?

3. How is rape an act of an overconforming male?
4. How are aggression and sexuality related for most men?
5. Why is it difficult to know accurately the incidence of rape?
6. Why do people tend to "blame the victim" of sexual assault?
7. Explain the difference between the "restrictive approach" and the "assertive approach" to rape prevention and what is wrong with each.
8. What social and institutional factors promote sexual violence?

Suggestions for Responding

1. Doyle proposes that the male role be changed to eliminate its emphasis on aggression. Do you think this is desirable or not? Why? How might we go about making such a change?
2. Doyle also proposes that eliminating violent pornography is one way to reduce violence against women, and he dismisses the claim that this would be an infringement of First Amendment rights. Do you agree or disagree with his position? Why? ✦

68

Fraternities of Fear

KATHLEEN HIRSCH

Some scenes from the ivory tower: Five lacrosse team buddies and another student at St. John's University in Queens, New York, allegedly invited friends in to watch, last March, while they brutally sodomized a female student. A full month went by before the police were notified by university officials, who claimed to be protecting the victim's privacy. Because of the charges, all six men were suspended for the duration of the academic year. The woman has withdrawn from school.

At Colgate University, in Hamilton, New York, two women reported that a student sexually harassed two women, then raped a third, during the course of one evening last February. A doctor presented physical evidence to the university's judicial board of the rape victim's condition, which was said to include severe bruising and a ripped vagina. The student was found "guilty." His punishment, suspension in abeyance, was changed following campus protest to suspension for two semesters. The public authorities were never contacted.

In 1987, two fraternity sophomores at the University of New Hampshire, in Durham, were accused of sexually assaulting a woman student in a dormitory. A university disciplinary board, comprised of students, faculty, and staff, found the men "not guilty" of sexual assault but suspended the men for a semester, because of disrespect to others. The lack of sterner sanctions led students to a sit-in protest at the dean of students' office; 11 activists were eventually arrested. In a criminal hearing, the accused men, pleading guilty to misdemeanor charges, were sentenced to what amounted to 90 days in jail. The woman withdrew from school; the men eventually graduated, their degrees safely in hand.

The bad news this fall is that college campuses are unsafe for women. This is not because violent crimes occur more frequently there than anywhere else—actually, in the case of sex crimes, the rate runs about the same as the general population. Rather, it is because colleges do almost nothing about their student aggressors. In case after case of campus rape, university officers rely on administrative judicial boards that mete out absurdly lenient punishments; they fail to file criminal complaints in an effort to ward off bad publicity; and they largely succeed in creating the impression that crimes against women are aberrations in otherwise civilized communities devoted to the refinement of the mind.

Here are the facts. One out of four women will be sexually assaulted on a college campus. At the very most, only one in ten of those will report it. Their attackers will be fellow students 80 percent of the time, and the most likely location of the attack will be a dormitory room or a fraternity house.

Fraternities in particular seem to be breeding grounds for campus sexual aggression, from jeering verbal abuse to acquaintance rape. A 1969 study by the dean's office at the University of Illinois at Urbana-Champaign found that frat men, a quarter of its male student population,

perpetrated 63 percent of student sexual assault at the institution. From such studies it is also becoming clear that fraternities promote the most heinous form of sexual assault, the gang rape. Unlike widely publicized gang rapes that conform to class and racial stereotypes, this crime, if committed behind a fraternity's doors, becomes a boy's prank—or even a sanctioned rite of passage into the grown-up world of male dominance, privilege, and power.

The fraternity gang rape almost always conforms to script. New, naive students, or women from a nearby college, are invited to their first frat party, usually early in the fall term (although gang rapes take place at *any* time of the year, with women of *any* age). Alcohol is plentiful. In some cases, drinking is a prerequisite to entering the actual party, either by consuming a few cocktails in an upstairs room or having successive ones in several rooms. The point is for women to become as inebriated as possible—without suspecting negative consequences.

The victim is selected, either before the party or soon after she arrives, by a frat brother, and is "worked over," in a perverse parody of seduction, relying on a variety of ruses from flattery to subtle threats. The woman may actually believe that the student is seriously interested in her, "unaware that the 'friendly' persuasion of the [brother] is actually a planned pursuit of easy prey," wrote Julie K. Ehrhart and Bernice R. Sandler, in the paper "Campus Gang Rape: Party Games?"

The woman is led to one of the frat rooms, under the impression that she'll be with one man, or left alone to "sleep off" the alcohol. She is assaulted as soon as she enters his room, where other brothers are waiting for her. Or, more frequently, she regains consciousness while she is being raped by several men.

It is not enough, sensitive observers say, to recognize the pattern of a gang rape in order to protect oneself or reduce its occurrence. Gang rape—like pornography—is pervasive, because it is a key feature of male bonding rituals within patriarchal societies.

Peggy Reeves Sanday, an anthropology professor at the University of Pennsylvania and the author of *Fraternity Gang Rape: Sex, Brotherhood, and Privilege on Campus* (New York University Press), found that fraternities attract a certain type of male, more insecure than average; men whose psychological and social bonds to parents, especially their mothers, have not yet been broken.

The security delivered by the fraternity "alter ego" is a powerful allure for these young men. They voluntarily endure humiliating and often physically painful initiations designed to break family allegiances. Forcibly torn from one set of norms, they are inducted into new ones that promise self-assurance—provided that they comply with the brotherhood's tightly enforced conformity.

These new norms have been described as "highly masculinist" by two Florida State University sociologists, Patricia Yancey Martin and Robert A. Hummer, writing in *Gender and Society*. The world of fraternities is characterized chiefly by "concern with a narrow, stereotypical conception of masculinity and heterosexuality; a preoccupation with loyalty . . . and an obsession with competition, superiority, and dominance."

"Almost always, male bonding turns against women," Sanday said. "It's a matter of degree, not kind. The way in which men extract loyalty from one another almost always means that they elevate male bonding by making women the despised other, and the scapegoat."

During Sanday's interviews, men degraded the women they slept with, "using such terms as gash, horsebags, heifers, scum, scum bags, queen, swanks, scum buckets, scum doggies, wench, life-support systems, beasts, bitch, swatches, and cracks." Laura McLaughlin, a resident adviser at Colgate, says it isn't unusual for women visiting with friends to be greeted at a fraternity house with comments like "Who's the chick? Who'd you bring us?"

Degrading women unites men in a culture that requires them to compete intensely. But, more important, at an age when their sexual identity is still fluid and a source of profound anxiety, frat men alleviate any insecurities about homoerotic attachments—and satisfy them—by having sex in front of each other, by abusing and dehumanizing women. In short, through gang rape.

Incredible amounts of time and energy go into planning, executing, documenting (in frat logs), and recollecting these bonding rituals. An entire underground lexicon of these practices exists: "rude-hoggering" (bedding the "ugliest" woman at a party), "landsharking" (kneeling on the floor behind a woman and biting her buttocks), and "baggings" (a group of men cornering a woman, dropping their trousers, wriggling their penises, and offering to gang rape her).

"Men rape for other men," contends Claire Walsh, director of Sexual Assault Recovery Services at the University of Florida. "It's a way of maintaining the myth of macho masculinity; a way to confirm their feelings of sexual adequacy. If a man in the room didn't participate, his sexual capacity could be called into question."

Kristen Buxton's assault at Colgate University in 1987 was horribly typical. Although Buxton, entering her junior year, was no newcomer to the university's social scene, she accepted an invitation to Sigma Chi's end-of-summer party because she was at emotional loose ends: her grandmother had just died, and she just had ended a serious relationship that had enabled her to avoid the more raucous "singles" side of Colgate life.

As nightfall approached, the weather in Hamilton, New York, that Saturday in late August was "great," Kristen remembers. In the company of old friends, she was glad to be at the party.

Twelve hours later she sat in her mother's living room north of Boston, unable to speak.

"Her face was all swollen from crying," Marah Buxton says. "I assumed she was upset over my mother. She wasn't able to get any words out of her mouth. I looked at Andrew [the friend who'd driven her home], and I said, 'I'm frightened. Give me a clue.'"

He answered, "This is going to take a while."

According to Kristen, shortly before midnight she was shown to a second-floor bedroom of Sigma Chi where the party was taking place, and went to sleep. She was awakened when two freshman athlete recruits gang raped her. Her screams, loud enough to break through the party noise below, brought friends to her aid.

If Buxton's experience was typical, her response, however, was not. For one thing, she was clear about what happened and decided, from the beginning, to prosecute. In part because she had the good fortune to be taken to a hospital emergency room near her hometown, she was immediately put in touch with police officers who pursued the criminal case.

The vast majority of sexual assault survivors on campuses keep it to themselves—blaming themselves, either because they were drinking or because they were "stupid enough" to have been in the wrong place at the wrong time. Women also believe, erroneously, that because the man was a friend, it couldn't have been rape.

Survivors' silence plays directly into the self-protective impulses of university officials. The morning after her daughter's rape, Marah Buxton phoned the school to inform them of the crime. In the three traumatic years that have passed since then, she says, "only one dean called. They distanced themselves completely."

Traumatized and often physically injured victims who deal directly with college clinics and officials may discover impassive bureaucracies instead of supportive advocates. "It's a syndrome," says Jeffrey Newman, Kristen Buxton's attorney and an expert on campus sexual assault. "We hear this over and again. The clinic head usually sends them to the school administration. The administration usually meets with the parents, probably with the attorney from the school present, to explain the benefits of undergoing the judicial process within the school, as opposed to the outside."

"What they're trying to do," says Newman's associate, Rosanne Zuffante, "is intimidate the young woman into backing off. And they succeed most of the time."

University tactics can violate a woman's due process, says Howard Clery, of Security on Campus, Inc., who insists that "a university cannot adjudicate a felony." But, typically, colleges attempt to do just this. Once a victim is persuaded to keep her accusations within the university, a judicial board hears testimony from all involved. The boards, normally composed of several faculty members, were originally established to review plagiarism cases and honor code violations. Now they determine the "innocence" or "guilt" of accused rapists, and dole out any punishments they deem fit.

On many campuses, the penalty for rape is identical to, or less severe than, the sanctions for plagiarism—one year's suspension. Frequently, confessed rapists are not even removed from campus. They are placed on "probation." (In Buxton's case, the athletes accused of rape withdrew from Colgate.)

Brave women who, like Buxton, press charges with the local authorities face several hurdles. Advocates say that district attorneys are reluctant to handle campus rape cases, and it's not only because they are difficult to win.

"It's a political game," says Newman. "Usually there are strong connections between the D.A.'s office and the higher-ups in the university. Most of the time you find the D.A.'s drop the case or they never take it. They say, look, there's just not enough evidence."

Buxton says she came under severe pressure from her D.A. to agree to a plea bargain that resulted in misdemeanor convictions, probation punishments, and, worst of all, no trace of the crime on her assailants' records.

Even more pressure is applied by peers. Buxton sometimes thought she was in hell after she returned to campus that fall—reading news accounts of the incident, feeling as if everyone was looking at her differently—but never more so than when she was finally persuaded by friends to join them at a downtown Hamilton pub.

"A bunch of fraternity members surrounded my table and just kind of stood there," she recounts. "Another time, I was standing in the middle of the room and a couple of them came over and were joking: 'Oh, look who's out.' They tried to intimidate me a lot."

This isn't uncommon. "Most women feel that if they make a public statement they have to leave," admits Ann Lane, founder of Colgate's women's studies program. "They receive threats from frat brothers, obscene phone calls. One woman [at Colgate] got a rock thrown through her window."

It is the rare victim who is offered adequate counseling. At best, institutions run a support group moderated by a faculty adviser or a clinic staffer.

"There was never any support," Buxton says of her own case. "Just kind of a blank stare."

It is the female students who pay the price for institutional passivity. Victims drop out of the classes they share with their assailants. Their grades go down. They experience chronic depression and have trouble concentrating. Eventually, many women, like Buxton, leave school for a period of time, or drop out altogether.

The code of silence exerts a ripple effect, observers say, through the entire female student population. It diminishes everything from classroom assertiveness and performance to confidence levels. Overall, says Professor Sanday, it suppresses a woman's initiative.

"There's a lot of anxiety," says Colgate resident adviser McLaughlin. "Almost every woman you talk to has a story."

And, interviews reveal, many have stories about a botched university clinic "rape kit" (the semen, blood, and other physical evidence of the assault) or a member of the judicial board unversed in the legal definition of rape. The unofficial negligence of universities reveals itself on many, mutually reinforcing levels.

By ignoring rape victims and their needs, universities succeed in minimizing adverse press. Sex crimes, characterized as "isolated incidents," keep consumers (students and their parents) and donors (alumni) ignorant and happy. The boat doesn't get rocked, and another generation learns the dynamics of domestic violence.

According to Sanday, what's at stake is "Brotherhood. That's older males protecting younger males, protecting their lost youth, and protecting their actual fraternity brothers. Protecting the American dream. The dream in which the young man goes out with his buddies, works his way up, becomes head of everything, and makes a fortune. Along the way, if he has to rape a few people—competitors, women—that's sort of what we expect. The American dream is very misogynistic."

But victims, feminists, and advocates on campus are fighting back. Victims are suing universities in civil court—successfully claiming, in many cases, that the institution is liable for security breaches or rule infractions that contributed directly to the rape. Colgate is currently defending itself in a $10 million civil damage suit filed by Buxton, who charges that the school should have forbidden the Sigma Chi party, because the fraternity had already been sanctioned for serving alcohol to minors. (Despite several requests, university officials were unavailable for comment.)

After lawsuits, the most sweeping effort to make universities responsible for campus criminal activity has been legislative. In June, the House of Representatives passed the "Student Right To Know and Campus Security Act"—despite keen back-room opposition from organized education lobbyists. If it becomes law, the act will require all institutions receiving federal aid to release their yearly crime statistics. It will also allow victims the right to know what happens to the perpetrators of crimes against them.

Howard and Connie Clery, whose own daughter was raped and murdered by a fellow student, urge any victim of campus rape to contact the police and the local district attorney's office. If possible, hire a lawyer. Security on Campus, their two-year-old organization in Gulph Mills, Pennsylvania, will provide the names of attorneys and other information needed to pursue a legal case.

Finally, protests, vigils, and marches by campus feminists have pushed administrators to take a more active stand against the abuse of women and overt institutional sexism. Thanks to them, and to a growing number of enlightened deans and college presidents, there is room for cautious optimism.

For example, at the University of Pennsylvania (the site of several highly publicized rapes) an ongoing rape education program, including films, regular discussions, and lectures, has increased the number of women reporting and asking for help.

After the 1987 protests at the University of New Hampshire, the institution developed the Sexual Harassment and Rape Prevention Program, geared toward averting sexual violence. The University of Illinois at Urbana-Champaign investigates every case of sexual assault and battery, whether the attack occurs on or off campus. The institution hired a victims' advocate, and requires all perpetrators found guilty of sexual assault to participate in counseling. It also is developing an educational program for men with a family history of domestic violence.

Inevitably, there is the question of the fraternities themselves. It would seem that women's obvious recourse is to avoid, even boycott, fraternity social events and seek entertainment elsewhere. But it isn't that simple. Most campuses with fraternities have virtually abdicated responsibility for social life to "the houses," which are among the few places where minors can find easy access to alcohol.

Instead of abolishing the system, some colleges have forced fraternities to grow up. At Bowdoin and Trinity colleges, coed frats have appeared. Colby College voted to abolish its eight fraternities and two sororities in 1984, and the University of Illinois has banned alcohol at after-hours frat parties, and a brother in most houses is trained to counsel and intervene when a potentially violent situation develops.

At Colgate, where fraternities have been an issue for the last ten years, more than 500 students and staff staged a protest last year against them; the faculty subsequently voted to abolish the system. "It's detrimental to humane learning in a very broad sense," says Colgate's Lane, who lobbied for change. "It's anti-intellectual in its core. Fraternities foster values that are in opposition to values we all uphold and respect."

In response, Colgate's board of trustees established a subcommittee to investigate the houses. Its report, with recommended solutions, should be delivered this fall.

One hopes that the board considers the many women who silently share Kristen Buxton's story. These are not alums who will remember their alma maters at giving time. Buxton graduated . . . a year behind the classmates with whom she entered. As she tries to assess her four years of college, she only begins to suggest the legacy of male aggression in America—even to society's most privileged and educated women:

"I'm a lot more hesitant about things, more cautious. I'm much more comfortable with things I'm used to. I think I'm probably more scared. Like, I'm much more comfortable just being home."   [1990]

Understanding the Reading

1. How do colleges and universities generally respond to rape and sexual assault? Why?
2. What is the "script" for a fraternity gang rape?
3. How are fraternity members characterized in this article?
4. How do fraternity members degrade women, and why?
5. Why are most campus rapes not prosecuted?
6. What effect does campus rape have on the victim and other women on campus?
7. Why don't universities play a more active role in fighting campus rape?
8. What steps have been taken to stop campus rape?

Suggestions for Responding

1. Why do colleges and universities treat rape differently than the law does? Should they?
2. Investigate and report on the procedures followed in sexual assault cases on your campus. ◆

69

"The Rape" of Mr. Smith

UNKNOWN

The law discriminates against rape victims in a manner which would not be tolerated by victims of any other crime. In the following example, a holdup victim is asked questions similar in form to those usually asked a victim of rape.

"Mr. Smith, you were held up at gunpoint on the corner of 16th & Locust?"

"Yes."

"Did you struggle with the robber?"

"No."

"Why not?"

"He was armed."

"Then you made a conscious decision to comply with his demands rather than to resist?"

"Yes."

"Did you scream? Cry out?"

"No. I was afraid."

"I see. Have you ever been held up before?"

"No."

"Have you ever given money away?"

"Yes, of course—"

"And did you do so willingly?"

"What are you getting at?"

"Well, let's put it like this, Mr. Smith. You've given away money in the past—in fact, you have quite a reputation for philanthropy. How can we be sure that you weren't *contriving* to have your money taken from you by force?"

"Listen, if I wanted—"

"Never mind. What time did this holdup take place, Mr. Smith?"

"About 11 P.M."

"You were out on the streets at 11 P.M.? Doing what?"

"Just walking."

"Just walking? You know that it's dangerous being out on the street that late at night. Weren't you aware that you could have been held up?"

"I hadn't thought about it."

"What were you wearing at the time, Mr. Smith?"

"Let's see. A suit. Yes, a suit."

"An *expensive* suit?"

"Well—yes."

"In other words, Mr. Smith, you were walking around the streets late at night in a suit that practically *advertised* the fact that you might be a good target for some easy money, isn't that so? I mean, if we didn't know better, Mr. Smith, we might even think you were *asking* for this to happen, mightn't we?"

"Look, can't we talk about the past history of the guy who *did* this to me?"

"I'm afraid not, Mr. Smith. I don't think you would want to violate his rights, now, would you?"

Naturally, the line of questioning, the innuendo, is ludicrous—as well as inadmissible as any sort of cross-examination—unless we are talking about parallel questions in a rape case. The time of night, the victim's previous history of "giving away" that which was taken by force, the clothing —all of these are held against the victim. Society's posture on rape, and the manifestation of that posture in the courts, help account for the fact that so few rapes are reported.   [n.d.]

Understanding the Reading

1. In what way are rape victims often discriminated against, when they are being questioned initially?
2. Why would an officer of the law imply that the victim was "asking for it"?
3. With present-day DNA technology, do you think that society's attitude toward investigating rape has changed? Why or why not?

Suggestion for Responding

1. Why do you think rape victims are treated so differently from victims of other crimes? ✦

70

1–2 Punch: A Major Blow to Roe

ALLISON STEVENS

Dr. Paul Blumenthal was preparing to perform an abortion for a woman who was 22 weeks pregnant and carrying a fetus with a congenital anomaly. A professor of obstetrics and gynecology at Stanford University, Blumenthal would have preferred to use a particular procedure he believed was the safest and most medically appropriate for the woman. But instead of going with his best medical instincts, he felt it necessary to recommend an alternative method that for the woman was more dangerous, more time-consuming and more painful.

The reason for the change? Blumenthal feared that by performing a "dilation and evacuation"— a quick, safe and legal procedure—he might be *perceived* as violating a federal law passed in 2003 that the Supreme Court has just ruled constitutional. It bans *intact* dilation and evacuation, a variant on the legal method, in which a physician partly delivers a fetus before completing the abortion procedure.

Passed by a Republican-controlled Congress and signed into law by President Bush, the ban has not been enforced until now, as it was stayed in lower courts by successful lawsuits from Planned Parenthood, the ACLU and the Center for Reproductive Rights on behalf of the National Abortion Federation, Dr. LeRoy Carhart and other physicians. They challenged the ban for its vague language, asserting it could apply to other procedures, and because it lacked an exception for the health of the woman—a precedent established more than three decades ago in *Roe v. Wade* and repeatedly reaffirmed in court cases since then.

This April, in the first abortion case since the retirement of legendary centrist Justice Sandra Day O'Connor, the U.S. Supreme Court—whose conservative flank is now bolstered by Bush appointees Chief Justice John Roberts and Justice Samuel Alito—ignored precedent and overturned lower-court decisions in voting 5–4 in favor of the abortion procedure ban. The ruling in

Gonzales v. Carbart revealed the rightward shift of the court in the absence of O'Connor, who had joined a 5–4 majority in 2000 that struck down a similar state ban because it lacked the requisite maternal health exception. With Alito now in O'Connor's seat, the court ruled the other way.

The law's vague language has had a chilling effect: Doctors like Blumenthal are shying away from performing procedures that remain legal because they fear they may *unintentionally* violate the law and face criminal penalties. Indeed, physicians found guilty of breaking the law can be sentenced with fines and prison terms of up to two years. "Ever since the Supreme Court decision came down, we've made efforts to steer clear of crossing the line, or even the perception of crossing the line," Blumenthal says.

The ramifications of the decision do not end there. Advocates on both sides of the issue see the court's departure from precedent—and the opinion's hostile tone toward abortion rights—as an invitation to anti-choice lawmakers around the country to continue their efforts to chip away at access to abortion and perhaps even criminalize the procedure altogether. Writing for the Supreme Court majority, Justice Anthony Kennedy peppered his ruling with language sympathetic to the anti-choice position—a point noted by Justice Ruth Bader Ginsburg in her biting dissent. In the ruling, Kennedy refers to obstetrician-gynecologists as "abortion doctors" and describes a fetus as an "unborn child"—terms that Ginsburg said reveals the court's "hostility" to the fundamental right to abortion.

Conservative legislators are already taking the high court's bait: On April 19, one day after the court handed down its ruling, a pair of state legislators in Louisiana introduced "copycat" versions of the federal abortion ban that would carry stiffer penalties (including prison terms of up to 10 years for physicians). Lawmakers in Michigan and North Carolina also introduced anti-choice measures in the weeks after the court announced its decision in the case, and the Iowa state Senate amended a health budget bill to prohibit state funding of the kind of abortion procedures banned by the Supreme Court. That provision died before becoming law.

Several other states enacted anti-choice laws in the aftermath of the decision: Georgia passed a measure requiring abortion providers to offer women the opportunity to see the fetus in an ultrasound before undergoing an abortion; North Dakota backed a nearly complete abortion ban that will take effect if the Supreme Court overturns *Roe v. Wade;* and Oklahoma passed a bill banning most abortions in state-funded hospitals. Meanwhile, the Missouri legislature approved a law requiring certain abortion clinics to meet more burdensome and more costly operating standards—which could force at least one clinic in the state to shut down if the governor signs it.

But the real legislative onslaught won't come until next year, experts say. That's because most state legislatures had already adjourned for the year or passed deadlines barring introduction of new legislation. "I think we're going to see again a flood of legislation at the state level in which they seek to add additional hurdles to women who are seeking abortion," said Nancy Northup, president of the Center for Reproductive Rights.

Clarke D. Forsythe, president of Americans United for Life, a group in Chicago that opposes abortion rights, predicted as much in a May 1 memo to supporters. He wrote that the decision "opens the door to more aggressive regulation of abortion" and specifically encouraged what he called "informed consent" restrictions. These types of laws, known by opponents as "biased counseling" restrictions, can even order doctors to give medically specious, state-scripted information to women about purported dangers associated with abortion and a fetus' ability to feel pain. Often, these laws are coupled with mandatory delays or waiting periods, which add to the cost of the procedure for women who need to pay for overnight accommodations, child care and transportation. Also predicted to be introduced in legislatures next year are a wave of state versions of the federal abortion ban, efforts to eliminate exceptions for a woman's health from existing laws, and some outright bans on abortion that could be used as legal vehicles to reverse *Roe v. Wade*.

The decision has emboldened some anti-abortion extremists. Signs of their renewed ardor came during two recent episodes of violence at clinics that provide abortion services. In April, a bomb was found in the parking lot of the Women's Health Center in Austin, Texas, and in May a fire was set at a Planned Parenthood family-planning clinic in Virginia Beach.

But the *Carbart* ruling has also galvanized supporters of abortion rights. On the day after the decision, federal lawmakers, led by Sen. Barbara Boxer (D-Calif.) and Rep. Jerrold Nadler (D-N.Y.), reintroduced the Freedom of Choice Act (FOCA), a measure that would codify in federal law the rights established in *Roe v. Wade.* If passed, the measure would likely lead to court challenges that could overturn the *Carbart* decision. Seven states—California, Connecticut, Hawaii, Maine, Maryland, Nevada and Washington—have already passed their own versions of the Freedom of Choice Act. The measure was also introduced in Rhode Island.

But the federal version, which would guarantee access to abortion across the land, is not likely to win passage anytime soon. Even though Congress is now controlled by Democrats, a party that officially backs abortion rights, the House of Representatives is still controlled by opponents of abortion: Of the 435 members of the House, a slight majority currently opposes abortion rights and another 10 percent of the chamber has a mixed record on the subject and supports some restrictions, according to NARAL Pro-Choice America. In the Senate, only about one-third of the members have strong records in support of abortion, and nearly half strongly oppose it; the rest have mixed records on reproductive rights and family planning, including Senate Majority Leader Harry Reid.

Even if the Freedom of Choice Act were to clear Congress, it would face certain death in the White House. Bush made that clear after the Supreme Court decision, when he issued a pre-emptive threat to veto "any legislation that weakens current federal policies and laws on abortion or that encourages the destruction of human life at any stage."

Pro-choice advocates can take some solace in the fact that they now have a staunch ally in the most powerful leader in the legislative branch. Speaker Nancy Pelosi—and many of her colleagues on House congressional committees—can be counted on to bottle up any anti-choice measures that might come before Congress. That will put at least a temporary stop to the sort of abortion restrictions that were enacted during the 12 years that Congress was controlled by religious conservative Republicans.

But proactive legislation protecting access to abortion will not win passage until voters send more pro-choice representatives to the Capitol and the White House. Until then, there is little hope for bills that would increase access to abortion (such as providing coverage of the procedure under Medicaid) or protect it by enshrining abortion rights in federal law.

Until then, there is also uncertainty over whether the basic right to abortion will be upheld by the Supreme Court. Currently, four justices are assumed to oppose abortion (Roberts, Alito, Antonin Scalia and Clarence Thomas), and one—Kennedy—was considered a swing vote until he sided with them in *Carbart.* Whether he supports a complete reversal of *Roe v. Wade* is unclear, but that may not matter if another staunch opponent of women's rights is appointed to the bench. Alarmingly, the two oldest members of the court—Justices John Paul Stevens, 87, and Ruth Bader Ginsburg, 74—are also strong backers of a woman's constitutional right to privacy.

The importance of elections, and their implications for the court, is a concept well understood by the political Right, which routinely uses a candidate's stance on abortion as a litmus test in primary elections. That is evident in the race for the Republican presidential nomination, where front-runner Rudy Giuliani of New York faces a mutiny from the party's conservative base now that his support for abortion rights has come under heavy media scrutiny.

Unlike the Right, Democratic candidates do not always place a high degree of importance on the issue of abortion when campaigning for votes. Feminists tried to make abortion rights an issue in the 2000 elections, when pro-choice advocates widely circulated campaign buttons at the Democratic National Convention in Los Angeles that blared: "It's the Supreme Court, Stupid!"—a riff on the "It's the Economy, Stupid!" catchphrase coined by Democratic strategist James Carville.

But both Al Gore and Bush downplayed abortion: Gore did not highlight his pro-choice position in his campaign, and Bush obfuscated his anti-abortion position, presenting a moderate front by using such politically soft terms as "culture of life," a phrase that allowed him to convey opposition to abortion without coming out directly for overturning *Roe v. Wade.* That stance allowed him to mollify social conservatives without alarming average voters, who also may have taken some relief when, in the days before Bush's first inaugural, Laura Bush appeared on NBC's *Today Show* and said she believed *Roe* should not be overturned.

Four years later, abortion-rights advocates again sounded the alarm, warning of the looming vacancies on the high court that could endanger access to abortion. Once again, both presidential candidates played down the issue of abortion, and voters—a majority of whom back the right to abortion—re-elected Bush and strengthened the Republican majorities in the House and Senate; paving the way for the appointments—and subsequent confirmations—of Roberts and Alito.

"The tragedy is that neither Gore nor [John] Kerry chose to make it a major issue in their campaigns," says Kim Gandy, president of the National Organization for Women. "Bush would never have been elected if they had."

In the 2006 elections, pro-choice forces fought back. Voters selected more pro-choice lawmakers, thus picking up seats in Congress; turned back an effort to ban abortion in South Dakota; and rejected initiatives that would have required parental notification in California and Oregon. And in a stunning defeat for abortion opponents, voters in Kansas ousted a zealous anti-choice attorney general who had subpoenaed the records of 90 women and girls who had abortions in order to scour them for evidence of illegal procedures.

"When choice was on the ballot in 2006, pro-choice voters prevailed," says NARAL Pro-Choice America president Nancy Keenan. That momentum will only grow over the next two years, now that the *Carhart* decision has put the threat to abortion in stark relief, she says: "The climate is changing a lot for us. The threat is much more real now. . . . People are concerned about the Supreme Court and they are concerned about what the next administration will look like. They're starting to connect the dots."   [2007]

Understanding the Reading

1. What is the *Carhart* ruling, and why does the author say that it shows no concern for women's health?
2. Give two reasons why this ruling was not passed earlier by the Supreme Court.

3. Why is it expected that the case that legalized abortion, *Roe v. Wade,* may be reversed?

Suggestion for Responding

1. Discuss the following issues in class— a woman's right to choose versus not being allowed to choose whether to terminate a pregnancy. Consider these contexts: the woman's life is in danger, or she is pregnant because she was raped. Do these contexts change your decision? ✦

71

Erosion of Unions Hurts Women, Particularly Latinas

LINDA CHAVEZ-THOMPSON AND GABRIELA LEMUS

Although women have made many gains since the 1960s, they must still catch up with men when it comes to equal pay and the benefits that generally accompany it, like educational attainment and access to health insurance, paid leave and other benefits. This is particularly true for women of color who have the highest levels of disparities in income in comparison to men. In 2006, women overall made 77 percent of men's annual earnings.

The wage gap is stark irrespective of one's ethnic group, but for Latinas it is singularly startling. Latinas earn only 52.4 percent when compared with men. In industries that are job-typed, such as teaching and nursing where many Latina workers are concentrated, unions have fostered change in closing the pay gap and given Latinas access to health insurance and other benefits. We must assess the remaining barriers to economic equality and push hard for policies that are even-handed and diminish gender- and racial-inequities. If ever there was an argument for joining a union, then this would be it. And if ever there was an argument for having the capacity to bargain collectively without retribution, this would definitely be it.

Women are struggling. As a result, their families are also facing challenges. Women are the foundation for family decisions and unfortunately, more and more, they carry the primary responsibility and are the sole decision-makers in their children's welfare. Latinas also often uphold their family and cultural traditions to take care of their elders. Women's role as caretakers in our society is one factor in pay inequity. Absent strong government-provided safety nets, like quality affordable day care, women will continue to be forced to choose between their families and their jobs.

Not everything is at the federal level. States have an important role to play in the shifts of women from poverty to economic prosperity. States can implement innovative programs that assist women by providing educational and training programs to maximize women's earning potential or alternatively, they could set their own minimum wage laws and strengthen pay equity at the state level. Yet, local, state and national policies continue to lag behind the changing realities of women's lives as they struggle to balance the need to work with their obligations to care for their families.

At the federal level, there is legislation in Congress that could potentially address part of the solution toward pay equity, and that is the Employee Free Choice Act. EFCA would restore workers' freedom to form unions and collectively bargain, while strengthening penalties for companies that coerce or intimidate employees. It is critical that women be allowed to form unions and be part of a process where they can express an opinion by the simple but deliberate signing of an authorization card. Union women earn 31 percent more in their median weekly earnings than those without a union, which translates into $758 per month in comparison to $579 without a union.

The freedom to join a union is a fundamental right protected by our country's constitutional freedom of association, its labor laws and the Universal Declaration of Human Rights. Yet, this right continues to be eroded, and as a result, more and more women have become the victims of harassment, discrimination and even termination for attempting to improve their lives by forming unions.

Clearly, women have the right to improve their economic well-being and the welfare of their families. By so doing, they also help to strengthen the communities they live in by being able to contribute more to their local and state economies. On this Equal Pay Day, government and employers have a unique opportunity to come together with workers to both create a better environment in the workplace and improve economic equality.   [2007]

Understanding the Reading

1. What is the wage gap between Latinas and men in the United States?
2. What are some of the barriers to economic equality for Latinas?
3. What is the Employee Free Choice Act, and how could it improve workers' lives?

Suggestions for Responding

1. Discuss the basic idea of unions. Why would a government be against unions when they strengthen economies?
2. Some people have spent their adult lives struggling to organize different kinds of unions: migrant farm workers, steel workers, and factory workers. Research some of these union organizers. What role do unions play in American life today? ✦

SUGGESTIONS FOR RESPONDING TO PART V

1. Write a research report on the male–female pay differentials in the field you have chosen as a career. If at all possible, try to control for differences in the education and experience of the two groups.

2. Investigate the federal Women's Education Equity Program to find out what kinds of research it conducts and the kinds of services it provides to public schools. If there is a similar agency in your state or area school district, learn about its activities and services.

3. Research the initial entry of women into higher education—in women's colleges such as Mount Holyoke in 1837 and Vassar in 1865 and at the coeducational Oberlin College in 1832. How did the educational and extracurricular experiences differ in the two kinds of institutions? How were women treated differently from men at Oberlin?

4. If you are heterosexual, attend a meeting of the gay and/or lesbian group or center on your campus. Find out what its priorities are, and explore ways that you could help reduce the prejudice and discrimination it faces.

5. Title IX of the Education Amendments of 1972 prohibits sex discrimination in all federally funded educational programs. Its intent is to encourage equity in athletic programs, requiring colleges and universities to provide and equally support comparable sports offerings for women and men. See if your school is in compliance. How many sports are offered for women and for men? How many women and men participate? Are budgets for the two overall programs equitable? Are scheduling and access to facilities fair to both women and men? Do the number and rank of the coaches reflect appropriate gender balance?

6. Investigate and report on a governmental or volunteer organization formed to protect rape victims or victims of domestic violence to learn what support is available to women in your area.

7. The Cleary Act demands that colleges disclose and *give full access to* rape statistics on campus. Is your college in compliance with the Cleary Act? If you have never seen these statistics, take action by inviting the appropriate administrators to your classroom. Make demands and write letters to your school newspaper.

VI
Power and Classism

Most Americans like to think of ours as a class-less society, and thus we tend to ignore class as an aspect of our lives. If we do think of class, most of us tend to identify ourselves as middle-class. Historically, the sense of a classless nation arose because most early European immigrants were neither nobility nor serfs but, rather, generally were "commoners"—farmers, artisans, trades workers, and such. Due to the abundance of land on this continent, these early immigrants could also become property owners and enjoy a substantial degree of autonomy. From the beginning, of course, this view of a middle-class nation was inaccurate because, among other things, it ignored slaves, indentured servants, Native Americans, and others whose reality did not meet this idyll. Additionally, in the colonial era, White land-owning males constituted only about 7 percent of the population.

Socioeconomic inequities became more generalized and pronounced with the nineteenth-century onset of the **industrial revolution,** the transformation of methods of production, transportation, and communication through the substitution of machines for hand labor. This mechanization of production systems brought about massive social and economic changes, and America began developing an identifiable class structure. More and more people moved from being self-sufficient and independent to being wage earners working for and dependent on factory and business owners.

This shift signaled the growth of **capitalism,** an economic system characterized by private (or corporate) ownership of capital assets and by free-market determination of prices, production, and distribution of goods. The capitalist system was reinforced by a belief in **free enterprise,** the freedom of private businesses to operate competitively for profit with minimal government regulation.

Satisfaction of capitalist interests inevitably resulted in an inequitable distribution of power, resources, and property. To realize maximum profits, it was in the employers' interest to pay the lowest possible wages to the workers and to require the highest possible production from them, an arrangement that seriously disadvantaged the workers. This inequality led wage earners, during the latter decades of the nineteenth century and the first half of the twentieth, to respond by organizing and forming **unions** to advance their interests, to collectively improve wages and working conditions, and to enhance job security. Union successes, however, were uneven as the owners often had the law (and private police forces) enforcing their interests.

Capitalism also created a number of "panics" and **depressions,** periods of drastic decline in the national economy characterized by decreasing business, falling prices, and rising unemployment.

Although both owners and workers suffered from these economic declines, hard times fell most heavily on the latter, especially during the Great Depression of the 1930s, which led to the social reforms of President Franklin D. Roosevelt's New Deal.

New Deal social policies included farm supports; federal reforms of the financial system; national control of the stock market, banking, and public utilities; the development of public works projects and housing programs; relief for the unemployed; minimum wage standards; and the Social Security system. Some people bitterly complained that these policies conflicted with the values of capitalism and free enterprise and that they moved this country toward socialism. They were not wholly misguided: **Socialism** is an economic system in which the producers (workers) possess both political power and the means of producing and distributing goods and in which government provides for human welfare needs, including health care, education, economic security, and so on.

Nonetheless, New Deal social programs and post–World War II economic prosperity led to the growth of a broad middle class during the 1950s and 1960s. But since then, wage growth for full-time wage and salary workers has been stagnant, with average weekly earnings of production falling from $450 in 1967 to $424 in 1997. (Economic data in this introduction are based on the U.S. Census Bureau, Official Statistics, as reported in *Statistical Abstracts of the United States,* October 1998.) Since 1980, there has been a definite redistribution of wealth upwards, with no evidence of the wealth "trickling down" to the middle and lower classes. The share of income going to the middle one-fifth of Americans in 2010 shrank to its lowest level ever (Center on Budget and Policy Priorities, June 25, 2010).

It is important to distinguish between *income* and wealth. Income is what one earns, whereas *wealth,* or *net worth,* is the total value of what one has. Recently, there has been apparent growth in the median (middle) household income in the United States. The median household income had regained its 1989 level by 1997. But this came about because the median family in 1997 worked more hours, equivalent to about six full-time weeks per year. According to the U.S. Census Bureau, the percentage share of aggregate income received by the poorest 20 percent of families fell from 5.4 percent in 1970 to 4.2 percent in 1996. By way of contrast, that received by the richest 5 percent rose from 5.6 percent in 1970 to over 20 percent in 1996.

By another measure of prosperity, **national wealth**—all of America's cash, real estate, stocks, bonds, factories, art, personal property, and anything else of financial value—the wealthiest have fared even better. In 1976, the wealthiest 1 percent of America's families owned 19.2 percent of the total of our national wealth. By 1983, those at this 1 percent tip of our economy owned 34.3 percent of our wealth and, by 1998, this top 1 percent controlled about 38 percent of the nation's wealth and possessed more wealth than the bottom 90 percent.

Most Americans are more conscious of the problems and impediments caused by race, gender, and sexual orientation than we are of those based on socioeconomic class. Class in America is difficult to define because we are reluctant to talk about it and because the boundaries between classes are blurred. **Class** is related to relative wealth, but socioeconomic culture is also a component, as is relative access to power. Roughly, we tend to speak of the upper class, upper middle class, middle class, working class, poor, and underclass, but in the United States these categories are fluid and dependent on context. (In some other cultures, "class" is a much more permanent idea, regardless of one's personal wealth.)

Despite definitional difficulties, class is a reality in the United States, as are the related stereotypes, prejudices, and discrimination that provide the basis for our classism. Because of **classism,** wealthy and financially better off people are privileged and assigned high status, whereas poor and working-class people and their cultures are stigmatized and disadvantaged simply because of their relative wealth. It should come as no surprise to anyone that those at the top of the economic hierarchy benefit most from classist values and those at the bottom suffer the most from classism.

Race has a substantial impact on economic prosperity. More specifically, the median **net worth** of White households in 2000 was $81,700, but it was only $10,000 for Black households. Thus, the median net worth of White households was roughly eight times that of Black households in 2000.

The official federal **poverty line** is based on the cost of a "Thrifty Food Plan," which is not considered nutritionally adequate for long-term use, multiplied by three to account for nonfood expenses and adjusted for family size and for changes in the consumer price index. In 1996, 7 percent of Whites and 26 percent of Blacks and Hispanics fell below the poverty line. Further, the trend is disturbing: The overall 1996 poverty rate for White children was 15.5 percent but almost 40 percent for Black children and Hispanic children.

Our social stereotype of the "lazy, freeloading poor" notwithstanding, 3.5 million people who worked full time, year-round in 1993 were below the official poverty line; over 7 million were at 150 percent of the poverty line, an alternative measure of poverty, which is still inadequate to cover such essential expenses as child care. In the 1970s, a full-time, minimum-wage worker with two children lived above the poverty line; in 2008, the same family ended up with $11,960 a year—far below the 2008 poverty line of $17,600.

In addition, the **Federal Reserve Board,** which controls the money supply, interest rates, and inflation, sets policies that keep millions of people unemployed in order to control inflation. In 2012, 13.1 million people were unemployed, and millions more were involuntarily working parttime as temporary and part-time jobs were substituted for full-time positions. In 2011, Black unemployment was 16.7 percent, 8.5 percent for Whites.

Gender is as critical a factor in determining socioeconomic class as race is. Nearly two-thirds of poor adults are women, probably for several reasons. For one thing, women in 2007, even with similar education and employment experience, still earn 77 percent of what men do. Furthermore, although the official 1993 unemployment rate for women maintaining families was 7.7 percent for Whites and 13.7 percent for Blacks, the real jobless and underemployment rates are much higher. It is also worth noting that women's standard of living drops 33 percent after divorce, whereas men's rises 10 to 15 percent; more than 60 percent of the fathers pay no child support after five years. Additionally, the number of households headed by women has more than doubled since 1970: in 1992, women maintained 12 million families on their own.

Contrary to common knowledge, single-mother families, both Black and White, increased at a higher rate in the 1970s than in the 1980s or 1990s. Unfortunately, in 1996 men had a median income of over $26,000, whereas women earned almost half that ($13,500). The typical woman behind the rise in never-married mothers in the 1980s, according to the U.S. General Accounting Office, was not an unemployed teenage dropout but, rather, a working woman between the ages of twenty-five and forty-four who had completed high school. Also contrary to image, the proportion of Black children born to unmarried mothers—most of them not teenagers—has grown mainly because the birthrates for married Black women have fallen dramatically.

Poverty does disproportionately affect women of color. Blacks are 38 percent of those on welfare, a percentage that has been going down since 1969, when it was 45 percent. Even though disproportionately more people of color are poor, unemployed and underemployed, they have disproportionately less access to government income support programs, such as unemployment insurance, workers' compensation, and Social Security.

A number of misconceptions about welfare are accepted as truths by American society. In contrast to our assumptions, about 72 percent of families on welfare have only one or two children; families with four or more children are just 10 percent of the total, and that number keeps going down. Equally inaccurate is the stereotype that the welfare mother is a fifteen-year-old with a new baby. In reality, 7.6 percent of mothers receiving Temporary Assistance for Needy Families (TANF) are under twenty. In 2008, about 35.2 percent of families receiving TANF were White, 35 percent African American, 23.3 percent Latino, 2 percent Asian, and 1.3 percent Native American. Despite the "welfare-as-a-way-of-life" stereotype, the typical recipient is a short-term user of TANF, and five years is the limit, as mandated.

The economic realities have substantial adverse effects on our nation's children. According to the American Community Survey (2006), 18.5 percent of children live below the poverty line. According to the Children's Defense Fund, poor children are twice as likely as other children to die from birth defects; three times as likely to die from all causes; four times as likely to die from fires; and five times as likely to suffer from infectious diseases and parasites. It seems clear that children are the greatest victims of poverty. According to economist Edward Wolff, we should be concerned with this huge disparity for two reasons: First, it is unethical to have such inequality. Also, "the divisiveness that comes out of large disparities in incomes and wealth, is actually reflected in poor economic performances of a country." ("The Wealth Divide: The Growing Gap in the United States Between the Rich and the Rest," *The Multinational Monitor* 24, no. 5 (May 2003): 6.)

To most of us, classism tends to be less visible than racism or sexism. Moreover, we also believe that we live in a **meritocracy,** in which advancement is based on ability or achievement. Thus, we hold to the myth that, although people cannot determine their race or sex, individuals can control their economic well-being and are responsible for their economic success or failure. As a result, we tend to blame poor people for their poverty. The readings in Part VI show that such beliefs and stereotypes misrepresent reality.

Part VI opens with several analyses of the current economic conditions in our society. First, in Reading 72, billionaire Warren Buffett urges the United States to "stop coddling the super-rich" by giving them a lower tax rate than most of the middle class. In Reading 73, Holly Sklar describes the socioeconomic realities of the United States that contradict our national self-image, our ideals, and our proclaimed values. In Reading 74, Albert Hunt analyzes the reasons behind our growing prison population. In Reading 75, Rick Ungar focuses on the increasing number of small businesses offering health care to their employees because of Obamacare. In Reading 76, David Moberg asks why Americans tolerate such extreme economic disparities in income, and especially in wealth, that characterize the country today, and he reports on the negative effects this inequality has on our nation.

Many of our social assumptions and practices contribute to class distinctions and classism and reinforce discrimination, which can be unconscious and unintentional. Robert Cherry (Reading 77), for example, examines how discrimination is **institutionalized**—that is, how the various parts of our social system work together to create a self-perpetuating cycle of discrimination and economic disadvantage. For instance, people with lower educational levels have limited access to good jobs with good pay, whereas affordable housing is available only in neighborhoods with poor schools, which means the next generation is doomed to lower educational levels and on and on.

Other economic practices intentionally discriminate against poor people. For example, "redlining," decisions by banks and insurance companies not to invest in certain areas—most often, older, inner-city, and minority neighborhoods—contributes to their increasing impoverishment and deterioration. In Reading 78 Leslie Brown reports on the judicial ruling against National Mutual Insurance Company for this practice; the company had refused to issue policies to Black individuals or in Black communities.

Then Hunter O'Hara's reading titled "The Spectre of Regionalism" (Reading 79) alerts us to the seldom discussed bigotry so often found among us—that of believing one's "region of origin is a primary determinant of the quality of one's standard of living" and inherent superiority. Renu Nahata (Reading 80) focuses on how the media inaccurately portray welfare recipients; she charges the media with the responsibility for perpetuating popular acceptance of these distorted images.

Reading 81 examines the growing problem of homelessness in this country. Doug A. Timmer, D. Stanley Eitzen, and Kathryn D. Talley begin their analysis of this problem with an overview of the general problems caused by poverty and then focus on homeless people themselves, challenging the belief that people are homeless as a result of personal disabilities. They conclude that lack of low-cost housing is a central factor in the increased rate of homelessness, as is the low level of public assistance. Part VI closes with an article on environmental justice: Aaron Frasier describes one family's experiences in "Orsted Speaks on Environmental Racism," which highlights the shocking story of a young trainer and body builder who discovers she and several members of her family have cancer because no one told the Black families in the area that a toxic chemical spill had compromised their safety. Only White families received this information.

These readings give us an unflattering image of ourselves as a society, making these class issues difficult for us to digest and making it even harder for us to do something about them. It is tempting to deny the structural and individual elements of classism and to hold onto the myths about poverty and the rewards of hard work and discipline. However, as citizens of the world in the twenty-first century, we must not comfort ourselves with a dismissive rationalization, such as "for ye have the poor always with you." Instead, we as a society must provide for the least privileged and most oppressed among us if the American community that we all value is to remain strong and a true world leader.

72

Warren Buffett Calls for Higher Taxes for US Super-Rich

GRAEME WEARDEN

Warren Buffett, at the 2010 meeting of his Berkshire Hathaway investment group, says that billionaires like himself have been "coddled" by Congress.

In the process of accumulating one of the greatest fortunes the world has ever seen, Warren Buffett stands apart from the average squillionaire. Not for him the clichés of lavish mansions and superyachts, preferring instead his modest home in Omaha, Nebraska and nights in with burger and cherry cola.

Now Buffett has added to his list of atypical pronouncements by saying that America's super-rich should pay more tax if the country's debt problems are ever to be solved.

Writing in the New York Times on Monday, Buffett argued that the richest members of US society are indulged with an unfairly generous tax regime and are not making a fair contribution to repairing the country's finances.

"While the poor and middle class fight for us in Afghanistan, and while most Americans struggle to make ends meet, we mega-rich continue to get our extraordinary tax breaks," wrote Buffett, whose personal fortune was estimated at $50bn (£30bn) by Forbes this year, making

him the third richest person in the world behind Carlos Slim and Bill Gates.

"These and other blessings are showered upon us by legislators in Washington who feel compelled to protect us, much as if we were spotted owls or some other endangered species. It's nice to have friends in high places," the 80-year old investor added.

Buffett, known as the Sage of Omaha, built his fortune on a no-frills investment strategy and was a fierce critic of the exotic financial investments that brought the banking system to its knees in 2008, dubbing them instruments of financial mass destruction.

A long-time critic of the US tax system, he has calculated that he handed over 17.4% of his income as tax last year—a lower proportion than any of the 20 other people who work in his office.

Under the debt ceiling deal agreed in Washington, a "super committee" of 12 congressmen and senators must find $1.5tn worth of savings and cuts to help cut America's national debt. Tax rises are hugely unpopular with elements within the Republican party, with the Tea Party movement adamant that America should balance its books by cutting public spending.

Buffett argues that this super-committee should raise the tax rate paid by those earning more than $1m a year, including earnings from capital gains which are currently taxed at a lower rate than ordinary income. Those raking in upward of $10m a year could then pay even more.

The package of tax cuts brought in by President George W. Bush are set to expire at the end of 2012, although they could be extended. Many of the leading Republicans who hope to challenge Barack Obama at the next presidential election have argued for lower taxation to stimulate the US economy.

On Saturday Rick Perry, the governor of Texas, argued that it was an "injustice" that almost a half of all Americans currently pay no federal income tax.

"Spreading the wealth punishes success while setting America on a course for greater dependency on government," Perry argued as he announced his bid for the 2012 Republican nomination.

Buffett argues that the US policymakers should be looking at the other end of the spectrum.

As he put it: "My friends and I have been coddled long enough by a billionaire-friendly Congress. It's time for our government to get serious about shared sacrifice."   [2011]

Understanding the Reading

1. In the context of this article, how does Warren Buffett disagree with Congress about how to solve our nation's debt crisis?
2. Why does the middle class pay a higher percentage of their income than the mega-wealthy in the United States?
3. With which statement do you agree: "Spreading the wealth punishes success",(i.e. the very wealthy should not pay more taxes); or "It is time for shared sacrifice", (i.e. the very wealthy have an obligation to pay higher taxes)?

Suggestions for Responding

1. Choose four European nations, (perhaps Germany, France, Denmark, and Spain)and compare what they get for their taxes, as opposed to what U.S. citizens get for their taxes.
2. Have a classroom discussion about where tax money should be spent to ensure a flourishing economy. ◆

73

Imagine a Country

HOLLY SKLAR

Stats?

Imagine a country where one out of four children is born into poverty, and wealth is being redistributed upward. Since the 1970s, the richest 1 percent of households has nearly doubled its share of the nation's wealth. The top 1 percent has more wealth than the bottom 90 percent of households combined.

It's not Jamaica.

Imagine a country whose national intelligence agency says, "Since 1975, practically all the gains in household income have gone to the top 20% of households."

Imagine a country where more and more jobs are keeping people in poverty instead of out of poverty.

Imagine a country where health care aides can't afford health insurance. Where food industry workers may depend on food banks to help feed their children. Where childcare teachers don't make enough to save for their own children's education.

Imagine a country where economic inequality is going back to the future circa the 1920s. In 1979, the bottom third of taxpayers had more than twice as much combined income as the top tenth of the richest 1 percent. In 2003, it was the other way around: The top tenth of the richest 1 percent of taxpayers had more income than the bottom third of taxpayers combined.

Imagine a country giving tax breaks to millionaires while cutting college tuition aid for students from low-income families. Imagine a country giving tax breaks to millionaires while cutting public health and safety, education, housing, economic development, environmental protection and other needed services.

It's not the Philippines.

Imagine a country with poverty rates higher than they were in the 1970s. Imagine a country that sets the official poverty line well below the actual cost of minimally adequate housing, health care, food and other necessities. On average, households need more than double the official poverty threshold to meet basic needs.

Imagine a country where the economy is increasingly not working for working people.

Imagine a country where productivity went up, but workers' wages went down. In the words of the national labor department, "As the productivity of workers increases, one would expect worker compensation [wages and benefits] to experience similar gains." That's not what happened. Between 1968 and 2005, worker productivity rose 111 percent, but the average hourly wage fell 5 percent, adjusting for inflation, and the minimum wage fell 43 percent.

Imagine a country where it takes nearly two minimum wage workers to make what one worker made four decades ago.

Imagine a country where the minimum wage has become a poverty wage instead of an anti-poverty wage. The minimum wage has lagged so far behind necessities that keeping a roof overhead is a constant struggle and family health coverage costs more than the entire annual income of a full-time worker at minimum wage.

Imagine a country where homelessness is rising for workers and their families, while federal housing assistance for low-income families is slashed. The largest federal housing support program is the mortgage interest deduction, which disproportionately benefits higher-income families.

It's not Mexico.

Imagine a country where some of the worst CEOs make millions more in a year than the best CEOs of earlier generations made in their lifetimes. In 1980, CEOs of major corporations made an average 45 times the pay of average full-time workers. In 1991, when CEOs made 140 times as much as workers, a prominent pay expert said the CEO "is paid so much more than ordinary workers that he hasn't got the slightest clue as to how the rest of the country lives." In 2003, a leading business magazine put a pig in a pinstriped suit on the cover and headlined its CEO pay roundup, "Have they no shame? Their performance stank last year, yet most CEOs got paid more than ever." In 2005, CEOs made even more—352 times the pay of average workers.

A leading business magazine observed, "People who worked hard to make their companies competitive are angry at the way the profits are distributed. They think it is unfair, and they are right."

It's not England.

Imagine a country where wages are falling despite greatly increased education. Since 1973, the share of workers without a high school degree has plummeted and the percentage with at least four years of college has more than doubled. But the 2005 average hourly wage was 11 percent below 1973, adjusted for inflation.

Imagine a country where households headed by persons under age 35 had lower median net worth (assets minus debt) in 2004 than in 1995, adjusted for inflation.

Imagine a country where more and more two-paycheck households are struggling to afford a home, college, health care and retirement. Middle-class households are a medical crisis, outsourced job or busted pension away from bankruptcy.

Imagine a country becoming a nation of Scrooge-Marts and outsourcers—with an increasingly low-wage workforce instead of a growing middle class.

Imagine a country whose corporate and government policy makers are running the economy into the ground. The nation is in record-breaking debt to other countries. It has a record trade deficit, hollowed-out manufacturing base,

and deteriorating research and development. The infrastructure built by earlier generations of taxpayers has eroded greatly, undermining the economy as well as health and safety.

Imagine a country where more workers are going back to the future of sweatshops and day labor. Corporations are replacing full-time jobs with disposable "contingent workers." They include temporary employees, on-call workers, contract workers and "leased" employees—some of them fired and then "rented" back at a large discount by the same company—and involuntary part-time workers, who want permanent full-time work.

It's not South Korea.

How do workers increasingly forced to migrate from job to job, at low and variable wage rates, without health insurance or paid vacation, much less a pension, care for themselves and their families, pay for college, save for retirement, plan a future, build strong communities?

Imagine a country where polls show a large percentage of workers would join a union if they could, but employers routinely violate workers' rights to organize. A leading business magazine observes, "While labor unions were largely responsible for creating the broad middle class after World War II . . . that's not the case today. Most . . . employers fiercely resist unionization, which, along with other factors, has helped slash union membership to just 13% of the workforce, vs. a midcentury peak of more than 35%." Full-time workers who were union members had median 2005 weekly earnings of $801 compared with just $622 for workers not represented by unions.

Imagine a country where the concerns of working people are dismissed as "special interests" and the profit-interests of globetrotting corporations substitute for the "national interest."

Imagine a country negotiating "free trade" agreements that help corporations trade freely on cheap labor at home and abroad.

One ad financed by the country's agency for international development showed a Salvadoran woman in front of a sewing machine. It told corporations, "You can hire her for 33 cents an hour. Rosa is more than just colorful. She and her co-workers are known for their industriousness, reliability and quick learning. They make El Salvador one of the best buys." The country that financed the ad intervened militarily to make sure El Salvador would stay a "best buy" for corporations.

It's not Canada.

Imagine a country where nearly two-thirds of women with children under age 6 and more than three-fourths of women with children ages 6–17 are in the labor force, but affordable childcare and after-school programs are scarce. Apparently, kids are expected to have three parents: Two parents with jobs to pay the bills, and another parent to be home in mid-afternoon when school lets out—as well as all summer.

Imagine a country where women working full time earn 76 cents for every dollar men earn. Women don't pay 76 cents on a man's dollar for their education, rent, food or childcare. The gender wage gap has closed just 12 cents since 1955, when women earned 64 cents for every dollar earned by men. There's still another 24 cents to go.

The average woman high school graduate who works full time from ages 25 to 65 will earn about $450,000 less than the average male high school graduate. The gap widens to $900,000 for full-time workers with bachelor's degrees. "Men with professional degrees may expect to earn almost $2 million more than their female counterparts over their work-life," says a government report.

Imagine a country where childcare workers, mostly women, typically make about as much as parking lot attendants and much less than animal trainers. Out of 801 occupations surveyed by the labor department, only 18 have lower median wages than childcare workers.

Imagine a country where more than 98 percent of the CEOs at the largest 500 companies are men, as are 95 percent of the top-earning corporate officers. Never mind that companies with a higher share of women in their senior management teams financially outperform companies with lower representation.

Imagine a country where discrimination against women is pervasive from the bottom to the top of the pay scale, and it's not because women are on the "mommy track." In the words of a leading business magazine, "At the same level of management, the typical woman's pay is lower than her male colleague's—even when she has the exact same qualifications, works just as many years, relocates just as often, provides the main financial support for her family, takes no time off for personal reasons, and wins the same number of promotions to comparable jobs."

Imagine a country where instead of rooting out discrimination, many policy makers are busily blaming women for their disproportionate poverty. If women earned as much as similarly qualified men, poverty in single-mother households would be cut in half.

It's not Japan.

Imagine a country where violence against women is so epidemic it is their leading cause of injury. Nearly a third of all murdered women are killed by husbands, boyfriends and ex-partners. Researchers say, "Men commonly kill their female partners in response to the woman's attempt to leave an abusive relationship."

The country has no equal rights amendment.

It's not Pakistan.

Imagine a country whose school system is rigged in favor of the already privileged, with lower caste children tracked by race and income into the most deficient and demoralizing schools and classrooms. Public school budgets are heavily determined by private property taxes, allowing higher income districts to spend more than poorer ones. In the state with the largest gap, state and local spending per pupil in districts with the lowest child poverty rates was $2,280 greater in 2003 than districts with the highest child poverty rates. The difference amounts to about $912,000 for a typical elementary school of 400 students—money that could be used for needed teachers, books, computers and other resources.

In rich districts, kids take well-stocked libraries, laboratories and state-of-the-art computers for granted. In poor districts, they are rationing out-of-date textbooks and toilet paper. Rich schools often look like country clubs—with manicured sports fields and swimming pools. In poor districts, schools often look more like jails—with concrete grounds and grated windows. College prep courses, art, music, physical education, field trips and foreign languages are often considered necessities for the affluent, luxuries for the poor.

It's not India.

Imagine a country where the infant death rate for children in the nation's capital is higher than for children in Kerala, India.

Imagine a country whose constitution once counted black slaves as worth three-fifths of whites. Today, black per capita income is about three-fifths of whites.

Imagine a country where racial disparities take their toll from birth to death. The black infant mortality rate is more than double that of whites. Black life expectancy is nearly six years less.

The official black unemployment rate is about twice that of whites and the black poverty rate is almost triple that of whites.

Imagine a country where the typical white household has about six times the net worth—including home equity—as the typical household of color. In 2004, median household net worth was $140,700 for white households and just $24,800 for households of color.

Imagine a country where the government subsidized decades of segregated suburbanization for whites while the inner cities left to people of color were treated as outsider cities—separate, unequal and disposable. Recent studies have documented continuing discrimination in education, employment, banking, insurance, housing, health care and criminal justice.

It's not South Africa.

Imagine a country that doesn't count you as unemployed just because you're unemployed. To be counted in the official unemployment rate you must be actively searching for work. The government doesn't count people as "unemployed" if they are so discouraged from long and fruitless job searches they have given up looking. It doesn't count as "unemployed" those who couldn't look for work in the past month because they had no childcare, for example. If you need a full-time job, but you're working part-time—whether 1 hour or 34 hours weekly—because that's all you can find, you're counted as employed.

A leading business magazine observed, "Increasingly the labor market is filled with surplus workers who are not being counted as unemployed."

Imagine a country where there is a shortage of jobs, not a shortage of work. Millions of people need work and urgent work needs people—from staffing after-school programs and community centers, to creating affordable housing, to strengthening levees, repairing bridges and building mass transit, to cleaning up pollution and converting to renewable energy.

It's not Germany.

Imagine a country with full prisons instead of full employment. The jail and prison population has more than quadrupled since 1980. The nation is Number One in the world when it comes to locking up its own people. In 1985, 1 in every 320 residents was incarcerated. By mid-year 2005, the figure had increased to 1 in every 136.

Imagine a country where prison is a growth industry. The government spends more than $25,000 a year to keep someone in prison, while cutting cost-effective programs of education, employment, community development, and mental illness and addiction treatment to keep them out. In the words of a national center on institutions and alternatives, this nation has "replaced the social safety net with a dragnet."

Imagine a country that has been criticized by human rights organizations for expanding rather than abolishing use of the death penalty—despite documented racial bias and growing evidence of innocents being sentenced to death.

It's not China.

Imagine a country that imprisons black people at a rate much higher than South Africa did under apartheid. One out of eight black men ages 25-29 are incarcerated in prisons or jails compared to one out of 59 white men in the same age group. The nation's bureau of justice statistics reports that incarceration rates for black men of all ages were five to seven times greater than those for white men in the same age groups. Incarceration rates for black women are generally four times higher than for white women.

Imagine a country where a national sentencing project reported in 2004, "Black women born today are five times more likely to go to prison in their lifetimes than black women born in 1974."

Meanwhile, nearly one out ten black men and women are unemployed according to the official count. This includes nearly one out of three black men and women ages 16–19 and one out of six, ages 20–24. Remember, to be counted in the official unemployment rate you must be actively looking for a job and not finding one. "Surplus" workers are increasingly being criminalized.

Imagine a country whose justice department observed, "The fact that the legal order not only countenanced but sustained slavery, segregation, and discrimination for most of our Nation's history—and the fact that the police were bound to uphold that order—set a pattern for police behavior and attitudes toward minority communities that has persisted until the present day." A newspaper headline reads, "GUILTY . . . of being black: Black men say success doesn't save them from being suspected, harassed and detained." Racial profiling and "driving while black" are well-known terms.

Imagine a country where from first arrest to third strikes resulting in lifetime sentences—often for nonviolent petty crimes—blacks and

Latinos are arrested and imprisoned in massively disproportionate numbers.

Imagine a country waging a racially biased "War on Drugs." Nearly three out of four drug users are white, according to government data, but more than three out of four state prisoners convicted of drug offenses are black and Latino.

A study in a prominent medical journal found that drug and alcohol rates were slightly higher for pregnant white women than pregnant black women, but black women were about ten times more likely to be reported to authorities by private doctors and public health clinics—under a mandatory reporting law. Poor women were also more likely to be reported.

It is said that truth is the first casualty in war, and the "War on Drugs" is no exception. Contrary to stereotype, "The typical cocaine user is white, male, a high school graduate employed full time and living in a small metropolitan area or suburb," says the nation's former drug czar. A leading newspaper reports that law officers and judges say, "Although it is clear that whites sell most of the nation's cocaine and account for 80% of its consumers, it is blacks and other minorities who continue to fill up [the] courtrooms and jails, largely because, in a political climate that demands that something be done, they are the easiest people to arrest." They are the easiest to scapegoat.

It's not Australia.

Imagine a country that ranks first in the world in wealth and military power, and 36th in child mortality (under age five), tied with Poland and Chile and well behind countries such as South Korea and Singapore. If the government were a parent, it would be guilty of child abuse. Thousands of children die preventable deaths.

Imagine a country where health care is managed for healthy profit. In many countries health care is a right. But this nation has health care for some instead of health care for all. Nearly one out of five people under age 65 has no health insurance, public or private.

Health care is literally a matter of life and death. Lack of health insurance typically means lack of preventive health care and delayed or second-rate treatment. The uninsured are at much higher risk for chronic disease and disability, and have a 25 percent greater chance of dying (adjusting for physical, economic and behavioral factors). Uninsured women with breast cancer have a 30 percent to 50 percent higher risk of dying than insured women, for example. Uninsured car crash victims receive less care in the hospital and have a 37 percent higher mortality rate than privately insured patients.

Imagine a country where many descendants of its first inhabitants live on reservations strip-mined of natural resources and have a higher proportion of people in poverty than any other ethnic group.

Imagine a country where five centuries of plunder and lies are masked in expressions like "Indian giver." Where the military still dubs enemy territory, "Indian country."

Imagine a country that has less than 5 percent of the world's population and less than 3 percent of world oil reserves, but consumes 25 percent of the world's oil. It is the number one contributor to global warming. While automakers from other countries raced to make more fuel efficient vehicles, this nation churned out bigger gas guzzlers. It has obstructed international action to protect the environment and avoid catastrophic climate change.

It's not Brazil.

Imagine a country whose senate and house of representatives are not representative of the nation. They are overwhelmingly white and male, and increasingly millionaire. One out of three house members are millionaires, according to financial disclosure records that don't even include the value of their primary residences. One out of two senators are millionaires, but no senators are women of color.

Imagine a country that lags behind 67 other countries when it comes to the percentage of women in national legislative bodies. Just 14 percent of its senate and 15 percent of its house of representatives were women in 2006.

If the 100-member senate reflected the population it would have 51 women and 49 men, including 67 whites, 14 Latinos, 13 blacks, 5 Asian and Pacific Islanders and 1 Native American. Instead, it has 14 women and 86 men, including 94 whites, 3 Latinos, 1 black, 2 Asian and Pacific Islanders and no Native Americans.

Imagine a country where the cycle of unequal opportunity is intensifying. Its beneficiaries often slander those most systematically undervalued, underpaid, underemployed, underfinanced, underinsured, underrated and otherwise underserved and undermined—as undeserving, underclass, impoverished in moral and social values and lacking the proper work ethic. The oft-heard stereotype of deadbeat poor people masks the growing reality of dead-end jobs and disposable workers.

Imagine a country where white men who are "falling down" the economic ladder are being encouraged to believe they are falling because women and people of color are climbing over them to the top or dragging them down from the bottom. That way, they will blame women and people of color rather than corporate and government policy. They will buy the myth of "reverse discrimination." Never mind that white males hold most senior management positions and continuing unreversed discrimination is well documented.

Imagine a country that spends about as much on the military as the rest of the world combined. It also leads the world in arms exports. Companies with close ties to the government are rewarded for war profiteering with new contracts.

Imagine a country whose leaders misuse a fight against terrorism as camouflage for trampling the bill of rights and undermining democracy. The most fundamental civil liberties, including the right not to be thrown into prison indefinitely on the secret word of government officials, are being tossed aside. An attorney general attacked critics of administration policy with McCarthyite words: "To those who scare peace-loving people with phantoms of lost liberty, my message is this: Your tactics only aid terrorists for they erode our national unity. . .They give ammunition to [our] enemies."

In this same country, a five-star general who became president had warned in 1961, "In the councils of government, we must guard against the acquisition of unwarranted influence, whether sought or unsought, by the military-industrial complex . . . We must never let the weight of this combination endanger our liberties or democratic processes. We should take nothing for granted. Only an alert and knowledgeable citizenry can compel the proper meshing of the huge industrial and military machinery of defense with our peaceful methods and goals, so that security and liberty may prosper together."

Imagine a country whose president "has quietly claimed the authority to disobey more than 750 laws enacted since he took office, asserting that he has the power to set aside any statute passed by Congress when it conflicts with his interpretation of the Constitution." A newspaper investigation reveals, "Among the laws [he] said he can ignore are military rules and regulations,

affirmative-action provisions, requirements that Congress be told about immigration services problems, 'whistle-blower' protections for nuclear regulatory officials, and safeguards against political interference in federally funded research."

It's not Russia.

It's the United States.

The words of Martin Luther King Jr. call down to us today.

A true revolution of values will soon cause us to question the fairness and justice of many of our past and present policies. We are called to play the Good Samaritan on life's roadside; but . . . one day the whole Jericho road must be transformed so that men and women will not be beaten and robbed as they make their journey through life. . . .

A true revolution of values will soon look uneasily on the glaring contrast of poverty and wealth. . . .There is nothing but a lack of social vision to prevent us from paying an adequate wage to every American citizen whether he be a hospital worker, laundry worker, maid or day laborer. [2006]

Understanding the Reading

1. Why, after each description, does Sklar choose to name a country that she is not describing?
2. Reread the selection with the knowledge that Sklar is describing the United States and reflect on what is unacceptable in a country with our ideals and values.

Suggestion for Responding

1. Write a personal essay in which you consider the impact these issues have had on you directly, either positively or negatively. ✦

74

Bulging Jails Are Other American Exception

ALBERT R. HUNT

One area where the U.S. indisputably leads the world is incarceration.

There are 2.3 million people behind bars, almost one in every 100 Americans. The federal prison population has more than doubled over the past 15 years, and one in nine black children has a parent in jail. Proportionally, the U.S. has four times as many prisoners as Israel, six times more than Canada or China, eight times more than Germany and 13 times more than Japan.

With just a little more than 4 percent of the world's population, the U.S. accounts for a quarter of the planet's prisoners, and has more inmates than the leading 35 European countries combined. Almost all the other nations with high per capita prison rates are in the developing world.

There's also a national election in America soon. This issue isn't on the agenda. It's almost never come up with Republican presidential candidates; one of the few exceptions was a debate in September when the audience cheered the governor of Texas, Rick Perry, because his state has carried out a record number of executions.

Barack Obama, the first black president, rarely mentions this question or how it disproportionately affects minorities. More than 60 percent of America's prisoners are black or Hispanic, though these groups comprise less than 30 percent of the population.

"We've had a race to incarcerate that has been driven by politics, racially coded, get-tough appeals," says Michelle Alexander, a law professor at Ohio State University who wrote "The New Jim Crow: Mass Incarceration in the Age of Colorblindness."

Escalating Costs

The escalating cost of the criminal-justice system is an important factor in the fiscal challenges around the country. Nowhere is that more evident than in California, which is struggling to obey a court order requiring it to reduce its overcrowded prisons by 40,000 inmates.

Today there are 140,000 convicts in California's state prisons, who cost about $50,000 each per year. The state spends more on prisons than it does on higher education.

Yet the prisons are so crowded—as many as 54 inmates have to share one toilet—that Conrad Murray, the doctor convicted in the death of the pop star Michael Jackson, may be able to avoid most prison time.

California isn't unique. In Raleigh County, West Virginia, the county commission has worried that the cost of housing inmates at its Southern Regional Jail may imperil basic services, including education. That problem is exacerbated as the state keeps more prisoners longer at such regional facilities to alleviate its overcrowding problems.

The prison explosion hasn't been driven by an increase in crime. In fact, the crime rate, notably for violent offenses, is dropping across the U.S., a phenomenon that began about 20 years ago.

The latest FBI figures show that murder, rape and robberies have fallen to an almost half-century low; to be sure, they remain higher than in other major industrialized countries.

There are many theories for this decline. The most accepted is that community police work in major metropolitan areas has improved markedly, focusing on potential high-crime areas. There are countless other hypotheses, even ranging to controversial claims that more accessible abortion has reduced a number of unwanted children who would be more likely to commit crimes.

However, one other likely explanation is that more than a few would-be criminals are locked up. Scholars such as James Q. Wilson have noted that the longer prison terms that are being handed down may matter more than the conviction rates.

This comes at a clear cost. For those who do ultimately get out, being an ex-con means about a 40 percent decrease in annual earnings. Moreover, research suggests that kids from homes where a father is in jail do considerably less well in life and are more prone to becoming criminals themselves.

"Without Fathers"

"People ask why so many black kids are growing up without fathers," says Alexander. "A big part of the answer is mass incarceration."

It seems clear that the U.S. penal system discriminates against minorities. Some of this is socioeconomic, as poorer people, disproportionately blacks and Hispanics, may commit more crimes.

Much of the inmate explosion and racial disparities however, grow out of the way America treats illegal drugs. It began several decades ago with harsher penalties for crimes involving crack cocaine, which was more widely used by blacks, than powder cocaine, which was more likely to involve whites. A larger issue is how the American criminal justice system differentiates in its treatment of drug sellers—who get the book thrown at them—versus drug users, who, at most, get a slap on the wrist.

A hypothetical example: A black kid is arrested for selling cocaine to the members of a fraternity at an elite university. The seller gets sent away for 25 years. The fraternity is put on probation for a semester by the university and nothing else.

In all likelihood, the convicted seller is quickly replaced and few of the fraternity kids change their drug-use habits. The lesson: neither the supply nor the demand has changed, and the prison population grows.

Given their budgetary difficulties, about half the states are actually reducing their prison populations. Smart selective policies are cost-effective. Many criminologists and sociologists believe the proclivity to commit crimes diminishes with age; the recidivism rate for convicts over 30 is relatively low, and most analysis suggests that parole and probation are far cheaper for taxpayers than incarceration.

Nevertheless, the politics of the crime issue cuts against any rational approach. Even if recidivism rates are low, it's the failures that attract attention. In 1988, the Democratic presidential nominee, Michael Dukakis, was savaged when it was revealed that one convict furloughed under his watch, the now infamous Willie Horton, committed a rape while at large. Four years ago, the former governor of Arkansas, Mike Huckabee, a Republican, was hurt in his bid for his party's nomination by reports of crimes committed by felons he had paroled.

"One case where a parolee does something very wrong is sensationalized," Alexander says, "and many, many others are kept behind bars for a long time."   [2011]

Understanding the Reading

1. Why does America have the highest prison population in the world proportionally?
2. If the violent crime rate is dropping in the United States, then why are the prisons bulging?

3. How will California solve its budgetary problems related to its prison system?

Suggestion for Responding

1. Have a classroom discussion on the fact that the United States spends more money on prisons than on education. ✦

75

More Small Businesses Offering Health Care to Employees Thanks to Obamacare

RICK UNGAR

The first statistics are coming in and, to the surprise of a great many, Obamacare might just be working to bring health care to working Americans precisely as promised.

The major health insurance companies around the country are reporting a significant increase in small businesses offering health care benefits to their employees.

Why?

Because the tax cut created in the new health care reform law providing small businesses with an incentive to give health benefits to employees *is working*.

"We certainly did not expect to see this in this economy," said Gary Claxton, who oversees an annual survey of employer health plans for the nonprofit Kaiser Family Foundation. "It's surprising."

How significant is the impact? While we won't have full national numbers until small businesses file their 2010 tax returns this April, the anecdotal evidence is as meaningful as it is unexpected.

United Health Group, Inc., the nation's largest health insurer, added 75,000 new customers working in businesses with fewer than 50 employees.

Coventry Health Care, Inc., a large provider of health insurance to small businesses, added 115,000 new workers in 2010 representing an 8% jump.

Blue Cross Blue Shield of Kansas City, the largest health insurer in the Kansas City, Mo. area, reports an astounding 58% increase in the number of small businesses purchasing coverage in their area since April, 2010—one month after the health care reform legislation became law.

"*One of the biggest problems in the small-group market is affordability,*" said Ron Rowe, who oversees small-group sales for the Kansas City operation for Blue Cross Blue Shield. "*We looked at the tax credit and said, 'this is perfect.'*"

Rowe went on to say that 38% of the businesses it is signing up *had not offered health benefits before*.

Whatever your particular ideology, there is simply no denying that these statistics are incredibly heartening. However, for those of you who cannot get past your opposition, even for a moment of universal good news, let's break it down.

The primary, most enduring complaint of the opponents of the ACA has been that the law is deathly bad for small business.

Apparently, small businesses, and their employees, do not agree.

The next argument has been that the PPACA is a job killer.

If these small businesses found the new law to be so onerous, why have so many of them *voluntarily* taken advantage of the benefits provided in the law to give their employees these benefits? They were not mandated to do so. And to the extent that the coming mandate obligations might figure into their thinking, would you not imagine they would wait until 2014 to make a move as the rules do not go into effect until that time?

Of course, there is the nagging banter as to how Obamacare is leading us down the road to socialism.

Let it go, folks.

Private market insurance companies are experiencing significant growth because of a tax break provided by the PPACA. I may have missed the day this was discussed in economics class, but I'm pretty sure this is not a socialistic result of federal legislation.

When data like this appears, we have the opportunity to really find out who is talking smack for political benefit and who actually cares about getting affordable and available health care to America's workers. Certainly, there will be elements of the new law that will not work out exactly as planned. That's simply reality when it comes to any new piece of landmark legislation. But if you cannot celebrate what appears to be an important early success, you really should give some thought as to where your true interests and intents lie.

If you're all about beating up on President Obama, you can conveniently forget this bit of data as if it never really happened. However, if your interest is to make health care available to more Americans, this should be a happy day for you—no matter what your ideological beliefs.

Understanding the Reading

1. Why are more small businesses offering health care benefits to their employees under Obamacare?
2. What are some reasons anyone would be against an incentive for small businesses?

Suggestion for Responding

1. Have a class discussion on health care benefits for all in the United States after researching the systems of other countries such as England and Taiwan. ◆

76

The Great Divide

DAVID MOBERG

It's time for this year's Dubious Distinction Award in economics, and once again the United States is the easy winner: It has far and away the greatest inequality in both wealth and income of all major industrialized countries, according to two recent studies. And it is growing more unequal at a faster rate than virtually everyone else, as well.

Such an achievement flies in the face of the image of the United States as an egalitarian country populated by one big happy middle class. Early in this century, extremes of wealth and poverty were far more pronounced in northern European countries than in the United States. Now, inequality in the United States is so extreme that New York University professor Edward N. Wolff argues it's far outside the mainstream of the industrialized world.

But does it really matter? Apologists for the status quo argue that such inequality is necessary to generate investment and reward risk-taking, thereby creating a prosperous economy. Besides, they say, Americans aren't bothered by the presence of an uprecedented number of millionaires in their midst. Certainly U.S. citizens are far less likely than most Europeans to favor government action to equalize incomes.

Today, many liberals have simply given up on the fight for income equality, while conservatives actively promote policies that will further concentrate both wealth and income in the hands of the upper class.

But it is wrong to celebrate or even ignore inequality. It's not just a question of fairness. As much as congressional Republicans may argue otherwise, inequality is bad for society and damaging to national economic performance.

In *Top Heavy,* a new study for The Twentieth Century Fund, Wolff reports that in 1989 the top 1 percent of U.S. households controlled 39 percent of the nation's "marketable wealth" (that is, real estate, securities and so on) and 48 percent of the financial wealth. If social security and pensions are included, the share of the top 1 percent declines, but the trend remains the same.

In many ways differences in wealth are more important than differences in income. As economists define it, "wealth" includes income-generating property, such as stocks and bonds, as well as personal assets, such as homes and cars. Income, by contrast, is the money received from wages, property, pensions or government programs. Wealth—especially in stocks, bonds and business shares—is crucial because it provides both economic and political power and family financial security.

Essentially, the study shows that the rich were able to capture almost all the new wealth and much of the income generated in the '80s. From 1983 to 1989, the richest 1 percent obtained 62 percent of the increase in marketable wealth.

During the same period, the bottom four-fifths of all American households captured only 1 percent of the nation's increase in wealth—and so its share of the wealth dropped by one-fifth. Looking only at financial wealth, the bottom four-fifths actually *lost* 3 percent, while the top 1 percent captured 66 percent of the increase.

In a new international comparative study on income inequality, economist Timothy Smeeding of Syracuse University reports that "America has the most inequality of any modern nation we've looked at." From 1983 to 1989, according to Wolff, the top 1 percent garnered 37 percent of the gains in real income, while the bottom 80 percent got only 24 percent. Only in Britain has the rise of inequality been greater, and there only slightly more. In the United States, Smeeding says, not only has the gap between the highest and lowest earners been greater than in any other industrial country, but welfare state policies that redistribute income have also been weakest. As a result, America's poorest are in absolute terms poorer than people in a comparable position in most European countries.

There's a link between the good fortune of the rich and the misfortune of the rest. "The rich have gotten richer because the middle class and poor have gotten poorer," Wolff explains. "Keeping wages low has caused property income and stock prices to increase, which has shown up in increased wealth and income of the rich." This was intensified in the takeover and leveraged buy-out craze, which enriched a handful of speculators while driving down wages of workers in debt-laden companies. Similarly, the boom in the stock market over the last decade and a half has served to further enrich the already rich, who tend to put their money in stocks. In contrast, the major investments of middle-class families are their homes—which have appreciated less in value than stock have.

Top Heavy relies on figures from the years before 1990. According to Wolff, inequality has increased even more rapidly since then. Since 1989, middle-class family incomes have declined in real terms. And ordinary Americans can no longer cope with the earnings squeeze by sending another family member off to work, because so many families already rely on two wage earners. Private pensions are less common, and Social Security is more insecure than ever. Republican policies, from tax breaks for the rich to cutbacks in welfare or middle-class student loan programs, will only make things worse.

What does the United States get in return for this inequality, which supposedly creates savings and rewards entrepreneurs? There is no more social mobility or economic growth in the United States than in other industrial countries. And our lower unemployment rate comes at a high price for workers: Nearly one-fourth of the workforce here now earns less in real terms than the 1968 minimum wage.

And there is a growing body of evidence that inequality, rather than promoting economic growth, actually hurts the economy. For both industrialized and developing countries, economists have found that where inequality is greatest, economic growth is slowest. For example, a recent study of 41 countries found that the countries that performed the best from 1960 to 1985 had the strongest educational systems and the lowest levels of inequality of income and wealth. A British study of industrialized countries from 1979 to 1990 similarly showed that the strongest performers typically had the most egalitarian distribution of income.

Economists are unsure why inequality has this negative effect, but University of Massachusetts–Boston professor Arthur MacEwan suggests four possible reasons. First, he argues, high inequality leads to conflict and social disorder, which is bad for business. Second, the relatively high wages in countries with more egalitarian distributions of income tend to push employers to purchase labor-saving machinery, which increases productivity. Third, workers are more motivated to work if they feel economic rewards are fairly distributed and wages are relatively high. Fourth, greater equality leads to more spending on health and education, since people are more likely to identify their own well-being with improving the health care and schooling of the whole society.

Currently, the opposite dynamic is at work in American society. New York University associate professor Roland Benabou notes that rich Americans may flee to the suburbs to get better education for their kids, then refuse to help pay for inner-city education. But, while their children gain an advantage, society overall becomes less efficient and productive because of the ill-trained city workers, and even the suburban children may lose. Several recent studies conclude that even within the United States, the metropolitan economies with the greatest disparity between urban and suburban incomes perform the worst. The "savage inequality" of our educational system (to borrow Jonathan Kozol's term) thus perpetuates and worsens income inequality in the broader society, especially at a time when only highly educated workers can hold their own.

None of the new critics of inequality would disagree with the importance of savings and investment. But, as Benabou has argued, it's "not just how much of national income is saved and invested in human capital" that counts, but to whom it goes. "How income gets distributed matters not just for justice but also for efficiency," he argues.

In short, inequality is not only wrong; it's bad business as well.   [1995]

Understanding the Reading

1. How do supporters of the status quo justify income inequality?
2. What is the distinction between wealth and income?
3. Why is it wrong to ignore income inequality?
4. What is the relationship between the increasing wealth of the richest people and the declining wealth of middle class and poor people?
5. Why does inequality hurt the economy?

Suggestions for Responding

1. Have you and/or your family benefited from or been hurt by the recent trend toward income inequality? Write a short paper describing how you have been affected.
2. Write a letter to Moberg agreeing or disagreeing with his analysis.
3. Investigate and report on one of the leveraged buy-outs of the past decade or so. ◆

77

Institutionalized Discrimination

Robert Cherry

Individuals and institutions may use decision-making procedures that inadvertently discriminate and reinforce inequalities. For example, income differentials can cause unequal access to education even though the school system does not intend to discriminate; locational decisions of firms may have the unintended impact of reducing access to jobs. Similarly, when housing is segregated by income (race), all individuals do not have equal access to job information, as higher-income (white) households will tend to have greater access to job information through personal contacts than lower-income (black) households. Thus, employers will have more higher-income white applicants than if housing was distributed without regard to race or income. Also, employers attempting to reduce their screening costs might rely on group stereotypes rather than more individualized information when deciding which applicants to interview.

In none of these instances is discrimination consciously undertaken, but disadvantaged groups, having unequal access to education, job information, and the interviewing process, are nonetheless harmed. Though unintentional, these problems reinforce the "vicious cycle" of poverty.

Income Differentials and Educational Attainment

Income constraints place heavy burdens on the allocation decisions of low-income households. Often they must "choose" to do without many necessities, such as education. In addition, children from low-income households often have explicit household responsibilities that take time away from school activities. This may involve responsibility for household activities (baby-sitting, shopping, and so on) or earning income. In either case, economists would argue that on average low-income students have a greater opportunity cost[1] on their time than high-income students.

Since their opportunity costs are greater, lower-income students rationally allocate less time to studying and school-related activities than equally motivated higher-income students.

At the college level, even the availability of low-cost public institutions does not necessarily equalize the economic cost of education to all students. Just as at the elementary and secondary school level, lower-income students have a greater opportunity cost on their time than comparable higher-income students. Even if family responsibilities are negligible, students still require income for their own support. This invariably requires lower-income students to work at least part-time while attending school and has often led to the sending of male but not female offspring to college.

The level of income required is influenced by whether the student can live at home while attending college. Historically, public colleges were located in rural areas. For example, none of the original campuses of the Big Ten or Big Eight colleges are located in the states' largest metropolitan areas. The original campus of the University of Illinois is not located in Chicago and the University of Missouri is not located in St. Louis or Kansas City. Thus, not only did lower-income students have to pay for room and board away from home, but it was usually difficult to find part-time employment in these rural communities. This implies that even the availability of low-cost public colleges did not necessarily place the lower-income student on an equal footing with more prosperous students.

Theoretically, low-income youths with appropriate abilities and motivation should be able to borrow money to finance their education. As long as the economic returns from schooling are greater than the interest rate, students will gain from borrowing rather than forgoing additional education. The equalizing of economic costs can occur only if all students of equal promise can borrow at the same rates. Financial institutions, however, cannot accept expectations or probabilities of future income as sufficient collateral for loans. They require bank accounts or other tradable assets, which are normally held by upper-income but not lower-income households. Thus, students from lower-income households cannot borrow readily for education without government intervention.

It also appears that schools in poorer neighborhoods tend to have larger classes and weaker teachers. John Owen found that within the same city, as the mean neighborhood income rose by 1 percent, class size decreased by 0.24 percent and the verbal ability of teachers rose by 0.11 percent. This inequality is even more glaring when comparisons are made between cities. Owen found that for each 1 percent increase in the mean income of a city, there was a rise of 0.73 percent in real expenditures per student and a 1.20 percent increase in the verbal ability of teachers. Thus, students living in poorer neighborhoods in poorer cities have a double disadvantage.

If higher opportunity costs and lower-quality education were not sufficient to discourage educational attainment, Bennett Harrison found that for black inner-city youths, incomes are hardly affected by increases in educational attainment. He notes, "[A]s their education increases, blacks move into new occupations, but their earnings are hardly affected at all by anything short of a college degree, and there is no effect whatever on their chances of finding themselves without a job over the course of the year." Thus, independent of conscious discrimination by the educational system, we should expect low-income minority youths to have lower educational attainment than white youths, even when ability and motivation are held constant.

During the 1970s, a number of policies were implemented in an attempt to compensate for the influence of family income on educational attainment. First, legislatures began funding state universities in larger urban areas. Second, court rulings forced states to change funding formulas so that per capita funding from wealthy and poor communities within each state would become more equal. Third, guaranteed student loans reduced the disadvantage low-income students faced when attempting to finance their education.

DIFFERENTIAL IMPACT
OF INCOMPLETE INFORMATION

In the most simplified labor models, it is assumed that workers and firms act with complete information: Workers know the jobs that are available, and firms know the productivity of job seekers. In this situation, competitive firms would hire the best applicants for the jobs available, and workers would gain the maximum wage obtainable.

Economists have recently developed models in which information has a price; it is only "purchased" up to the point at which its benefits are at least as great as its costs. Neither firms nor workers rationally attempt to gain complete information concerning the labor market opportunities available. Workers find that some additional job information is not worth its cost, while firms find that some information on the productivity of applicants is not worth the additional personnel expenses. Liberals have argued that when workers and firms rationally decide to act on the basis of optimal rather than complete information, biases are generated.

Let us begin by analyzing how firms decide the optimal productivity information they should obtain. A firm benefits from additional productivity information if it translates into hiring a more profitable work force. A firm must weigh this increased profitability against the cost involved in seeking the additional information. After some point, it is likely that the benefits from additional information are insufficient to outweigh its cost. Even though the firm realizes additional information would probably result in hiring a somewhat more productive worker than otherwise, it knows that the added screening expenses would be even greater.

When a strong profit motive and wide productivity differentials among applicants are present, extensive screening will occur. This is the case with professional sports teams, especially since television revenues have transformed ownership from a hobby to a profit-making activity. Liberals believe, however, that in the vast majority of situations, productivity differentials among applicants are quite small and benefits from extensive screening are minimal.

Liberals suggest that the initial screening of applicants is often done with very little individual productivity information available. For firms with a large number of relatively equally qualified applicants, there is no reason to spend much time determining which applicants should be interviewed. These firms simply take a few minutes (seconds) to look over applications and select a promising group to interview. The employer realizes that such a superficial procedure will undoubtedly eliminate some job applicants who are slightly more productive than those selected for interviews. Since productivity differentials are perceived to be minor, however, this loss is not sufficient to warrant a more extensive (expensive) screening procedure.

There would be no discrimination if the job applicants victimized were random, but let us see why the screening method might cause the consistent victimization of individuals from disadvantaged groups. Suppose a firm considering college graduates for trainee positions decides that it has many equally qualified candidates. Looking at résumés, the firm can quickly identify each applicant's race, sex, and college attended. If the firm has enough applicants from better colleges, it is likely to say, "All things being equal, students from these colleges are likely to be more qualified than applicants who attended weaker colleges." Thus, the firm dismisses applicants from the weaker colleges, even though it realizes that weaker schools produce some qualified applicants. The firm has nothing against qualified graduates of weaker colleges. It simply reasons that the extra effort required to identify them is not worth the expense.

However unintentional, highly qualified graduates from weaker schools are discriminated against. Discrimination occurs because this screening method determines the selection for interviews on the basis of group characteristics rather than individual information. More generally, highly qualified applicants from any group that is perceived to have below-average productivity would be discriminated against by this superficial screening method.

Suppose employers believe that black and female applicants are typically less productive than their white male counterparts. If the firm has sufficient white male applicants, it will not interview black or female applicants. The firm will decide that although there are some black and female applicants who are slightly more productive than some white male applicants, it is not worth the added expense to identify them. The process by which individuals are discriminated against when firms use group characteristics to screen individuals is usually called statistical discrimination.

Statistical discrimination can occur indirectly. A firm hiring workers for on-the-job training may be primarily interested in selecting applicants who will stay an extended period of time. The firm does not want to invest training in individuals who will leave the firm quickly. Presumably, if the firm had a sufficient number of applicants who worked more than four years with their previous employer, it would not choose to interview applicants with more unstable work experience. Again, the firm reasons that although there are likely to be some qualified applicants among those with an unstable work record, it is too costly to identify them. This method of screening is likely to discriminate because of the nature of seniority systems, which operate on a "last hired, first fired" basis. Many minorities and women have unstable work records because they are hired last and fired first. Thus, even when firms do not use racial or gender stereotypes, they discriminate, since women and minorities are more likely to come from weaker schools and have more unstable work records than equally qualified white male applicants.

FINANCIAL AND OCCUPATIONAL EFFECTS

Many economists believe the job market is divided between good (primary) and bad (secondary) jobs. Good jobs have characteristics such as on-the-job training and promotions through well-organized internal labor markets. Bad jobs have little on-the-job training and minimum chance for promotions; they are dead-end jobs. Since on-the-job training is a significant aspect of primary-sector jobs, employment stability and behavioral traits are often more important than formal education and general skills. Both conservative and liberal economists agree that workers who do not possess the proper behavioral traits, such as low absenteeism and punctuality, will not be employed in the primary sector. Most liberals believe that many women and minority workers who possess the proper behavioral traits also will not find jobs in the primary sector as a result of statistical discrimination.

Facing discrimination in the primary sector, many qualified female and minority workers shift to secondary labor markets. As a result, secondary employers have a greater supply of workers and can reduce wages and standards for working conditions. Primary employers and majority workers also benefit from statistical discrimination.

Since majority workers face less competition, more of them will gain primary employment than they would in the absence of statistical discrimination.

Primary employers may have to pay somewhat higher wages and employ somewhat less productive workers as a result of statistical discrimination, but the reduced screening costs more than compensate for the higher wages and productivity losses. Moreover, many primary employers also hire secondary workers. For them, the higher cost of primary employees will be offset by the resulting reduction in wages paid to secondary workers and their somewhat higher productivity.

Since primary workers, primary employers, and secondary employers benefit from statistical discrimination, there are identifiable forces opposed to change. Thus, rather than the market disciplining decision makers, statistical discrimination creates groups having a financial stake in its perpetuation.

APPLICANTS AND THEIR SEARCH FOR JOB INFORMATION

For job seekers, the cheapest source of job information is personal contacts, including neighbors and relatives and their acquaintances. Additional information can be obtained from newspaper advertisements and government employment offices. The most costly information is obtained from private employment agencies. A significant difference in the cost of job information would occur if one individual had few personal contacts and was forced to use private employment services, while another individual had extensive personal contacts. All things being equal, the individual with the lower cost of obtaining information would be better informed and hence more likely to obtain higher earnings.

The job information minorities receive from their search effort is likely to be less valuable than the job information received by their white counterparts. The fact that an individual is recommended by a personal contact might be sufficient reason to grant the person an interview. Those who obtain information from newspaper ads or government employment services do not have this advantage. This distinction is summed up in the adage "It's not what you know but who you know that counts."

Low-income (minority) individuals tend to have fewer contacts than high-income (white) individuals of equal abilities and motivation. High-income (white) individuals tend to have many neighbors or relatives who have good jobs, own businesses, or are involved in their firm's hiring decisions. Low-income (minority) individuals, having few personal contacts, are forced to spend additional time and money to obtain job information. Even if the job information is as valuable as that obtained by their white counterparts, minorities might give up searching for employment sooner because it is more costly. They do not do so because they are less able or less motivated; they simply face greater expenses.

AFFIRMATIVE ACTION

Affirmative action legislation is the major government attempt at counteracting the discriminatory features of the hiring process. Affirmative action assumes that discrimination results from employment decisions based on incomplete information. The role of the government is simply to encourage firms to hire all qualified applicants by forcing them to gather individualized productivity information.

Guidelines stipulate that all government agencies and private firms doing business with the government must publicly announce job openings at least forty-five days prior to the termination of acceptance of applications. This provision attempts to offset the information inequality disadvantaged workers face. More importantly, these employers must interview a minimum number of applicants from groups that tend to be victims of statistical discrimination.

It is important to remember the difference between affirmative action and quotas. Under affirmative action, there is no requirement to hire; employers are required only to interview female and minority applicants and make sure they have access to job information. Quotas are more drastic actions reserved for situations in which firms are not making good faith efforts to seek out and hire qualified female and minority applicants. For example, if a firm attempts to circumvent affirmative action guidelines by announcing job openings in papers that reach only the white community or, after interviewing applicants, uses discriminatory procedures to eliminate women from employment, the government can impose quotas. Thus, quotas are imposed only when it is demonstrated that the lack of female or minority employment reflects something more conscious than the unintentional effects of incomplete information.

Besides the government, some private groups have attempted to compensate for unequal access to information. Women's groups have attempted to set up networks to aid female job applicants for management positions. Female executives are encouraged to share as much information as possible with other women to offset the traditional networking done by men. In many areas, male networking is referred to as the old boy network, and entry into it has historically been critical to obtaining the most desirable jobs. Thus, the lack of personal contacts is at least partially offset by networks that direct job information to disadvantaged workers and provide low-cost productivity information to firms.

SKILL AND LOCATIONAL MISMATCHES

Many individuals reject the view that groups are held back due to external pressures by noting that "when we came to America, we faced discrimination but were able to overcome it." In particular, these individuals often believe that internal inadequacies are responsible for the seemingly permanent economic problems minorities face. One response is to argue that the discrimination minorities face is more severe and their economic resources fewer than those of European immigrants at the turn of the century. Another response dominated the U.S. Riot Commission's assessment of black poverty. This presidential commission, which was created to study the causes of the urban rebellions of the late 1960s, noted,

> When the European immigrants were arriving in large numbers, America was becoming an urban-industrial society. To build its major cities and industries, America needed great pools of unskilled labor. Since World War II . . . America's urban-industrial society has matured: unskilled labor is far less essential than before, and blue-collar jobs of all kinds are decreasing in numbers and importance as sources of new employment. . . . The Negro, unlike the immigrant, found little opportunity in the city; he had arrived too late, and the unskilled labor he had to offer was no longer needed.

This commission, commonly known as the Kerner commission, avoided blaming either the victims (culture of poverty) or society (discrimination) for black economic problems; they were simply the result of technological change. To compensate for the higher skill levels required for entry-level positions, the Kerner commission recommended extensive job-training programs. Supposedly, once these skills were obtained, blacks would enter the employment mainstream and racial income disparities would diminish.

Job-training programs became the centerpiece of the liberal War on Poverty initiated during the Johnson administration. To an extent, these job-training programs complemented compensatory educational programs. Whereas the compensatory programs attempted to develop general skills, job-training programs attempted to develop specific job-related skills. Whereas the compensatory programs were attempts to increase white-collar skills, job-training programs were attempts to increase blue-collar skills.

The government's involvement in job-training programs was pragmatic; it sought upward mobility in ways that would not conflict with the interests of other groups. Thus, it did not aggressively institute training programs that would conflict with the objectives of many craft unions. This meant that in many of the construction trades, which had historically restricted membership, the government accepted union prerogatives. Job-training success also was impeded by the seeming irrelevance of many of the skills taught, and there were complaints that training programs did not use the latest equipment and the newest methods.

Many liberals discounted these complaints. They agreed with conservatives that the problems disadvantaged groups faced stemmed from their internal inadequacies. These liberals thought the actual technical skills developed were irrelevant; what was critical was the development of the proper behavioral traits of punctuality and low absenteeism. These liberals also recommended more restrictive programs that would train only the least deficient of the disadvantaged group. In contrast, those liberals who believed that external pressures, particularly discrimination, were dominant proposed costly training programs and a more aggressive approach to craft unions.

Job-training success also was impeded by the shifting of blue-collar jobs out of Northeastern and Midwestern urban areas. After World War II, technological changes decreased the viability of central city locations. First, trucking replaced the railroads as the major transportation mode. When firms delivered their output (and received their input) on railcars, central city locations were ideal. When trucking became dominant, traffic tie-ups made those locations too costly. Indeed, recognizing these costs, the federal government built a new interstate highway system so that travelers could bypass congested central city areas.

Second, new technologies emphasized assembly-line techniques that required one-level production. No longer could manufacturing firms use factory buildings in which they operated on a number of floors. High land costs made it too expensive to build one-level plants in urban centers, so manufacturing firms began to locate in industrial parks near the new interstate highways on the outskirts of urban areas. This intensified minority employment problems, as most minorities continued to live in the inner city.

Minorities with the proper behavioral requirements, education, and skills have difficulty obtaining employment due to these locational mismatches. Inner-city residents are likely to lack the financial ability to commute to suburban jobs. They are unlikely to own a car or to earn a sufficient income to justify the extensive commuting required, even if public transportation is available. Minorities also are less likely to have access to these jobs because they have fewer personal contacts working in suburban locations.

Liberals have offered a number of recommendations to offset locational mismatches. Some economists have favored government subsidies to transportation networks that would bring inner-city workers to suburban employment locations. These subsidies would be cost-effective if the added employment generated greater income tax revenues and government spending reductions. Other economists have favored subsidizing firms to relocate in targeted inner-city zones. This approach was even endorsed by President Reagan under the catchy name "Free Enterprise Zones."   [1989]

Term

1. OPPORTUNITY COST: The relative proportion of time or resources that can be invested in a given activity.

Understanding the Reading

1. In what ways does having a lower income level limit one's educational attainment?
2. Explain what Cherry means by "purchasing information" and how it affects discriminatory employment practices or statistical discrimination.
3. What causes higher wages in the primary sector and lower wages in the secondary sector?
4. How are low-income people disadvantaged in their job searches?
5. Explain how affirmative action is supposed to work and how it differs from quotas.
6. What were the objectives and problems of job training as a solution to minority unemployment or underemployment?

Suggestions for Responding

1. Apply Cherry's analysis to the circumstances described in one of the selections in Part VI.
2. Write a brief essay in which you speculate on how the "cycle of poverty" that Cherry describes might be broken. ◆

78

Jury Whops Insurer

LESLIE BROWN

On October 26, the Richmond Circuit Court awarded a $100 million judgment against Nationwide Mutual Insurance Company upon finding that the company had discriminated against blacks in the city. The judgment was the largest civil rights verdict in U.S. history.

The ruling closed the first case in the nation where an insurance company was brought to trial for redlining—the illegal practice of avoiding business in minority neighborhoods. During the two-week trial, the plaintiff, Housing Opportunities Made Equal of Richmond (HOME), argued that the insurance company restricted its target market to predominately white neighborhoods, overcharged blacks for coverage and made race-based decisions in deciding whom to target for premium sales. "Nationwide was deaf and blind to its own obvious racial bigotry," says attorney Thomas Wolf, a senior member of the legal team that represented HOME. "The lesson here for large corporations is that if they don't root out their racism—conscious or subconscious—they may pay a heavy price for it."

This was not the first time Nationwide had been accused of racial discrimination. In 1992, the National Fair Housing Alliance conducted an investigation after widespread reports began surfacing that the company regularly turned down blacks for premiums. The group eventually filed a complaint with the Department of Housing and Urban Development (HUD).

In 1994, HUD began giving grants to local fair housing groups across the country to investigate racial discrimination by Nationwide and other insurance companies. HOME received three grants for $1.2 million to investigate 30 companies in the Richmond area. Eleven testers—both black and white—were trained to pose as home-buyers and seek rate quotes for home insurance.

The testing began in June 1995. During the following 15 months, HOME conducted approximately 220 tests. The probe quickly began to focus on Nationwide. "We found problems in other companies but the most egregious was with Nationwide," says Connie Chamberlin, executive director of HOME and president of the National Fair Housing Alliance.

In 15 paired tests of similar houses, black testers seeking homes in black neighborhoods received only six insurance quotes while white testers seeking homes in white neighborhoods received 12 quotes. In the nine cases in which black testers were denied quotes, Nationwide agents told them their homes were too old, did not meet minimum value standards and that there was not enough time until the closing on the house to permit the required inspection. When

blacks were able to obtain coverage, they were charged as much as 15 percent more for their premiums.

HOME also discovered that Nationwide targeted zip codes in the largely white suburbs of Richmond, ignoring those with a significant black population. Additionally, the investigation uncovered that Nationwide was moving all of its agents outside of the city of Richmond—which has a predominately black population—into the white suburbs. The company justified the decision by saying they were trying to target people who were more likely to buy both homeowners and auto insurance policies.

Nationwide denies that they violated state insurance regulations or federal laws regarding racial discrimination. However, company officials were unable to answer why there was a higher rate of blacks turned down for coverage than whites. Moreover, Nationwide had admitted in marketing documents that they excluded affluent, predominately black neighborhoods, but included trailer parks that they determined were more than 90 percent white.

"The plaintiffs have not presented any factual evidence to support their claims against Nationwide," says a company statement issued after the verdict. "Instead, they swayed the jury by relying on insinuations and emotionally charged allegations which have no place in a court of law."

Nationwide spokesman Bob Sohovich says the company thought the facts were clear and convincing in the trial and maintains that the company has not violated any laws. "We are committed to marketing in all areas, including the urban market," he says. "We took this to court because we thought we had done nothing wrong."

Lawyers for Nationwide said the company will appeal the verdict to the Virginia Supreme Court.

In addition to the $100 million in punitive damages, the jury awarded HOME $500,000 in compensatory damages to reimburse the group for the cost of investigating Nationwide. "The ruling signifies a couple of things," Wolf says. "Institutional racism can be proven when it is laid out before a jury. The jury sent a strong message to corporate America that this type of corporate racism is not going to be tolerated."   [1998]

Understanding the Reading

1. What is redlining?
2. How did HOME gather evidence against Nationwide?

Suggestion for Responding

1. To combat redlining in banking, Congress passed the Community Reinvestment Act in 1977; research and report on its regulations, and try to develop a comparable plan to combat insurance redlining. ◆

79

The Spectre of Regionalism

HUNTER O'HARA

I am a native Appalachian. My roots are in southern West Virginia, Saint Albans, near Charleston. When I left West Virginia in 1994, I was to encounter *regionalism* in Maryland, Florida and elsewhere. I define regionalism as a belief that one's region of origin is a primary determinant of the quality of one's standards of living, social forms, customary beliefs, levels of sophistication, intellect and aesthetic development and that regional differences produce an inherent superiority of persons from particular regions. In particular, I noticed regionalism directed at West Virginia, i.e., WV trailer jokes, a WV Governor's Mansion with axles joke, WV poverty jokes, WV incest jokes and on and on. On occasion, when I mentioned my state of origin, comments such as "bet you're glad you're out of there" and "oh, I'm sorry" were made.

I am a professor of Education at The University of Tampa. My Learner Diversity class recently discussed celebrities who changed their last names for professional advantage. One student noted that another celebrity had changed his accent. "Why would someone change their accent?" I mentioned that I had changed my West Virginia accent. "But why?" another student asked. Baiting them, I said, "Because West Virginians are uncultured, uneducated, poverty-stricken, inbred hillbillies who don't wear shoes and who live in trailers.

They took the bait, swallowing it whole. One student began to laugh and tell how she and her telephone operator peers noticed that West Virginians did not know what a telephone was called. At one point in her life she drove through part of West Virginia on a regular basis but would not have dreamed of stopping. Another student said that she had applied for admission to West Virginia University but decided not to go. A third added that West Virginia University, my alma matter, would "take anyone." She then revealed, tongue dead center in her month, that WVU had accepted her sister. She added that her sister had decided not to go because the nearby mall had only one store. "One store?" I queried. Hmmm, I thought, the malls I visited in West Virginia were all fully stocked. The only trouble was they had the same tired stores that all other American malls have.

My experience with West Virginia's culture and fine arts was resoundingly counterstereotype. As a boy, then undergraduate, then teacher, I never imagined that some would be surprised at my West Virginia–nurtured aesthetic development. On West Virginia stages I heard singers Sills, Pavoratti, Peters, Alexander and Price, pianists Watts and Van Cliburn, saw the Canadian Ballet, the Charleston Ballet, the West Virginia Symphony, the Charleston Light Opera Guild and so on.

I sang with the Charleston Civic Chorus and West Virginia Opera Theatre productions of *La Boheme* and *La Traviata*. I performed in a master class for Metropolitan Opera star Jerome Hines at West Virginia State College. When my West Virginia music students competed successfully at New York University against students from all over the country we must have surprised regionalists.

As for education in West Virginia, 25 years ago I never thought that my extraordinary elementary school principal or the compelling music teacher I adored, both of whom I have written about, or all of the National Merit Scholarship semifinalists in my class did not match, nay were in stark contrast to, poor West Virginia–education stereotypes. When I moved away from home, I began to be exposed to West Virginia incest and trailer jokes in "proper" environments in other states. Recently, one of my UT colleagues made a West Virginia incest comment. I never understood how the incest stereotype emerged. What is the source of claims that West Virginians have higher incest rates than individuals in other states, I have wondered. Do researchers really study and document such things, and if so, how? "Excuse me. We're conducting a study: are you molesting or have you impregnated your daughter? Thank you. I'll be sure to mark you in the 'yes' column."

Seriously, what valid measure of incest rates could possibly exist? If valid measures do not exist, who creates such stereotypes, and for what purpose? It is clear that some enjoy any situation in which they elevate themselves over large populations of people. Hitler made a career out of the elitist predilections of some of his people (we see such phenomena today in the United States). Some individuals would surely be disappointed that I was not molested by a parent or other family member. It is interesting to note that in recent years incest, in other states, is referred to as child abuse.

I am amazed at how tenaciously people cling to derogatory stereotypical information about others but how correspondingly irresponsible they are about confirming the data. One of my students asked why I dropped my West Virginia accent. Was it so that I could be given opportunity? I noted that my objective was not to be given opportunity but rather to avoid being denied opportunity by narrow-minded individuals who would judge my intellect or competence by the way I pronounced my vowels. One of my African American students nodded in agreement. In the past I had used the dialect gear shift when I sensed a particular tone in a gatekeeper's manner.

Consider: Mississippi, Arkansas, Alabama, Kentucky, Montana and some other states—what images come to mind, and what are their sources? Are those images from our own experience or have we willingly accepted the negative portrayals and images seen on television and film and in literature as factual? How many stereotypes were reinforced by the Beverly Hillbillies series alone? Who stands to gain from such large-scale stereotyping? Someone must.

One thing is for certain: Americans are too willing to allow the media to dictate to them their opinions, tastes, preferences and biases. When people buy into and perpetuate myths, such as when they disparage West Virginia, they belittle themselves and my family.

During the course of the 20th Century, expressions of prejudice in public and private forums, against African Americans, certain religions, the disabled, for example, have become less acceptable. Other groups have not fared as well, however. The expression of region-related, age-related and size-related bigotry is common. It occurs frequently and without apology. The dilemma of coping with bigotry and all of its negative consequences remains.

On a rainy day in 1962, J.F.K. told a Charleston, West Virginia, crowd, "The sun may not always shine in West Virginia, but the people always do," a lovely tribute from a President from Massachusetts. What Kennedy said is true.

I am proud of West Virginia and the struggle of its people to overcome oppression. I applaud their courage and their wisdom. While other states are threatened by crime for example, West Virginia has maintained its refusal to execute poor (or rich) criminals, while maintaining the lowest crime rate in the nation.

Meanwhile, the mountains and valleys of West Virginia, the most wooded state in the nation, are lush, green and majestic, impervious to the unflattering machinations of timid minds.

As a teacher preparer who teaches a diversity course, I encourage my students to think about diversity in a broadly inclusive way, i.e., race, class, gender, ethnicity, age, sexual orientation, gender identification, religion, culture, physically challenged individuals, left handed individuals and so on. I also want them to regard regionalism as another form of bigotry to be avoided in their daily lives and particularly when they enter the classroom.   [2008]

Understanding the Reading

1. Define regionalism as you understand it.
2. Why would someone consciously change his or her accent?
3. What details about the author's life would surprise regionalists?
4. What does a regionalist gain by expressing and perpetuating stereotypes?

Suggestion for Responding

1. Ponder the states and regions you have commented on in your lifetime. Then do the same for foreign countries. Have you made elitist remarks and jokes? If so, why do you think you have done so? ✦

80

Persistent Welfare Stereotypes

RENU NAHATA

"There is now a fairly widespread feeling, justified or not, that some welfare recipients are not doing enough to get off the dole." Thus began *ABC World News Tonight*'s "American Agenda" segment on welfare reform (4/14/92). While Peter Jennings' opening statement acknowledges that there may be disparities between public perception and reality, this segment and many others continue to rely heavily on widely held misconceptions about welfare.

With few exceptions, the mainstream media have portrayed the issue of welfare in terms and images not too far removed from Ronald Reagan's "welfare queens." Following news coverage, one might believe that most welfare recipients are black, unwed, unemployed, teenage mothers of several children, living in the inner city. She might be, as one article suggested, "a walking statistic: a single mother of five who dropped out of high school at 17, pregnant with her first child" (*Newsday,* 9/23/90). But the statistic she represents is quite small, since only two percent of all poor children live in such households (*Washington Post,* 6/3/91).

In fact, as Jack Smith acknowledged on *This Week With David Brinkley* (4/12/92), "most recipients of welfare are white, not black; most live in the suburbs, not the inner city; most want to work and stay on welfare less than two years." According to a Health and Human Services report, the average number of children in AFDC (Aid to Families with Dependent Children) families is only 1.9—well under the national average.

Whether "justified or not," several states have based their reform measures on the perception that the welfare system's failures derive from women abusing its benefits. In response, state legislatures have taken aim at those receiving assistance, while media have further fueled these concerns by offering up a parade of mothers, unwed, unrepentant and most often black.

The Wisconsin program, considered a model for other states, reduces benefits for a second child and eliminates them for a third, on the assumption that increased benefits will encourage women to have more children. However, according to the House Ways and Means Committee's 1991 Green Book, the average size of AFDC families has been decreasing steadily for 20 years. More to the point, the Center on Budget and Policy Priorities argues that there is no significant relationship between AFDC benefit levels and birth rates. Although these statistics are readily available, most news reports about such welfare "reforms" fail to use them.

ABC World News' April 14 [1992] segment on welfare relied on the "decline in values" critique made by many of welfare's detractors. Correspondent Rebecca Chase tried to demonstrate the corrosive social impact of welfare by interviewing several black mothers, most of them unwed and in their teens, one a mother of six who has been on welfare for the past 20 years. The two questions put to these women were, "How many of you are married?" and "Do you feel like you owe the taxpayers anything for them helping you support your children?"

Chase seemed to find the moral dilemma of unmarried motherhood, and the issue of gratitude for public support, far more compelling than soaring black unemployment (particularly for males), absence of affordable child care and discriminatory hiring practices. Instead of addressing these kinds of issues, poverty and welfare are studied through the narrow lens of individual responsibility and moral double standards.

The same lens is used by *U.S. News and World Report*'s David Whitman (4/20/92), who approvingly describes the latest attitude toward those on welfare as the "new paternalism," i.e., "rewarding them for doing right and fining them for doing wrong." Given these absolute terms, Whitman's conclusion is not surprising: "No federal intervention . . . is likely to prompt legions of unwed, chronic welfare mothers to marry the fathers of their children."

This Week With David Brinkley (4/12/92), in a lengthy segment on Wisconsin's reform experiment, made an effort to dispel long-standing myths. But the show managed to undermine those facts by loading both the taped segment and the discussion that followed with repeated images of and references to urban blacks. Despite one guest's effort to raise the question of incentive in the absence of employment opportunities, larger societal factors lost ground to George Will's concern over "illegitimacy in our cities."

Even while attempting to dispel "social myths" about welfare, an Ellen Goodman column (*Boston Globe,* 4/16/92) focused on poor women with a sense of "entitlement" as the main problem with welfare. "Americans instinctively believe that the welfare poor should play by the same rules as the rest of us. A family that works does not get a raise for having a child. Why then should a family that doesn't work?"

The headline chosen by the *Globe* for Goodman's column, "Welfare Mothers With an Attitude," played up the worst aspects of the piece. And the graphic that accompanied the article, while apparently intended satirically, could just as easily be read as endorsing the stereotype of the African-American welfare mother with too many kids and too much money. At some point, repetition of stereotypical imagery merely hardens perceptions, rendering corrective caveats effectively useless.

Although most polls show that Americans still support public spending on the poor, James Patterson, a historian of social policy at Brown University, points out that "people support programs when they imagine the beneficiaries look a lot like themselves" (*New York Times,* 5/17/92). As if to substantiate this premise, just one month earlier the *Times* (4/13/92) ran "From Middle Class to Jobless: A Sense of Pride Is Shattered."

The primary concern of this article was the suffering, fear and loss of pride felt by recently unemployed white-collar workers (illustrated by a photograph of a white accountant). Mounting welfare rolls in predominantly middle-class areas like Westchester, New York, inspired the writer to feel compassion. In this case, the rise in chronic unemployment, family breakdowns, vanishing spouses, substance abuse and domestic violence are seen to stem from economic circumstances rather than vaguely defined social pathologies.

However, most welfare recipients we see in the media are black. And most efforts to reform welfare are directed at inner cities. There is little room for compassion here. The panacea generally offered for inner-city poverty and family breakdowns comes most often in the form of imposing "values."

Lawrence Mead, the author of an influential new book, *The New Politics of Poverty: The Non-working Poor in America,* demonstrates this tendency. One of the main sources in the *U.S. News* article about the "new paternalism," Mead argued in a *New York Times* op-ed (5/19/92) that "if poor adults behaved rationally, they would seldom be poor for long in the first place. Opportunity is more available than the will to seize it." Child care, he believes, can usually be found if one only looks for it, and "the ghetto mentality," more than racism or any other factor, is the main cause of unemployment. His solution to these personal failings is "a more authoritative social policy in which the needy are told how to live instead of merely being subsidized."

When President Bush can blame the L.A. uprising on Lyndon Johnson's Great Society programs, the official view is not far from Mead's. Stories like "White House Links Riots to Welfare" (*New York Times,* 5/5/92) display a certain skepticism, yet media assumptions about welfare and poverty—focusing on inner-city black women, their supposed unchecked fertility and lack of "individual responsibility"—differ little from the administration's. Despite the fact that most media outlets recognize the prevalence of stereotypes, few seem willing to give up those stereotypes as the basis for their coverage.   [1992]

Understanding the Reading

1. How are welfare recipients portrayed in the media?
2. In what ways does the welfare stereotype not fit reality?
3. What does Nahata think causes welfare dependence?
4. What economic circumstances affect welfare?

Suggestions for Responding

1. Interview someone who is or has been on welfare and describe how he or she differs from the welfare stereotype.
2. Find an op-ed article about welfare and write a brief essay about its use of stereotypes and myths. ✦

81

The Root Causes of Homelessness in American Cities

Doug A. Timmer,
D. Stanley Eitzen,
and Kathryn D. Talley

The facts concerning poverty in the United States are grim. Data from 1991 reveal that 14.2 percent of the population (about 35.7 million Americans) were below the official poverty line (the data in this section are taken from U.S. Bureau of the Census). Over one-fifth of all children (21.8 percent) were poor. About one-third of all African Americans (32.7 percent) and almost three out of ten Hispanics (28.7 percent) were poor.

The poor face a number of obstacles. They are rejected and despised by others. They are looked down upon as lazy, shiftless, dirty, and immoral. They often receive inferior educations because they live in economically depressed school districts. They often are exposed to toxic chemicals. Many of the poor are malnourished and have health problems. In 1991 some 35.4 million Americans had no health insurance and many were refused medical care for financial reasons. The result is that on average low-income families pay one-fifth of their incomes toward health care—twice as much as the one-tenth paid by high-income families.

Whereas misery, ill health, malnutrition, and discrimination are endemic among all the poor, the most disadvantaged among them also live in substandard housing without adequate plumbing, heat, or other facilities. The poorest of the poor are often just an illness, accident, divorce, or other personal disaster away from homelessness. During the 1980s and the early 1990s the proportion of poor people who became homeless increased dramatically. An ever-increasing number of homeless were visible on the streets as the demand on shelters far outstripped the supply. Much more than at other times in U.S. history, the homeless are experiencing a severe housing shortage, which is forcing many of them to sleep in temporary shelters or even in doorways, on heating grates, in dumpsters, in cardboard boxes, and in abandoned buildings.

Three questions are raised and answered in this section: (1) What is the extent of homelessness in America? (2) Is homelessness caused by personal disabilities? and (3) Are the "new" homeless different from the "old" homeless?

The homeless are typically defined as those who have no permanent home and who must resort to streets, shelters, or other makeshift quarters. The number of homeless is impossible to determine accurately since they may be living with relatives or friends or hidden beneath bridges, in alleys, in abandoned buildings, in shelters and are therefore difficult to find and count. The low estimate, by the U.S. Department of Housing and Urban Development (HUD) during the Reagan administration, was that between 250,000 and 350,000 Americans were homeless. Political conservatives find appeal in this low figure because it means that the problem is relatively insignificant and not in need of additional public programs and resources to ameliorate it. Estimates at the high end come from advocacy groups like the National Coalition for the Homeless, which put the figure at between 3 and 4 million. Reformers, convinced of the magnitude and seriousness of the problem, are prone to accept these higher figures.

Whatever the actual numbers of the homeless, three points must be underscored. *First,* the proportion of Americans who are homeless is the highest since the Great Depression, with a rapid rise in the past fifteen years or so and still climbing. *Second,* the numbers actually minimize the seriousness of the problem because so many of the urban poor are on the brink of homelessness and many who lack housing are hidden by doubling or tripling up with relatives or friends. Jonathan Kozol estimates that there are over 300,000 hidden homeless in New York City alone and that nationwide more than 3 million families are living doubled up. When these households are added to those poor people paying more than half of their monthly income for rent, more than 20 million families are living near the edge of homelessness in the United States. And *third,* we should not become unduly focused on the numbers because they deflect us from the problem itself and the homeless themselves.

A recurrent belief among politicians, journalists, social scientists, and the public is that homelessness is a consequence of personal disabilities. That is, homeless persons tend to suffer from chronic alcoholism or from chronic physical or mental disorders and these disabilities explain their homelessness. This is a myth with damaging consequences. Although some homeless persons suffer from alcoholism, most do not. Some suffer severe mental or emotional disturbances, but most do not.

Typically, the recent rise in homelessness is seen as a consequence of the deinstitutionalization of mental patients that began in the 1950s. The data appear to support this notion, since the average daily census of psychiatric institutions dropped from 677,000 in 1955 to 151,000 in 1984. Almost all of the reduction in mental patients had occurred by 1978, yet the homeless did not begin overflowing the streets and shelters until 1983.

Several other cautions must be raised concerning the emphasis on the homeless as mentally ill. First, most of the homeless are *not* mentally ill: there is solid research evidence to indicate that no more than 10 to 15 percent of persons living on the street are mentally impaired in some way. Researcher James Wright, using data from the national Health Care for the Homeless (HCH) program, has concluded that as many as one-third of the homeless probably are mentally ill. But more recent research has confirmed the 10 to 15 percent estimate.

A second caution concerns context. Elliot Liebow, in his description and analysis of homeless women, argues that judgments about the homeless often involve descriptions of them as deviant—mentally ill, alcoholic, drug addicted—descriptions that would receive more positive judgments if they were in another setting.

Like you, I know people who drink, people who do drugs, and bosses who have tantrums and treat their subordinates like dirt. They all have good jobs. Were they to become homeless, some of them would surely also become "alcoholics," "addicts," or "mentally ill." Similarly, if some of the homeless women who are now so labelled were to be magically transported to a more usual and acceptable setting, some of them—not all, of course—would shed their labels and take their places with the rest of us somewhere on the spectrum of normality.

In short, there is a class bias involved here. When homeless people do have mental difficulties or problems with alcohol, these situations are identified as the cause of their homelessness. But when well-housed middle-class and upper-middle-class people are mentally ill or alcoholic it is identified as an unfortunate situation requiring attention and treatment.

A third caution has to do with cause and effect. Does mental illness cause homelessness or do the stresses induced by extreme poverty and homelessness cause mental illness? Although some argue that mental illness is a cause of homelessness, there are no data to support this claim. The much stronger argument is that mental illness is a probable consequence of homelessness. This is based on the assumption that a stable life leads to mental stability and an unstable one to mental instability.

A fourth caution is that the emphasis on the personal sources of homelessness blames the victims for their problem and deflects attention away from its structural sources. To do so leads to faulty generalizations and public policies doomed to fail.

In this regard, sociologist Michael Sosin's recent study of homeless persons in Chicago is instructive. Comparing a sample of homeless persons to a sample of "vulnerable" persons—not homeless but impoverished and precariously close to losing their shelter—Sosin found the lack of access to various social and institutional supports and resources to be a much better predictor of homelessness than any personal disabilities or "deficits."

People are homeless not because of their individual flaws but because of structural arrangements and trends that result in extreme impoverishment and a shortage of affordable housing in U.S. cities. The extent to which the homeless population is made up of the mentally ill, the physically handicapped and disabled, alcoholics, and drug abusers and addicts results from their being more vulnerable to the kind of impoverishment that excludes them from the urban housing market. Their vulnerabilities mean that they may be the first to lose permanent shelter. But the absolute shortage of low-income, affordable housing in the United States ensures that even if no one were plagued with these personal disabilities, the size of the homeless population would be roughly the same.

The current and expanding crisis of urban homelessness results from the convergence of two contradictory and proximate forces: the rapidly dwindling supply of low-income housing and the increased economic marginality among the poor and the near poor, caused by the changing economy, changes in family structure, and shifts in government policies. These proximate causes of urban homelessness, it must be remembered, are in turn embedded in and derived from the structure of a historically changing corporate capitalist economy and society.

Our analysis of housing does not focus exclusively on the homeless. To do so risks adding to the deviant identity homeless persons have thrust upon them. Singling out homeless people exacerbates their supposedly "special" character. To do so encourages a view that they are considerably different from those who are housed. In truth, the homeless are not distinct persons, nor do they have a completely distinct problem. They happen to be at the extreme end of a shelter continuum—ranging from those who are sufficiently housed, through those who are ill-housed, to those who have no housing at all. Thus, the urban homeless problem is fundamentally a housing problem.

There is not enough low-cost housing available for the economically marginal in U.S. cities. The low-income housing supply has shrunk dramatically in recent years. The inflation of the 1980s is one source of this shrinkage: The cost of housing at all levels rose rapidly. The median price of a single-family dwelling sold in 1970, for example, was $23,000; in 1980 it was $62,200; in 1989 it was $92,900; and by 1993 it was $104,000. This varied by locality, of course, with the cost of a median house in Honolulu, San Francisco, and Anaheim well over double the median and Los Angeles, San Diego, Newark, Boston, and New York City just below double the national median.

The cost of renting followed the inflationary trend of the 1970s and 1980s; in fact, it rose faster than renters' incomes. This was partly a function of the high cost of home purchases, which floods the rental market, putting upward pressure on rents. Between 1970 and 1990, for example, rents tripled while renters' incomes only doubled. This inflation in the housing market at all levels has placed increased pressures on the poor, who

simply cannot afford the increased rents or must sacrifice essentials such as food to pay the higher rents. The federal standard for affordable housing is less than 30 percent of household income for rent. A survey of forty-four cities by the Center on Budget and Policy Priorities found that 75 percent of low-income households (those earning less than $10,000 annually) paid more than 30 percent of their incomes in rent. In thirty-nine of the forty-four cities surveyed, housing costs alone normally exceeded the entire grant for a family of three receiving assistance from the Aid to Families with Dependent Children (AFDC) program. Data from 1989 indicated that nearly one-half (47 percent) of those households below the poverty line *spent more than 70 percent of their incomes for housing.* Paying such a high proportion of their low income for rent places these households on the brink of homelessness, one medical crisis, one layoff, or one pay cut away from losing their shelter.

One factor explaining the increasing lack of affordable rental housing is the "rent squeeze" caused by concentrated ownership of rental housing in U.S. cities. In both New York City and Houston, for example, 5 percent of all landlords control more than one-half of the rental housing stock. In Boston, only twenty individuals own 40 percent of the city's rental units. When rental housing is controlled by a few, rents rise.

Although the rising cost of low-income housing is an important reason for the increased rates of homelessness, other factors are also important. Foremost, there has been an absolute loss in low-income units. From 1970 to 1989 the number of rental units for the poor declined 14 percent to 5.5 million while the number of poor renters—those who made less than $10,000 in 1989 dollars—increased from 7.3 million to 9.6 million.

Conspicuous among the reasons for the decline of low-income housing has been the loss of single-room occupancy (SRO) hotels, often the housing of last resort for the economically marginal in cities. About a million SRO units have been torn down nationwide since the 1970s. In New York City, for example, the stock of SROs shrunk from 127,000 units in 1975 to 14,000 in 1985.

SROs and other low-cost rental housing have disappeared because of two related trends. One is gentrification—the process of converting low-income housing to condominiums or upscale apartments for the middle and upper-middle classes. Condominium conversion involves taking rental units and turning them into apartments for sale. This practice often replaces those who cannot afford a down payment or qualify for a home mortgage with those more affluent persons who can. Gentrification typically includes buying up older and sometimes rundown property in poor and working-class neighborhoods and rehabilitating it into middle-class condominiums, townhouses, single-family dwellings, and upscale lofts and apartments. Often, the original residents of the area are displaced because they cannot afford the increased rents, purchase prices, and insurance and property taxes associated with the neighborhood's rising property values. The poor, who once had housing, are left out. Especially harmed by this process are non-whites. Research by Phillip Clay studied fifty-seven gentrifying neighborhoods in thirty cities and found that before gentrification about half the neighborhoods were predominantly black. After gentrification, 80 percent were dominated by whites and only 2 percent were predominantly nonwhite.

Slumlords have also contributed to the inner-city housing shortage. Slumlording occurs when investors buy rental properties in poor neighborhoods and purposefully fail to maintain them. Typically, the slumlords are middle class and white, the tenants poor and black. Over time serious housing code violations develop as roofs leak, stairways deteriorate, plumbing fails, and electrical wiring becomes dangerous. Slumlords simply squeeze whatever rents they can for as long as they can. The end point of this process is when the city condemns the buildings, evicts the residents, and takes over the property for delinquent taxes and unpaid utility bills.

Another market mechanism that leads to the urban housing crisis is "warehousing." Here, real estate speculators buy property on the edges of gentrifying areas and gradually empty them of their occupants by not maintaining them or by not renting them when renters leave. The goal is selling these properties to other developers for a profit. Developers are especially attracted to "warehoused" properties since they spare them the difficulties of removing poor and working-class leaseholders who will not be able to afford the newly gentrified property.

A comparison of all blacks with all whites in U.S. society showed that blacks spend more on rent than whites do. This is because African Americans are concentrated in urban areas where rents tend to be higher and because their housing options are limited by discrimination.

Rollbacks in public housing have further reduced the supply of low-income housing in U.S. cities. Federal low-income housing programs, including government subsidies for its construction, declined dramatically during the Reagan presidency. Federal support for subsidized housing dropped from $32.2 billion in 1981 to $6 billion in 1989. The U.S. Department of Housing and Urban Development (HUD) authorized the construction of 183,000 subsidized dwellings in 1980 but only 20,000 in 1989. Ameliorating the problems of the poor and the homeless was clearly not a priority of the Reagan administration: "When Reagan came to office in 1981, the federal government spent seven dollars on defense for every dollar on housing. When he left office in 1989, the ratio was forty-six to one."

These recent cutbacks in public housing exacerbate an already meager public housing sector. When compared to the industrial democracies of Europe, for example, U.S. public housing makes up a paltry share of the total housing stock. In Europe, urban public housing often accounts for as much as 40 percent of the total housing stock, compared to only 1.3 percent in the United States. Only 6 percent of U.S. households qualifying for low-income housing assistance receive it from the government. And only one-fifth of the poor live in government-subsidized housing of any kind, whether public housing run by local housing authorities, privately owned projects subsidized by HUD, or private apartments for which tenants pay rent with government vouchers. This is the lowest rate of assistance of any industrial nation in the world.

The Department of Housing and Urban Development estimates that as many as 13 million more families qualify for housing assistance but cannot be helped because of a shortage of federal funds. Of the 13 million lacking assistance, 5.1 million are considered to have "worst-case needs" because they spend more than 50 percent of their incomes on rent or live in "severely substandard" conditions.

To summarize, the dramatic shrinkage in the supply of low-cost housing is both a problem of affordability and supply. Clearly, market forces, which, according to conservative analysts should work to solve social problems, have *not* worked to furnish an adequate supply of low-cost housing in America's cities. In reality, market forces are the source of, not the solution to, the problem. Nor did the federal government step in to meet this need. The result was a shortage of affordable housing units for the poorest of the poor. And this structural change in urban housing markets was occurring at the very time that the numbers of the very poor were increasing.

The dramatic rise in homelessness over the past decade and a half is the result of a severe contradiction unfolding in the United States: As the supply of low-income housing is being reduced, increasing numbers of Americans, especially women, children, and minorities, are becoming more and more economically marginal. Just as too much money chasing too few goods causes inflation, so, too, does too many poor and marginal people chasing too few affordable apartments cause homelessness. Or, to switch the metaphor, think of this as a game of musical chairs, in which the chairs represent apartments affordable to the poor and the players are the poor seeking permanent shelter in those apartments. As the game has been played over the past fifteen years in American cities, the number of chairs has been systematically reduced by failed government policies and private-sector investment decisions. Meanwhile, the transformation of the economy and work, changes in family structure, and cutbacks in public-sector supports for the poor continue to add players to the game. The outcome of this game is that an increasing number of players are losers; they cannot find "chairs" and become homeless.   [1994]

Understanding the Reading

1. Describe poverty in the United States.
2. How many American people are homeless, and who are the hidden homeless?
3. Do disabilities cause homelessness?
4. What are the reasons for the increase in homelessness?

Suggestions for Responding

1. Investigate public assistance payments in your area and then search the "For Rent" ads in local newspapers to see what kind of housing is available for 30 percent of this payment.
2. Write an essay speculating about why low-income assistance and supported housing that is government-supported in the United States are so far below those of most other industrialized nations. ✦

82

Orsted Speaks on Environmental Racism

AARON FRASIER

Sheila Holt Orsted was shocked when she learned that she had stage two breast cancer.

Orsted was a bodybuilder and personal trainer who taught five aerobics classes and played basketball on a women's league. She later found out that the cancer was caused by toxic chemicals near her home.

Orsted spoke in the Garrett Conference Center auditorium on Wednesday evening about environmental racism and how it has affected her life. Orsted's speech was among Constitution Week events this week.

Orsted's story began in 2002, when she was traveling home to Dickson, Tenn., for Christmas. When she arrived home, she learned that her father, aunt and two cousins had cancer.

After traveling back home, she scheduled a physical, only to learn of her breast cancer.

Orsted's father received a letter from the county explaining that their family farm was 57 feet from the site of a chemical spill.

A manufacturing company that produced valves for automobiles and boats had been dumping their degreaser, trichloroethylene (TCE) near the farm. Orsted's father was told that this chemical had gotten into the water supply but that it wouldn't cause any health problems.

In between chemotherapy treatments, Orsted began investigating the situation and found that the white families in the area had also received a letter—but one that told them to discontinue their water because it was dangerous for their health.

This introduced Orsted to the issue of environmental racism: informing one race of people about something for their protection but leaving the other group out in the cold.

Orsted began rallying against the issue. She received [help] from Robert Bullard, director of the Environmental Justice Resource Center at Clark Atlanta University, as well as two non-profit law firms.

Orsted, with the help of the firms, filed lawsuits against the manufacturing company. The company went bankrupt as a result of the suit.

But the chemical spill has polluted the entire water supply of Dickson and spreads about a mile a year.

Orsted told students that everyone needs to do something to help stop environmental racism.

She has been featured on CNN and in the Washington Post. After seeing an article about her, Hillary Clinton contacted her and asked her to speak at the United States' first environmental justice meeting.

"I believe this is my calling," Orsted said. "I was put on this earth to tell my story."

Now in remission, Orsted has been traveling to different college campuses to speak on the topic of environmental justice. She wants to get people involved and stop the oppression of blacks.

"Getting a black president did not solve all of the racial issues," she said.

Dickson sophomore Caitlin Bowen and Harlan senior Kelsey Middleton both attended the speech to write papers for their African American Studies class. Bowen was left thinking about the possibility that TCE could be in her own hometown water supply.

Orsted said she wants others to get involved and work for equality.

"We will not be victims, but victors," she said.

[2010]

Understanding the Readings

1. What is Sheila Orsted's family's health story concerning a chemical spill?
2. Why is this story about racism?
3. Describe Sheila's activism.

Suggestions for Responding

1. Research toxic sites in your county.
2. Invite Sheila Orsted or a fellow activist to your campus to speak on environmental racism. ✦

SUGGESTIONS FOR RESPONDING TO PART VI

1. Write an autobiographical analysis of your economic life from as far back as you can remember. Besides describing changing circumstances over time, analyze the impact economic class has had on your sense of self-worth, feelings, opportunities, and experiences—as well as the effects change has had on others' responses to you.

2. Alternatively, imagine a twenty-one-year-old woman, divorced and with a three-year-old child. She has graduated from high school but has not gone to college. She has not worked since her child was born. While she was in high school, she worked during the summers and sometimes after school for minimum wage in retail stores and fast-food restaurants. Her ex-husband has not paid any child support, though legally he is required to do so. Her parents are no longer living, and she has no sisters or brothers. How is she going to support herself and her three-year-old child?

Looking at the classifieds of a local newspaper, find this woman a job. Find out what her yearly salary would be, and calculate her monthly income from that projected salary. Do not forget how much she will have to pay for income taxes and FICA deductions. (Information about the percentages for these deductions should be available in your library.)

After you write your report on your findings, draw some conclusions from comparing her finances with the poverty line, which is approximately $15,130 a year for a two-person family in 2012, and with your local welfare payment for a two-person family. What do these comparisons show?

3. In 1995, federal politicians from both parties committed themselves to "ending welfare as we know it." From what you *know* (not believe) about welfare and from the readings in Part VI, try (either alone or with a small group) to create a policy that would improve our welfare system or social safety net.

4. After reading Part VI, identify what you feel is the central economic problem facing our nation today. Research this problem either in the library or in your community and write a paper concretely describing the problem and what you think should be done to address it.

VII

Race, Class, and Gender after 9/11 and Post-Katrina

MOST OF US HAVE HEARD IT SAID—"AFTER 9/11, everything changed." Certainly for the broken families who lost loved ones in the World Trade Center, the Pentagon, and all the hijacked planes that crashed, life is immeasurably changed. But the sentence implies more—it refers to how we feel about ourselves and others in the world, and from this has issued a large debate nationwide and worldwide. Whether or not "everything changed" depends on the reactions of individual citizens and of governments. As for individual behavior, after 9/11, there were basically three ways of carrying on day-to-day. One was to "cocoon"— basically, to go about one's business with very little social interaction and to stay close to home. The second way was to want revenge and, so, to direct anger toward those nearby and afar. The third way was to become very involved with some sort of community service or cause that the person highly valued. Many people wanted to do something to heal themselves and the world. As for national reactions, the global outpouring of sympathy and grief quickly changed when the United States announced that there were ties between Saddam Hussein and Al Qaeda and that Iraq had weapons of mass destruction. Ignoring the warnings from the United Nations Security Council, the United States invaded and occupied Iraq, at great loss of American and Iraqi life,

based on false claims of Iraq having weapons of mass destruction and ties to Al Qaeda.

What happened within the United States was equally upsetting and designed to quell any critics. With the passage of the Patriot Act, the federal government was given more power than any other administration to do surveillance on our own people, circumvent due process and First Amendment rights, prevent citizens from traveling, incarcerate whomever it sees fit, and demand access to student records from universities. Combine these policies of no checks and balances with deep troubles in the United States economy and anxiety over the safety of family members serving in Iraq and Afghanistan, and we see a movement of citizenry ready for change. The dialogues and "town meetings" going on all over America have been about revisiting our core values. Do we have a greater sense of unity as Americans now, or not? Does this sense cross racial, ethnic, and gender boundaries, or do we use these boundaries to structure how people see themselves and others in the world? Has being afraid made us **xenophobic**—highly fearful of anyone of foreign origin? Or perhaps mistrusting the dramatic, military approach to global and domestic problem solving, do we look forward to the time when we can again call on each other for resources, healing many of the rifts, especially with those living within America and with our traditional allies? As for law-abiding immigrants, who have been recently marginalized by an atmosphere of fear, we definitely look forward to the time when we will not feel *compelled* to fly or wear an American flag, as an attempt to not be targeted because of our accent, color of skin, or country of origin. This part of the text is dedicated to Americans, new and old, who are willing to help heal a wounded nation and world, by active citizenship and faith that we can learn from our history.

We begin Part VII with Reading 83 where Tram Nguyen takes us into a "Public's Truth" forum, one of several discussions planned throughout the United States, focusing on the effect the war on terrorism and change in domestic laws have had "on the lives of immigrants, refugees, and communities of color." Reading 84 is by Muzaffar A. Chishti, Doris Meissner, Demetrios G. Papademetriou, Jay Peterzell, Michael J. Wishnie, and Stephen W. Yale-Loehr from the Migration Policy Institute, a nonpartisan, independent, nonprofit think tank that devotes its time to studying the common ground of national security, civil rights, and immigration policy. This article analyzes the effectiveness and impact of our war on terrorism (which is primarily done through immigration control) and gives recommendations for sound immigration policy. In Reading 85, we focus on culturally appropriate mental health care for American Muslims, by Amber Haque.

Readings 86 and 87 focus on two very vulnerable groups that have been adversely affected by the aftermath of 9/11. Donovan Slack describes the efforts of a refugee and relocation center in Trenton, New Jersey. After the terrorist attacks, no refugees were allowed to enter the United States for several months, even though they had been approved, and many were in great danger in refugee camps or in hiding. As a result, many died. Farai Chideya then asks, "Wouldn't it be great if people like [Jessica] Lynch and [Shoshana] Johnson didn't have to go to war to get a job or an education?" Both women came from towns with 20 percent and 24 percent unemployment, where the per capita incomes are between $13,000 and $14,000 a year. Chideya suggests that we

could do better by investing as a nation in local service corps, where young people can give back to their country while gaining skills.

Reading 88 by Mary Sue Ply titled "Phoenix Rising from the Waters: The Post-Katrina Renewal of the New Orleans East Vietnamese Community" gives us an unusually close description of New Orleans East's Vietnamese village, and its resilience in the aftermath of Hurricane Katrina. Defying Mayor Nagin's orders to resettle, the Vietnamese residents returned, bringing redevelopment experts from other parts of the United States and Vietnam. Reading 89 by Human Rights Watch describes the nature of the September 11 backlash violence and the responses of local, state, and the federal government.

These articles challenge us all to share ideas, analyze, and make proposals for serious problem solving—much as the Migration Policy Institute does. If every classroom becomes a temporary think tank, our country will have made great strides, here and in the world.

83

Immigrant Families Condemn Racial Targeting

TRAM NGUYEN

Abdul Hatifie hosts a weekly radio show broadcast to the Afghan community in the Bay Area and Los Angeles. Along with announcements of community events and discussions of Afghan culture, the Alameda doctor tries to talk about discrimination and anti-immigrant scapegoating.

"(Listeners) hear me talk of people's stories and politics and they ask, 'Why do you say these things? Why can't you just stay quiet?'" I try to explain to them that to say the truth is not a crime, Hatifie said. "I am a person who has the right to speak, but now, in this country, we are taking out the Constitution, we are taking away our rights. The U.S. is not supposed to be like this."

Hatifie was one of 14 immigrants who shared their stories during a public hearing May 10 hosted at Buena Vista United Methodist Church, a Japanese American congregation in Alameda,

California. Organized by the Applied Research Center, the testimonials were the first in a series of "Public's Truth" forums planned around the country to highlight the impact of the "war on terrorism" and national security on the lives of immigrants, refugees, and communities of color.

At least 1,200 immigrants have been secretly detained in the last two years, and the federal government still hasn't released any information on their names and whereabouts. Thousands more [have been] deported or forced to flee "special registration" requirements, FBI interrogations, and INS raids. More than 10,000 immigrant workers have lost their jobs as a result of Operation Tarmac raids at airports, citizenship requirements for screeners, and social security "no-match letters" used to fire workers.

Despite widespread fear in their communities, participants at the forum were outspoken in condemning the policies and practices that have unjustly targeted them.

"Why is it acceptable for our government to tear families apart?" asked Theresa Allyn, a student at UC Berkeley whose mother was deported to the Philippines after 30 years in the U.S. Allyn's mother, a teacher, fell "out of status" with immigration authorities after she lost her green card during a 1999 robbery. Complications over replacing her green card status eventually led to her deportation in January 2003.

Other speakers related stories of attacks across a spectrum of ethnic communities and social sectors. Marwa Rifahie, an 18-year-old Egyptian American, described harassment at her high school from a teacher who called her a "Nazi." Former airport worker Erlinda Valencia recalled English-proficiency tests and citizenship requirements that resulted in her lay-off after 14 years as a screener at San Francisco airport. Community activists Kawal Ulanday and Rebecca Gordon described government scrutiny of their political activities—being visited by the FBI and put on a "no-fly" list for profiling at airports, respectively—that pointed to a larger "clamping down on all our freedoms."

The setting of the hearing, in a Japanese American Methodist church, held particular significance for audience members as Rev. Michael Yoshii drew parallels between the post-9/11 climate and the climate that led to World War II internment. This hearing, along with its antecedent

held by the Hate Free Zone of Seattle last year, is modeled after national hearings held during the Japanese American redress movement during the 1980s.

One of the Public's Truth testimonials belonged to Alba Witkin, an 83-year-old resident of Berkeley, Calif. who worked with American Friends' Service Committee during the 1940s to help Japanese American internees eligible to leave the camps for placement at colleges and universities.

"I know that it is hard to understand why people didn't seem to react to the Japanese internment. A lot of people ask me how could average citizens sit back and let that happen," she recalled. "But a lot of people didn't know the full extent of what was happening. The press didn't report it. I think that is a commentary on the media in 1942 as well as the media today. I still don't think we're getting all the stories."

Future Public's Truth forums are planned for San Jose, Los Angeles, and other cities nationwide.

According to Rev. Yoshii, "We need to establish a public record of these egregious violations and take action to protect the civil liberties and human rights of all families, regardless of their race, religion, or country of origin."   [2003]

Understanding the Reading

1. What is the purpose of the "Public's Truth" forums?
2. Why is the U.S. government detaining immigrants?
3. Why was Theresa Allyn's mother deported after thirty years in the United States?
4. What kind of harassment are some community activists experiencing?
5. What are the parallels between the post-9/11 atmosphere and what happened to Japanese Americans during World War II?

Suggestions for Responding

1. Collect testimonials from your own community of how immigrants are being treated.
2. Research what policies the Homeland Security Department has changed that have made it especially difficult or impossible for thousands of law-abiding immigrants to stay in the United States. ◆

84

America's Challenge: Domestic Security, Civil Liberties, and National Unity After September 11

Muzaffar A. Chishti, Doris Meissner, Demetrios G. Papademetriou, Jay Peterzell, Michael J. Wishnie, and Stephen W. Yale-Loehr

Summary

The U.S. government's harsh measures against immigrants since September 11 have failed to make us safer, have violated our fundamental civil liberties, and have undermined national unity.

The devastating attacks of September 11 demanded a wide-ranging response. The United States has responded with military action, as in Afghanistan; through intelligence operations to disrupt al Qaeda and arrest its members; and by re-organizing homeland security.

But our new security measures must be effective rather than merely dramatic, and must not destroy what we are trying to defend. The government's post–September 11 immigration measures have failed these tests.

These actions have not only done great harm to the nation; they have also been largely ineffective in their stated goal of improving our domestic security. Despite the government's heavy-handed immigration tactics, many of the September 11 terrorists would probably be admitted to the United States today.

Al Qaeda's hijackers were carefully chosen to avoid detection: all but two were educated young men from middle-class families with no criminal records and no known connection to terrorism. To apprehend such individuals before they attack requires a laser-like focus on the gathering, sharing, and analysis of intelligence, working hand-in-glove with well-targeted criminal and immigration law enforcement.

Instead, the government conducted round-ups of individuals based on their national origin and religion. These roundups failed to locate terrorists, and damaged one of our great potential assets in the war on terrorism: the communities of Arab- and Muslim-Americans.

We believe it is possible both to defend our nation and to protect core American values and principles, but doing so requires a different approach. It is too easy to say that if we abandon our civil liberties the terrorists win. It is just as easy to say that without security there will be little room for liberty. What is hard is to take both arguments with equal seriousness and to integrate them within a single framework. We set out to reach that important balance in this report.

As we worked on this project we became convinced that more than security and civil liberties—that is, the rights of individuals—are at stake. There is a third element: the character of the nation. Our humblest coin, the penny, bears the words *e pluribus unum*, or "from many, one." The phrase goes to the heart of our identity as a nation and to the strength we derive from diversity. We strongly believe that fully embracing Muslim and Arab communities as part of the larger American society would not only serve this American value but help break the impasse between security and liberty, strengthening both.

Harsh Measures Against Immigrants Have Failed to Make Us Safer

Our 18-month-long review of post–September 11 immigration measures determined that:

- The U.S. government overemphasized the use of the immigration system;
- As an antiterrorism measure, immigration enforcement is of limited effectiveness; and
- Arresting a large number of noncitizens on grounds not related to domestic security only gives the nation a false sense of security.

In some cases, the administration simply used immigration law as a proxy for criminal law enforcement, circumventing constitutional safeguards. In others, the government seems to have acted out of political expediency, creating a false appearance of effectiveness without regard to the cost.

Our research indicates that the government's major successes in apprehending terrorists have not come from post–September 11 immigration initiatives but from other efforts such as international intelligence activities, law enforcement cooperation, and information provided by arrests made abroad. A few noncitizens detained through these immigration initiatives have been characterized as terrorists, but the only charges brought against them were actually for routine immigration violations or ordinary crimes.

Many of the government's post–Sept. 11 immigration actions have been poorly planned and have undermined their own objectives. For example, the goals of the special call-in registration program have been contradictory: gathering information about nonimmigrants present in the United States, and deporting those with immigration violations. Many nonimmigrants have rightly feared they will be detained or deported if they attempt to comply, so they have not registered.

Our research also found serious problems at the Federal Bureau of Investigation (FBI) that are hampering our nation's counterterrorism efforts and damaging other key national interests. The State Department has tried for 10 years to get access to FBI information to add to its terrorist watchlists; those discussions are still going on. Automating this process would help to overcome long delays in visa approvals that are damaging U.S. political and economic relations abroad. It would also allow agencies to focus on a more in-depth risk assessment of visa applicants who raise legitimate security concerns.

Finally, the Justice Department's efforts to enlist state and local law enforcement agencies into enforcing federal immigration law risks making our cities and towns more dangerous while hurting the effort to fight terrorism. Such action undercuts the trust that local law enforcement agencies have built with immigrant communities, making immigrants less likely to report crimes, come forward as witnesses, or provide intelligence information, out of fear that they or their families risk detention or deportation.

GOVERNMENT IMMIGRATION ACTIONS THREATEN FUNDAMENTAL CIVIL LIBERTIES

The U.S. government has imposed some immigration measures more commonly associated with totalitarian regimes. As this report details, there have been too many instances of long-time U.S. residents deprived of their liberty without due process of law, detained by the government and held without charge, denied effective access to legal counsel, or subjected to closed hearings. These actions violate bedrock principles of U.S. law and society.

Take the experience of Tarek Mohamed Fayad, an Egyptian dentist arrested in southern California on Sept. 13, 2001, for violating his student visa. During Fayad's first 10 days of incarceration he was not allowed to make any telephone calls. Thereafter, he was allowed sporadic "legal" calls and only a single "social" call per month. The "legal" call was placed by a Bureau of Prisons counselor either to a designated law office or to one of the organizations on the INS's[1] list of organizations providing free legal services in the region. The privilege of making a call was deemed satisfied once the call was placed, regardless of whether the call was answered. Of the agencies on the list provided to Fayad, only one number was a working contact for an agency providing legal counseling to detainees and none of the organizations agreed to provide representation. In the meantime, Fayad's friends had hired an attorney for him, but the attorney was unable to determine his location for more than a month. Even after the attorney found out that Fayad was being detained at a federal facility in New York, the Bureau of Prisons continued to deny that Fayad was in custody.

Rather than relying on individualized suspicion or intelligence-driven criteria, the government has used national origin as a proxy for evidence of dangerousness. By targeting specific ethnic groups with its new measures, the government has violated another core principle of American justice: the Fifth Amendment guarantee of equal protection.

The government also conducted a determined effort to hide the identity, number and whereabouts of its detainees, violating the First Amendment's protection of the public's right to be informed about government actions. This right is at the heart of our democracy, and is crucial to maintaining government accountability to the public.

The government's post–September 11 actions follow a repeating pattern in American history of rounding up immigrant groups during national security crises, a history we review as part of this report. Like the internment of Japanese-Americans during World War II, the deportation of Eastern-European immigrants during the Red Scare of 1919–20, and the harassment and internment of German-Americans during World War I, these actions will come to be seen as a stain on America's heritage as a nation of immigrants and a land where individual rights are valued and protected.

REPORT PROFILES 406 DETAINEES, DESPITE GOVERNMENT SECRECY

More than 1,200 people—the government has refused to say exactly how many, who they are, or what has happened to all of them—were detained after September 11. Despite the government's determined efforts to shroud these actions in secrecy, as part of our research we were able to obtain information about 406 of these detainees . . . :

- Unlike the hijackers, the majority of noncitizens detained since September 11 had significant ties to the United States and roots in their communities. Of the detainees for whom relevant information was available, over 46 percent had been in the United States at least six years. Almost half had spouses, children, or other family relationships in the United States.
- Even in an immigration system known for its systemic problems, the post–September 11 detainees suffered exceptionally harsh treatment. Many were detained for weeks or months without charge or after a judge ordered them released. Of the detainees for whom such information was available, nearly 52 percent were subject to an "FBI hold," keeping them detained after a judge released them or ordered them removed from the United States. More than 42 percent of detainees were denied the opportunity to post bond. Many of the detainees were subjected to solitary confinement, 24-hour lighting of cells, and physical abuse.
- Although detainees in theory had the legal right to secure counsel at their own expense and to contact family members and consular representatives, the government frequently denied them these rights, especially in the first weeks after September 11.
- Many of the detainees were incarcerated because of profiling by ordinary citizens, who called government agencies about neighbors, coworkers, and strangers based on their ethnicity, religion, name, or appearance. In Louisville, KY, the FBI and INS detained 27 Mauritanians after an outpouring of tips from the public; these included a tip from a suspicious neighbor, who called the FBI when a delivery service dropped off a box with Arabic writing on it.

In New York, a man studying airplane design at the New York Institute of Technology went to a Kinko's store to make copies of airplane photos. An employee went into the wastebasket to get his information and then called the FBI; after nearly two months in detention, he accepted voluntary departure. Nearly 28 percent of the detainees were arrested because of a tip to the authorities by private citizens.

Most important, immigration arrests based upon tips, sweeps, and profiling have not resulted in any terrorism-related convictions against these detainees. Of the four detainees in our sample who had terrorism-related charges brought against them, all four were arrested based on traditional investigative techniques, not as the result of immigration enforcement initiatives. One has since been convicted and two have been acquitted; charges were dropped against the fourth individual, and he was deported.

GOVERNMENT TARGETING OF ARAB- AND MUSLIM-AMERICANS UNDERMINES NATIONAL UNITY

The government's actions against Arabs and Muslims have terrified and alienated hardworking communities across the nation.

President Bush's visit to a Washington mosque shortly after September 11 had a temporary positive impact on Arab- and Muslim-American communities. But the subsequent failure of government leaders to speak out on a sustained basis against discrimination, coupled with the Justice Department's aggressive immigration initiatives, sent a message to individuals and companies that discrimination against Arabs and Muslims was acceptable, leaders of these communities said. These views emerged in a coast-to-coast series of interviews that the Migration Policy Institute conducted to gauge the impact of the crisis on Arab- and Muslim-Americans.

"September 11 has created an atmosphere which suggests that it is okay to be biased against Arab-Americans and Muslims," said a regional director of an Arab-American civil rights organization.

The Justice Department's decision to conduct closed immigration proceedings for many of the detainees only increased suspicion that Arab- and Muslim-Americans were being treated under a different standard of due process. "The automatic association with terrorism is present in all these proceedings," said a prominent Arab-American lawyer in Michigan.

There is a strong belief among Arab- and Muslim-Americans that these measures are ineffective in responding to threats of terrorism, but are being undertaken for political expediency or public relations at a huge price to their communities. "This is political smoke to make people feel good," said the spokesman of a national Arab-American organization.

In a striking consensus, however, many leaders of the community have developed a positive reaction to law enforcement agencies since September 11, especially to local police. "The local police are our friends," said the chief imam of a New York Islamic center, citing their constant presence to protect his mosque.

Discrimination in the workplace soared after September 11. So overwhelming was the number of complaints it received that the Equal Employment Opportunity Commission (EEOC) created a new category to track acts of discrimination against Middle Eastern, Muslim and South Asian workers after September 11. In the 15 months between Sept. 11, 2001, and Dec. 11, 2002, the EEOC received 705 such complaints. Many more went unreported. And to add insult to injury, some of those who were detained after September 11 have been fired by their employers as a result.

Yet the experience of Arabs and Muslims in America post–September 11 is more than a story of fear and victimization. It is, in many ways, an impressive story of a community that at first felt intimidated but has since started to assert its place in the American body politic. Naturalization applications from Arab and Muslim immigrants have jumped and voter registration has risen since September 11.

September 11 and its aftermath have ushered in what could be called the "Muslim moment": a period of rising Muslim self-consciousness, new alliances outside their own communities, interfaith dialogue, and generational change. The sense of siege has strengthened some Muslim- and Arab-American political organizations and has led them to a greater focus on civil rights, social services, economic development, and engagement with government agencies. The notion of a distinct "American Muslim" identity has gained new currency. It is an identity that seeks to assert its independence from forces abroad, one that combines the essential elements of Islam and the values of U.S. constitutional democracy.   [2003]

Term

1. INS: Immigration and Naturalization Service.

Understanding the Reading

1. Why does the Migration Policy Institute say that the government's post–September 11 actions have failed to be effective and have been very destructive?
2. What was one of our best local assets in our war on terrorism?
3. How can we have both security and liberty?
4. Why hasn't the call-in registration program worked?
5. Why shouldn't local law enforcement enforce federal immigration law, according to this report? Do you agree or disagree?
6. How have our First Amendment rights been harmed?
7. Describe what the article calls the "Muslim moment."

Suggestions for Responding

1. Mayor Bloomberg of New York City has told local law enforcement not to enforce certain federal immigration laws. Find which other cities have responded in the same way and which make a point of enforcing federal immigration law.
2. Invite Arab Americans or Muslim Americans to your class to discuss practical ways of balancing security with liberty. ✦

85

Religion and Mental Health: The Case of American Muslims

AMBER HAQUE

Surveys of the general population in America show that 95% of the people believe in God and a majority also identify themselves with a religion (Hoge, 1996). There is an increased amount of research in the West that shows the influence of religion on mental health. More recently, multiculturalism, religious diversity, and a concern regarding inequalities in health care delivery between mainstream Americans and ethnic minorities are making researchers particularly interested in religion and its influence on mental health (AMA, 2002). A realization that different people need different treatment, especially help that is religious in nature is also acknowledged by the American Psychological Association's Ethical Code of Conduct, which specifies that psychologists need to respect and consider the religious views of a client and, in case they cannot, that the client should be referred to a psychologist who can (APA, 1992). Lothstein (2002) points out that "the alienation that has existed between the mental health professions and religion for most of the 20th century is ending. The influence of the naturalistic, anti-religious assumptions that once gripped the field has weakened, and there is now a more spiritually open *Zeitgeist*" While there is a growing interest in examining the role of religion and mental health in religious minorities of America, no research work is presently available on the mental health of American Muslims. The September 11 attacks on America have brought Muslims to the forefront of American attention and the issues arising from this event may very well exacerbate the already existing mental health concerns of these people. Who are the Muslims and what is their religion? How do Muslims perceive mental health and what factors threaten their mental health in a culture that is alien to their own? How does their religion deal with mental health and how are Muslims responding to such challenges? Do Muslim clients have

different role expectations of their psychologists and counselors [than] the mainstream population does? These questions are pertinent for academicians, researchers and practitioners of all helping professions as the Muslim population grows and is encountered in professional settings. This paper attempts to familiarize the non-Muslim audience about American Muslims and their belief systems, factors affecting their mental health, how the Muslim community is responding to such challenges, and what expectations Muslims have of their mental health professionals. The paper also outlines a set of recommendations for future planning and the increased well-being of this growing minority.

MUSLIMS OF AMERICA

Although claims of the first Muslim arrival in America are reported as early as 1178 when a group of Chinese Muslim sailors landed on the West coast (DawaNet, 2003), history books record the Muslim arrival in 1312 when Mansa Abu Bakr came from Mali to South America (Nyang, 1999). Many sea voyages to the "New World" were made between the 15th and 16th centuries when an estimated 10 million African slaves came to America of whom around 30% were Muslims. Again, in the 18th century, the Moors from Spain were reported to be living in the Carolinas and Florida. It is believed that most of these early migrants were uneducated and due to various reasons, including forced conversions to Christianity over the years, they assimilated into the mainstream American culture (Nyang, 1999; Shamma, 1999). Muslim migration to the US in the 19th and 20th centuries occurred in several waves. The first wave was from the Arab world between 1875 and 1912 and was comprised of unskilled people who left the Middle East mainly for economic reasons; the second was from 1918–1922 after World War I; the third from 1930–1938 was of American Muslim relatives conditioned by US immigration laws; the fourth from 1947–1960 included many immigrants from Eastern Europe, India, Pakistan, Soviet Union and other parts of the world; and the fifth was from 1967 until the present (Haddad, 1991). For reasons, including discriminatory practices towards African Americans, an Afro-American leader named Noble Timothy Drew Ali founded the Moorish Science Temple Movement in 1913 in New Jersey and claimed that he was chosen by God to restore the true identity of the blacks who are descendants of Muslim Moors from Morocco. In 1930, the *Nation of Islam* was born, headed by Wallace Ford from Detroit, who was succeeded by his disciple Elijah Muhammad. These organizations did not preach the teachings of mainstream *Sunni* Islam and were soon challenged from within by prominent figures like Malcolm X and Warith Deen Mohammad, Elijah's son. These influential personalities abandoned the *Nation of Islam* and together with their followers joined the mainstream group of Muslims of America that follows the teachings of the Qur'an, the Muslim holy book, and *Sunnah* or the traditions of Prophet Muhammad. Conversion of non-Muslims occurred not only among Afro-Americans but also among many persons of Anglo-Saxon origin and Native Americans who embraced Islam for varied reasons (Lang, 1997). The name of Muhammad Alexander Russell Webb, a white American and one of the pioneers of Islamic *dawah* efforts towards the end of the 19th century is familiar to many American Muslims. The white American intellectuals converting to Islam were largely attracted by the growing Sufi orders in America. The more educated immigrant Muslims who came from different parts of the globe in the 1940s through the '60s became especially concerned about the religion and cultural values of their young and in 1972 established the Muslim Students Association (MSA) on almost all university campuses throughout North America. Presently, the estimated population of Muslim Americans ranges from 3 to 6 million residing throughout the United States, concentrated mostly in urban areas of the East and West Coast, Midwest, and parts of the South, especially Texas and Florida (Haddad, 1991; Husain & Husain, 1996).

Recent polls show that 22% of American Muslims are US born, 78% are immigrants, 27% are of Middle East origin, 25% are from South Asia, 24% are African Americans and the rest are from Europe, the Far East, or other parts of the world (Zogby International, 2002). Another survey sponsored by Georgetown University in 2001 and conducted on urban Muslims shows that half of the American Muslims earn more than $50,000 a year and 58% are college graduates. Seven in 10 Muslims are active in their mosques; 35% of men and 26% of women attend religious and/or community services weekly (Project MAPS, 2001).

Although Muslims come from different national and ethnic backgrounds, there are very few basic differences among them in matters of religion. They generally stick to the same worldview based on the Qur'an and *Sunnah*. Muslims believe in the existence of One God who depends on no one, and no one is like Him. Muslims firmly believe in the existence of angels who do things as commanded by God. They believe in the Messengers of God from Adam to Abraham, Moses, Christ, and finally Muhammad who brought the same messages of worshipping one God. Muslims also believe in the Books of God including the Bible, but the Qur'an is the final revelation. They believe in the Day of Judgment (one will be paid his/her due for actions in this world—God will do justice to all), and destiny or fate, and life after death.

THE ISLAMIC CONCEPT OF MENTAL HEALTH

The Islamic view of man is dualistic, as man possesses both body and soul (Q38:71–72).[1] While the body is perishable, the soul is everlasting; the body is only a vehicle for the human soul. It is primarily the individual soul that is responsible for human behavior and it will be questioned in the life hereafter. The soul functions at three different levels and should be kept pure and be guided according to the injunctions given in the Qur'an.[2] Thus, the soul becomes the focus of attention for practicing Muslims and care of the body although essential, becomes secondary to the care of the soul. The Qur'an says, "Guard your own souls. If you follow guidance, no harm can come to you from those who stray" (Q5:108). The soul is comprised of the *ruh* (spirit), the *qalb* (heart), and the *aql* (intellect). The spirit is a quality of God, which He has breathed into man (Q38:71–72) and which exalts man above all other creations. The spirit also possesses the inherent knowledge of oneness of God and the ability to acquire true knowledge (Unity of God).

The heart or *Qalb,* which is the cognitive faculty in humans, is the seat of volition, intention, and wisdom. The Qur'an talks about the illnesses of the heart in many places, referring to errors in man's thinking that lead to man's own destruction.[3] Intellect or *Aql* is the faculty of reasoning of the highest order. In Islam, faith is not blind and does not stand above reason, to the extent that the Qur'an invites man to reflect on all that it says. These combined faculties are bestowed upon man to reach the ultimate truth that will bring out ultimate wisdom and happiness, preconditions to good mental health. Happiness in Islam relates to the present world as well as the hereafter; the latter being more meaningful and permanent and a gift of God to those who spend their lives in submitting to His commands. Muslim scholars explain that virtues and good character can be produced by training *Nafs al Ammarah* (animal soul) and its bodily faculties by *Nafs al Lawwamah* (rational soul) that guides human actions based on thinking and reflection (Al Attas, 1993).

The Qur'an declares that man is created in the best of moulds that can make him surpass the angels in positive qualities. This is because man is given the knowledge that angels do not have (Q2:31) and freewill, unlike angels who must follow the commandments of God. Man is given freewill to seek the true reality and self-understanding that will lead him to foster divine attributes in himself. However, if man does not use his faculties in the prescribed manner, he may fall prey to his bodily desires and become lowlier than animals (Q95:4–5). The innate disposition or *fitrah* is a source of guidance and is centered in the soul, telling humans when they are wrong. It is the deviation from *fitrah* or a corruption of the original positive nature by following one's own whims that can lead to mental health problems. Illness is also looked upon as the will of God and problems of life may be trials from God (Q2:155–156, 21:35) and a means of washing away sins if dealt with patiently. In Islam, man is viewed as a microcosm of the entire universe, meaning that as the cosmos follows its own nature prescribed by God, man must also follow the divine injunctions or suffer consequences. If man submits to the will of God, he will not experience a conflict in life or will be psychologically and morally equipped

to deal with such conflicts. Islam views mental health not only as the absence of pathology but presence of virtues that can lead man to his own well-being.

The Qur'an is explicit about the virtues that preserve mental health and vices that can bring various mental health problems. Virtues can be external or internal. External virtues refer to the fulfillment of divine commandments like acts of worship, doing good to others and following Islamic rules of attire, eating, cleanliness, relationships, etc. Internal virtues arise from reasoning based on the Qur'anic revelations and include good intentions, a desire to seek knowledge of self and knowledge of God, which can be attained through sincere contemplation. External and internal virtues complement one another and are necessary for the attainment of happiness and the well-being of the individual.

Besides the corruption of the *fitrah* based on one's own volition, other factors that may cause mental health problems include interventions from the *Jinn* (genie), black magic and effects of the evil eye. Such factors would especially affect those people who have lost faith and attach more value to the present world. The Qur'an and *Sunnah* give details on the existence of these variables in human life and the manner in which they can be treated. However, it should be noted that such beliefs and practices are found in other religions as well and are often reflective of cultures rather than religion.

One also needs to distinguish between the Islamic concept of mental health based on religion and the western concept based on the secular and scientific theories of human nature and illness. Muslims perceive scientific development as a successive or cumulative effort leading towards discovering the laws of God; they believe that science can be flawed if not based on faith. The integration of science and religion is a primary component of Muslim scholarly belief (Haque, 1998). It is also important to know that modern social science disciplines emerged out of a struggle between scientists who emphasized observation and experimentation in all phenomena and the religionists who resorted to divine scriptures for everything. In this struggle, science eventually came out victorious over religion resulting in the secularization of knowledge.[4] Religion and metaphysical elements were eliminated from explaining human behavior. When psychology separated from philosophy, it also emerged as a scientific discipline where religion played almost no role or a negative role in explaining human behavior. Although some psychologists took interest in the psychology of religion, their influence remained minimal because of the strong influence of psychodynamic and behavioral theories. However, due to factors including a religious revival in America, psychologists are now showing more interest in the influence of religion on mental health.

MENTAL HEALTH STRESSORS

Living in a society that is in contrast to one's values and belief systems can be highly stressful and challenging. Muslims face ongoing stressors in the American society that may negatively affect their mental health. Although no research is currently available on identifying sources of stress for American Muslims, the following stand out as major challenges.

Religious beliefs and observance of religious rituals. The Muslim religious beliefs rooted in the Qur'an and *Sunnah* not only carry a different worldview but also compete with the dominant religions of America. Despite being an Abrahamic religion like Judaism and Christianity, Islam negates certain elements found in these religions and prescribes a code of life incompatible with the Western outlook. For those Muslims who perform their religious rituals like the five daily prayers and observe fasting in the month of Ramadan, the American context presents particular problems at the workplace as it may result in inconvenience for both the employees and the employer. Ablutions that should be made before each prayer, the offering of prayers in a prescribed manner and in a particular place with a prayer mat can all become difficult. Friday prayers that are obligatory and must be offered in a mosque may not always be possible due to work schedules or the unavailability of a mosque in the area.[5]

Sense of alienation and identity crisis. For Muslims, American living presents various challenges ranging from food (pork and alcohol products are strictly prohibited) to the religious and cultural belief systems. For newer immigrants, even the dress, weather and language can cause adjustment problems. American-born children raised in Muslim homes face ongoing challenges to the Islamic code of life. Thus, Muslims may not feel themselves to be a part of the mainstream society. While this cannot be generalized for all, it is true of Muslims who stick to their religion and cultural norms and values and end up forming their own rigid communities. It is also true that while immigrants face more challenges upon entering America, their American-born children find it easier to assimilate in the mainstream culture. However, if the children move away from or discard Islamic values, conflicts between the older and newer generations develop.

Misconceptions about Muslims and Islam. The media bashing of Muslims over the years is another major source of stress. An interesting article by Shaheen (1999) outlines how Muslims have been portrayed by the Western media over the years. Movies like Lawrence of Arabia (1962), Black Sunday (1977), Rollover (1981), and Delta Force (1986) create a negative image of Muslims resulting from the Arab-Israel conflict, a secular bias against Islam, a political agenda or plain ignorance on the part of the media. The main misconception about Islam is that it is a religion of violence, including the belief that Muslims are terrorists and that Islam is anti-American. Such beliefs have certainly been reinforced by a small group of radical individuals who generally have their own personal agendas. A major misconception also is that Islam is a religion of the Arabs, although many immigrants from Eastern Europe, Russia and China are also Muslims. Immigrants from Pakistan, Bangladesh, Malaysia, Indonesia, and the African continent and many other non-Arab countries are Muslims as well. Members of the Muslim community, especially young adults and children, find it difficult to cope with such stressors.

Prejudice and discrimination. Media bashing and stereotyping has led to a stigmatization of the Muslims resulting in prejudice as well as discrimination in all walks of life, especially after the September 11 attacks on America. Factors like high unemployment and the presence of right-wing movements based on ethnic and religious biases are other sources of psychological stress for Muslims and members of other minority groups. Hate mail and threat notes are a common occurrence at local Islamic centers in the U.S.[6] Muslim women face ongoing discrimination for wearing the *hijab* (headscarf), which is a part of their culture and religious faith. There are also incidents of prejudice reported in schools.

Social issues. Islam is not a religion in the narrow sense of the term but a way of life. It prescribes behaviors in all areas of life including family relationships (where member roles as well as gender roles are defined, e.g., children must obey parents except when parents go against religion), upbringing of children (parental role is crucial and there is emphasis on education and discipline), socialization (clear rules are laid down and free mixing of the sexes is prohibited), dietary issues (alcohol, pork and their by-products are strictly prohibited, which makes grocery shopping difficult—a devout Muslim must read the ingredients of all products to ensure compliance with dietary prohibitions), and monetary practices (poor-due is compulsory and interest is prohibited). Islamic injunctions often come in direct conflict with American living, which is highly liberal and permits many behaviors unacceptable in Islam.

Education of children. Although this issue is not voiced openly, Muslims are concerned about what is taught in the schools. Since American education is secular in nature, children may learn things that are in conflict with the Islamic worldview. For example, the Darwinian theory of evolution is in clear contrast to the Islamic story of creation and may change the mindset of a Muslim child against religion unless a proper analysis of such materialistic theories is explained to the children by their parents.

Islamic counseling services. While there is some effort on the part of certain Muslim organizations to establish counseling services for Muslims, formal services or agencies tailored for the needs of Muslim clients are severely lacking. This may be partly because there are very few therapists who are well grounded in Islamic approach to treatment and also due to a lack of Muslim professionals interested in starting such services. In Muslim countries, it is generally the Imam (one who leads the prayer at a mosque or a knowledgeable person of Islamic tenets) who treats mental health problems but such

persons in the U.S. would not qualify for counseling certification because of lack of training/education in the American/secular based mental health professions. Problems of broken homes, joblessness, and discrimination, religiosity, and relationship issues are left untreated because many Muslims may not feel comfortable working with secular therapists who do not understand Muslim culture or the religious contexts of Muslim issues.

Another way to look at such challenges is by age group. For example, at school, children are generally expected to comply with cultural norms in dress code, food habits, socialization and even accent. Secular holidays like Halloween and Valentine's Day do not exist in Islam, and Muslim children are in a dilemma when their parents do not approve of participation in these events. Further complications arise during adolescence when dating becomes the social norm. Muslim youths are supposed to stay away from such activities as premarital free mixing between the genders is prohibited. Selecting partners for marriage is a more serious issue because parents prefer their grown-up children to marry in their own cultures. Adult couples also have to make Islamic versus non-Islamic choices when buying a home or even a car that is financed on interest as interest is considered *haram* (prohibited) in Islam. Leaving children at babysitters or day care centers may not adhere to Islamic values and choosing between sending children to public schools that suffer from "secular" problems or Islamic schools that are private but expensive or simply unavailable is problematic. Women's issues of work, education and role expectations within Islam and different Muslim cultures pose significant challenges to Muslim women. Old age brings its own peculiar problems, prominent among which is loneliness that is increased because of being an ethnic as well as a religious minority. Even going to mosques for religious services can become difficult at this age due to transportation problems or the unavailability of mosques in the area.

A growing area of concern is the new converts who come to the fold of Islam. The number of Muslim converts is increasing but there is hardly any system of social support for them. While they are isolated from their native groups, the integration of these converts into Muslim societies remains a challenge. Muslims originating from countries like Iran, Iraq and Afghanistan are facing threats on a wider scale due to the political tensions between America and these nations. Muslim refugees from Bosnia, Palestine and Kashmir suffer from PTSD symptoms. Islamic rulings are clear on managing the affairs of society but such rules cannot be applied in a non-Muslim country. Muslims may feel cheated by the law of the land in cases of inheritance, child custody, child upbringing, and so forth, as American laws may violate the basic Qur'anic injunctions on family and social-related matters.[7] Such factors give rise to stress, anxiety, fear, insecurity, helplessness and depression among Muslims.

FACING THE CHALLENGES

Realizing the social and religious challenges that would arise in an un-Islamic culture, the MSA addressed some of these issues on its formation in the 1970s. Because MSA was basically a students' association, the Islamic Society of North America (ISNA) was established in 1981 as an umbrella organization with a mission to serve "the diverse needs of Muslims in North America . . . and provide a unified platform of expression for Islam, to develop educational, outreach and social services that translate the teachings of the Qur'an and the *Sunnah* into everyday living, and to enhance Islamic identity in society." Over the years, ISNA has developed many services for the Muslims including the establishment of Islamic Centers and Islamic schools, financial planning of Muslim funds from an Islamic perspective, management of charity monies, youth activities, matrimonial services, religious services, conferences, publications, etc. Although these activities may incorporate Muslim needs at a macro level, there are no direct services that are geared towards addressing mental health issues, per se. After the establishment of ISNA, many other smaller Muslim organizations have cropped up in America but few address specific mental health concerns and if they do, it is primarily the religious leader of the Islamic Center who counsels the client or family from an Islamic perspective. In the last few years, organizations like the Association of Muslim Social

Scientists (AMSS) have shown interest in conducting conferences and workshops on Islamic counseling. Two agencies that work towards the general social welfare of Muslims in a limited geographical area were established in the 1990s—the Islamic Health and Human Services (IHHS) was founded in Detroit in 1991 and the Islamic Social Services Association was founded in Virginia in 1999. Considering the large number of Muslims in America and their complex mental health issues, it can be stated that mental health services for Muslims and by Muslims are almost non-existent.

What approach does Islam take towards the treatment of mental health? Islam takes a two-pronged preventive approach to protect humans from sacrificing their mental health. The emphasis is on both building positive qualities in oneself that would prevent mental health problems and avoiding negative qualities that may lead to various mental health problems. There are numerous verses throughout the Qur'an emphasizing the development of three main positive qualities, i.e., faith, repentance and patience. Islamic faith refers to belief in God that gives the client a sense of acceptance especially when things are going against one's wishes. The Qur'anic verse 2:216 states, "It may be that you dislike a thing which is good for you and that you like a thing which is bad for you. God knows but you do not know." The Qur'an also points out that to return to faith and a need for higher assistance is in man's nature (Q17:67, 30:30). Faith in God is enhanced by praying and developing God-consciousness that will provide a sense of security and protection and on the other hand, a sense of apprehension that will prevent oneself from wrongdoings (Q91:7–8). The Qur'an also exhorts man to purify one's *nafs* through prayer and remembrance of God (Q2:152,2:186, 13:28, 27:62, 29:45, 40:60, 63:9)—this act is also called *Dhikr*. Reading the Qur'an in itself is healing (Q10:57, 17:82, 41:44). Muslims believe in finding solace by simply listening to or reciting the verses of the Qur'an and the Qur'an confirms this belief. Perhaps this is why many Muslims carry a copy of the Qur'an even when they are traveling. Repentance is asking God for forgiveness after which a person finds relief from psychological turmoil after breaking God's rules and regains self-integration. Repentance over mistakes is encouraged, as God loves to forgive (Q4:110, 6:54, 73:20). However, they reminded that a sin for which one asks forgiveness should not be repeated. Developing qualities of patience and perseverance is seen as an unfailing cure for all kinds of illnesses (Q2:153, 3:200, 3:146, 8:46, 8:66, 12:83, 16:96, 16:126, 23:111, 28:54, 31:17, 32:24). Gratitude and contentment are other virtues emphasized as they lead to satisfaction with what one has and prevent one from being greedy (3:145, 4:147, 6:53, 14:5, 14:7,14:32–34, 31:31, 34:19, 42:33, 93:11). Justice for all is reiterated in many places as it will lead to a balanced and just society (Q16:90).[8]

Other virtues that the Qur'an emphasizes are avoiding negative behaviors, e.g., avoiding extravagance that leads to a spendthrift character and other negative consequences (Q39:53); avoiding envy or jealousy that may lead one to anger and depression (Q2:109, 4:32)—envy is only permissible towards a person of better character or one who has spiritual qualities that takes one closer to God; avoiding passionate bodily desires that will lead to illegitimate sex or other unhealthy behaviors leading to the destruction of one's overall health and family/social relationships (Q3:142, 21:102, 43:71). The Qur'an also stresses avoiding pride as it may lead to a sense of elation, which stops one from moving ahead and leads one to look down upon others (Q4:49); avoiding temptation as it may lead toward injustice for oneself or others (Q57:14); avoiding corruption because it is unjust for others and will lead to chaos in the society (Q91:7–8) and avoiding anger because it is a major cause of physical illness and self-destruction (Q3:134). Many injunctions from the Prophet are given to overcome anger, some of which include: taking a few sips of water, making ablution, sitting down or lying down, leaving the area that arouses a person's anger; avoiding evil thinking as it is not beneficial for anyone (Q48:12). The Qur'an uses the word *waswas* meaning a whispering into the heart from Satan and prescribes certain verses for recitation that will also keep Satan away.

Faith, prayer, hope, patience, and taking responsibility can be integrated into therapy in dealing with Muslim clients. While we have seen the benefits of faith in the previous section,

regarding prayer one is assured that if the prayer is not answered it will earn a better reward in the hereafter and God knows what is best for a person. Group prayer is mandatory at least on Fridays and attains a sense of belongingness for Muslims even if they do not personally know anyone in their congregation. For a problem that afflicts the community, group prayers are often performed asking God for help. Patience refers to finding satisfaction at the end-result of an event especially when the outcome is negative. A great amount of reward is promised in the hereafter for the person who endures hardship with patience and this results in the emotional adjustment of the client. Islam places great emphasis on individual responsibility for all actions since human nature is given the ability to differentiate between right and wrong. The Qur'an even states, "Verily, never will God change the conditions of the people until they change it themselves" (Q13:11). Primarily, any treatment in Islam leads toward building strong faith in the client and reinforcing *fitrah*. A treatment without religious blend would be only partially effective, if at all.

Muslims coming from the Arab and South Asian cultures anticipate qualities in a therapist that may be quite opposite to the expectations one may have in western cultures. According to Al Issa (2000), the Muslim therapist needs to be assertive in telling a client what the problem is, unlike Western cultures where the choice to do something may be offered by the therapist but the client is not obligated to do it. In Islam the therapist plays an advisory and a teacher's role and the client is a learner or a disciple. The client may not challenge what the therapist has to say. The therapist may also express personal situations, problems, and anecdotes, from which the client is supposed to pick up lessons. The therapist emphasizes interdependence in the family rather than independence. This of course, reflects the collectivistic nature of Muslim society in general. Behavioral functioning is given more value than emotional states (e.g., there is less emphasis on feelings and more on behavior). Feelings have to be subdued in the interest of benefiting others. Moral values play a very distinct and important role. Emphasis is placed upon seeking help from the Qur'an, praying to God, keeping faith and hope, and of course, patience. It is a different issue if the Muslim therapist is trained in the Western paradigm and follows the scientific, non-judgmental, and value-free approach. Such therapists may not have a following within their own culture groups unless they incorporate Islamic values in their therapies.

CONCLUSIONS AND RECOMMENDATIONS

The Muslim presence in America dates back to pre-Columbian times and has grown consistently due to immigration, births, and conversions. American Muslims are not limited to a particular ethnic group and come from almost all races and nations from around the globe. The American Muslim population comes from the indigenous peoples as well as Whites, African-Americans and American Indians. Considering the growing population of Muslims in North America and their unique mental health needs, it is essential that the mental health professionals understand and treat Muslims as an important part of the multicultural fabric of the American society. The professionals need to understand the culture, customs, and religious beliefs of Muslims in order to serve them on an equal footing with other Americans. This could be achieved by providing cultural sensitivity training to professionals in areas including the religious faith of Muslims, their sociopolitical contexts and an awareness of the cultural differences among the Muslim people. A major problem that currently exists is the lack of research on Muslims in general and their mental health in particular, without which it is difficult to devise sound treatment plans. This issue becomes more complicated when mental health is studied in relation to religion. American journals like the *International Journal for the Psychology of Religion* and the *Journal for the Scientific Study of Religion* cover some studies on Muslim issues and may be good reference points for interested researchers. While doing research or assessment, psychological tests meant for the general population may not be suitable for Muslims. Culture free tests may be used to assess the general nature, level and extent of their mental health concerns, but emphasis should be placed on developing tests that are standardized for Muslims themselves. While education on multicultural issues is given to the professionals, it is also important that such knowledge be given to the students at the university level, training them to deal with these issues later on. Muslim scholars and health professionals can play a major role in disseminating such knowledge. Muslim students must also enter the human and social service professions in order to serve the people of their own cultures. More importantly, there is a need to develop a comprehensive and conceptual understanding of the Islamic perspective on mental health that can guide the professionals to appropriate treatment methods. A combination of useful modern approaches and religious treatments could go a long way to helping Muslim clients. Analysis of the interplay between religion and indigenous culture on the one hand and American life-style on the other hand is a serious area of research.

Notes

1. 'Q' indicates a reference from the Qur'an followed by the chapter and then the verse(s). A translation of the Qur'an by Abdullah Yusuf Ali (1996) is used as reference.

2. *Nafs Ammarah (Q12:53)*—free indulgence in gratifying passions and the tendency to do evil, *Nafs Lawwamah (Q75:2)*—conscience that directs man towards right or wrong, and *Nafs Mutmainnah (Q89:27)*—self that reaches the ultimate peace. Islamic teachings emphasize overcoming the passions of *Nafs Ammarah* to achieve *Nafs Mutmainnah* by using *Nafs Lawwamah* throughout one's life. The conflict of *Nafs Ammarah and Nafs Lawwamah* is a basic psychological conflict that a person goes through. Najati (2002) surmises that perhaps, it is God's will that the way man adopts in solving this conflict becomes the real test in this world. The successful ones are those who have the ability to reconcile these two needs and establish some sort of equilibrium between them. Islam educates people on how to establish this equilibrium by way of strengthening the spiritual component in man by inviting him to believe in one God and to worship Him. The other approach for man is to dominate his material component by

controlling his drives, emotions, and sexual desires. By these approaches of education, Islam teaches people to attain equilibrium between the material and the spiritual components of their personalities and thus enjoy good mental health. Although some scholars compare Freudian division of the mind to the three levels of the self given here, such comparison is flawed as the Islamic description arises out of the spiritual essence while Freud's description comes out of biological instincts in humans.

3. The heart is one of three types, the healthy heart, the dead heart and the sick heart. The healthy heart is cleansed from any desire that challenges God's commands, commits totally and relies fully on God only. The dead heart is unaware of its Creator, listens to its desires and whims and is immersed in worldly pleasures. The sick heart is somewhere in the middle with its love of God as well as love of the material world, engulfed in self-admiration and wavering between safety and destruction depending on which way it tilts itself.

4. The word "secular" is derived from the Latin root word *saeculum* meaning the present age. Thus, secular connotes this world or contemporary times. Secularization refers to rescuing man from the world beyond or a turning away from religious and metaphysical control of man. A distinction must also be made between secular and Western. There are many people in the West belonging to different religions and are not secular in their outlook. Even non-religious persons may not agree to all the concepts that secularism has to offer. West also is not totally synonymous with secularism, an error commonly made in academic circles, especially in the Muslim world. In the secular system, concern with God is a private matter at best, thereby leaving the notion of religion outside the scope of society's interest.

5. Ablution involves washing of the hands, rinsing out the mouth, cleansing the nostrils, washing face and arms up to the elbows, wiping the head, inner sides of the ears, neck and finally washing the feet up to the ankle. All five prayers are preferred at the mosque where one should go walking because there is a reward at each step taken.

At the mosque besides the religious aspect of remembering God, one gets to meet the fellow Muslims that strengthen social bonding and brotherhood. Fasting during Ramadan is a form of self-control in areas including anger, envy, sexual desire, etc. and develops a sense of gratitude for what one has and understanding and sympathy for others who do not have food. *Zakat* or alms giving is a built-in social security system for the poor and increases sympathy for the needy.

6. The Council of American Islamic Relations (CAIR) reports the following anti-Muslim incidents after the September 11 attacks until February 2002: Public harassments (372), Physical assaults (289), Deaths (11), Death threats (56), Bomb threats (16), Discrimination at workplace (166), Discrimination at school (74), Airport profiling (191), FBI/Police intimidation (224), and Hate mail (315). This is of course a very conservative report, as most incidents do not get reported due to a fear of backlash, etc. Other organizations of Muslims also maintain such records on the Internet. An annual report released by CAIR indicated an 18 percent increase in total incidents and a 60 percent rise in discrimination cases. The 60-page report, called "Patterns of Discrimination," details more than 280 incidents and experiences of anti-Muslim violence, discrimination, stereotyping, bias, and harassment. CAIR, February, 2002 (http://www.cair-net.org/). These figures have not been updated since February 2002.

7. For inheritance, male children get a larger share of property than female children or even more than the wife of the deceased husband. This is because males are given full responsibility of supporting their families in financial matters, whereas females are not. Children are considered minors until they reach adulthood and may not have access to their inherited property. For child custody, it is the father who generally remains the custodial parent. However, in Islam child custody has two forms, residential care and legal guardianship. The former covers the child's daily living needs and the latter includes important decisions about the child's life. It is the latter for which the father is responsible.

8. One may ask if there is complete justice in the Muslim world and the answer is a definite "no" because not all Muslims follow the injunctions of Islam causing immense lawlessness in many Muslim countries. There is definitely a lack of understanding of true Islam among Muslims themselves, which leads to more misconceptions of Islam and Muslims among non-Muslims. It is interesting that many Muslim converts report that their conversion was based on the religion of Islam and not on the behaviors of the present-day Muslims (see for example, Lang, 1996).   2004

References

Al Attas, S.M.N. (1993). The concept of happiness in Islam. International Institute of Islamic Thought and Civilization: Kuala Lumpur, Malaysia.

Al Issa, I. (2000). Mental Illness in the Islamic World. London: International University Press.

Ali, A. Y. (1996). The meaning of the Holy Qur'an. Beltsville: MD, Amana Publication.

American Psychological Association (1992). Ethical Principles of Psychologists and Code of Conduct. *American Psychologist,* 47, 1597–1611.

American Medical Association (2002). American Medical News, Editorial. July 8/15, 2002. American Disparities in treatment: Closing the health care gap. AMA *Health Disparities* site, offering information on the Association's policies, resources and partnerships (http://www.ama-assn.org/go/healthdisparities).

DawaNet (2003). American Muslim History. http://www.dawanet.co./history/amermuslimhist.asp.

Haddad, Y.Y. (1991). *The Muslims of America.* New York: Oxford University Press.

Haque, A. (1998). Psychology and Religion: Their Relationship and Integration from Islamic Perspective. *The American Journal of Islamic Social Sciences,* 15, 97–116.

Husain, A. and Husain, I. (1996). A brief history and demographics of Muslims in the United States. In Asad Husain, John Woods and Javed Akhtar (eds.). *Muslims in America: Opportunities and Challenges.* Chicago: International Strategy and Policy Institute.

Hoge, R.D. (1996). Religion in America: The demographics of beliefs and affiliation. In E.P. Shafranske (ed.), *Religion and the clinical practice of psychology* (pp. 21–41). Washington, D.C.: American Psychological Association.

Lang, J. (1996). Even Angels Ask: A Journey to Islam in America. Pp. 230. Beltsville, MD: Amana Publications.

Lothstein, L.M. (2002). Review on Handbook of psychotherapy and religion by P. Scott (ed.). http://www.proquest.umi.com.

Najati, M.O. (2000). The concept of mental health in the Holy Qur'an and the Hadeeth. Kuwait: www.islamnet.com.

Nyang, S.S. (1999). *Islam in the United States of America.* Chicago: ABC International Group, Inc.

Projects MAPS (2001). Results of Poll of American Muslims. Georgetown University, http://communications.georgetown.edu/press_releases/12200l/maps_study.html

Shaheen, J. (1999). Hollywood's Reel Arabs and Muslims. In A. Haque (ed.), *Muslims and Islamization in North America* (pp. 179–202). Beltsville, MD: Amana Publishers.

Shamma, F. (1999). The curriculum challenge for Islamic schools in America. In A. Haque (ed.), *Muslims and Islamization in North America* (pp. 273–296). Beltsville, MD: Amana Publishers.

Zogby International (2002). http://www.zogby.com/index.cfm

Understanding the Readings

1. According to this article, name a few basic essentials that would be needed for giving "culturally appropriate counseling" to an American Muslim.

2. Why is it important to know that in Islam "faith is not blind and does not stand above reason"?

3. What are challenges for Muslims living in America? Are there any possible solutions?

Suggestion for Responding

1. Read selected portions of the Qur'an and look for a panel of young Muslims who are willing to talk with your class about faith, social relations, and living in the United States. ✦

86

"Empty Seats in the Lifeboat": 9/11 Fallout Stalls Refugees

DONOVAN SLACK

Trenton [N.J.]—Elvis Gojkic looks like a typical teenager, but the Trenton High School student with the spiked brown hair and smiling brown eyes has seen much more than the average American teen.

"From my family, 17 men are dead," said the 18-year-old Bosnian refugee.

Growing up in Tuzla, Gojkic witnessed the worst of the Balkan conflict before he and his mother, Melvija, settled in Trenton 18 months ago, seeking refuge from their war-torn homeland.

The Gojkics were lucky.

More than 220 refugees are "languishing" in Bosnian and West African camps, held up from joining family members in New Jersey by bureaucratic fallout from 9/11, according to local aid workers.

The displaced people were screened, rescreened and ultimately approved for transport to New Jersey, but only 14 of 225 slated arrivals have made their way to the States since September.

President Bush pledged in November to bring 70,000 refugees to the United States before September 30 this year, but as of May 31, only 13,763 have arrived, said Elizabeth Morley, Director of Immigration and Refugee services for Lutheran Social Ministries of New Jersey.

Morley joined about 40 locally settled refugees in marking World Refugee Day in June with an informal luncheon at the Lutheran Church of the Redeemer in Trenton. While many attendees expressed happiness and gratitude for their new lives—away from war and death—a gauze of sadness obscured the festive atmosphere.

"I miss my country, my people," said Elvis Gojkic, sipping cola from a plastic cup. "My home is empty, it's broken."

Broken homes worry Morley as well. The U.S. State Department has only a few more months to bring in thousands more refugees, hundreds destined to be reunited with family members in New Jersey, she said. If the government fails to transport the approved refugees before the deadline, Morley said, "they may not survive the wait."

"Every year they only set a certain number of slots," she said. "They represent lives—empty seats in the lifeboat."

Burlington City resident Fofi Baimba has been waiting since January 1999 for six family members to join him from Sierra Leone. At least one of them has already missed the boat.

Mamie Kormah Baimba, Fofi's 58-year-old mother, died in January 2001 after spending two weeks lost in the bush. She had been trying to return home from a refugee camp.

"She just couldn't take it anymore," Fofi said. "She was too tired."

A U.S. State Department official said the department has mounted a "super-human" effort to bring in as many people as possible, but enhanced security measures since 9/11 have hampered that effort.

While scores of refugees have been waiting abroad, agencies who normally help them settle in New Jersey have faced problems of their own.

"We can't do refugee resettlement when there's no refugees coming in," said Sister Janet Yurkanin, director of immigration and refugee services for the Catholic Diocese of Trenton.

Lutheran Social Ministries had to cut its case management staff in half when the flow of refugees slowed to a trickle, Morley said.

For those refugees lucky enough to be part of the trickle, life in America has presented hardships of another sort.

Elvis Gojkic and his mother have maintained grueling schedules, trying to support themselves and a handful of family members left behind in Bosnia. Until recently, Elvis worked in a sponge factory from 3:30 p.m. until midnight every weekday after attending classes from 8 a.m. to 3 p.m. at Trenton High. His mother, who named Elvis after the rock 'n' roll icon, works six days a week in a North Brunswick factory, taking on as many hours as her bosses will give her.

Their daily schedules are punctuated by reminders of the lives and people they left behind.

Tuesday marked the 10th anniversary of the bomb blast that killed Melvija's husband, Elvis' father.

"I hate to think about all the losses," said Melvija, looking over at Elvis, who was dressed like a typical American teen in baggy jeans and an over-sized Phillies jersey.

"I'm lucky I have him. I'm lucky I had the opportunity to get him out of that country." [2002]

Understanding the Reading

1. Why did Elvis come to America with his mother?
2. Why are some approved refugees held up from immigrating?
3. Why did Fofi Baimba's fifty-eight-year-old mother die?
4. Describe the daily schedules of Elvis and his mother in the United States.

Suggestion for Responding

1. Refugee and relocation agencies, such as the Lutheran Social Ministries, enable refugees to leave their countries, usually in the midst of a war, by doing the legal work for entry; loaning money for plane tickets, rent, and food; and helping the family find work, enter school, get health insurance, and take language classes, if possible. Refugees must repay everything, enabling the next family to immigrate. Research Canada's national policies for refugees and compare its benefits with those of the United States. ✦

87

Working Class Women as War Heroes

FARAI CHIDEYA

Private Jessica Lynch is a hero, the kind who in her hopefully long life will never escape her youthful fame. The baby-faced 19-year-old fought off Iraqis in an ambush, endured broken bones, gunshot and stab wounds, and went eight days without food. This movie played in real time has all the elements that make fast-paced war flicks like "Behind Enemy Lines" box office magic. Her face, frozen with what must have been shock, pain and relief during her rescue, is already one of the most haunting images of the war.

Lynch is linked in more ways than one to Shoshana N. Johnson, a 30-year-old mother from El Paso, Texas. Johnson, who left her 2-year-old daughter with her parents when she deployed, joined the army to get training to be a chef. She ended up one of the first American prisoners of war in Iraq. Lynch—well, she wanted to be a kindergarten teacher.

How did a chef-in-training and a future teacher end up toting guns in the desert? Both of these female war heroes come from hometowns fighting their own battles, economic ones. Lynch comes from the you-can't-make-this-stuff-up town of Palestine, in Wirt County, a farm community in western West Virginia of 5,900 people, 99 percent of them white. Wirt has a 15 percent unemployment rate; 20 percent live below the poverty line; and the average income per person is $14,000.

El Paso County is huge by comparison—nearly 700,000 people—but no more prosperous. Seventy-eight percent of El Pasans are Latino, and 24 percent live below the poverty line. The border city, hit hard by the impact of NAFTA,[1] has a per capita income of just $13,000.

The folks in Wirt and El Paso are separated by half a country, but they have a lot in common. In both places, the economy has collapsed. The military is probably one of the best games in town. Jessica Lynch's family says she joined to get an education, something she probably couldn't have gotten otherwise. Now that she's a hero, a group of colleges have stepped forward to offer her a scholarship.

Wouldn't it be great if people like Lynch and Johnson didn't have to go to war to get a job or an education? At the same time that Americans are protesting against the war, thousands this week protested in favor of affirmative action, which faces its latest Supreme Court challenge. Working-class women and African-Americans like Lynch and Johnson will be among those to lose if affirmative action is ended. But affirmative action, as useful as it is, only gives a fraction of Americans the chance they deserve. Schools in working-class neighborhoods are becoming more like truly impoverished ones. In other words, they've become places where too many bright students lose hope.

Yale graduate and notably lackluster student George W. Bush got the benefits of an affirmative action program called "legacy admission," i.e., preference for the kids of alums (particularly the rich ones). For all his hawkishness, Bush went AWOL[2] from his National Guard duty during the Vietnam War, 1972–1973. His father was a war hero. But these days rich men (and women) don't fight.

That's left to the working class. A New York Times article titled "Military Mirrors Working-Class America" notes, "With minorities overrepresented and the wealthy and the underclass essentially absent, with political conservatism ascendant in the officer corps and Northeasterners fading from the ranks, America's 1.4 million-strong military seems to resemble the makeup of a two-year commuter or trade school outside Birmingham or Biloxi far more than that of a ghetto or barrio or four-year university in Boston."

Don't get me wrong—I'm not saying money's the only reason people join the military. A lot of enlistees are following their dreams of serving their country. Others, like a 27-year-old interviewed in the Times article, like to blow things up (though not necessarily people). And some, like a friend of mine who spent ages 17–20 in the military, think it's a great way to grow up and find your mission in life.

There are a few other options for young Americans seeking a way to give to their country, earn money for college and get skills; in particular, the service corps like City Year and Americorps. In these programs, young Americans the same age as Lynch can spend a year or two giving back to a local community—working on buildings, serving the elderly, even helping teach kindergarten. With school budgets being slashed, there's plenty of need and plenty of room for young recruits to lend a hand.

But these programs are still modest compared to the size and stability of the military. Before the motto an "Army of One," the Navy boasted the slogan, "It's Not Just a Job, It's an Adventure." Some people just want a job. What they get is far more uncertain.   [2003]

Terms

1. NAFTA: North American Free Trade Agreement. This agreement went into effect on January 1, 1994, linking Canada, the United States, and Mexico in a free trade sphere. Although most tariffs have been eliminated among the three nations, NAFTA is very controversial as to whether the economies of its members are benefiting.

2. AWOL. Absent without leave. In military contexts it is deserting your post without permission.

Understanding the Reading

1. Why did Jessica Lynch and Shoshana Johnson join the army if they wanted to become a kindergarten teacher and a chef, respectively?
2. Why does the author say that George W. Bush got the benefits of an affirmative action program, and how does that relate to Jessica and Shoshana?
3. Which Americans fight wars now?
4. What other kind of service, other than military, could be an alternative if the government expanded these programs?

Suggestion for Responding

1. There has been much controversy surrounding the capture and rescue of Jessica Lynch. Research the BBC story that sharply conflicted with the U.S. government's story. Also contrary to the government rendition, Lynch has said that she would not be alive today had it not been for the care she received in the Iraqi hospital. Discuss why you think the government made a video of her rescue. ◆

88

Phoenix Rising from the Waters: The Post-Katrina Renewal of the New Orleans East Vietnamese Community

MARY SUE PLY

When the evacuees from the Vietnamese community in New Orleans East returned to homes and businesses ravaged by Hurricane Katrina's winds and the floods resulting from broken and overtopped levees, the older generations faced the second and, in some cases, the third challenge to rebuild their lives. As they cleaned and gutted their families' properties and hauled out ruined, stinking, moldy appliances, furniture, clothing, photographs, and heirlooms, the younger generation gained a deeper understanding and appreciation of how hard their elders had worked after they arrived in New Orleans in 1975. Despite the one to eight feet of water in almost every building, despite city plans to turn their neighborhood into uninhabited green space, despite attempts to make their environs a waste dumping ground, despite the slow response from the federal, state, and local governments, the Vietnamese community in New Orleans East was the first seriously flooded neighborhood to be repopulated and revitalized. The residents did not wait for federal "Road Home" money or SBA loans or nonexistent insurance payments. As a community, they rebuilt their lives, yet again.

"War and political adversity" (Faciane A1) forced the elders to move from North to South Vietnam after the Communist Viet Minh defeated the French colonial army in 1954, and then to emigrate to the United States after Communist military and guerrilla forces defeated the South Vietnamese armed forces in 1975. Some of the Vietnamese expatriates were airlifted out of Saigon by the American military. Some sneaked across the border into Cambodia. Others, called "boat people," paid huge fees to be smuggled out of Vietnam in small, leaky boats, which were often attacked by pirates, who stole their few remaining possessions. If the boats didn't sink or they weren't caught by the Vietnamese navy, the "boat people" spent months in crowded refugee camps in Thailand and Cambodia before being allowed to come to the United States (Faciane A6).

The first Vietnamese in New Orleans East settled a large subdivision fittingly called Village de l'Est. Vietnamese culture revolves around the family and the village in which their relatives have lived, worked, and been buried for generations. The Vietnamese in New Orleans East had created a new "village," and no hurricane could drive them away. After Katrina their community "bounced back with a vigor surpassed by few areas of New Orleans that were as heavily flooded" (Faciane A1).

After the defeat of South Vietnam in 1975, Associated Catholic Charities settled 1000 Vietnamese expatriates in the cheap housing in Village de l'Est on the far eastern edge of New Orleans, including the Versailles Arms apartments (hence, the designation of their neighborhood as "Versailles"). In 1976 another 2000 relocated from other states as a result of communication through "ethnic networks rather than official resettlement policy" (Zhou 828). Some of the new residents were Buddhists, but most were Catholic. Thirty percent of the early residents of Versailles had come from two northern villages, which had moved south en masse after Vietnam was divided in 1954 (Zhou 828).

In 1980, one third of the Vietnamese immigrants in the United States were poor. "[C]lustered in the poorest part of a poor area in a poor city in a poor State," the Vietnamese in New Orleans East were no exception (Zhou 826, 828). More friends and relatives of the original residents were drawn to Versailles, and by 1990 the Vietnamese community represented 43 percent of the population of the two census districts in which they lived (Zhou 828). A 1979 survey reported that a majority of the Vietnamese residents in New Orleans East were "'agriculturists and fishermen'"; while some of the residents became commercial fishermen, many more took low-paying jobs, often in the service and tourist industries (Zhou 830). In 1994, the Versailles community was described as "a rapidly deteriorating working-class suburb" (Zhou 828). Despite financial problems, the residents had roots—the family and the church—that provided stability. By 1990 "married-couple families" represented 81 percent of the Vietnamese families, and 37.3 percent of the families owned homes (Bankston 459). By 2005, the year Katrina struck the region, the Vietnamese ranked as "the third largest ethnic group in eastern New Orleans" (Williams B2).

In the ten years before the hurricane, the economic status of the neighborhood had improved as more residents built and expanded businesses and younger residents became educated professionals. Along Chef Menteur Highway and Alcee Fortier Street, the main entrance corridor into Versailles, the shops and restaurants catered to a Vietnamese clientele. Stores offered Vietnamese-language CD's and videos, including the operas enjoyed by the older residents. The grocery stores stocked *nuoc mam* fish sauce, cellophane noodles and vermicelli, rice paper for spring rolls, seafood, special herbs for hot and sour soup—all of the ingredients necessary for traditional Vietnamese cuisine. These stores also sold incense, Catholic statuary and icons, and small Buddha statues. The Dong Phuong bakery's scrumptious French breads and pastries drew customers from all over New Orleans. In other parts of the city, Vietnamese families opened businesses, including small grocery stores, convenience stores with gas pumps, salons, construction companies, and restaurants.

The increasing prosperity was mirrored in the dwellings. The earliest residents had lived in the dilapidated Versailles Arms apartments and small, one-story brick tract homes with fenced yards near the Alcee Fortier/Dwyer Boulevard corridor (Bankston 459). In the 1980's larger ranch-style dwellings were built on streets a Vietnamese developer had named *Tu-Do* ("Freedom") and *My-Viet* ("America-Vietnam") (Bankston 459). Before Katrina, still more streets with Vietnamese names became the sites of large, expensive two-story homes.

Prosperous residents chose to stay in Village de l'Est so as to maintain their cultural identity. In one tradition that grew out of the residents' "socioeconomic heritage" as village farmers in Vietnam, many of the older female residents created "a market-gardening landscape" either in their backyards or in communal plots along a canal near Alcee Fortier Street (Airriess 1). Beginning in 1979, vegetables and herbs, as well as traditional Vietnamese clothing and live birds, were sold early on Saturday mornings in the courtyard of a local grocery store in a quieter imitation of the bustling markets older residents had patronized in Vietnam (Yee, "Market" B1-2).

Another powerful unifying influence was the Mary Queen of Vietnam Catholic Church. Responding to applications from community leaders, the Archdiocese of New Orleans in September 1983 granted permission for the construction of the church. The current large, but plain prefabricated metal building was completed in May 1985. Funded by Vietnamese Catholics from all over New Orleans, Mary Queen of Vietnam became a "personal parish . . . that [was] determined not by the place of residence of parishioners but by their rite[s], language, or nationality" (Bankston 460). The church was the epicenter of the hous-

ing developments, as well as the mechanism for maintaining the Catholic faith as well as traditions like the annual Tet lunar New Year celebration (Bankston 460). To sustain their native culture, the parishioners built the Child Development Center, in which volunteers taught "classes in Vietnamese language, literature, and culture." The Vietnamese Educational Association decided that the center should also help children to succeed in American schools (Bankston 460). Thus, in Versailles, the church, family, and neighborhood were intertwined:

> . . . children in this community are not supported by their families alone, but by the entire community, which forms the social context in which individual families function. . . . [The large extended families] are instilled with the idea that "the family always goes first." They honor mutual, collective obligations to one another and to their relatives to attain respect, cooperation, and harmony within . . . a web of social and kinship relations. . . . The Vietnamese have come to believe that education is the chief means for their children to achieve [success], and they have thus adjusted their cultural patterns to orient the younger generation toward educational and occupational attainment. (Zhou 830)

One of the risks in encouraging the children to gain an American education was the possible erosion of the sense of culture and community. However, the church and the older generations remaining in Versailles held the allegiance of the young people, who attended mass at Mary Queen of Vietnam even if their apartments and jobs, offices, or university classes were closer to central New Orleans.

On Sunday, August 28, 2005, as Katrina bore down on Louisiana, the *Times-Picayune* ran a feature story on a $20 million project to construct a larger sanctuary for the church with architecture influenced by traditional Vietnamese structures, plus a shrine and a nursing home/retirement community to house aging residents (Yee, "Church" B1-2). Because of Vietnamese family traditions and respect for elders, a nursing home would ensure that younger generations would still gravitate to the neighborhood and the church.

Even as readers were perusing that *Times-Picayune* story, residents from all over New Orleans, including the Versailles community, were fleeing from Katrina, taking a little food and water, and a few changes of clothing but leaving behind important documents and mementos of a lifetime. The appendix details the horrific experience of the parish priest, Father Vien The Nguyen, his staff, and several hundred parishioners after Katrina made landfall on August 29. The priest's leadership ensured the survival of hundreds of people who had not evacuated, often because of age or ill health. In an interview on November 5, 2005, Father Vien expressed his sadness over the death of a lady whose home he and helpers had visited before they were finally rescued on September 2. For some reason—fear or deafness—she had not responded when they knocked on the door and called her name, leading them to believe she had already left. She was the only parishioner that wasn't evacuated to safety.

About 15,000, or 50 percent, of Louisiana's Vietnamese population went to Houston, where, rather than going to official shelters, most stayed with friends and relatives, in Catholic churches, convents, and temples (Phan 1), or in the homes of Vietnamese Houstonians who heard about the refugees' plight on Radio Saigon Houston (Grayczyk A11) and picked up evacuees—total strangers—at the Hong Kong 4 shopping center (Vien in Vollen 176). Some Versailles residents went to Austin, San Antonio, and Arkansas; Father Vien assigned assistant pastors to parishioners in the larger cities and then shuttled back and forth to check on his flock (Vien in Vollen 176).

Less than three weeks after the storm, some residents came home on the weekend to assess the damage, secure some valuables, and clean their properties. A *Times-Picayune* article on September 18 cited residents' concerns that, while the church and community ties would draw the older people back, the younger people were "gone" (MacCash A14). But the older generations, the neighborhood leaders, and the priests and the nuns would not let their American "village" die.

Rebuilding home is difficult when there is no electricity, gas, land-line telephone service, sewerage, or water (Williams B2). When the mayor authorized a "look and leave" visit for residents on Wednesday, October 5, many of the Versailles Vietnamese looked and *stayed*. Mai Nguyen and her family "'stayed in a house without electricity

and no water for three months.'" But, digging deep into their own pockets rather than waiting for insurance money or Road Home funds, the Nguyens reopened their Ba Mien restaurant on Chef Menteur Highway (Faciane A5).

Summing up the Vietnamese residents' determination to return, Father Vien noted, "At our own peril we are here. At our own joy we are here" (Vollen 190). By coming back first just on weekends and then permanently, Vietnamese residents like Mai Nguyen were "breaking the law. The resettlement of New Orleans East was civil disobedience, a mass act of defiance against Mayor Ray Nagin's orders barring residents from returning to great stretches of the city" (Kromm 22). In October 2005, well before the mayor's Bring Back New Orleans Commission had even met, church leaders were planning the revitalization process and demanding that water and electricity be restored (Howley 1).

In early November, six weeks after Katrina, Father Vien was back in the church's rectory, with electricity provided by a small, noisy generator, although Entergy had restored power to residences which had experienced less flooding. Vietnamese-American students from other states were helping with the cleanup. The Red Cross still brought food to be shared on the church's outdoor stage, and parishioners cooked huge quantities of Vietnamese food in the rectory. Father Vien had water for drinking, bathing, and scrubbing hauled in from the West Bank of New Orleans, which had escaped the flooding that had devastated so much of the city. He was concerned that city officials were planning to stop the community's recovery—a valid fear given the Urban Land Institute's recommendation later that month that severely flooded parts of New Orleans should not be rebuilt but instead turned into "green spaces" (Kromm 23). The war for the survival of Village de l'Este had begun. Working with leaders of other communities in New Orleans, the Vietnamese resisted plans to raze their homes and destroy their way of life. Local publicity as well as articles in national publications galvanized support for the survival of traditional neighborhoods, ranging from the Lower Ninth Ward to Versailles to middle-class Broadmoor, to wealthy Lakeview. Given such widespread opposition from citizens of all races and classes, the mayor scuttled the "green spaces" plan.

By February 27, 2006, there was a 45 percent rate of return of Vietnamese to New Orleans, compared to about one third of the rest of the population. Many of the homes and businesses of the Versailles community had been refurbished, prompting a *Village Voice* writer to describe it as "an oasis in a desert of abandonment." Yet, six months after the storm, a food distribution center still operated on church land (Shaftel). By late March 2006, moldy dry wall, useless appliances, construction debris, and destroyed possessions were piled on the "neutral ground" between the lanes on the main boulevards. This trash, awaiting removal by federal contractors, proved that the residents were back to stay, as did the crusty French bread and gooey macaroons sold by the Dong Phuong bakery, which had reopened in January 2006. However, some residents were still waiting for FEMA trailers, where they could live while repairing their homes. On June 11, 2006, over nine months after the hurricane, the *Times-Picayune* reported that some residents would move into 199 FEMA trailers in "a matter of days" (Nolan, "Making" A12).

According to Father Vien, the redevelopment of Village de l'Est was not haphazard or accidental: "We were the first community in all of New Orleans to come forth with a development plan. . . . Out of our own pockets, we brought in thirty-three experts from all over the country and two architects from Vietnam to design the redevelopment of our area. We unveiled [the plan] on the third of February [2006], and on the fourteenth of February, our Valentine's gift was a waste dump" (Vien in Vollen 202). The opening of this landfill for hurricane debris, including lead-based paint and asbestos, resulted in immediate protest. The dump was located nearby, on the opposite side of an 80-foot wide canal flowing from the Bayou Savage Wildlife Refuge, "the largest urban wildlife refuge in the continental U.S. . . . " The canal was connected to the lagoon that Versailles residents used to water their vegetable gardens (Vien in Vollen 202-203). The planned 80-foot high mound of trash was in the direct path of any future storm surges, which would wash all of the toxic waste into the Versailles neighborhood. A coalition of the parishioners of Mary Queen of Vietnam, the National Alliance of Vietnamese Service Agencies, and the Louisiana Environmental Action Network contested the Louisiana Depart-

ment of Environmental Quality's ruling that the landfill was safe. They commissioned studies by scientists at Louisiana State University, and enlisted support from city council members and the U.S. Wildlife and Fisheries Department (Schwinn 1–2). In one demonstration, Vietnamese residents, including one tiny Vietnamese nun, marched with protest signs in front of city hall. In July 2006 the mayor acceded to the residents' wishes and closed the dump (Schwinn 2). But the leaders of [the] Vietnamese community continued to negotiate with the city to remove the garbage that had been dumped prior to the closure of the landfill.

The number of people returning to Village de l'Est steadily grew. Father Luke Nguyen, another pastor at Mary Queen of Vietnam, reported that, by October 2006, "80 percent of the community of 7,000 had come home and 95 percent of their businesses were up and running" (Howley 1). So many Latino construction workers were in New Orleans East that a *taqueria* and a Central American import store had opened among the Vietnamese businesses. On March 30, 2007, the mayor finally announced a plan for investing money to revitalize selected neighborhoods in New Orleans, with the bulk of the money slated for New Orleans East and the Lower Ninth Ward (Krupa and Donze A1, 8–10). The Vietnamese community would receive a small grant for "beautification on the Alcee Fortier corridor" (Krupa and Russell A1, 5–6). The inclusion of the Vietnamese community in the plan suggested that city officials had finally recognized their importance in New Orleans. The comparatively small sum allocated to Versailles probably reflected how much the Vietnamese had already accomplished in rebuilding their neighborhood, their lives, without much government assistance.

On May 21, 2007, Father Vien noted that, based on church attendance, the return of the Vietnamese residents was about 90 percent complete. As a result of the repopulation of Village de l'Est, the city reopened the fire station, and an elementary school run by the Recovery School District and a charter high school were holding classes. To secure a greater police presence in the neighborhood, the church provided rooms in one of its properties so that officers could open a substation (Vien). The elders had planted new vegetable gardens, and the Saturday morning market was back in business. Father Vien explained the significance of the gardens: "We really feel that with what these elders know about growing, they are real teachers for us, and we hope to keep learning from them. They have great wisdom in growing beautiful food year-round" (Walker C1, 6). Even more valuable were the elders' strength, courage, and wisdom gained from surviving war and natural disasters.

The neighborhood was the proverbial hive of activity. Multiple cars were parked outside the repaired homes (only a few white FEMA trailers remained); bags of fertilizer were piled beside the neat yards and flower gardens. A few stores sold furniture, cabinets, and counter tops to remodelers. Almost everything necessary to sustain an independent life could be found at nearby businesses: gas station, pharmacy, grocery store, dry cleaners, restaurants, entertainment venues. The resurgence of the Vietnamese population encouraged their non-Vietnamese neighbors to return and even to send their preschool-age children to the reopened Child Development Center, where they, too, learned Vietnamese (Vien). While a few medical clinics had opened in New Orleans East, the nearest emergency room or hospital bed was at least 30 minutes away (Moran A6). To improve access to health care, Father Vien sought to attract Vietnamese-speaking doctors to the clinics.

Viewing the wreckage caused by Katrina as an opportunity to truly renew their community, the church formed the Mary Queen of Vietnam Community Development Corp., and other residents created Vietnamese Initiative and Economic Training (Faciane A6). Church leaders planned to expand the Child Development Center and, eventually, construct the new sanctuary (Vien). In response to American-style "political adversity," the Vietnamese developed American-style political savvy. Capitalizing on their economic stability and social unity, their leaders negotiated with government officials at all levels. In September 2007, two years after the hurricane, the city was planning to allocate grants and tax credits not only to beautify the Alcee Fortier corridor ($1.5 million) but also to create "a sustainable community urban farm," an open market, a boardwalk over the bayou, and an "84-unit senior housing complex" ($15.2 million) ("Targeted" A14). But rather than waiting for government funds, the Community Development Corp. went forward

with the plans for the farm and secured foundation grants to purchase 20 acres next to the church. Several universities will donate "planning or agricultural aid" for the farm, which should be operating in 2009. A combination of small family plots and larger commercial plots will "knit the generations together" as the elder "master gardeners" pass their knowledge to "younger, thoroughly Americanized Vietnamese," who could then use the profits to "raise capital and launch small businesses . . . " (Nolan, "Vietnamese" B1-2).

The Vietnamese in Village de l'Est will build their post-Katrina lives on the foundation of ancient cultural values and traditions, passing to each new generation the wisdom of the past and the vision for a better future. According to Father Vien, the Vietnamese expression "que huong" refers to "homeland or ancestral birthplace. 'In the pre-Katrina days, when we say 'que huong' we mean Vietnam. . . . Now when [we] say it, [we] mean New Orleans. There's a shift in [our] hearts. We have buried our loved ones here. We are connected to the land'" (Cohen B4). This connection is so powerful that no politician, no hurricane, no floodwaters, no hardship can ever break it. [2008]

APPENDIX
HURRICANE KATRINA AND
AFTERMATH IN NEW ORLEANS EAST:
NOTES FROM ORAL HISTORY
INTERVIEWS OF FATHER VIEN THE
NGUYEN, PASTOR OF MARY QUEEN
OF VIETNAM CATHOLIC CHURCH*

Sunday, August 28, 2005: At the 9:30 a.m. mass, VTN encourages parishioners to evacuate since Katrina has been upgraded to Category 5—175 + mph winds. VTN opens two-story school building as a shelter and tells the 100–120 evacuees to bring food and water. Staff and residents bring an invalid and other elders, some on walkers and in wheelchairs, to the rectory, where there is a generator.

Monday, August 29: Katrina comes ashore early in morning and dies down by 5:30 p.m. There is minimal flooding at 2:30, but considerably more by 5:30. VTN hears that a levee has been breached and decides to bring any parishioners who haven't evacuated back to the shelter. He can't use 15-passenger van because the water is too high, so he borrows an unmotorized boat without proper paddles. After he returns to shelter in darkness (electricity out hours before), he says mass.

Tuesday, August 30: Evacuees are housed in the rectory, in the school building, and on an outdoor covered stage. Attempts to seal levee breaches with giant sandbags airlifted by helicopters are not working well. VTN organizes evacuees to gather boats and ropes, with plans to climb on the roof and pull others up if the water gets too high.

Wednesday, August 31: Approximately 200 evacuees are in church facilities. The men barbecue a drowned deer; they ration water, food, and propane. Rescuers in boats take the elderly and children; others wade about a mile to Chef Menteur Highway. VTN stays with an invalid and her wheelchair-bound daughter, as well as a few of his own family. Cell phones still work; a state trooper promises to send a rescue helicopter for the invalid and her family, but no helicopter comes. The church is running out of gasoline for the generator.

Thursday, September 1: Approximately 350–400 evacuees who had gone to the highway wade back; no one had picked them up. Some were invalids whose wheelchairs had been left on the highway. VTN organizes food for these people. Evacuees set up 55-gallon drums for toilets. Some people are being picked up in trucks at the highway; a few are fighting for space. VTN goes to the highway to calm them; he is given a motorized boat, which he doesn't know how to operate (he can't swim either!).

Friday, September 2: Evacuees still on church grounds fear they won't be rescued. Finally two concerned citizens from Lafayette use their personal boats to rescue VTN and the remaining evacuees. VTN surveys the damage to N.O. East and sees many people who still have not been rescued. VTN is driven to Catholic Church in Lafayette (~120 miles away).

October 5: Mayor allows evacuees a "look see" visit to their property. VTN sets up office on the West Bank on Wednesday and holds mass at Mary Queen of Vietnam on the following Sunday. Attendance at mass increases steadily every Sunday as evacuees come back to clean their homes on weekends despite having no water, sewage, gas, electricity, or land-line phones. Resurrection of New Orleans East service is held on the Sunday after All Saints Day, with 1500–1600 in attendance.

*Lola Vollen and Chris Ying, eds. *Voices from the Storm.* Voice of Witness Series. Canada: McSweeney's, 2006.

References

Airiess, Christopher, and David L. Clawson. "Vietnamese Market Gardens in New Orleans." *Geographical Review* 84 (1994): 1 p. *Questia Online Library.* 23 March 2007 <http://www.questia.com>.

Bankston, Carl L., III, and Min Zhou. "De Facto Congregationalism and Socioeconomic Mobility in Laotian and Vietnamese Immigrant Communities: A Study in Religious Institutions and Economic Change." *Review of Religious Research* 41.4 (2000): 453–470. *JSTOR.* 23 March 2007 <http://www.jstor.org/search>.

Cohen, Sarah. "Vietnamese Priest Serves Neighborhood, City." *Advocate* [Baton Rouge] 27 Nov. 2005: B4.

Faciane, Valerie. "Vietnamese Community Thriving in Eastern N.O." *Times-Picayune* [New Orleans] 23 April 2007: A1+.

Graczyk, Michael. "Vietnamese Evacuees Find Rest, Hope in Texas." *Advocate* [Baton Rouge] 6 Sept. 2005: A11.

Howley, Kerry. "Vietnamese Resistance." *Reason* 38.8 (Jan. 2007): 1 p. *Academic Search Premier.* 23 March 2007 <http://www.ebscohost.com>.

Kromm, Chris. "Grassroots Gumbo." *The Nation* 18 Sept. 2006: 22–26. *Google.* 23 March 2007 <http://www.thenation.com/doc/20060918/kromm>.

Krupa, Michelle, and Frank Donze. "Leaders Unite Behind Recovery Plan." *Times Picayune* [New Orleans] 30 March 2007: A1+.

Krupa, Michelle, and Gordon Russell. "N.O. Post-K Concept Unveiled." *Times Picayune* [New Orleans] 29 March 2007: A1+.

MacCash, Doug. "Vietnamese Businesses Must Start Over—Again." *Times-Picayune* [New Orleans] 18 Sept. 2005: A14.

Moran, Kate. "City Considering Buying Hospital in Eastern N.O." *Times-Picayune* [New Orleans] 11 April 2007: A1+.

Nolan, Bruce. "Making All Things New: Mary Queen of Vietnam." *Times-Picayune* [New Orleans] 11 June 2006: A12.

———. "Vietnamese Church Resowing Tradition." *Times-Picayune* [New Orleans] 25 Nov. 2007: B1+.

Phan, Aimee. "Vietnamese Lose All, This Time to Katrina." *USA Today* 16 Sept. 2005: 2 pp. *Academic Search Premier*. 23 March 2007 <http://www.ebscohost.com>.

Schwinn, Elizabeth. "Charity Coalition Helps Shut Down Katrina Landfill." *Chronicle of Philanthropy* 18.21 (17 Aug. 2006): 2 pp. *Academic Search Premier*. 23 March 2007 <http://www.ebscohost.com>.

Shaftel, David. "The Ninth Re-Ward: The Vietnamese Community in New Orleans East Rebuilds after Katrina." *Village Voice Online* 27 Feb. 2006: 5 pp.

"Targeted Recovery Areas." *Times-Picayune* [New Orleans] 13 Sept. 2007: A13+.

Vien, Father Nguyen The. Personal interview. 5 Nov. 2005.

———. Personal interview. 21 May 2007.

Vollen, Lola, and Chris Ying, eds. *Voices from the Storm: The People of New Orleans on Hurricane Katrina and Its Aftermath*. Voice of Witness Series. San Francisco: McSweeney's Books, 2006.

Walker, Judy. "Vietnamese, If You Please." *Times-Picayune* [New Orleans] 12 April 2007: C1+.

Williams, Leslie. "Under the Radar." *Times-Picayune* [New Orleans] 27 November 2005: B1+.

Yee, April. "Church of Change." *Times-Picayune* [New Orleans] 28 Aug. 2005: B1+.

———. "Market Saigon Style." *Times-Picayune* [New Orleans] 31 July 2005: B1+.

Zhou, Min, and Carl L. Bankston, III. "Social Capital and the Adaptation of the Second Generation: The Case of Vietnamese Youth in New Orleans." *International Migration Review* 28.4 (1994): 821–845. *JSTOR*. 23 March 2007 <http://www.jstor.org/search>.

Understanding the Reading

1. The Vietnamese refugees who relocated to New Orleans East were very poor. What gave stability to the community?

2. What actions did the community take to ensure its culture was kept intact, yet its children would succeed in America?

3. Describe Father Vien's leadership.

4. Describe the community's development plan.

Suggestions for Responding

1. Research the latest news and developments of the Vietnamese community in New Orleans East.

2. Instead of receiving help from local and federal government, the residents had to find ways to stop several of their actions. As one example, research and discuss who decides where toxic waste dumps should be located? Are there any near your neighborhood? ✦

89

"We Are Not The Enemy": Hate Crimes Against Arabs, Muslims, and Those Perceived to Be Arab or Muslim After September 11

HUMAN RIGHTS WATCH

A HISTORY OF BACKLASH ATTACKS AGAINST ARABS AND MUSLIMS IN AMERICA

Long before September 11, the stereotype of the Arab or Muslim as a "terrorist" had taken hold in the American imagination and fueled anti-Arab and anti-Muslim prejudice. That prejudice sometimes led to hate crimes, particularly after acts of violence ascribed rightly or wrongly to Arab or Muslim terrorists. In light of the history of backlash violence against Arabs and Muslims in the United States before September 11 2001, the hate crimes that followed September 11 were all too predictable. Government officials should be aware that there is a danger of an anti-Arab or anti-Muslim backlash anytime terrorism is linked to these communities.

The victims of this violence have not been limited to one nationality or religion. Those who have been attacked include persons who only appear— at least to some Americans—to be Middle Eastern, Arab, or Muslim. South Asians, for example, have regularly been attacked. So have people who "appear" Muslim—even though Muslims are found among all races, ethnic groups, and nationalities. In the context of U.S. hate-violence, however, "Muslim" has been equated with Middle Eastern or Arab. Sikh men who wear turbans have also been lumped with "Arab" terrorists and victimized. In short, a confluence of events in U.S. history has led to the construction of a new racial stereotype and target for bias, fear, and hate crimes: persons who are or appear to be "Middle Eastern, Arab or Muslim." For brevity's sake, in this report we refer to this violence as anti-Arab and anti-Muslim, while fully cognizant of the heterogeneous composition of the victims.[1]

Middle East Tensions in the 1970s and 1980s

Though neither government agencies nor Arab or Muslim nongovernmental organizations tracked incidents of bias-motivated crime in the 1970s,[2] Arab and Muslim activists point to the 1973 Arab-Israeli war and oil embargo as a starting point for increased prejudice and hostility against their communities in the United States.[3] An Arab-American from Dearborn, Michigan described the change in public attitudes towards Arab-Americans after 1973 in the following way: "suddenly we were being held responsible for things we had nothing to do with and no control over and maybe didn't even support in the first place."[4] Activists contend that hostility increased during the Iran hostage crisis in 1979. According to Albert Mokhiber, former President of the American Arab Anti-Discrimination Committee (ADC), the oldest Arab-American civil rights organization, "Iranians were being targeted for hate crimes at that point . . . so were Arab-Americans, and Arabs and Iranians aren't the same. . . ."[5]

Arab-American activists also believe the ABSCAM scandal of 1980 heightened negative stereotypes of Arabs.[6] ABSCAM, short for "Arab Scam," was a federal political corruption sting operation in which federal agents posed as wealthy sheiks and offered bribes to politicians. As one Arab-American noted, after ABSCAM: "[A]ll Arabs were bad. Everybody was lumped together. You became that horrible, hook-nosed, terrorizing murderer. You were not to be trusted."[7]

The founders of the ADC credit the negative publicity surrounding the ABSCAM scandal as the impetus for the group's creation.[8]

The hijacking of TWA Flight 847 by Shiite militants on June 14, 1985 and the hijacking of the Italian cruise liner the Achille Lauro on October 7, 1985 by the Palestinian Liberation Organization were followed by a spate of violent crimes against Arab and Muslims in the United States. On October 11, 1985, the regional director of the ADC Southern California office, Alex Odeh, was killed when a bomb exploded outside the front door of his office.[9] The day before, Odeh had been on local television denying PLO involvement in the hijacking.[10] The ADC office in Washington, D.C., was firebombed two months after Odeh's death.[11] Two months before Odeh's murder, a bomb outside the ADC's Boston office injured a policeman when it detonated while the officer was trying to defuse it.[12] In the same time period, a Houston mosque was pipebombed (causing $50,000 in damage),[13] the windows of the Islamic Institute in Dearborn, Michigan were broken,[14] and a mosque in Potomac, Maryland was vandalized.[15] In 1986, the day the United States attacked Libya, five Arab students at Syracuse University were beaten while their attackers yelled anti-Arab epithets.[16] Arab-American businesses in Dearborn, Michigan were also vandalized soon after the attack on Libya.[17]

Persian Gulf War

The beginning of the Persian Gulf crisis in August 1990 led to a major wave of hate crimes nationwide against Arabs and Muslims in the United States. The ADC recorded four anti-Arab hate crimes, from January to August 1990, before the crisis began[18]; between August and the start of the war on January 16, 1991 it recorded forty hate crimes. During the first week of the war, it recorded another forty-four.[19]

In Los Angeles, fires destroyed the businesses of a Lebanese-American and an Iranian Jew.[20] In Cincinnati, a store owned by an Arab-American was firebombed.[21] In New York, ten men with a bottle beat a man who looked Arab on the subway.[22] In Baltimore, four or five men yelling "filthy Arab" attacked and broke the car window of a Polynesian Jew.[23] In San Francisco, vandals smashed the windows of four Arab-American businesses.[24] In Tulsa, Oklahoma, the house of an Iraqi native was burned down.[25] Threats against Arab and Muslim Americans were so numerous in Detroit that Mayor Coleman Young asked

Michigan's Governor to assign National Guard troops to protect the city's Arab and Muslim population.[26]

The severe nature and extent of the crimes prompted the first efforts by public officials to address violence against Arab and Muslim Americans. President George H.W. Bush strongly called for an end to hate attacks against Arab-Americans, insisting on September 24, 1990 that "death threats, physical attacks, vandalism, religious violence and discrimination against Arab-Americans must end."[27] In California, noting that the current "wave of hate crimes is greater than we have seen since the brutal heyday of the Ku Klux Klan," Lieutenant Governor Leo McCarthy introduced hate crimes legislation that proposed to increase civil and criminal penalties for those who commit bias-motivated crime.[28] In Los Angeles, the district attorney's office released a public service announcement asking viewers to call the Los Angeles County district attorney's office if they had any knowledge of crimes against Arabs, Muslims or Jews.[29] In Chicago, the Human Relations Commission helped Arab and Muslim shopkeepers post signs warning against committing hate crimes.[30]

Oklahoma City Bombing and TWA Flight 800

On April 19, 1985, a bomb destroyed the Alfred P. Murrah Federal Building in Oklahoma City, Oklahoma, killing 168 people. In the two days before federal authorities stated that foreign terrorists were not responsible, many Americans assumed Arab terrorists were behind the attack.[31] The Council on Islamic Relations (CAIR), a Muslim civil rights organization, recorded over two hundred incidents of anti-Muslim harassment, assault, or property damage in the days immediately following the bombing.[32]

In Oklahoma City, a Muslim woman who was seven months pregnant suffered a miscarriage after a brick thrown through her window traumatized her the morning after the bombing.[33] At a Muslim day care center in Texas, a teacher and sixty young students were frightened when a passing driver shouted to the teacher, "Here's a bomb for you lady," and then threw a bag of soda cans at her.[34] In New York City, callers threatened to bomb Arab-owned business and attack the families of the owners.[35] In Richardson,

Texas, a mosque received ten threatening phone calls.[36] Just one day after the bombing, as reports of backlash attacks began to surface, President Bill Clinton called on Americans not to rush to any judgments or blame any religion for the attack.[37]

On July 17, 1996, TWA Flight 800 exploded soon after leaving New York, killing all its passengers. As with the Oklahoma City bombing, there was public speculation in the media that Muslim or Arab terrorists were responsible for the explosion.[38] Ultimately, the downing of TWA Flight 800 was blamed on a mechanical failure.[39] Nevertheless, CAIR received ten reports of anti-Muslim verbal harassment and threats of violence prompted by anger against Muslims after the plane exploded.[40]

September 11: Expectations of Backlash Violence

The past history of backlash violence left many of Arabs, Muslims, and those perceived to be Arab or Muslim, apprehensive that they would be targets of backlash violence whenever a terrorist incident was blamed on Arabs or Muslims. This fear was vividly expressed in messages sent by Muslims, Arabs, and Sikhs to community e-mail groups in the hours immediately after the September 11 attacks. A few of the messages are excerpted below:

- "Both towers of the World Trade Center are burning. In the coming hours (minutes?), the finger pointing will start just as it did after Oklahoma City."[41]
- "I apologize for this haphazard email. I am shocked beyond belief as our great country is going through crisis as none before. At this time we stand with our hands folded in Ardas (Sikh prayer) to all victims of this dastardly attack. However . . . it is critical that we as Sikh-Americans do not become victims of this terror. . . . What I am saying is very simple, "though we are peace loving people with no connections whatsoever to . . . (Osama bin Laden et al. [sic]), there are individuals which may not see the difference". . . . Everyone's work or school situation is different but no one [sic] should go under any bullying or even be made uncomfortable by fellow colleagues."[42]

- "I'm sure we've all heard of the tragedy this morning. . . . Needless to say, we all realize that no Muslim in their right mind would condone such an action. I'm only writing to be sure you are all aware of the unavoidable atmosphere that will rise as a result of this attack: we're non-white, we're Arab . . . we're Muslims. . . . There will be some 'serious' anti-Arab, anti-Muslim sentiment running rampant through this country. . . . So be careful, stay with your families, stay off the streets unnecessarily, and watch your fellow sisters and brothers."[43]
- "During this period of time in which events unfold in NY and Washington, we urge Arabs and Muslims to be watchful and proactive in handling what may result in backlash against our communities, property and persons."[44]

THE SEPTEMBER 11 BACKLASH

The September 11 hate crime backlash confirmed the fears of Arabs and Muslims in the United States: a major terrorist attack gave rise to a nationwide wave of hate crimes against persons and institutions perceived to be Arab or Muslim. Unlike previous hate crime waves, however, the September 11 backlash distinguished itself by its ferocity and extent. The violence included murder, physical assaults, arson, vandalism of places of worship and other property damage, death threats, and public harassment. Most incidents occurred in the first months after September 11, with the violence tapering off by December.

Not surprisingly, the persons most vulnerable to September 11–related hate crimes were those easily identified as Arabs or Muslims, including Muslim women who wear hijabs.[45] Sikhs who wear turbans also appear to have been disproportionately targeted, presumably because of the erroneous assumption by many Americans that men wearing turbans are Arab or Muslim. Similarly, bias-motivated property attacks were often directed at property that could easily be identified with Muslims or Arabs, such as mosques.

Many Arabs and South Asians who have come to the United States seem to have clustered in certain jobs, including driving taxis, or have

become small business owners, running gas stations, convenience stores, and motels. This may account for the prevalence of backlash victims among persons with these occupations. Two of the three September 11–related murders for which charges have been brought were of convenience store workers.[46] The other September 11–related murder for which charges have been brought was of a gas station owner.[47] In Tulsa, Oklahoma and Seattle, Washington, taxi dispatch services noted that after September 11 they had received threatening calls saying that their Muslim and Arab taxi workers would be killed.[48]

Polls conducted by national Arab and Muslim advocacy groups measured the cumulative perceptions created by September 11–related criminal and non-criminal bias incidents in the Arab and Muslim communities. In July 2002, CAIR polled 945 Muslim Americans on how September 11 and its aftermath affected them. The poll found that 48 percent believed their lives had changed for the worse since September 11.[49] While 79 percent said they experienced an act of kindness or support from friends or colleagues of other faiths since September 11, 57 percent experienced an act of bias or discrimination, ranging from a disparaging remark to employment discrimination to a hate crime.[50] A poll of Arab-Americans conducted in May 2002 found that that 20 percent had personally experienced discrimination since September 11.

The full dimensions of the backlash may never be known. There are two reasons for what amounts to a systemic gap in public knowledge about the extent of hate crimes in the United States. First, the federal hate crimes reporting system contains significant limitations, including the voluntary nature of the reporting system and the failure of some local law enforcement agencies that ostensibly participate in the federal reporting system to furnish information on hate crimes to federal authorities. These gaps in the federal hate crimes reporting system were detailed in a September 2000 U.S. Department of Justice–funded study, which estimated that almost six thousand law enforcement agencies in the United States likely experience at least one hate crime that goes unreported each year.[51] Second, the racial or ethnic identity of a crime victim without more is an insufficient basis on which to determine whether a crime is hate-related. Absent specific indicia of bias— e.g, statements made by the perpetrator—hate-based crimes may not be recorded as such.

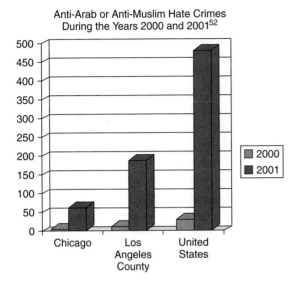

Anti-Arab or Anti-Muslim Hate Crimes During the Years 2000 and 2001[52]

Murder

> *I stand for America all the way! I'm an American. Go ahead. Arrest me and let those terrorists run wild!*[54]
> —Frank Roque, after being arrested for the murder of Balbir Singh Sodhi

At least three people were murdered as a result of the September 11 backlash. There is reason to suspect four other people may also have been murdered because of anti-Arab and anti-Muslim hatred.

BALBIR SINGH SODHI

Balbir Singh Sodhi, a forty-nine-year-old turbaned Sikh and father of three, was shot and killed while planting flowers at his gas station on September 15, 2002. Police officials told Human Rights Watch that hours before the crime, Sodhi's alleged killer, Frank Roque, had bragged at a local bar of his intention to "kill the ragheads responsible for September 11."[55] In addition to shooting Sodhi three times before driving away, Roque also allegedly shot into the home of an Afghani American and at two Lebanese gas station clerks.[56] The Maricopa County prosecutor's office was due to try Roque for Sodhi's murder on November 12, 2002.

VASUDEV PATEL

On October 4, 2001, Mark Stroman shot and killed Vasudev Patel, a forty-nine-year-old Indian and father of two, while Patel was working at his convenience store in Mesquite, Texas.[57] A store video camera recorded the murder, allowing law enforcement detectives to identify Stroman as the killer. Stroman said during a television interview that anger over the September 11 attacks caused him to attack any store owner who appeared to be Muslim. He further stated during the interview: "We're at war. I did what I had to do. I did it to retaliate against those who retaliated against us."[58] In addition to killing Patel, Stroman also shot and killed Waquar Hassan on September 15, 2001 (see below), and also shot Rais Uddin, a gas

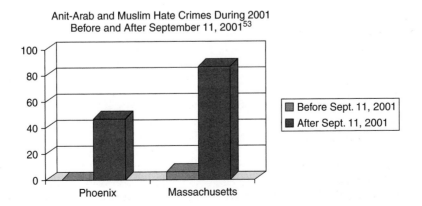

Anit-Arab and Muslim Hate Crimes During 2001 Before and After September 11, 2001[53]

station attendant, blinding him.[59] Stroman was tried and convicted of capital murder for killing Patel and sentenced to death on April 3, 2002.[60]

WAQUAR HASSAN

Waquar Hassan, a forty-six-year-old Pakistani and father of four, was killed while cooking hamburgers at his grocery store near Dallas, Texas on September 15, 2001. Although no money was taken from Hassan's store, police in Dallas initially believed that he was killed during a robbery because he had been robbed twice that year.[61] Hassan's family, however, believed his murder was a hate crime because nothing was stolen by the assailant and the murder had occurred so soon after September 11.[62] His family also pointed out that customers visiting Hassan's store after September 11 subjected him to ethnic and religious slurs.[63] The case remained unsolved until Mark Stroman admitted to killing Hassan to a fellow prison inmate in January 2002.[64] Murder charges against Stroman were dropped once he was convicted and sentenced to death for Vasudev Patel's murder.[65]

ALI ALMANSOOP

On September 17, 2001, Ali Almansoop, a forty-four-year-old Yemini Arab, was shot and killed in his home in Lincoln Park, Michigan after being awoken from his sleep by Brent David Seever. At the time of his murder, Almansoop was in bed with Seever's ex-girlfriend.[66] Immediately before killing Almansoop, Seever said that he was angry about the September 11 terrorist attacks. Almansoop pleaded that he did not have anything to do with the attacks.[67] Seever shot Almansoop anyway. Seever acknowledged to police investigators that he killed Almansoop in part because of anger related to September 11. Prosecutors chose to prosecute the matter as a murder, rather than a bias-motivated murder, because they believe Mr. Seever's motivation for murdering Almansoop was motivated in part by jealousy over Almansoop's relationship with is ex-girlfriend. Mr. Seever had been stalking his ex-girlfriend before the murder.[68]

ABDO ALI AHMED

On September 29, 2001, Abdo Ali Ahmed, a fifty-one-year-old Yemini Arab and Muslim, and father of eight, was shot and killed while working at his convenience store in Reedley, California.[69] Cash in two registers and rolled coins inside an open safe were left untouched. In addition, Ahmed's gun, which he kept for protection, reportedly remained in its usual spot, indicating that he may not have felt in mortal danger.[70] Two days before his murder, Ahmed had found a note on his car windshield which stated, "We're going to kill all of you [expletive] Arabs."[71] Instead of contacting the police, Ahmed threw the note away.[72]

Ahmed's family and local Muslim leaders have told the local press that they believe his killing was a hate crime.[73] However, largely because no perpetrator or perpetrators have been found for whom a motive can be established, police have not classified the murder as a hate crime. California Governor Gray Davis offered a $50,000 reward for information leading to the conviction of Ahmed's killers.[74] At the time of this writing, the investigation into Ahmed's murder was stalled because police had run out of leads.[75]

ADEL KARAS

On September 15, 2001, Adel Karas, a forty-eight-year-old Arab and Coptic Christian, and father of three, was shot and killed at his convenience store in San Gabriel, California. According to press reports, his wife, Randa Karas, believes he was murdered because he was mistaken for a Muslim. She points out that no money was taken from the cash register and that her husband had a thick wad of bills in his pocket. Local police told Human Rights Watch that they do not believe his murder was bias-motivated because there is no evidence to indicate anti-Arab or anti-Muslim bias. The murder remained unsolved at the time of this writing.[76]

ALI W. ALI

Ali W. Ali, a sixty-six-year-old Somali Muslim, died nine days after being punched in the head while standing at a bus stop in Minneapolis, Minnesota on October 15, 2002.[77] According to press reports, the only known witness to the attack saw the assailant walk up to Ali, punch him, stand over him, and then walk away.[78] His son and Somali community members attributed the attack against Ali to anger created against Somalis by a front page local newspaper article that appeared two days before the attack.[79] The article said that Somalis in Minneapolis had given money to a Somali terrorist group with links to Osama Bin Laden.[80] After originally finding that Ali had died of natural causes, the Hennepin County medical examiner's office on January 8, 2002 ruled Ali's death a homicide.[81] Ali's family regards his murder as a hate crime. Both local police and the FBI have been unable to find Ali's assailant.[82]

Assaults

Violent assaults related to September 11 were numerous and widespread. A review by the South Asian American Leaders of Tomorrow (SAALT) of news articles published during the week following September 11 found reports of forty-nine September 11–related assaults.[83] CAIR received 289 reports from Muslims of assaults and property damage incidents across the United States from September 11 until the second week of February.[84]

ISSA QANDEEL

On the morning of September 13, 2001, Issa Qandeel, a Palestinian Muslim and an Arab, was leaving the Idriss Mosque in Seattle, Washington when he smelled gas near his jeep and saw a man, subsequently identified as Patrick Cunningham, come out from behind his jeep. Cunningham was carrying a can of gasoline and a gun. When Qandeel asked Cunningham what he was doing behind the jeep, Cunningham walked away.

When Qandeel tried to stop him, Cunningham shot at Qandeel three times, although his gun did not discharge any bullets. Cunningham then started running away and Qandeel chased him. Cunningham shot at Qandeel again and this time a bullet did discharge, although it missed Qandeel. Cunningham was apprehended when he crashed his car trying to get away. Police later discovered that Cunningham planned to burn cars in the mosque driveway because of anger at the September 11 attacks. Federal authorities prosecuted Cunningham for attacking Qandeel and attempting to deface a house of worship. He pled guilty on May 9, 2002 and was scheduled to be sentenced on October 18, 2002. He faces a minimum of five years of incarceration.[85]

KULWINDER SINGH

On September 13, 2001, Raymond Isais Jr. allegedly assaulted Kulwinder Singh, a turbaned Sikh taxi worker, in SeaTac, Washington. After getting into the back seat of Singh's taxi, Isais told Singh, "You have no right to attack our country!" He then started choking Singh. After both men then got out of the taxi, Isais started punching Singh, pulled out tufts of his beard and knocked off his turban. Isais called Singh a terrorist during the assault. Local police were able to apprehend Isais Jr. the same day using a description provided by Singh. He was charged with a hate crime by local country prosecutors.[86]

SWARAN KAUR BHULLAR

On September 30, 2001, Swaran Kaur Bhullar, a Sikh woman, was attacked by two men who stabbed her in the head twice as her car was idling at a red light in San Diego. The men shouted at her, "This is what you get for what you've done to us!" and "I'm going to slash your throat," before attacking her. As another car approached the traffic light, the men sped off. Bhullar felt that she would have been killed by the men if the other car had not appeared. She was treated at a local hospital for two cuts in her scalp and released later that same day. Local police and federal law enforcement officials have been unable to identify Bhullar's attackers.[87]

FAIZA EJAZ

On September 12, 2001, Faiza Ejaz, a Pakistani woman, was standing outside a mall in Huntington, New York waiting for her husband to pick her up from work. According to press reports, Adam Lang, a seventy-six-year-old man sitting in his car outside the mall, allegedly put his car in drive and started driving towards her. Ejaz was able to avoid the car by jumping out of the way and running into the mall. Lang then jumped out of his car and screamed that he was "doing this for my country" and was "going to kill her." Mall security agents seized Lang. Sergeant Robert Reecks, commander of the Suffolk County Bias Crimes Bureau, told reporters: "if she hadn't jumped out of the way, he would have run right over her."[88] Lang was charged with first-degree reckless endangerment, which requires an enhanced penalty if the crime is bias-motivated.

CRYSTAL ALI-KHAN

On June 18, 2002, Crystal Ali-Khan, a American Muslim woman who wears a hijab, was allegedly assaulted by a woman in a drug store near Houston, Texas. Before assaulting Khan, the woman told her that she had learned about "you people" over the last ten months and doesn't trust "a single damn one of you." Before Khan could get away from the woman, she slammed Khan to the floor and began pulling at her headscarf, which had the effect of choking her. Though Khan told the woman she could not breathe, she kept pulling at the headscarf. Khan then pulled off her headscarf, in violation of her religious obligations in a desperate effort to alleviate the choking. The woman then dragged Khan by her hair to the front of the store. When police arrived, the woman was holding Khan by her ponytail on the front sidewalk of the store. She told police that she was making a citizen's arrest. The police told her to let Khan go, at which point Khan was able to put her headscarf back on.[89]

KARNAIL SINGH

Karnail Singh is a Sikh man who owns a motel in SeaTac, Washington. In mid-October, 2001, John Bethel, a local vagrant who sometimes came into Singh's motel for coffee and food, told Singh, "You better go back to your country. We're coming to kick your ass." A few days later, on October 19, Bethel entered Singh's motel and shouted, "You still here? Go back to Allah!" before hitting Singh with a metal cane while he stood behind the counter in the motel lobby. Singh, who bled profusely from the blow, spent half a day in the hospital and required ten stitches on his head. Bethel was sentenced to nearly two years in prison for assault with a deadly weapon.[90]

SATPREET SINGH

On September 19, 2001, Satpreet Singh, a turbaned Sikh, was driving in the middle lane of a two lane highway in Frederick County, Maryland. A pickup truck pulled up close behind Singh and the driver started making profane gestures towards him. The pickup truck then moved alongside Singh's car on his left and the driver took out a rifle. Singh increased his speed to get away from the pickup truck. Seconds later he heard rifle shots. No bullets hit Singh or his car.

The pickup truck then turned around and started traveling in the opposite direction. Singh filed a criminal complaint with the local police. At the time of this writing, local authorities have not been able to ascertain the identity of the person who shot at Singh.[91]

FEDERAL, STATE, AND LOCAL HATE CRIME PREVENTION EFFORTS BEFORE AND AFTER SEPTEMBER 11

Government officials face a complex challenge in seeking to prevent spontaneous, unorganized bias-motivated acts of violence. The experiences discussed below reveal the importance, first of all, of a serious commitment to act decisively before, during, and after outbreaks of such violence. They also reveal the efficacy of specific steps taken in some jurisdictions that may serve as a model for others.

Public Condemnation

Hate crimes are symbolic acts conveying the message that the victim's religious, ethnic, or racial community is unwelcome.[92] Animosity against Arabs, Muslims, and those perceived to be Arab or Muslim, reflects a belief that persons from these communities are "foreigners" who are not "loyal" Americans and who are intrinsically linked to an Arab and Muslim terrorist enemy.

Public statements embracing the millions of law-abiding Arabs and Muslims as part of American society and communicating that hate crimes would not be tolerated were among the most effective measures that countered and contained September 11–related violence.[93] Arab and Muslim activists believe that anti-backlash "messages" by prominent political and civil society leaders helped stem the number of backlash attacks.

Though the overwhelming majority of public figures in the United States condemned acts of bias after September 11, there were a few who expressed contempt for or bias against Arabs and Muslims. Just a week after September 11, a member of Congress, John Cooksey, told a Louisiana radio station, "If I see someone [who] comes in that's got a diaper on his head and a fan belt wrapped around the diaper on his head, that guy needs to be pulled over."[94] Similarly, while speaking to law enforcement officers in Georgia, Representative C. Saxby Chambliss stated: "just turn [the sheriff] loose and have him arrest every Muslim that crosses the state line."[95] Representatives Cooksey and Chambliss both eventually apologized for their remarks.[96]

In addition, a few significant religious commentators publicly expressed distrust or anger against Muslims. Franklin Graham, son of the well-known Reverend Billy Graham, called Islam: "wicked, violent and not of the same God."[97] Televangelist Pat Robertson, also speaking about Islam, said: "I have taken issue with our esteemed President in regard to his stand in saying Islam is a peaceful religion. . . . It's just not."[98] In the same vein, former Southern Baptist President Jerry Vines told conventioneers at the June 2002 annual gathering of the Southern Baptist Convention that the Muslim prophet Muhammad was a "demon-possessed pedophile." Unlike Representatives Cooksey and Chambliss, these religious leaders have stood by their comments.[99]

Public messages were also used proactively as a tool to prevent future hate crimes. Two weeks before the September 11 one-year anniversary, the San Francisco district attorney's office embarked on a campaign promoting tolerance by placing anti-hate posters on city buses and bus stops.[100] The poster includes the faces of four Arab or Muslims persons or persons who may be perceived as Arab or Muslim under the heading, "We Are Not the Enemy."[101] The campaign was prompted by concerns the September 11 anniversary might rekindle backlash animosity and anti-Arab and anti-Muslim violence. According to San Francisco District Attorney Terence Hallinan, "With war heating up in the Middle East, we're launching a pre-emptive strike against any backlash against Arab-Americans and Muslims."[102] Eight hundred posters were placed on the outside and inside of San Francisco buses. In addition to promoting a message of tolerance, they also encourage citizens to report hate crimes to the San Francisco district attorney's office.

MIXED MESSAGES

While acknowledging the importance of official condemnation of hate crimes and messages supporting tolerance, Arab and Muslim community leaders have expressed concern about federal government "mixed messages."[103] Official statements exhorting the public not to view Muslims or Arabs differently than anyone else were countered by measures taken as part of the anti-terrorist campaign that cast a cloud of suspicion over all Arabs and Muslims in the United States. Those measures have included, for example, the detention of some 1,200 persons of almost exclusively Arab, Muslim, or South Asian heritage because of "possible" links to terrorism;[104] the FBI requests to interview over eight thousand men of Arab or Muslim heritage; and the decision that visitors to the United States from certain Middle Eastern countries would be fingerprinted. Activists believe these actions reinforce an image of Arabs and Muslims as potential terrorists or terrorist sympathizers. Referring to the effect of these policies on the perception of Muslims and Arabs in the general public, Joshua Salaam, of CAIR, said: "Most people are probably asking, 'If government doesn't trust these people, why should I?'"[105]

APPENDIX

Backlash Preparation
Center for the Prevention of Hate Violence
Stephen L. Wessler
(207) 780-4756
e-mail: CPHV@usm.maine.edu
website: http://www.cphv@usm.maine.edu

Hate Crimes Prosecution
Michigan Attorney General's Taskforce on Hate Crimes
Michigan Attorney General Hate Crimes Prosecution Team
(517) 335-0804

Hate Crime Tracking
Los Angeles County Commission on Human Relations
Marshall Wong
Hate Crimes Coordinator
(213) 974-7617
www.LAHumanRelations.org

Affected Community Outreach
Special Counsel to the Assistant Attorney General on Backlash Discrimination
Joseph Zogby
(202) 514-6534

e-mail: Joseph.Zogby@usdoj.gov
website: www.usdoj.gov/crt/nordwg.html

Corporal Daniel Saab
Community Policing Officer
Dearborn Police Department
(313) 943-2800

Hate Crimes Investigation Support
Office of the Maine Attorney General
Civil Rights Team Project
Attorney General Thomas Harnett
(207) 626-8800
website: www.maine.gov/ag/civilrights.html

ACKNOWLEDGMENTS

This report was written by Amardeep Singh, U.S. Program researcher at Human Rights Watch, based on research he undertook in Washington, D.C. and five other cities across the United States. It was edited by Jamie Fellner, director of the U.S. Program, and Joe Saunders, interim program director, with legal review provided by Dinah Pokempner, general counsel. Jonathan Horowitz, program coordinator, provided significant research and production assistance.

Human Rights Watch would like to thank the many public officials and community activists who provided us with information, documentation, and insights about backlash crimes and government responses to it following September 11.

Human Rights Watch is grateful to the William and Flora Hewlett Foundation and to Atlantic Philanthropies for providing the funding that made this report possible.

Notes

1. See Leti Volpp, "The Citizen and the Terrorist," 49 UCLA Law Review 1575 (2002).
2. The federal government began tracking hate crimes data with the passage of the Hate Crime Statistics Act in 1990.
3. David Lamb, "Loyalty Questioned; U.S. Arabs Close Ranks Over Bias," *Los Angeles Times,* March 13, 1987.
4. David Lamb, "Loyalty Questioned; U.S. Arabs Close Ranks Over Bias," *Los Angeles Times,* March 13, 1987.
5. Albert Mokhiber, "American Arab Anti-Discrimination Committee News Conference," National Press Club, Washington, D.C., Federal News Service, February 20, 1992.
6. Patrick Cooper, "Daschle's Proud Mentor Looks Back," *Roll Call,* July 19, 2001: "Human Rights: American-Arab Committee Fights Discrimination," Inter Press Service, August 20, 1985; Alan Achkar and Michele Fuetsch, "Taking Pride In Their Heritage; Arab-Americans Battle The Sting Of Stereotypes As They Work To Open Others' Eyes To Reality Of Their Culture," *Plain Dealer,* November 26, 1995.
7. Alan Achkar and Michele Fuetsch, "Taking Pride In Their Heritage; Arab-Americans Battle The Sting Of Stereotypes As They Work To Open Others' Eyes To Reality Of Their Culture," *Plain Dealer,* November 26, 1995.
8. Chris Tricarico and Marison Mull, "The Arab: No More Mister Bad Guy?" *Los Angeles Times,* September 14, 1986.
9. Steve Lerner, "Terror Against Arabs in America: No More Looking the Other Way," *New Republic,* July 28, 1986.
10. Steve Lerner, "Terror Against Arabs in America: No More Looking the Other Way," *New Republic,* July 28, 1986.
11. Thomas Lerner, "Cover Story Language, incidents increasingly [sic]," *United Press International,* December 15, 1985.
12. Thomas Lerner, "Cover Story Language, incidents increasingly [sic]," *United Press International,* December 15, 1985.
13. "Terror Against Arabs in America: No More Looking the Other Way," *New Republic,* July 28, 1986.
14. "Human Rights: American-Arab Committee Fights Discrimination," *Inter Press Service,* August 20, 1985.
15. Ibid.
16. "Arab-Americans Are Targets Of Terrorism In U.S.," *Seattle Times,* September 7, 1986.
17. Murray Dubin, "Hate acts' against minorities are on the rise, experts say," *Houston Chronicle,* December 7, 1986.
18. "American Arab Anti-Discrimination Committee News Conference," Federal News Service, February 20, 1992. The ADC data is based on reports of hate crimes filed by victims with its national office. Unlike a law

enforcement agency, the ADC does not conduct an investigation to confirm whether a report of a bias incident is true. In classifying a criminal act and as a hate crime, the ADC used the federal definition of a hate crime.

19. Albert Mokhiber, "American Arab Anti-Discrimination Committee News Conference," National Press Club, Washington, D.C., Federal News Service, February 20, 1992.

20. Kenneth Reich and Richard A. Serrano, "Suspicious Fires Probed for Ties to Gulf Tension Crime: An Arson Unit studies a West Los Angeles Market Blaze and Police Label the Torching of a Sherman Oaks Store a Likely Hate Crime. Owners of Both Businesses are of Mideast Descent," *Los Angeles Times,* January 24, 1991.

21. Adam Gelb, "War's Backlash: Two Communities Torn by Conflict; Arabs Emerge as New Target of Prejudice," *Atlanta Journal and Constitution,* January 19, 1991.

22. Cynthia Ducanin, "Crisis in the Middle East: American Sentiment: Threats Against Arab-Americans Rise, Hotline Set up for Victims; Savannah Station Stirs Outcry," *Atlanta Journal and Constitution,* September 1, 1990.

23. Adam Gelb, "War's Backlash: Two Communities Torn by Conflict. Arabs Emerge as New Target of Prejudice," *Atlanta Journal and Constitution,* January 19, 1991.

24. "Vandals Strike at Arabs in The City," *San Francisco Examiner,* January 25, 1991.

25. Ted Bridis, "Suspected 'Hate Crime' Yields to Flood of Support," Associated Press, February 23, 1991.

26. Rick Hampson, "Arab-Americans: Dual Loyalties and Nagging Worries," Associated Press, January 20, 1991.

27. "Home-Grown Hatemongers," *New York Times,* February 27, 1991.

28. "McCarthy, Lockyer Announce Legislation to Battle Hate Crimes," *Business Wire,* February 6, 1991. The California State Legislature enacted the legislation that year.

29. "Southland: Briefly TV Ads to Fight Hate Crimes," *Los Angeles Daily News,* February 1991.

30. Frank Burgos and Zay N. Smith, "Shops Asked to Help Fight Hate Crimes," *Chicago Sun-Times,* January 30, 1991.

31. Bonnie Miller Rubin, "U.S. Muslims Are Looking For Apology," *Chicago Tribune,* April 22, 1995. Timothy McVeigh, a U.S. citizen who was neither Arab or Muslim, was eventually tried and executed for the bombing.

32. Farhan Haq, "United States: Terrorism Fears Put Muslims on the Alert," *Inter Press Service,* August 17, 1995. CAIR data is based on reports of bias incidents filed by victims with its national office. These incidents include everything from verbal harassment to discrimination to bias-motivated criminal acts. CAIR accepts the facts reported to it as true.

33. Charles M. Sennott, "After the bombings, America Faces up to Prejudice," *Boston Globe,* June 21, 1995.

34. Hamzi Moghradi, "A Rush to Judgment—Again," *Plain Dealer,* April 23, 1995.

35. Laura Outerbridge, "American Muslims Articulate Fear of Backlash," *Washington Times,* April 21, 1995.

36. Hamzi Moghradi, "A Rush to Judgment—Again," *Plain Dealer,* April 23, 1995.

37. John Nichols, "Bumbling Analysis Of Bombing Promoted Ethnic Stereotypes," *Capital Times,* April 24, 1995.

38. David Johnston; "Terror In Oklahoma City: The Investigation; At Least 31 Are Dead, Scores Are Missing After Car Bomb Attack In Oklahoma City Wrecks 9-Story Federal Office Building," *New York Times,* April 20, 1995; Stewart M. Powell and Holly Yeager, "FBI Issues Bulletin for 3 Suspects," *Seattle Post-Intelligencer,* April 20, 1995.

39. Rick Hampson, "Another Grim Task," *USA Today,* November 1, 1999.

40. Suzanne Cassidy, "Muslim Report Validates Local, National Aura of Bias: Pervasive Bigotry Alleged to Arise from Unjust, Constant Media Pairing of Islam with Terrorism," *The Harrisburg Patriot,* August 5, 1997.

41. Alex Khalil, September 11, 2001, written to Global Network of Arab Activists Yahoogroup at 9:49 a.m.

42. "Sikh-Americans: we need to be proactive During this Crisis!!!!!!," retrieved on September 11, 2001, from http://groups.yahoo.com/group/sikh-sewa/. Accessed by subscribing to Sikh-Sewa Yahoogroup and viewing archives.

43. "Bismillah," retrieved on September 11, 2001, from http://groups.yahoo.com/group/yma-online. Accessed by subscribing to Young Muslim Association Yahoogroup and viewing archives.

44. "Action Alert: Report Hate Crimes and Contact Media Outlets," from http://groups.yahoo.com/group/adcsf. Accessed by subscribing to American Arab Anti-Discrimination Committee Yahoogroup and viewing archives.

45. Hijab is the practice among Muslim women of covering the head and body.

46. Vasudev Patel and Waquar Hassan were killed while working in convenience stores.

47. Balbir Singh Sodhi was killed while working at his gas station.

48. Curtis Killman, "Tulsa-area Muslims feel fear," *Tulsa World,* September 16, 2001; "Bush Appeals For Calm Amid Incidents Of Hate; Threats And Attacks Have Targeted Mosques, Arab Americans," *Seattle Post-Intelligencer,* September 14, 2001.

49. "Poll: Majority of U.S. Muslims suffered post September 11 bias," Council on American-Islamic Relation, August 21, 2002, retrieved on August 28, 2002, from http://www.cair-net.org/asp/article.asp?articleid=895&articletype=3.

50. Ibid.

51. "Improving the Quality and Accuracy of Bias Crime Statistics Nationally: An Assessment of the First Ten Years of Bias Crime Data Collection," The Center for Criminal Justice Policy Research College of Criminal Justice, p. 61 (2000).

52. Anti-Muslim hate crimes in the United States increased from twenty-eight during 2000 to 481 during 2001. See "Crime in the United States—2001," Federal Bureau of Investigation, retrieved on October 30, 2002, from http://www.fbi.gov/ucr/01cius.htm. Anti-Arab and anti-Muslim hate crimes in Los Angeles County increased from twelve during 2000 to 188 during 2001. See "Compounding Tragedy: The Other Victims of September 11," Los Angeles County Commission on Human Relations, pp. 12 and 14, retrieved on September 24, 2002, from http://humanrelations.co.la.ca.us/Our_publications/pdf/2001HCR.pdf. Anti-Arab and anti-Muslim hate crimes in Chicago increased from four during 2000

53. During 2001, Massachusetts had five anti-Arab or anti-Muslim hate crimes before September 11 and eighty-six after. See Marie Szaniszlo, "Study: 9/11 fuels anti-Arab crime," *Boston Herald,* September 25, 2002. During 2001, Phoenix had no anti-Arab or anti-Muslim hate crimes before September 11 and forty-six after. See "Bias Incident Statistics," Phoenix Police Department, retrieved on October 29, 2002, from http://www.ci.phoenix.az.us/POLICE/hatecr2.html.

54. Human Rights Watch interview with Sergeant Mike Goulet of the Mesa, Arizona police department, August 6, 2002.

55. Ibid.

56. Ibid.

57. Michael Tate, "Mesquite seeks clues in killing of gasstore owner," *Dallas Morning News,* October 5, 2001.

58. "News Roundup," *San Antonio Express-News,* February 14, 2002.

59. Ibid.

60. "Death Sentence for Revenge Killing," United Press International, April 4, 2002. While Human Rights Watch believes all bias-motivated crimes should be prosecuted, it does not condone the death sentence in this or any other criminal matter.

61. Alan Cooperman, "Sept. 11 Backlash Murders and the State of 'Hate'; Between Families and Police, a Gulf on Victim Count," *Washington Post,* January 20, 2002.

62. Human Rights Watch telephone interview with Zahid Ghani, brother-in-law of Waquar Hassan, August 25, 2002.

63. Ibid.

64. Ibid.

65. The prosecution used Stroman's confession that he killed Hussain during sentencing portion of his trial for the murder of Vasudev Patel.

66. Alan Cooperman, "Sept. 11 Backlash Murders and the State of 'Hate'; Between Families and Police, a Gulf on Victim Count," *Washington Post,* January 20, 2002.

to sixty during 2001. See "Hate Crimes in Chicago: 2001," Chicago Police Department, p. 13, retrieved on September 24, 2002, from http://www.ci.chi.il.us/CommunityPolicing/Statistics/Reports/HateCrimes/HateCrimes01.pdf.

67. Ibid.

68. Ibid.

69. Evelyn Nieves, "Slain Arab-American May Have Been Hate-Crime Victim," *New York Times,* October 6, 2001

70. Karen de Sa, "Local Muslims Convinced Central Calif. Killing was hate crime," *San Jose Mercury News,* December 6, 2001.

71. Karen Breslav, "Hate Crime," *Newsweek,* October 15, 2001.

72. Ibid.

73. Jennifer Fitzenberger, "Family sees hate crime in Reedley homicide; Relatives say victim was shot because he was Muslim; officials draw no conclusions," *Fresno Bee,* October 1, 2001.

74. "Police," *Fresno Bee,* November 29, 2001.

75. Human Rights Watch telephone interview, Sergeant Tony Reign, Fresno Police Department, California, September 16, 2002.

76. Human Rights Watch telephone interview, Lieutenant Joe Hartshorne, Los Angeles County Sheriff's Department, September 16, 2002.

77. "Somalis discuss freedom and fear, U.S. flags, worries of backlash abound as community meets," *Star Tribune* (Minneapolis, MN), October 25, 2001.

78. David Chanen, "FBI questions witness in alleged hate assault," *Star Tribune* (Minneapolis, MN), November 16, 2001.

79. Lou Gelfand, "Readers say Sunday article spurred unfair attacks on local Somalis," *Star Tribune* (Minneapolis, MN), October 21, 2002.

80. "Somalis, Muslims denounce paper's story," *Star Tribune* (Minneapolis, MN), October 16, 2001.

81. David Chanen, "Bus stop assault is ruled homicide; Somali victim's family maintains it was hate crime," *Star Tribune* (Minneapolis, MN), January 9, 2002.

82. "FBI questions witness in alleged hate assault," *Star Tribune* (Minneapolis, MN), November 16, 2001.

83. "American Backlash: Terrorists Bring War Home in More Ways Than One," South Asian American Leaders of Tomorrow, p. 7, retrieved on August 28, 2002, from http://www.saalt.org/biasreport.pdf. SAALT is a national South Asian advocacy organization.

84. "Number of Reported Incidents by Category," Council on American-Islamic Relations,

retrieved on August 30, 2002, from http://www.cair-net.org/html/bycategory.htm.

85. Human Rights Watch interview with Issa Qandeel, July 31, 2002.

86. Human Rights Watch telephone interview with Kulwinder Singh, August 3, 2002.

87. Human Rights Watch telephone interview with Swaran Kaur Bhullar, June 27, 2002.

88. Pat Burson, "Terrorist Attacks; Driver Arrested in Hate Crime at Mall," *Newsday,* September 13, 2001.

89. Human Rights Watch telephone interview with Crystal Khan, August 21, 2002.

90. Human Rights Watch interview with Karnail Singh, August 2, 2002.

91. Human Rights Watch telephone Interview with Satpreet Singh, August 19, 2002. The Sikh Coalition, a Sikh civil rights organization formed in the wake of the September 11 backlash, received nineteen reports of turbaned Sikhs being harassed by other motorists while driving since September 11. Human Rights Watch telephone interview with Prabhjot Singh, director, Sikh Coalition, August 16, 2002.

92. Human Rights Watch telephone interview with Jack Levin, Professor, Northeastern University, August 18, 2002.

93. Human Rights Watch interview with Raed Tayeh, director, American Muslims for Global Peace and Justice, February 21, 2002; Human Rights Watch telephone interview, Deepa Iyer, South Asian American Leaders of Tomorrow, February 26, 2002.

94. Joan McKinney, "Cooksey: Expect Racial Profiling," *Advocate* (Baton Rouge, LA), September 19, 2001.

95. "Lawmaker Tries to Explain Remark; Rep. Chambliss, a Senate Hopeful, Commented on Muslims," *Washington Post*, November 21, 2001.

96. "Hall of Shame," *Washington Post,* November 22, 2002; Eli Sanders, "Understanding Turbans: Don't Link Them to Terrorism," *Seattle Times,* October 9, 2002.

97. Kevin Eckstrom, "Graham heir keeps stance on Islam talk," *The Times Union* (Albany, NY), November 24, 2001.

98. "Mr. Robertson's Incitement," *Washington Post,* February 24, 2002.

99. Kathy Shaidle, "Full Pews and Empty Gestures," *Toronto Star,* December 23, 2001; Richard N. Ostling, "Falwell labels Muhammad 'terrorist' in TV interview," *Chicago Tribune,* October 4, 2002.

100. "Anti-hate campaign begins in S.F. / Posters urge tolerance as Sept. 11 nears," *San Francisco Chronicle,* August 27, 2002.

101. The title of this report was taken from the title of this poster.

102. Human Rights Watch telephone interview with Terrence Hallinan, San Francisco district attorney, August 28, 2002.

103. Human Rights Watch interview with Pramila Jaypal, executive director, Hate Free Zone, July 31, 2002; Human Rights Watch interview with Raed Tayeh, director, American Muslims for Global Peace and Justice, February 21, 2002; Human Rights Watch interview with Joshua Salaam, Civil Rights Coordinator, Council on American-Islamic Relations, February 21, 2002.

104. Human Rights Watch, "Presumption of Guilt: Human Rights Abuses of Post-September 11 Detainees," *A Human Rights Watch Report,* vol. 14, no. 4(G), August 2002.

105. Human Rights Watch interview with Joshua Salaam, Civil Rights Coordinator, Council on American-Islamic-Relations, February 21, 2002.

Understanding the Reading

1. What in our history has caused backlash attacks against Arabs and Muslims in the United States?
2. Why did many Americans assume that Arab terrorists were responsible for the Oklahoma City bombing in 1985?
3. What percentage of Arab Americans have experienced discrimination since 9/11, according to this report?
4. What can government and citizenry do to stop this?

Suggestion for Responding

1. Research what kind of hate-crime tracking and hate-crime prevention entities exist in your area. ◆

SUGGESTIONS FOR RESPONDING TO PART VII

1. Read an American newspaper of note (e.g., *New York Times, Washington Post, L.A. Times,* or *Chicago Tribune*) at least three times a week, looking for news of world interest and opinion pieces on the Op-Ed page. Also read a foreign newspaper (onlinenewspapers.com) and compare news coverage of the same story. Divide the class so that some are especially responsible for each continent or region of the world. Take note of which newspapers are state-controlled (*Arab News* or *China Daily,* for example). Also note that the rest of the world seems to know much more about the United States than we do about the rest of the world.

2. Research whether your surrounding community has received refugees from abroad. Find creative ways to discover how they are faring. Are the children happy in school? Are the parents working? Are they underemployed? Are these families considered an integral part of the community? Research how other parts of the country react toward their refugees.

3. Research two activist groups: the Feminist Majority and Women's International League for Peace and Freedom (WILPF). The Feminist Majority, founded in 1987, has a very useful human rights watch newswire (feminist.org), which includes world news as well as national news. WILPF is nearly one hundred years old (Jane Addams was its first president) and is an official nongovernmental organization, recognized by the United Nations. It, too, works locally, nationally, and worldwide.

Invite speakers to your class representing each of these two agencies. Ask the WILPF representative about "The Raging Grannies."

4. Have a class discussion on ways of balancing national security with respect for civil rights. Compare America's ideals with what you see implemented by our different levels of government.

5. Compare the United States with other countries' reactions and solutions to "difference" as they struggle with their rapidly changing population. For example, Europe has a debate about religious symbols and religious articles of clothing worn in public schools; and there are debates about female circumcision as a religious rite imported with some immigrant groups.

6. As of 2012 much of New Orleans remains physically devastated, with little evidence that local, state, or federal government values the people, culture, and history of this unique part of America as a nation. What has developed are corporate strip clubs instead. What development plans can we create to ensure that those who wish to return can do so?

SUGGESTIONS FOR RESPONDING TO POWER

Research one manifestation of racism and sexism or classism that you read about in this book. As an individual, you will want to focus on what may seem to be a very small part of the problem, but a group could investigate a broader problem, breaking it into its component parts, with each group member assuming responsibility for one aspect.

As a group, you could investigate sexual harassment; as an individual, you could focus on something like sexual harassment on your campus. A group could look at housing segregation; individually, you could consider redlining (refusing credit to residents and businesses in certain locations) in your community. A group could research the issue of domestic battery, but individually you could research the cycle of violence. Or a group could examine current incidents of racial or homophobic harassment, but one person could concentrate on his or her campus or community.

Other broad areas for research include government policies affecting Native Americans; "scientific proof" of the inferiority of a racial, religious, or gender group; racist, sexist, or homophobic social policies; the race and/or gender wage gap; one facet of the history of racism or sexism in American law; organized racism, historically or at present; a manifestation of discrimination in education or employment; or the federal government's response or nonresponse to a community in crisis—one affluent and another with a large poor population.

Report on both the causes and the effects of the problem. Also include information about efforts that have already been made to alleviate or at least ameliorate the problem, and discuss how effective or unsuccessful they have been and why.

If your instructor plans to have you develop a "plan for action" in response to "Power," you probably want to select a topic for this assignment that particularly concerns you and that you would like to see changed.

As with earlier assignments, your instructor may ask you or your group to present your findings orally to your classmates. If this makes you uncomfortable, review the suggestions at the end of Part I on how to prepare for such a presentation.

C hange is not only possible but is also an inevitable part of life. Seasons pass. We grow older. This kind of natural change is beyond our control. We adjust to many changes without taking much notice. On the other hand, there is **social change,** caused and controlled by people acting individually and collectively.

Most of us think of social change as resulting from mass **social movements,** coalitions of groups and individuals seeking to revise social policies and transform social institutions. We recognize the strategies and achievements of the major American social movements that have affected the groups we have been reading about: abolition and civil rights, labor unions and consumer rights, woman suffrage and women's liberation, and gay and lesbian rights. This kind of direct collective action is probably the most effective way to promote social change, but it requires the strong commitment of many people who agree and will act on common objectives. However, social change does not necessarily depend on large-scale political activism. In fact, each of us in our daily life participates in the processes of social change.

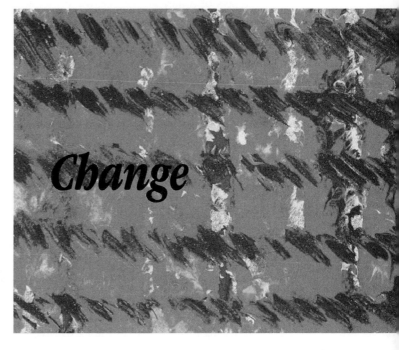

You may think this does not apply to you. For example, you may never have been interested in social issues, much less consider yourself a social activist, but this does not mean you have no impact on the shape of society. You may not consider yourself prejudiced, but when a friend tells you a racial joke, you might laugh so you will not offend her. Your laughter, however, indicates your approval of the joke's racist assumptions and, without your being aware of it, you have added one more stitch to the racist fabric of our society. In contrast, had you made a quiet comment that you do not care for that kind of joke, you could have begun to unravel at least one little thread. Both what you do and what you do not do influence social values.

Many of the issues raised in the first two divisions of this book are very disturbing. Because stereotypes are arbitrary oversimplifications, they blind us to the individuality of members of stereotyped groups and the rich potential of our diverse society. Prejudice, in turn, rests on such stereotyped thinking and encourages discrimination, sexism, heterosexism, racism, and classism. These "isms" support the beliefs and behaviors that lead to the pervasive neglect, exploitation, subordination, and oppression of women, minorities, lesbians, gay men, and the poor. This is a problem not just for members of these groups but for all Americans because systemic exclusion of so many people from full participation diminishes society by depriving us of their full skills, talents, wisdom, and creativity. Moreover, prejudiced convictions, and the behaviors that grow out of them, violate the most basic tenets of American society, the principles of freedom, equality, and justice. In other words, the practice of marginalizing groups is *a way of thinking*—it is not because of the presence of that group that discrimination occurs. Without a "traditional" group to oppress, another must be found, unless this behavior is no longer tolerated.

As troubling and discouraging as an awareness of these social problems may be, we do not need to accept them as inevitable or unalterable. They can be changed, and we can be instrumental in the process of effecting such change. We already have begun that process by learning about these issues, for we cannot begin to address a problem until we see and understand it. But such knowledge is only the first step.

This division, "Change," is intended to show how to make the changes we want. Part VIII, "Taking Action," gives us an understanding of the nature and dynamics of social change. By learning the step-by-step process of creating social change, we can see how to be more effective contributors to society. Of course, not everyone desires or supports certain social changes. In fact, some people will try to obstruct our efforts; others will resort to direct action to inhibit certain changes. However, people continue to exert their energies to make things better, at least according to their values. Part IX, "Change Makers," explores how people have worked to change their own lives and the world around them. This final section of the text challenges us to apply the knowledge we have gained and to articulate problems and possible solutions to the specific circumstances of this millennium. Together these readings will increase our sense of our ability to control our own lives and to influence the society in which we live.

VIII
Taking Action

AT ONE TIME OR ANOTHER, WE ALL WANT TO change something—our looks, our behavior, what happens to us or to others. This is one reason you are in school: You want your life to be different than it otherwise would be. Part VIII provides information about how to make change occur— how to think about problems, how to plan what we want to do, and how to do it. When we understand the way to approach change logically, we are better able to initiate and effect change ourselves.

This part describes a six-step process to effect change. By the end of Part VIII, you will understand both how social change is created and how to make such change yourself.

The first basic step in the process is **identifying the problem.** We tend initially to see a problem in its broadest form, such as the general issue of homelessness. But that problem is so extensive that it feels overwhelming, so we are likely just to shrug our shoulders and dismiss it. After all, "what can one person do?" We *can* do something, though. First, we must learn as much as we can about the specific issues that underlie the larger problem. This information will help us identify and define a specific, concrete issue to work on. Homelessness, for example, has numerous causes for us to consider: an apartment fire, high rents and low incomes in the community, job loss, and family breakups.

Another way of thinking about this issue is to think about its consequences, such as lack of economic resources, sanitary facilities, or safety.

The first selection (Reading 90) focuses on the Attorney General of the United States, Eric Holder, Jr., who has promised to use the full weight of his office's authority to protect the basic right of U.S. citizens to vote in the next election. Meanwhile, some states are instituting laws that target minorities, the poor, and students. Preventing these groups from voting has become an important strategy for certain power holders.

This brings us to the second step in the change process: **identifying the desired outcome**— that is, defining what specific change we would like to see. In Reading 91 Arturo Madrid considers his personal experiences of being seen as the "other" and concludes that America and Americans must come to terms with the diversity of our society, his desired outcome. In Reading 92, Derek Schork, as a teenager, tries (in a very dramatic way) to elicit an apology from a middle-aged man, who mistakenly concludes that he is parking in a handicapped space illegally. Alaina Love (Reading 93) analyzes "What Occupy Wall Street Demands of Our Leaders."

The third step is **developing strategies** for realizing the goal. Our first idea is probably not our best idea. We are better off considering many alternatives. Brainstorming—letting our minds wander freely—is a good approach. Take plenty of time, alone or with a group, to generate as many different ideas as possible. At this stage, do not censor yourself in any way; in fact, try to be as imaginative and creative as possible because what might at first seem an unrealistic strategy can sometimes trigger an original, workable solution. This is what Charlotte Bunch is doing in Reading 94 as she explores ways of bringing her feminist vision to bear on the public arena. Her "anything is possible" approach results in her suggesting many inventive tactics that most of us never would have dreamed of. Similarly, Andrew Kimbrell (Reading 95) explores ways that men can work for change in their relationships with their families, with the environment, and in the community. Try brainstorming tactics that could be used to help homeless persons get jobs; see how many you can list. You might realize, for instance, that, without a home, even qualified people have nowhere to receive responses to job applications. You could help solve this problem by figuring out a way to provide them with a mailing address.

Step four is **developing a plan for action.** Select the most appropriate strategies from your brainstorming and figure how to implement them. Be realistic. Consider what resources you have access to: time, energy, people, money, materials, and so on. Think about how you can augment them. After brainstorming about everything that needs to be done, develop a time line—a schedule of what needs to be done and in what order.

What could you do to help homeless people receive mail service? Probably very little by yourself, but if you interested others in working with you, you might create an effective solution. For example, you could solicit funds to pay rent on a post office box and distribute its contents at a prearranged location once a day. You could approach a church that already has a soup kitchen to feed homeless persons and offer to help church members establish a mail service for homeless jobseekers at the church's address. There are many other ways to tackle this problem. Once you settle on your approach, develop

your plan: the resources you need, your time frame, whom you need to work with you, and so on.

Once you have carefully mapped out your action project, your next step, the fifth, is **implementing the plan.** One major difficulty you will face at this stage is motivating people, getting them to act, to agree with you or your analysis of the problem, to support or perhaps even just to accept the desirability of the change you wish to implement. This is often the most crucial part of effecting social change. People resist change because we all tend to be more comfortable with the familiar, even when we realize that it is not perfect; we all value the security of living with what we already know. As Kathleen Ryan points out in Reading 96, people show resistance in a number of ways, but she also suggests ways to deal with it.

Taking action and creating social change is easiest, of course, if you have the power and authority to require people to change their attitude and behavior. However, seemingly powerless people can also create tremendous changes by organizing and working together. For example, in Reading 97 Cynthia Diehm and Margo Ross describe how people have identified the problem of domestic violence and taken steps to alleviate it through grass-roots activism. Throughout the country, small groups of people have worked together to set up shelters and to change laws and even the criminal justice system.

The final step in any good plan for social change is **evaluating your actions**—assessing the effectiveness of your endeavor and identifying the reasons for its successes and its disappointments. This is a very important step. Appraising the degree of your achievement can enhance your sense of a job well done, contributing to the satisfaction of everyone working with you. Identifying weaknesses in your project can help you plan better strategies to use in future actions. Evaluation is not simply a matter of determining whether or not the plan worked; it is much more a function of one's beliefs and expectations. People determine the relative success of a project based on a wide variety of standards, values, attitudes, and expectations. What one person considers a success another may perceive to be a failure.

Evaluative judgments differ when they rest on different priorities or value systems. In Readings 98 and 99, two law professors evaluate college and university policies that prohibit racist, sexist, and other types of harassing language or acts on their campuses. Gerald Gunther opposes them because he believes they violate our constitutional freedom of speech. In the final reading Charles R. Lawrence III supports them on the grounds that such offensive speech deprives its targets of constitutionally protected equal educational opportunities. Each presents a persuasive case for his point of view and is clearly convinced that his policy is better, based on his values.

An awareness of these six steps makes it easier for us to work for social changes that we desire. However, change is never easy. Each step requires a substantial investment of time and thought, and the more basic or extensive the desired change is, the more difficult it will be to achieve. Successful action demands thorough research, careful thought, strong motivation, extensive planning, and lots of time. If you commit yourself, however, you can do more than you probably think you can.

90

Attorney General Eric Holder Speaks at the Lyndon Baines Johnson Library and Museum

Eric Holder

Thank you, Mark [Updegrove]. It is a pleasure to be with you—and to join so many friends, colleagues, and critical partners in welcoming some of our nation's most dedicated and effective civil rights champions—as well as the many University of Texas law students who are here, and who will lead this work into the future.

I'd also like to thank Mark and his staff, as well as the Lyndon Baines Johnson Library and Museum's board members and community of supporters, for providing a forum for today's conversation—and for all that you do, not only to honor the life and legacy of our 36th commander-in-chief, but also to build upon his historic efforts to ensure the strength, integrity, and future of our democracy.

Nearly half a century has passed since a national tragedy catapulted Lyndon Johnson to the presidency, and at the same time launched a new chapter in America's story. Those of us who lived through those painful days will never forget LBJ's first presidential speech—to a nation in mourning, and in desperate need of strong and steady leadership. After quoting the 1961 inaugural address in which President Kennedy famously declared, "Let us begin," President Johnson outlined the unfinished business of the civil rights agenda. Then—with three simple words—he gave voice to the goals of his presidency, and issued a challenge that has echoed through the ages: "Let us continue."

In fulfilling this directive, President Johnson—and the many leaders, activists, and ordinary citizens who shared his vision and determination—set our country on a course toward remarkable, once-unimaginable, progress. Together, they opened new doors of opportunity, helping to ensure equal access to schools and public spaces, to restaurants and workplaces, and—perhaps most important of all—to the ballot box. Our great nation was transformed.

In 1965, when President Johnson signed the landmark Voting Rights Act into law, he proclaimed that, "the right to vote is the basic right, without which all others are meaningless."

Today, as attorney general, I have the privilege—and the solemn duty—of enforcing this law, and the other civil rights reforms that President Johnson championed. This work is among the Justice Department's most important priorities. And our efforts honor the generations of Americans who have taken extraordinary risks, and willingly confronted hatred, bias, and ignorance—as well as billy clubs and fire hoses, bullets and bombs—to ensure that their children, and all American citizens, would have the chance to participate in the work of their government. The right to vote is not only the cornerstone of our system of government—it is the lifeblood of our democracy. And no force has proved more powerful—or more integral to the success of the great American experiment—than efforts to expand the franchise.

Despite this history, and despite our nation's long tradition of extending voting rights—to non-property owners and women, to people of color and Native Americans, and to younger Americans—today, a growing number of our fellow citizens are worried about the same disparities, divisions, and problems that—nearly five decades ago—LBJ devoted his presidency to addressing. In my travels across this country, I've heard a consistent drumbeat of concern from many Americans, who—often for the first time in their lives—now have reason to believe that we are failing to live up to one of our nation's most noble, and essential, ideals.

As Congressman John Lewis described it, in a speech on the House floor this summer, the voting rights that he worked throughout his life—and nearly gave his life—to ensure are, "under attack . . . [by] a deliberate and systematic attempt to prevent millions of elderly voters, young voters, students, [and] minority and low-income voters from exercising their constitutional right to engage in the democratic process." Not only was he referring to the all-too-common deceptive practices we've been fighting for years. He was echoing more recent concerns about some of the state-level voting law changes we've seen this legislative season.

Since January, more than a dozen states have advanced new voting measures. Some of these new laws are currently under review by the Justice Department, based on our obligations under the Voting Rights Act. Texas and South Carolina, for example, have enacted laws establishing new photo identification requirements that we're reviewing. We're also examining a number of changes that Florida has made to its electoral process, including changes to the procedures governing third-party voter registration organizations, as well as changes to early voting procedures, including the number of days in the early voting period.

Although I cannot go into detail about the ongoing review of these and other state-law changes, I can assure you that it will be thorough—and fair. We will examine the facts, and we will apply the law. If a state passes a new voting law and meets its burden of showing that the law is not discriminatory, we will follow the law and approve the change. And where a state can't meet this burden, we will object as part of our obligation under Section 5 of the Voting Rights Act.

As many of you know—and as I hope the law students here are learning—Section 5 was put in place decades ago because of a well-documented history of voter discrimination in all or parts of the 16 states to which it applies. Within these "covered jurisdictions," any proposed change in voting procedures or practices—from moving a polling location to enacting a statewide redistricting plan—must be "precleared"—that is, approved—either by the Justice Department, or by a panel of federal judges.

Without question, Sections 5's preclearance process has been a powerful tool in combating discrimination for decades. In 2006, it was reauthorized with overwhelming bipartisan support —passing the House by a vote of 390 to 33, and the Senate by a vote of 98 to zero—before being signed into law by President Bush.

Despite the long history of support for Section 5, this keystone of our voting rights laws is now being challenged five years after its reauthorization as unconstitutional in no fewer than five lawsuits. Each of these lawsuits claims that we've attained a new era of electoral equality, that America in 2011 has moved beyond the challenges of 1965, and that Section 5 is no longer necessary.

I wish this were the case. The reality is that—in jurisdictions across the country—both overt and subtle forms of discrimination remain all too common. And we don't have to look far to see recent proof.

For example, in October, the Justice Department objected to a redistricting plan in East Feliciana Parish, Louisiana, where the map-drawer began the process by meeting exclusively with white officeholders—and never consulted black officeholders. The result was a map that diminished the electoral opportunity of African Americans. After the Justice Department objected, the parish enacted a new, nondiscriminatory map.

And, here in Texas, just two months ago, the department argued in court filings that proposed redistricting plans for both the state House and the Texas congressional delegation are impermissible, because the state has failed to show the absence of discrimination. The most recent Census data indicated that Texas has gained more than 4 million new residents—the vast majority of whom are Hispanic—and that this growth allows for four new congressional seats. However, this state has proposed adding zero additional seats in which Hispanics would have the electoral opportunity envisioned by the Voting Rights Act. Federal courts are still considering this matter, and we intend to argue vigorously at trial that this is precisely the kind of discrimination that Section 5 was intended to block.

To those who argue that Section 5 is no longer necessary—these and other examples are proof that we still need this critical tool to combat discrimination and safeguard the right to vote.

As concerns about the protection of this right and the integrity of our election systems become an increasingly prominent part of our national dialogue—we must consider some important questions. It is time to ask: what kind of nation—and what kind of people—do we want to be? Are we willing to allow this era—our era—to be remembered as the age when our nation's proud tradition of expanding the franchise ended? Are we willing to allow this time—our time—to be recorded in history as the age when the long-held belief that, in this country, every citizen has the chance—and the right—to help shape their government, became a relic of our past, instead of a guidepost for our future?

For me—and for our nation's Department of Justice—the answers are clear. We need election systems that are free from fraud, discrimination, and partisan influence—and that are more, not less, accessible to the citizens of this country.

Under this administration, our Civil Rights Division—and its Voting Section—have taken meaningful steps to ensure integrity, independence, and transparency in our enforcement of the Voting Rights Act. We have worked successfully and comprehensively to protect the voting rights of U.S. service members and veterans, and to enforce other laws that protect Americans living abroad, citizens with disabilities, and language minorities. As part of our aggressive enforcement of the "Motor Voter" law, this year alone, we filed two statewide lawsuits to enforce the requirement that voter registration opportunities be made available at a wider variety of government offices—beyond

just the local Department of Motor Vehicles. And we're seeing promising results from this work. For example, after filing a lawsuit in Rhode Island, we reached an agreement with state agencies that resulted in more voters being registered in the first full month after our lawsuit than in the entire previous two-year reporting period.

We're also working to ensure that the protections for language minorities included in the Voting Rights Act are aggressively enforced. These protections now apply to more than 19 million voting-age citizens. These are our Spanish-speaking friends and neighbors, our Chinese-speaking friends and neighbors, and a large and growing part of all our communities. In just the past year, we've filed three lawsuits to protect their rights. And, today, we're actively reviewing nationwide compliance.

But the Justice Department can't do it all. Ensuring that every veteran, every senior, every college student, and every eligible citizen has the right to vote must become our common cause. And, for all Americans, protecting this right, ensuring meaningful access, and combating discrimination must be viewed, not only as a legal issue—but as a moral imperative.

Just as we recently saw in Maine—where voters last month overturned a legislative proposal to end same-day voter registration—the ability to shape our laws remains in the hands of the American people.

Tonight, I'd like to highlight three areas where public support will be crucial in driving progress—and advancing much-needed reforms. The first involves deceptive election practices—and dishonest efforts to prevent certain voters from casting their ballots.

Over the years, we've seen all sorts of attempts to gain partisan advantage by keeping people away from the polls—from literacy tests and poll taxes, to misinformation campaigns telling people that Election Day has been moved, or that only one adult per household can cast a ballot. Before the 2004 elections, fliers were distributed in minority neighborhoods in Milwaukee, falsely claiming that "[I]f anybody in your family has ever been found guilty [of a crime], you can't vote in the presidential election"—and you risk a 10-year prison sentence if you do. Two years later, 14,000 Latino voters in Orange

County, California, received mailings, warning in Spanish that, "[If] you are an immigrant, voting in a federal election is a crime that can result in jail time." Both of these blatant falsehoods likely deterred some eligible citizens from going to the polls.

And, just last week, the campaign manager of a Maryland gubernatorial candidate was convicted on election fraud charges for approving anonymous "robocalls" that went out on Election Day last year to more than 100,000 voters in the state's two largest majority-black jurisdictions. These calls encouraged voters to stay home—telling them to "relax" because their preferred candidate had already wrapped up a victory.

In an effort to deter and punish such harmful practices, during his first year in the U.S. Senate, President Obama introduced legislation that would establish tough criminal penalties for those who engage in fraudulent voting practices—and would help to ensure that citizens have complete and accurate information about where and when to vote. Unfortunately, this proposal did not move forward. But I'm pleased to announce that—tomorrow—Senators Charles Schumer and Ben Cardin will reintroduce this legislation, in an even stronger form. I applaud their leadership—and I look forward to working with them as Congress considers this important legislation.

The second area for reform is the need for neutrality in redistricting efforts. Districts should be drawn to promote fair and effective representation for all—not merely to undercut electoral competition and protect incumbents. If we allow only those who hold elected office to select their constituents—instead of enabling voters to choose their representatives—the strength and legitimacy of our democracy will suffer.

One final area for reform that merits our strongest support is the growing effort—which is already underway in several states—to modernize voter registration. Today, the single biggest barrier to voting in this country is our antiquated registration system. According to the Census Bureau, of the 75 million adult citizens who failed to vote in the last presidential election, 60 million of them were not registered and, therefore, not eligible to cast a ballot.

All eligible citizens can and should be automatically registered to vote. The ability to vote is a right—it is not a privilege. Under our current system, many voters must follow cumbersome and needlessly complex voter registration rules. And every election season, state and local officials have to manually process a crush of new applications—most of them handwritten—leaving the system riddled with errors, and, too often, creating chaos at the polls.

Fortunately, modern technology provides a straightforward fix for these problems—if we have the political will to bring our election systems into the 21st century. It should be the government's responsibility to automatically register citizens to vote, by compiling—from databases that already exist—a list of all eligible residents in each jurisdiction. Of course, these lists would be used solely to administer elections—and would protect essential privacy rights.

We must also address the fact that although one in nine Americans move every year, their voter registration often does not move with them. Many would-be voters don't realize this until they've missed the deadline for registering, which can fall a full month before Election Day. Election officials should work together to establish a program of permanent, portable registration—so that voters who move can vote at their new polling place on Election Day. Until that happens, we should implement fail-safe procedures to correct voter-roll errors and omissions, by allowing every voter to cast a regular, nonprovisional ballot on Election Day. Several states have already taken this step, and it's been shown to increase turnout by at least three to five percentage points.

These modernization efforts would not only improve the integrity of our elections, they would also save precious taxpayer dollars.

Despite these benefits, there will always be those who say that easing registration hurdles will only lead to voter fraud. Let me be clear: voter fraud is not acceptable—and will not be tolerated by this Justice Department. But as I learned early in my career—as a prosecutor in the Justice Department's Public Integrity Section, where I actually investigated and prosecuted voting-fraud cases—making voter registration easier is simply not likely, by itself, to make our elections more susceptible to fraud. Indeed, those on all sides of this debate have acknowledged that in-person voting fraud is uncommon. We must be honest about this. And we must recognize that our ability to ensure the strength and integrity of our election systems—and to advance the reforms necessary to achieve this—depends on whether the American people are informed, engaged, and willing to demand commonsense solutions that make voting more accessible. Politicians may not readily alter the very systems under which they were elected. Only we, the people, can bring about meaningful change.

So speak out. Raise awareness about what's at stake. Call on our political parties to resist the temptation to suppress certain votes in the hope of attaining electoral success and, instead, encourage and work with the parties to achieve this success by appealing to more voters. And urge policymakers at every level to reevaluate our election systems—and to reform them in ways that encourage, not limit, participation.

Today, we cannot—and must not—take the right to vote for granted. Nor can we shirk the sacred responsibility that falls upon our shoulders.

Throughout his presidency, Lyndon Johnson frequently pointed out that, "America was the first nation in the history of the world to be founded with a purpose—to right wrong, [and] to do justice." Over the last two centuries, the fulfillment of this purpose has taken many forms—acts of protest and compassion, declarations of war and peace, and a range of efforts to make certain that, as another great president said, "government of . . . by . . . [and] for the people shall not perish from the Earth."

Today, there are competing visions about how our government should move forward. That's what the democratic process is all about—creating space for thoughtful debate, creating opportunity for citizens to voice their opinions, and ultimately letting the people chart their course. Our nation has worked, and even fought, to help people around the world establish such a process—most recently during the wave of civil rights uprisings known as the Arab Spring. Here at home, honoring our democracy demands that we remove any and all barriers to voting—a goal that all American citizens of all political backgrounds must share.

Despite so many decades of struggle, sacrifice, and achievement—we must remain ever vigilant in safeguarding our most basic and important right. Too many recent actions have the potential to reverse the progress that defines us—and has made this nation exceptional, as well as an example for all the world. We must be true to the arc of America's history, which compels us to be more inclusive with regard to the franchise. And we must never forget the purpose that—more than two centuries ago—inspired our nation's founding, and now must guide us forward.

So, let us act—with optimism and without delay. Let us rise to the challenges—and overcome the divisions—of our time. Let us signal to the world that—in America today—the pursuit of a more perfect union lives on.

And, in the spirit of Lyndon Baines Johnson, let us continue.   [2011]

Understanding the Reading

1. Why is there so much attention on voters' rights in this speech?
2. What are a few ways to intentionaly discriminate against certain United States voters?
3. Why does Eric Holder say that our voting system is antiquated, and how could it be modernized?

Suggestions for Responding

1. Have a class discussion on patterns of discrimination against voters and voter identification fraud.
2. What are your state's laws about students voting? ✦

91

Diversity and Its Discontents

ARTURO MADRID

My name is Arturo Madrid. I am a citizen of the United States, as are my parents and as were my grandparents and my great-grandparents.

My ancestors' presence in what is now the United States antedates Plymouth Rock, even without taking into account any American Indian heritage I might have.

I do not, however, fit those mental sets that define America and Americans. My physical appearance, my speech patterns, my name, my profession (a professor of Spanish) create a text that confuses the reader. My normal experience is to be asked, "And where are *you* from?" My response depends on my mood. Passive-aggressive, I answer, "From here." Aggressive-passive, I ask, "Do you mean where I am originally from?" But ultimately my answer to those follow-up questions that will ask about origins will be that we have always been from here.

Overcoming my resentment I try to educate, knowing that nine times out of ten my words fall on inattentive ears. I have spent most of my adult life explaining who I am not. I am exotic, but—as Richard Rodriguez of *Hunger of Memory* fame so painfully found out—not exotic enough . . . not Peruvian, or Pakistani, or whatever. I am, however, very clearly the *other,* if only your everyday, garden-variety, domestic *other.* I will share with you another phenomenon that I have been a part of, that of being a missing person, and how I came late to that awareness. But I've always known that I was the *other,* even before I knew the vocabulary or understood the significance of otherness.

I grew up in an isolated and historically marginal part of the United States, a small mountain village in the state of New Mexico, the eldest child of parents native to that region, whose ancestors had always lived there. In those vast and empty spaces people who look like me, speak as I do, and have names like mine predominate. But the *americanos* lived among us: the descendants of those nineteenth-century immigrants who dispossessed us of our lands; missionaries who came to convert us and stayed to live among us; artists who became enchanted with our land and humanscape and went native; refugees from unhealthy climes, crowded spaces, unpleasant circumstances; and, of course, the inhabitants of Los Alamos,[1] whose sociocultural distance from us was accentuated by the fact that they occupied a space removed from and proscribed to us. More importantly, however, they—*los americanos*—were omnipresent (and almost exclusively so) in newspapers, newsmagazines, books, on radio, in movies, and, ultimately, on television.

Despite the operating myth of the day, school did not erase my otherness. It did try to deny it, and in doing so only accentuated it. To this day what takes place in schools is more socialization than education, but when I was in elementary school—and given where I was—socialization was everything. School was where one became an American, because there was a pervasive and systematic denial by the society that surrounded us that we were Americans. That denial was both explicit and implicit.

Quite beyond saluting the flag and pledging allegiance to it (a very intense and meaningful action, given that the United States was involved in a war and our brothers, cousins, uncles, and fathers were on the front lines), becoming American was learning English, and its corollary: not speaking Spanish. Until very recently ours was a proscribed language, either *de jure*—by rule, by policy, by law—or *de facto*—by practice, implicitly if not explicitly, through social and political and economic pressure. I do not argue that learning English was not appropriate. On the contrary. Like it or not, and we had no basis to make any judgments on that matter, we were Americans by virtue of having been born Americans and English was the common language of Americans. And there was a myth, a pervasive myth, to the effect that if only we learned to speak English well—and particularly without an accent—we would be welcomed into the American fellowship.

Sam Hayakawa[2] and the official English movement folks not with standing, the true text was not our speech, but rather our names and our appearance, for we would always have an accent, however perfect our pronunciation, however excellent our enunciation, however divine our diction. That accent would be heard in our pigmentation, our physiognomy, our names. We were, in short, the *other.*

Being the *other* involves contradictory phenomena. On the one hand, being the *other* frequently means being invisible. Ralph Ellison wrote eloquently about that experience in his magisterial novel, *Invisible Man.* On the other hand, being the *other* sometimes involves sticking out like a sore thumb. What is she/he doing here?

For some of us being the *other* is only annoying; for others it is debilitating; for still others it is damning. Many try to flee otherness by taking on protective colorations that provide invisibility, whether of dress or speech or manner or name. Only a fortunate few succeed. For the majority of us otherness is permanently sealed by physical appearance. For the rest, otherness is betrayed by ways of being, speaking, or doing.

The first half of my life I spent downplaying the significance and consequences of otherness. The second half has seen me wrestling to understand its complex and deeply ingrained realities; striving to fathom why otherness denies us a voice or visibility or validity in American society and its institutions; struggling to make otherness familiar, reasonable, even normal to my fellow Americans.

I spoke earlier of another phenomenon that I am a part of: that of being a missing person. Growing up in northern New Mexico I had only a slight sense of us being missing persons. *Hispanos,* as we called (and call) ourselves in New Mexico, were very much a part of the fabric of the society, and there were *hispano* professionals everywhere about me: doctors, lawyers, schoolteachers, and administrators. My people owned businesses, ran organizations, and were both appointed and elected public officials.

My awareness of our absence from the larger institutional life of the society became sharper when I went off to college, but even then it was attenuated by the circumstances of history and geography. The demography of Albuquerque still strongly reflected its historical and cultural origins, despite the influx of Midwesterners and Easterners. Moreover, many of my classmates at the University of New Mexico were *hispanos,* and even some of my professors. I thought that would pertain at UCLA, where I began graduate studies in 1960. Los Angeles had a very large Mexican population and that population was visible even in and around Westwood and on the campus. Many of the groundskeepers and food-service personnel at UCLA were Mexican. But Mexican-American students were few and mostly invisible, and I do not recall seeing or knowing a single Mexican-American (or, for that matter, African-American, Asian, or American Indian) professional on the staff or faculty of that institution during the five years I was there. Needless to say, people like me were not present in any capacity at Dartmouth College, the site of my first teaching appointment, and of course were not even part of the institutional or individual mind-set. I knew then that we—a we that had come to encompass American Indians, Asian-Americans, African-Americans, Puerto Ricans, and women—were truly missing persons in American institutional life.

Over the past three decades the *de jure* and *de facto* types of segregation that have historically characterized American institutions have been under assault. As a consequence, minorities and women have become part of American institutional life. Although there are still many areas where we are not to be found, the missing persons phenomenon is not as pervasive as it once was. However, the presence of the *other,* particularly minorities, in institutions and in institutional life resembles what we call in Spanish a *flor de tierra* (a surface phenomenon): we are spare plants whose roots do not go deep, vulnerable to inclemencies of an economic, or political, or social nature.

Our entrance into and our status in institutional life are not unlike a scenario set forth by my grandmother's pastor when she informed him that she and her family were leaving their mountain village to relocate to the Rio Grande Valley. When he asked her to promise that she would remain true to the faith and continue to involve herself in it, she asked why he thought she would do otherwise. "Doña Trinidad," he told her, "in the Valley there is no Spanish church. There is only an American church." "But," she protested, "I read and speak English and would be able to worship there." The pastor responded, "It is possible that they will not admit you, and even if they do, they might not accept you. And that is why I want you to promise me that you are going to go to church. Because if they don't let you in through the front door, I want you to go in through the back door. And if you can't get in through the back door, go in the side door. And if you are unable to enter through the side door I want you to go in through the window. What is important is that you enter and stay."

Some of us entered institutional life through the front door; others through the back door; and still others through side doors. Many, if not most of us, came in through windows, and continue to come in through windows. Of those who entered through the front door, some never made it past the lobby; others were ushered into corners and niches. Those who entered through back and side doors inevitably have remained in back and side rooms. And those who entered through windows found enclosures built around them. For, despite the lip service given to the goal of the integration of minorities into institutional life, what has frequently occurred instead is ghettoization, marginalization, isolation.

Not only have the entry points been limited, but in addition the dynamics have been singularly conflictive. Gaining entry and its corollary, gaining space, have frequently come as a consequence of demands made on institutions and institutional officers. Rather than entering institutions more or less passively, minorities have of necessity entered them actively, even aggressively. Rather than waiting to receive, they have demanded. Institutional relations have thus been adversarial, infused with specific and generalized tensions.

The nature of the entrance and the nature of the space occupied have greatly influenced the view and attitude of the majority population within those institutions. All of us are put into the same box; that is, no matter what the individual reality, the assessment of the individual is inevitably conditioned by a perception that is held of the class. Whatever our history, whatever our record, whatever our validations, whatever our accomplishments, by and large we are perceived unidimensionally and dealt with accordingly. I remember an experience I had in this regard, atypical only in its explicitness. A few years ago I allowed myself to be persuaded to seek the presidency of a well-known state university. I was invited for an interview and presented myself before the selection committee, which included members of the board of trustees. The opening question of that brief but memorable interview was directed at me by a member of that august body. "Dr. Madrid," he asked, "why does a one-dimensional person like you think he can be the president of a multidimensional institution like ours?"

Over the past four decades America's demography has undergone significant changes. Since 1965 the principal demographic growth we have experienced in the United States has been of peoples whose national origins are non-European. This population growth has occurred both through birth and through immigration. A few years ago discussion of the national birthrate had a scare dimension: the high—"inordinately high"—birthrate of the Hispanic population. The popular discourse was informed by words such as "breeding." Several years later, as a consequence of careful tracking by government agencies, we now know that what has happened is that the birthrate of the majority population has decreased. When viewed historically and comparatively, the minority populations (for the most part) have also had a decline in birthrate, but not one as great as that of the majority.

There are additional demographic changes that should give us something to think about. African-Americans are now to be found in significant numbers in every major urban center in the nation. Hispanic-Americans now number over 15 million people, and although they are a regionally concentrated (and highly urbanized) population, there is a Hispanic community in almost every major urban center of the United States. American Indians, heretofore a small and rural population, are increasingly more numerous and urban. The Asian-American population, which has historically consisted of small and concentrated communities of Chinese-, Filipino-, and Japanese-Americans, has doubled over the past decade, its complexion changed by the addition of Cambodians, Koreans, Hmongs, Vietnamese, et al.

Prior to the Immigration Act of 1965,[3] 69 percent of immigration was from Europe. By far the largest number of immigrants to the United States since 1965 have been from the Americas and from Asia: 34 percent are from Asia; another 34 percent are from Central and South America; 16 percent are from Europe; 10 percent are from the Caribbean; the remaining 6 percent are from other continents and Canada. As was the case with previous immigration waves, the current one consists principally of young people: 60 percent are between the ages of 16 and 44. Thus, for the next few decades, we will continue to see a growth in the percentage of non-European-origin Americans as compared to European-Americans.

To sum up, we now live in one of the most demographically diverse nations in the world, and one that is increasingly more so.

During the same period social and economic change seems to have accelerated. Who would have imagined at mid-century that the prototypical middle-class family (working husband, wife as homemaker, two children) would for all intents and purposes disappear? Who could have anticipated the rise in teenage pregnancies, children in poverty, drug use? Who among us understood the implications of an aging population?

We live in an age of continuous and intense change, a world in which what held true yesterday does not today, and certainly will not tomorrow. What change does, moreover, is bring about even more change. The only constant we have at this point in our national development is change. And change is threatening. The older we get the more likely we are to be anxious about change, and the greater our desire to maintain the status quo.

Evident in our public life is a fear of change, whether economic or moral. Some who fear change are responsive to the call of economic protectionism, others to the message of moral protectionism. Parenthetically, I have referred to the movement to require more of students without in turn giving them more as academic protectionism. And the pronouncements of E. D. Hirsch and Allan Bloom[4] are, I believe, informed by intellectual protectionism. Much more serious, however, is the dark side of the populism[5] which underlies this evergoing protectionism—the resentment of the *other*. An excellent and fascinating example of that aspect of populism is the cry for linguistic protectionism—for making English the official language of the United States. And who among us is unaware of the tensions that underlie immigration reform, of the underside of demographic protectionism?

A matter of increasing concern is whether this new protectionism, and the mistrust of the *other* which accompanies it, is not making more significant inroads than we have supposed in higher education. Specifically, I wish to discuss the question of whether a goal (quality) and a reality (demographic diversity) have been erroneously placed in conflict, and, if so, what problems this perception of conflict might present.

As part of my scholarship I turn to dictionaries for both origins and meanings of words. Quality, according to the *Oxford English Dictionary,* has multiple meanings. One set defines quality as being an essential character, a distinctive and inherent feature. A second describes it as a degree of excellence, of conformity to standards, as superiority in kind. A third makes reference to social status, particularly to persons of high social status. A fourth talks about quality as being a special or distinguishing attribute, as being a desirable trait. Quality is highly desirable in both principle and practice. We all aspire to it in our own person, in our experiences, in our acquisitions and products, and of course we all want to be associated with people and operations of quality.

But let us move away from the various dictionary meanings of the word and to our own sense of what it represents and of how we feel about it. First of all we consider quality to be finite; that is, it is limited with respect to quantity; it has very few manifestations; it is not widely distributed. I have it and you have it, but they don't. We associate quality with homogeneity, with uniformity, with standardization, with order, regularity, neatness. All too often we equate it with smoothness, glibness, slickness, elegance. Certainly it is always expensive. We tend to identify it with those who lead, with the rich and famous. And, when you come right down to it, it's inherent. Either you've got or you ain't.

Diversity, from the Latin *divertere,* meaning to turn aside, to go different ways, to differ, is the condition of being different or having differences, is an instance of being different. Its companion word, diverse, means differing, unlike, distinct; having or capable of having various forms; composed of unlike or distinct elements. Diversity is lack of standardization, of regularity, of orderliness, homogeneity, conformity, uniformity. Diversity introduces complications, is difficult to organize, is troublesome to manage, is problematical. Diversity is irregular, disorderly, uneven, rough. The way we use the word diversity gives us away. Something is too diverse, is extremely diverse. We want a little diversity.

When we talk about diversity, we are talking about the *other,* whatever that other might be: someone of different gender, race, class, national origin; somebody at a greater or lesser distance from the norm; someone outside the set; someone who possesses a different set of characteristics, features, or attributes; someone who does not fall within the taxonomies we use daily and with which we are comfortable; someone who does not fit into the mental configurations that give our lives order and meaning.

In short, diversity is desirable only in principle, not in practice. Long live diversity . . . as long as it conforms to my standards, my mind set, my view of life, my sense of order. We desire, we like, we admire diversity, not unlike the way the French (and others) appreciate women; that is, *Vive la différence!*—as long as it stays in its place.

What I find paradoxical about and lacking in this debate is that diversity is the natural order of things. Evolution produces diversity. Margaret Visser, writing about food in her latest book, *Much Depends on Dinner,* makes an eloquent statement in this regard:

> Machines like, demand, and produce uniformity. But nature loathes it: her strength lies in multiplicity and in differences. Sameness in biology means fewer possibilities and therefore weakness.

The United States, by its very nature, by its very development, is the essence of diversity. It is diverse in its geography, population, institutions, technology; its social, cultural, and intellectual modes. It is a society that at its best does not consider quality to be monolithic in form or finite in quantity, or to be inherent in class. Quality in our society proceeds in large measure out of the stimulus of diverse modes of thinking and acting; out of the creativity made possible by the different ways in which we approach things; out of diversion from paths or modes hallowed by tradition.

One of the principal strengths of our society is its ability to address, on a continuing and substantive basis, the real economic, political, and social problems that have faced and continue to face us. What makes the United States so attractive to immigrants is the protections and opportunities it offers; what keeps our society together is tolerance for cultural, religious, social, political, and even linguistic difference; what makes us a unique, dynamic, and extraordinary nation is the power and creativity of our diversity.

The true history of the United States is one of struggle against intolerance, against oppression, against xenophobia, against those forces that have prohibited persons from participating in the larger life of the society on the basis of their race, their gender, their religion, their national origin, their linguistic and cultural background. These phenomena are not consigned to the past. They remain with us and frequently take on virulent dimensions.

If you believe, as I do, that the well-being of a society is directly related to the degree and extent to which all of its citizens participate in its institutions, then you will have to agree that we have a challenge before us. In view of the extraordinary changes that are taking place in our society we need to take up the struggle again, irritating, grating, troublesome, unfashionable, unpleasant as it is. As educated and educator members of this society we have a special responsibility for ensuring that all American institutions, not just our elementary and secondary schools, our juvenile halls, or our jails, reflect the diversity of our society. Not to do so is to risk greater alienation on the part of a growing segment of our society; is to risk increased social tension in an already conflictive world; and, ultimately, is to risk the survival of a range of institutions that, for all their defects and deficiencies, provide us the opportunity and the freedom to improve our individual and collective lot.

Let me urge you to reflect on these two words—quality and diversity—and on the mental sets and behaviors that flow out of them. And let me urge you further to struggle against the notion that quality is finite in quantity, limited in its manifestations, or is restricted by considerations of class, gender, race, or national origin; or that quality manifests itself only in leaders and not in followers, in managers and not in workers, in breeders and not in drones;

or that it has to be associated with verbal agility or elegance of personal style; or that it cannot be seeded, nurtured, or developed.

Because diversity—the *other*—is among us, [it] will define and determine our lives in ways that we still do not fully appreciate, whether that other is women (no longer bound by tradition, house, and family); or Asians, African-Americans, Indians, and Hispanics (no longer invisible, regional, or marginal); or our newest immigrants (no longer distant, exotic, alien). Given the changing profile of America, will we come to terms with diversity in our personal and professional lives? Will we begin to recognize the diverse forms that quality can take? If so, we will thus initiate the process of making quality limitless in its manifestations, infinite in quantity, unrestricted with respect to its origins, and more importantly, virulently contagious.

I hope we will. And that we will further join together to expand—not to close—the circle.

[1990]

Terms

1. Los Alamos: The military installation where scientists developed the atomic bomb.
2. Sam Hayakawa: The former president of San Francisco State University and an outspoken opponent of bilingual education.
3. Immigration Act of 1965: The federal law that abolished the national-origins quota system of immigration.
4. E. D. Hirsch and Allan Bloom: The authors, respectively, of *Cultural Illiteracy* and *The Closing of the American Mind*, both of which advocate a traditional curriculum.
5. Populism: A political philosophy that gives primacy to the needs of common people.

Understanding the Reading

1. Why does Madrid resent being asked where he is from?
2. What does he mean by being "other"?
3. What does he mean by referring to himself as "invisible" or a "missing person"?
4. What is the distinction between a school's erasing otherness and denying it?

5. Why did his grandmother's pastor feel that it was important for her to enter the church and stay?
6. What does Madrid mean by saying he is perceived unidimensionally?
7. Why does he find *breeding* an offensive term?
8. What point is Madrid making by giving the various dictionary meanings of *quality* and *diversity*?

Suggestion for Responding

1. Do you agree or disagree with Madrid that diversity is the basis for the "quality" of the United States? Why? ✦

92

Breakfast at Perkins

Derek Schork

Yes, stereotypes and prejudices have been a part of my thinking. I don't think anyone can honestly say that they have not had a prejudiced thought at one time or another, especially in the wake of 9/11. I'd rather not go into detail about these thoughts, as I am not particularly proud of them. However, there was one time that comes to mind when I was victimized by a stereotype. It made me very angry at the time, but now almost three years later, it's very easy for me and my friends, especially those who were there, to laugh about.

This story takes place on an early spring morning of my senior year in high school. You must know that I have a below-the-knee amputation of my left leg. This particular morning I was wearing jeans. Keep that in mind as you read on. A group of friends and I decided to go out for breakfast, instead of going to school on time. When I pulled into the parking lot at Perkins Restaurant I saw that there weren't any available parking spots on this side of the lot. Legally I am allowed to park in a handicapped spot and I have the designation that hangs from my mirror. I was running late and all of my friends were already inside so I parked in one of the handicapped spots. As I got out of my car with my friend Jamie, an older man (mid 50's) was walking into the restaurant, when he stopped and looked at us and said, "Which one of you is handicapped? You should be ashamed of yourselves." This made me irate. Who was he to question us about where we parked? He made the stereotype of seeing two kids wearing long pants (so he couldn't see my prosthesis) and he assumed that there was no way a kid could be handicapped. Well, I started yelling at him to turn around, as I rolled up my pant leg. He wouldn't turn around, which made me even madder. At this point I think he realized that he had made a mistake, but wouldn't admit it. So I continued to try to get his attention, this time by taking off my leg and hopping after him into the restaurant. Perkins Restaurant was not prepared for this scene—evident by the stunned looks on the faces of everyone as a cursing kid hopped in with leg in hand. The hostess tried to calm me down as the man walked to his seat and I reattached myself. My friends were having a good laugh as I went and sat down, and explained to them what happened. If the old man had asked me nicely instead of making a stupid assumption, I would have had no problem explaining to him why I parked there. This story is now legendary among my friends. At least now it's a good story to tell.   [2002]

Understanding the Reading

1. Why weren't Schork and his friends in school on this particular morning?
2. Why did the man outside Perkins Restaurant assume he was parking illegally?
3. What made Schork so angry? What did he do?
4. What could have solved this problem?

Suggestion for Responding

1. Share memories with your classmates of someone making erroneous assumptions, about you or someone else, because of a physical aspect of that person. Share your own mistaken judgments as well. ◆

93

What Occupy Wall Street Demands of Our Leaders

ALAINA LOVE

Occupy Wall Street began in mid-September with a group of 1,000 protestors marching through the streets and has now grown into a global movement in search of sanity in our political and economic system. Many in the group, unemployed and disheartened, are quietly demanding a new breed of leadership in Washington and on Wall Street—leaders measurably committed to the average individual struggling to make ends meet.

In the U.S., the movement has emerged as the yin to the Tea Party's yang, but itself is a form of chaos in the process of coalescing into a new order. Both Wall Street and Washington have an opportunity to influence the direction of that new order if leaders in both camps seriously address the overarching demand of Occupy Wall Street, which is for greater equality in our economic system and the political decisions that drive it.

And that is where both Wall Street and Washington have failed miserably in the eyes of the unemployed or underemployed protestors. In the various divisions of the movement sprouting up around the world, the cry is for hope, for economic opportunity, for soul in our business and politics, and for promise that the American dream will not be denied to today's young people.

What might influence protestors and propel them into positive action? Evidence that our most influential business leaders are demonstrating a true sense of purpose, which extends beyond greed and self-serving motives. It would make a meaningful difference if leaders in Washington enacted legislation that focuses more on the needs of the struggling middle class than on positioning for the next election campaign. Yet, this would mark a return to values embracing the higher good rather than the good of a chosen few—and that, unfortunately, is the

© Dave Moyer

antithesis of the economic and political leadership these protestors have come to know.

To the participants in Occupy Wall Street, business and political leaders have lost their footing. They have detoured the country away from the basic tenets of our government: life, liberty, equality and the pursuit of happiness.

This is, however, a movement in need of unified leadership. Washington and Wall Street have the potential to transform this nascent movement into a platform for positive action, rather than a hotbed of rage that ultimately leads to violence. It will require a revolution in the governance of our corporations and our country, with the leaders of companies, boards, states and the nation owning their part in the decisions that have led to the current quagmire. While Occupy Wall Street is a fledgling movement, it should remind all of us that we have a say in what happens in our economy. More than that, we have a responsibility to hold our leaders accountable.

The direction of the movement is not clear at this time, but a kind of disruptive innovation

could result from Occupy Wall Street that will demand new actions from Wall Street and Washington leaders as this movement evolves.

What types of demands?

They will want leaders who accept responsibility and accountability for their actions, and who have value sets that prompt them to care more about those they represent than they do about themselves.

They will want an end to taxpayer bailouts, and an end to corporate governance structures that allow the positions of CEO and president of the board to be held by the same individual. It also has not been lost on protestors that back in 1965 CEO pay was 24 times greater than the average employee's pay—and today is 300 times greater.

These protestors will also want our media to assume better responsibility for providing accurate, complete information rather than poisoning sound bites that fuel political frenzy and divert attention from critical matters that shape our nation's future.

And finally, they'll likely look for stiff penalties for offshore jobs creation while unemployment festers in the United States, and an end to the abdication of political leadership that has led to Washington gridlock.

Protestors may not yet define a unifying goal, but they are not confused about the fact that living conditions for the average American are rapidly deteriorating. And, what's more, no one appears to be listening.

Understanding the Reading

1. What is the main demand of the Occupy Wall Street Movement that stretches across the United States?
2. What does the author mean when she writes that "the cry is for . . . soul in our business and politics"?
3. What kind of basic change of values, and therefore public policies, does this movement demand?

Suggestion for Responding

1. Have a class discussion on how the United States, through political action, could bring hope to the unemployed and underemployed. ✦

94

Going Public with Our Vision

CHARLOTTE BUNCH

TRANSFORMATIONAL POLITICS AND PRACTICAL VISIONS

To bring the feminist vision to bear on all issues and to counter the right-wing agenda for the future, require that we engage in multiple strategies for action. We must work on many fronts at once. If a movement becomes a single issue or single strategy, it runs the danger of losing its overall vision and diminishing its support, since different classes of people feel most intensely the pressure of different issues. So while we may say at any given moment that one issue is particularly crucial, it is important that work be done on other aspects of the changes we need at the same time. The task is not finding "the right issue," but bringing clear political analysis to each issue showing how it connects to other problems and to a broad-based feminist view of change in society.

Feminist concerns are not isolated, and oppression does not happen one-by-one-by-one in separate categories. I don't experience homophobia as a separate and distinct category from economic discrimination as a woman. I don't view racism as unconnected to militarism and patriarchal domination of the world.

In order to discuss the specific strategies necessary to get through this transition and bring feminism into the public arena more forcefully, we must first be clear that feminism is a transformational politics. As such, feminism brings a perspective to *any* issue and cannot and must not be limited to a separate ghetto called "women's issues." When dealing with any issue, whether it is budgets or biogenetics or wife battering, feminism as a political perspective is about change in structures—about ending domination and resisting oppression. Feminism is not just incorporating women into existing institutions.

As a politics of transformation, feminism is also relevant to more than a constituency of women. Feminism is a vision born of women that we must offer to and demand of men. I'm tired of letting men off the hook by saying that we don't know whether they can be feminists. Of course they can struggle to be feminists, just as I can and must struggle to be antiracist. If feminism is to be a transforming perspective in the world, then men must also be challenged by it.

This does not mean that we do not also need spaces and organizations for women only. Women need and want and have the right to places where we gather strength and celebrate our culture and make plans only with women. But as a political vision, feminism addresses the future for men as well as for women, for boys as well as for girls, and we must be clear that it is a politics for the future of the world, not just for an isolated handful of the converted.

If we are clear about feminism as a transformational politics, we can develop viable public alternatives to Reaganism and all patriarchal policies. These would be policy statements of how we think the world could be organized in various areas if a feminist approach is taken.

We need feminist budgets for every town, state, and nation. For example, you could take the state budget in Montana, whatever it is, take the same amount of money and prepare a budget of how you would reorganize the use of that money if feminists had control of the state government. When you finish that one, you can do a federal budget. And when you finish that, take on the UN budget! Budgets are good indicators of priorities. If we publicized our approaches, people could see that there are alternatives, that we are talking about something different, and they would get a clearer idea of what a feminist perspective means in practical terms.

I would also like to see feminist plans for housing, transportation, criminal justice, child care, education, agriculture, and so on. We need serious discussion as feminists about how we deal with the issues of defense, not only by doing critiques of militarism, but also by deciding how to cope with the competing powers and threats in this world, as they exist right now. We're not going to solve many of the problems immediately, but we have to put forward other policies and practices, so people can see the difference. If we start with how things are now, then we can talk about how to move, step-by-step, toward policies that are based on very different assumptions and values.

To use such feminist policy statements, when we engage in electoral politics for example, would give people a clear and public statement of what it means to elect a feminist. We would also have something concrete to hold a candidate accountable to after election. To work to elect feminists with clear policy content makes a campaign focus on feminism as a transforming politics rather than just on personality or on adding women without clear political statements of what they represent. It can make electoral politics part of a strategy for change rather than isolated from the movement or a substitute for other action.

Developing such policies is particularly important now because the Reagan crowd is also about a "revolution" in social policies. We could call it reactionary, but if revolution means massive change in government policies, that is what Reagan is pulling off right now. We need a creative counter to these policy changes that is not just a return to where we were in the past. We have to put forward approaches that both deal with the problems that we had before Reagan, and reveal the antiwoman, patriarchal, racist, and sexist assumptions of the right wing.

ORGANIZING FOR ACTION

Perhaps the most important thing that we need to do, which underlies everything I've said, is organize. Organize. Organize. Organize. All the great ideas in the world, even feminist budgets, will mean little if we don't also organize people to act on them. We have to organize in a variety of ways.

We need to take what has been the decentralized strength of the women's movement—a multitude of separate women's projects and individuals whose lives have been radically affected by feminism—and find lasting forms for bringing that to more political power. The feminist movement has a wonderful array of creative small groups and projects. Nevertheless, when these don't have any voice in something larger, a lot of their potential power is lost simply because what is learned and done is limited to a small circle and has no larger outlet to affect the public. I don't want to abandon the small-group approach to working,

but those groups need to band together into larger units that can have a political impact beyond their numbers. This can take the form of citywide or issue-based alliances, which still preserve each group's autonomy. Such feminist alliances then become the basis for coalitions—as a feminist force—with other progressive groups. If we organize ourselves to join coalitions as a community, rather than having women going into other groups one by one, we have a better chance of keeping our feminist values and perspectives in the forefront of that coalition work.

We can utilize the grass-roots decentralized nature of feminism well in organizing around policy changes today, because it is at the state and local level where most of the battles with the right wing are presently focused. But to do that effectively we have to learn how to get our supporters out—to be visible about their politics. If we are trying to influence policy, the policy-makers must know that our people are reliable; if we say that a hundred thousand women will be in Washington, D.C., or a thousand in Billings, Montana, they have to know that they will be there.

The agenda for change is often set by the kind of organizing that goes on around specific issues—particularly ones that are very visible and of considerable interest to people, such as reproductive rights or the Family Protection Act.[1] Whatever the issue, as long as it is one that affects people's lives, the task of the organizer is to show how it connects to other issues of oppression, such as racism, and also to illustrate what that issue means in terms of a vision for the future. The Family Protection Act has demonstrated well these connections as its supporters have sought to bring back the patriarchal order through policies against gays, against assistance to battered women and children, against freedom in the schools, and against the organizing of workers into unions, and so on. It provides a clear case for discussing feminist versus antifeminist perspectives on life.

Another task of organizers is to devise strategies to activate people who care, but who aren't politically active. I saw a chain letter circulating among women artists, which instead of having people send a dollar, said: "Write a letter to

Senator So and So (participating in the hearings on abortion), and then send this letter to eight of your friends who want reproductive rights but who aren't doing anything about it."

One mistake we often make is to act as if there is nothing that supporters can do politically if they can't be activists twenty-four hours a day, seven days a week. We must provide channels of action for people who have ten minutes a day or an hour a week, because that very action ties them closer to caring and being willing to risk or move toward a feminist vision. We must mobilize the constituency we have of concerned individuals, recognizing that many of them are very busy just trying to survive and care for their children or parents.

One of Jerry Falwell's[2] organizations sends a little cardboard church to its local supporters, who deposit a quarter a day, and at the end of the week, they dump the money out and send it to Falwell. We can learn something from this approach, which provides a daily connection to one's supporters. When I see community resources—health clinics, women's centers, whatever—closing because they're no longer getting outside support, I worry about our connections to our supporters. This movement did not start with government money. This movement started in the streets and it started with the support of women, and it can only survive if it is supported by us.

I have no objections to feminists getting government money or applying for grants as long as we remember that when they don't give us the money, we have to figure out other ways to do what has to be done by ourselves. We have to go back to our own resources if we believe in what we're doing. If the peasants of Latin America have supported the Catholic Church over the centuries, I don't see any reason why the feminists and gay men and lesbians of North America cannot support our movements.

COALITIONS: THE BOTTOM LINE

Coalitions with other progressive groups are important, but we must be clear about what makes them viable. The basis of coalitions is integrity and respect for what each group describes as its bottom line. Now that's not always easy. But with honest struggle over what each group feels is its necessary, critical minimum demand, coalitions can work. If we are to make compromises on where we put our time and energy, it has to be within that framework. Coalitions don't succeed simply for ideological or charitable reasons. They succeed out of a sense that we need each other, and that none of our constituencies can be mobilized effectively if we abandon their bottom-line concerns. Therefore, we have to know where the critical points are for each group in a coalition.

This is a difficult process, but I saw it work in Houston at the National Women's Conference[3] in 1977. As one of the people organizing the lesbian caucus, I can tell you there were moments in that process when I was ready to scream over the homophobia we encountered. But we knew our bottom line and were clear about what compromises we could and could not accept. If it had been an event comprised only of feminists, we would have said more about lesbianism. But as a large, diverse conference, we saw our task as coalescing a critical mass recognition and support of the issue of sexual preference through working as part of the broad-based feminist coalition there.

In order to get this recognition, we had to organize our constituency so that other groups would want our support. We were clear that we would not support a compromise that left us out—that we had to have that mutual respect to make the coalition work. But the success of lesbians was based on the fact that we had organized at the state and local level as well as nationally. Our people were there and others knew we had the numbers. Many women realized that they had a lot more to gain by mobilizing our support for the overall plan by including us, than by alienating us, and creating a very public nuisance. Coalitions are possible, but they are only effective when you have mutual respect; when you have a clearly articulated bottom line; and when you have your own group mobilized for action. If you haven't got your own group organized, your own power base, when the crunch comes, no matter how politically correct or charitable people feel, they are going to align with the groups they feel will make them stronger.

We need more feminist alliances or coalitions that do not coalesce around only one event, but that establish themselves over time as representing a variety of groups and types of action, from electoral and media work to demonstrations or public education. Such ongoing political action groups are usually multi-issue and their strength lies in bringing groups together for concerted action on a city- or state-wide basis. These groups then become a reliable basis for coalitions with other progressive organizations.

GOING PUBLIC

I think that it is crucial for the feminist movement to become more public. By going public, I mean we need to move beyond the boundaries of our subculture. This does not mean giving up the women's community, which remains our strength, our base, the roots of our analysis and of our sustenance. But to go more public in actions that are visible beyond our circles, demonstrating to the world that feminists have not rolled over and played dead as the media sometimes implies.

Going public involves statements about our visions for change. This can be through vehicles such as feminist policy statements on housing or the budget, as well as by demonstrating the passion of our visions with militancy, such as the civil disobedience and fasting women did in the struggle for ratification of the ERA.[4] Such actions make our issues dramatically visible, seen as matters of life and death. These also capture the public imagination and re-create some of that spirit of discovery that accompanied the early years of women's liberation. We need more creative community or media-oriented events that bring that instant recognition of what is at stake and inspire people to talk about those issues.

One of the important things that I remember about the early days of the women's movement is that we talked about feminism—incessantly. We talked in the laundromat, we talked on our jobs, we talked to everybody because we were so excited about what we were discovering. And that talk spread—it excited other women, whether they agreed with us or not. The primary method by which women have become feminists is through talk, through consciousness-raising, and through talk with other feminists. It was not through the government or even the media, but through ourselves. And they cannot take that away. They can deny us money, but they cannot take away ourselves, and the way that this movement has grown is through our "beings"—through being active in the world and being visible.

We have to go public by moving out of what may be comfortable places and engage with women who don't necessarily call themselves feminists. You can go public a hundred different ways—whether that is through media-oriented action or by talking to women on the job or at established women's places. In going public, we risk the vulnerability that goes with such interaction, but the rewards are worth it. The challenge to our ideas that comes with it enables us and our ideas to expand and be more inclusive and more powerful. The interaction that comes with seeing feminism in relation to situations that are not familiar to us, or seeing women of different class or race or geographic backgrounds taking feminism in new directions, is a very good tonic for "tired feminists."

The growth of feminism depends precisely on this interaction—of different generations of feminists and of challenges that make our ideas change and go farther than when they started. If we believe that our visions are visions for the world and not just for a cult, then we have to risk them. For if our ideas cannot survive the test of being engaged in the world more broadly, more publicly, then feminism isn't developed enough yet, and that engagement will help us to know how to remold feminism and make it more viable. For if feminism is to be a force for change in the world, it too must grow and change; if we hoard it or try to hang onto it, we will only take it to the grave with us.

Going public with our visions is ultimately the only way that feminism can become a powerful force for change. There is no way that we can get more people wanting to be feminists and supporting and expanding our visions, if they can't even see them, if they never even hear about feminism from feminists rather than the media, and if they don't sense what we care about and believe in. To be seen as an alternative vision for the world, we first have to be seen. It's that simple and it's that important.

Another part of going public is coming out as feminists—in places where we might feel more comfortable not using the word or even discussing the ideas. An academic study has shown what movement activists have said for years—that the most effective counter to homophobia is "knowing one"—that is, people's antigay ideas change most when they realize that they know and care about someone who is gay. But this change would never occur if no one came out, and therefore most people could go on not realizing that they know one of "us" and accepting society's homophobia unchallenged.

"Coming out" as feminists has a similar power. It forces people to get beyond their media stereotypes and deal concretely with a feminist person and with ideas and visions as embodied by that person. Just as coming out for lesbians and gay men has to be decided on a personal basis, so too does coming out as a feminist. Still, it is important to recognize the political power of the personal action and to see that it is useful in advancing feminism and combating the power of the right wing, which includes the effort to intimidate us into going back into closets of fear and adopting apolitical life-styles.

Coming out and going public make it possible for us to communicate our feminist visions to people—the majority of whom I believe would welcome alternatives to the state of the world and have not necessarily accepted the right-wing's visions. They want alternatives to living behind closed doors in fear of violence on the streets and contamination in the air; they want decent work that does not destroy or demean them; they want to be able to affirm freedom and justice, but they may not believe that it is possible. We have to show them that we care about those same things and that our movement is about feminist struggles to create visions of new possibilities in the world, beginning with the struggle for possibilities for women and moving outward from there.

We need to invite people to join us in this struggle, approaching them with something to offer, rather than rejecting them as if they were enemies, or ignoring them as if they were not what we think they should be. If we invite them to join us in trying to become and create something different, we engage in politics as a process of seduction as well as of confrontation. Feminism must be a process of seeing and invoking the best in people as well as in confronting the worst. In this we may discover new ways of moving politically that will enable feminist visions to emerge and to provide the leadership so desperately needed to prevent the patriarchal militaristic destruction of the planet.

This is our challenge in the '80s. It is the particular moment that we have been given in human evolution and in the struggle between the forces of justice and domination. We are the inheritors of a proud and living tradition of creators, dreamers, resisters, and organizers who have engaged in the struggle before us, and we shall pass it on to the next generation. However long each of us lives, that's how much time we have, for this is a lifetime process and a lifetime commitment.   [1987]

Terms

1. FAMILY PROTECTION ACT: A 1981 congressional bill to repeal federal laws that promote equal rights for women, including coeducational school-related activities and protection for battered wives, and to provide tax incentives for married mothers to stay at home.
2. JERRY FALWELL: The founder of the Moral Majority, a conservative political organization.
3. NATIONAL WOMEN'S CONFERENCE: As part of the United Nations Decade for Women, each member country held a meeting to establish its national priorities for improving the status of women.
4. ERA: Equal Rights Amendment.

Understanding the Reading

1. Why does Bunch believe that feminism should not be limited to women's issues?
2. What does *transformational politics* mean?
3. List Bunch's strategies for achieving a feminist transformation.
4. What actions does she suggest?
5. What advantages does she see in "going public"?

Suggestion for Responding

1. Choose one strategy Bunch suggests, such as a feminist budget or coalition formation, and explore the social effects it could have. ◆

95

A Manifesto for Men

Andrew Kimbrell

As many of us come to mourn the lost fathers and sons of the last decades and seek to reestablish our ties to each other and to the earth, we need to find ways to change the political, social, and economic structures that have created this crisis. A "wild man" weekend in the woods, or intense man-to-man discussions, can be key experiences in self-discovery and personal empowerment. But these personal experiences are not enough to reverse the victimization of men. As the men's movement gathers strength, it is critical that this increasing sense of personal liberation be channeled into political action. Without significant changes in our society there will only be continued hopelessness and frustration for men. Moreover, a coordinated movement pressing for the liberation of men could be a key factor in ensuring that the struggle for a sustainable future for humanity and the earth succeeds.

What follows is a brief political platform for men, a short manifesto with which we can begin the process of organizing men as a positive political force working for a better future. This is the next step for the men's movement.

Fathers and Children

Political efforts focusing on the family must reassert men's bonds with the family and reverse the "lost father" syndrome. While any long-term plan for men's liberation requires significant changes in the very structure of our work and economic institutions, a number of intermediate steps are possible: We need to take a leadership role in supporting parental leave legislation, which gives working parents the right to take time from work to care for children or other family members. And we need to target the Bush administration for vetoing this vital legislation. Also needed is pro-child tax relief such as greatly expanding the young child tax credit, which would provide income relief and tax breaks to families at a point when children

need the most parental care and when income may be the lowest.

We should also be in the forefront of the movement pushing for changes in the workplace including more flexible hours, part-time work, job sharing, and home-based employment. As economic analyst William R. Mattox Jr. notes, a simple step toward making home-based employment more viable would be to loosen restrictions on claiming home office expenses as a tax deduction for parents. Men must also work strenuously in the legal arena to promote more liberal visitation rights for non-custodial parents and to assert appropriateness of the father as a custodial parent. Non-traditional family structures should also be given more recognition in our society, with acknowledgment of men's important roles as stepfathers, foster fathers, uncles, brothers, and mentors. We must seek legislative ways to recognize many men's commitments that do not fit traditional definitions of family.

Ecology as Male Politics

A sustainable environment is not merely one issue among others. It is the crux of all issues in our age, including men's politics. The ecological struggles of our time offer a unique forum in which men can express their renewed sense of the wild and their traditional roles as creators, defenders of the family, and careful stewards of the earth.

The alienation of men from their rootedness to the land has deprived us all of what John Muir[1] called the "heart of wilderness." As part of our efforts to re-experience the wild in ourselves, we should actively become involved in experiencing the wilderness first hand and organize support for the protection of nature and endangered species. Men should also become what Robert Bly[2] has called "inner warriors" for the earth, involving themselves in non-violent civil disobedience to protect wilderness areas from further destruction.

An important aspect of the masculine ethic is defense of family. Pesticides and other toxic pollutants that poison our food, homes, water, and air represent a real danger, especially to children. Men need to be adamant in their call for limitations on the use of chemicals.

Wendell Berry[3] has pointed out that the ecological crisis is also a crisis of agriculture. If men are to recapture a true sense of stewardship and husbandry and affirm the "seedbearing," creative capacity of the male, they must, to the extent possible, become involved in sustainable agriculture and organic farming and gardening. We should also initiate and support legislation that sustains our farming communities.

MEN IN THE CLASSROOMS AND COMMUNITY

In many communities, especially inner cities, men are absent not only from homes but also from the schools. Men must support the current efforts by black men's groups around the country to implement male-only early-grade classes taught by men. These programs provide role models and a surrogate paternal presence for young black males. We should also commit ourselves to having a far greater male presence in all elementary school education. Recent studies have shown that male grade school students have a higher level of achievement when they are taught by male teachers. Part-time or full-time home schooling options can also be helpful in providing men a great opportunity to be teachers—not just temperaments—to their children.

We need to revive our concern for community. Community-based boys' clubs, scout troops, sports leagues, and big brother programs have achieved significant success in helping fatherless male children find self-esteem. Men's groups must work to strengthen these organizations.

MEN'S MINDS, MEN'S BODIES, AND WORK

Men need to join together to fight threats to male health including suicide, drug and alcohol abuse, AIDS, and stress diseases. We should support active prevention and education efforts aimed at these deadly threats. Most importantly, men need to be leaders in initiating and supporting holistic and psychotherapeutic approaches that directly link many of these health threats to the coercive nature of the male mystique and the current economic system. Changes in diet, reduction of drug and alcohol use, less stressful work environments, greater nurturing of and caring for men by other men, and fighting

racism, hopelessness, and homelessness are all important, interconnected aspects of any male health initiative.

MEN WITHOUT HOPE OR HOMES

Men need to support measures that promote small business and entrepreneurship, which will allow more people to engage in crafts and human-scale, community-oriented enterprises. Also important is a commitment to appropriate, human-scale technologies such as renewable energy sources. Industrial and other inappropriate technologies have led to men's dispossession, degradation—and increasingly to unemployment.

A related struggle is eliminating racism. No group of men is more dispossessed than minority men. White men should support and network with African-American and other minority men's groups. Violence and discrimination against men because of their sexual preference should also be challenged.

Men, who represent more than four-fifths of the homeless, can no longer ignore this increasing social tragedy. Men's councils should develop support groups for the homeless in their communities.

THE HOLOCAUST OF MEN

As the primary victims of mechanized war, men must oppose this continued slaughter. Men need to realize that the traditional male concepts of the noble warrior are undermined and caricatured in the technological nightmare of modern warfare. Men must together become prime movers in dismantling the military-industrial establishment and redistributing defense spending toward a sustainable environment and protection of family, school, and community.

MEN'S ACTION NETWORK

No area of the men's political agenda will be realized until men can establish a network of activists to create collective action. A first step might be to create a high-profile national coalition of the men's councils that are growing around the country. This coalition, which could be called the Men's Action Network (MAN), could call for a national conference to define a comprehensive platform of men's concerns and to provide the political muscle to implement those ideas.

A MAN COULD STAND UP

The current generation of men face a unique moment in history. Though often still trapped by economic coercion and psychological co-option, we are beginning to see that there is a profound choice ahead. Will we choose to remain subservient tools of social and environmental destruction or to fight for rediscovery of the male as a full partner and participant in family, community, and the earth? Will we remain mesmerized by the male mystique, or will we reclaim the true meaning of our masculinity?

There is a world to gain. The male mystique, in which many of today's men—especially the most politically powerful—are trapped, is threatening the family and the planet with irreversible destruction. A men's movement based on the recovery of masculinity could renew much of the world we have lost. By changing types of work and work hours, we could break our subordination to corporate managers and return much of our work and lives to the household. We could once again be teaching, nurturing presences to our children. By devoting ourselves to meaningful work with appropriate technology, we could recover independence in our work and our spirit. By caring for each other, we could recover the dignity of our gender and heal the wounds of addiction and self-destruction. By becoming husbands to the earth, we could protect the wild and recover our creative connections with the forces and rhythms of nature.

Ultimately we must help fashion a world without the daily frustration and sorrow of having to view each other as a collection of competitors instead of a community of friends. We must celebrate the essence and rituals of our masculinity. We can no longer passively submit to the destruction of the household, the demise of self-employment, the disintegration of family and community, and the desecration of our earth.

Shortly after the First World War, Ford Madox Ford, one of this century's greatest writers, depicted 20th century men as continually pinned down in their trenches, unable to stand up for fear of annihilation. As the century closes, men remain pinned down by an economic and political system that daily forces millions of us into meaningless work, powerless lives, and self-destruction. The time has come for men to stand up.   [1991]

Terms

1. JOHN MUIR: An American naturalist and conservationist.
2. ROBERT BLY: The author of *Iron John* and advocate of the men's movement, which emphasizes men's exploring their inner maleness and bonding with other men.
3. WENDELL BERRY: A contemporary American writer and university professor who has a special interest in the environment.

Understanding the Reading

1. Why does Kimbrell think men need to focus on family?
2. Why would environmental activism be especially beneficial to men?
3. What can men do to improve their communities?
4. How can men improve their health?
5. Why should men be concerned about war?
6. What does Kimbrell see as the benefits men would gain by implementing his program?

Suggestion for Responding

1. Do you agree or disagree with Kimbrell that men have been victimized by society? Why? ✦

96

Resistance to Change

KATHLEEN RYAN

Resisting change is a very natural behavior; it is neither "good" nor "bad." Everyone does it from time to time. In many ways, resisting change is like driving in fog. When drivers enter a patch of fog, they should slow down, get a feel for the conditions, and then proceed at an appropriate pace. People making their way through the ambiguity and disorder of change have similar reactions. Their attitude is affected by their past experiences, their confidence in their skills, and by whether they interpreted the situation as an adventure or a problem. Their pace is influenced by how much they can learn about the change, their freedom to make decisions, and their ability to take action. In an ideal situation, past and present circumstances combine to give individuals the necessary confidence, freedom, and skills to move successfully and comfortably through a time of change. Unfortunately, few of us operate within ideal situations; we are often slowed down and encumbered by a variety of unanswered questions and unsettled concerns.

Handling resistance effectively is the unspoken challenge faced by anyone who wants to do things differently. Never knowing when it might actually surface, the change agent nevertheless needs to be ready for resistance. He or she needs to be able to:

1. Recognize resistance when it occurs;
2. Respond to the resistant person(s) in ways that identify the reasons behind the resistance;
3. Work, to whatever degree possible, with the resistant person(s) to answer the questions and ease the concerns which form the source of the resistance.

RECOGNIZING RESISTANCE

To recognize resistance when it occurs, one needs to have a sense of how resistance looks, feels, and sounds. Language and behavior are two of the primary means for identifying the source of resistance. At times the clues they give are very visible, allowing the underlying issue to be recognized easily. At other times, the source of the resistance is essentially hidden, hard to identify or connect to an event or situation.

To better understand *visible resistance,* imagine a discussion of the way the advertising media influence current images of men and women. As the conversation becomes increasingly animated, one person becomes quite hostile in [her] comments. Finally, in a burst of frustration, she suddenly stands and shouts, "This is the most ridiculous discussion I've ever

been in!" She leaves the room and slams the door on her way out. The exclamation of frustration, the departure, and the slamming of the door are all rather dramatic signs of resistance to a particular point or issue being discussed. They are *visible* signs of resistance.

The less obvious, *hidden resistance* is of course more difficult to identify. Consider the hypothetical case of a supervisor and a male employee. Because of a recent decision to rotate jobs temporarily, the male employee will be assigned to an all-female work crew for three months. After announcing the decision, the supervisor notices that the employee's participation in staff meetings is less enthusiastic. Even though the employee has sometimes spoken positively about the change, his general attitude on the job is less pleasant, he is less patient, and he does not seem to produce the usual amount or quality of work. In this case, the employee's small changes in attitude and behavior—extended over a period of time—can be interpreted as signs of resistance to the new job assignment. Until the supervisor confronts the employee, however, he or she has no way of knowing whether the resistance actually exists, and if so, what its cause might be.

The more skilled you become at listening and watching for signs of resistance to change, the better you will be at managing change. Simply put, if you are unable to recognize resistance when it occurs, it will be very difficult for you to take action to overcome it.

REASONS AND CLUES

People resist change for a variety of reasons. The first clues about resistance are usually found in the words people speak and in their behavior. While behavioral signs of resistance are more general, language often gives very direct clues to the reasons for resistance. The material presented in this section is designed to expand your awareness of how people's language and behavior can be tied to very specific reasons for resisting change. As you read through the following lists, think of those with whom you live and work. Think of yourself as well. Note any familiar linguistic or behavioral clues to resistance to change.

REASONS FOR RESISTANCE	WORDS OF RESISTANCE	REASONS FOR RESISTANCE	WORDS OF RESISTANCE
1. Information. People don't have enough or accurate information about the change.	"I've never heard of a man who's been very successful in that kind of role." "Well, I'm sorry, but I won't go along with this until somebody can show me an example of where she's been successful with this idea before."		"You want me to be the first woman to go out on the line? Forget it. I don't need that kind of hassle."
2. Influence. People have a strong desire to influence what happens to them in their work and their environment. If they cannot influence these decisions, they may resist because they feel left out.	"Nobody consulted me before bringing these women down here in the shop." "I'll never understand why they don't talk to the people who are really doing the work before they make their decisions."	7. Desire to be right. People think that if they change, all their previous effort will be "wrong." They have a strong desire to be "right" in their thinking and behavior.	"I told you all along, women don't want this 'sensitive male' stuff. They want a man who can tell them what to do." "I don't know exactly what to do. I'd hate to take a position that really upsets the way things are done around here."
3. Feelings. People have emotional reactions to change. For example, they may become angry, frustrated, or scared by something new. These feelings often remain unspoken and trigger resistance.	"I'm worried about how those guys are going to react to me. I frankly don't know if it's worth the effort or not." "My child is not going through any program like that. I'll take him out of school before I let them teach him about *those* kinds of things."	8. Ability. People are not confident about their ability to handle new responsibilities or perform new tasks required by a change.	"Oh, I could never do that!"
4. Control. People have a need to control information, decisions, or other people. If they cannot do so, they may resist.	"How do you expect me to do my part when I don't have access to the information I need?" "I haven't had enough time to coach her on the budgeting issues. I don't think she's ready for the promotion just yet."		"Nobody told me that when I volunteered for this position I'd have to play nursemaid to a bunch of prima donnas. I just want to get the job done. They keep slowing things down with all their new ideas. I don't know how to handle them."
5. Benefits. People don't see any advantage to changing.	"I wish someone would tell me what they think is so great about this new plan." "Why in the world do you want to go back to school? You're already overqualified for half the jobs you apply for!"	9. Routine. People don't want to alter their living or working conditions or routine.	"You mean to tell me we may have to talk different around here?" "There's something you need to know if you're going to fit in here. There are certain things that have always been done certain ways."
		10. Status. People don't want to lose their status, authority, or power.	"What do you mean they want a female engineer out there in the field? Don't you know what they will do to morale?" "Why do we need all these experts to tell us what to do? We're doing just fine."
6. Stress. People feel overloaded; they don't want the added stress of another change.	"If you tell the line managers that they've got to be responsible for this EEO[1] training, you'll have a revolt on your hands. They've already got too much to handle."	11. Structure. People have a need for structure. Change can create confusion about roles, responsibilities, and procedures.	"The new policy is clear on this issue. You can't expect me to ignore it." "Was this your father's idea?"

REASONS FOR RESISTANCE

12. Values. People disagree with the basic values or concepts behind the change. They may think that the change violates a basic belief about people or work, or that the change will have an undesirable effect.

WORDS OF RESISTANCE

"But what about the person who'll use this law to damage someone's career? If we tell our employees about this, all we're going to be doing is investigating complaints."

"Schools should not have anything to do with teaching children about sexuality and family decision-making. That's the parents' job."

While words are an important part of any-one's communication, they are not the only way we communicate. Behavior—nonverbal communication—can be just as important as words in identifying the source of resistance to change. Behavioral signs of resistance, especially when unaccompanied by words, are often very difficult to tie to resistance. Because of this, it is wise to become familiar with some of the behavioral clues to visible and hidden resistance. Some of those clues are listed here:

Behavioral Clues to Resistance to Change

VISIBLE RESISTANCE

- name-calling
- loud sighing
- unusual non-participation
- unexpected cool, aloof manner
- argumentative behavior
- obvious avoidance
- walking away
- walking out
- deliberately changing the subject
- missing appointments
- no follow-through on specific commitments
- sullen posture
- critical jokes
- quitting
- angry outbursts
- telling others it won't work
- poor attendance
- constant excuses for poor performance
- deliberately distorting information

HIDDEN RESISTANCE

- increased illnesses
- acting "dumb"
- blasé, disinterested attitude
- delaying tactics
- losing things
- pretending to lack information
- not passing along information
- work slow-down
- indirect communication (innuendo)
- not returning phone calls
- being placed last on a busy agenda
- unnecessarily referring a question to someone else
- consistent day-dreaming
- lack of thorough preparation
- tardiness
- forgetting
- procrastination
- appearing agreeable, but taking no action

- cynical expression and tone
- complaining to others
- signs of depression or sadness
- unusual swearing
- negative facial expressions
- spreading gossip

If we were physicians, we would look for the symptoms of a disease or illness. We would observe those symptoms carefully and use them as a basis for our diagnosis. We would not treat the disease without first considering its underlying cause. The words and behaviors listed above should be regarded in the same manner—as symptoms of resistance and clues to its cause, clues that must be considered in context of the situation in which they appear.

The most direct way to understand why a person is resisting a change is to ask the person. For example:

You are a mid-level manager working in a large organization which has become increasingly public about its commitment to equal opportunity for women and minorities. You have been asked to join a task force which will investigate possible pay discrepancies between job classifications—including those which have been traditionally held by female employees. You become aware that your task force meetings seem to get bogged down with reports and discussions of procedures, rather than with defining critical problems and addressing questions that need attention. The task force chair-person is a colleague of yours and is known for her skillful facilitation of meetings, and it is more and more difficult to find a time when everyone can meet. You decide, because of her behavior, that the task force chairperson is somehow resisting the potential changes involved in this work. You decide to investigate further, to see if you are right.

In such a case, you might say:

"Jane, I get the feeling you're not very comfortable with your role on this task force. You don't seem to be approaching the facilitation with your usual flair."

Or:

"Tell me what you think about where all this work will lead."

Or:

"I'll bet you're feeling some extra pressure because of chairing this task force, Jane. Do you have the kind of clerical support to be able to handle this and your regular work too?"

In cases such as these, you want to create an opportunity for the person who you think is resisting to talk. If this person trusts and respects you, you have a relatively good chance to discover whether your suspicions about the resistance are correct or not. Once you confirm that resistance exists, you should identify the reason for it. This information is critical for any action you subsequently take to overcome the resistance. In this case, Jane may be resisting because of:

Values. She believes the organization could work on other issues which would better, and more immediately, promote equal opportunity.

Benefits. Because of previous experiences with other task forces, Jane believes that in the end, no one will benefit from all this work, and no substantial changes will really take place.

Stress. She has too many other responsibilities to give this project the attention it needs.

Because you are not Jane's superior, your role in helping her to overcome her resistance is somewhat limited. There are some very positive things you could do, however:

Values. If you believe the work of this task force *is* critical for developing equal opportunity, say so. Present your reasons, along with information about studies in other organizations which have increased wage equity and reduced the risk of a disruptive, painful strike for recognition of comparable worth.

Benefits. Talk with Jane to find out her past experiences. If you agree that there's a good chance nothing will come of your current work, raise that issue with the entire task force. With Jane, or in the task force, brainstorm strategies for overcoming that likelihood. Play an active part, behind the scenes or visibly, to act on those strategies.

Stress. Work with Jane to identify the time and resource problems that are increasing her stress. Once again, develop strategies to overcome the problems, including a proposal to Jane's boss which outlines the problems and asks for additional resources. Offer to do what you can to ease the burden of her responsibilities. Follow through on those commitments.   [1985]

Term

1. EEO: Equal Employment Opportunity.

Understanding the Reading

1. Explain the difference between visible resistance and hidden resistance.
2. Explain the twelve reasons for resistance.
3. How do information, feelings, and influence affect resistance?

Suggestions for Responding

1. Describe a time when someone tried to impose a change on you that you did not like. In what ways did you resist? How was the conflict finally resolved?
2. Explain what kinds of resistance to your plan of action you anticipate and how you plan to handle them. ✦

97

Battered Women

Cynthia Diehm and Margo Ross

Any examination of the status of American women cannot ignore the plight of the estimated three to four million or more women who are beaten by their intimate partners each year. The home, once seen as a sanctuary for women, is increasingly being recognized as a place where females may be at risk of psychological and physical abuse.

Abusive and violent behavior among people who are married, living together, or have an ongoing or prior intimate relationship is referred to as spouse abuse, battering, or domestic violence.

It occurs among people of all races, age groups, religions, lifestyles, and income and educational levels. Approximately 95 percent of the victims of such violence are women.

A battering incident is rarely an isolated occurrence. It usually recurs frequently and escalates in severity over time. It can involve threats, pushing, slapping, punching, choking, sexual assault, and assault with weapons. Each year, more than one million women seek medical assistance for injuries caused by battering. Battering may result in more injuries that require medical treatment than rape, auto accidents, and muggings combined.

A typical response to domestic violence is to question why women remain in abusive relationships. Actually, many women do leave their abusers. In one study of 205 battered women, 53 percent had left the relationship. Moreover, there is no way to know how many women have chosen not to identify abuse as the reason they ended their marriages.

Divorce proceedings can be particularly difficult for battered women, especially when child custody litigation is involved. If a battered woman has left the home without her children, she may lose custody of them because her action may be perceived as desertion. If the batterer is established in the community, the court may see him as a better custodial parent, regardless of his wife's accusations of violence, because she may appear to be in transition and unstable. If the woman is granted custody, the abuser usually is given child visitation rights—a situation that continually places the woman at risk of abuse. Some states have passed legislation that mandates consideration of spouse abuse as evidence in custody litigation.

Battered women, in general, do not passively endure physical abuse, but actively seek assistance in ending the violence from a variety of sources, including police, lawyers, family members, and the clergy. Frequently, it is the failure of these individuals and systems to provide adequate support that traps women in violent relationships. A study of more than 6,000 battered women in Texas found that, on average, the women had contacted five different sources of help prior to leaving the home and becoming residents of battered women's shelters.

Certainly, many battered women suffer in silence. These women endure physical abuse for a variety of reasons:

- A woman may feel that it is her duty to keep the marriage together at all costs because of religious, cultural, or socially learned beliefs.
- A woman may endure physical and emotional abuse to keep the family together for the children's sake.
- A woman may be financially dependent on her husband and thus would probably face severe economic hardship if she chose to support herself and her children on her own.
- A battered woman frequently faces the most physical danger when she attempts to leave. She may be threatened with violence or attacked if she tries to flee. She fears for her safety, her children's safety, and the safety of those who help her.

THE LEGACY OF INDIFFERENCE

Despite the severity of domestic violence, it is a problem that, until quite recently, has been cloaked in secrecy. Up to the early 1970s, battered women had few options but to suffer in silence or to attempt single-handedly to leave controlling and violent men. To understand why society is just beginning to confront domestic violence, it is essential to view the problem within its historical context.

Domestic violence is not a new phenomenon; historically, husbands had the legal right to chastise their wives to maintain authority. In the United States, wife beating was legal until the end of the nineteenth century. Alabama and Massachusetts were on record as rescinding the "ancient privilege" of wife beating in 1871, but most states merely ignored old laws.

While battering was no longer legally sanctioned by the early part of the twentieth century, the spirit of the law remained and abuse was still common. Social and justice systems have viewed domestic violence as a private family matter and have been reluctant to intervene.

CHANGE THROUGH GRASSROOTS ACTIVISM

The legacy of society's indifference to violence in the home fueled a grassroots "battered women's movement," which gained nationwide momentum in the mid-1970s. Inspired by the feminist anti-rape movement's analysis of male violence against women as a social and political issue, battered women began to speak out about the physical abuse they were suffering in their marriages and intimate relationships.

At first, battered women helped one another individually by setting up informal safe homes and apartments. In such an environment—free from intimidation by their abusers—battered women could speak openly and thus soon discovered the commonality of their experiences. As the issue was publicized, women of all races, cultures, ages, abilities, and walks of life began to expose the violence they suffered. It quickly became clear that woman battering was a pervasive problem, and a nationwide movement started to take shape.

The early experience of the movement revealed the acute need of safe shelter for battered women and their children. Unless a woman could feel truly safe, she could not effectively evaluate her situation and make clear decisions about her future. Operating on shoestring budgets, battered women's advocates began to establish formal programs around the country. Only a handful of such programs existed in the mid-1970s; today, there are more than 1,200 shelters, hot-lines, and safe-home networks nationwide. Grassroots lobbying efforts at the federal level led to congressional passage of the 1984 Family Violence Prevention and Services Act, which earmarked federal funding for programs serving victims of domestic violence.

Creating and expanding a network of shelters and services for battered women and their children, while essential, was not the only goal of the grassroots movement. Equally important was the task of promoting changes in the criminal justice system that would hold abusers accountable for their violence and uphold the rights of battered women.

In 1984, the report of the Attorney General's Task Force on Family Violence reaffirmed the need for an improved criminal justice response to domestic violence, stating: "The legal response to family violence must be guided primarily by the nature of the abusive act, not the relationship between the victim and the abuser." The report focused on the role of the criminal justice system and recommended actions for each of its components that would increase the effectiveness of its response and better ensure the victim's safety. Across the country advocates continue to work with law enforcement personnel, prosecutors, judges, and legislators to implement new policies and enact legislation.

THE CRIMINAL JUSTICE RESPONSE

Domestic violence is now a crime in all 50 states and the District of Columbia, either under existing assault and battery laws or under special legislation. However, the true extent of crimes involving domestic violence remains largely unknown, since no accurate statistics on the number of battered women exist. Neither of the two sources of national crime statistics—the Federal Bureau of Investigation's Uniform Crime Report (UCR) and the federal Bureau of Justice Statistics' National Crime Survey (NCS)—is specifically designed to measure the incidence of crime in the domestic setting.

The UCR, which is based on police department reports, only collects information on the victim-offender relationship in the homicide category. Despite the UCR's limitations, it does provide a chilling picture of the potential lethality of domestic violence. According to the latest report, 30 percent of female homicide victims were killed by their husbands or boyfriends.

To supplement the UCR, the Bureau of Justice Statistics conducts an ongoing national telephone survey of some 60,000 American households to glean information on crimes not reported to police. Originally designed to collect data on such crimes as burglary and aggravated assault, the NCS also asks respondents about their relationships to offenders and thus inadvertently obtains information on domestic violence. Results of the 1978–82 NCS led analysts to estimate that 2.1 million women were victims of domestic violence at least once during an average 12-month period. This estimate is not intended to portray the true extent of the problem; rather, it is an indication of the number of women who believed domestic violence to be criminal and who felt free to disclose such information over the telephone to an unknown interviewer.

National crime statistics are based primarily on local police department reports, which traditionally have not included a discrete category for domestic violence. Police departments in a number of jurisdictions are just beginning to develop methods to report domestic violence crimes separately. It will be many years before this practice becomes universal and a more accurate picture of the nature and incidence of domestic crimes is available.

Law enforcement has traditionally operated from a philosophy of nonintervention in cases of domestic violence. Unless severe injury or death was involved, police rarely arrested offenders. Expert police opinion was that there was little law enforcement could do to prevent such crimes. Moreover, it was believed that even if an offender were arrested, cases would never go to trial because of the victim's fear of testifying against her abuser.

The police response to domestic violence has been altered significantly in the last few years. In 1982, a study in Minneapolis found that arrest was more effective than two nonarrest alternatives in reducing the likelihood of repeat violence over a six-month follow-up period. Interestingly, only two percent of abusers who were arrested in the study went before a judge to receive court punishment. Thus, the Minneapolis study showed that arrest appears to reduce recidivism, even if it does not lead to conviction. The results of the study were widely publicized and have contributed to a more aggressive law enforcement response to domestic violence.

Research results, however, have been only partially responsible for changes in police policies. Class action lawsuits brought by victims against police departments for lack of protection also have effected policy change. In 1985, for example, a battered woman in Torrington, Connecticut, won a multimillion dollar settlement from the city for the failure of the police department to protect her from her husband's violence. *Thurman v. Torrington* was a catalyst for the state's passage of the 1986 Family Violence and Response Act, which mandates arrest in domestic violence cases when probable cause exists.

For the past several years, the Crime Control Institute has conducted a telephone survey of police departments serving jurisdictions with populations of 100,000 or more. In 1986, 46 percent of these departments indicated they had a proarrest policy in cases of domestic violence, as compared with 31 percent in 1985 and 10 percent in 1984. In addition, the percent of urban police departments reporting more actual domestic violence arrests appears to have risen from 24 percent in 1984 to 47 percent in 1986.

Other components of the criminal justice system have also begun to take a tougher stance on domestic violence. Many district attorneys' offices have established separate domestic violence units to encourage more vigorous prosecution of offenders. Judicial training on domestic violence has been promoted so that stronger court sanctions are imposed against abusive men.

The changes in the criminal justice system's response to domestic violence are quite new, however, and have not occurred universally. Although states have enacted various types of statutes to promote more aggressive treatment of domestic violence as a crime, whether this approach is upheld by individual actors within the system varies from jurisdiction to jurisdiction.

In many jurisdictions, courts can order batterers to attend special counseling programs either before the case is adjudicated or as a condition of probation. Frequently, criminal charges are dismissed if the defendant "successfully" completes the program. Unfortunately, the effectiveness of special programs for abusive men is hard to measure, and little information exists on the effectiveness of intervention.

LEGAL PROTECTION FOR THE VICTIM

In the early 1970s, few legal remedies existed for the battered woman seeking protection from abuse. If married, she could file for divorce, separation, or custody, and in some states obtain an injunction ordering her husband not to abuse her while domestic relations proceedings were pending.

Since that time, 47 states and the District of Columbia have enacted legislation allowing battered women to obtain civil protection or restraining orders. Depending on the state, through such legislation the court can order the abuser to move out of the residence, refrain from abuse of or contact with the victim, enter a batterers' treatment program, or pay support, restitution, or attorney's fees. However, "a protection or restraining order is meaningful only if violation of the order constitutes a crime and police are able to verify the existence of an order when a violation is alleged."

The ability of such orders to protect all domestic violence victims is inconsistent across jurisdictions. Some areas require the victim to be married to and currently cohabitating with the abuser. Abuse may be narrowly defined as an attempt or infliction of bodily injury or serious bodily injury, providing no protection from threats of violence or destruction of property. The duration of protection orders can range from 15 days to no more than one year, thereby forcing many women to relocate to avoid abuse. Moreover, it is believed that protection orders are poorly implemented and enforced. It may be quite difficult for low-income women, women of color, and women who have defended themselves against physical abuse to obtain this type of protection. The use and enforcement of civil protection orders is now under study through funding from the Justice Department.

THE IMPORTANCE OF PREVENTION

Clearly, just responding to domestic violence is not sufficient. An improved criminal justice response and the development of court-ordered programs for abusive men are not panaceas for the problem. Battered women's advocates believe that to bring an end to domestic violence, it is necessary to examine how the culture teaches young men and women to play roles that lead to such violent behavior, and how restricted access to economic resources can trap women in the potentially lethal cycle of violence.

If the cycle of violence is to be broken, advocates on behalf of battered women stress that young women must be encouraged to go beyond traditionally passive, dependent roles, while young men must be taught that abusive, violent, and controlling behavior is never acceptable. To this end, battered women's advocates have established children's programs in many shelters, as well as curricula on domestic violence for use in elementary, middle, and high schools.

Finally, equal access to employment, housing, and economic resources must be available to all women. This situation is particularly acute for battered women, who frequently remain in abusive relationships simply because of economics. Thus, a critical determinant of whether a battered woman will live without violence or be forced to return to an abusive partner often is the availability of decent affordable housing, adequate pay, and other forms of economic assistance.

Violence in the home is a problem with serious repercussions for the battered woman, her children, and the entire community. Breaking the cycle of violence requires financial support for services to battered women, a strong criminal justice response that holds abusive men accountable for their violence, and, most important, ongoing social activism that focuses on improving the status of all women.   [1988]

Understanding the Reading

1. Why do women stay in abusive relationships?
2. What actions have battered women undertaken to combat domestic violence?
3. What legal action has been taken to respond to the problem of domestic violence?
4. What can be done to *prevent* domestic violence?

Suggestion for Responding

1. How would you respond to someone you know who is in an abusive relationship? Be sure you take into account the resistance that the person may express. ✦

98

Freedom for the Thought We Hate

GERALD GUNTHER

I am deeply troubled by current efforts—however well-intentioned—to place new limits on freedom of expression at this and other campuses. Such limits are not only incompatible with the mission and meaning of university; they also send exactly the wrong message from academia to society as a whole. University campuses should exhibit greater, not less, freedom of expression than prevails in society at large.

Proponents of new limits argue that historic First Amendment rights must be balanced against the university's commitment to the diversity of ideas and persons. Clearly, there is ample room and need for vigorous university action to combat racial and other discrimination. But curbing freedom of speech is the wrong way to do so. The proper answer to bad speech is usually more and better speech—not new laws, litigation, and repression.

Lest it be thought that I am insensitive to the pain imposed by expressions of racial or religious hatred, let me say that I have suffered that pain and empathize with others under similar verbal assault. My deep belief in the principles of the First Amendment arises in part from my own experiences. I received my elementary education in a public school in a very small town in Nazi Germany. There I was subjected to vehement anti-Semitic remarks from my teacher, classmates, and others—"Judensau" (Jew pig) was far from the harshest. I can assure you that they hurt.

More generally, I lived in a country where ideological orthodoxy reigned and where the opportunity for dissent was severely limited.

The lesson I have drawn from my childhood in Nazi Germany and my happier adult life in this country is the need to walk the sometimes difficult path of denouncing the bigots' hateful ideas with all my power, yet at the same time challenging any community's attempt to suppress hateful ideas by force of law.

Obviously, given my own experience, I do *not* quarrel with the claim that *words* can do harm. But I firmly deny that a showing of harm suffices to deny First Amendment protection, and I insist on the elementary First Amendment principle that our Constitution usually protects even offensive, harmful expression.

That is why—at the risk of being thought callous or doctrinaire—I recently opposed attempts by some members of my university community to enlarge the area of forbidden speech to prohibit not only "personal abuse" but also "defamation of groups"—expression "that by accepted community standards . . . pejoratively characterizes persons or groups on the basis of

personal or cultural differences." Such proposals, in my view, seriously undervalue the First Amendment and far too readily endanger its precious content. Limitations on free expression beyond those established by law should be eschewed in an institution committed to diversity and the First Amendment.

In explaining my position, I will avoid extensive legal arguments. Instead, I want to speak from the heart, on the basis of my own background and of my understanding of First Amendment principles—principles supported by an ever larger number of scholars and Supreme Court justices, especially since the days of the Warren Court.[1]

Among the core principles is that any official effort to suppress expression must be viewed with the greatest skepticism and suspicion. Only in very narrow, urgent circumstances should government or similar institutions be permitted to inhibit speech. True, there are certain categories of speech that may be prohibited; but the number and scope of these categories has steadily shrunk over the last fifty years. Face-to-face insults are one such category; incitement to immediate illegal action is another. But opinions expressed in debates and arguments about a wide range of political and social issues should not be suppressed simply because of disagreement with those views, with the content of the expression.

Similarly, speech should not and cannot be banned simply because it is "offensive" to substantial parts of a majority of the community. The refusal to suppress offensive speech is one of the most difficult obligations the free speech principle imposes upon all of us; yet it is also one of the First Amendment's greatest glories—indeed it is a central test of a community's commitment to free speech.

The Supreme Court's 1989 decision to allow flag-burning as a form of political protest, in *Texas v. Johnson,* warrants careful pondering by all those who continue to advocate campus restraints on "racist speech." As Justice Brennan's majority opinion in *Johnson* reminded, "If there is a bedrock principle underlying the First Amendment, it is that the Government may not prohibit the expression of an idea itself offensive or disagreeable." In refusing to place flag-burning outside the First Amendment, moreover, the

Johnson majority insisted (in words especially apt for the "racist speech" debate): "The First Amendment does not guarantee that other concepts virtually sacred to our Nation as a whole—*such as the principle that discrimination on the basis of race is odious and destructive*—will go unquestioned in the marketplace of ideas. We decline, therefore, to create for the flag an exception to the joust of principles protected by the First Amendment." (Italics added.)

Campus proponents of restricting offensive speech are currently relying for justification on the Supreme Court's allegedly repeated reiteration that "fighting words" constitute an exception to the First Amendment. Such an exception has indeed been recognized in a number of lower court cases. However, there has only been *one* case in the history of the Supreme Court in which a majority of the justices has ever found a statement to be a punishable resort to "fighting words." That was *Chaplinsky v. New Hampshire,* a nearly fifty-year-old case involving words which would very likely not be found punishable today.

More significant is what has happened in the nearly half-century since: Despite repeated appeals to the Supreme Court to recognize the applicability of the "fighting words" exception by affirming challenged convictions, the court has in every instance refused. One must wonder about the strength of an exception that, while theoretically recognized, has for so long not been found apt in practice.

The phenomenon of racist and other offensive speech is not a new one in the history of the First Amendment. In recent decades, for example, well-meaning (but in my view misguided) majorities have sought to suppress not only racist speech but also anti-war and anti-draft speech, civil rights demonstrators, the Nazis and Ku Klux Klan, and left-wing groups.

Typically, it is people on the extremes of the political spectrum (including those who advocate overthrow of our constitutional system and those who would not protect their opponents' right to dissent were they the majority) who feel the brunt of repression and have found protection in the First Amendment; typically, it is well-meaning people in the majority who believe their sensibilities, their sense of outrage, justify restraints.

Those in power in a community recurrently seek to repress speech they find abhorrent, and their efforts are understandable human impulses. Yet freedom of expression—and especially the protection of dissident speech, the most important function of the First Amendment—is an anti-majoritarian principle. Is it too much to hope that, especially on a university campus, a majority can be persuaded of the value of freedom of expression and of the resultant need to curb our impulses to repress dissident views?

The principles to which I appeal are not new. They have been expressed, for example, by the most distinguished Supreme Court justices ever since the beginning of the court's confrontations with First Amendment issues nearly seventy years ago. These principles are reflected in the words of so imperfect a First Amendment defender as Justice Oliver Wendell Holmes: "If there is any principle of the Constitution that more imperatively calls for attachment than any other it is the principle of free thought—not free thought for those who agree with us but freedom for the thought that we hate." This is the principle most elaborately and eloquently addressed by Justice Louis D. Brandeis, who reminded us that the First Amendment rests on a belief "in the power of reason as applied through public discussion" and therefore bars "silence coerced by law—the argument of force in its worst form."

This theme, first articulated in dissents, has repeatedly been voiced in majority opinions in more recent decades. It underlies Justice Douglas's remark in striking down a conviction under a law banning speech that "stirs the public to anger": "A function of free speech [is] to invite dispute. . . . Speech is often provocative and challenging. That is why freedom of speech [is ordinarily] protected against censorship or punishment."

It also underlies Justice William J. Brennan's comment about our "profound national commitment to the principle that debate on public issues should be uninhibited, robust and wide-open, and that it may well include vehement, caustic and sometimes unpleasantly sharp attacks"—a comment he followed with a reminder that constitutional protection "does not turn upon the truth, popularity or social utility of the ideas and beliefs which are offered."

These principles underlie as well the repeated insistence by Justice John Marshall Harlan, again in majority opinions, that the mere "inutility or immorality" of a message cannot justify its repression, and that the state may not punish because of "the underlying content of the message." Moreover, Justice Harlan, in one of the finest First Amendment opinions on the books, noted, in words that we would ignore at peril at this time:

"The constitutional right of free expression is powerful medicine in a society as diverse and populous as ours. . . . To many, the immediate consequence of this freedom may often appear to be only verbal tumult, discord and even offensive utterance. These are, however, within established limits, in truth necessary side effects of the broader enduring values which the process of open debate permits us to achieve. That the air may at times seem filled with verbal cacophony is, in this sense, not a sign of weakness but of strength."

In this same passage, Justice Harlan warned that a power to ban speech merely because it is offensive is an "inherently boundless" notion, and added that "we think it is largely because governmental officials cannot make principled distinctions in this area that the Constitution leaves matters of taste and style so largely to the individual." (The Justice made these comments while overturning the conviction of an antiwar protestor for "offensive conduct." The defendant had worn, in a courthouse corridor, a jacket bearing the words "Fuck the draft.")

I restate these principles and repeat these words for reasons going far beyond the fact that they are familiar to me as a First Amendment scholar. I believe—in my heart as well as my mind—that these principles and ideals are not only established but right. I hope that the entire academic community will seriously reflect upon the risks to free expression, lest we weaken hard-won liberties at our universities and, by example, in this nation.   [1990]

Term

1. WARREN COURT: The Supreme Court under Chief Justice Earl Warren, which passed down such decisions as the prohibition of school segregation.

Understanding the Reading

1. Why does Gunther describe his childhood in Germany?
2. Why does he argue that speech "should not . . . be banned simply because it is "offensive"?
3. What connection does Gunther make between flag-burning and racist speech?
4. Why does he object to the use of the concept of "fighting words" to prohibit racist speech?
5. Explain each of the quotations of the five Supreme Court justices.

Suggestion for Responding

1. Gunther presents a persuasive advocacy of freedom of speech. Develop an argument in favor of some restrictions. ◆

99

Acknowledging the Victims' Cry

CHARLES R. LAWRENCE III

I have spent the better part of my life as a dissenter. As a high-school student, I was threatened with suspension for my refusal to participate in a civil-defense drill, and I have been a conspicuous consumer of my First Amendment liberties[1] ever since. There are very strong reasons for protecting even speech that is racist. Perhaps the most important is that such protection reinforces our society's commitment to tolerance as a value. By protecting bad speech from government regulation, we will be forced to combat it as a community.

I have, however, a deeply felt apprehension about the resurgence of racial violence and the corresponding increase in the incidence of verbal and symbolic assault and harassment to which African-Americans and other traditionally excluded groups are subjected. I am troubled by the way the debate has been framed in response to the recent surge of racist incidents on college and university campuses and in response to some universities' attempts to regulate harassing speech. The problem has been framed as one in which the liberty of free speech is in conflict with the elimination of racism. I believe this has placed the bigot on the moral high ground and fanned the rising flames of racism.

Above all, I am troubled that we have not listened to the real victims—that we have shown so little understanding of their injury, and that we have abandoned those whose race, gender, or sexual orientation continues to make them second-class citizens. It seems to me a very sad irony that the first instinct of civil libertarians has been to challenge even the smallest, most narrowly framed efforts by universities to provide African-Americans and other minority students with the protection the Constitution, in my opinion, guarantees them.

The landmark case of *Brown v. Board of Education*[2] is not a case that we normally think of as a case about speech. But *Brown* can be broadly read as articulating the principle of equal citizenship. *Brown* held that segregated schools were inherently unequal because of the message that segregation conveyed: that African-American children were an untouchable caste, unfit to go to school with white children. If we understand the necessity of eliminating the system of signs and symbols that signal the inferiority of African-Americans, then we should hesitate before proclaiming that all racist speech that stops short of physical violence must be defended.

University officials who have formulated policies to respond to incidents of racial harassment have been characterized in the press as "thought police," even though such policies generally do nothing more than impose sanctions against intentional face-to-face insults. Racist speech that takes the form of face-to-face insults, catcalls, or other assaultive speech aimed at an individual or small group of persons falls directly within the "fighting words" exception to First Amendment protection. The Supreme Court has held in *Chaplinsky v. New Hampshire* that words which "by their very utterance inflict injury or tend to incite an immediate breach of the peace" are not protected by the First Amendment.

If the purpose of the First Amendment is to foster the greatest amount of speech, racial insults disserve that purpose. Assaultive racist speech functions as a preemptive strike. The invective is experienced as a blow, not as a proffered idea. And once the blow is struck, a dialogue is unlikely to follow. Racial insults are particularly undeserving of First Amendment protection, because the perpetrator's intention is not to discover truth or initiate dialogue but to injure the victim. In most situations, members of minority groups realize that they are likely to lose if they fight back, and are forced to remain silent and submissive.

Courts have held that offensive speech may not be regulated in public forums (such as streets, where the listener may avoid the speech by moving on). But the regulation of otherwise protected speech has been permitted when the speech invades the privacy of the unwilling listener's home, or when the unwilling listener is a "captive audience" and cannot avoid the speech. Racist posters, flyers, and graffiti in dormitories, bathrooms, and other common living spaces would seem to fall within the reasoning of these cases. Minority students should not be required to remain in their rooms in order to avoid racial insult. Minimally, they should find a safe haven in their dorms and in all other common rooms that are a part of their daily routine.

I would also argue that the university's responsibility for ensuring that these students receive an equal educational opportunity provides a compelling justification for regulations that ensure them safe passage in all common areas. A minority student should not have to risk becoming the target of racially assaulting speech every time he or she chooses to walk across campus. Regulating vilifying speech that cannot be anticipated or avoided need not preclude announced speeches and rallies—situations that would give minority-group members and their allies the opportunity to organize counterdemonstrations or avoid the speech altogether.

The most commonly advanced argument against the regulation of racist speech proceeds something like this: We recognize that minority groups suffer pain and injury as the result of racist speech, but we must allow this hate-mongering for the benefit of society as a whole. Freedom of speech is the lifeblood of our democratic system. It is especially important for minorities, because often it is their only vehicle for rallying support for the redress of their grievances. It will be impossible to formulate a prohibition so precise that it will prevent the racist speech you want to suppress without catching in the same net all kinds of speech that it would be unconscionable for a democratic society to suppress.

Such arguments seek to strike a balance between our concern, on the one hand, for the continued free flow of ideas and the democratic process dependent on that flow, and, on the other, our desire to further the cause of equality. There can, however, be no meaningful discussion of how we should reconcile our commitment to equality with our commitment to free speech until it is acknowledged that racist speech inflicts real harm, and that this harm is far from trivial.

To engage in a debate about the First Amendment and racist speech without a full understanding of the nature and extent of that harm is to risk making the First Amendment an instrument of domination rather [than] a vehicle of liberation. We have not all known the experience of victimization by racist, misogynist, and homophobic speech, nor do we equally share the burden of the harm it inflicts. We are often quick to say that we have heard the cry of the victims when we have not.

The *Brown* case is again instructive, because it speaks directly to the psychic injury inflicted by racist speech by noting that the symbolic message of segregation affected "the hearts and minds" of African-American children "in a way unlikely ever to be undone." Racial epithets and harassment often cause deep emotional scarring and feelings of anxiety and fear that pervade every aspect of a victim's life.

Brown also recognized that African-American children did not have an equal opportunity to learn and participate in the school's community when they bore the additional burden of being subjected to the humiliation and psychic assault contained in the message of segregation. University students bear an analogous burden when they are forced to live and work in an environment where at any moment they may be subject to denigrating verbal harassment and assault. The same injury was addressed by the Supreme Court when it held that, under Title VII

of the Civil Rights Act of 1964, sexual harassment which creates a hostile or abusive work environment violates the ban on sex discrimination in employment.

Carefully drafted university regulations could bar the use of words as assault weapons while at the same time leaving unregulated even the most heinous of ideas provided those ideas are presented at times and places and in manners that provide an opportunity for reasoned rebuttal or escape from immediate insult. The history of the development of the right to free speech has been one of carefully evaluating the importance of free expression and its effects on other important societal interests. We have drawn the line between protected and unprotected speech before without dire results. (Courts have, for example, exempted from the protection of the First Amendment obscene speech and speech that disseminates official secrets, defames or libels another person, or is used to form a conspiracy or monopoly.)

African-Americans and other people of color are skeptical about the argument that even the most injurious speech must remain unregulated because, in an unregulated marketplace of ideas, the best ones will rise to the top and gain acceptance. Experience tells quite the opposite. People of color have seen too many demagogues elected by appealing to Americans' racism, and too many sympathetic politicians shy away from issues that might brand them as being too closely allied with disparaged groups.

Whenever we decide that racist speech must be tolerated because of the importance of maintaining societal tolerance for all unpopular speech, we are asking African-Americans and other subordinated groups to bear the burden for the good of all. We must be careful that the ease with which we strike the balance against the regulation of racist speech is in no way influenced by the fact that the cost will be borne by others. We must be certain that those who will pay that price are fairly represented in our deliberations and that they are heard.

At the core of the argument that we should resist all government regulation of speech is the idea that the best cure for bad speech is good— that ideas that affirm equality and the worth of all individuals will ultimately prevail. This is an empty ideal unless those of us who would fight racism are vigilant and unequivocal in that fight. We must look for ways to offer assistance and support to students whose speech and political participation are chilled in a climate of racial harassment.

Civil rights lawyers might consider suing on behalf of African-Americans whose right to an equal education is denied by a university's failure to ensure a nondiscriminatory education climate or conditions of employment. We must embark upon the development of a First Amendment jurisprudence grounded in the reality of our history and our contemporary experience. We must think hard about how best to launch legal attacks against the most indefensible forms of hate speech. Good lawyers can create exceptions and narrow interpretations that limit the harm of hate speech without opening the floodgates of censorship.

Everyone concerned with these issues must find ways to engage actively in actions that resist and counter the racist ideas that we would have the First Amendment protect. If we fail in this, the victims of hate speech must rightly assume that we are on the bigot's side.   [1990]

Terms

1. FIRST AMENDMENT LIBERTIES: Freedom of worship, speech, press, and assembly.
2. *BROWN V. BOARD OF EDUCATION:* A case in which the United States Supreme Court declared segregated schools unconstitutional.

Understanding the Reading

1. What are "fighting words"?
2. Why does Lawrence feel that universities should regulate racist speech?
3. How does he answer opponents of regulation?
4. What connection does he see between *Brown v. Board of Education* and current policies on racist speech?

Suggestions for Responding

1. Lawrence presents a persuasive advocacy of some restrictions on "racist speech." Develop an argument against such restrictions.
2. Explain how you will evaluate your plan of action after you have implemented it. If you already have undertaken the action, write an evaluation of it. ✦

SUGGESTIONS FOR RESPONDING TO PART VIII

ACTION PROJECT FOR SOCIAL CHANGE

The readings in Part VIII have tried to show that you can actually do something to effect social change. Now it is time to put what you have learned into practice. Simply follow the steps described in the introduction to Part VIII, commit yourself, and take action.

First, identify something as a problem, such as becoming aware of sexism in the media. You then need to have a desire to do something about the problem, and you need to figure out specifically what it is that you find offensive and what you want to achieve. Then, alone or together with whoever else is going to join you in your action, brainstorm about possible actions you could realistically take. You could write to the producers of videos or to a specific network; you could try to organize a boycott; or you could undertake other, different actions. Then, plan your action project, considering what you will do, when you will do it, and how you will evaluate the success of your project. Finally, do it and become a change maker yourself.

IX
Change Makers

We usually think of change makers as the movers and shakers of the world, those larger-than-life people who "really make a difference." On everyone's list would be major figures such as George Washington, Abraham Lincoln, Dwight Eisenhower, Andrew Carnegie, Henry Ford, Martin Luther King, and just maybe social worker Jane Addams. Part IX is not about people of such heroic proportions, however. Instead, it is about people like ourselves, not necessarily wealthy, privileged, or from influential families. This is not to imply that all those previously listed had these advantages; it is simply that their achievements are so embedded in our understanding of American history that they no longer seem to be "real" people like us.

The people we will read about here are young and old. In "Boys State," Reading 100, is by Michael Moore as he recounts his decision as a teenager to confront the Elks Club on their all-white members policy. Mother Jones (Reading 101) was a fifty-year-old widow when she first became a union organizer of coal miners. César Chávez (Reading 102), founder of the United Farm Workers Union, was a young man when he began work as a labor organizer. Reading 103 details the Matthew Shepard and James Byrd, Jr. Hate Crimes Prevention Act signed by President Obama.

Readings 104, 105, and 106 give some insight into the civil rights movement, possibly the most enveloping and dynamic social movement of the past century, one that has transformed American society. Over a century ago, Ida B. Wells-Barnett, who was orphaned at age fourteen and who took responsibility for her younger siblings, challenged the practice of White lynching of Blacks; she earned an international reputation and eventually became a co-founder of the National Association for the Advancement of Colored People. The ultimate successes of the civil rights movement depended on similar dedication and commitment of many people whose names are not widely known today. For example, the report by the Southern Poverty Law Center summarizes the decades-long struggle of hundreds of individuals, taking stands by themselves, but more often cooperating in groups, to demonstrate the unfair policies and practices that kept Blacks subordinate in most areas of society.

Anne Moody, a college student from an impoverished southern Black family, was willing to face violence from White high school students—taking beatings, being sprayed with paint and condiments—to stand up for the right of Blacks to eat at a public lunch counter. Similarly, college student Muriel Tillinghast risked rape and other violence to assert Blacks' rights during the Freedom Summer activism.

Readings 107, 108, and 109 introduce change makers from the most impoverished group in the United States, Native American women. Despite their lack of resources, they are improving life on their reservations. Michael Ryan tells how, despite obstructive government regulations and lack of funds, three women created on their Yakima, Washington, reservation a college that in eight years graduated over 400 students. As Valerie Taliman reports, JoAnn Tall, a mother of eight who lives on the Pine Ridge Indian Reservation in South Dakota, has spent much of her life organizing against environmental destruction on Indian reservations simply because she has reverence for "Grandmother Earth." Next, Ann Davis introduces us to the indefatigable Cecilia Fire Thunder, who has organized her tribal sisters to transform life and politics on their Lakota reservation. Reading 110, "Claiming Respect for Ancestral Remains," describes the dedicated work of the Repatriation Committee of the Caddo Nation of Oklahoma.

Middle-class people are also effective change makers. Standing up for the civil rights of another oppressed group is Frank Kameny; Deb Price (Reading 111) reports on how he fought back against governmental policy that fired workers, regardless of their competence, simply because they were homosexual.

All of us can learn important lessons from the change makers who speak in these pages. They show that everyday people who are committed to fighting social injustice can make a difference. Following their examples, any of us can do the same if we just care enough and make the effort to leave the world a better place for our having been here.

100

Boys State

Michael Moore

I HAD NO IDEA why the principal was sending me to Boys State. I had broken no rules and was not a disciplinary problem of any sort. Although I was a high school junior, it was only my second year in a public high school after nine years of Catholic education, and not having nuns or priests to direct me still took some getting used to. But I thought I had adjusted quite well to Davison High School. On the very first day of my sophomore year, Russell Boone, a big, good ol' boy who would become one of my best friends, took his fist and knocked the books out of my hands while I was walking down the hall between fourth- and fifth-hour classes.

"That's not how you hold em," he shouted at me. "You're holdin' 'em like *a girl.*"

I picked up the three or four books and looked around to see if anyone had stopped to laugh at the boy who carried his books like a girl. The coast seemed clear.

"How'm I supposed to carry' em?" I asked.

Boone took the books from me and held them in the cup of his hand with his arm fully extended toward the floor, letting the books hang by his side.

"Like this," he said while walking a manly walk down the hallway.

"How was I holding' em?" I asked.

"Like this," he barked as he mocked me, holding my books up to the center of his chest like he was caressing breasts.

"That's how girls do it?" I asked, mortified that for the first half of my first day in public school, everyone had seen me walking around like a pansy.

"Yes. Don't do it again. You'll never survive here."

Check. So, half a day impersonating a girl. What else had I done to deserve Boys State?

Well, there was that time a few months later on the band bus. Boone had fallen asleep with his socks and shoes off. Honestly I can't say he had socks. But there he was, barefoot, his leg propped up on the armrest of the seat in front of him. Larry Kopasz had his cigarettes with him and it was decided that in order to solve the riddle "How long does a cigarette take to burn all the way down if being smoked by a foot?" he lit one and placed it between Boone's toes to find out. (Answer: seven and a half minutes.) Boone let out quite a yell when the hot cinder of the Lucky Strike reached his toes, and he didn't miss a beat from dreamland to wrestling

Kopasz to the floor of the bus, which caught the attention of the driver. (In those days, as most adults and bus drivers smoked all the time, student smoking often went undetected because their smoke simply went into the same smoky air we were all breathing.) Some how I got implicated in this brawl, as Boone held us all collectively responsible. (On that same overnight band trip, we snuck into Boone's room to run an other science experiment: "Does placing one's hand while asleep in a warm bowl of water make one piss himself?" Answer: yes. And this time we took a Polaroid so we'd have proof to hold against him should Boone, the bedwetting tuba player, turn us in.)

But that was it. Seriously. I got good grades, was on the debate team, never skipped school and other than a skit I wrote for Comedy Week about the principal living a secret life as Pickles the Clown, I had not a smirch on my record.

As it turned out, Boys State was not a summer reformatory school for hoodlums and malcontents. It was a special honor to be selected to attend. Each June, after school ended, every high school in the state sent two to four boys to the state capital to "play government" for a week. You were chosen if you had shown leadership and good citizenship. I had shown the ability to come up with some very funny pranks to play on Boone.

Michigan's Boys State was held three miles from the Capitol Building on the campus of Michigan State University (the girls held a similar event called Girls State on the other side of the campus). Two thousand boys were assembled to elect our own pretend governor of Michigan, a fake state legislature, and a made-up state supreme court. The idea was for us boys to break down into parties and run for various offices in order to learn the beauties of campaigning and governing. If you were already one of those kids who ran for class office and loved being on student council, this place was your crack house.

But after campaigning for "Nixon-the-peace-candidate" as a freshman, I had developed an early allergy to politicians, and the last thing I wanted was to be one. I arrived at the Michigan State dormitories, was assigned my room and, after one "governmental meeting," where a boy named Ralston talked my ear off about why he should be

state treasurer, I decided that my best course of action was to hole up in my room for the week and never come out except at feeding times.

I was given a small single room that belonged to that floor's resident advisor. He apparently had not moved all of his stuff out. I found a record player and some record albums sitting near the window-sill. I had a few books with me, plus a writing tablet and a pen. It was all I needed to make it through the week. So I essentially deserted Boys State and found refuge in this well-stocked fifth-floor room in the Kellogg Dorms. The album collection in my room included James Taylor's *Sweet Baby James,* The Beatles' *Let It Be,* the Guess Who's *American Woman,* and something by Sly and the Family Stone. There was a big coin-operated snack machine down at the end of the hall, so I had everything I needed for the week.

In between listening to the records and writing poems to amuse myself (I called them "song lyrics" to make them seem like a worthwhile endeavor), I became enamored with a new brand of potato chip that I heretofore had not encountered. The snack machine offered bags of something called "Ruffles" potato chips. I was amazed at how they were able to put hills and valleys into a single chip. For some reason, these "hills" (they called 'em "ridges") gave me the impression that I was getting more chip per chip than your regular potato chip. I liked that a lot.

On the fourth day inside my NO POLITICS ALLOWED/FIRE AND RAIN bunker, I had completely run out of Ruffles and made a run down the hall for more. Above the snack machine was a bulletin board, and when I got there I noticed some-one had stuck a flyer on it. It read:

BOYS STATERS!
SPEECH CONTEST
on the life of
ABRAHAM LINCOLN
Write a speech on the life of Abe Lincoln
and win a PRIZE!
Contest sponsored by the
ELKS CLUB

I stood and stared at this flyer for some time. I forgot about my Ruffles. I just couldn't get over what I was reading.

The previous month, my dad had gone to the local Elks Club to join. They had a golf course just a few miles from where we lived, and he and his linemates from the factory loved to golf. Golf, the sport of the wealthier class, was not normally played by the working class in places like Flint. But the GM honchos had long ago figured out ways to lull the restless workers into believing that the American Dream was theirs, too. They understood after a while that you couldn't just crush unions—people would always try to start unions simply because of the oppressive nature of their work. So the GM execs who ran Flint knew that the best way to quell rebellion was to let the proles have a few of the accoutrements of wealth—make them think that they were living the life of Riley, make them believe that through hard work they, too, could be rich some day!

So they built public golf courses in and around the factories of Flint. If you worked at AC Spark Plug, you played the I.M.A. or Pierce golf courses. If you worked at Buick you headed over to the Kearsley course. If you worked at the Hammerberg Road plant, you played at Swartz Creek. If you worked in "The Hole," you played the Mott course.

When the factory whistle blew at 2:30 p.m. every day, our dads grabbed their bags from the car and started whacking balls around (they'd play nine holes and be home for dinner by five). They loved it. Soon working class became "middle class." There was time and money for month-long family vacations, homes in the suburbs, a college fund for the kids. But as the years went on, the monthly union hall meetings became sparsely attended. When the company started asking the union for givebacks and concessions, and when the company asked the workers to build inferior cars that the public would soon no longer want, the company found they had a willing partner in their demise.

But back in 1970, thoughts like that would get you locked up in the loony bin. Those were the salad days (though I'm certain it was illegal to offer a salad anywhere within a fifty-mile radius of Flint). And the guys in the factory grew to believe that golf was *their* game.

The Elks Club owned a beautiful course that was not as crowded as the Flint public courses, but you had to be a member. So it was with some disappointment when my dad went out to the Elks Club to join that he was confronted with a line printed at the top of the application:

CAUCASIANS ONLY

Being a Caucasian, this should not have been, a problem for Frank Moore. Being a man of some conscience, though, it gave him pause. He brought the form home and showed me.

"What do you think about this?" he asked me.

I read the Caucasian line and had two thoughts:

1. Are we down South? (How much more north can you get than Michigan?)
2. Isn't this illegal?

My dad was clearly confused about the situation. "Well, I don't think I can sign this piece of paper," he said.

"No, you can't," I said. "Don't worry. We can still golf at the I.M.A."

He would occasionally go back to the Elks course if invited by friends, but he would not join. He was not a civil rights activist. He generally didn't vote because he didn't want to be called for jury duty. He had all the misguided racial "worries" white people of his generation had. But he also had a very basic sense of right and wrong and of setting an example for his children. And because the union had insisted on integrating the factories as early as the 1940s, he worked alongside men and women of all races and, as is the outcome of such social engineering, he grew to see all people as the same (or at least "the same" as in "all the same in God's eyes").

Now, here I was, standing there in front of this Elks Club poster next to the vending machine. The best way to describe my feelings at that moment is that I was seventeen. What do you do at seventeen when you observe hypocrisy or encounter an injustice? What if they are the same thing? Whether it's the local ladies' club refusing to let a black lady join, or a segregated men's club like the Elks that has the audacity to sponsor a contest on the life of the Great Emancipator, when you're seventeen you have no tolerance for this kind of crime. Hell hath no indignation like that of a teenager who has forgotten his main mission was to retrieve a bag of Ruffles potato chips.

"They want a speech?" I thought, a goofy smile now making its way across my face. "I think I'm gonna go write me a speech."

I hurried back to my room, sans the bag of Ruffles, got out my pad of paper, my trusty Bic pen, and all the fury I could muster.

"How dare the Elks Club besmirch the fine name of Abraham Lincoln by sponsoring a contest like this!" I began, thinking I would lead with subtlety and save the good stuff for later. *"Have they no shame? How is it that an organization that will not allow black people into their club* **is** *a part of Boys State, spreading their bigotry under the guise of doing something good? What kind of example is being set for the youth here? Who even allowed them in here? If Boys State is to endorse any form of segregation, then by all means, let it be the segregation that separates these racists from the rest of us who believe in the American Way! How dare they even enter these grounds!"*

I went on to tell the story of my dad going to join the Elks and refusing to do so. I quoted Lincoln (my mother's continual stops at Gettysburg whenever we drove to New York would now pay off). And I closed by saying, *"It is my sincere hope that the Elks change their segregationist policies—and that Boys State never, ever invites them back here again."*

I skipped dinner, putting the final touches on the speech, rewriting it a couple times on the pad of paper, and then fell asleep listening to Sly Stone.

The next morning, all speech contestants were instructed to show up in a School of Social Work classroom and give their speech. There were fewer than a dozen of us in the room and, much to my surprise (and relief), there was no one present from the Elks Club. Instead, the speeches were to be judged by a lone high school forensics teacher from Lansing. I took a seat in the back of the room and listened to the boys who went before me. They spoke in laudatory tones of Lincoln's accomplishments and his humanity, but mostly how he won the Civil War. It was the type of stuff the mayor might say at a town's Fourth of July picnic. Sweet. Simple. Noncontroversial.

Few in the room were prepared for the barrage of insults about to be hurled at the Elks Club. Take William Jennings Bryan, add some Jimmy Stewart, and throw in a healthy dose of Don Rickles, and I'm guessing that's what it must've sounded like to the assembled as I unleashed my invective disguised as a speech.

About halfway through my rant, I looked over toward the teacher/judge. He sat there without expression or emotion. I felt my heart skip a beat, as I was not used to being in trouble—and the last thing I wanted was for my parents to have to drive down to East Lansing and haul me home. I occasionally glanced at the other Boys Staters in the room to see how this was going down. Some looked at me in fear, others had that "boy-is-he-gonna-get-it" look on their faces—and the black kid in the room . . . well, what can I say, he was the only black kid in the room. He was trying to cover the smile on his face with his hand.

When the speeches were over, the teacher/judge went to the head of the class to issue his verdict. I slunk down in my seat, hoping that he would simply announce the winner and not issue any rebukes.

"Thank you, all of you, for your well-thought-out and well-written speeches," he began. "I was impressed with each and every one of you. The winner of this year's Elks Club Boys State Speech Contest is . . . Michael Moore! Congratulations, Michael. That was a courageous thing to do. And you're right. Thank you."

I didn't realize it, but he was already shaking my hand, as were about a third of the other boys.

"Thank you," I said somewhat sheepishly. "But I really didn't wanna win anything. I just wanted to say something."

"Well, you sure said something," the teacher replied. "You'll receive your award tomorrow at the closing ceremonies with all two thousand boys in attendance."

"Oh—and you'll have to give the speech to them." *What?* Give what to whom?

"It's the tradition. The winner of the Elks Club speech gives his speech at the closing assembly, where they announce the election results and hand out all the awards."

"Um, no, I don't really wanna do that," I said, distressed, hoping he would take pity on me. "You don't really want me to give that speech, do you?"

"Oh, yes I do. But it's not up to me, anyway. You have to give it. That's the rule."

He also told me that for my own good, he wasn't going to mention to anyone the content of the speech before tomorrow. *Oh, yes, that's much better,* I thought. Let them all be hit with it fresh, like a big surprise, the kind which has the speaker being chased from the great hall, his prize in one hand, his life in the other.

After winning the speech contest, my night went something like this: "Fire and Rain," bathroom. "Across the Universe," bathroom. "Hot Fun in the Summertime," bathroom. And when you're seventeen and you don't have a car and you aren't prone to walking long distances—and you live in a state where mass transit is outlawed—there is a sense of imprisonment. That's it—I was in Boys State Prison! By morning, I had said my final prayers and made a promise to myself that if I got out of this alive, I'd never cause trouble like this again.

The time came and thousands of Boys Staters were ushered into the university hall. On the stage sat various officials, including, I believe, the real governor of Michigan. I took a seat near the front, on the side, and quickly scanned the place for guys who enjoyed being white. There was virtually no long hair here in 1971, and way too many of them had that clean-cut, disciplined, aggressive look that would probably serve them well after a year or two in the Hanoi Hilton, if not the U.S. Congress.

You will have to forgive me for the order of what came next because the event became a blur. My basic survival instincts had kicked in, and that was all that mattered. Someone was elected lieutenant governor or attorney general or Most Likely to Be Caught in the Senate Bathroom Someday. Somewhere in the middle of those announcements I heard my name. I lifted myself out of the chair (against the better advice of my excretory system) and made my way to the stage. The few boys I made eye contact with had that bored "Oh, shit another speech" look on their faces. For an instant I felt like I was soon going to be doing them a huge favor. This was certainly not going to sound like anything they were used to in third-hour civics class. That much I knew.

I ascended to the stage and walked past the dignitaries settled in their comfortable chairs. As I looked at them one by one, I noticed a man who was wearing antlers. A hat with *antlers*. It was not Bullwinkle and this was not Halloween. This man was the Chief Elk, the head of all Elks, and he held in his lap the Elks Club Boys State speech trophy. He had a big, wide smile, a smile more appropriate for a Kiwanis or a Rotarian, with more teeth than I thought humanly possible, and he was so proud to see me take the podium. Oh, man, I thought, this guy is about to have a very bad day. I hope they did a patdown.

Unrolling my pages of paper, I peered out at the mass of newly minted testosterone. Sixteen- and seventeen-year-olds who should have been doing anything right now—shooting hoops, kissing girls, gutting trout—anything but sitting here listening to me. I took a deep breath and began the speech.

"How dare the Elks Club . . ." I remember it was somewhere around that point when I could feel a *whoosh* of tension in the room, hundreds murmuring, snickering under their breath. *Please God,* I thought, *could some responsible adult come up to the podium immediately and put an end to this!*

No one did. I motored onward, and near the end I could hear the cadence in my voice and I thought this wouldn't be half bad if I were singing it in a rock band. I finished with my plea that the Elks change their ways and, as I turned my head to see the crimson tide that was now the face of the Chief Elk, his teeth resembling two chainsaws ready to shred my sorry self, I blurted out, "And you can keep your stinkin' trophy!"

The place went insane. Nearly two thousand boys leapt to their feet and whooped and hollered and cheered me. The hollering wouldn't stop and order had to be restored. I jumped off the stage and tried to get out of there, my escape route having been preplanned. But too many of the Boys Staters wanted to shake my hand or slap my back locker-room style, and this slowed me down. A reporter began to make his way toward me, notebook in hand. He introduced himself and said that he was astonished at what he had just seen and was going to write something and put it over the wire. He asked me a few questions about where I was from and other things that I didn't want to answer. I broke away and headed quickly out a side door. Keeping my head down and avoiding the main campus path,

I made it back to the Kellogg Dorms, checked the vending machine for Ruffles, rushed to my room and bolted the door.

The machine was out of Ruffles, but there was the Guess Who, and I turned it up so I could have some time to figure out what in hell's name I'd just done.

At least two hours passed, and it seemed like I was in the clear. No authorities had come to take me away, no Elks militia had arrived seeking revenge. All seemed to be back to normal.

Until the knock on the door.

"Hey," the anonymous voice barked. "There's a call for you."

The dorm rooms had no phones.

"Where's the phone?" I asked without opening the door.

"Down at the end of the hall."

Ugh. That was a long walk. But I needed Ruffles, and maybe they had restocked the machine. I opened the door and headed down the long hallway to the one public phone. The receiver hung dangling by its cord, like a dead man swinging from the gallows. What I didn't know was that on the other end of the line was the rest of my life.

"Hello?" I answered nervously, wondering who would even know where I was or how to reach me.

"Hello, is this Michael Moore?" the voice on the line asked.

"Yes."

"I'm a producer here at the *CBS Evening News* with Walter Cronkite in New York. We got this story that came over the wire about what you did today, and we'd like to send a crew over to interview you for tonight's newscast."

"Huh?" *What was he talking about?*

"We're doing a story on your speech exposing the Elks Club and their racial policies. We want you to come on TV."

Come on TV? There wasn't enough Clearasil in the world to get me to do that.

"Uh, no thank you. I have to get back to my room. Bye."

I hung up and ran back to the room and locked the door again. But it didn't matter. This became my first-ever media lesson: *I* don't get to decide what goes in the morning paper or on the nightly news. That night, I was introduced to the world.

"And today in Lansing, Michigan, a seventeen-year-old boy gave a speech that took on the Elks Club and their segregationist practices, shedding light on the fact that it is still legal for private clubs in this country to discriminate on the basis of race. . . ."

The next day the dorm phone rang off the hook, even as I was packing up to leave. I didn't answer any of the calls, but I heard from the other boys that there were reporters phoning from the Associated Press, two TV networks, the NAACP, a paper in New York and another in Chicago. Unless it involved them offering me free food or an introduction to a girl who might like me, I did not want to be bothered.

My parents were waiting outside in the car to take me back home. This much I'll say: my parents were not unhappy with my actions.

When I got home, the phone continued to ring. Finally, a call came from the office of Michigan senator Phil Hart. He wanted to talk to me about coming to Washington. The aide said it was something about a bill that would be introduced, a bill to out-law discrimination by private entities. A congressman would be calling me about testifying in front of a congressional committee. Would I be willing to do that?

No!! Why were they bothering me? Hadn't I done enough? I didn't mean to cause such a ruckus.

I thanked him and said I would discuss it with my parents (though I never told them; they would have wanted me to go!). I went outside to mow the lawn. We lived on Main Street, on a corner, across the street from the town fire station and kitty-corner from the town bowling alley. Over the din of the mower's engine I could faintly hear the honk of a horn.

"Hey, Mike!" shouted Jan Kittel from the car that had just pulled up to the curb. With her was another girl from our class. I had known Jan since fifth grade in Catholic school. In the past year she and I were partners on the debate team. I loved her. She was smart and pretty and very funny. I waved.

"Hey, c'mere! We heard about what you did at Boys State!" she said excitedly. "Man, that was something! You rocked it! I'm so proud of you."

I was ill equipped to handle the range of feelings and body temperature I was experiencing.

I had absolutely no clue where to go with this other than to stutter out a "thanks." They got out of the car and she made me tell them the whole story, complete with the near riot I caused, which resulted in a lot of "right-ons!" and "farm outs!"—and, yes, a big hug for my efforts. They were running an errand and had to get going, but not before she said she hoped see me again that summer.

"You and I will kick ass in debate this year," she offered, as I glanced in relief at the EMS unit parked in front of the fire station. "It'll be fun."

They drove off and I finished the lawn. It dawned on me that doing something political had brought me both a lot of grief *and* a girl who stopped by to see me. Maybe I was too harsh on the class officer types who populated Boys State with their geek-like love of all things political. Maybe they knew a certain secret. Or maybe they would all just grow up to populate Congress with their slick, smarmy selves, selling the rest of us out at the drop of a dime. Maybe.

The following year was not a good one for the Elks Clubs of America. Many states denied them their liquor licenses (the unkindest cut of all). Grants and funds became scarce. Various bills in Congress to stop them and other private clubs were debated. And then the federal courts in D.C. dealt them a death blow by taking away their tax exempt status. Facing total collapse and the scorn of the majority of the nation, the Elks Club voted to drop their Caucasians Only policy. Other private clubs followed suit. The ripple effect of this was that now racial discrimination *everywhere* in America, be it public or private, was prohibited.

My speech was occasionally cited as a spark for this march forward in racial fixing in the great American experiment, but there were other speeches far more eloquent than mine. Most important for me, I learned a valuable lesson: That change can occur, and it can occur *anywhere,* with even the simplest of people and craziest of intentions, and that creating change didn't always require having to devote your every waking hour to it with mass meetings and organizations and protests and TV appearances with Walter Cronkite.

Sometimes change can occur because all you wanted was a bag of potato chips.   [2011]

Understanding the Reading

1. Why did the author decide to enter the speech contest on the life of Abraham Lincoln, sponsored by the Elks Club, while at Boys State?
2. What was the reaction to his speech?
3. How did the author's speech change America?

Suggestion for Responding

1. Research changes in racist policies in the late 1960s and early 1970s in the U. S. Try to find who or what caused these changes. ✦

101

Victory at Arnot

MARY HARRIS "MOTHER" JONES[1]

Before 1899 the coal fields of Pennsylvania were not organized. Immigrants poured into the country and they worked cheap. There was always a surplus of immigrant labor, solicited in Europe by the coal companies, so as to keep wages down to barest living. Hours of work down under ground were cruelly long. Fourteen hours a day was not uncommon, thirteen, twelve. The life or limb of the miner was unprotected by any laws. Families lived in company owned shacks that were not fit for their pigs. Children died by the hundreds due to the ignorance and poverty of their parents.

Often I have helped lay out for burial the babies of the miners, and the mothers could scarce conceal their relief at the little ones' deaths. Another was already on its way, destined, if a boy, for the breakers; if a girl, for the silk mills where the other brothers and sisters already worked.

The United Mine Workers decided to organize these fields and work for human conditions for human beings. Organizers were put to work. Whenever the spirit of the men in the mines grew strong enough a strike was called.

In Arnot, Pennsylvania, a strike had been going on four or five months. The men were becoming discouraged. The coal company sent the doctors, the school teachers, the preachers and their wives to the homes of the miners to get them to sign a document that they would go back to work.

The president of the district, Mr. Wilson, and an organizer, Tom Haggerty, got despondent. The signatures were overwhelmingly in favor of returning on Monday.

Haggerty suggested that they send for me. Saturday morning they telephoned to Barnesboro, where I was organizing, for me to come at once or they would lose the strike.

"Oh Mother," Haggerty said, "Come over quick and help us! The boys are that despondent! They are going back Monday."

I told him that I was holding a meeting that night but that I would leave early Sunday morning.

I started at daybreak. At Roaring Branch, the nearest train connection with Arnot, the secretary of the Arnot Union, a young boy, William Bouncer, met me with a horse and buggy. We drove sixteen miles over rough mountain roads. It was biting cold. We got into Arnot Sunday noon and I was placed in the coal company's hotel, the only hotel in town. I made some objections but Bouncer said, "Mother, we have engaged this room for you and if it is not occupied, they will never rent us another."

Sunday afternoon I held a meeting. It was not as large a gathering as those we had later but I stirred up the poor wretches that did come.

"You've got to take the pledge," I said. "Rise and pledge to stick to your brothers and the union till the strike's won!"

The men shuffled their feet but the women rose, their babies in their arms, and pledged themselves to see that no one went to work in the morning.

"The meeting stands adjourned till ten o'clock tomorrow morning," I said. "Everyone come and see that the slaves that think to go back to their masters come along with you."

I returned to my room at the hotel. I wasn't called down to supper but after the general manager of the mines and all of the other guests had gone to church, the housekeeper stole up to my room and asked me to come down and get a cup of tea.

At eleven o'clock that night the housekeeper again knocked at my door and told me that I had to give up my room; that she was told it belonged to a teacher. "It's a shame, mother," she whispered, as she helped me into my coat.

I found little Bouncer sitting on guard down in the lobby. He took me up the mountain to a miner's house. A cold wind almost blew the bonnet from my head. At the miner's shack I knocked.

A man's voice shouted, "Who is there?"

"Mother Jones," said I.

A light came in the tiny window. The door opened.

"And did they put you out, Mother?"

"They did that."

"I told Mary they might do that," said the miner. He held the oil lamp with the thumb and his little finger and I could see that the others were off. His face was young but his body was bent over.

He insisted on my sleeping in the only bed, with his wife. He slept with his head on his arms on the kitchen table. Early in the morning his wife rose to keep the children quiet, so that I might sleep a little later as I was very tired.

At eight o'clock she came into my room, crying.

"Mother, are you awake?"

"Yes, I am awake."

"Well, you must get up. The sheriff is here to put us out for keeping you. This house belongs to the Company."

The family gathered up all their earthly belongings, which weren't much, took down all the holy pictures, and put them in a wagon, and they with all their neighbors went to the meeting. The sight of that wagon with the sticks of furniture and the holy pictures and the children, with the father and mother and myself walking along through the streets turned the tide. It made the men so angry that they decided not to go back that morning to the mines. Instead they came to the meeting where they determined not to give up the strike until they had won the victory.

Then the company tried to bring in scabs.[2] I told the men to stay home with the children for a change and let the women attend to the scabs. I organized an army of women housekeepers. On a given day they were to bring their mops and brooms and "the army" would charge the scabs up at the mines. The general manager, the sheriff and the corporation hirelings heard of our plans and were on hand. The day came and the women came with the mops and brooms and pails of water.

I decided not to go up to the Drip Mouth myself, for I knew they would arrest me and that might rout the army. I selected as leader an Irish woman who had a most picturesque appearance. She had slept late and her husband had told her to hurry up and get into the army. She had grabbed a red petticoat and slipped it over a thick cotton night gown. She wore a black stocking and a white one. She had tied a little red fringed shawl over her wild red hair. Her face was red and her eyes were mad. I looked at her and felt that she could raise a rumpus.

I said, "You lead the army up to the Drip Mouth. Take that tin dishpan you have with you and your hammer, and when the scabs and the mules come up, begin to hammer and howl. Then all of you hammer and howl and be ready to chase the scabs with your mops and brooms. Don't be afraid of anyone."

Up the mountain side, yelling and hollering, she led the women, and when the mules came up with the scabs and the coal, she began beating on the dishpan and hollering and all the army joined in with her. The sheriff tapped her on the shoulder.

"My dear lady," said he, "remember the mules. Don't frighten them."

She took the old tin pan and she hit him with it and she hollered, "To hell with you and the mules!"

He fell over and dropped into the creek. Then the mules began to rebel against scabbing. They bucked and kicked the scab drivers and started off for the barn. The scabs started running down hill, followed by the army of women with their mops and pails and brooms.

A poll parrot in a near by shack screamed at the superintendent, "Got hell, did you? Got hell?"

There was a great big doctor in the crowd, a company lap dog. He had a little satchel in his hand and he said to me, impudent like, "Mrs. Jones, I have a warrant for you."

"All right," said I. "Keep it in your pill bag until I come for it. I am going to hold a meeting now."

From that day on the women kept continual watch of the mines to see that the company did not bring in scabs. Every day women with brooms or mops in one hand and babies in the other arm wrapped in little blankets, went to the mines and watched that no one went in. And all night long they kept watch. They were heroic women. In the long years to come the nation will pay them high tribute for they were fighting for the advancement of a great country.

I held meetings throughout the surrounding country. The company was spending money among the farmers, urging them not to do anything for the miners. I went out with an old wagon and a union mule that had gone on strike, and a miner's little boy for a driver. I held meetings among the farmers and won them to the side of the strikers.

Sometimes it was twelve or one o'clock in the morning when I would get home, the little boy asleep on my arm and I driving the mule. Sometimes it was several degrees below zero. The winds whistled down the mountains and drove the snow and sleet in our faces. My hands and feet were often numb. We were all living on dry bread and black coffee. I slept in a room that never had a fire in it, and I often woke up in the morning to find snow covering the outside covers of the bed.

There was a place near Arnot called Sweedy Town, and the company's agents went there to get the Swedes to break the strike. I was holding a meeting among the farmers when I heard of the company's efforts. I got the young farmers to get on their horses and go over to Sweedy Town and see that no Swede left town. They took clotheslines for lassos and any Swede seen moving in the direction of Arnot was brought back quick enough.

After months of terrible hardships the strike was about won. The mines were not working. The spirit of the men was splendid. President Wilson had come home from the western part of the state. I was staying at his home. The family had gone to bed. We sat up late talking over matters when there came a knock at the door. A very cautious knock.

"Come in," said Mr. Wilson.

Three men entered. They looked at me uneasily and Mr. Wilson asked me to step in an adjoining room. They talked the strike over and called President Wilson's attention to the fact that there were mortgages on his little home, held by the bank which was owned by the coal company, and they said, "We will take the mortgage off your home and give you $25,000 in cash if you will just leave and let the strike die out."

Reply

I shall never forget his reply:

"Gentlemen, if you come to visit my family, the hospitality of the whole house is yours. But if you come to bribe me with dollars to betray my manhood and my brothers who trust me, I want you to leave this door and never come here again."

The strike lasted a few weeks longer. Meantime President Wilson, when strikers were evicted, cleaned out his barn and took care of the evicted miners until homes could be provided. One by one he killed his chickens and his hogs. Everything that he had he shared. He ate dry bread and drank chicory. He knew every hardship that the rank and file of the organization knew. We do not have such leaders now.

The last of February the company put up a notice that all demands were conceded.

"Did you get the use of the hall for us to hold meetings?" said the women.

"No, we didn't ask for that."

"Then the strike is on again," said they.

They got the hall, and when the President, Mr. Wilson, returned from the convention in Cincinnati he shed tears of joy and gratitude.

I was going to leave for the central fields, and before I left, the union held a victory meeting in Bloosburg. The women came for miles in a raging snow storm for that meeting, little children trailing on their skirts, and babies under their shawls. Many of the miners had walked miles. It was one night of real joy and a great celebration. I bade them all good bye. A little boy called out, "Don't leave us, Mother. Don't leave us!" The dear little children kissed my hands. We spent the whole night in Bloosburg rejoicing. The men opened a few of the freight cars out on a siding and helped themselves to boxes of beer. Old and young talked and sang all night long and to the credit of the company no one was interfered with.

Those were the days before the extensive use of gun men, of military, of jails, of police clubs. There had been no bloodshed. There had been no riots. And the victory was due to the army of women with their mops and brooms.

A year afterward they celebrated the anniversary of the victory. They presented me with a gold watch but I declined to accept it, for I felt it was the price of the bread of the little children. I have not been in Arnot since but in my travels over the country I often meet the men and boys who carried through the strike so heroically. [1925]

Terms

1. MARY HARRIS "MOTHER" JONES: After the loss of her four children and her husband in a yellow fever epidemic and the destruction of her dressmaking shop in the Chicago fire of 1871, "Mother" Jones became a legendary labor union organizer.
2. SCABS: Strike breakers.

Understanding the Reading

1. What were the miners' lives like?
2. Why was Mother Jones not called down to supper, and what was the real reason that she had to give up her room at the hotel?
3. What was the effect of the sheriff's putting the family who sheltered her out of their house?
4. Why did Mother Jones organize an "army of women" rather than men to face the scabs?
5. Why did the miners finally win the strike?

Suggestion for Responding

1. Describe a time when you joined with others to organize for change. ✦

102

The Organizer's Tale

CÉSAR CHÁVEZ

It really started for me 16 years ago in San Jose, California, when I was working on an apricot farm. We figured he was just another social worker doing a study of farm conditions, and I kept refusing to meet with him. But he was persistent. Finally, I got together some of the rough element in San Jose. We were going to have a little reception for him to teach the *gringo*[1] a little bit of how we felt. There were about 30 of us in the house, young guys mostly. I was supposed to give them a signal—change my cigarette from my right hand to my left, and then we were going to give him a lot of hell. But he started talking and the more he talked, the more wide-eyed I became and the less inclined I was to give the signal. A couple of guys who were pretty drunk at the time still wanted to give the *gringo* the business, but we got rid of them. This fellow was making a lot of sense, and I wanted to hear what he had to say.

His name was Fred Ross, and he was an organizer for the Community Service Organization (CSO) which was working with Mexican-Americans in the cities. I became immediately really involved. Before long I was heading a voter registration drive. All the time I was observing the things Fred did, secretly, because I wanted to learn how to organize, to see how it was done. I was impressed with his patience and understanding of people. I thought this was a tool, one of the greatest things he had.

It was pretty rough for me at first. I was changing and had to take a lot of ridicule from the kids my age, the rough characters I worked with in the fields. They would say, "Hey big shot. Now that you're a *politico*, why are you working here for 65 cents an hour?" I might add that our neighborhood had the highest percentage of San Quentin graduates. It was a game among the *pachucos*[2] in the sense that we defended ourselves from outsiders, although inside the neighborhood there was not a lot of fighting.

After six months of working every night in San Jose, Fred assigned me to take over the CSO chapter in Decoto. It was a tough spot to fill. I would suggest something, and people would say, "No, let's wait till Fred gets back," or "Fred wouldn't do it that way." This is pretty much a pattern with people, I discovered, whether I was put in Fred's position, or later, when someone else was put in my position. After the Decoto assignment I was sent to start a new chapter in Oakland. Before I left, Fred came to a place in San Jose called the Hole-in-the-Wall and we talked for half an hour over coffee. He was in a rush to leave, but I wanted to keep him talking; I was scared of my assignment.

There were hard times in Oakland. First of all, it was a big city and I'd get lost every time I went anywhere. Then I arranged a series of house meetings. I would get to the meeting early and drive back and forth past the house, too nervous to go in and face the people. Finally

I would force myself to go inside and sit in a corner. I was quite thin then, and young, and most of the people were middle-aged. Someone would say, "Where's the organizer?" And I would pipe up, "Here I am." Then they would say in Spanish—these were very poor people and we hardly spoke anything but Spanish—"Ha! This *kid?*" Most of them said they were interested, but the hardest part was to get them to start pushing themselves, on their own initiative.

The idea was to set up a meeting and then get each attending person to call his own house meeting, inviting new people—a sort of chain letter effect. After a house meeting, I would lie awake going over the whole thing, playing the tape back, trying to see why people laughed at one point, or why they were for one thing and against another. I was also learning to read and write, those late evenings. I had left school in the 7th grade after attending 67 different schools, and my reading wasn't the best.

At our first organizing meeting we had 368 people: I'll never forget it because it was very important to me. You eat your heart out; the meeting is called for 7 o'clock and you start to worry about 4. You wait. Will they show up? Then the first one arrives. By 7 there are only 20 people, you have everything in order, you have to look calm. But little by little they filter in and at a certain point you know it will be a success.

After four months in Oakland, I was transferred. The chapter was beginning to move on its own, so Fred assigned me to organize the San Joaquin Valley. Over the months I developed what I used to call schemes or tricks—now I call them techniques—of making initial contacts. The main thing in convincing someone is to spend time with him. It doesn't matter if he can read, write or even speak well. What is important is that he is a man and second, that he has shown some initial interest. One good way to develop leadership is to take a man with you in your car. And it works a lot better if you're doing the driving; that way you are in charge. You drive, he sits there, and you talk. These little things were very important to me; I was caught in a big game by then, figuring out what makes people work. I found that if you work hard enough you can usually shake people into working too, those who are concerned.

You work harder and they work harder still, up to a point and then they pass you. Then, of course, they're on their own.

I also learned to keep away from the established groups and so-called leaders, and to guard against philosophizing. Working with low-income people is very different from working with the professionals who like to sit around talking about how to play politics. When you're trying to recruit a farmworker, you have to paint a little picture, and then you have to color the picture in. We found out that the harder a guy is to convince, the better leader or member he becomes. When you exert yourself to convince him, you have his confidence and he has good motivation. A lot of people who say OK right away wind up hanging around the office, taking up the workers' time.

During the McCarthy era[3] in one Valley town, I was subjected to a lot of redbaiting.[4] We had been recruiting people for citizenship classes at the high school when we got into a quarrel with the naturalization examiner. He was rejecting people on the grounds that they were just parroting what they learned in citizenship class. One day we had a meeting about it in Fresno, and I took along some of the leaders of our local chapter. Some redbaiting official gave us a hard time, and the people got scared and took his side. They did it because it seemed easy at the moment, even though they knew that sticking with me was the right thing to do. It was disgusting. When we left the building they walked by themselves ahead of me as if I had some kind of communicable disease. I had been working with these people for three months and I was very sad to see that. It taught me a great lesson.

That night I learned that the chapter officers were holding a meeting to review my letters and printed materials to see if I really was a Communist. So I drove out there and walked right in on their meeting. I said, "I hear you've been discussing me, and I thought it would be nice if I was here to defend myself. Not that it matters that much to you or even to me, because as far as I'm concerned you are a bunch of cowards." At that they began to apologize. "Let's forget it," they said. "You're a nice guy." But I didn't want apologies. I wanted a full discussion. I told them I didn't give a damn, but that they had to learn to distinguish fact from what appeared to be a fact because of fear. I kept them there till two in the morning. Some of the women cried. I don't know if they investigated me any further, but I stayed on another few months and things worked out.

This was not an isolated case. Often when we'd leave people to themselves they would get frightened and draw back into their shells where they had been all the years. And I learned quickly that there is no real appreciation. Whatever you do, and no matter what reasons you may give to others, you do it because you want to see it done, or maybe because you want power. And there shouldn't be any appreciation, understandably. I know good organizers who were destroyed, washed out, because they expected people to appreciate what they'd done. Anyone who comes in with the idea that farm-workers are free of sin and that the growers are all bastards, either has never dealt with the situation or is an idealist of the first order. Things don't work that way.   [1966]

Terms

1. GRINGO: A disparaging term used in Mexico and elsewhere in Latin America for North Americans.
2. PACHUCOS: A nickname for Mexican American youth, especially delinquents and gang members.
3. McCARTHY ERA: In the 1950s, Senator Joseph McCarthy used his office to crusade against internal subversion and to charge high governmental and military officials, including several presidents, with being Communists or "fellow travelers" of Communism.
4. REDBAITING: The act of attacking or persecuting someone, accusing them of being Communist or communistic.

Understanding the Reading

1. What made Chávez interested in organizing the Mexican Americans?
2. What steps did he take to organize the new CSO chapter in Oakland?
3. What techniques did he use to make initial contacts?
4. What tactics were used to discredit Chávez?

Suggestion for Responding

1. What leadership qualities does Chávez display? ✦

103

The Matthew Shepard and James Byrd, Jr. Hate Crimes Prevention Act

RAMON JOHNSON

The Matthew Shepard and James Byrd, Jr. Hate Crimes Prevention Act, signed by Pres. Barack Obama[1] expands federal hate crimes legislation to include gender, sexual orientation, gender identity and disability.

HOW DOES THE MATTHEW SHEPARD AND JAMES BYRD ACT CHANGE PREVIOUS LAWS?

The bill expands previous hate crime legislation by:

- removing the current prerequisite that the victim be engaging in a federally protected activity, like voting or going to school;
- giving federal law enforcement agencies greater ability to engage in hate crimes investigations that local authorities choose not to pursue;
- providing $10 million in funding for 2008 and 2009 to help state and local agencies pay for investigating and prosecuting hate crimes; and by
- requiring the FBI to track statistics on hate crimes against transgender people.

HISTORY

The Federal Bureau of Investigations didn't begin tallying national crime statistics[2] or investigating hate crimes until 1924 under the direction of J. Edgar Hoover. And according to the FBI, the term "hate crime" didn't enter the national vocabulary until the 1980s.

In April of 1968, a week after the assassination of Martin Luther King, President Lyndon Johnson signed the Civil Rights Act of 1968, expanding the previous 1964 act to include race, color, religion or national origin.

Human rights activists and legislators began pushing for an additional expansion of hate crimes legislation after the brutal killings of James Byrd, Jr., an African American man in Texas, and Matthew Shepard, a gay Wyoming youth. Numerous bills—the most notable being the Federal Law Enforcement Hate Crimes Prevention Act[3]—have been introduced, but failed in conservative-led sessions.

However, on October 28, 2009, eleven years after the death of Byrd and Shepard, the Matthew Shepard and James Byrd, Jr. Hate Crimes Prevention Act was signed into law by President Barack Obama following successful House[4] and Senate[5] votes. The act widens federal hate crimes laws to include crimes based on gender, sexual orientation, gender identity and disability bias.   [2011]

Notes

1. http://gaylife.about.com/b/2009/10/29/barackobamagayhatecrimes.htm
2. http://gaylife.about.com/od/hatecrimes/a/statistics.htm
3. http://gaylife.about.com/od/hatecrimes/p/matthewshepard.htm
4. http://gaylife.about.com/b/2009/10/09/house-expands-hate-crime-legislation.htm
5. http://gaylife.about.com/b/2009/10/26/senate-passes-the-matthew-shepard-and-james-byrd-jr-hate-crimes-prevention-act.htm

Understanding the Reading

1. How does this Act change our previous laws?
2. When did the term "hate crime" come into being in the United States?
3. Why is it important to track statistics on hate crimes?

Suggestion for Responding

1. Research the crimes perpetrated on Matthew Shepard and James Byrd, Jr. ✦

104

Free at Last

SOUTHERN POVERTY LAW CENTER

By 1910, blacks were caught in a degrading system of total segregation throughout the South. Through "Jim Crow" laws (named after a black minstrel in a popular song), blacks were ordered to use separate restrooms, water fountains, restaurants, waiting rooms, swimming pools, libraries, and bus seats.

The United States Supreme Court gave its approval to Jim Crow segregation in the 1896 case of *Plessy v. Ferguson.* The Court said separate facilities were legal as long as they were equal. In practice, Southern states never provided equal facilities to black people—only separate ones.

Frederick Douglass[1] tried to expose the inherent contradictions in the law of the land: "So far as the colored people of the country are concerned," he said, "the Constitution is but a stupendous sham . . . fair without and foul within, keeping the promise to the eye and breaking it to the heart."

Despite Douglass' eloquent arguments, it would be generations before the nation lived up to its promises.

FIGHTING JIM CROW

Just as slaves had revolted against being someone else's property, the newly freed blacks revolted peacefully against the forces of racism. Ida B. Wells began a crusade against lynching at age 19 that inspired a national gathering of black leaders in 1893 to call for an anti-lynch law.

George Henry White, the only black U.S. congressman at the turn of the century, was a bold spokesman for equal rights. The former slave from North Carolina sponsored the first anti-lynching bill and insisted that the federal government enforce the constitutional amendments. In a speech to his fellow congressmen, White asked, "How long will you sit in your seats and hear and see the principles that underlie the foundations of this government sapped away little by little?"

One of the strongest critiques of American racism was offered by W. E. B. DuBois, a Harvard-educated sociologist. In *The Souls of Black Folk,* DuBois said American society had to be transformed if blacks were to achieve full equality.

DuBois, along with other black and white leaders, established the National Association for the Advancement of Colored People [NAACP] in 1910. The NAACP launched a legal campaign against racial injustice, began documenting racist violence, and published a magazine called *Crisis.* By 1940, NAACP membership reached 50,000.

As blacks were organizing for reform, white supremacists were organizing to stop them. By the time the NAACP was 10 years old, two million whites belonged to the Ku Klux Klan. During the 1920s, Klansmen held high positions in government throughout the country.

In the South, Klan violence surged. Blacks moved North in record numbers, hoping to escape racial terrorism and to find better jobs. Although they faced poverty, unequal education, and discrimination in the North as well, racial restrictions there were less harsh. Blacks could even vote in Northern states. Indeed, by 1944, the black vote was a significant factor in 16 states outside the South.

BRINGING DEMOCRACY HOME

With the election of President Franklin Delano Roosevelt, black Americans finally had an ally in the White House. Black leaders were included among the president's advisers. Roosevelt's New Deal made welfare and jobs available to blacks as well as whites. A more liberal Supreme Court issued rulings against bus segregation and all-white political primaries. Black labor leader A. Philip Randolph scored a major victory when he convinced President Roosevelt to issue an Executive Order banning racial discrimination in all defense industries.

The demand for equal rights surged after World War II, when black soldiers returned from battling the racist horrors of Nazi Germany only to find they remained victims of racism at home.

Determined to bring democracy to America, blacks sought new strategies. Seeing Mahatma Gandhi[2] lead the Indian masses in peaceful demonstrations for independence, the Congress of

Racial Equality [CORE] decided to put the philosophy of nonviolence to work in America.

After much training and discussion, black and white members of CORE entered segregated restaurants, quietly sat down, and refused to leave until they were served. They did not raise their voices in anger or strike back if attacked. In a few Northern cities, their persistent demonstrations succeeded in integrating some restaurants.

After the Supreme Court outlawed segregation on interstate buses in 1946, CORE members set out on a "Journey of Reconciliation" to test whether the laws were being obeyed. Blacks and whites rode together on buses through the South and endured harassment without retaliating.

While the sit-ins and freedom rides of the 1940s served as models for the next generation of civil rights activists, they did not capture the broad support that was necessary to overturn segregation. The CORE victories were quiet ones, representing the determination of relatively few people.

The major battles against segregation were being fought in courtrooms and legislatures. Growing pressure from black leaders after World War II forced President Harry Truman to integrate the armed forces and to establish a civil rights commission. In 1947, that commission issued a report called *To Secure These Rights* that exposed racial injustices and called for the elimination of segregation in America.

By that time, half a million blacks belonged to the NAACP. Lawsuits brought by the NAACP had forced many school districts to improve black schools. Then, in 1950, NAACP lawyers began building the case that would force the Supreme Court to outlaw segregated schools and mark the beginning of the modern civil rights movement.

A MOVEMENT OF THE PEOPLE

Linda Brown's parents could not understand why their 7-year-old daughter should have to ride long distances each day to a rundown black school when there was a much better white school in their own neighborhood of Topeka, Kansas. Harry Briggs of Clarendon, South Carolina, was outraged that his five children had to attend schools which operated on one-fourth the amount of money given to white schools. Ethel Belton took her

complaints to the Delaware Board of Education when her children were forced to ride a bus for nearly two hours each day instead of walking to their neighborhood high school in Claymont. In Farmville, Virginia, 16-year-old Barbara Johns led her fellow high school students on a strike for a better school.

All over the country, black students and parents were angered over the conditions of their schools. NAACP lawyers studied their grievances and decided that it was not enough to keep fighting for equal facilities. They wanted all schools integrated.

A team of NAACP lawyers used the Topeka, Clarendon, Claymont and Farmville examples to argue that segregation itself was unconstitutional. They lost in the lower courts, but when they took their cause to the Supreme Court, the justices ruled they were right.

On May 17, 1954, the Supreme Court unanimously ruled that segregated schools "are inherently unequal." The Court explained that even if separate schools for blacks and whites had the same physical facilities, there could be no true equality as long as segregation itself existed. To separate black children "solely because of their race," the Court wrote, "generates a feeling of inferiority as to their status in the community that may affect their hearts and minds in a way very unlikely ever to be undone."

The *Brown v. Board of Education* ruling enraged many Southern whites who did not believe blacks deserved the same education as whites and didn't want their children attending schools with black children. Southern governors announced they would not abide by the Court's ruling, and White Citizens' Councils were organized to oppose school integration. Mississippi legislators passed a law abolishing compulsory school attendance. A declaration called the Southern Manifesto was issued by 96 Southern congressmen, demanding that the Court reverse the *Brown* decision.

Despite the opposition by many whites, the *Brown* decision gave great hope to blacks. Even when the Supreme Court refused to order immediate integration (calling instead for schools to act "with all deliberate speed"), black Americans knew that times were changing. And they were eager for expanded rights in other areas as well.

WALKING FOR JUSTICE

Four days after the Supreme Court handed down the *Brown* ruling, Jo Ann Robinson wrote a letter as president of the Women's Political Council to the mayor of Montgomery, Alabama. She represented a large group of black women, she said, and was asking for fair treatment on city buses.

Blacks, who made up 75 percent of Montgomery's bus riders, were forced to enter the buses in front, pay the driver, and re-enter the bus from the rear, where they could only sit in designated "colored" seats. If all the "white" seats were full, blacks had to give up their seats.

Women and children had been arrested for refusing to give up their seats. Others who challenged the bus drivers were slapped or beaten. Hilliard Brooks, 22, was shot dead by police in 1952 after an argument with a bus driver.

Every day, black housekeepers rode all the way home after work, jammed together in the aisles, while 10 rows of "white" seats remained empty.

Blacks could shut down the city's bus system if they wanted to, Jo Ann Robinson told the mayor. "More and more of our people are already arranging with neighbors and friends to ride to keep from being insulted and humiliated by bus drivers."

The mayor said segregation was the law and he could not change it.

On December 1, 1955, Rosa Parks was riding home from her job as a department store seamstress. The bus was full when a white man boarded. The driver stopped the bus and ordered Mrs. Parks along with three other blacks to vacate a row so the white man could sit down. Three of the blacks stood up. Rosa Parks kept her seat and was arrested.

Jo Ann Robinson and the Women's Political Council immediately began to organize a bus boycott with the support of NAACP leader E. D. Nixon. Prominent blacks hurriedly formed the Montgomery Improvement Association and selected a newcomer in town, Dr. Martin Luther King Jr., to be their leader.

On the night of December 5, a crowd of 15,000 gathered at Holt Street Church to hear the young preacher speak. "There comes a time that people get tired," King told the crowd. "We are here this evening to say to those who have mistreated us so long that we are tired—tired of being segregated and humiliated; tired of being kicked about by the brutal feet of oppression. . . . We have no alternative but to protest.

"And we are not wrong in what we are doing," he said. "If we are wrong, the Supreme Court of this nation is wrong. If we are wrong, God Almighty is wrong!"

If the bus boycott was peaceful and guided by love, King said, justice would be won. Historians in future generations, King predicted, "will have to pause and say, 'There lived a great people—a black people—who injected new meaning and dignity into the veins of civilization.'"

For 381 days, black people did not ride the buses in Montgomery. They organized car pools and walked long distances, remaining nonviolent even when harassed and beaten by angry whites. When Dr. King's home was bombed, they only became more determined. City officials tried to outlaw the boycott, but still the buses traveled empty.

On December 21, 1956, blacks returned to the buses in triumph. The U.S. Supreme Court had outlawed bus segregation in Montgomery in response to a lawsuit brought by the boycotters with the help of the NAACP. The boycotters' victory showed the entire white South that all blacks, not just civil rights leaders, were opposed to segregation. It demonstrated that poor and middle class blacks could unite to launch a successful protest movement, overcoming both official counterattacks and racist terror. And it showed the world that nonviolent resistance could work—even in Montgomery, the capital of the Confederate States during the Civil War.

King went on to establish an organization of black clergy, called the Southern Christian Leadership Conference, that raised funds for integration campaigns throughout the South. Black Southern ministers, following the example of King in Montgomery, became the spiritual force behind the nonviolent movement. Using the lessons of Montgomery, blacks challenged bus segregation in Tallahassee and Atlanta.

But when they tried to integrate schools and other public facilities, blacks discovered the lengths to which whites would go to preserve white supremacy. A black student admitted to the University of Alabama by federal court order was promptly expelled. The State of Virginia closed all public schools in Prince Edward County to avoid integration. Some communities filled in their public swimming pools and closed their tennis courts, and others removed library seats, rather than let blacks and whites share the facilities.

Blacks who challenged segregation received little help from the federal government. President Eisenhower had no enthusiasm for the *Brown* decision, and he desperately wanted to avoid segregation disputes.

Finally, in 1957, a crisis in Little Rock, Arkansas, forced Eisenhower to act.

NINE PIONEERS IN LITTLE ROCK

On September 4, 1957, Governor Orval Faubus ordered troops to surround Central High School in Little Rock, to keep nine black teenagers from entering. Despite the *Brown* ruling which said black students had a right to attend integrated schools, Governor Faubus was determined to keep the schools segregated.

That afternoon, a federal judge ordered Faubus to let the black students attend the white school. The next day, when 15-year-old Elizabeth Eckford set out for class, she was mobbed, spit upon and cursed by angry whites. When she finally made her way to the front steps of Central High, National Guard soldiers turned her away.

An outraged federal judge again ordered the governor to let the children go to school. Faubus removed the troops but gave the black children no protection. The nine black children made it to their first class, but had to be sent home when a violent white mob gathered outside the school. Faubus said the disturbance proved the school should not be integrated.

President Eisenhower had a choice: he could either send in federal troops to protect the children or allow a governor to defy the Constitution. Saying "our personal opinions have no bearing on the matter of enforcement," the president ordered in troops. For the rest of the school year, U.S. soldiers walked alongside the Little Rock nine as they went from class to class.

The next year, Governor Faubus shut down all the public schools rather than integrate them. A year later, the U.S. Supreme Court ruled that "evasive schemes" could not be used to avoid integration, and the Little Rock schools were finally opened to black and white students.

Although the Little Rock case did not end the long battle for school integration, it proved the federal government would not tolerate brazen defiance of federal law by state officials. It also served as an example for President John F. Kennedy who in 1962 ordered federal troops to protect James Meredith as he became the first black student to attend the University of Mississippi.   [1989]

Terms

1. FREDERICK DOUGLASS: An escaped slave, who became a leading abolitionist.
2. MAHATMA GANDHI: A Hindu nationalist and spiritual leader, who led the "passive resistance" movement to get the British out of India.

Understanding the Reading

1. What were Jim Crow laws?
2. How did the newly freed Blacks respond to them?
3. How did Franklin Roosevelt's presidency benefit Black Americans?
4. What gains did CORE achieve?
5. Explain the Supreme Court ruling in *Brown v. Board of Education.*
6. What made the Montgomery bus boycott effective?
7. What tactics did Whites use to avoid school desegregation?

Suggestions for Responding

1. Imagine that you were an African American in the South in the first half of the twentieth century. Choose one example of Jim Crow segregation (separate schools, restrooms, waiting rooms, drinking fountains; prohibitions on voting; rules about having to ride in the back of the bus) and describe your experience. What would you realistically do in such circumstances?
2. Learn more details about one specific example of southern White resistance to school integration, and write a brief report on it. ✦

105

The Movement

Anne Moody

I had counted on graduating in the spring of 1963, but as it turned out, I couldn't because some of my credits still had to be cleared with Natchez College. A year before, this would have seemed like a terrible disaster, but now I hardly even felt disappointed. I had a good excuse to stay on campus for the summer and work with the Movement, and this was what I really wanted to do. I couldn't go home again anyway, and I couldn't go to New Orleans—I didn't have money enough for bus fare.

During my senior year at Tougaloo, my family hadn't sent me one penny. I had only the small amount of money I had earned at Maple Hill. I couldn't afford to eat at school or live in the dorms, so I had gotten permission to move off campus. I had to prove that I could finish school, even if I had to go hungry every day. I knew Raymond and Miss Pearl were just waiting to see me drop out. But something happened to me as I got more and more involved in the Movement. It no longer seemed important to prove anything. I had found something outside myself that gave meaning to my life.

I had become very friendly with my social science professor, John Salter, who was in charge of NAACP[1] activities on campus. All during the year, while the NAACP conducted a boycott of the downtown stores in Jackson, I had been one of Salter's most faithful canvassers and church speakers. During the last week of school, he told me that sit-in demonstrations were about to start in Jackson and that he wanted me to be the spokesman for a team that would sit-in at Woolworth's lunch counter. The two other demonstrators would be classmates of mine, Memphis and Pearlena. Pearlena was a dedicated NAACP worker, but Memphis had not been very involved in the Movement on campus. It seemed that the organization had had a rough time finding students who were in a position to go to jail. I had nothing to lose one way or the other. Around ten o'clock the morning of the demonstrations,

NAACP headquarters alerted the news services. As a result, the police department was also informed, but neither the policemen nor the newsmen knew exactly where or when the demonstrations would start. They stationed themselves along Capitol Street and waited.

To divert attention from the sit-in at Woolworth's, the picketing started at J. C. Penney's a good fifteen minutes before. The pickets were allowed to walk up and down in front of the store three or four times before they were arrested. At exactly 11 A.M., Pearlena, Memphis, and I entered Woolworth's from the rear entrance. We separated as soon as we stepped into the store, and made small purchases from various counters. Pearlena had given Memphis her watch. He was to let us know when it was 11:14. At 11:14 we were to join him near the lunch counter and at exactly 11:15 we were to take seats at it.

Seconds before 11:15 we were occupying three seats at the previously segregated Woolworth's lunch counter. In the beginning the waitresses seemed to ignore us, as if they really didn't know what was going on. Our waitress walked past us a couple of times before she noticed we had started to write our own orders down and realized we wanted service. She asked us what we wanted. We began to read to her from our order slips. She told us that we would be served at the back counter, which was for Negroes.

"We would like to be served here," I said.

The waitress started to repeat what she had said, then stopped in the middle of the sentence. She turned the lights out behind the counter, and she and the other waitresses almost ran to the back of the store, deserting all their white customers. I guess they thought that violence would start immediately after the whites at the counter realized what was going on. There were five or six other people at the counter. A couple of them just got up and walked away. A girl sitting next to me finished her banana split before leaving. A middle-aged white woman who had not yet been served rose from her seat and came over to us. "I'd like to stay here with you," she said, "but my husband is waiting."

The newsmen came in just as she was leaving. They must have discovered what was going on shortly after some of the people began to leave the store. One of the newsmen ran behind the woman who spoke to us and asked her to identify herself. She refused to give her name, but said she was a native of Vicksburg and a former resident of California. When asked why she had said what she had said to us, she replied, "I am in sympathy with the Negro movement." By this time a crowd of cameramen and reporters had gathered around us taking pictures and asking questions, such as Where were we from? Why did we sit-in? What organization sponsored it? Were we students? From what school? How were we classified?

I told them that we were all students at Tougaloo College, that we were represented by no particular organization, and that we planned to stay there even after the store closed. "All we want is service," was my reply to one of them. After they had finished probing for about twenty minutes, they were almost ready to leave.

At noon, students from a nearby white high school started pouring in to Woolworth's. When they first saw us they were sort of surprised. They didn't know how to react. A few started to heckle and the newsmen became interested again. Then the white students started chanting all kinds of anti-Negro slogans. We were called a little bit of everything. The rest of the seats except the three we were occupying had been roped off to prevent others from sitting down. A couple of the boys took one end of the rope and made it into a hangman's noose. Several attempts were made to put it around our necks. The crowds grew as more students and adults came in for lunch.

We kept our eyes straight forward and did not look at the crowd except for occasional glances to see what was going on. All of a sudden I saw a face I remembered—the drunkard from the bus station sit-in. My eyes lingered on him just long enough for us to recognize each other. Today he was drunk too, so I don't think he remembered where he had seen me before. He took out a knife, opened it, put it in his pocket, and then began to pace the floor. At this point, I told Memphis and Pearlena what was going on. Memphis suggested that we pray. We bowed our heads, and all hell broke loose. A man rushed forward, threw Memphis from his seat, and slapped my face. Then another man who worked in the store threw me against an adjoining counter.

Down on my knees on the floor, I saw Memphis lying near the lunch counter with blood running out of the corners of his mouth. As he tried to protect his face, the man who'd thrown him down kept kicking him against the head. If he had worn hard-soled shoes instead of sneakers, the first kick probably would have killed Memphis. Finally a man dressed in plain clothes identified himself as a police officer and arrested Memphis and his attacker.

Pearlena had been thrown to the floor. She and I got back on our stools after Memphis was arrested. There were some white Tougaloo teachers in the crowd. They asked Pearlena and me if we wanted to leave. They said that things were getting too rough. We didn't know what to do. While we were trying to make up our minds, we were joined by Joan Trumpauer. Now there were three of us and we were integrated. The crowd began to chant, "Communists, Communists, Communists." Some old man in the crowd ordered the students to take us off the stools.

"Which one should I get first?" a big husky boy said.

"That white nigger," the old man said.

The boy lifted Joan from the counter by her waist and carried her out of the store. Simultaneously, I was snatched from my stool by two high school students. I was dragged about thirty feet toward the door by my hair when someone made them turn me loose. As I was getting up off the floor, I saw Joan coming back inside. We started back to the center of the counter to join Pearlena. Lois Chaffee, a white Tougaloo faculty member, was now sitting next to her. So Joan and I just climbed across the rope at the front end of the counter and sat down. There were now four of us, two whites and two Negroes, all women. The mob started smearing us with ketchup, mustard, sugar, pies, and everything on the counter. Soon Joan and I were joined by John Salter, but the moment he sat down he was hit on the jaw with what appeared to be brass knuckles. Blood gushed from his face and someone threw salt into the open wound. Ed King, Tougaloo's chaplain, rushed to him.

At the other end of the counter, Lois and Pearlena were joined by George Raymond, a CORE[2] field worker and a student from Jackson State College. Then a Negro high school boy sat down next to me. The mob took spray paint from the counter and sprayed it on the new demonstrators. The high school student had on a white shirt; the word "nigger" was written on his back with red spray paint.

We sat there for three hours taking a beating when the manager decided to close the store because the mob had begun to go wild with stuff from other counters. He begged and begged everyone to leave. But even after fifteen minutes of begging, no one budged. They would not leave until we did. Then Dr. Beittel, the president of Tougaloo College, came running in. He said he had just heard what was happening.

About ninety policemen were standing outside the store; they had been watching the whole thing through the windows, but had not come in to stop the mob or do anything. President Beittel went outside and asked Captain Ray to come and escort us out. The captain refused, stating the manager had to invite him in before he could enter the premises, so Dr. Beittel himself brought us out. He had told the police that they had better protect us after we were outside the store. When we got outside, the policemen formed a single line that blocked the mob from us. However, they were allowed to throw at us everything they had collected. Within ten minutes, we were picked up by Reverend King in his station wagon and taken to the NAACP headquarters on Lynch Street.

After the sit-in, all I could think of was how sick Mississippi whites were. They believed so much in the segregated Southern way of life, they would kill to preserve it. I sat there in the NAACP office and thought of how many times they had killed when this way of life was threatened. I knew that the killing had just begun. "Many more will die before it is over with," I thought. Before the sit-in, I had always hated the whites in Mississippi. Now I knew it was impossible for me to hate sickness. The whites had a disease, an incurable disease in its final stage. What were our chances against such a disease? I thought of the students, the young Negroes who had just begun to protest, as young interns. When these young interns got older, I thought, they would be the best doctors in the world for social problems.

Before we were taken back to campus, I wanted to get my hair washed. It was stiff with dried mustard, ketchup and sugar. I stopped in at a beauty shop across the street from the NAACP office. I didn't have on any shoes because I had lost them when I was dragged across the floor at Woolworth's. My stockings were sticking to my legs from the mustard that had dried on them. The hairdresser took one look at me and said, "My land, you were in the sit-in, huh?"

"Yes," I answered. "Do you have time to wash my hair and style it?"

"Right away," she said, and she meant right away. There were three other ladies already waiting, but they seemed glad to let me go ahead of them. The hairdresser was real nice. She even took my stockings off and washed my legs while my hair was drying.

There was a mass rally that night at the Pearl Street Church in Jackson, and the place was packed. People were standing two abreast in the aisles. Before the speakers began, all the sit-inners walked out on the stage and were introduced by Medgar Evers.[3] People stood and applauded for what seemed like thirty minutes or more. Medgar told the audience that this was just the beginning of such demonstrations. He asked them to pledge themselves to unite in a massive offensive against segregation in Jackson, and throughout the state. The rally ended with "We Shall Overcome" and sent home hundreds of determined people. It seemed as though Mississippi Negroes were about to get together at last.   [1968]

Terms

1. NAACP: National Association for the Advancement of Colored People.
2. CORE: Congress of Racial Equality.
3. MEDGAR EVERS: The NAACP field secretary in Mississippi, who was assassinated a few weeks after this event.

Understanding the Reading

1. How do you account for the various reactions of the Whites at the lunch counter when the demonstrators sat down?
2. Why did the high school students respond differently than these people did?
3. Explain the reaction of the women in the beauty shop.

Suggestion for Responding

1. Explain how Moody's experience illustrates the various features of nonviolent resistance. ◆

106

Freedom Is a Constant Struggle

MURIEL TILLINGHAST

Three days after I graduated, I decided I was going to Mississippi. I didn't know what was going to happen after that, but I was definitely going to go. Now, it was already bad enough that I had let my hair grow natural—that eliminated about 90 percent of the discussion in my house—but when I decided to go to Mississippi, everyone got on my case. My parents, my family—people weren't *talking* to me.

We knew that something momentous was occurring down South. People were operating in very small groups, but they were operating in many different places. At that point the press had not yet decided what political perspective they were going to take on events in the South, so they were actually showing all this activity on television. This was a source of encouragement for us and helped to tie the lines of communication together. Of course, that didn't last. Later on, I'm sure the press boys sat down in a large room and said, "Enough of this, let's move on."

Now, I was basically a Northerner—folks from Washington, D.C., like to think that they're from the North. I had already had some experiences on the eastern shore of Maryland, which will let you know immediately that you're not North, but I hadn't really gotten ready for Mississippi. We all spent a week at the orientation center in Oxford, Ohio. SNCC[1] sent up its people, who told us all these tales about what folks had to go through just in terms of a normal life struggle. We knew that Mississippi was going to be a special place. And for all of us who went, we know we didn't come back the same.

HEADING SOUTH

So we went to Mississippi after spending a week getting ready for something you really couldn't get ready for. We headed in on Greyhound buses. People were singing and talking and joking around on the bus, but when we hit that Mississippi line there was silence. People got dropped off at various projects one by one in the dead of night. I was dropped off in Greenville. We made a point of distinguishing Greenville from Greenwood. Green*ville* was relatively liberal. If you were in Green*wood,* you were in deep. I still had hope.

In all honesty I spent my first two weeks in the office upstairs because I didn't know quite how I was going to be able to survive Mississippi. After a while it dawned on me that I would never get anybody to register that way, so I started coming downstairs and cautiously going out into the town. I functioned like a shadow on the wall, just getting used to walking in the streets.

Charles Cobb was my project director. About a month after I got to Mississippi, Charles looked at me and said, "You know, I want to do something else. So I'm going to leave you in charge of this project. You look like you can handle it." Right, sure thing . . .

I was in charge of three counties: Washington, Sharkey, and Issaquena. In Mississippi, you learn the county structure like the back of your hand, because the basis of power politics is the county structure. Greenville, which was the base of our operations, was the Washington County seat. It was the town in a county of hamlets. Sharkey County was the home of the Klan in that part of Mississippi. Issaquena was a Black county, and it was sort of discounted at the time.

By and large we took our mandate from Stokely Carmichael [Kwame Toure], who was the project chief in our area. We were young, and we were just beginning to learn what politics and power were all about. We began to find out that power is monolithic, particularly in places where there is not a lot of competition.

People in Mississippi knew about us long before we had even gotten there. We didn't realize it at first, but we were under constant surveillance. For instance, a young white volunteer was doing some research at the library, which was in the same building as the police station, on the second floor. As she was coming out of the library, the police chief said to her, "Come here, I want to show you something." He took her to a room, and in that room was a file drawer, and in that file drawer were pictures of everybody in our project. We had no idea that they were watching us this closely. And they had pictures of every kind of activity, taken day and night, because they were using infrared.

se pictures may not mean anything
, but there were times when the politi-
ssure really got to us. For example, we
some young gay men who were in our
project, and I remember very tearfully putting
one of them on the bus. He said, "Muriel, I can't
have those pictures shown." I didn't even know
that anything was going on, but the bottom line
is that everybody's privacy was invaded. And
that's *before* we had even registered anybody
to vote.

In these little country towns, as soon as a
foreign-sounding motor comes across the road
in the middle of the night, people know that
a stranger is there. You need never make an
announcement. You can stay in the house all
day—someone knows. "I heard a different
motor last night. It stopped about two doors
down the street." And they start making inqui-
ries. There were instances when the police just
opened the door and came through the house
looking for us and never said a word to any of
the people who lived there. Not that they were
going to rough us up at that point, but someone
knew that someone was keeping company with
people who weren't local.

In order to encourage people to vote, we
had to explain what was going on in the country and why they were in the situation that
they were in. We tried to convince them of the
importance of their participation in the voting
process by showing them who was actually
on the voting rolls—for instance, half the local
cemetery! Sometimes we were able to register
only a few people—why risk your life simply to
sign a piece of paper or register at the county
courthouse—but as people gradually came to
trust us, they would talk to their neighbors, and
the numbers swelled.

THE HEART OF THE BLACK BELT

Later I moved out of Greenville and into
Issaquena County. Until I got to Mississippi,
I didn't know anything about Black counties.
I began to find out that there were these towns
like Mound Bayou outside of Holly Springs
where Blacks had settled after the Emancipation Proclamation and established their own
base.

Most people in the North don't understand
why Blacks are so poor. They don't realize that
when Black people left slavery, they left with
nothing—I mean *nothing*. Whatever they were
wearing, those were the clothes that they took
with them into their new life. Whatever beans
or seeds they could gather, that was going to
be food. They didn't own the land they were
standing on—they were immediately trespassing. And in Mississippi trespassing was a serious
crime—as serious as selling a kilo of cocaine
in New York City today. You were going to go
to jail and your minimum time was going to be
five years—just for standing on the land.

So the people had to move, and when
they moved, they moved under pain of death,
because the same people who had always kept
Black people enslaved were again at work
hunting down those bands of Blacks who were
leaving by foot. Black people had no way of
defending themselves. They had to travel by
night, gathering up at certain places—word
gets around on the grapevine. And they began
to establish themselves in various places, even
in the state of Mississippi. Issaquena was one
of those places. It was sort of a long county,
and very sparsely settled. Counting everybody
standing up, the county seat at Mayersville had
50 people.

Some of you may be familiar with the name
of Unita Blackwell. She made a name for herself over time as the mayor of Mayersville and
as an activist, but when I met Unita, she was
just an ordinary housewife. She and her husband, Jeremiah Blackwell, were the first ones to
offer us a safe haven in Issaquena. That's really
how we operated. We would be invited in by
one household, and based on that household's
sense of us as individuals and where we were
going as an organization—because they knew
that we were not alone—they would introduce
us to someone else. This would be our next
contact. And if this sounds like we were operating under war conditions, we were. You did
not talk to *anybody* unless someone said it was
okay. And it wasn't that obvious who was safe
to talk to, because you never knew if you were
talking to the State Sovereignty Commission.

The State Sovereignty Commission was
an intelligence-gathering force. It was set up
by the government of the state of Mississippi.

Hundreds of thousands of dollars of state tax-payers' money—including Black taxpayers' money—was used to finance all this surveillance. It was responsible for gathering and spreading disinformation early in the game. Early on we thought it was *mis*information—that they just didn't get it straight—but it was really *dis*information that was deliberately designed to undermine public support for the activities that we were engaged in.

You had to be careful about who you spoke to because you could be trailed back to your base. Wherever you were staying, those people were as vulnerable to midnight raids as you were on the streets. So when they allowed you to sleep on their floor or in their best bed in the corner of their house, whatever the accommodations were, they were putting themselves in jeopardy. As Bob Moses used to say, "Mississippi needs no exaggeration." It was its own exaggeration.

I remember one family of cotton pickers that I stayed with—two adults and five kids. They were in Hollandale, a nasty little town on the highway between Greenville and Mayersville. This family was at the very bottom of the economic ladder. They worked by permission on someone else's land. They worked from sun up to sun down with no breaks. It was as close to slavery as I hope I ever see in life. I usually made a point of eating somewhere else, but one night they said, "No, you eat with us." I'll never forget that dinner. It was cornbread and a huge pot of water into which they cut three or four frankfurters. For them that was a *good* dinner.

FOUNDING A FREEDOM SCHOOL

We also started a Freedom School. Why? Well, out of natural curiosity schoolchildren wanted to know, "Why can't we vote?" So there was a need to put this particular situation into some sort of historical context. And as you talked about the history of Black people in this country, you began to see another kind of development taking place in the young people. Before they would let certain things in school go by unchallenged. They might not like something, but they wouldn't question it. Our presence gave them a support base, and they began to

have the courage to say certain things, or not to read certain things, or to bring other materials to the classroom. This was unheard of. And it wouldn't take long before those kids would be sent home, first one kid, then another, and by the time a week had passed, there would be 20 kids who had been told by the principal, "Don't come back!"

Now the school system was segregated—these were Black kids in Black schools—so how could this be happening? To understand that you have to understand the power relations in the South. You don't get to be a Black principal in a Black school in Mississippi unless you are an acceptable political commodity—pure and simple. And you quickly become *un*acceptable when you start having alien thoughts—like why can't we register to vote and what is this Grandfather Clause anyway—just normal conversation. But that wasn't considered normal conversation, that was considered subversive, and these young people had to be plucked out before they spread the cancer to the rest of the student population. So even though most of us tried to maintain a low profile, it didn't take long for brush fires to occur.

SHERIFF DAVIS BUILDS A JAIL

Even though Issaquena was a Black county, all the people who had any power were white, including Sheriff Davis. When our paths crossed, which they did all too frequently, we would greet each other—"How ya doin',"—because Mississippi is country-like in that way. The first time I saw Sheriff Davis coming down the road he had a pickup truck. By the next week the pickup truck had a kind of metal grating on the top. One day he stopped me and said, "You like that, you like what I got? Well, that's for y'all."

And then Sheriff Davis told us that he was building a one-room jail out of cinder blocks—just for us! And did we like that? It was big enough to stand up in, you could sit down, and of course it was out there in the middle of the hot sun. When we told him he was really wasting his time, Sheriff Davis said, "Well, I know you're gonna do something. I know you are, and I'll keep up with you." Sometimes when we would go walking down the street, there was Sheriff

Davis's car, coming right behind us. He'd sit in the front and wait, and sometimes we'd go past the person's house and go to somebody else's house in the back, because we didn't want to lead him directly to our next possible registrant.

I don't think we understand what people risked when they took those steps. As soon as we had made contact with people, as soon as they went to the courthouse to register, their boss would be right there. If they worked in the cotton fields, oftentimes they were dismissed immediately. Or they'd be cut off of their welfare rations. The power system was consolidated on the notion that no, you will not move up, you will not challenge us in any way.

Welcoming the Klan

Then we began to look at other things that were going on. Why could some people plant cotton when others couldn't? There were these gentlemen farmers who planted nothing but made an awful lot of money, and then there were people who were planting cotton but were barely able to get it ginned. So early on, we began to deal with the cotton allotment system. Well, when we began to run people for the cotton allotment board, we hit the economic bell. And that brought out the Klan.

Sometimes the Klan seemed benign compared to some of the other rabid, racist organizations, like the Association for the Preservation of the White Race, who made no bones about the fact that if they saw you, they were going to kill you.

One time I called a meeting of tractor workers, thinking that I was going to organize *Black* tractor workers, and I walked right dead into a nest of Klansmen who had gotten the same word. I don't know who had told them, but they were there. As I approached them in my car—carefully—I was wondering who were all these white men standing at the church steps. They knew something was wrong because the place of the meeting was a Black church, and they didn't look happy. I kind of looked at them. They kind of looked at me. I said, "You here for the meetin'?" and they said, "Yeah. You called the meetin'?" I said, "No. I'm just looking for the person who called the meetin'." And I kind of backed on out and left.

All of us learned how to be patient, how to play for the occasion, because your life could turn on a dime. Later you might laugh, but at the time it wouldn't seem so funny. Like the time I ran into the police car. Now, you should have seen me jump out of my car all incensed, carrying on about this and that, with this poor white volunteer sitting next to me. He just knew we were dead. But this policeman was so disgusted with me that he just told me to get a move on.

Life Lessons

One of the things I have learned about doing political work is that you may not be serious, or you may not know how serious a step you're taking, but when the opposition see anybody treading on their territory, they're *always* serious.

We had so many near misses, so many close calls, and we had nobody to depend on but ourselves. If you had a problem you sure couldn't call a cop! Which is almost the same situation [in which] the Black community finds itself in the inner cities today. If you have a problem and you call the cop, the cop is going to give you a *bigger* problem. So we learned to handle things ourselves as best we could.

Most of all we learned that people in Mississippi were a very special group of people. They were our country's peasant base. They were incredible in their wisdom, and many had extreme courage. I can remember this guy, Applewhite. Now Applewhite was a placid, nondescript kind of guy. You were never quite sure whether what you had to say registered or not. I didn't like riding with Applewhite because I felt that if I was going to get pushed into something, I was going to be on my own. One day we were riding down the road, and I said to Applewhite, "Do you have anything in this car in case we get stopped?" Well, you would never know what was going on in Applewhite's head—he had a perfect poker face. "Open up the glove compartment," he said. "Check down underneath the seat on my side. And on your side. Listen, we may not survive, but we sure could blaze a few holes." I said, "That's the way I want to go."

I learned that people aren't always what they appear. At the same time you're trying to organize them, they're trying to figure out where you are in this constellation of players. Are you going to be around when the action goes down? Am I talking to the State Sovereignty Commission? And essentially, is what you're telling me true? That's why we always encouraged people to read. We always encouraged people to discuss. Nothing that we did was cloaked in any kind of secrecy, which is the way I've continued to operate.

So that was my life for two years. It was about day-to-day survival but it was also about how you transform a community that really had not been touched in over 100 years by any outside force—how you get it to join the twentieth century and get enough players inside that loop to be able to carry it on after you leave. On the whole, I think we were very successful. We paid some very, very high prices for it, but I think most of us would have done it again.   [1994]

Term

1. SNCC: Student Nonviolent Coordinating Committee.

Understanding the Reading

1. How were the volunteers prepared for going to Mississippi?
2. What were Tillinghast's responsibilities in Mississippi?
3. In what ways were the volunteers threatened by law enforcement?
4. How did the volunteers persuade people to register to vote?
5. Why were southern Blacks so poor?
6. What was the State Sovereignty Commission?
7. What was the Freedom School, and why was it established?
8. What tactics did Sheriff Davis use to intimidate the volunteers?
9. Why did Tillinghast feel the volunteers had to handle problems on their own?
10. How did she feel about the Mississippi Blacks?

Suggestions for Responding

1. List the various resistance tactics White Mississippians used, and rank-order them based on your sense of their effectiveness, justifying your choices.

2. Consider one of the experiences Tillinghast describes, and write a short narrative or essay describing how you think you might have reacted to it. Comment on how you wish you might have reacted instead. ✦

107

"Don't Tell Us It Can't Be Done"

MICHAEL RYAN

Martha Yallup, Sister Kathleen Ross and their colleagues made something wonderful happen on the Yakima Indian Reservation in Washington State a decade ago. In a poor area where higher education was almost inaccessible, they began to train Head Start[1] teachers from the Indian communities. It was hard work, but it was doubly rewarding. Not only did the program give adults new skills, but it also helped provide a leg up for the children born into the grueling poverty of the reservation. For Martha, the tribe's Head Start director, and Sister Kathleen, the academic vice president of Fort Wright College in Spokane, the program was a splendid example of how a private college and a community group could work together to change lives.

Then disaster struck.

"In 1980, the board of Fort Wright decided to close the college," Sister Kathleen recalls. "I had the job of coming down here and telling Martha that we were going to have to end the program because the home campus was closing. I gave her the bad news, and I remember she just looked at me and said: 'No, it's not closing.'"

Instead of sitting by and watching their dream die, Martha Yallup got together with a colleague, Violet Rau, and Sister Kathleen and decided on a plan of incredible daring: They would start a college on their own.

The idea seemed as doomed as it was courageous. The reservation was no place to raise the funds needed to start a college from scratch. And Fort Wright was in no position to help much. A small liberal-arts school run by the Catholic Sisters of the Holy Names of Jesus and Mary, it had been driven out of business by competition from larger, better-financed schools. And, although Martha and Violet were confident, virtually nobody believed in them—except Sister Kathleen. "People on the reservation said, 'You're crazy. It's going to fail," Martha recalls.

But Martha and Violet went to work on the reservation, lining up community leaders, public officials and business people to form a board of directors for the new college—and to start raising money for it. Back in Spokane, Sister Kathleen persuaded college officials to keep Fort Wright open through the spring of 1982. Then the hard work began.

First, the new college needed recognition from the IRS[2] so that it could accept donations. Sister Kathleen fought her way through the agency's bureaucracy and emerged with official recognition. Then the women tried to persuade the authorities to transfer Fort Wright's accreditation to their new school. "Our philosophy had always been, 'If you don't ask, you don't get," Martha says with a laugh. They failed, but they made a strong enough case that they were granted candidate status—the last step before full accreditation. That meant that their new school's courses could be recognized for full credit by other institutions.

But they had one more obstacle to clear: A college designed for some of the poorest people in the country would have to be able to offer financial aid. And the federal government's rule held that a school must be in business two years before its students qualify for federal loans. "We went to the top person in the Seattle office," Sister Kathleen says, "and he said, 'There's got to be a way,' so I asked him if I could see the book of regulations." She found a section that allowed the government to authorize financial aid when a school is sold to a new owner. It was clearly intended to cover vocational schools, but the rule didn't say that explicitly. "The guy looked at me like I was crazy," Sister Kathleen recalls. "Then he said, 'Why not?" Sister Kathleen and her board of directors purchased their education program from Fort Wright for $1, and a new college was born.

The day I went to visit, Heritage College had been in business for eight years. It is a nondenominational institution—although a small group of nuns still holds key administrative positions at the school. Sister Kathleen Ross has been the president since before the college opened its doors. Martha Yallup, now the deputy director of the Yakima tribe's Department of Human Services, was the board's first chair and still serves as its secretary.

But the story that began with the determination of a handful of courageous women has become a story of courage and determination on the part of hundreds. This year, Heritage College will confer 199 degrees and certificates. The average Heritage student is 35 and, as the faculty likes to say, "place-bound"—inhibited by family and work commitments from traveling the 90 minutes it takes to get to the nearest college off the reservation. For most of the students, college is a dream which could never have come true without Heritage.

If you want to know how great the accomplishment of Sister Kathleen, Martha Yallup and the others is, meet Hipolito Mendez. He may be the typical Heritage student—an industrious, outgoing man who works part-time to pay his tuition and speaks eagerly of his planned career as a high school teacher. He is also a 47-year-old father of five. "My wife and I had a business, and it went down the tubes," he says. "We decided, 'Now's the time to go back to school and do something with our lives.' But we discovered we just couldn't afford to go to the state university. There wasn't much hope for us. Then we heard about Heritage."

Admittedly, he says, it felt strange for a man in middle age to become a college student, but Mendez found that Heritage's emphasis on personalized education eased his transition. "The first week, I was apprehensive," he says. "After that, I fit right in." Next fall, he will begin a new life as an educator—and his wife, Paula, will start teaching elementary school as well.

Or look at how Heritage has changed the life of Edith Walsey, 32. "If this college wasn't here, I wouldn't have gone to college, because of my family and my tradition and my husband," she confides. "I'm from the Warm Springs reservation in Oregon. The teachers here understand my customs. At first, it was kind of hard for me. My husband wasn't for me going to school. We have three children. Now he takes care of them while I'm in class and working part-time. I'm a junior studying computers. When I graduate, I hope to go home and work with my tribe."

In its eight years of existence, Heritage has grown from a three-room cottage to a set of buildings on the campus of a former elementary school in the reservation town of Toppenish. It now has 25 full-time faculty, an additional 70 or so part-time, and more than 400 degree-holding alumni. These are impressive statistics, but not as impressive as the testimonial one recent graduate gave Sister Kathleen last year. A native of the reservation, she had gone away to college but dropped out, feeling uncomfortable in an alien culture. Then she heard about Heritage. She enrolled and finished her degree. In one sentence, she summed up the magic of the school. As she told Sister Kathleen: "You allowed me not to be a failure."   [1991]

Terms

1. HEAD START: A federal program for disadvantaged preschoolers.
2. IRS: Internal Revenue Service.

Understanding the Reading

1. What problems did Yallup, Rau, and Sister Kathleen face in starting Heritage College?
2. How did they overcome each of them?
3. Evaluate the effectiveness of the project.

Suggestion for Responding

1. Describe a time when you faced what seemed to be impossible obstacles, and explain how you tackled them, alone or with the help of others. ✦

108

Saving Native Lands

VALERIE TALIMAN

When JoAnn Tall drives past the Wounded Knee burial site near her home on the Pine Ridge Indian Reservation in South Dakota, she remembers the more than 300 Lakota people—mainly unarmed women and children—who were gunned-down there by the U.S. military in the winter of 1890. The massacre forever changed the lives of the Lakota; not only were vast homelands stolen through subsequent broken treaties, but the slaughter marked the beginning of nearly a century of U.S. government suppression of Lakota religious and cultural practices.

This tragic legacy has fueled much of Tall's commitment to resisting the continued oppression and exploitation of her people. Tall, an Oglala Lakota mother of eight, has long been active in the struggle to sustain and nurture Native communities. Still, she was surprised last April when the San Francisco-based Goldman Environmental Foundation awarded her $60,000 as one of 1993's seven "environmental heroes" from around the world, who have, despite extreme hardships, committed themselves to grassroots activism.

Tall, 41, was chosen for her organizing efforts to stop toxic waste dumps and nuclear weapons testing on Indian lands. Her activism spans more than 20 years, much of it focused on the environment, most of it done behind the scenes without credit. She speaks modestly of her accomplishments, noting that "there are a lot of strong women doing this work that you never hear about. Every now and then we get lucky and one of us gets an award. But a lot more never get recognized, and yet they continue."

Tall says her dedication to environmental work is grounded in the Lakota's reverence for the natural world. To her people, Grandmother Earth (Unci Maka) is not owned, much less bought and sold. Generations upon generations of Lakota are buried throughout the Northern Plains, and many sacred places lie within their homelands. Unci Maka has sustained Her children throughout creation and must be granted reciprocal respect, according to the Lakota worldview.

Guided by a spiritual commitment that came to her over the years in Lakota ceremonies and in dreams, Tall has spent a lifetime grappling with conflict and poverty, confronting government, corporate, and even military forces that threaten Native lives and land. At 20, she was involved in the 1973 armed occupation of Wounded Knee, where elder Oglala women had assumed leadership of a resistance movement against U.S. domination over tribal government, lands, and rights.

"It was a war, an invasion of our homeland," Tall remembers. "Federal agents were shooting at us, even women and children, and I knew I could get killed. But I thought, 'How dare they—this is *our* land!' I learned how to deal with fear at Wounded Knee."

This resolve has served her in subsequent confrontations. For example, in 1987 the defense contractor Honeywell announced plans to conduct weapons tests in a Black Hills canyon that is an ancient burial and ceremonial site. Tall strode into a hearing where corporate officials were courting the Lakota residents with a slick public relations presentation. "I tore into the PR guy," she recalls. "I said, 'How dare you try to desecrate our church? That's what the Black Hills mean to us; they're our church.' I told him, 'We're going to win this war.'"

Tall immediately helped organize a resistance camp of about 150 people, who refused to leave the canyon for three months until Honeywell backed out. "During one of our ceremonies, I had a vision that symbolized the seven generations to come and I knew this missile testing would be the beginning of the end for us," Tall said. "With the help of our medicine people, we made a spiritual commitment to protect the canyon, and we won."

Inspired by this triumph, Tall cofounded the Native Resource Coalition, which stopped Connecticut-based O & G Industries from building a 5,000-acre landfill and incinerator on the Pine Ridge reservation. The coalition later found that more than 60 Indian communities had been targeted for toxic-waste sites within a two-year period.

The powerful waste industry had discovered that there are often fewer regulations governing toxic waste on Indian reservations than on land under state, county, and municipal jurisdictions. Attempting to exploit the sovereign status of tribal governments, many waste merchants began offering deals disguised as "economic development" to poverty-stricken tribes desperately in need of jobs. To make matters worse, the waste industry chose communities where language barriers exist. In many Native languages, there are no words for dioxins, PCBs, or other poisons, so the dangers are impossible to explain and translators' high-tech rhetoric makes the million-dollar waste deals sound safe.

Outraged by the idea that tribal lands were being targeted as dumping grounds, the Native Resource Coalition joined with other grassroots groups in 1991 to host a national environmental conference in the Black Hills. The meeting was designed to alert tribes to the environmental racism and economic blackmail directed at Native people, who retain only 4 percent of U.S. land. At this gathering, Tall helped form the Indigenous Environmental Network, which now boasts more than 50 member organizations helping to educate and protect Native people in the U.S. and Canada.

Tall is but one of many Native women who are doing this work. "Our women come from a long line of resistance," she notes. "History tells us that we are the backbone of everything that is." Indeed, in Native societies women are not only life-givers, caretakers, clan mothers, and matriarchs, but they are truly the center of Indian communities.

"Contrary to those images of meekness, docility, and subordination to males with which we women typically have been portrayed by the dominant culture's books and movies, anthropology, and political ideologues . . . it is women who have formed the very core of indigenous resistance to genocide and colonization since the first moment of conflict between Indians and invaders," says Juaneño/Yaqui scholar M. Annette Jaimes.

Protecting the environment is fundamental to the survival of Native peoples, many of whom still depend on their aboriginal rights to hunt, fish, and harvest natural foods and medicines. The identities, spiritual ways, cultures, and health of more than 500 Native nations in the U.S. hinge on their ability to live in a respectful interdependent relationship with their homelands.

Destruction of Native lands caused by government and industry includes strip-mining, coal-burning power plants, unregulated dumps, intensive logging, hydroelectric dams, uranium mining, contamination of rivers and waterways, and more than 800 nuclear bombs exploded as "tests." In every instance of activism against this destruction, Native women have been on the front lines. From the Navajo grandmothers fighting relocation at Big Mountain, Arizona, to the Dann sisters' stand to save Western Shoshone homelands in Nevada, to Onondaga clan mothers in New York fighting James Bay Hydro, they persevere in the resistance.   [1994]

Understanding the Reading

1. Why did JoAnn Tall receive an award for being an "environmental hero"?
2. Why did Tall oppose the Honeywell test plans?
3. What did the Native Resource Coalition accomplish?
4. Why has the waste industry targeted reservations?
5. What role do Native American women play in their society?
6. Why are Native Americans especially concerned about their homelands and the environment?

Suggestion for Responding

1. Research and report on the 1973 armed occupation of Wounded Knee. ✦

109

Cecilia Fire Thunder: She Inspires Her People

Ann Davis

Cecilia Fire Thunder hunches over a doll she's making, clamping one more silver buckle on the belt before she fastens it to a dark blue, shell-decorated dress. The kitchen table where she works is a cluttered stage of tall, elegant Plains Indian women, hands outstretched with an eagle wing fan or holding a fringed shawl close in to their waists.

Her small trailer home on the Pine Ridge reservation in South Dakota is a Frankenstein's[1] laboratory—plastic bags full of arms, legs, and torsos bulge beneath the planter, overflow

behind the TV. Corpses waiting for heads line the sofa.

Fire Thunder sits back and studies the doll, reading glasses perched at the end of her nose. "Some of that old stuff is ugly," she mutters, attaching a small buckskin bag to the belt. "I like my bodies to resemble bodies—they don't have to look like stuffed tamales."

When Fire Thunder started making dolls a few years ago, her original impetus was simple: to reflect contemporary Plains Indian women, the friends she dances with at pow-wows around the Midwest. When her foot-high dolls won her awards and trips to Washington, D.C., to demonstrate dollmaking techniques at the Smithsonian, she took it in stride. Making art is part of her life, and speaking in public goes with the territory.

You might think dollmaking an utterly apolitical activity. Not for Fire Thunder. Even her dolls are lessons in history and cultural values. The cowrie shells on her traditional dolls reveal the extensive trade routes existing between tribes on the West Coast and the Great Plains. The tanned hides are a vehicle to talk about the Lakota's relation to other life forms and their philosophy of natural harmony.

When she talks to non-Indian audiences, Fire Thunder uses the dolls to clear away misconceptions about Native Americans. When she speaks in local schools, she uses her dolls to talk about traditional values and the problems of drugs and alcohol.

"I talk to high school kids, not about how it should be, but about how it is," Fire Thunder said. Instead of lecturing about the evils of substance abuse, Fire Thunder asks them point-blank how many still do drugs, even after years of being preached at in the schools. Most raise their hands. Then they tell her about growing up in alcoholic homes, about nights of no sleep, worrying whether they'll get beat up by a drunk adult.

Even though students understand that drugs and alcohol are bad for them, Fire Thunder believes they will not change their behavior until adult problem drinkers admit it and share their experiences with younger people.

Fire Thunder says that part of the reason she can reach Indian people at a gut level is because she is one of them. She can tell jokes that non-Indians could never get away with, jokes that in a humorous way reveal people's dysfunctional behavior to themselves. For instance, What is Indian love? Answer: a black eye and a hickie.

"The gift I have is my humor, my gift to communicate," Fire Thunder said. "No white person can say what I say." She believes it is up to Indian people to solve their own problems.

When asked if she ever gets overwhelmed by all the work, Fire Thunder says no. "My passion is what I do. The most important thing I have is that I know who I am," she says. "I still have a lot of quirks, but my identity is pretty strong. And I know when to play."

Out on the dance floor in the Rapid City Civic Center, Fire Thunder wears her traditional women's dress, decorated with cowrie shells and a handsome silver belt. Like the Pied Piper,[2] she breaks away from the movement of the group and leads a long snakeline of women in and out around a kaleidoscope of feathers and swirling fringe. She bends her head to hear a joke, laughs and continues her swinging walk, head tilted back elegantly, like one of her dolls. She's easy to pick out among hundreds of dancers. "If you feel good about yourself, you're just going to shine," says Cecilia Fire Thunder, and she does.

Fire Thunder goes non-stop. A dazzling public speaker, organizer in her home community of the Pine Ridge reservation, a founder of the Oglala Lakota Women's Society, registered nurse, mother, political lobbyist, pow-wow enthusiast, traditional dollmaker, KILI radio personality: you might think this enough for a lifetime or two. But this summer, Fire Thunder, who ran for tribal president—and lost—was also appointed tribal health planner for the Pine Ridge reservation and charged with building the first comprehensive plan to fight alcoholism.

Many community groups approved when Fire Thunder was appointed to the sensitive political post. "If anyone can do it, she can," was the comment heard frequently around the tribal office, according to Taylor Little White Man, executive director of the Oglala Sioux Tribe.

Like her dolls, she is tall and captivating with deep brown eyes, a brilliant smile and abundant energy. And some internal switch seems to have locked in the "on" position when Fire

Thunder was born. It's an intensity that delights some and frustrates others. Her rebelliousness infuriated the nuns at Red Cloud Indian School, a Catholic boarding school she attended until tenth grade. The nuns tried to convince the head priest not to let her come back; she was too influential with the other girls.

She rebelled most against the violence: How the religious brothers beat boys with thick belt-straps outside the girls' classroom windows. How the nuns humiliated "bad" girls by forcing them to bend over a big piano in front of the class, pulling down their panties and smacking them with rulers. How they did things so bad that Fire Thunder won't tell me about them.

"They hurt us to make us cry because once you cried, they'd defeated you," she said.

It took Fire Thunder years to undo the emotional damage caused by the boarding school, an internalized violence she feels she carried into her relationship with her children. "In order to do what I do, you have to confront your own devils, because something or someone will remind you of your past," Fire Thunder said. Fire Thunder's attempts at easing children's suffering is a constant in her work as community organizer, health planner, speaker, even dollmaker.

Inspired by her meeting with organizer Eileen Iron Cloud at a pow-wow in Colorado, and their discussions about empowering women and influencing state legislation at Pine Ridge, Fire Thunder, along with Iron Cloud, formed the Oglala Lakota Women's Society in 1987.

Fire Thunder recounts Lakota spiritual tradition, saying that thousands of years ago a woman gave her people a pipe and told them how to pray with it in ceremonies. This woman who came among the people was the inspiration for the women's society, says Fire Thunder. Through the society, women are able to air their concerns about community and tribal affairs.

Repeatedly, the number one issue on the nine reservations was alcohol. Not a surprising statistic, since some nine out of ten people on Pine Ridge are alcoholic.

"Part of community organizing is getting people to tell you what you already know," Fire Thunder said.

Now that women had identified their major focus, the group decided to take on the candidates for tribal election. Fire Thunder talked about sober leadership on her radio show; the women's society sent out 1,000 mailings urging voters to support sober leaders. At stump speeches, women badgered the candidates to state whether they still drank. "We didn't care who you were, what you did, what kind of past you had," Fire Thunder said. "If you were sober, we were gonna vote for you."

Though their criteria were crude, their results were impressive: after the smoke cleared on election night, 11 of the 16 new tribal council members were declared non-drinkers.

The domestic violence was next. Tribal law had required that women sign a complaint against abusive partners before the police would act. In 1988, the women's society lobbied for and won a mandatory arrest law for domestic violence. Since fall of last year, whenever there is probable cause of domestic abuse, the perpetrator automatically spends the night in jail. The complaint is signed by the arresting officer. At first, a lot of "men in shock" were sitting in jail cells, Fire Thunder said. The women's society was criticized as "manhaters" and the trial court briefly tried to overturn the law. But most have now come to accept mandatory arrest as reality.

Part of the women's focus was on helping abusive men to change. Through their efforts, they won a grant to provide counseling to men who batter. "We did this because we also love our men," Fire Thunder said. "We want them to understand their rage and anger."

The society's other main concern was child sexual abuse. In 1988, the group staged a candlelight march in support of National Child Abuse Prevention Month. Last year, they went one step further by letting abused children speak out about their experience. In a two-hour show broadcast live on radio station KILI, six children talked about how it felt to be beaten, raped, ridiculed and neglected. "In those two hours, we reached more people in the listening audience than with anything else we ever did," Fire Thunder said.

Such confrontational tactics have not always made her a popular figure. She and others in the women's society have been accused of butting into other people's business. Some reservation people have complained that women's groups are not "traditional."

But Fire Thunder brushes off the criticism, saying she is motivated more by the pain of children than the fear of criticism. "When oppression is so great, there's no nice way to get to the heart of the people," she said. "The only way was 'shock treatment'—hit 'em hard and shake 'em up. Now that they've accomplished an awareness of issues on Pine Ridge, their tactics can change," she said.

The fierce pace of the women's society has slowed in the past year. Iron Cloud says the group lost its focus. She has been studying organizing models and believes that [the] women's society needs to reorient itself to keep all women involved, rather than having a few do all the work.

Fire Thunder believes everyone just got worn out. "We pulled back because we had to. For three years, we gave 150 percent of everything in our lives" to the women's society, she [says]. Fire Thunder agrees the group needs to restructure itself for the next phase of work.

Some say Fire Thunder sold out when she accepted a position with the tribal government this summer. "They say, 'Oh, they're gonna shut her up,'" Fire Thunder says. "But I took the position with the understanding that I could do more."

Though Iron Cloud counseled her not to take the new job, she believes Fire Thunder has the strength to hang in there and not sell out to political interests.

Perhaps she will. Fire Thunder has already written grants for half a million dollars and taken charge of the committee overseeing a new plan to house all alcohol programs under one roof. She says the tribe has a lot of catching up to do to enable people to face the pain of their addictions.   [1991]

Terms

1. FRANKENSTEIN: A fictional scientist who created a monster that destroyed its maker.
2. PIED PIPER: A legendary piper whose music charmed first the rats and then the village children into following him out of town forever.

Understanding the Reading

1. What tactics does Fire Thunder use in her work with high school students?
2. What is the purpose of the Oglala Lakota Women's Society?

3. What tactics did Fire Thunder employ to combat alcoholism on the Lakota reservation?
4. How did she address the problem of domestic violence?
5. What did she do about the problem of child abuse?

Suggestion for Responding

1. The article reports that the Women's Society has lost its earlier momentum. Using your knowledge about the change process, what advice would you give them (or a similar group working on some community problem) about the one specific outcome that you feel is most necessary? Explain its priority and the strategies you would recommend to realize that outcome. ◆

110

Claiming Respect for Ancestral Remains: Repatriation and the Caddo Nation of Oklahoma

ROBERT L. CAST,
BOBBY GONZALEZ, AND
TIMOTHY K. PERTTULA

Since the passage of the Native American Graves Protection and Repatriation Act (NAGPRA) in 1990, the Caddo Nation of Oklahoma has repatriated hundreds of sets of prehistoric and historic Caddo human remains and thousands of associated and unassociated funerary objects. At least 130 museum facilities have human remains and funerary objects culturally affiliated to the Caddo. In this article, we discuss the importance of repatriation to the Caddo Nation and the role of the Caddo Repatriation Committee within the tribal government, and we provide concrete examples of several repatriation efforts and accomplishments.

The Caddo have one primary burial tradition with particularly important implications for the repatriation and reburial of human remains and funerary objects.

Caddo spiritual belief dictates that funerary objects (such as ceramic vessels) are to be placed in the grave of the deceased person as containers to hold and provide sustenance for them on their journey in the afterlife. If these objects are separated from the person, the Caddo believe that this journey has been interrupted. A large part of our NAGPRA work is spent obtaining information and documentation to reunite funerary objects with human remains so they can then be reburied to fulfill this traditional Caddo need. Sometimes, unfortunately, this cannot be accomplished because of the great dispersion of human remains and funerary offerings from sites and burials among several different museum facilities.

ORGANIZATION

The Caddo peoples lived in contiguous portions of Arkansas, Louisiana, Oklahoma and Texas (an area of about 180,000 square km) from time immemorial until they were removed—first by treaty with the United States of America in 1835, and then through force of arms from the Brazos Reserve by Texans in 1859—from their traditional homelands and forced to resettle in western Oklahoma. This painful history of forced migration gives contemporary repatriation efforts particular significance.

The Caddo Nation Repatriation Committee was formed through a tribal resolution in 1996. The committee consists of traditional elders that still speak the language and actively participate in hosting and attending annual dances; teaching Caddo songs and dances to young people; and performing the reburial ceremonies of human remains and associated funerary objects culturally affiliated to the Caddo Nation under NAGPRA. The committee has been instrumental in providing insight and guidance by attending regular meetings with Caddo Nation Cultural Preservation Department (CPD) staff and addressing the sensitive issues of repatriation, burial practices and traditions, reburial of human remains and associated funerary objects, and the education of the general public about the Caddo through exhibits in the Caddo Nation Heritage Museum in Binger, OK.

Through input from the Repatriation Committee, the Caddo's CPD has developed agreements with museums and repositories that have collections in their possession and control that fall under NAGPRA regulation. These agreements focus on the treatment, care and handling of Caddo funerary objects, objects of cultural patrimony, and sacred objects, with an emphasis on insuring the traditional treatment of items in the collections. For example, the Caddo believe that a light of some sort should be left on where any human remains are being housed. To date, the Caddo have agreements with Northwestern State University (in Natchitoches, LA), the Sam Noble Oklahoma Museum of Natural History at the University of Oklahoma, the Texas Archeological Research Laboratory at the University of Texas, and the Arkansas Archeological Survey.

CONSULTATION

Through these agreements, the Repatriation Committee has had an important role in consultations addressing the analysis of human remains and funerary objects in archeological research being done on Caddo sites and with collections from the Caddo Nation's original homelands. One of the stipulations of the agreements addresses the need for students and researchers interested in doing work with any collections defined as being culturally affiliated with the Caddo to consult with the Caddo before beginning a research project where these collections may be needed as part of ongoing research or comparative analysis. There are a handful of archaeologists and anthropologists with an interest in the Caddo who have requested input on a variety of research proposals, ranging from documenting the temporal and spatial distributions of Caddo pottery found in burials; to determining the importance of maize in the prehistoric Caddo diet; and to bioarcheological analysis of human crania, especially the distinctive Caddo practice of cranial modeling.

The Repatriation Committee makes its recommendations of support or opposition to these proposals and analyses on a case-by-case basis. Oftentimes, a researcher may presuppose that the Repatriation Committee will deny any request involving the analysis of human remains; however, this historically has not been the case. Any types of destructive analysis of human remains (for purposes of radiocarbon dating or isotope analysis) certainly tend to be taboo, but there have been several instances where the Repatriation Committee has approved destructive analysis.

Through this collaborative process, researchers who plan to work with collections that are culturally affiliated to the Caddo quickly learn they must communicate effectively, be ready to ask and answer many questions, and be prepared to consult appropriately about their specific research interests. They must also be prepared to share their results with the committee, and to have their findings scrutinized by the CPD and our archeological consultants. This collegial process of consultation and information-sharing helps to not only better prepare graduate students for their future in the discipline, but also to better prepare our staff and committee members for understanding the variety of complex research approaches being proposed by universities and repositories continuing to work with collections affiliated with Native American tribes.

REPATRIATION

The actual repatriation of human remains, funerary objects, sacred objects, and objects of cultural patrimony has been variable. In some cases putting all the pieces of a NAGPRA puzzle back together, such as finding which institution has human remains and which institution (that just happens to be a thousand miles away) has associated funerary objects, is a daunting task. We have completed NAGPRA repatriations that took years of careful negotiation to accomplish, and we have also repatriated skulls and funerary objects while standing in a parking lot. In that particular non-NAGPRA case, the human remains and objects had been given to an individual from a known looter, who then returned them to us.

We have also repatriated human remains and funerary objects under the National Museum of the American Indian Act from the Natchitoches National Fish Hatchery in Louisiana, and have collaborated with a wide variety of other government entities on repatriation efforts in recent years. Working in conjunction with representatives of the Federal Highway Administration and the Texas Department of Transportation, after five years of consultation the Caddo were able to see that 27 individuals and their associated funerary objects, recovered in excavations at a sixteenth- and seventeenth-century Caddo cemetery, were reburied in a local cemetery in Mount Pleasant, TX. These repatriations are milestones for the Caddo people. Having ancestral Caddo remains and funerary objects finally treated with some modicum of respect is a large part of what the CPD, the Repatriation Committee and the Caddo Nation strive to achieve.   [2010]

Understanding the Reading

1. What is NAGPRA and why is it important to Native Americans and non–Native Americans?
2. Name some burial traditions that are especially important to the Caddo Nation of Oklahoma.
3. Besides working in cooperative relationships with many governmental and educational entities and with other native tribes, has the Repatriation Committee had success in returning remains and funerary objects to their burial sites?

Suggestion for Responding

1. Discuss why this is such an important topic, especially for Native Americans. ◆

111

Friends of Justice: Take Heart

DEB PRICE

Decade after decade, federal workers fired for being homosexual left quietly, without protest. That was until 1957, when Uncle Sam decided to kick out Frank Kameny, then a meek astronomer working for the Army Map Service.

"I took that as a declaration of war by my government upon me," Kameny recalls. "And I don't grant my government the right to declare war on me."

Suddenly radicalized, Kameny did the unthinkable: He fought back.

He poured all his meager financial resources into a long-shot appeal. Despite a doctorate from Harvard, he was impoverished by the federal blackball, which kept him from entering the young aerospace industry or returning to academia. For months he survived on 20 cents' worth of food a day.

Teaching himself the intricacies of law, he pursued his case in the courts, finally writing his own petition to the Supreme Court. Turned away by the "supreme injustices," as he calls them, he never was reinstated. His career as an observational astronomer was over. Yet he ultimately won what turned out to be an 18-year war.

Federal personnel officials "surrendered to me on July 3, 1975," Kameny says gleefully in his Washington, D.C. home. The Civil Service Commission announced homosexuality was no longer grounds for dismissals.

That historic change followed years of successful battles that Kameny waged for other gay workers fired from their federal jobs or denied security clearances. The nominal fees he charged his gay clients for his renowned expertise largely supported him.

"I've stabbed myself in the back," he jokes in his booming voice. "By killing the (anti-gay) issue as an activist, I have deprived myself of an income as a self-characterized paralegal."

Kameny credits his days as an Army private at World War II's front lines for his pit-bull activist style. "I dug my way across Germany . . . slit trench by slit trench," the former mortar-shell loader says.

That tenaciousness has served Kameny well in his many protracted battles to ensure gay people full equality. Now 68, the cheerfully dogged Kameny, surrounded by stacks of documents from his paper wars, ticks off his awesome victories with the pride of a four-star general.

His most recent triumph was the . . . repeal of Washington, D.C.'s sodomy law. While actual prosecutions are rare, sodomy laws are indirectly used to tar gay people and deny them jobs and even their own children in custody disputes. He began that fight 30 years ago as the first person to publicly denounce D.C.'s antiquated law in testimony before Congress.

Even in his defeats, Kameny gained gay ground by staking out new territory: In 1971, for example, he became the first openly gay person to run for public office when he competed for D.C. congressional delegate. Today, 128 openly gay people hold elective public office.

Kameny laid the groundwork for his most profound success in 1961 when he founded the D.C. branch of the Mattachine Society, an early gay rights group. The gay movement of that pre-Stonewall[1] era was "bland and apologetic and unassertive," Kameny recalls. He opted instead for "militancy and activism."

Kameny soon realized that a major stumbling block was the theory that gay people were mentally ill. Drawing on his formidable scientific skills, he dove in and found "shoddy . . . and just plain sleazy research in which moral, cultural and theological value judgments were cloaked in the language of science."

And so began his 10-year war with the American Psychiatric Association [APA]. "They surrendered about noontime on Dec. 15, 1973," Kameny notes with his characteristic precision, when APA's trustees voted that homosexuality was not an illness. "In one fell swoop, 15 million gay people were cured!"

Today, with his eyes fixed not on the stars but on the earthly territory yet to be won, the former astronomer is mapping a new strategy for his 31-year-old assault on the military's gay ban. "I tend not to lose my wars," he says confidently. Friends of justice should take heart.   [1993]

Term

1. PRE-STONEWALL: In 1969, gays rioted in response to a police raid on a homosexual bar in New York City, initiating the gay rights movement.

Understanding the Reading

1. How did Kameny cause the federal government to change its policy on homosexuality?
2. Why did he fight Washington's sodomy law?
3. On what grounds did Kameny attack the American Psychiatric Association's labeling of homosexuality as a mental illness?

Suggestions for Responding

1. Write a short essay explaining your reaction to Kameny's accomplishment.
2. Research and report on the Stonewall riot. ◆

SUGGESTIONS FOR RESPONDING TO PART IX

1. Write a personal essay describing yourself as a change maker. Make clear what problem you decided to work on, how you chose to attack it, what happened, and how successful (or unsuccessful) your effort was.
2. Make an oral presentation to the class about your action project, briefly covering the points raised in question 1.
3. Research a civil rights activist or organization, focusing on one particular action he, she, or they undertook. Write an essay describing and evaluating the project.
4. Investigate a group on your campus or in your community that is working to implement a change you consider desirable. Write an article for your local newspaper publicizing the group's efforts.
5. Explain how you are personally affected by our diverse, multicultural American society.
6. In the 1890s, Ida B. Wells-Barnett exposed and fought the racist use of lynching to control Black males, especially those who were perceived as economic threats to local Whites. Report on her work, including statistics on the incidence of lynching when she initiated her campaign and after it was underway.

SUGGESTIONS FOR RESPONDING TO CHANGE

Throughout history, important social and economic change has been the result of organized movements. The following assignments are intended to give you a better understanding of organized nongovernmental forces that have changed life in America.

1. Research the origins of a specific labor union, such as the American Federation of Labor and Congress of Industrial Organizations (AFL-CIO); Actors' Equity Association; Knights of Labor; National Women's Trade Union League; National Consumers League; International Workers of the World; National Education Association; Longshoremen's and Warehousemen's Union; United Farm Workers of America; 9–5; Teamsters; Association of Federal, State, County and Municipal Employees; International Ladies' Garment Workers Union; and so on. Write a report on the forces that led to the initial organizing and the obstacles the organizers faced.

2. Research and report on the strategies used by the abolition movement, and analyze their effectiveness.

3. Research and report on the strategies used by the National Woman Suffrage Association, the American Woman Suffrage Association, or the National American Woman Suffrage Association, and analyze the effectiveness of the organization.

4. In the post–Civil War years, women organized for a number of purposes. Research one of these organizations, such as the women's club movement, the temperance movement, settlement houses, or the National Consumer League, and report on their short-term and long-term achievements.

5. Write a biography of a major historical change maker, focusing on his or her contributions to the larger movement of which he or she was a part. Consider such activists as Lucretia Mott, Sarah and Angelina Grimké, William Lloyd Garrison, Frederick Douglass, Elizabeth Cady Stanton, Susan B. Anthony,

Carrie Chapman Catt, Mary McLeod Bethune, Frances Willard, Mary Church Terrell, Jane Addams, Florence Kelley, Lillian Wald, Louis Brandeis, Sophie Loeb, Emma Goldman, Elizabeth Gurley Flynn, Rose Schneiderman, Mary Anderson, Abigail Scott Duniway, Thurgood Marshall, or Morris Dees.

6. Research and report on the goals and strategies used by one of the civil rights organizations of the 1950s and 1960s—for example, the Student Non-Violent Coordinating Committee, Southern Christian Leadership Conference, National Association for the Advancement of Colored People, Congress of Racial Equality, Black Panthers, American Indian Movement, La Raza Unida, National Organization for Women, National Abortion Rights Action League, or National Association for the Legalization of Marijuana.

7. Identify someone in your community who has effected a change that has had a direct impact on you, your family, or your friends or neighbors. Go to your local library or newspaper morgue and review the clipping file on this person; arrange for an interview if you can. Report on what motivated the person, what resources he or she had to make this effort effective, and what obstacles he or she had to overcome; assess the value of this person's efforts.

8. Invite one or more members of an Arab American association or a Muslim American community to speak to your class or university. If possible, combine this with a member of a Japanese American community who was imprisoned in a relocation camp during World War II or who had a family member imprisoned in the camps. Discuss the consequences to all Americans when civil liberties are suspended for any group.

9. As a class, watch at least the first twenty minutes of the film *Skokie* and discuss the following questions: (a) As a citizen (Jew or non-Jew) of the town of Skokie, Illinois, home to many Holocaust survivors and their

descendants, how would you react if neo-Nazis marched down your street? (b) As the judge responsible for issuing or denying permits for public demonstrations, would you give a permit to these neo-Nazis to demonstrate in Skokie? (c) As the mayor of Skokie, how would you react? (d) As the head of the American Civil Liberties Union, would you accept the neo-Nazis' demand for protection of their First Amendment rights, even though many of your members would consequently leave, and also knowing that if the neo-Nazis ever came to power, the first thing they would do would be to suspend freedom of speech? Remember, as head of the ACLU you are dedicated to the protection of the liberties outlined in the Bill of Rights.

10. Be in touch with a church organization, mosque, temple, or nongovernmental organization that can guide your class to help residents in distress, be it homelessness, illiteracy, or other needs. Find out what is needed and encourage your community to help.

CREDITS

INDEX